Praise for *British Children's Fiction in the Second World War*

'vast, comprehensive, polymorphous and wholly captivating'
Nicholas Barker, *The Spectator*

'a clear labour of love, full of amusement and insight'
Ann Martin, *The Scotsman*

'By the end, the reader has read not only a fascinating analysis of the subject, but also an invaluable anthology.'
A. N. Wilson, *The Times Literary Supplement*

'The war was, in some ways, a gift to those writers prepared to make the most of it. And *British Children's Fiction in the Second World War* provides the last word on all of them.'
Patricia Craig, *The Irish Times*

'Omnivorously well read, intelligently speculative, occasionally cavalier with detail while always succeeding with the bigger picture, [Owen Dudley Edwards] is an unashamed enthusiast for most of the authors he has quarried so extensively.'
Nicholas Tucker, *Books for Keeps*

'This is without doubt one of the most stimulating and enjoyable books I have read for some time.'
Mary Cadogan, Children's Book History Society newsletter

Titles available and forthcoming in the *Societies at War* series

War Damage in Western Europe
Nicola Lambourne

War Aims in the Second World War
Victor Rothwell

The Battle of Britain on Screen:
'The Few' in British Film and Television Drama
S. P. MacKenzie

British Children's Fiction in the Second World War
Owen Dudley Edwards

The Second World War and Forced Migration Movements in Europe
Rainer Schulze

Britain, Ireland and the Second World War
Ian S. Wood

Sweden, the Swastika and Stalin:
The Swedish Experience in the Second World War
John Gilmour

Prisoners of War in the Far East, 1942–45
Kent Fedorowich

Propaganda and War, 1939–45
Robert Cole

World War

Owen Dudley Edwards

© Owen Dudley Edwards, 2007, 2009

Transferred to Digital Print 2011

First published in hardback in 2007 by
Edinburgh University Press Ltd
22 George Square, Edinburgh

This paperback edition published 2009

Typeset in Melior by
Iolaire Typesetting, Newtonmore

Printed and bound in Great Britain by
CPI Antony Rowe, Chippenham and Eastbourne

A CIP record for this book is available from the British Library

ISBN 978 0 7486 1650 3 (paperback)

The right of Owen Dudley Edwards
to be identified as author of this work
has been asserted in accordance with
the Copyright, Designs and Patents Act 1988.

Published with the support of the
Edinburgh University Scholarly Publishing Initiatives Fund.

Contents

Figures

For our children
Leila, Sara, Michael

With eternal gratitude

'One of ours!' said know-all Ted.
Bombs came down and killed him dead;
Cried his wife with laughter merry
'There, I *said* it was a Jerry!'
Nancy Gunter, after Harry Graham[1]

Whoohoo go the goblins, coming back at nightfall,
Whoohoo go the witches, reaching out their hands for us,
Whoohoo goes the big bad wolf and *bang* go his teeth.
Are we sure we shall be the lucky ones, the princess, the
    youngest son,
The third pig evading the jaws? Can we afford to laugh?
They have come back, we always knew they would, after
    the story ended . . .
Naomi Mitchison, 'Siren Night' (1940)[2]

Part One

The School of War

FIGURE 1 The road to *Animal Farm* – see p. 71 n. 21.

1

Orwell v. Richards:
Children's Fiction to 1940

Chips had told some big brass hat from the War Office that bayonet-fighting was vulgar. Just like Chips. And they found an adjective for him – an adjective just beginning to be used: he was pre-War.
James Hilton, *Good-bye, Mr Chips* (1934), p. 99

Once upon a time, there was a United Kingdom in an archipelago off the coast of Europe. One day when its children woke up, their country was at war. A lot of these children read stories; and this is a book about the stories written for them while the war was on.

John Ronald Reuel Tolkien was a writer of a book for children, *The Hobbit* (1937), and he spent much of the war writing its sequel, *The Lord of the Rings* (1954–5). At the same time, he was crafting into shape for publication a lecture 'On Fairy-Stories' which he had delivered as the Andrew Lang Lecture to the University of St Andrews on 8 March 1939 (it was published in 1947). In his last note to it, Tolkien wrote: 'As for the beginning of fairy-stories: one can scarcely improve on the formula *Once upon a time*. It has an immediate effect . . . It produces at a stroke the sense of a great uncharted world of time.'[3]

The book you are reading is supposed to be history, seeking to chart a world of time from that same year when Tolkien lectured on fairy-stories, 1939, until 1945, the year when another great writer and critic of fiction for young minds, George Orwell, published his *Animal Farm: A Fairy Story*.[4] But historians who want to be useful should sometimes begin: 'Once upon a time'. Our first paragraph, beginning like that, relates to 1939. But it would do just as well for 1914: the United Kingdom was larger in 1914, and covered all the archipelago; but, despite that, there was much in common among the assumptions in the stories held by their writers, their publishers, their sellers and their readers. Our first paragraph could even relate to 1899. A smaller proportion of the archipelago's children read books in those days, and a smaller proportion of the stories were written with poorer children in mind, but many of the big questions behind these stories were still the same, even if the views on them changed in many ways between 1899 and 1939.

Many of the writers we meet in our book were alive in 1899. Tolkien was born in 1892, and served in the First World War. William Earl Johns was born in 1893, and so did he. In very different ways their writing in the Second World War would reflect their experiences in the First World War, but transformed and globalised by the war that surrounded them, and the peace that had led up to it. (The First World War helped Tolkien realise the working-class Sam Gamgee as a character, but the Second World War explains why Sam proved the only Ring-bearer to hold to the Quest; the First World War enabled Johns to create Biggles, but it took the Second World War to make him give birth to his feminist female pilot, Worrals.) Richmal Crompton Lamburn was born in 1890, her William being brought to his first print in February 1919. Gladys Eleanor May Dyer was born in 1894, and would publish (as Elinor M. (or Mary) Brent-Dyer) from 1922, founding her fictional School at the Chalet in 1925. Enid Mary Blyton was born in 1897, and her first book, *Child Whispers* (verse), also appeared in 1922. George Orwell was born as Eric Blair in 1903, but his first published work, a poem calling for youth enlistment in HM Forces, appeared in the *Henley and South Oxfordshire Standard* on 2 October 1914. And the giant who dominated juvenile fiction between the two World Wars, Charles Harold St John Hamilton (who also wrote as Martin Clifford, Owen Conquest, Hilda Richards and so on, but above all by the name used here, Frank Richards), was born in 1876.

We will find continuities between 1939 (or 1938) and 1945–7, or mutations, or even resumptions. We will find revolutions more apparent than real, and revolutions more real than apparent. Juvenile fiction has its equivalents for A. J. P. Taylor's remark that the Second World War began with the Polish cavalry crossing the ice with swords drawn, and ended with the atomic destruction of Hiroshima and Nagasaki. Tolkien's Frodo and Sam on Mount Doom might be atomic fiction – the horrors of atomic warfare were one of Tolkien's harshest indictments of his age. Enid Blyton's last war-born series, *The Island of Adventure* (1944) and its sequels, climaxes (1949) in *The Mountain of Adventure*'s boy animal-lover Philip symbolically crucified between two wings on which Science demanded he fly to what would certainly prove his death. (He is rescued, unhurt.) Unlike Tolkien,[5] Blyton had no specific religious intent in writing, so far as we know (she sometimes denied any awareness of what she was writing at all). But, as recent author of a life of Christ,[6] her caricature of insane experiment for alleged new freedom harmonised with her revulsion at the destruction of children in Science's name, and naturally she expressed herself in the rich paraphernalia of the angel-sponsored birth of Jesus (surrounded by animals) and His sacrifice at the hands of corrupt men. Philip is anything but Christ-like most of the time, fighting his corner against crooks or his sister Dinah with verve, but here he does not resist the death he anticipates.[7]

Biggles Hunts Big Game (1948) drew a more explicit but equally pessimistic verdict. W. E. Johns had been a brave advocate of air-power build-up and resistance to Nazi aggression, thereby in post-Munich months losing editorships in journals he had founded; but he put some grim post-war conclusions into the mouth of his intrepid hero, Biggles:

> 'Two world wars have nearly caused the earth to seize up on its axis. . . . What have scientists done to help matters? They've been so busy producing lethal weapons that they've forgotten how to do the simple things – like providing food to feed the people. The man in the street doesn't want atomic bombs. He wants bread and butter. The world has gone cockeye and he knows it. He also knows there is nothing he can do about it. Tomorrow, he says, some clueless sabre-rattler will start another war, or, maybe, set loose a bunch of irritated atoms that will send the whole universe up in a cloud of dust and small pebbles. Result? He shrugs his shoulders and says, "What's the use of working? What's the use of doing anything? Let's go out and play games."'
>
> Bertie nodded. 'What you mean is, the whole bally world is round the bend?'
>
> Biggles smiled faintly. 'That's what it's coming to. . . .'

Frank Richards was still denouncing US–UK nuclear submarines in the last year of his life:[8]

> 'Holy Loch' certainly is a misnomer, in the circumstances: for a more unholy beast of a thing it would be hard to imagine. It does seem strange that nearly two thousand years of Christianity have produced no better result than this.

George Orwell had evangelised his early Second World War readers with a gospel of English Revolution as chief war aim;[9]

but, nearing war's end, *Animal Farm* satirised the Russian Revolution's degeneration into the Stalinist state, and both it and its dystopian sequel, *1984* (1949), had obvious morals for the UK as well as the USSR. Orwell's hopes of an egalitarian 'English' revolution, like the Bolsheviks' and the animals' hopes in theirs, received their epitaph in his fairy-story's final reduction of all revolutionary laws and slogans to 'ALL ANIMALS ARE EQUAL BUT SOME ANIMALS ARE MORE EQUAL THAN OTHERS'. (The illiteracy is vital, symbolising conformity as the enemy of literature.) His hero, Winston Smith, sole surviving rebel against totalitarian rule in *1984*, ends up loving the quintessence of despotism, Big Brother. Both books were written in the assumption that they would influence adolescent minds – as they did – and this assumption logically followed from Orwell's essay 'Boys' Weeklies' published at the beginning of the war, demanding revolutionary emancipation from what its author saw as the reactionary intention of publishers of children's weekly magazines or comics. The comics' authors Orwell seems to have regarded as factory workers, churning out conformist valorisation of public-school elites for deferential consumption by acceptant little proletarians, very much as the various kinds of writers in the service of the state in *1984* churn out pornography or propaganda at their rulers' behest. His main target in 'Boys' Weeklies' was the Amalgamated Press, publishing house of the *Magnet*, *Gem*, *Modern Boy* and so on. Like the children's stories, and the warborne public, he needed a hate object, such as the Kaiser in 1914–18, or (much more justifiably) Hitler in 1939–45: *1984* shows the modern state's technologisation of the process. The essay in its book text pointedly levelled its Parthian shot at William Ewert Berry, first Baron (later Viscount) Camrose (1879–1954), controller of press relations at the Ministry of Information in autumn 1939, as well as owner of the *Daily Telegraph*, the *Financial Times* and the Amalgamated Press:[10]

> *All* fiction from the novels in the mushroom libraries downwards is censored in the interests of the ruling class. And boys' fiction above all . . . is sodden in the worst illusions of 1910. The fact is only unimportant if one believes that what is read in childhood leaves no impression behind. Lord Camrose and his colleagues evidently believe nothing of the kind, and, after all, Lord Camrose ought to know.

The demonisation was pointed enough to alarm the author's fellow-Etonian, Cyril Connolly, whose new monthly magazine *Horizon* had contracted to publish 'Boys' Weeklies' in its third issue, March 1940, which appeared a few days before Victor Gollancz published Orwell's *Inside the Whale* containing 'Boys' Weeklies' together with his essays on Henry Miller (the title-essay) and on Charles Dickens. The *Horizon* text substituted an anodyne 'The proprietors of these papers' for the name of Camrose.[11]

In some respects, it was Orwell more than the comics who reflected assumptions of 1910. The *Gem* (founded on 16 March 1907), starring St Jim's school, and the *Magnet* (15 February 1908), chronicling Greyfriars, commenced their thirty-two-year-long lives under Alfred Harmsworth, Lord Northcliffe (1865–1922), who does seem to have subjected them to proprietorial scrutiny and intervention from time to time. Thus on 7 November 1914 the *Magnet* featured Harry Wharton (the captain of the Remove), Herbert Vernon-Smith (the millionaire's son and Bounder of Greyfriars) and Peter Todd (the schoolboy lawyer and study-mate of Billy Bunter) resolutely facing a German firing-squad (and, of course, surviving). Shortly afterwards, a directive was issued forbidding schoolboy involvement in the European battlefield. The proprietorial ukase may have followed difficulties with war censorship, which during that war forced deletions on writers of boys' stories such as Percy F. Westerman. The spectacle of Northcliffe studying Wharton and the Bounder, whose characters were as intrepid, and tempers as uncertain, as his own, may be incongruous but not impossible: Max Aitken, Lord Beaverbrook (1879–1964), was credited with daily consumption of his *Daily Express* comic strip featuring the anthropomorphic little bear Rupert, who faced endless adventures with a stoicism rising far above the doggerel in which many were related.[12] Orwell may have remembered that the *Magnet* in the first months of the First World War made constant allusions to its Northcliffe stablemate the *Daily Mail*: the Greyfriars schoolmaster Mr Quelch was shown reading it and conning its maps for war news. The Camrose proprietorship (from 1926)[13] brought no such obsessive flaunting of its *Daily Telegraph*, however superior its harmony with Mr Quelch's *gravitas*. Instead, there were constant allusions to a closer-related publication, the *Greyfriars Holiday Annual*, inducing a rough magic self-containment as well as author's and characters' solipsism. The rivals of the Amalgamated Press, the Dundonian D. C. Thomson, copied this convention among many others: house creations read house products. But the practice did not indicate intrusive proprietorial concern, as was made pointedly clear when the Germans invaded Norway in April 1940. The supply of pulp for paper slowed dramatically, with

Canadian timber also at risk from Atlantic submarine warfare, and the *Magnet* was sacrificed along with almost all of Camrose's comics to save the *Telegraph* and the *Financial Times*. (The *Gem* and several others had fallen from October to December 1939.) If Camrose was in conspiracy to make acquiescent cannon-fodder and wage-slaves of the youthful UK proletariat, he was the most frivolous conspirator since Mark Twain's Tom Sawyer.[14]

But, by that time, Orwell's case had received a devastating blow. *1984* even posits the authorship of 'proletfeed' as ultimately reaching a post-human technological origin:[15]

> There was a whole chain of separate departments dealing with proletarian literature, music, drama and entertainment generally. Here were produced rubbishy newspapers containing almost nothing except sport, crime and astrology, sensational five-cent novelettes, films oozing with sex, and sentimental songs which were composed entirely by mechanical means on a special kind of kaleidoscope known as a versificator.

And just as 'Boys' Weeklies' had shrewdly noted that the future in comics seemed to lie more with Thomson's products – *Adventure* (founded 17 September 1921), *Rover* (4 March 1922), *Wizard* (22 September 1922), *Hotspur* (2 September 1933) and the largely car-toon-strip *Dandy* (4 December 1937) and *Beano* (30 July 1938)[16] – Thomson's comics had anonymous writers for the masses of printed fiction-texts (although their most famous artist, Dudley D. Watkins, creator of the Broons and Oor Wullie, Desperate Dan and Lord Snooty, was already widely known). But Orwell took mass-produc-tion authorship as axiomatic for all boys' weeklies from publishing empires:[17]

> not only the characters but the whole atmosphere of both *Gem* and *Magnet* has been preserved unchanged, partly by means of very elaborate stylisation. The stories in the *Magnet* are signed 'Frank Richards' and those in the *Gem*, 'Martin Clifford' but a series lasting thirty years could hardly be the work of the same person every week. Consequently they have to be written in a style that is easily imitated – an extraordinary, artificial, repetitive style, quite different from anything now existing in English literature.

What he had not anticipated was that the cog in the machine or the slave from the chain-gang would indignantly surface and demand space in *Horizon* as a human being and fellow-author. Richards's reply was printed for the fifth issue (May 1940), and after wicked play with his unexpected pulpit –[18]

> From the fact that *Horizon* contains a picture that does not resemble a picture, a poem that does not resemble poetry, and a story that does not resemble a story, I conclude that it must be a very high-browed paper indeed: and I was agreeably surprised, therefore to find in it an article written in a lively and entertaining manner, and actually readable. I was still more interested as this article dealt chiefly with my work as an author for boys.

– Richards opened devastatingly elegant fire:

> Mr Orwell finds it difficult to believe that a series running for thirty years can possibly have been written by one and the same person. In the presence of such authority I speak with diffidence: and can only say that, to the best of my knowledge and belief, I am only one person, and have never been two or three.

The wound inflicted by this lay not in its argument (which was very slightly mendacious)[19] but in its humour. The man who wrote that had survived because his intellectual resources of wit, debate, satire, social comment, human psychology and classical literary range could match any that *Horizon* could throw against him: he might be asinine in specifics, but his range was very hard to equal. In fact, did he but know it, Orwell and he between them may have rescued *Horizon* from a highbrow grave. Some readers found the rediscovery of fun an irresistible bonus.[20] Richards was also giving Orwell a perfect illustration of what values he was actually transmitting: he was giving the British child what it would need more than anything else in the years ahead – a capacity for laughter, a pursuit of the comic, a belief in community. Richards hereby struck up the overture for the grand comic writing and artistry to overcome the gloom – indeed blackout – of the future: Crompton's William and Watkins's Wullie, Johns's feminist banter and Blyton's cliché-mangling parrot, Brent-Dyer's schoolgirls' deflation of pompous men and Eric Linklater's metamorphoses of difficult children. Orwell's constriction of comics to serve his current left-wing dogma carried with it the dehumanisation of the producer, however proletarian: Richards was forcing him to confront the writer as human being.[21]

The question Orwell's 'Boys' Weeklies' had intended to ask was:

what values are the children of 1938 being given? The question it ended up asking was: what values had the children of 1940 been given? Between its conception and its publication, desiderata in those values had conspicuously changed. In 1938, both Richards and Orwell were supporters of Munich. In 1940, they rallied to the cause of war. Both men had become critical of their First World War chauvinism (more measured in the *Magnet* and *Gem* than in what has survived by the teenage Eric Blair). 'Boys' Weeklies' noted the absence of Officers' Training Corps from Greyfriars and St Jim's; in fact, they had had them, but they had been silently dropped since the Great War. Richards recorded privations of ex-soldiers, including a subsequent criminal, ultimately jailed, whose narrative of his road to crime invited sympathetic reading. He had also given his readers ugly reminders of Nazi and Fascist challenges to isolation. After the Nazi agent and Greyfriars Old Boy Franz Kranz has kidnapped Bob Cherry to get his father's aircraft designs in January 1934, he successively adds Vernon-Smith and Redwing to his victims, step by step, as Churchill would say. *Magnet* readers were being told after Hitler's rise to power that the Nazis sought air supremacy and had no scruples about the means to acquire it. Fascist agents try to rob Vernon-Smith's father in December 1935 to finance Mussolini's rape of Ethiopia, and to murder him in April 1937 to grab his tin holdings on the Ethiopian border. Smithy's ordeal at his father's danger was an inoculation for readers of what they might have to sustain themselves, should war come in the next few years.[22]

The previous September, 1936, the neo-Falstaffian Billy Bunter had been in mortal peril from a Fascist spy, rather pointedly named Muccolini, who mixed his circus proprietorship with photography of British air installations. Orwell insisted in 'Boys' Weeklies' that the stories were written in the Edwardian convention that 'over in Europe the comic foreigners are jabbering and gesticulating, but the grim grey battleships of the British Fleet are steaming up the Channel'.[23] But the *Magnet* in the 1930s fostered no such isolationist illusions (although many of its imitator 'Public School' stories and magazine serials may have done). Richards's anti-Fascism meant that when a story demanded high-ranking local support for Greyfriars schoolboys in Rome, they come under the protection of 'Cardinal Colonna' rather than of a state official. Orwell would not necessarily have read those particular issues (although he was vulnerable to Richards's riposte that he 'flicks off his condemnations with so careless a hand'). His journey to the real Spanish Civil War began shortly before the *Magnet* endangered some of its own heroes from arms-smugglers running the blockade and defying Non-intervention to supply arms to Franco (or, less likely, to the Spanish government). He missed the series on the Vernon-Smiths' peril from Fascist bullets because he was serving with the Spanish POUM, to be wounded in the throat by a Fascist bullet about two weeks after it had finished. He was convalescing in French Morocco from September 1938 when he gave the *Magnet* and *Gem* to British recruits in the French Foreign Legion (responding to their preference for them over all other British magazines), and would not have seen them again until March 1939 when he returned. He would thus have missed Richards's neo-Gilbertian version of post-Munich politics as heard by Greyfriars on the BBC:

'Herr Hitler addressed a crowd of ten thousand persons this afternoon at —'

Sudden silence again.

Smithy, it seemed, was not interested in the chin-wag of the Fuhrer. . . .

'I'm getting the ten o'clock news!' said Vernon-Smith. 'The football results will be given over again — when that gabblin' ass has finished talking about Hitler and Mussolini. . . .'

'In a speech at Turin this afternoon, Signor Mussolini stated that the just aspirations of the Italian people —

Sudden silence again as Smithy shut off! He did not want to hear about the aspirations of the Italian people, just or unjust! All this dreary stuff was simply irritating to Smithy.

'Bother the blithering asses!' the Bounder was heard to growl. 'Do they really think that people are interested in such stuff?' . . .

'The honourable member for Muddycombe stated that he repudiated with scorn any such suggestion! This ship was not a foreign ship. It was a purely British ship. It was true that the captain was a Greek, the mate a Swede, and the crew wholly composed of Lascars, but —' . . .

'Mr Chinwag challenged that statement', droned the announcer. 'Peace, he admitted, was the universal desired but he could not help feeling that peace would be most easily obtained by declaring war upon practically everybody.'

That may be lampoon on Churchill, still in the wilderness.

'The member for Popping hoped that the Government would remember that their first and greatest duty was to concern themselves with the inhabitants of any country but their own –' . . .

'He hoped, and he trusted, that no British statesman would ever so far forget what was due to foreign peoples as to waste a single thought upon the inhabitants of these islands –' . . .

'That is the end of the speech by the honourable member for Popping. We have now to announce that Sir Noodle Balmycrumpet has been appointed minister at Hankey-Pankey –'

This was published on 28 January 1939 and ably represents the ostrich *Zeitgeist*, showing isolationism at its deepest in the months after Munich, in strong contrast to the *Magnet* in the years before it.[24]

In this isolationist mood, Richards was far from ready to concede altruism to its critics. Two months later, *Magnet* readers were given firm indications that war-fear was the fodder of publicity-hunters and self-centred neurotics such as Horace Hacker ('the Acid Drop'), Master of the Greyfriars Shell:[25]

The Acid Drop was a worrying man by nature; he worried his Form and he worried himself; he indulged in worry as if it were a sort of entertainment.

He worried about whether the Income Tax was going to rise, and whether Consols were going to fall. He worried about whether there was going to be a war – and even about whether he would get damaged if there was a war! Hacker's personal safety seemed an important thing – to Hacker – and he worried about it. He worried about whether there would be a food shortage if there was a war. He worried about whether the banks would break, and paper money lose its value. No doubt that was why he had parked that fistful of quids [gold sovereigns] secretly – like other nervous and uneasy people. . . .

Banks might be bombed if there was a war. And Hacker, like so many worriers, always fancied that war was just around the corner. Every time there was a crisis Hacker fancied that the crash was coming. It never came – but he always expected it at the next crisis. . . .

Really it was quite an awkward situation for a worrying gentleman whose thoughts and cares were wholly concentrated on himself.

Unknown to his readers, there was brave self-mockery in this. When the war came, Richards was left virtually destitute on the disappearance of the papers whence came his income, and the following year produced income-tax demands on his empty coffers. He was perhaps crushing down fears of his own, as was much of the general isolationist bluster. Unlike Hacker, he was brave, and his bachelor concerns extended to his sister, his niece, his housekeeper, her father, and his cats: his garden would be a war casualty when he was forced to retreat from the North Foreland of Kent, in the Thanet area, to a rented Hampstead flat (his first choice was bombed after he had proved unsuccessful in his attempt for it). Orwell seems to have missed the study of Hacker's psycho-economics but noted the Cornwall series of April–May 1939, in which the Bounder's father 'cashed in on the general panic by buying up country houses in order to sell them to "crisis scuttlers". But that is probably as near to noticing the European situation as the *Gem* and *Magnet* will come, until the war actually starts.'[26] But the observation deserved more acknowledgement than Orwell would accord. Richmal Crompton, the satirical chronicler of the scapegrace William in short stories since 1919, was as ruthless in her dissection of bomb-dodgers when the war came as Richards would be on its eve.[27]

When the war did come, it hardened as a theme. Crompton was a little earlier than Richards, drawing William catastrophically into Air Raid Precaution in May 1939, with a hint of phoney war precaution before phoney war. William was annoyed at not being allowed to play with his gas-mask:[28]

> 'I told 'em I ought to be able to wear it a bit each day jus' for practice', went on William. 'I told 'em I wouldn't be much use in a war 'less I did. Why, anyone'd think they *wanted* me to get killed, keepin' my gas mask where I can't get at it. It's same as murder. Just 'cause of us playin' gladiators in 'em the first day we got 'em! Well, the bit of damage it did was easy to put right. It was a jolly good thing really, 'cause it sort of showed where it was weak. They said I'd been *rough* on it. Well, if war's not s'posed to be *rough* I don't know what is. Seems cracked to me to have somethin' for a war you can't be *rough* in. . . .'

The remorselessness of William's logic makes one wonder if O'Brien in *1984* could have stood up to it. Billy Bunter, of course, would have capitulated to O'Brien immediately, and promptly lied his way out of capitulation at the first opportunity. He found the gas-mask a useful adjunct when disguised as an African prince and beginning to lose pigmentation.[29] Evacuation was required for schools roughly in

Greyfriars's supposed area of Kent – the North Foreland seems an obvious candidate, since Richards's choice of it as a domestic background after he had been writing Greyfriars for many years suggests he found the landscape sufficiently congenial to what his imagination had drawn. But Richards had little interest in the pursuit of a theme demanding technical knowledge of modern government which his reclusive life could hardly resource. Other school-story writers made much of evacuation, most notably Elinor M. Brent-Dyer, Angela Brazil, Gunby Hadath and L. A. G. Strong. Crompton had anticipated it as early as August 1938, when William pretends to be a visitor to his own village from the London slums:[30]

> He pointed over the hedge to a cow that was pleasantly ruminating in the next field.
> 'What's that?' he gruffed.
> 'That's a cow.'
> 'What's a cow?'
> Miss Milton sighed. But, of course, it was quite natural that a slum child should never have seen a cow.
> 'It's – just a cow, dear', she said. 'A cow is – well, it's a cow.'

But evacuation sometimes involved very grim stories. There were the lonely flights in twos and threes chronicled by Olive C. Dougan, Agnes M. Miall, Josephine Elder and Major Charles Gilson, cases given a horrific potential when Jewish children are involved.[31] Brent-Dyer, having long ago set her English school in the Austrian Tyrol, had to make refugees of her characters and firmly did so around Nazi persecution of the Jews. *The Chalet School in Exile* appeared in April 1940, taking its story almost to Christmas 1939. Unlike Richards's stories and their imitators in weekly comics and magazines, and unlike Crompton's William stories (collected in books, but magazine-born), the Chalet School saga allowed its cast of characters to grow older, although more slowly than real time allowed. There had been little discussion of the rise of Nazism beyond ominous allusions to undesirable new national spirit in Germany (*The Exploits of the Chalet Girls*, 1933) and the expulsion of the sister of an enthusiast for it (*The Chalet School and the Lintons*, 1934). Chambers of Edinburgh, Brent-Dyer's publishers, had in fact suggested the end of the series on its twelfth instalment (*Jo Returns to the Chalet School*, 1936), so that the Second World War, which would terminate the *Gem* and *Magnet*, was to give a new (and thirty-year) lease of life to the Chalet School.[32] *The Chalet School in Exile* is one of the best books for children – in all senses – to appear in the Second World War, none the worse because Brent-Dyer (who had not revisited the continent in ten years) had hard research to do on the upsurge and nature of Austrian lynch-mob tactics against Jews, which she brought to unforgettable life. The probability is that this part of the book had been written before the outbreak of war, but it is noteworthy that very little hostile comment on Nazi anti-Jewish practices reached British child audiences in peacetime: Elder's *Strangers at the Farm School*, Gilson's *Out of the Nazi Clutch* and Dougan's *The Schoolgirl Refugee*, sensitive explorations of Jewish suffering, are all from 1940 even though their supposed events are sometimes set much earlier in Nazi days of power. Some may have preceded the war in serial form: W. E. Johns's *Biggles – Secret Agent* was published in 1940, but first appeared in the *Magnet*'s stablemate *Modern Boy* between 12 August and 14 October 1939, and its depiction of the effects of persecution of the Jews is flesh-creeping. Some books may have been withheld or postponed by publishers before the war: Johns set *Biggles – Secret Agent* in an imaginary principality, 'Lucrania', although it is wholly under German influence and has Biggles's old enemy Erich von Stalhein as its Chief of Secret Police, or, as children would now be learning in its German name, Gestapo. Tolkien found his proposed German publishers of *The Hobbit*, Rütten & Loening of Potsdam, writing in July 1938 to demand proof of his Aryan descent. He asked Stanley Unwin, his publisher:[33]

> do their lunatic laws require a certificate of 'arisch' origin from all persons of all countries?
> Personally I should be inclined to refuse to give any *Bestatigung* (although it happens that I can), and let a German translation go hang. In any case I should object strongly to any such declaration appearing in print. I do not regard the (probable) absence of Jewish blood as necessarily honourable; and I have many Jewish friends, and should regret giving any colour to the notion that I subscribed to the wholly pernicious and unscientific race-doctrine.
> You are primarily concerned, and I cannot jeopardize the chance of a German publication without your approval.

So he sent Unwin two drafts in reply to Rütten & Loening, the surviving one of which told them:

> I regret that I am not clear as to what you intend by *arisch*. I am not of *Aryan* extraction: that is Indo-iranian; as far as I am aware none

of my ancestors spoke Hindustani, Persian, Gypsy, or any related dialects. But if I am to understand that you are enquiring whether I am of *Jewish* origin, I can only reply that I regret that I appear to have *no* ancestors of that gifted people.

He added that, though his German ancestry was five generations distant, he had looked on 'my German name with pride' and had done so when serving 'in the English army' in 'the late regrettable war', but 'I cannot, however, forbear to comment that if impertinent and irrelevant enquiries of this sort are to become the rule in matters of literature, then the time is not far distant when a German name will no longer be a source of pride'. We can take pride in Tolkien; but we should also notice the pressures on British publishers in the Munich era.

Ironically, one publisher who seems seriously to have more or less consistently sought to welcome and celebrate Jewish presence in Britain between 1910 and 1940 was the Amalgamated Press, notably in the *Gem* and the *Magnet*. Richards produced some charming stories of cultivated Jews shaming stupid and ill-mannered anti-Semitism.[34] The irony was that Orwell's 'Boys' Weeklies' denounced the magazines and their imitators as racist and xenophobe while ignoring anti-Semitism (explored by him elsewhere). In fact, the situation was far more complex than he recognised, but the question was important, and racism on one front often betokened racism on all, coupled with resultant failure to take up the supreme issue against Hitler. Richards's reply to Orwell gave little help on this score, preferring satirically to agree with some of Orwell's charges, much as Harry Wharton or Herbert Vernon-Smith when under unjust attack practically incite further injustice by apparently admitting while actually denying the charges:[35]

As for foreigners being funny, I must shock Mr Orwell by telling him that foreigners *are* funny. They lack the sense of humour which is the special gift of our own chosen nation: and people without a sense of humour are always unconsciously funny. Take Hitler, for example, – with his swastika, his 'good German sword', his fortifications named after characters from Wagner, his military coat that he will never take off until he marches home victorious: and the rest of his fripperies out of the property-box. In Germany they lap this up like milk, with the most awful seriousness; in England, the play-acting ass would be laughed out of existence. . . . The fact that Adolf Hitler is deadly dangerous does not make him less comic.

This is wonderful in its way. The war began to get very ugly while Richards was writing, with the German invasions of Denmark and Norway on 9 April 1940, and Richards had only obtained agreement that *Horizon* would give space for his reply by the beginning of April. This would be Richards's only chance for non-fictional defiance of Hitler, in hopes that his name would be on some Nazi death-list in the event of a successful invasion of the UK. He was also proclaiming a theme in which almost all British literature for children met the Second World War: it was to be brave, and it was to be funny.

But heroics, however heart-warming, seldom supply critical analysis. Of course, Richards made fun of foreigners, just as he made fun of every single person to appear in his texts. Orwell had certainly seen the passage in the Cornwall story when Redwing, having rescued Bunter from the ocean, very slowly extracts information that Smithy's life in in danger: we know that Redwing will strain every nerve to save his adored Smithy, and yet we are invited to convulse ourselves with laughter at his wild frustration at Bunter's opaqueness, ignorance, indifference and, above all, greed. Seldom if ever has a matter of life and death been made so hilarious. But Richards's actual use of foreigners involved considerable pains to show respect for their dignity, however funny they might be, just as he respected the dignity of the heroic Redwing. The crucial question would be how persons from countries threatened by the rise of Nazism, Fascism, Stalinism and Japanese imperialism were respected. Japanese aggression in China began in 1931. Orwell asserted:[36]

> The assumption all along is not only that foreigners are comics who are put there for us to laugh at, but that they can be classified in much the same way as insects. That is why in all boys' papers, not only the *Gem* and *Magnet*, a Chinese is invariably portrayed with a pigtail.

Richards was not actually replying to this charge at all when he defied Hitler and Mussolini by lampoon. And Orwell was right to denounce the absurdity of Richards's retention of the pigtail thirty years after it had been discarded in China. But what he missed was Richards's emphases on the superiority of Chinese respect for elders in contrast to British youth, the absurdity of British conventions as

fully as Chinese when taken literally, and the death-defying comradeship between white and Chinese Greyfriars boys. Richards
wrote in the Dickensian/Trollopeian convention of absurd names,
and hence his Chinese boys are 'Wun Lung' and 'Hop Hi'; but Bob
Cherry's readiness to risk his life for Wun Lung and vice versa
testifies to Richards's fundamental principle of schoolboy mutual
respect and affection across racial divides. Similarly, Johns in 1933–4
has Biggles, rescuing a Chinese from a watery grave, receive a
courteous rebuke when his 'Speekee Engleesh?' is answered by
'Not that sort'. The new acquaintance ultimately proves to be an
Oxonian Chinese pirate, countered some eight years later by Arthur
Ransome's Cambridge-educated female Chinese pirate, the eponymous Missee Lee. Above all, Major Charles Gilson turned out a
series of stories where the intrepid hero with whom readers were to
identify was a young Chinese, including thrilling accounts of the
Japanese conquest of Shanghai in November 1937. The obvious
progenitor of Gilson's plots is Rudyard Kipling's masterpiece Kim
(1901); but Kim, while devoted to his Indian guru, is himself white
(Irish, admittedly). The Chinese boys are also granted a white hero to
serve, rescue and be rescued by; but, as with Kim, the story is theirs,
not the white master's.[37] But implicit in Kipling and Gilson is
affection and respect for the bright native boy, and for the strong
native fighting man (in Gilson's stories often the boy's big brother),
while not noticeably anticipating native officer material. Tactics
might well be managed by native hands and minds, but strategy
needed whites.[38]

Children's literature, when not isolationist, involved international
adventures (frequently violent) either directly or for British interests,
or for some acceptable protégé of British preference or of the heroes'
choice. The classic formula remained one of boy or girl protagonist(s)
with whom the reader could identify or whom s/he might imagine as
a personal friend – or replace, as Sandy Stranger replaces David
Balfour as ally of Alan Breck Stewart when under the spell of
Stevenson's Kidnapped, in Muriel Spark's The Prime of Miss Jean
Brodie (unmatched in its analytical recall of childhood in the 1930s).
The boy(s) or girl(s) were usually linked to adult heroes of the Kipling
imperial type, as Kim is to Colonel Creighton, and is usually a waif
proving to be of notable if not always reputable parentage. Sometimes the child hero exists – and may even have been added to an
existing series – to make the chief (adult) hero more accessible to a
child audience (Sexton Blake's Tinker, Nelson Lee's Nipper, Biggles's
Ginger). Sometimes, as indeed in Kim, the adult master is offstage for

much of the action. The genre was diagnosed, and denounced, by Virginia Woolf's cousin J. K. Stephen, who died, curiously enough, nine years before *Kim* appeared, but who maliciously prayed for the day[39]

> When there stands a muzzled stripling,
> Mute, beside a muzzled bore:
> When the Rudyards cease from Kipling
> And the Haggards Ride no more.

But even he could not escape a heroic resonance in the final line; and what he perceived in 1891–2 inaugurated a half-century of its kind, Kipling and Rider Haggard waxing strong for most of it. Richards's schoolboys had many a vacation international adventure, initially under imperial hero leadership (Captain Corkran, Major Cherry, Colonel Wharton), then guarded by Richards's version of Sexton Blake, Ferrers Locke, and in the 1930s much more on their own. In the Blytonian world – and in the Second World War in general – adults were ruthlessly removed, whether by accidents, war service, ailments or appropriate miscreants. A crucial question on the race front was whether the child protagonist might bond with a foreigner, especially a non-white, sometimes adult (as in Kim's case) but more frequently child. Richards was a pioneer in such inter-racial unity by cementing the friendship between Harry Wharton, Frank Nugent, Bob Cherry and Hurree Jamset Ram Singh from the *Magnet's* second month; and Wun Lung also appeared in 1908. Both were figures of fun but also invited affection and respect, Hurree Singh being more intelligent and Wun Lung more resourceful than the white boys. Hurree Singh's place derived in part from the great cricketer Ranjitsinhji Vibhaji maharaha jam saheb of Nawanagar (which in Richards's variations became nabob of Bhanipur), and his nomenclature and partnership with whites derive from Conan Doyle's *The Sign of Four* (and its precursor *The Mystery of Cloomber*).[40] Wun Lung, unlike Hurree Singh, is not one of the Famous Five, but is Bob Cherry's study-mate, a place he holds with a mischievous (and exceptionally explicit) devotion to 'handsome Bob Chelly'. In 1909, John Finnemore introduced a Japanese schoolboy, Ito Nagao (*His First Term* 1909) into his Slapton school saga starring Teddy Lester (apparently the first schoolboy book series, 1907–21). Ito's equality with Lester is more of the Hurree Singh than the Wun Lung variety of comradeship.

The Sino–Japanese conflict necessarily divided orientals into allies and enemies, the most striking case appearing in the Belgian comic strip by Georges Remi (1907–83), drawing his adventures of the boy reporter Tintin as 'Hergé' (French pronunciation of his initials, reversed). Beginning in 1929 with crudely racist depiction of non-European peoples, Remi was converted to international brotherhood in 1934 when he formed a devoted friendship in Brussels with another 27-year-old, the Chinese sculptor Chang Chong-chen, whom he promptly introduced eponymously in his series as Tintin's only coeval friend, for whom alone Tintin weeps. The real Chang transformed Remi's ideas on art, 'friendship, poetry and nature':[41]

> For me up to then China was peopled by a vague, slit-eyed people who were very cruel, who would eat swallows' nests, wear pigtails and throw children into rivers . . . I was influenced by the pictures and stories of the Boxer Uprising [of 1900] where the accent was always on the cruelty of the yellow people, and this made a deep impact.

So, in Le Lotus Bleu, when Chang is saved from the river by Tintin, they exchange absolutions:

> '. . . why did you save my life?'
> '?'
> 'I thought all white devils were wicked, like those who killed my grandfather and grandmother long ago. During the War of Righteous and Harmonious Fists my father said.'
> 'The Boxer Rebellion, yes. But Chang, all white men aren't wicked. You see, different peoples don't know enough about each other. Lots of Europeans still believe that all Chinese are cunning and cruel and wear pigtails, are always inventing tortures, and eating rotten eggs and swallows' nests. . . .'

This was published in book form in Belgium in 1936. We cannot say how many copies may have made their way to British children (although it would clearly have been an attractive – and therefore possibly suspect – way for children to learn French). The story covers Japanese penetration of China from Mukden (September 1931) to Japan's announcement of withdrawal from the League of Nations (March 1933), and is credited with helping to turn western European opinion against Japan. In practice, this meant that much of the melodramatic fear and loathing against the Chinese was now diverted increasingly against the Japanese, with few writers (other than Gilson) showing anything like the personal affection for the Chinese now animating Hergé.[42] Whether from Hergé (and he was a frequent visitor to France if not Belgium), or from his own observations of news and League of Nations debates, W. E. Johns switched to suspicion of Japan, identified in all but name as mastermind of covert operations against Britain in *Biggles – Air Commodore* (1937, serialised in Amalgamated Press's *Modern Boy* in 1936). Johns was prescient on one point: the unnamed Japanese mobilise many local peoples in Malaya in their service. Johns also enjoyed himself in preliminary satire on self-protective British politicians, but unlike Hergé he did not go the length of suggesting that western residents in China collaborated with the Japanese in the cause of 'teach[ing] that yellow [Chinese] rabble to mind their manners . . . It's up to us to civilise the savages . . . look what we've done for them, all the benefits of our superb western civilisation . . . yellow scum!' Johns would have repudiated such collaborators with disdain, yet he hardly realised what aid he gave the Japanese claims of liberation with throwaway narrator lines such as 'if the fate of a Malay Dyak is ever human'. Major Gilson knew better.[43]

Mussolini's Roman Empire raises comparable questions for the Arab and African peoples, and here once more Orwell's 'Boys' Weeklies' over-generalised: Spaniards, Mexicans, Arabs, Afghans and Chinese 'conform more or less exactly' to patterns 'sinister, treacherous', and Africans to 'comic, very faithful'. The last may have been the boy Blair rather than the comics of the 1930s testifying to such reactions. It fits in with early *Gem* and *Magnet* up to 1922. But, in September–October 1931, Richards produced a heroic African for the *Magnet*, following but improving on Rider Haggard in *King Solomon's Mines*. Once again, mutual respect and love dissolve notions of racial supremacy, in particular when the great Kikuyu hunter Kikolobo and Vernon-Smith save one another's lives time after time in Kenya and the Congo. It is savagely contrasted with Bunter's racism.

The purist could nevertheless find racialist language in the various battles of schoolboys and cannibals; but, whatever devil might be in the detail, the series had its magnificent hero in Kikolobo, very much a black Alan Breck without Alan's Dumas-style affection for gambling and drink. Richards was certainly correct in asserting that the Congo still had its cannibals in 1931, and probably in assuming what schoolboy reactions when enslaved by the cannibals might be, on hearing of their captors' chagrin at some tidings:[44]

> 'Might be white men coming!' said Nugent hopefully. 'This king-
> dom will be mopped up some day by the Belgian Congo govern-
> ment.'
>   'Oh, my hat! That would be too ripping!' sighed Bob. 'Too jolly
> good to be true, I'm afraid.'

The government was now that of the Belgian people, not of their
atrocious King Leopold II, whose regime far outdid that of any
cannibal ruler in the extent of its excesses, as Richards must have
remembered from a quarter-century earlier. The citation was a trifle
insensitive, but it was absolutely true of its time and circumstances.

New colonialism was another matter, especially in non-British
hands. Richmal Crompton naturally gave William and his rival
Hubert Lane a spot of imitation of would-be dictators in the summer
of 1937. William, leading the Green Shirts, outlines his programme:

> 'You've gotter have a dictator . . . you've all gotter be Green shirts
> same as us. . . . We're goin' to fight everyone that isn't. . . . We're
> goin' to fight everyone in the world. . . . We're goin' to conquer the
> world. . . . We're goin' to be dictators over the world.'

This no doubt did duty as Crompton's disrespects to *Mein Kampf*;
but Hubert's bulk suggested Mussolini, which meant an equivalent
of Ethiopia (invaded in 1935 and annexed in 1936) and Libya
(independence revoked in 1927). Hubert's Blue Shirts proclaim a
colony ('Well, all these shirt people want col'nies'), and William
privately seeks information from Henry, who reports: 'They want
col'nies . . . 'cause there's food and stuff there'. But, when William
manages to get food for his colony, in the tradition of the Empire as
Britain's bread-basket, the lady who provides it confuses his polity
with a fairy feast:

> 'I shall always think of you as the Little Boy who Believes in
> Fairies.' An agonised spasm passed over William's face at this, but
> she was too shortsighted to notice it. 'So kind and helpful. And so
> interesting – all you told me about the colonial question, though
> I'm afraid I don't know as much about politics as I should.'

At all events, they prove their colony superior to Hubert but privately
agree with him that they are tired of the shirt war, despite their
satisfaction in ending with a good feed 'that had turned so strangely
. . . from a colony into a fairy feast. After all, what did it matter what

it was called?' In other words, Fascists and their colonial adventures were sissies. Crompton naturally denied attempting to mould her readers, but she certainly seems to have done her bit in this instance.[45]

Arabs were ambiguous. Were they white or not? The prime villain who sells Smithy and the Famous Five into Congo slavery is 'half German and half-Arab, though he calls himself a white man' (according to the Bounder's father): his death at heroic black hands is intended to win universal applause, and saves all the Greyfriars boys.[46] The pattern of Arabs as 'sinister, treacherous' is negated in the first instance by the Famous Five taking a young sheikh, Ali ben Yusef, to their hearts (August–October 1924) so that he also is bonded unshakeably with them. They do find a treacherous Arab guide who tries to murder them, but Bob Cherry saves him from a lion; therefore he uses tracking skills to save Bob at all costs when an avenging Arab enemy ties him to a camel and forces him on a Mazeppa-ride[47] in the Sahara. Equally, Harry Wharton had previously refrained from killing Ibrahim when he was found to have poisoned their coffee. It is precisely the point on which *The Lord of the Rings* would later turn, Gollum saving Frodo from himself when he becomes enslaved to the Ring after Frodo has spared Gollum's life when his homicidal malice had forfeited it. Tolkien worked on the instruction in the Lord's Prayer 'Forgive us our trespasses as we forgive those who trespass against us', but the silently religious Richards seems to have acted on the same text.[48] It is pointedly clear that it is at variance with the philosophy of vengeance animating all Arabs in the story, friend, foe or mixture. But, in other respects, Arab characters are as varied as those of the boys in Richards's schools. The cult of T. E. Lawrence after the First World War romanticised young Arab sheiks and boys and the Rudolph Valentino movie of 1922, *The Sheik*, had its impact on the *Magnet*. On the other hand, a severe critic of Lawrence who knew and disliked him in his RAF days, W. E. Johns, had his own desert background, as did Charles Gilson. Gilson in general valorised Arabs, to starry heights when they were on the British side in the Second World War. Johns was less sympathetic, although he could make an Arab or an Egyptian a likeable partner for his heroes.[49]

If a historian's interrogations of inter-war authors for children on such questions as race – and class – are peculiarly justified in the light of the war and peace to follow, they are anachronistic. However much William might despise Hubert Lane for believing in fairies,[50] all children's literature had fairy origins. E. Nesbit may have been the most influential predecessor to overshadow Richards before the First World War, and she narrowed the gap between child characters and preternatural ones such as the Psammead and the Phoenix, more so than her intellectual ancestor Lewis Carroll. Carroll's Alice is a credible, memorable figure; in Nesbit's writings, to be memorable it is usually necessary to be mythical.[51] Her most prolific disciple before and during the Second World War, Enid Blyton, had some of the same problems: apart from her self-portrait in George of the 'Five' series, and clever development of the boy detective and his girl Watson, the boy animal-lover, the boy sailor, the boy waif and so on, her memorable characters were half-preternatural, such as Kiki the parrot, Timmy the dog, the Saucepan Man and (from 1949) Noddy.[52] We may regard Noddy as a degenerate figure; but, however deplorably, he remains in the line of descent from such characters as Bill the Lizard in *Alice*, whose identity reminds us that Noddy's genealogy would also include Kenneth Grahame's Toad and *his* degenerate offspring, A. A. Milne's Pooh and Piglet. Similarly, Kiki, while less formally rational, reworks convincingly some of Carroll's logic-become-nonsense, as well as the discourse of the Psammead and the Phoenix, where her lack of their magic is offset by her mockery of order (for example, the use of 'God Save the King' for satirical purposes to deflate loss, grief or fear).[53] The great folklorist Alan Bruford showed time and again the reappearance of the fairy-story, cunningly disguised, in popular culture. Many comic strips, even if formally dismissing fairies, made themselves dealers in magic and spells, in purely literary or iconic terms of course: such themes might try to legitimise their themes via science fiction, but then again they mightn't. But Bruford showed how activity innocent of magic intent played the old game. For example, the old folk-tale question from the cruel king, 'tell me tomorrow what I am thinking or I'll cut off your head' (answered by sending a substitute who says 'you think I'm X but I'm not'), is revived as a Pat-and-Mike identical-twins gag from a stand-up comedian (just possibly via the *Eagle* comic's and BBC Radio's PC 49 in the early 1950s). The old Gaelic story of the misanthropic Conán Maol, whose backside sticks to the floor in an enchantment, Bruford points out is retained in stories in comic strips (and in the *Magnet*), where someone who deserves it finds themselves sitting in glue.[54] Orwell was really in favour of that kind of comic-strip material, and in fact praised Mickey Mouse (also Charlie Chaplin, Popeye the Sailor and so on) as the little man standing up to the bully or misanthrope or giant or – clearly – Fascist;[55] and in this respect excellent training for the Second World War. Orwell also recognised the fairy-tale roots of this: the little man wins because of his good deeds despite his small power, but these may require a magic reward to give him victory.

The aeroplane, apparently the most modern of all devices available to the Second World War writer for children, was actually the strongest link to the fairy-tale heritage. Perseus with the winged shoes of Hermes flying to kill the Gorgon Medusa; Phrixus on the golden-fleeced flying ram thus saved from being sacrificed; Bellerophon on Pegasus killing the Chimera; Dedalus escaping from Crete on the wings he had made – all seemed more real when flying-machines began to fill the sky. So too did their frequent darker sides: Phrixus's sister Helle falling into the Hellespont; Dedalus's son Icarus flying too near the sun and melting the wax of *his* wings. Some of the children who first read Nesbit's *The Phoenix and the [magic] Carpet* (1904) must have known that, in the December preceding its publication, the first aeroplane had been flown by Orville and Wilbur Wright. By 1910, the readers of *Little Folks* were able to choose between fairy flights with Agnes Grozier Herbertson and *Round the World in an Aeroplane* with Olaf Baker (who by 1914 was writing 'a Tale of 2000' in which '*We were rapidly approaching the appalling height of Fifteen Thousand Feet!*').[56] By the eve of the Second World War, the children who had been reading about flights in Blyton's *Adventures of the Wishing Chair* (1937) might graduate to Bob Cherry's desperate rescue of Wun Lung and his aged uncle from a plane-crash, and so to Biggles in its publishers' *Modern Boy*, *Biggles Flies West* being on offer the same year. This last was exceptionally derivative of traditional children's literature, albeit pirate rather than fairy, since it drew too obviously on Stevenson's *Treasure Island*: Johns could never have equalled Long John Silver, but his villains in this book were among the weakest he drew, clearly doomed by inferiority complex. But Johns's real magic was the air, which he connected perfectly the next year when *Modern Boy* serialised *The Rescue Flight*, about two schoolboys running away to the First World War where they fly with Biggles.[57] Yet Blyton's wishing chair, only airborne when it grows wings, offered a more real base for take-off being closer to the known world. It took the Second World War to make aircraft almost domestic, as boys collected pieces of crashed planes, relatives entered the RAF to serve at home even more than overseas, and the still semi-mythical idea of man in the air might result in the reader's death without moving from her or his book.[58]

Time-travel was another matter. The Orwell–Richards debate

turned on it. 'The year is 1910 – or 1940, but it is all the same', Orwell defined for the 'mental world of the *Gem* and the *Magnet*'. 'His most serious charge against my series', noted Richards,

> is that it smacks of the year 1910: a period which Mr Orwell appears to hold in peculiar horror. Probably I am older than Mr Orwell: and I can tell him that the world went very well then. It has not been improved by the Great War, the General Strike, the out-break of sex-chatter, by make-up or lipstick, by the present discontents, or by Mr Orwell's thoughts upon the present discontents!

The last was apparently gentle fogeyism; it was in fact blazing pride driving in its first palpable hit. For all of Orwell's Socialist dogmatism and Richards's *panache* of conservatism, the rapiers were here firmly exchanged: the Old Etonian Orwell was dismissing the Amalgamated Press scribe or scribes as derivative hacks writing stories 'fantastically unlike life at a real public school' – and Richards, from a poorer background without a public-school education, threw in the common shortened title of Edmund Burke's essay of 1770[59] as a contemptuous rejoinder to the opponent who intellectually undervalued him. He went on to answer the charge of plagiarism by flaunting cultural debts to great literature far beyond the limits by which Orwell had bound himself. Orwell charged Richards with snobbery: Richards, without bothering to spell out his most respectful portrait as that of the factory boy Mark Linley, and his most unrelieved blackguard as the nauseatingly aristocratic Cecil Ponsonby, largely amused himself with trivial fencing. But his defence clearly meant that his opponent's arguments had shown up Orwell as the greater snob, whose charges concealed his own lack of literary range ('Mr Orwell, is so very modern, that I cannot suspect him of having read anything so out of date as Chaucer . . . Has Mr Orwell never read "Alice"? . . . as Dryden – an obsolete poet, Mr Orwell – has remarked'). And the *coup de grâce* at the end was the Richards version of class:[60]

> a man can believe that the 'tenth possessor of a foolish face' has certain qualities lacking in the first possessor of a sly brain, without being a snob. I am very pleased to be an author, and I think I would rather be an author than a nobleman; but I am not fool enough to think that an author is of such national importance as a farmer or a farm labourer. Workmen can, and often do, get on

quite well without authors; but no author could continue to exist without workmen. They are not only the backbone of the nation: they *are* the nation: all other classes being merely trimmings.

To this out-Marxing Marx, he added the economic argument that his paper could never ridicule or demonise the working class since his readers came from there, as they must for every paper apart from, say, *Horizon* ('I have often wondered how so many young men with expansive foreheads and superior smiles contrive to live at all on bad prose and worse poetry').

Orwell in fact took the argument for the papers as plagiarism of the archaic rather farther than 1910: 'All literature of this kind is partly plagiarism . . . without doubt the main origin of these papers is *Stalky & Co.*' So did Richards, who (concealing initial minor points of obligation to *Stalky*) enjoyed making intellectual mincemeat of Orwell's arguments by vocabulary and by showing the antiquity of names and expressions supposedly coined in Kipling's autobiographical school story. But where Richards really demolished this argument was in turning it against Orwell:[61]

what I dislike most is Mr Orwell telling me that I am out of date. Human nature, Mr Orwell, is dateless. A character that lives is always up to date. If, as Mr Orwell himself says, a boy in 1940 can identify himself with a boy in *The Magnet*, obviously that boy in *The Magnet* is a boy of 1940. . . . The oldest flying story I have read was written in Greek about three thousand years ago; but I don't suppose it was the earliest: I have no doubt that when they finish sorting over the Babylonian bricks they will find a flying story somewhere among the ruins, and very likely a death-ray and an invisible man keeping it company. If this stuff is new, Mr Orwell, what is old?

Tradition meant the reader's being confronted by old friends in new clothes. So far from its being plagiarism, most writers would want their intellectual forebears remembered.[62] Not all of the books deemed appropriate for boys and girls by L. M. Alcott, Lewis Carroll, Mark Twain, Captain Marryat, R. M. Ballantyne, W. H. G. Kingston, Susan Coolidge, James Fenimore Cooper and R. L. Stevenson were available in 1939, still less during the war with its dwindling stocks, bombed warehouses and restricted paper; but, when the war was over, they roared back into availability, clearly indicating that the demand was firm even when the famine was fiercest. What Orwell had diagnosed as the survival and self-perpetuation of the values of 1910 was more invocation than ineptitude. Stevenson himself was almost openly vague in the supposed dating of *Treasure Island*'s events: it will be an exceptionally alert young historian who deduces which King George Jim Hawkins annoys pirates by calling on God to save (George II, but conclusively so only from Dr Livesey's having served at Fontenoy). In twentieth-century stories, it became more deliberately opaque. Despite Orwell's mockery, the *Gem* and *Magnet* stories are carefully set in the year, and month, of their appearance. But, when the schoolboys embark on travel outside Europe, the clock whizzes back for decades. South Seas narratives occupy common time and space with Conrad, perhaps even with Melville. So does their stablemate as serial, *Biggles in the South Seas*, not published as a book until the Second World War had broken out. Shell-Breaker and Full Moon, its adorable Polynesian boy and girl, could have walked (or at least swum) from the pages of Melville's *Typee*.[63] Richards's King of the Islands, and his Rio Kid of Texas, while zealously to the rescue of Greyfriars boys in 1938, are natural figures from late nineteenth-century fiction (if too clean for late nineteenth-century fact). In clear homage to *Treasure Island*, Richards in 1927 succeeded where Johns was to fail, producing a credible modern version of Long John Silver – the pirate hidden in the sea-cook became the sea-lawyer concealed in the millionaire's valet, until the moment when Soames threw off his disguise to blackmail the treasure map from Tom Redwing as the price of the life of Herbert Vernon-Smith. The servant with his own agenda is an old device: Richards made it his. It might be found in Beaumarchais's Figaro, in Barrie's Crichton, in Wodehouse's Jeeves; and, by reworking them for the *Magnet*, Richards was less anachronistic than custodial of the past, to anticipate the future. And, when the Second World War had begun, Soames is brought back to save the lives of Bunter and the Famous Five during an air raid, having previously menaced them yet again to further his latest crookery:[64]

Wharton was listening, with a beating heart.

'If that's a Hun –' he breathed.

'That', came Soames' icy voice, 'is a Heinkel bomber. If the light was still on, Master Wharton, the ruins of this building would be our tomb.'

'Thank Heaven we were in time!'

Soames stood beside him – a shadow in the gloom. His face was tilted up – he watched the sky with icy coolness. . . .

Wharton dragged him towards the doorway
'Quick!' he panted. 'The next may –'
'Oh, quite!' drawled Soames. He stepped aside at the little doorway, in his half-mocking, deferential manner. 'You first, sir – I trust I know my place!'

That was partly to ensure that he himself would have a rapid exit from the bomb-shelter. This, too, was a salute to Stevenson's Silver making his end-of-story escape from his new but transient allies, Jim Hawkins and his friends. In the *Magnet* for 24 September 1927, Soames, trying to get the treasure from Redwing, reminisces about Redwing's uncle who had willed it to him, 'Black Peter as I remember him . . . the blackest scoundrel that ever sailed the Pacific': it links the testator to Stevenson's deceased pirates Flint and Billy Bones. But his name comes from Conan Doyle's eponymous Sherlock Holmes 1904 story, concerning a modern pirate whose ill-gotten gains bring his own death after torturing his family when in sadistic retirement.[65] And just as Conan Doyle, when a recent author of several remarkably brutal historical pirate stories, drew the theme into his own times, Richards in early 1940 used Soames to bridge his 1927 landfall in pirate country with the recruitment of even a modern Long John Silver against the Nazis:

'Listen!' muttered the spy. 'You are a rogue – a rascal – on your own confession. All I carry shall be yours – and twice as much if I go free.'
Harry Wharton caught his breath.
Soames shook his head gently.
'Even a rogue may have his limit!' he said. 'I may be no credit to the country to which I belong, Herr Braun – little more, perhaps, than you are to yours! Yet there is something in the call of one's country that stirs even a rogue like myself! Now –'
He did not finish the sentence. The desperate man before him tore at the revolver in his pocket – and Soames fired on the instant.
'You asked for it, mein herr!' said Soames grimly.
The man from the Gestapo, with a groan, sank to the floor.

The moral comparison was plain: a crook, thief, murderer still considered himself less of a disgrace to Britain than Germany was disgraced by its Nazis. Any schoolboy could read that meaning, and sympathise with its logic. Many would know the Stevensonian origin. But fewer would see the salutation to sea stories of a century before, when Soames introduces himself to the spy: 'My name is Soames – but it might be Ishmael, for my hand is against every man, and every man's hand is against me.'

As usual, Richards was putting down markers for his young readers to recall when they graduated to the classics, in this case the opening of Herman Melville's *Moby-Dick*.[66]

Naturally, Richards, here as elsewhere, observed the rule that in a story for children, children must prove themselves superior to adults (or at least satisfactory substitutes) most of the time – if possible morally, in any case practically. Soames might rescue Harry Wharton from the Nazi, as here, but readers knew their Wharton would not lightly accept adult usurpation of his leadership. He might be right or wrong in this, in specific stories. Sometimes Wharton – and even more, Richmal Crompton's William – might be declared wrong by his author; but stories sometimes – not always – worked out for the best because of his defiance of the deference to adults he should show. The author for children is entitled to any morality it wants and can justify, but to succeed it must show it is covertly or openly on the child's side. Even a tale of a bad child getting its deserts must cater to the self-respect of children, the bad child being shown adverse to children's needs (Blyton, for instance, seldom let a story of a bad child become mere adult propaganda: her memory of adult treachery in her childhood stood her in good stead).[67] The hero child is very old and was obviously a natural resource for storytellers wanting to please children, especially at bedtime, from the earliest stages of human speech. David killing Goliath is the obvious Biblical example. There were problems about encouraging child self-assertion in wartime, when blind obedience might be a necessity and (much more often) was stated to be. Apart from all else, young soldiers still reading children's fiction might be ill-advised to develop too much initiative in response. So, in *Biggles & Co.* (1936), Ginger could save Biggles's life by flagrantly disobeying his orders not to follow him on the flight to negotiate with Algy's kidnappers, but in *Biggles Sweeps the Desert* (1942) he has to be severely reprimanded for disobeying orders and shown how it nearly brought about his own death. All the same, if he had not got lost in the desert, Biggles would not have gone in search of him so that they both found where the Nazi base was. J. K. Rowling salutes the convention with gentle satire by having Harry Potter and his friends fiercely enjoined not to break some regulation; and, when the taboo has been violated, the authorities seem to take it for granted that it clearly would have been, boys (and girls) being boys (and girls) or wizards or heroes. J. K. Stephen in 1891 testified to the antiquity of the convention by yearning for the day

> [When] a boy's egregious blunder
> Will *not* bring success to pass . . .

The implication, especially in pre-Christian cultures, that the child hero is a *predestined* hero (Heracles, David, Cú Chulainn, Siegfried, Arthur, Romulus) links the convention to time-travel in its most straightforward form. All fiction for children is time, travel in that, consciously or otherwise, the author is writing for children of one time while remembering itself at another time (Richards in 1940 would be still shadowed by Richards – still Hamilton – in 1890 when he was 16 and had his tragic break with the boy on whom he based Harry Wharton, never mind about 1910). Yet, whether in memoir or in fictional creation, the author is time-travelling, not just coldly studying some other entity, separate as that other entity – the child who will become the author – might in reality want to be. Max Beerbohm's cartoon series of many contemporaries in which 'The Old Self' is suddenly and dismayingly confronted by 'The Young Self' captures the chasms between them.

Time played its most obvious part in preparing British children for the Second World War where revival of the First World War in one form or another was concerned. First of all, there were the veterans, if not of combat (and several Second World War writers for children had seen First World War combat), then at least of creativity. By 1918 Dorita Fairlie Bruce, Violet M. Methley, Elsie J. Oxenham, Angela Brazil, Bessie Marchant, Christine Chaundler, Ethel Talbot, Doris A. Pocock, Agnes M. Miall, Percy F. Westerman, Gunby Hadath, Charles Gilson and Frank Richards were seasoned writers of books or at least magazine stories under their own or other names, some for more than a decade. This made for very different senses of the First World War among them. Richards in retrospect became rapidly disillusioned with politicians' posturings and promises, to the extent that the Greyfriars Officer Training Corps disappeared, as Orwell noted (forgetting that it had been a prominent feature). Percy F. Westerman, by contrast, had the officers of a destroyer remark to one another just after participating in the sinking of the *Bismarck* (27 May 1941):

'there are facts about the last war that should not be allowed to sink into oblivion. That's where we as a nation made a great mistake. Instead of Peace Pledge Unions and other probably well-meaning but crank-controlled parties, one-sided disarmament and all that sort of thing, we should have kept a strong Navy and Air Force. If we had, my lad, we shouldn't be limping home, practically easy meat for the first U-boat or bomber that comes our way. And remember again, Germany, a signatory to the Treaty of Versailles, was, under its terms, forbidden to possess either warplanes or submarines.'

'Yet there were people at home who agreed with the Germans that the terms were harsh and unjust.'

'Exactly; but what would be Hitler's terms supposing he did win this war? What terms did he give to those countries he's overrun?'

This, from a lifelong Portsmouth-and-Poole resident active in navy support work, probably reflected local (and retired) naval officer chit-chat, however vulnerable to Johns's wartime comment:[68]

'Are you suggesting', inquired Biggles icily, 'that we arrange our code of behaviour by what a Nazi would do?'

Writers whose First World War memories were from their pre-publication lives might take a cooler attitude to the Second World War than old sweats at the same stand for a third of a century. Perhaps Benjamin Gwillim Aston, the Glasgow Academy schoolmaster who wrote his eleven school stories as Jeffrey Havilton, gave the most considered reflection on the First World War to appear in a story for children in the Second World War:[69]

The fact of war should perhaps have overpowered all the petty interests of schoolboys. Certainly they themselves had thought it would; games and books and school societies and private hobbies would be flat and tame; you would be conscious all the time that the real thing was going on outside in the world, and it would seem babyish and somehow a kind of blasphemy to enjoy a game of rugger. . . . Your father had told you of the great surging crowds in London in 1914, the queues at the recruiting offices, the thrill of being commissioned, the greater thrill of action. He hadn't, per-haps, told you of the disillusion that followed the enthusiasm as bitter month followed bitter month. . . . Father had fought in the last war; it was a man's job to fight when the right time came. Nothing else would matter but the war.

But when the business started it was amazingly different from what you had expected. There were no singing crowds, there were no recruiting offices, there was no enthusiasm. . . . But there was something finer; the solid unity of men and women in agreement on a duty which was not to be shirked. Nobody at all thought that war was a fine adventure; but everybody knew grimly that it would not be scamped for that. Father had done this job once, and he could be pardoned for feeling bitter that it had all to be done again; but he was willing to help in the doing of it.

It was a queer war. No enthusiasm and, for a time, no war. . . . It was rather like shutting your eyes and jumping over a precipice only to find that the drop was two feet.

Havilton was writing at the end of the 'phoney war' about the mood of its beginning. He continued to write the other four-fifths of his story, *School versus Spy* (1940), and, when he finished it, entered the army (as Aston) and served for the duration of the war. As Aston, he retired from his school at 65 in 1967 and died in 1991, not having written another school story in fifty years. He was writing after Orwell's 'Boys' Weeklies' and probably after Richards's reply; more decisively than either of them, he had written the epitaph for an era.[70]

The contrast would express itself readily and well in the stories written for British children in each World War. The First World War was close enough to the nineteenth century to retain the touch of *Kindertötenlieder*, the wallowing lamentation for dead infants from Dickens's Little Nell in *The Old Curiosity Shop* to Harriet Beecher Stowe's Little Eva in *Uncle Tom's Cabin*. It might be an author's therapy – Stowe had lost a child before starting her novel – but in any event Dickens was by then supplying what American publishers would thereby make standard requirements. Even the early *Magnet* fell back on it. The convention hardly survived the First World War (its first really notable use later is in the hard realism of Susan Cooper's retrospective novel of the Second World War, *Dawn of Fear* (1970), utterly free from the pre-war mawkishness).[71] But, in December 1914, C. Priscilla Raydon was drenching readers of *Little Folks* with 'For England's Sake', in which crippled little Jennifer throws herself in front of a German officer's gun so that her French cousin can alert French troops to cut down the invaders (disguised as 'British soldier-men'). And afterwards,

> French and English they gathered round,
> In a dim-eyed silence no man could break,
> Honouring her with a last salute –
> A little maid dead for England's sake.

The symbolism here was as artful as the verse, whatever the quality of the artistry. Jennifer's parents are dead of unexplained causes (in England), requiring her adoption by 'the big French uncle with mother's smile'. *Little Folks* in the First World War had plenty of stories whose readers were expected to identify with heroic French and Belgian children, and indeed dogs, who disclose the enemy, open the dykes, and fetch the Red Cross, respectively – thus greatly differing from Second World War reading matter whose British readers were usually left to identify with their fellow-nationals only, first by isolationism, then by isolation. But little Jennifer must assert both her kinship with the French in living and her Englishness in dying – to die for the French in December 1914 was to die for the British. Whether the hero children were British or French, they were much closer to the firing-line in the First World War: W. E. Johns's 'Cub' Peters, caught up in the French resistance after fruitlessly trying to rescue his father at Dunkirk, is a rarity for the Second World War, whose drifting children on the continent in other authors' hands are refugees and fugitives. Schoolchildren finding spies on the staff was another matter – this echoed the First World War stories of sinister German governesses, to which James Hilton had made an elegant reply in the 1930s in a school story for adults partly set in World War I:[72]

> 'Those few of you who were here before the War will remember Max Staefel, the German master. He was in Germany, visiting his home, when war broke out. He was popular while he was here, and made many friends. Those who knew him will be sorry to hear that he was killed last week, on the Western Front.'
>
> He was a little pale when he sat down afterwards, aware that he had done something unusual. He had consulted nobody about it, anyhow; no one else could be blamed. Later, outside the chapel, he heard an argument:
>
> 'On the Western Front, Chips said. Does he mean that he was fighting for the Germans?'
>
> 'I suppose it does.'
>
> 'Seems funny, then, to read his name out with all the others. After all, he was an *enemy*.'
>
> 'Oh, just one of Chips's ideas, I expect. The old boy still has 'em.'
>
> Chips, in his room again, was not displeased by the comment. Yes, he still had 'em – those ideas of dignity and generosity that were becoming increasingly rare in a frantic world.

But they were not entirely absent from children's literature even in the height of War Fever in 1914. If *Little Folks* had plenty of German officers as zealous to shoot children as (in the *Magnet*) the Bounder, Peter Todd and Harry Wharton find, Lilian Gask's 'A Hero of the Marne' shows the dog hero's master Pierre pushing a water-flask into the hand of a German even more badly wounded than himself; and yet another German, 'human wolf, gaunt with fear and hunger . . . craving for vengeance as for food' and about to kill Pierre, sees the empty French water-flask in the dead German's hand and puts back his sword. Understandably, such charity was as rare as realism. By October 1915, John Clendennan's fictional sea scouts were saving British cruisers from destruction by getting themselves picked up by German submarines whose 'torpedo-man' is 'leaped upon' by our hero ('I think I struck him on the head with my fist first and then clung about his body'). Although Percy F. Westerman in the First World War shared some of the Sinbad seamanship on offer here, it contrasts profoundly with the grim realities dominating his *Sea Scouts at Dunkirk* (1941), whose boys do not die, but where they are likely to have been wounded, they are wounded.[73]

Eileen Colwell's review of Enid Blyton's *The Sea of Adventure* in the *School Librarian* (July 1948) became famous for its attempted witticism: 'But what hope has a band of desperate men against four children?' So few of Blyton's critics showed signs of having read her that the remark won its celebrity as the work of one who apparently had; but the case was badly chosen, in that the four children end the story with but half-victory, their failures partly due to their own mistakes. In any case, a comparison between Blytonian intrepid infants and the First World War child heroes of children's fiction leaves her firmly on the side of realism, death excepted. There was also more humour in *The Sea of Adventure*, when the children set out for their confrontation of the enemy destined to elicit such mixed results:[74]

> 'Well, good luck to us all!' said Dinah. 'May we rescue Bill – and Horace too – defeat the enemy – and get back home in safety!'
> 'God save the King', said Kiki devoutly, in exactly the same tone of voice, and everyone laughed.

The reassurance of the parrot's prayer would have been taboo in the First World War, sinning as it did against divinity and monarchy alike (not that Blyton had the slightest known objection to either). The *Sea of Adventure*'s crooks are gun-runners, another emblem of

Blyton's hatred of war; and few Second World War fictional children saw so many guns, while counterparts in the First World War were frequently one jump from cannon-fodder. Flora Sidney Woolf captured the fairy-tale horror of a battlefield discovered by a small Belgian girl:[75]

> The sky was like a dark giant in a passion, intermittently flushing an angry red. Out of his mouth came a cruel roar. In the flashes Marie saw figures moving and running here and there in a confused mass, as if they were trying in vain to escape him.

Schoolgirls seem to have been more prevalent choices for death-defying fictional visits to stricken fields than the boys from whom Northcliffe withdrew authorisation. Child fiction with any adult consumption needed to use the propaganda possibilities of martyrdom. A war which had made so much of German atrocities in Belgium used literature of girl danger much more successfully than that of brave boys blasting off bombs. The child hero must not be superhero: even if male, vulnerability was all. Some of these stories might be reprinted in the neutral USA before April 1917. Children themselves took such points. When F. Knowles Campling, the former editor of Little Folks, writing a series (as Eric Wood) 'Six Brave Deeds of the War', inspired a competition directed by his successor Herbert D. Williams, child choices plumped heavily for Campling's girl heroes rather than his men – the French serving-maid who hid and fed ten British soldiers in the convent in which the Germans had quartered themselves, and the two Belgian telephone operators who kept the lines from Louvain open in the early days of German invasion. These were identifications cutting across conventions of class, country and (evidently for some readers) gender. Dorothea Moore replayed the old 'Not really a Coward' theme for a story of a little Belgian refugee, in which the British girls ultimately prove inferior, not simply equal, in courage and humanity to their hitherto despised ally and visitor.[76]

Little as graphic happens in stories for children written in the Second World War: various writers (Elinor Mordaunt, Elisabeth Kyle, I. A. Shead, M. Frow, Kitty Barne) pictured homes after being bombed, and Richmal Crompton sardonically described expectations of being bombed, but the process of being bombed was too close to many readers' experience to encourage reproduction. Gunby Hadath would be one of the few to pursue it, in the school story whose title ages with painful anachronism, Grim and Gay (1942):[77]

One of the August bombs had gone crashing through the roof of the Old Library, which, replaced just before the war started by the more spacious new one at the corner between Terry's House and the Armoury, had already been ear-marked for demolition. Accordingly, it was decent of Hitler, the School said, as soon as it returned for the September term, to save them the cost and trouble of breaking it up.

. . . when these early birds discovered as well a crater or two in the middle of the cricket ground, they said, 'sold again, Adolph, you ought to have gone for the rugger ground. For in England, you twerp, we don't play cricket in winter!'

The appropriate place for such stiff upper lip was obviously the sexagenarian *Boy's Own Paper*, where it was serialised from October 1941 before book publication: the opening salvo gave fair warning of the exceptional mayhem to follow. The *BOP* had sworn its own continuance despite paper shortage, size truncation, blitz and so on, and it was only fair that as one of the few surviving serial outlets it had heady stuff from which to continue in its next. But, even in child fiction with adult characters, Second World War writers preferred combat bombardment. The boy (or girl) who wanted blitz would find in John Buchan's *Mr Standfast* (1919) the most dramatic use of an air raid – although its most obvious disciple in the Second World War was firmly classifiable as adult fiction, Graham Greene's *The Ministry of Fear* (1943), whose hero had murdered his wife. Even Hadath's jests-while-the-old-school-is-bombed had its First World War origin:[78]

'I suppose you haven't forgotten that a Zeppelin flew over the place, and dropped a bomb on us?'
    'Well, it only blew up the gym', said Potter. 'Those blessed Huns can't drop bombs for toffee . . .'

First World War stories during its course certainly reshaped vocabulary. Its usages ensured that thirty years later, William would 'do his bit', Biggles would 'see it through' and Worrals would 'carry on'. The Second World War was perhaps rather less self-conscious in the laughter it needed and provided, its writing more self-dependent, its manner less corporate. But some themes vanished. John Clendennan, he of the superboy sea scouts, had also shown peacetime interests in ambiguity of loyalties in stories of Amerindian–white hostility, with marginal figures flitting between both cultures: 'In

Spite of War' (*Little Folks*, January 1916) was a touching Christmas tale of the love of an English and a German boy, surviving the ostracism of the German child in contemporary England. The most that the Second World War would make of such conventions would be in unhappiness in Brent-Dyer at internment camps into which anti-Nazi refugees were thrown. Equally, First World War stories frequently exempted German air pilots from the habitual charges of treachery and brutality hurled against the 'Uhlans', Prussians and Kaiserlics in general. Johns tried to retain a little of this in the duel between Biggles and von Zoyton in *Biggles Sweeps the Desert* (and some of his former descriptions of First World War dogfights with it), but both there and elsewhere the horror of Nazism made the spirit very hard to sustain.

Nor did the Second World War echo the disillusion setting into the most orthodox fictional channels by the end of the First World War. Mary Cadogan and Patricia Craig point out that by August 1916 Richards (as Martin Clifford) was already allowing some barbed comment from his heroes in the *Gem*:[79]

> [*Arthur Augustus D'Arcy*:] 'the wah has been dwaggin' on long enough . . . our gweat statesmen are so busy lookin' aftah their jobs and their salawies that they haven't weally time for we-flection.'
>
> [*Tom Merry*:] 'the war is a permanent institution. Under the new law, we're going to be conscripted when we grow up, and then we shall have to take our turn in the trenches. We've got to keep ourselves fit, or we shan't be allowed to go out and get killed'.
>
> [*another junior*:] 'all countries will be governed by the same kind of silly idiots in the future as in the past, so there will always be another war, on and off.'

If the boy Blair, later Orwell, was still reading the *Gem* by that point, this might have lodged in his cranium to inspire the theme of perpetual war for perpetual peace in *1984*. By September 1918, the editor of *Little Folks* was toying with the same subversive ideas in his own column 'The Editor's Den', foreseeing the First World War still happening in 1968. The Second World War might ultimately get bored with its own fighting, in some domestic British eyes, but its children's fiction never gets cynical about the war. The phoney war acted as counterpart to the disillusion of 1918, and the emotion in both periods was one of grim waiting made tolerable by gaiety of mockery, rather than any general wish to capitulate.

To Enid Blyton, 1939 gave means to gather her forces. In 1937, Blyton had taken her first substantial steps in serial creative writing by starting her *Sunny Stories*, published by her husband's employers, George Newnes, as a weekly begun on 15 January 1937 (paper supplies cut it down to fortnightly after 27 March 1942, a compromise made by several publishers whose interest in their weeklies was greater than that of Lord Camrose). Fairies were not necessarily escapist in her columns: she preached conventional morality for children, frequently by stories in which good fairies or bad intervened either through justice or self-interest to make some child's crimes fit an appropriate punishment. A child not wanting to brush its hair agrees to its removal by a fairy seeking hair to make dolls, and is then upset at being (temporarily) bald. Here, the fairy agency is pointedly unethical; but other stories involve moral arbiters, notably Mr Pink-Whistle, half-human, half-brownie and invisible at will. The parentage, however improbable, obviously derives from Greek divine procreation, as with Perseus, Heracles, Achilles and Aeneas: Blyton's years at work in 'retelling' old stories for Newnes gave her a strong classical base, from the fabulist Aesop above all. Strikingly independent of the short stories were successive serials, afterwards made books with no change. These began with the discovery of a wishing chair in an old shop by two children who quickly join forces with a pixie and visit magic lands when the chair sprouts its wings. This lasted for two-thirds of a year and was succeeded by a very different escapism: children, turned into drudges by ruthless guardian aunt and uncle, finding a secret island to which they escape under the guidance of a Huckleberry Finn figure. The drudge children are of middle-class origin, the ragged leader lower-class but firmly acknowledged as their 'Captain' – and adopted by their parents in their ultimate return *ex machina* (an aeroplane crashed on a much more inaccessible island). The convention of the lower-class leader was one to which Blyton returned, for Andy in *The Adventurous Four* (1940) and Barney in *The Rockingdown Mystery* (1949). It is in part homage to what would be a useful principle for evacuees in wartime, the value of Nature-wise locals. It acknowledges that Huckleberry Finn is actually a more admirable and more sympathetic figure than Tom Sawyer (although not necessarily the most reliable choice in civilised matters, such as criminal trials). Blyton seems exceptional in the deference due to her lower-class leaders: she derived much from Mark Twain, Louisa Alcott, Frances Hodgson Burnett and other (primarily) American sources, but none of them has the lower-class boy assuming permanent leadership over his more ignorant contemporary social betters.

April 1938 saw *Sunny Stories* begin Blyton's third serial, *Mr Galliano's Circus*, about a bourgeois English family (the Browns) which finds security and vocation in a circus led by a firm and likeable authority figure: a stage Italian whose peculiarities of English are intended to make readers laugh, though clearly with affection rather than ridicule. October 1938 produced *The Enchanted Wood*, whose unexpectedly ruralised children find a great tree on whose topmost branches temporarily rest magic lands, each with a new morality. May 1939 brought a fresh instalment of Mr Galliano's circus. October 1939 brought back the *Secret Island* children, now once more thrown largely on their own resources, this time to rescue the heir to a Ruritanian kingdom.[80]

March 1940 opened the serial whither all the predecessors had been leading, the natural expression of Blyton's Froebel-taught search for a new education: *The Naughtiest Girl in the School*, ostensibly the selfish spoiled child being led (rather than made) to come to terms with society, but more profoundly celebrating a society – Whyteleafe School – run by the children with money held in common and the lightest of adult supervision over the child-made order and discipline. The trend of the succession of serials was to prepare children for a world in which traditional forms of authority had broken down or been usurped or discarded. Even the supportive moralistic short stories or fables usually turned on judgement by peers (not always justified) or pixies or Pink-Whistle, to which parents when present are chiefly affirmations. It was in part a covert reassertion of religious discipline by positing preternatural or alien authority alongside or alternative to child authority – modern versions of guidance from angels, exemplification from saints (including sinners-turned-saints such as Paul of Tarsus, Patrick of Ireland or Augustine of Hippo), and church community from early Christian to post-Reformation Kirk. Blyton's politics were probably highly simplistic; but, if she had thought out a child psychological survival kit for security in a coming war, she could hardly have been more apposite. The arrival of the war itself and its accompaniment of child dispersal and exile naturally sharpened the urgency of her activity, and hence the message to protect the weak, civilise the wealthy and so on codified itself in the communism of Whyteleafe. That it also sidelined parents was all too appropriate for the war years.

But it was not timeless. The aeroplane played important roles in Blyton fiction from the first major non-magic book, *The Secret Island*, neatly accounting for the Cinderella condition of the children by their parents' somewhat manic air exploration, also destined to determine *The Secret Mountain* (1941). Blyton knew she was in the age of Biggles, and would use minor authority figures named Johns, stolid like the Captain. Air adventures came increasingly from Richards, Johns's stablemate in *Gem* and *Modern Boy*. Second World War fiction might – and frequently did – ignore the war, but few authors risked entrapment in a rapidly forgotten pre-war past. Arthur Ransome is the conspicuous exception: his aquatic *Swallows and Amazons* sailed through the war regardless of any interruption by outside events taking place after their first appearance in 1930. He really became a historical novelist, most notably in the pirate tales *Peter Duck* and *Missee Lee*, but more and more in the other books as well.[81] Yet an equally perennial formula, the horse opera, confronted its nemesis in the Second World War when a young publisher, saturated with the genre, recorded the Nazi conquest of an imaginary Channel Island, and her fictitious children learned to put their pony obsession into the perspective of human endurance: Mary Treadgold's *We Couldn't Leave Dinah* (1941). It harmonises with A. J. P. Taylor's signification of the Polish cavalry beginning Second World War. Treadgold was fed up with professionally reading 'a staggering number of manuscripts about Ponies and Pony Clubs', and worked on her alternative in an air-raid shelter while above her the Blitz on London began. The real Channel Islands which she had known as a girl were taken by Germany on 1 July 1940; and, while they supplied as much locale as she wanted for her make-believe Clerinel, their fall inspired her to confront British complacency with a metaphor for invasion potential (Clerinel is distanced from the real islands and is invaded later). She later described the book as 'a mixture of escape and wish-fulfilment', but admitted that[82]

> If anything extra got into the book – anything in the way of pity and courage that has never appeared in other more recent books that I have published – it was, I think, because it was written in a time when to be a Londoner was to look gladly out from the windows of a fortress and to find that along with everybody else one had for a little while become far-sighted.

That brief far-sight in her case meant a view of pre-war illusion almost tangible from the device of imaginary space for the recovery of time. The book itself seems to have been welcomed by its readers for its charm and honesty in telling them whence they had come to where they now were, and it is hard to see much escape for author or reader in it, or in the demand that forced its publisher Jonathan Cape to put out four editions in three paper-famined years in which their allotment for juvenile fiction was heavily husbanded for Arthur Ransome – whose appeal was escapist and nostalgic while also celebratory of the endangered Britain. The absurdity of the child obsessions is convincingly asserted from Treadgold's title onwards: they cannot leave the beloved, privileged pony, and are temporarily marooned in a Nazi-ruled former homeland. At the end of the story, some children escape – others do not, and may be doomed – and the lucky fugitives judge their pre-war selves:[83]

> 'Good-bye, Dinah, good-bye', called Caroline. She stood knee-deep in the heather with one hand shading her eyes, watching until Dinah's flying form disappeared between the hills.
>
> There had been no time to bid the romantic and tearful farewell to Dinah. But it didn't matter, thought Caroline, not feeling at all tearful. It didn't seem so bad leaving Dinah behind on the island this time. . . . Caroline blushed as she remembered her distress at leaving Clerinel. All that somehow seemed feeble and sentimental now, just like her feelings about Dinah.
>
> . . . Funny, even that last ride over the hills with Dinah was already beginning to seem like a dream.

Of course the reader acquiesced in this, perhaps with more thought of those left to face the Nazis: Caroline has learnt much, but her imagination remains fortunately limited, and it was for child readers to make the most of theirs. The reader no doubt felt fonder of Dinah at the end than at the beginning, where her fetish status was intended to irritate; but the reader knew s/he also would have to leave Dinah. (And, in retrospect, Taylor would confirm that Tread-gold's perception of the Channel Islands as a parable was 'not encouraging' in the real-life subsequent history.)

Blyton's apprenticeship in American Black folklore gave her access to the Brer Rabbit stories and the ground they held in common with fairy and human actors, and she also strengthened her child readers challenged by transplantation to rural landscapes when their eyes fell on her *Birds of Our Gardens* (1940), *Enid Blyton's Book of the Year* (1941), *Shadow the Sheep-dog* and *The Children of Willow Farm* (1942) and so on. But, in 1908, Kenneth Grahame's *The Wind in the Willows* had reached a peak to which all future workers in the anthropomorphic could only partly ascend in reverential wonder as they reached their own limits – A. A. Milne, Blyton, Alison Uttley, even the poet of countryside and sea, John Masefield. W. W. Robson argued for a professional proficiency in Grahame beyond the rest:

> The characters belong to the timeless ideal world of children, freed from adult cares and responsibilities. Yet they have the independence of adults. The indispensable ingredient of 'messing about in boats', and the whole River Bank way of life, is freedom. The Wind in the Willows is an artistic expression of the human longing to 'have it both ways', to break down the antithesis of the Grecian Urn, to take the coldness out of the 'cold pastoral'.

The children's world before 1940 needed such solutions, however much the actual children in the Second World War may have had ugly occasion to learn more.[84]

The Wind in the Willows conquered Time, and Mole, Rat, Badger and Toad survived to make radio-listening children brave against Hitler and proud of the River Bank they themselves were defending. But Time was under attack in another way from the British pre-war writers for children. Alison Uttley had told humanised animal stories of Brock the Badger and the Four Pigs, of Little Grey Rabbit, Squirrel and Hare. When war came, she even allowed appropriate metaphor to enter into these series. She built on the wartime appositeness of The Wind in the Willows having culminated in the liberation of Toad Hall by Badger, Rat, Mole, Toad and Otter, who defeat the invaders occupying it. (Wireless must have made that a highly inspiring climax, bringing real hope to wartime child listeners.) Uttley's story 'The Boat' first appeared in October 1940. Sam Pig is given a boat built by Brock the Badger; it is then stolen and occupied by the Fox. He uses it to seize and kill fowl and rabbits who think Sam still controls it. Sam has to call in the otters to sink the once-loved boat. This could be easily analogised to Axis seizure of British craft and their subsequent destruction, not to speak of Axis possession of innocent European countries requiring possible punitive raids, or subversion from local resistance. Even more explicit, both in derivation from The Wind in the Willows and in relevance to the conflict at hand, was Uttley's Hare Joins the Home Guard (1942). An army of weasels menaces Little Grey Rabbit's home. Initially factionalism and incompetence, conceit and disunion endanger them (much as Sam's and Brock's over-confidence lost their boat to the Fox). But, as in the Battle of Britain, salvation comes from the air, and Wise Owl carries off 'the big Weasel in the front of the army'. Once war was on, Uttley rallied her standard anthropomorphs in countryside dear to her. Although Grahame's River Bank is evidently on the Thames, Uttley's scenes are set in her childhood paradise, central Derbyshire, with the river presumably the Derby Derwent.[85] That her war was spent in Beaconsfield, Buckinghamshire, thrusting her into irritated proximity with Enid Blyton, strengthened her yearning for her lost land all the more, just as Blyton herself, sealed off from seaside holidays at Swanage by its mined beaches, reconquered her former stamping-ground on the Dorset coast for *Five on a Treasure Island* (1942), psychologically *her* most emotive book. Uttley's masterpiece, written on the eve of war, luxuriated in the Derbyshire of Matlock, Crich and the ruined Wingfield Manor, where Mary Queen of Scots had been held more than once as her cousin Elizabeth I's prisoner between 1568 and 1587. *A Traveller in Time* can join Blyton's yearning for Dorset, Malcolm Saville's children's discovery of Shropshire, Brent-Dyer's happiness on the Welsh borders of Herefordshire (whither came the refugee Chalet School), Percy F. Westerman's lifetime in Portsmouth, Poole, Wareham and the seas beyond, Richards's beloved Kent coast from whose real and imaginary delights he was driven into wartime exile, Ransome's various water-wonderlands from Cumbria to East Anglia, and the strange mixture of her childhood Lancashire home and her present North Kent domicile into which Richmal Crompton stirred William and his village. Explicit or not, these were the places for love of which they rallied their child forces in the war. Is it coincidence that the most distinguished – and courageous – pacifist to emerge as a writer for children during the war, the Rev. W. Awdry of Tank Engine Thomas celebrity, should have invented the country through which his railway engines made their rural and romantic way? Johns's country was of course the air; and the ground terrain for which his poetic vision wept in the Second World War was martyred and enslaved France.[86]

André Maurois was perhaps the greatest literary friend the British and Irish (when united) had had in early twentieth-century France. Born in 1885 as Émile Herzog into a family of Alsatian Jews now settled in Normandy, he was a liaison officer with the British army in the First World War, resulting in the deeply affectionate *Les Silences du Colonel Bramble* (1918) and *Les Discours du Docteur O'Grady* (1920). The 1920s saw his biographies of Shelley (*Ariel*, later in translation (1936) the first Penguin book ever published), of Disraeli, of Byron; 1937 produced his history of England. But, like many another writer, Maurois felt increasing retrospective doubts about the World War he had known, and in 1930 he produced a story for children, *Patapoufs et filifers*, which in fact was a pacifist fable. Two brothers, one fat, one thin, supposedly based on Maurois's sons, find their way to *Les Empires de Sous-Sol*, where two deeply contrasting peoples dwell far below the Earth's crust: Edmond goes to the fat, cultured, greedy, indolent, and Thierry to the thin, Philistine, austere, regimented. War breaks out between the two polities. The thin win, but the fat corrupt them and infect their overlords with their way of life and (particularly) leisure. The boys play important parts as observers, translators, mediators and so on. It was illustrated with vigour and imagination by Jean Bruller, who wrote as 'Vercors'. Eleven years later, it was translated as *Fattypuffs and Thinifers* and published in London by John Lane. To the *Times Literary Supplement* on 27 December 1941, 'This most amusing fantasy' won pride of place in a review of many juveniles, but purely as comedy:

> Are you a Thinifer? Are you lean, energetic, punctual and perhaps a little short-tempered because you care so little about eating? If so, you will, like the people of M. ANDRÉ MAUROIS'S imaginary country, have little patience with the amiable, rotund, goodnatured Fattypuffs, whose attention is concentrated on the pleasures of food and rest. But if, like many of us nowadays, you find your mind dwelling more and more on thoughts of nourishment, then you will sympathise with the Fattypuffs.

Some joke about wartime rationing was clearly trembling anachronistically in the ether. That Maurois had intended the *Patapoufs* as caricatures of the French and the *Filifers* of the Germans may be obvious today, and seems to have been obvious in 1930; but 1941 ignored any clues. Even a recognition of Athens and Sparta as remote models was apparently beyond the wartime British critics, however normally thrustful with classical allusions to exhibit public-school antecedents. Maurois, now a refugee in the USA, was hardly likely to disabuse them, and 'Vercors' in the French underground even less so.[87]

But the ironies imposed by Time were hideous. So far from the latest occupation by conquering Thinifers finding itself corrupted by the defeated Fattypuffs, the signs were that the Nazi tyrants bred enough craven imitators to feel all too secure in the France they ruled and the France they controlled. Little sons of André Maurois who came to Thinifer attention in 1941 would have been sent to concentration camps, and might well be handed over to such

imprisonment and extinction had they shown their faces prominently among Fattypuffs. As it was, his mother, still in occupied
France, was phenomenally lucky to survive. Certainly the basic
truths were unanswerable: that war is silly, that excessive nationalism is homicidal, that force easily produces the converse of its
victor's aims. But those morals were now stifled, or at least shelved.
They were highly relevant to the Franco–German post-war *rappro-
chement*, with differential allowance for a Fattypuff win (or at least
token presence among the winners). By that stage, Maurois could
muse in comfortable retrospection:[88]

> For me, the child's book has an essential direction: it must have a
> child as the hero and that child must be able to achieve in the
> world of great people a heroic action impossible for it in real life:
> for instance, to bring an end to a war. A child is happy if the hero
> of the book, who is of his/her age, does great things. He must
> always perform either in the issues of his times or in eternal issues,
> eternal myths.

It was a fine agenda for the writers for children in the Second World
War, but it was incapable of realisation. Not only were the tasks too
great, but also the questions to be begged were too great.[89] Orwell
insisted in 'Boys' Weeklies' that the *Magnet* and *Gem* 'characters are
so carefully graded as to give almost every type of reader a character
he can identify himself with.'

Richards usually turned his masters into caricatures, often ruthless and obtuse totalitarians, all too ready to misjudge a boy in utter
neglect of a good record and in frequent contempt of evidence
adverse to the thesis. Richards had built up Greyfriars following
close scrutiny of the Archer-Shee stolen postal-order case at Osborne
Naval College (1908–11), used it for one two-week Greyfriars episode
(*Magnet*, 3 and 10 May 1911), and retained much of what he had
learned of arbitrary magisterial conduct. Individual masters may be
sympathetic: Mr Quelch's ill-judged feud against Wharton in October–December 1932 is very moving in the ultimate reconciliation, a
scene built ably on Hugh Walpole's story of a schoolmaster's mistaken feud against a young colleague, *Mr Perrin and Mr Traill* (1911),
and in the subsequent series the repentant Quelch actually aids
the boys to conceal a reformed criminal lad fleeing from the police.
But the stories certainly perpetuate the great child–adult divide,
in a (largely benign) totalitarian system, relieved by occasional
rebellion.[90]

Identification is more uncertain than Orwell made out. What Orwell showed was that *he* identified with a Greyfriars character, clearly the 'Byronic' Vernon-Smith, and hence was working him up to play the part Orwell's fictional human heroes had so often played, viz. being George Orwell. Flory in *Burmese Days*, Gordon Comstock in *Keep the Aspidistra Flying* and George Bowling in *Coming Up for Air* all anticipate *1984*'s Winston Smith as divergent Orwell versions of Orwell. But we cannot say that this was universal: it is not clear for instance, that the boy Eric Blair identified with Vernon-Smith or anyone else. What children's stories seem much more to do is to provide an enrapturing comrade for the readers. Nobody caught it as well as Muriel Spark in *The Prime of Miss Jean Brodie*, almost certainly recalling little Millie Camberg as she was in Edinburgh around 1930:[91]

Sandy, who had been reading *Kidnapped*, was having a conversation with the hero, Alan Breck . . .

'Sandy, you must take this message o'er the heather to the Macphersons', said Alan Breck. 'My life depends upon it, and the Cause no less.'

'I shall never fail you, Alan Breck', said Sandy 'Never.'

'Mary', said Miss Brodie, from behind, 'please try not to lag behind Sandy.'

Sandy kept pacing ahead, fired on by Alan Breck whose ardour and thankfulness, as Sandy prepared to set off across the heather, had reached touching proportions.

This is not an identification with Stevenson's narrator in *Kidnapped*, the Lowlander Whig Presbyterian David Balfour, but a supplanting, Sandy having none of David's misgivings about Jacobites, Highlanders or Catholicism (she – and her creator Muriel Spark – would adopt Roman Catholicism). What is less clear is whether readers played the game of 'who do you think you really are?' as well as 'who would you like to be your friend?' and 'who would you like to be?' Earlier, Orwell had tackled this question in 'The Art of Donald McGill':[92]

There is one part of you that wishes to be a hero or a saint, but another part of you that is a little fat man who sees very clearly the advantages of staying alive with a whole skin. He is your unofficial self, the voice of the belly protesting against the soul. His tastes lie towards safety, soft beds, no work, pots of beer and women with 'voluptuous' figures. He it is who punctures your fine attitudes and urges you to look after Number One, to be unfaithful to your wife, to bilk your debts, and so on and so forth.

Horizon printed this in September 1941, eighteen months after 'Boys' Weeklies': and what it means is that Orwell – unstinted in his admiration for that 'really first-rate character . . . the fat boy, Billy Bunter' – would have found Bunter in all of us. So did Richards. Even our readiness (in defiance of all reason) to imagine ourselves as a football star when reading the *Magnet* is a Bunterian folly, illustrated when Bunter wheedles or blackmails his way into a match, convinced of his own games mastery, or else when he explains his exclusion from match-play as victimisation by jealous rivals. Orwell's (and Richards's) denial of a sex-motif in the stories does not apply to Bunter, always ready to make nauseous claims as to girls being smitten with his charms. Bunter was eminently useful to Richards to ridicule and thus denounce repulsive traits and conduct: boasting, racism, sexism, treachery, scandalmongering, greed, cadging, snobbery and so on. But the reader could jeer at Bunter while silently squashing the internal Bunterisms never to be acknowledged.

Thus Richards's appeal was particularly strong in terms of identification, offering a canvas of largely convincing characters with whom to identify, in whom to find company and from whom to dissociate. If Richards had been a Roman Catholic, it might be tempting to identify Bunter as a form of confession. But the urge to confess hardly needs formal religious commitment. It has, after all, greatly enriched modern psychiatry. Arguably, Crompton pulled off the same effect with one single character, since most children loved to think they were William, would want to be friends with William, and would be invited by the author to laugh at and learn from hilarious mistakes by William, particularly in taking things literally. Nevertheless Crompton, like Richards, told children that however unwise, wrong-headed, absurd and even repulsive they might be, they deserved more respect than adults did – apart from those of them whose obnoxious characteristics were adult ones, such as William's enemy the snobbish, ingratiating sneak Hubert Lane, Bunter himself (whose vocabulary, and verification, had an adult orotundity), the American boy capitalist Fisher T. Fish, and the senior 'sportsmen' who abuse prefect status in Greyfriars and St Jim's. The psychological blow to over 15,000 habitual weekly buyers and innumerable borrowers when the *Gem* ended its days on 30 December 1939, and to over 40,000 purchasers and untold borrowers when the *Magnet* was cut off in mid-serial in late May 1940, can scarcely be imagined. We have records of the thunderstruck grief of adults like Professor Denis Brogan; and the deprivation of children, so dependent on Greyfriars, was heart-rending. Many of them were already cruelly strained by personal evacuation, parental enlistment, nocturnal darkness and so on, and now the closest friends in their imaginations may have gone, perhaps shortly to be followed by some of their closest friends in life. The bombs were already falling: *Happy Mag*, where William's triumphs and disasters had made their monthly appearance since December 1922, vanished the same May, George Newnes's premises – which housed its production – receiving a direct hit. William survived, in book form and (from August) in *Modern Woman*, and the regular multi-serial comics held on in some cases, with publishers less callous than Camrose about children's emotional needs.

Certainly, one of the clearest images through the early months of the Second World War is the child sheltering behind its comic. In retrospect, the protective comic loomed large, sometimes distorting historical reality. Jim Davidson in Peterhead, Aberdeenshire, remembered the beginning of the war:

A mannie named Chamberlain had said on the wireless that a state of war now existed between Great Britain and Germany. It had a disastrous effect on my parents. Everyone was very serious. . . . And that reminds me of a question I've often wondered about: when the *Magic* comic was launched and mother brought a copy for Alex and me, how did the comic manage to give away a small lollipop with the introductory copy? I could have sworn sweeties were rationed from early in the war. In fact, I remember when war was first declared that I saved up about half a dozen assorted sweets to enable me to cope with the wartime shortages that would come. Though my cache of sweets only lasted a day or two.

Davidson's *A Bairn's War – 1939–45* (2002) is one of the best memoirs of Second World War childhood that Britain produced, and the mistake is instructive about images and priorities. But it is a mistake. The *Magic* was launched on 22 July 1939 by D. C. Thomson of Dundee, to join its sister tabloids, the *Dandy* and the *Beano*, respectively eighteen and twelve months older: it added Koko the Pup on its front cover to follow the *Dandy*'s Korky the Cat and the *Beano*'s Eggo the Ostrich. Koko's first episode in fact took an anti-militarist complexion, perhaps in the afterglow of Munich; it would have been less likely with war declared. Koko, kicking a football (in good anthropomorphic style), has its bladder punctured by a snooty guardsman's bayonet; Koko then fills it with water, puts it between the guardsman's legs, and expels contents in superior officer's face, leaving officer furiously chasing guardsman out of picture. Thomson's was puritanical as to the obvious, but adult editors might miss implications that children would gleefully deduce: that the white-moustached captain or colonel or knight-at-arms would think his (black-moustached) subordinate had pee'd in his face. The want of military consciousness, in assuming that the result of such conduct was a chase with a view to retaliatory physical violence rather than court-martial, also suggests a doomed peacetime popular culture. Soldiers in comics became much more protagonist-friendly (and hence reader-friendly) as war advanced. But the *Magic* had little time to see it, being one of Thomson's very few war casualties (the *Skipper* was its other comic to fall, both in 1941). Koko did some useful war work, being parachuted on to a torpedo on 16 November 1940, diverting it from its target (a British warship), and sending it to blow up its parent swastika'd submarine (somewhat maliciously named 'U8'). But Davidson was left to lament: 'What happened to the *Magic* comic, anyway? . . . I really enjoyed that comic.' Sweet-rationing was not imposed for over a year, but sweet scarcity had driven William into stomach-churning amateur production of Sardine Toffee by April 1941.[93]

Comics might increase escapism, or merely dismay by their distance from grim realities, at least when the war began. One little girl in Crompton's Bromley vividly remembered her *Girls' Crystal* happily retailing the endless adventures of Sally Warner and Co. (any nomenclatural resemblance to Harry Wharton was certainly not coincidental) in their endless voyages through a peaceful globe (give or take local crises in remote points flashing little local difficulties), while she waved cheerio 'on a lovely sunny morning' to her father, called up for army service. (He survived; one of her schoolmates was killed, watching for 'incendiary bombs at Bromley Parish Church with her father. We had three minutes' silence.') Once the war had started, many comics with regular features shared the *Magnet*'s anxiety to let its boy heroes be heroic against Hitler, at least by spring 1940. But Sally Warner and her fellow-Merrymakers continued their rollicking career (under the authorship of G. C. Graveley, known to his girl readers as Daphne Grayson) so cheerfully that finally the episode in the *Girls' Crystal Annual 1944* was subheaded as from 'those carefree days when luxury cruising was all the rage', and its 1945 successor dated itself from 'those happy-go-lucky days before the war'. More was expected of more proletarian-conscious products (the *Girls' Crystal* was one of Lord Camrose's survivors). Davidson recalled that D. C. Thomson's *Sunday Post* was rapidly off the mark in 1939, with 'the Broons' responding to the blackout:

> They had been forced to stay in because of it, and make their home entertainment, playing snakes and ladders and table-tennis and 'Postman's Knock' with Joe and Hen's soldier pals. [Koko the Pup, please note.] Needless to say 'Postman's Knock' was Daphne's idea – and poor Maw and Paw had to leave their game of draughts and go out into the blackout to get peace and quiet. The last drawing on that particular page was just a black square, a real blackout picture, with two conversation bubbles which said:
>
> Paw: Ye canna get peace in yer ain hame, the picters are a' full up – whaur are ye, Maw?
>
> Maw: I'm here, Paw! Haud ma hand!
>
> That's how black the blackout was.

When you think about it, it wasn't a bad vision of war's blackness, and blessings. That was probably why Davidson held on to the memory.[94]

If the Broons entered the war in a spirit of resignation, so did others. W. E. Johns's first 'Tale of the Second Great War', *Biggles in the Baltic*, was published by June 1940 and by Oxford, having been serialised in the *War Thriller* from 9 March to 18 May 1940, its final issue. It duly began:

> As the momentous words 'England is now, therefore, in a state of war with Germany' [in contrast with what Davidson heard in Scotland] came sombrely over the radio, Major James Bigglesworth, D.S.O., better known as Biggles, switched off the instrument and turned to face his friends, Captain the Honourable Algernon Lacey, M.C., and 'Ginger' Hebblethwaite. There was a peculiar smile on his face.
>
> 'Well, that's that. It looks as if we are in for another spot of war flying', he murmured with an affected unconcern which did not

deceive the others, who realized full well the gravity of the situation.

'Seems sort of unreal, as if something which you thought had only been a dream had suddenly come true', remarked Algy quietly.

Algy was evidently autobiographical for his author, as well as for himself: Biggles and Co. had engaged themselves in operations to prevent the conquest of a Ruritania doing duty for Austria or Czechoslovakia or Poland, and had been drawn into the Spanish Civil War so as to witness German and Italian presence in effective supervision of Franco's officers, contrary to Chamberlain's Non-Aggression pact, as Chamberlain refused to see. Johns, as a good soldier, did not imply that the dreams in which he had made Algy and the others participate were undertaken to prevent the Second World War, although Biggles had been forthright in *Biggles Goes to War* about ways in which to make the League of Nations work and aggressor nations be forced to confront the realities of their conduct. On the other hand, Biggles was entitled to a peculiar smile.

Yet a poetic passage in the story seems intended for a metaphor on the UK's situation. Biggles, occupying a tiny island secretly owned and fortified by Britain near the Kiel canal, carries out some operations but falls into the hands of his old enemy von Stalhein, is tried and is found guilty of espionage on a ship which, however, is torpedoed by Algy. Biggles gets back to base but does not realise that von Stalhein has his marked map:[95]

His eyes closed, and he sank into a heavy dreamless sleep of utter weariness.

The hour hand of the clock on the mantelpiece ticked its way slowly round the dial, and still he did not awake. Another hour went by and still he slept, unaware that the sun had been blotted out by a dark indigo curtain that rose swiftly from the northern horizon. Presently, too, this curtain was blotted out by whirling flakes of snow that eddied about the entrance to the cave before dropping silently on the sullen water. And still he slept on, unaware of the silence, a sinister silence broken only by the relentless ticking of the clock on the mantelpiece.

He did not hear the tramp of feet that came cautiously along the catwalk. He neither heard nor saw the door open as Erich von Stalhein, an automatic in his hand, entered the room.

The German counter-espionage officer fitted a cigarette into a long holder, lighted it, and blew a smoke ring into the air. On his face was an expression of supreme contempt. For a little while he considered the sleeping figure thoughtfully; then, reaching forward, he tapped him on the shoulder with the pistol.

Biggles's eyes opened. A shadow of amazement swept through them as they came to rest on the German's austere face. Slowly he raised himself on one elbow.

'You know, von Stalhein, you're becoming a positive pest', he muttered petulantly. 'Why can't you let a fellow sleep?'

Von Stalhein smiled sardonically, 'Don't worry' he purred. 'Very soon you shall go to sleep for a long, long time.'

If Johns was continuing the metaphor, he did so in Biggles then being rescued by Ginger, the symbol of youth, all too recently of childhood. In fact, Ginger is around to rescue, having got lost on a boyish exploring expedition. For all his previous experience of air warfare, he is still very much the apprentice in this book. This is no longer simply keeping him up as the identification/comradeship target for the reader. Johns was naturally endowing Ginger with his own memories of beginner's luck in the First World War (Johns was lucky: he wasn't killed). And he was also finding his way of telling his young readers – all too likely to be participants in this war before they were much older – that the future, if there was to be one, meant rescue of 'England' by them. But, apart from writers with serious agendas such as Johns, or writers whose location absolutely necessitated their absorption in anti-Nazism such as Brent-Dyer, or writers whose stock characters left them no choice but to stand up and be counted such as Frank Richards, how serious were children's writers about the war theme, and how long did it take such seriousness to develop?

Quite a few writers and weeklies reran First World War material, perhaps to dodge censorship, perhaps because it was cheaply on hand, perhaps because they had never grown out of it. Johns cannibalised old stories and worked up good passages. The Gem went out of business featuring a First World War pilot named 'Mad' Carew (presumably avoiding little yellow gods), who was transferred to the Triumph to begin the remaining six months of its existence. The Triumph in 1940 was also incorporating old St Jim's stories warmed up from the First World War with 'Nazi' substituted for 'Prussian'. Frank Elias played the same game in book form with a First World War story slightly updated. He did manage a couple of

Second World War books, his self-cannibalisation having evidently given him sufficient nourishment to revive his flagging productivity. Hal Wilton (in reality Frank S. Pepper) continued his *Champion* series of the boxing First World War pilot Rockfist Rogan, who took his time about changing wars. The phoney war seemed to discourage literary investment. Percy F. Westerman continued to pour out titles from Blackie's, but the Second World War was on by well over a year before he began to put it in his books. Biggles was in print hearing Chamberlain's words by 9 March 1940, but it was six months more before the same broadcast effectively began *The War – and Alan Carr*, and before it prefaced the capture of a Nazi ship disguised as a neutral Norwegian in *At Grips with the Swastika*. Of Westerman's six books published in autumn 1940, one was set during the Spanish Civil War and two others in Ruritanias of uncertain time. Dorita Fairlie Bruce conscientiously declared war for the participation of her (now married) favourite schoolgirl, but *Dimsie Carries On* did not appear until 1942, however scrupulously it began in September 1939. If it did, the two World Wars were impressively connected in its first words:

'But how on earth', asked Dimsie, gazing up at her husband with startled brown eyes, 'do you expect to do all that and run the practice too?'

Dr Peter Gilmour propped one shoulder against the drawing-room mantelpiece, and passed his hand across his thick unruly thatch of hair in which grey threads were beginning to show. Nature had intended it for a strong capable hand, to match the other, at present thrust into his pocket; but a German shell-splinter in 1918 had spoiled the work of Nature in depriving it of two fingers, while another fragment of the same shell had gone further and smashed up one of his legs. The doctor's friends and patients never regarded him as a maimed cripple but there were times when the fact came home to Peter himself, and this particular day in September, 1939, was one of them.

Dimsie and he have children. Hemingway it isn't. But the plot turns on a very First World War point – the treacherous governess, in this case of British birth and hence traitor in law as well as fact. The device was so famous in First World War thrillers that *1066 and All That* declared one of the two causes of the war to be German governesses, a wave of whom penetrated British homes (the other cause being the Kaiser).[96]

All of this was respectful of the British government, even from Johns, with every motive to avenge himself on the Prime Minister and his cronies whose response to Johns's warnings over Munich was to get him fired by George Newnes Ltd from the journals he had built up and edited, *Popular Flying* and *Flying* (Camrose, whose papers serialised Johns's Biggles stories, was a Chamberlain crony but an adverse critic of Munich). 'Storm Troops of the Baltic Skies', as *Biggles in the Baltic* was named when serialised in the *War Thriller* in March–May 1940, even began with assertions of British war-preparedness 'Some time ago, perceiving that war might not be averted' (as Colonel Raymond of the Air Ministry puts it). There would be bitter irony in the serialisation of Biggles's successful Baltic operations and their June book publication coinciding with the utter collapse of actual British Baltic strategy in the disasters which sealed German control of Norway. A year later, Johns even turned the Norwegian disaster into a personal triumph for Biggles, in *Biggles Defies the Swastika*, although most of the book is an Odyssey up and down Norway to stave off capture (by von Stalhein) until Ginger prevents the British fleet from sailing into the Westfiord at Narvik after the Nazis have 'stuffed' it with magnetic mines. The effect of this would naturally be to leave child readers with a sense of Norway as some sort of British triumph (much as Dunkirk had been trans-formed in the popular mind). Norway had brought the downfall of Chamberlain, whom Johns loathed; but the great culprit in its case was in fact Churchill, whom he respected – and by now probably revered. The book was probably begun in autumn 1940 but did not appear until August 1941, in troika with *Biggles Sees it Through*, set in the last days of the Russo–Finnish war of 1939–40, and *Spitfire Parade*, largely cannibalised from First World War stories. Their publisher, Oxford University Press, had lost staff during the war and never satisfactorily replaced the two stars gone just before it, their joint editors of books for children, themselves writing as 'Herbert Strang' and (occasionally) 'Mrs Herbert Strang'. Oxford was now losing its grip, and before the end of the war would have lost Johns to Hodder & Stoughton. The publication delay meant that Johns antici-pated Orwell in writing a book critical of the USSR when it had become an ally of the UK, so recently that Oxford saw it through with no known demurrers: *Animal Farm* met its rejections from publishers on both left and right when the Grand Alliance had hardened from mere goodwill between fellow-victims. But *Biggles Sees it Through* (again, presumably intended to show serious British commitment in Scandinavia) was thus confusingly distanced from where the war had reached, in contrast to *Phantom Patrol* by A. R. Channel (Arthur Catherall), which Orwell hailed enthusiastically if inaccurately in *Time and Tide* on 7 December 1940. The Finns scarcely enter Johns's story; they are credible characters in Catherall's.

Biggles Sees it Through excited no attention to its seventeen-month-old theme from a forgotten war: the *Times Literary Supplement* (13 September 1941) thought that it and its Norway-set companion

> are pretty improbable but not so much so as to be utterly fantastic and on the whole are told in a happily realistic style that makes the maddest adventures seem quite plausible while one is lost in them. These books are very good of their type, being suitably full of excitement but devoid of horrors.

That was almost sound enough to have been written by a schoolgirl or boy, and neatly sums up the Johns appeal from 1932 to 1952. It also asserted the conventional limits of supposed parental desiderata in wartime fiction for children. Both stories have distinction, if unequal to that reached in *Biggles in the Baltic* – notably Biggles's 'beginning to suspect that the British Intelligence Service had been mistaken in thinking that the Germans were contemplating an attack on Norway', only to discover that it has just happened, and Biggles and his friends' return halfway through their Finnish adventure to hand over crucial documents which each wrongly assumes that one of the others is holding. Johns immunised his young readers against disillusion with their leaders by injecting, with as much humour as possible, blunders by their heroes. But the map of Scandinavia on the actual cover-boards of *Biggles Defies the Swastika* accurately symbolised the limits of Johns's acquaintance with the area. Catherall in contrast might lack the schoolboy intimacy of Johns: Johns knew Walter Scott's trick of giving the reader the eyes of an observer conscripted by the plot, while Catherall's reader has a ringside seat without being a player. But Catherall knew the Arctic and the North Sea (as he would show the same year in *Raid on Heligoland*). Being thirteen years junior to Johns, he set his war books aside for wartime service in the RAF from 1940. Orwell's praise for *Phantom Patrol* saw its quality:

> Some English Boy Scouts have been spending their holidays in Finland, and they are just due to go home when the war breaks out and they are trapped in the country. Their Finnish and Lapp

friends are all taking part in the war, so the English boys join and accompany the famous sky-fighters who put up such a wonderful fight against the Russians. This is a real war story, with none of the horrors shirked, even the bombing of Helsinki, but there are also first-class descriptions of the reindeer, the snow-huts, the birch-forests and all the other wonders of the frozen north.

But his testimony shows that it was the landscape and the Lapps which were memorable. There is only one English Boy Scout; his involvement arises from his father's wounding in a Russian bomb attack; and the heavy slaughter is in Petsamo (a.k.a. Pechenga), which is as far from Helsinki as John o' Groats is from Land's End. It was careless of Orwell; but, with eleven books for review that week in different journals (and with broadcast, book proof and so on), it was understandable. If he didn't know his Arctic from his Helsinki, Catherall apparently didn't help him, where the map-bound Johns kept his reader straight. Clearly, Catherall had made the non-British lads so sympathetic that Orwell vaguely assimilated some of them to British status: that events are sometimes described as through their eyes must have exacerbated this. This cosmopolitanism of identity (especially noteworthy in Gilson and Brent-Dyer) seems to have vanished during the war, although at its end Puffin Books would reprint several pre-war books by Dutch, Swedish and other authors about children of their lands. This is distinct from the popularity of post-war narratives of real children in the Second World War such as *The Diary of Anne Frank* or Ian Serraillier's *The Silver Sword*.[97]

How far was the Finnish theme indicative of a political agenda? Orwell certainly sought to make it so, on his way to politicise children's literature in *Animal Farm* now that Lord Camrose had clearly given up his efforts in that direction, if any. A. J. P. Taylor would demonstrate how Biggles's presence in Finland reflected the irrational realities of March 1940: he was evidently an advance guard of what Taylor saw as the 'Anglo-French expeditionary force of 100,000 men hastily assembled' but not despatched before peace broke out on 12 March. Johns phrased this as the Air Ministry having 'allowed Biggles to accompany a party of volunteers to help the Finns in their struggle against Soviet aggression' — but the speed with which Johns's air heroes are put back on intelligence track is a clear metaphor for British official involvement. Taylor would remark that 'The motives for the projected expedition to Finland defy rational analysis' but that 'The decisive argument was simply the need for some action, never mind where or who against'. This is consistent

with Johns. That a German spy masquerading as 'a member of the
International Squadron fighting for Finland' is taken aback when
von Stalhein tells him that Biggles is a British agent seems deliberately to convey the lunacy of the business: why else should British
air pilots of war experience be in Finland with their own country at
war, however phonily? Johns makes it clear that there was nothing
phoney about the Finnish war: Algy at one point speaks of 'ten
thousand men . . . dying every day along the Mannerheim Line',
which had become the chief battle-front, and where the Russians had
lost most of their 200,000 casualties by 12 March. Catherall (as
Channel) understandably ends his book (set at the opening of the
Finnish Winter War) with the protagonist's wounded father having
to tell him:

> 'There is one thing you must not forget, Stuart. The British Empire
> is at war. We are fighting Germany, Britain needs men, and in
> another twelve months you may be called upon to stand shoulder
> to shoulder with Britons in a fight quite as desperate as this
> Russo–Finnish struggle.'
>   'Yes, a man must fight for his own country first', Juhani said.
> 'You have fought well for Finland . . .'

Taylor mused in this connection:

> For Great Britain and France to provoke war with Soviet Russia
> while already at war with Germany seems the product of a
> madhouse, and it is tempting to suggest a more sinister plan:
> switching the war on to an anti-Bolshevik course, so that the war
> against Germany could be forgotten or even ended. . . . Still, their
> main impulse was simply a vague longing for action. The 'phoney'
> war discredited ministers and exasperated the public. Finland
> seemed to offer an opening to start fighting somewhere, with the
> added advantage of being far from the Western front.

Johns caught this neatly: for Biggles, Algy and Ginger the chance to
make their war a fighting one, for the Air Ministry something else,
undefinable to pilots and readers, and probably to itself. But Catherall makes his illiterate Lapp have no doubt whom he is fighting and
why:

> The biting north wind whipped his face, and after the heat of the
> burning town the sting of the blast, forty degrees below zero, was

all the keener. If Juhani felt it he gave no sign. After a moment or so he murmured his thoughts aloud.

'M'sieur Stalin, you are the big bull of the herd just now. But men and countries are like animals. One day they grow strong, they challenge the herd bull, overthrow him, and are master of the herd. You may taste victory, M'sieur Stalin, but there will come a day, as there comes a day to the big herd bull, when a younger bull will challenge thee. Thou shalt feel the rip of the antler in thy shoulder, and the burning pain from a stabbing hoof in thy chest.'

Juhani spat out, then turned and headed south. He sped across the snow in graceful fashion. There were few to equal him on skis. The snow hissed in powder under his powerful gliding strokes.

The ski-fighter is thus another figure on the road to *Animal Farm*.[98]

But, however ambiguous the intentions of the British government in February and March 1940, Richmal Crompton gave her verdict on Neville Chamberlain by April. 'William Takes Charge' appeared in *Happy Mag*, for May, turning on William's efforts to get his fellow-children of the village treated as evacuees with such benefits as might accompany the status. He perpetually compares himself to Chamberlain, logically in his eyes, ludicrously in those of his readers. But it is not William who suffers by the comparison:[99]

He made one last attempt, and, approaching a smallish house that he thought optimistically might afford shelter to a couple or so of his clients, knocked at the door. A very old woman opened it. She smiled at him pleasantly and said: 'Yes dear? What do you want?'

'Mr Chamb'lain's sent me to ask if you've got any rooms vacant.'

'No, dear', she replied. 'I didn't order bacon. Just a pound of sausages as usual, and tell him to send before dark.'

She was closing the door on him.

'No, wait', he said loudly. 'I din' mean that. Listen.' He raised his voice still more. 'Mr Chamb'lain's sent me to ask if you c'n take in any 'vacuees.'

She looked at him pityingly.

'What a shame to send a child like you touting for orders!' she said. 'No, dear, tell him I've never used a vacuum. I use an old-fashioned broom just as my mother did – with tea leaves if the carpet's very bad. And tell your mother from me that it's a great mistake to let a child of your age take up this sort of work. For one thing it's a blind alley, and for another you're far too young for it.'

She vanished for a moment, to reappear with a biscuit which she thrust into his hand. 'And now go home and get your tea.'

With that she disappeared, leaving him staring at the closed door, the biscuit in his hand. There seemed nothing to do but eat the biscuit, so he proceeded to do that as he walked slowly down to the gate and along the road. . . . After all, even Mr Chamberlain, he told himself, would have eaten a biscuit if anyone had given him one. . . .

The date of composition is uncertain, but it was certainly after Christmas and probably before the Nazi invasions of Denmark and Norway on 9 April. It must be unusual in its malice at the expense of the Prime Minister of a writer's country in the Second World War, and was evidently intended as a contribution to pressure for Chamberlain's ousting in Churchill's interest (Crompton could easily remember the removal of Asquith in the First World War). It is unusual in making so much of a living politician. Churchill would sound offstage as an affectionately identifiable voice involuntarily aiding William in mid-1941. But Crompton clearly decided to ridicule Chamberlain openly. The skit on his personal diplomacy, the highlighting of his ineptitude and inability to make himself and his political intent understood, the sneer at his aggrandisement of worthless concession, the reiteration of his unfitness for the responsibilities he flaunted, the dwelling on his deliberation for ludicrous results, the ultimate stress on his empty optimism, the 'blind alley' – all would win the bitter smiles they deserved from sophisticated child readers and from the parents who either read it or were asked to explain it.

Dunkirk itself was decisive in reality (as an ominous defeat) and in imagination (as a glorious victory), but in children's fiction its necessarily mythical status may have been too fragile for much interference, quite apart from Norway's and its disastrous impacts on what were foolishly deemed luxury activities like publishing for children. Percy F. Westerman took it on, and largely staffed his *Sea Scouts at Dunkirk* with young teenagers (not as young as most of its readers) rather than the very late teenagers who normally supplied his heroes. It closed (on a visit to a wounded Scout in hospital) with covert instructions to readers as to their own duty (a message in several other Westerman Second World War books):

'That's the rotten part about it. We've been under fire at Dunkirk – they didn't bother about our age then, and we didn't do so badly –

and yet we aren't considered old enough to fight in defence of our country.'

'What are the age-limits?' asked Peter.

'Sixty-five', replied Jimmy. 'And my Uncle Bill, who's turned sixty-eight, put his name down and said he was sixty. They knew all about him, but they took him all right.'

'But the lower limit?'

'I don't know exactly; 'bout seventeen, I reckon. They get us sea scouts to dig trenches and sand-bags and they won't let us man them when they're finished', he added resentfully. 'Well, we'll wait another month, and by that time, Peter, you'll be fit. Then we'll make out we're over seventeen and jolly well sign on. Game?'

'Game!' replied Patrol-leader Peter Ross.

This may be idealised, but Westerman apparently worked closely with Sea Scouts at Dunkirk time in or near Portsmouth – and perhaps beyond ('you aren't allowed to get under way without a certificated skipper . . .'). Westerman simultaneously, if very briefly, redeemed Norway while valorising Dunkirk ('the brilliant epic of Narvik . . . inspired the Easthaven sea scouts'). Westerman grappled with the British psychological triumph in making a victory out of Dunkirk being apparently at odds with the 'stiff upper lip' tradition of so much British imperial fiction (including his own 116 or so titles to date – having a Scottish publisher, Blackie, his stocks were in less danger):

> It has often been said that the British are a very unemotional people. Undoubtedly they take news of grave set-backs with praiseworthy calm; but there are numerous occasions when their pent-up emotions are let loose . . . [such as] the rescue of the betrayed Expeditionary Force from their vastly outnumbering foes.
>
> The Easthaven folk let themselves go 'good and proper'. The cliffs echoed and re-echoed to the tumultuous cheering, hats were thrown in the air and scarves waved welcome home the modern counterpart of the 'Merchant Adventurers' [i.e. Francis Drake and the English maritime opposition to the Spanish Armada].

As to the betrayals, Sea Scouts at Dunkirk introduces the local poacher as its Fifth Columnist. But treachery was not limited to him. Westerman told his readers that 'the British troops . . . found themselves in a trap caused solely by the traitorous defection of

King Leopold, the recreant son and successor to the lion-hearted Albert of the Belgians' (not having been the editor of a popular journal, as Johns had been, Westerman saw no need for sophistication).[100]

Westerman certainly knew his boats and their crews, even if the personnel seldom evolved beyond a chorus-line. But the destruction of Richards's *Magnet* and similar journals meant a hard division between book fiction with some claim to quality, and tabloids whose aesthetic value was almost wholly non-literary or at best cleverly captional. Richards received a small sum from the Amalgamated Press for the survival of Bunter and Greyfriars as repulsive caricatures by other hands in the *Knockout* comic. In place of Richards's elegant ironies and classical comedies appeared 'BILLY BUNTER – THE FATTEST SCHOOLBOY ON EARTH', capturing a 'Nasti U-boat' by sticking in its hatch. Orwell's thesis that the *Magnet* and its satellites affirmed and enlarged class difference was chiefly relevant in the effects of their demise. A literacy gap was created between children whose people could afford books and those who could only afford comics. The D. C. Thomson *Adventure*, *Hotspur*, *Wizard* and above all *Rover* fought for the principle of extensive reading-matter in working-class hands, retaining in less lofty terms the Richards respect for the worker, but about a decade after the war they followed the principle of *Magnet*-into-*Knockout*. Literature for the child masses was doomed, and the image had ultimately devoured the word. And money set the book–comic division at the very moment when politically the class structure was supposedly dissolving. Westerman's war was a war about people, however characterless; the *Knockout*, the *Beano*, the *Dandy* and their fellow-tabloids could be very amusing, but their basic assumption was of a readership too stupid to know war as much more than inevitable defeat of a moron or a monster. At least Westerman, and still more Gilson and Johns, made it clear to the book-readers that victory was problematic.[101]

Comic-book caption-and-picture methods were by their nature anti-intellectual in British publications. This seems unique to them, and a case might even be made for Scots-language comic strips such as 'Oor Wullie' and 'The Broons' for sometimes turning on jokes which could deepen for the reader with greater learning – the bonus which Richards had provided. Hergé's 'Tintin', after it had matured past its early racism and reaction, would make for sophisticated humour. After the war, René Goscinny and Albert Uderzo drew 'Astérix' from 1959 with firm intellectual prerequisites, beginning with Caesar's Gallic Wars. In America, Mickey Mouse performed the title-role of Paul Dukas's *The Sorcerer's Apprentice* for Walt Disney's *Fantasia* (1940) and shook hands with Leopold Stokowsky conducting it for the Philadelphia Orchestra. Walt Kelly's 'Pogo' was highly intellectual, incisively satirising current affairs, Al Capp's 'Li'l Abner' frequently wandered into vigorous social satire (less successfully when he drifted to the right), and from 1950 Charles Schulz's 'Peanuts' even seemed to have Beethoven as an offstage character, occasionally the most tragic in comics. In Ireland, the anthropomorphic 'Curly Wee' supported Roland Clibborn's imaginative drawings by Maud Budden's verse, which demanded previous appreciation of writers as varied as Marco Polo and Charles Dickens. One episode aboard ship sent up Coleridge rotten:

> 'An Albatross!' sneered Mr Fox, 'Pooh! what an ugly thing!'
> He threw his heavy scrubbing brush and caught it on the wing.
> 'You've brought bad luck upon our ship', the Coxswain cried,
>   'you cur!'
> (The Coxswain knew, because he'd read *The Ancient Mariner*.)

The spectacle of hoary old salts having to get up their superstitions by reading Coleridge should keep the postmodernist busy for pages. But the death of the *Magnet* seemed the knell for intellectualism in the English comic strip. A late exception from 1950 was the work of John Ryan in the *Eagle*, laughing at the Great Detective Harris Tweed, whose success is almost entirely due to his much-patronised boy assistant; but even that required little preliminary reading save Sexton Blake and his imitators.[102]

Richards himself eked out a wartime living as best he could, having given himself little preparation for his sudden loss of income: his generosity from time to time had been matched by gambling fever of the kind he condemned so forcefully in Herbert Vernon-Smith, Ralph Reckness Cardew and others of his literary offspring. If he joined the anonymous writers for D. C. Thomson, no record has come to light. He invented Greyfriars lookalikes such as Carcroft, Sparshott and Topham, and he began work on series about a runaway waif constantly threatened by a mysterious peer whose minions are always trying to kidnap and ruin him – Jack Nobody, later Jack Free. The London *Evening Standard* ran an interview with him in October 1943, possibly inspired by Michael Foot's memories of boyhood reading, possibly also with effects on a somewhat repentant Orwell. Leonard Russell of the *Sunday Times* drew Richards into the fifth

Saturday Book to write one of the essays on one's profession, his being 'Boys' Writer'. Orwell's review in the *Manchester Evening News* for 6 December 1945 gave Richards's essay pride of place, as well he might, for it had singled him out: 'George is a very good writer in his own line – but in this matter ['Boys' Weeklies'] he simply did not know what he was talking about'. It virtually put him up there with George Figgins and George Herries of St Jim's, even with the godlike George Wingate, captain of Greyfriars (and not, please not, with William George Bunter of the Greyfriars Remove). Orwell, in reply, came out of his puritanical closet and admitted that as prophet he was among the Sauls:

> All lovers of the 'Gem' and the 'Magnet' – and both papers have their followers in tens of thousands, both here and in the Dominions – will be delighted to see that Frank Richards is back on the job and has written a long autobiographical article in this year's 'Saturday Book'.
>
> We may hope that the 'Gem' and 'Magnet' themselves, after having been 'amalgamated' with other papers for the last five years owing to the paper shortage, will reappear before long.

It is possible that Richards's geniality to Orwell may have owed something to *Animal Farm*, published in August 1945 and widely reviewed, subsequently arousing much interest in Orwell's *Critical Essays*, whose appearance in January 1946 included 'Boys' Weeklies' with a graceful note of apology to Richards for doubting his single authorship. Various reviewers including Evelyn Waugh were to nostalgise about Richards's lost glories. *Picture Post* ran a three-page piece about him, Charles Skilton was inspired to publish books by him, and Monty Haydon of the Amalgamated Press permitted him to put Greyfriars and his schoolboys into them. But, as Orwell's review of the *Saturday* had noted, Bunter buoyed up the trade:

> In Bunter – with his vast, spherical form, his spectacles, his endless search for food and his postal orders which never turn up – Mr Richards has achieved something that is denied to most imaginative writers: he has created a character able to travel outside the bounds of the reading public.
>
> I have known a barrage balloon nicknamed Billy Bunter by its crew and I have known the same name given to a promising porker on a farm.

(Here was definite, if anachronistic, evidence of Orwell's connection of Bunter and pig relevant to *Animal Farm*.)

The *Knockout* Billy Bunter must (reluctantly) be credited with some contribution to Bunter's continuing wartime fame. Inevitably, the post-war series commissioned by Skilton played Bunter in its titles even when his relevance to the main plot was firmly subordinate. Orwell's 'Boys' Weeklies' had seen the genius of the stories partly lying in the variation in their spotlights:

> First there will be a series of rollicking adventure stories, featuring the Famous Five and Billy Bunter; then a run of stories turning on mistaken identity, with Wibley (the make-up wizard) in the star part; then a run of more serious stories in which Vernon-Smith is trembling on the verge of expulsion.

This greatly diminished, and inevitably the grotesque Bunter's domination of the stories accelerated. By 1949, Mandeville Publications were reviving *Gem* characters, and here the limelight could vary from D'Arcy to Tom Merry to Cardew the Cad to Talbot (haunted by his criminal past) to Skimpole (imbecile intellectual); and, while less successful than the Greyfriars revivals, they ran to 21 titles. But Bunter, like Apollyon, straddled the way of the Greyfriars series. Blyton, in some ways Richards's most notable wartime supplanter (her publisher Hodder & Stoughton even purloined the name 'Famous Five' for Julian, Dick, George, Anne and Timmy the dog), ended in the same quagmire: her better characters dwindled into comparative insignificance before the all-conquering grotesque, Noddy. Heroes declined and boobies advanced. It was a fair comment on the Britain of the 1950s. In adult literature, Kingsley Amis was taken for comedy in place of Wodehouse and Waugh. Poetry listened to the empty Larkin displacing the abundant Auden. On the stage, John Osborne proclaimed the realism of the kitchen sink, and audiences fought shy of Sean O'Casey, whose characters could not have afforded one.[103]

And Orwell was dead. Yet Richards, surviving him, responded to a *Punch* commission in his last year of life, to show what really had been the ethos behind the school stories. He chose the 'viewpoint not so much of pedagogue as of the pupil': 'This I acknowledge is somewhat revolutionary. But we live in an age of revolution. Let us keep up with the times' (the times were beginning the 1960s). His brief was to announce his policy as 'Minister for Education'. He wanted to take a firm stand against the age-old superstition that young people exist chiefly for the purpose of being tormented by well-meaning elders. The urge to worry the young for their own good is latent in all of us. It seems to be ineradicable. But like other deleterious impulses it can and must be kept in check. Better for a child to drop H's than tears. Better for the boy to perpetrate howlers than to howl. Education must no longer be the Moloch on whose grisly altar the young are ruthlessly, though conscientiously, immolated. In ancient Carthage they used to tip little ones into a fiery furnace, no doubt from the best of motives. The progress of civilization has modified and mollified the method without abolishing the system, which in our own time takes the milder but still painful form of Homework and 11-plus exams. We must progress further. These relics of barbarism I propose to abolish entirely.

The history of hitherto existing society was the history of generation struggle. Richards at the end of his career came out as having been essentially on the child's side. It was a choice many of his successors after the fall of the *Magnet* would have had to make during the Second World War, if – under Richards's influence – they had not made it earlier. The war would help shape many of their choices, and those choices help shape the child's retention of confidence in facing the challenges of war. In his lifelong struggle against tyranny, Orwell made enemies and mistakes; but he profited by his mistake over Richards both in his subsequent open generosity and in his secret derivation. For Richards, like so many colleagues, had fought long and well against tyranny in a most insidious and widely accepted form. In the process, he had trained his readers in comedy, courage and comradeship, all of which they would need.[104]

Notes

1. G. W. Stonier (ed.), *New Statesman Competitions* (1946), 31; the original entry appeared during the war. It entered the vernacular: I heard it from my mother, who didn't read the *New Statesman*. Graham's *Ruthless Rhymes for Heartless Homes* (1899) had its sequel *More Ruthless Rhymes . . .* in 1930. The common enjoyment of mock-celebration of Victoriana linked child and adult tastes in the Second World War: Hilaire Belloc's complete *Cautionary Verses* for children and T. S. Eliot's *Old Possum's Book of Practical Cats* appeared in 1939 (the first instalment of Belloc dating from 1896).
2. Epigraph for Chapter 3, 'The First Siren', in Tom Harrisson, *Living Through the Blitz* (1976), quoted by permission of Professor Murdoch Mitchison.
3. 'On Fairy Stories', *Tree and Leaf* ([1964] 2001), 81.

4. For the saga of *Animal Farm*'s struggle for publication, see Peter Davison et al. (eds), *The Complete Works of George Orwell* (1998), XVI, XVII. The edition is indispensable to any historian of culture or intellect in Second World War Britain.

5. *The Lord of the Rings* is in the strict sense a Catholic novel. Frodo loses his faith (i.e. instead of destroying the fatal Ring he seeks to usurp its ownership, thus falling prey to the sin of Pride), but, because of his good deeds – specifically in sparing Gollum when he might have killed him as a reasonable measure of self-protection – the Ring is destroyed and Frodo is saved (physically, with Sam, but, more important, spiritually). This follows the late medieval tradition of the Everyman plays. Luther insisted on justification – i.e. salvation – by faith alone. To put it another way, Frodo's love is greater than self-love, and he forgives his intended murderer. See Tolkien to Michael Straight, [?January/February 1956,] Tolkien, *Letters*, ed. Humphrey Carpenter and Christopher Tolkien ([1981] 1995), 232–7; and (on A-bomb) Tolkien to his son Christopher, 9 August 1945, *Letters*, 116.

6. *The Children's Life of Christ* (1943). 1943 saw nineteen books by her in that year apart from the three short stories in the now fortnightly *Sunny Stories*. The *Life of Christ* was reverent without being mawkish, and fitted in with the protective aura that Blyton's wartime work threw around her readers. 1942's eighteen titles had included the first of her works of formal religious origin, *The Land of Far-Beyond*, based on John Bunyan's *The Pilgrim's Progress* (template for Louisa M. Alcott's *Little Women*, all of whose protagonists supplied models for Blyton characters).

7. *Mountain of Adventure* (1949). Stuart Tresilian (one of the best children's book-illustrators of the 1940s) eloquently realised the crucifixion posture with realistic schoolboy above chapter 24. Dinah's unexpected affection for Philip when marked for sacrifice, and Lucy-Ann's offer to fly and die in his stead, hint at the supportive women at Calvary, for which C. S. Lewis would use somewhat similar girls Susan and Lucy the following year in *The Lion, the Witch and the Wardrobe*. Blyton's awareness of scientists was heightened during the Second World War when her usual holiday at Swanage was forbidden because of mined beaches; and the surrounding terrain including limestone-tunnelled Purbeck was reminiscently used to create her mainland locale for *Five on a Treasure Island* (1942) and its sequels, the initially repulsive father/uncle Quentin being made a scientist while the forbidden Swanage/Purbeck was heavily settled with scientists in real life, including the future Sir Bernard Lovell. Their presence was officially secret, but wartime gossip travelled, and the coincidence is greater than Blyton normally expected her own readers to digest. See Rodney Legg, *Dorset's War Diary* (2004), 21, 150, 182 and passim.

8. *Biggles Hunts Big Game*, 14–15. Johns reasserted this in his space series begun with *Kings of Space* (1954): the books are much inferior to his war fiction, but they denounced misuse of science as forcefully as C. S. Lewis *Out of the Silent Planet* (1938), which probably influenced him. Richards to Joe Wark, 5 January 1961, in Richards, *Letters to a Friend*, ed. Mary Cadogan and John Wernham (n.d. [2001]), n.p.

9. Notably in *The Lion and the Unicorn* (1941) in Orwell, *Complete Works*, XII. 391–432.

10. For 'Boys' Weeklies', see Orwell, *Complete Works*, XII, 57–79, followed by Frank Richards's reply, 79–85.

11. Orwell, *Complete Works*, XII, 76, 79. Connolly afterwards became chief reviewer to the *Sunday Times*, owned by Camrose's brother James Gomer Berry, first

Viscount Kemsley, so the precaution from his point of view was wise. Indirectly, therefore, Camrose exercised more control over Orwell's essay in *Horizon* than he seems to have done over Richards in the *Gem* and *Magnet*.

12. Westerman, *The Secret Channel and Other Stories* (1918), made it clear that it had been censored (possibly in original magazine publication, if any). Its publishers, A. & C. Black, now operating in London, having moved from Edinburgh, may have been more deferential to nearby censors than Westerman's usual publishers, Blackie of Glasgow. P. G. Wodehouse, *Heavy Weather* (1933), chapter 2, satirises the newspaper magnate reading the comics he publishes for children.

13. The last allusions to the *Daily Mail* in the *Magnet* seem to be in July 1926.

14. For Camrose, see Duff Hart-Davis, *The House the Berrys Built* (1990), a fascinating book, but concerned with the *Telegraph*, not the Amalgamated Press. The *Gem*, by now with far fewer readers than the *Magnet*, was wound up at the end of a St Jim's serial in the final issue for 1939; allegedly it continued in the *Triumph*, which ran ill-edited St Jim's stories, including plots evidently from before the First World War. The *Modern Boy* finished the serialisation of W. E. Johns's 'Castle Sinister' (to be published in June 1940 as *Biggles: Secret Agent*) and folded with that issue, 14 October 1939. Johns's *Biggles in the South Seas*, published in September 1940, had been serialised in the *Gem* to its conclusion on 9 December 1939, three weeks before termination of the paper. But the *Magnet* was brutally truncated after 18 May 1940, when a new serial had been started, and its destruction without warning was truly bitter for readers, some of whom still tasted their betrayal sixty years later. The *Triumph* went then also. The *Magnet* supposedly continued in the *Knockout*, but all that remained of Greyfriars was an infantile Bunter-based comic strip, not by Richards. Similarly, the Amalgamated Press's 'Schoolboy's Own Library' (reprinting, and sometimes abridging and conflating old stories from the *Magnet*, *Gem* and so on, most by Richards) were raised from fourpence (their price since 1930) to fourpence and a halfpenny (always pronounced 'haypnee') per item from January 1940, when the ninety-six-page pocket books were reduced to sixty-four pages. Their last publication was on 2 June 1940, when an old Greyfriars story had reached its second instalment and the third was announced but never appeared.

15. Orwell, *Complete Works*, XI.

16. Orwell, *Complete Works*, XII, 67–75. In the hardening of the Second World War, the ferociously anti-trade-union D. C. Thomson's comics became strongly left-wing, the *Rover* in particular running serials in 1942–3 in which Russian Communist commandos fighting in Romania were the heroes; but, if he was aware of it, the anti-Stalinist Orwell would hardly have been gratified at such an answer to his call in 'Boys' Weeklies' for left-wing comics. But, just as Richards personally evinced an anti-racist, anti-snob conservatism, Thomson's had a paternalist reformism, anti-snob, variable on race. The ethos of all the papers was in general anti-capitalist, probably following lines established by Richards.

17. Orwell, *Complete Works*, XII, 59 and note.

18. Orwell, *Complete Works*, XII, 79. The items thus described in the March issue of *Horizon* seem to have been respectively 'Association of Oaks' by Graham Sutherland, 'In Memory of Sigmund Freud' by W. H. Auden, and Philip Toynbee's opening chapter for a sour novel of school life, *A School in Private* (1941), not the short story it purported to be. Richards would naturally have detested it: it had little humour.

19. Richards wrote of himself as author in the third person during the article, but this passage is in a cunning first. In the previous ten years, all *Magnet* weekly

tales but two (one in 1930, one in 1931) had been by Charles Hamilton, the real Frank Richards. In all, Hamilton wrote 1,380 out of 1,683 stories of Greyfriars School printed in the *Magnet* since its foundation on 15 February 1908, and he wrote much less of the *Gem*; but the *Gem* from mid-1931 to Easter 1939 had been stocked with old St Jim's stories, often rewritten and abridged, Hamilton writing as Clifford being in nearly all cases of these reprints the original author. At worst, his mendacity was venial: his accomplishment was still extraordinary and included literally countless serials and stories in many other journals.

20. Both *Horizon*'s financial angel and *Horizon*'s readers seem to have found the magazine a success from the printing of 'Boys' Weeklies', and circulation stepped up from March 1940 when it appeared. Richards thus kept the high-brow higher. Orwell's pioneer work in literary sociology gave *Horizon* a meaning for the war years and after. It also became more readable.

21. Paradoxically, its major effect on Orwell may have been to help make his fictional characters animals. His citations from the *Magnet* in 'Boys' Weeklies' make it clear that he gave particularly close study to the issues of the *Magnet* from 15 April to 5 August 1939. The artist Leonard Shields gave the issue of 15 April a *Magnet* cover showing Billy Bunter confronted by a pig's head which he has taken from a luncheon-basket, captioned that Bunter is the one with the spectacles. The last two sentences of *Animal Farm* are:

> No question, now, what had happened to the faces of the pigs. The creatures outside looked from pig to man, and from man to pig, and from pig to man again; but already it was impossible to say which was which.

Bunter's twisted logic to prove the truth of his lies could have influenced Squealer's, and is indeed often compared to Goebbels's by Bunter's school-mates. The second serial, begun on 20 May, involved an attempt to have Vernon-Smith replaced at Greyfriars by a lookalike cousin, from which he is saved by the devotion of his friend Tom Redwing; Winston Smith's personality is ultimately replaced in *1984* by that of a conformist (which Vernon-Smith's replacement would have been), when he betrays and is betrayed by his supposedly devoted friend Julia. Orwell was clearly attracted by 'Vernon-Smith, "the Bounder of the Remove", a Byronic character' and also by 'the scholarship-boy (Tom Redwing), an important figure in this class of story because he makes it possible for boys from very poor homes to project themselves into the public-school atmosphere' (Orwell, *Complete Works*, XII, 65, 64).

22. Ex-soldier crook, *Magnets* 1,140–1 (December 1929); Franz Kranz, *Magnets* 1,354–8 (January–February 1934); Fascist robbery, *Magnets* 1,452–5 (December 1935 to January 1936); Fascist murder plots, *Magnets* 1,522–5 (April–May 1937).

23. Muccolini, *Magnets* 1,481–90 (July–September 1936). Orwell, *Complete Works*, XII, 67. In fact, during the war, the image of the invincible navy was reasserted in juvenile literature at some distance from reality: 'far out on the silver streak of Channel moved the dark shapes of a passing convoy – one of those convoys that went by, night and day, on their lawful occasions, to the great glory of the British Navy' (Dorita Fairlie Bruce, *Toby at Tibbs Cross* (1942), 133). Her fellow-writer of schoolgirl stories, Elinor M. Brent-Dyer, was franker about vulner-ability in *The Chalet School Goes to It* (1941), first chapters, especially '[Naval] War at First-Hand'. The implications of Percy Westerman's navy yarns recalled the tradition Orwell cites, notably in such titles as *When the Allies Swept the Seas* (1940); but in practice he had to concede much more uncertain outcomes.

24. Colonna, *Magnet* 1,388 (September 1934: the serial has a few frivolous allusions

to Mussolini); gun-running to Spain, *Magnets* 1,505–9 (December 1937 to January 1938).

25. Hacker, *Magnet* 1,617 (February 1939).

26. Orwell, *Complete Works*, XII, 66 and note. [Charles Hamilton], *The Autobiography of Frank Richards* ([1952] 1962), 179–82.

27. Crompton, 'William Makes a Corner', *Modern Woman* (December 1940), and *William Does His Bit* (April 1941), 138:

> Mr and Mrs Jones were professional bomb-dodgers. They had left London for Scotland at the outbreak of war. They had left Scotland for the south coast after the first Scottish raid. They had left the south coast for Cornwall after the fall of Belgium, and Cornwall for Wales after the fall of France. . . . After each move they had left behind them a household of shattered and exhausted friends or relations, on whom they had parked themselves and who generally considered the raid that had finally relieved them of their guests not too high a price to pay.

28. Crompton, 'William and A.R.P.', *Happy Mag* 204 (May 1939), and *William and A.R.P.* (May 1939), 1–2.

29. African prince, *Magnet* 1,654 (October 1939).

30. Brent-Dyer, *The Chalet School in Exile* (1940), *The Chalet School Goes to It* (1941; recently retitled *The Chalet School at War*). Brazil, *The Mystery of the Moated Grange* [1942], *The Secret of the Border Castle* ([1943]), *The School in the Forest* ([1944]). Hadath, *From Pillar to Post* (1940: on which see Orwell, *Complete Works*, XII, 302–3), *The Swinger* (1942), *What's in a Name?* (1945). Strong, *Wrong Foot Foremost* (1940: see Orwell, ibid.). Brazil grasped one nettle in this forcefully:

> 'It's an evacuated school, from Gloucestershire.'
> 'Evacuated? Like the slum children they sent to the village from Leeds?'
> 'Of course not! It's a very select school, with nice girls. They've been turned out of St Hilda's because it has been taken over for Canadian soldiers. . . .' (*Forest*, 10).

Crompton, 'William's Day Off', *Happy Mag* (August 1938), and *William and A.R.P.*, 73–4.

31. Dougan, *The Schoolgirl Refugee* (1940), *Schoolgirls in Peril* (1944). Miall, *The Schoolgirl Fugitives* (1942). Elder, *Strangers at the Farm School* (1940). Gilson, *Out of the Nazi Clutch* (1940). All of these are tense and realistic, very different from the brittle heroics of soldiers' escapes popular near the war's end.

32. On Brent-Dyer, see Sue Sims and Hilary Clare, *The Encyclopaedia of Girls' School Stories* (2000), 73–81, and works therein cited.

33. Tolkien to Unwin, 25 July 1938; Tolkien to Rütten & Loening Verlag, 25 July 1938, *Letters*, 37.

34. *Gem* 394 (1915), reprinted, *Greyfriars Holiday Annual 1975* (including *Gem* advertisement telling readers to pass issue on to a Jewish chum): the story is the more telling in that the anti-Jewish boy is Monty Lowther, close friend of the hero Tom Merry but here left looking contemptible until he repents when the Jew, Dick Julian (origin of Blyton's two boys' names in her 'Five'?), saves his life and they become friends. In *Magnets* 1,126–8 (September–October 1929), the nobility of the Jew, Monty Newland, contrasts with the anti-Jew whose grievance against Jews in general arises from parental injuries from a swindler

supposed to be Jewish but eventually proved to be his own cousin. This may have been intended as a parable on the baselessness of current anti-Jewish prejudice and the likelihood that grievances mask guilt among the anti-Jews themselves.

35. Orwell, *Complete Works*, XII, 84.

36. Orwell to Geoffrey Gorer, *Complete Works*, XII, 137. Ibid., 66. Richards's *Magnet* illustrators had dropped the pigtail by 1930; he had not.

37. Chinese, *Magnets* 1,175–85 (August–October 1930), 1,541–4 (September 1937). W. E. Johns, 'The Oriental Touch', *Biggles Flies Again* (1934: issued as Penguin, November 1941). Ransome, *Missee Lee* also appeared in November 1941; she was supposedly based on Madame Sun Yat-sen, encountered by Ransome fifteen years earlier, but the Leeds-educated Ransome's contribution to the usually tedious Oxford v. Cambridge rivalry is when Missee Lee, serving Cooper's Oxford Marmalade, says: 'Better scholars, better plofessors at Camblidge but better marmalade at Oxford' (p. 186). The lady is bellicose, but over a decade away from the Second World War.

38. For example, Gilson, *Sons of the Sword* (1941), *The Yellow Mask* (1942), but also many short stories, notably 'Exchange No Robbery', in [']Herbert Strang['] (ed.), *Highway to Adventure* (1941), 180–201. Gilson seems to have influenced W. E. Johns; and *Biggles Sweeps the Desert* (November, 1942) alludes to a 'master pilot' named Gillson [*sic*], who appears at the end of the story (set in Libya) stating: 'This is my machine. Let me have her. Where are we bound for?' (p. 169). This may have been a disciple's homage to a dying man: Gilson died on 18 May 1943. Gilson's *Libyan Patrol* appeared in late 1942.

39. Stephen, *Lapsus Calami* (1896: posthumous), 3; it first appeared in *Cambridge Review* (February 1891) and is entitled 'To R.K.'

40. Kipling died in 1936, Haggard in 1925. The convention of much imperial fiction, including Haggard's, Kipling's and Buchan's (especially *Prester John*, 1910), that, however civilised, the native returns to his natural ethics when his own country calls, is maintained in Ransome's *Missee Lee*, Johns's 'The Oriental Touch' and its Second World War sequel *Biggles Delivers the Goods* (April 1946), and in Richards's stories of the Arab boy leader of Greyfriars (*Magnets* 862–9, August–October 1924) and of Hurree Singh's return to his own Indian kingdom (*Magnets* 960–70, July–September 1926).

41. Remi to Numa Sadoul, in Sadoul, *Entretiens avec Hergé* (1989), quoted in Michael Farr, *Tintin the Complete Companion* (2001), 51.

42. Hergé, *The Blue Lotus* (1983), 43. The original comic strip was serialised in *Le Petit Vingtième* in Brussels, 1934–5. The story is so firmly set in history that it was not published in London by Methuen until the year of its artist/author's death, although English translations of other works had been available since 1953–66.

43. Hergé, *The Blue Lotus*, 7. *Biggles – Air Commodore*, 191. Benoit Peeters, *Hergé fils de Tintin* (2002), 118–24.

44. *Magnets* 1,228–38 (August–October 1931). Richards drove home the lesson of Bunter's contemptible racism in other stories, for example in India where Bunter's kicking of an Indian servant ends with the servant robbing him of valuables, irreparably (*Magnets* 968–70, August–September 1926), and in the South Seas where his 'faithful nigger' thumbs his nose at him from a safe tree, cover-illustrated (*Magnets* 1,588–98, July–September 1938).

45. Crompton, 'William the Dictator', *Happy Mag* (August 1937), reprinted as 'What's in a Name?', *William the Dictator* (June 1938).

46. *Magnet* 1,238.

47. *Magnets* 862–9. The Arab guide saves Bob as a matter of honour, and which also animates Kikolobo in saving Smithy; but Ibrahim, the guide, is animated by obligation, whereas Kikolobo is increasingly driven by love, reciprocated.

48. Richards was very hostile to dragging the God in whom he believed to buttress fictional characters (*Saturday Book 1945*).

49. Gilson, *Libyan Patrol* (1942). Johns, *Biggles Flies East* (1935) has a very Lawrence-like figure, Major Sterne (a clear association of names via the author of *Tristram Shandy*), who proves to be the German master spy von Stalhein on his first appearance. On Lawrence, see the invaluable *By Jove, Biggles! The Life of W. E. Johns* by Peter Berresford Ellis and Piers Williams (1981), 107–11. Biggles and Co. have an Egyptian partner in *Biggles Flies South* (1938) and an Arab assistant in *Another Job for Biggles* (1951); both are attractive and knowledgeable. Johns seems to have had Middle East experience in the 1920s, probably in Iraq and India, but its nature is unknown.

50. Crompton, 'William's Midsummer Eve', *Modern Woman* (July 1941), and *William Carries On* (May 1942).

51. An exception has to be made in the case of Oswald Bastable, partly from his dual personae, actor and narrator. 'As with Henry Adams and Norman Mailer, Oswald's use of the third person gives him both a commanding and an irritating quality as narrator. It would be interesting to know, but hard to find out, to what extent boys (or girls) find it easy to identify with him' (W. W. Robson, 'E. Nesbit and *The Book of Dragons*', in Robson, *Critical Enquiries* (1993), 211–12). Noel Streatfeild, *Magic and the Magician: E. Nesbit and her Children's Books* (1958) is a useful though not brilliant indication of Nesbit's impact on a writer of this period.

52. *Five Children and It* (Nesbit) would seem to have originated the Blyton Five inclusion of the dog: it is a simple reversal, the Psammead ('It') distanced from the children, the dog integrated with them (and introduced in *Five on a Treasure Island* after cousinly suspicion that he might be a fisher-boy deemed desirable by George, undesirable by her parents: as Blyton had just made a fisher-boy the hero of *The Adventurous Four* (1941), the implied snobbery is being ridiculed, not endorsed).

53. Kiki is in *The Island of Adventure* (1944) and sequels (*Castle, Valley* and so on). The Saucepan Man is in *The Enchanted Wood* (1939) and its Faraway Tree sequels.

54. Bruford's arguments begin in his *Gaelic Folk-Tales and Medieval Romances* (1969), 4–7. The king/think motif may be best known in the ballad 'King John and the Abbot of Canterbury'. About 1951, the *Eagle* introduced two identical twins who converse in rhyme ('Take your pick' 'Pat or Mick') and who, after initial anti-social attitudes, become pillars of PC 49's youthful crook-catching support ('Mike! What the dickens?' '49! The plot thickens!'). PC 49 was originally the protagonist of a music-hall song before the First World War.

55. For example, Orwell, *Complete Works*, XII, 315 (reviewing the Chaplin film *The Great Dictator*, 21 December 1940); also *The English People* (1947), written c. 22 May 1944 (Orwell, *Complete Works*, XVI, 205). The argument applies all the more to the child heroes of books for children – and, as Enid Blyton and others would remind us, the animal heroes. Indeed, all the 'little man' heroes listed by Orwell were child favourites. For a similar thesis to Orwell's in fiction for children, see Johns, *Biggles Goes to War* (1938), 30.

56. Herbertson, 'Be-by and the Things he Did', *Little Folks* (December 1909 to April 1910): her last book of poems appeared during the Second World War. (Another serial in the same months, Ralph Simmons, 'The Buccaneers of Swan Lake',

anticipates the plot of Ransome's *Swallows and Amazons*, 1930.) Baker, 'The New Planet', *Little Folks* (November 1913 to April 1914).

57. *Magnet* 1,544 (September 1937). *Modern Boy* (26 June to 11 September 1937, 1 October to 3 December 1938).

58. For boy competition on relics of crashed aircraft, Crompton 'William's Midsummer Eve', *William Carries On*; on family members in forces, 'Reluctant Heroes', ibid.; 'Feasts for Heroes', *William and the Brains Trust* (April 1945), 'The Outlaws and the Parachutist', *William Does His Bit*; 'William – The Salvage Collector', ibid. Orwell, *Complete Works*, XII, 67, 79–80.

59. *Thoughts on the Cause of the Present Discontents.*

60. Orwell, *Complete Works*, XII, 61, 62, 80, 81, 82–3.

61. Ibid., 84–5.

62. See, for example, Robert Louis Stevenson, 'To the Hesitating Purchaser', opening *Treasure Island.*

63. Serialised as 'Biggles' South Sea Adventure', *Gem*, 14 October to 9 December 1939, book publication September 1940. Whatever Melville critics have sought to make of his friendships in *Typee*, Johns – and Biggles – clearly assume that Ginger's friendship with Full Moon is deep but childlike in camaraderie. This is in contrast to Ginger's love for Jeanette Ducoste during the Second World War in *Biggles 'Fails to Return'* (August 1943). Dorita Fairlie Bruce followed the same pattern of sudden adulthood and serious romance as a feature of the Second World War (*Toby at Tibbs Cross*; and *Nancy Calls the Tune* (1944), her third eponymous schoolgirl heroine being already married by *Dimsie Carries On* [no pun imagined], 1941). Elinor M. Brent-Dyer married off Jo, her series heroine, between *Anschluss* in Austria and the outbreak of war (*Chalet School in Exile*).

64. *Magnets* 1,017–26 (July–October 1927), 1,676–82 (March–May 1940). Quotation from 1,681 (4 May 1940). Richards, whose self-defence in *Horizon* had appeared a few days earlier, had first-class proof of topicality here.

65. Arthur Conan Doyle, *The Return of Sherlock Holmes*: 'Black Peter'. 'The Three Students', the next story but two, gives Holmes a (non-criminal) client named Soames. *Magnet* 1,682 (11 May 1940).

66. But both Melville and Soames also invoke Ishmael as a miraculous survivor.

67. Enid Blyton, *The Story of My Life* (1952), could not conceal her love for her father and her disappointment with him – nor her hostility to her mother, who is pointedly sidelined apart from her being 'not very fond of animals' following the description of a beloved kitten taken away after two weeks. Barbara Stoney, *Enid Blyton* (1974), reveals that Blyton's adored father left home for ever when she was 12: 'the shock to the highly-strung girl of what she felt was her father's rejection of her for someone else, was incalculable' (p. 20).

68. Westerman, *Destroyer's Luck* (1942), 157. Johns, *Biggles Sweeps the Desert*, 72. See also ibid., p. 123.

69. Havilton, *School versus Spy* ([1940]), 44–5.

70. I am greatly obliged to Brian Doyle and Robert J. Kirkpatrick for their courtesy in sending me data on Aston/Havilton. See also Doyle's notice in Kirkpatrick, *The Encyclopaedia of Boys' School Stories* (2000), 159–61.

71. One Second World War story turning on a child's death, Violet Needham's *The Stormy Petrel* (1942), is Ruritanian and may have been written much earlier (its precursor, *The Black Riders*, 1939 certainly was). Needham's work has considerable integrity and faces children with hard choices, above all psychological: this one ends in an assassin killing his own son, who is preventing his regicide. But the boy is then identified with Bunyan's Mr Standfast, in error for

Mr Valiant-for-Truth, which indicates that Needham's inspiration here was the First World War story by John Buchan, *Mr Standfast* (1919).

72. Johns, *King of the Commandos* (October 1943), chapters 1–2. Havilton, *School versus Spy*, rises impressively above the herd of the spy-schoolmaster genre. James Hilton, *Goodbye, Mr Chips* (1934), 97–8. The quotation salutes the anti-war classic *Im Westen Nichts Neues* (1929; later burnt by the Nazis) by the German First World War veteran Erich Maria Remarque, whose English title is *All Quiet on the Western Front.*

73. Admittedly, one effect of this is the last chapter being entitled 'Game', as in 'Tell Mother I died game': 'Just fancy: two of the 1st Easthaven Sea Scouts wounded in action with the enemy! I was the first, though! Does Peter's mother know? She is somewhere about.' But all survive.

74. *Sea of Adventure* (1948), 260. Colwell's review is variously quoted by Frank Eyre, *20th-Century Children's Books* (1952), 53, Crouch, *Treasure Seekers and Borrowers* (1962), 97, and Sheila Ray, *The Blyton Phenomenon* (1982), 52.

75. Flora Sidney Woolf, 'A Night on The Battlefield', *Little Folks* (January 1916), 156.

76. 'Competition Corner', *Little Folks* (August 1916), 'Wood' series running November 1915 to April 1916. Editor Williams endorsed the choices of French and Belgian girl heroes. Moore, 'A Coward's Courage', *Little Folks* (April 1918), 410.

77. Mordaunt, *Blitz Kids* ([1941]); Kyle, *The Seven Sapphires* (1944); Shead, *They Sailed by Night* (1943); Frow, *The Intelligence Corps and Anna* (1944); Barne, *Three and a Pigeon* (1944). Crompton, 'William and the Bomb', *Modern Woman* (June 1941) and *William Carries On*; 'William Makes a Corner'; 'William – The Salvage Collector'; 'William and the Air Raid Shelter', *Happy Mag* (January 1940) and *William and the Evacuees* (May 1940); 'William Helps the Spitfire Fund', *Modern Woman* (March 1941), and *William Does His Bit.* Hadath, *Grim and Gay* (1942), 9 (beginning of book).

78. Richards, *Magnet* 375 (17 April 1915) – it counters Orwell's notion that Richards derived from Gunby Hadath, in fact his literary junior.

79. Mary Cadogan and Patricia Craig, *Women and Children First* (1978), 83–4, quoting *Gem* 445 ([August?] 1916). I am most grateful to this pioneer work.

80. *The Secret of Spiggy Holes* (1940). This coincided almost exactly in time with Noel Streatfeild, *The House in Cornwall* (1940), also concerned with saving an endangered heir of a Ruritania. *The Times Literary Supplement* (7 September 1940) was not surprised to find certain elements in the present political situation being utilised for what are termed children's 'Thrillers'. Both seem obscurely activated by Hitler's destruction of Czechoslovakia and the natural readiness to seek personal solutions rather than political.

81. One neat moment of contemporary relevance occurs in the miniature epic *We Didn't Mean to Go to Sea* (1937), when the children are nearly sunk by a German vessel with no sign of compunction. Ransome's politics were mostly anti-Stalin at this point (his wife having been Trotsky's secretary), but it seems a very deliberate tilt at Hitlerian aggression, which in foreign affairs was then most evident in Spain (the Nazis bombed Guernica on 27 April 1937 when the book was being written).

82. Marcus Crouch, *Chosen for Children* (1967), 25–9, quotation at pp. 28–9.

83. Treadgold, *We Couldn't Leave Dinah* (1941), 260, 269. Taylor, *English History 1914–1945* (1964), 493. A useful extrapolation of the possible fate of Britain in the light of the Channel Islands experience is Norman Longmate, *If Britain had Fallen* (1972), based on a BBC TV film. The title for *Dinah* imposed by Treadgold's American publishers Doubleday, *Left Till Called For* (1941), has the gallant confidence in ultimate military success which was a useful message

to send to a USA on the verge of entry into the war, but it misses the haunting element of a lost world and the childhoods that the ironies of the British title acknowledge to be gone forever.

84. Robson, 'On *The Wind in the Willows*', *The Definition of Literature and Other Essays* (1982), 123, 125. Masefield is the sole figure of literary stature comparable to Grahame among those mentioned above, and both were reassuring favourites on BBC Children's Hour during the Second World War. Masefield's *The Midnight Folk* (1927) wins for his protagonist, the boy Kay Harker, allies who would be largely at home in Grahame land: Kay is threatened by adults, and ultimately rescued by other adults, but comes close to adult independence and childish freedom while never fully possessed by either. *The Box of Delights* (1935), being a dream, ultimately keeps Kay's adventures and independence excluded from reality; but, as transmitted at Christmas 1943, partly adapted by the folklorist John Keir Cross, Kay acquired more command, performed by the future ballet dancer John Gilpin, then aged 13.

85. For Uttley's 'The Boat', see *The Adventure of Sam Pig* (1940) and *Six Tales of Brock the Badger* (1941). Her war years are well documented in her biography: Denis Judd, *Alison Uttley* (1986), 157–87.

86. For a typical Johns lament for France, see the opening of *Gimlet Goes Again* (November 1944), but also *Worrals Carries On* (1942), *Worrals Flies Again* (1942), *Worrals on the War-Path* (1943) and (for Monaco and the Riviera) *Biggles 'Fails to Return'*. Awdry's cleric status did not protect him from victimisation on the grounds of his pacifism: one vicar deprived him of a curacy when his wife was in advanced pregnancy, leaving him in serious economic straits for a time. See B. Sibley, *The Thomas the Tank Engine Man* (1995).

87. For Maurois, see Jack Kolbert, *The World of André Maurois* (1985).

88. Maurois, in spring 1956 (Bibliothèque l'Heure Joyeuse, *À Propos de André Maurois, Patapoufs et Filifers*, 1999), 39. My translation.

89. Crouch (*Treasure Seekers and Borrowers*, 92) also failed to understand the book and thus found it 'a little too cerebral to make a successful story for young children', but in labelling it a 'comic fantasy full of exact circumstantial detail' he stumbled on a Maurois genre. The only notable book in which children are responsible for killing Hitler, or an obvious caricature of Hitler, also merited the Crouch label for Maurois: Eric Linklater, *The Wind on the Moon* (1944).

90. Orwell, *Complete Works*, XII, 64. *Magnets* 173–4 (the Archer-Shee imitation with Bob Cherry as victim, Harry Wharton and the working-class Mark Linley as his only friends, Nugent as the alienated money-loser – and a thesis which may very well have been true of the original case, that there was a conspiracy to frame the alleged thief). *Magnets* 1,285–304 (Quelch v. Wharton).

91. Spark, *The Prime of Miss Jean Brodie* (1961), 34, 38–9.

92. Orwell, *Complete Works*, XIII, 29.

93. Crompton, 'Claude Finds a Companion', *Modern Woman* (April 1941) and *William Does His Bit*. Davidson, *A Bairn's War*, 5, 12. I am most grateful to Dr Tom Barron for the latter.

94. Doris Turner (née Ricketts), in Paul Rason (comp.), *Memories of the Many: 50 years on . . . from . . . Bromley reflecting on their war* ([1995]), 34–5. Davidson, *A Bairn's War*, 14.

95. *Biggles in the Baltic* (June 1940), 9, 184–6. The Ruritania story is *Biggles Goes to War*, and the Spanish Civil War *Biggles in Spain* (May 1939), serialised in *Modern Boy* (21 January to 1 April 1939). Johns was at first anti-Communist about the Spanish War (probably revolted by the initial massacres of clerics), but became very anti-Franco during 1937: Biggles and Algy are neutral in

Biggles in Spain, but Ginger fights for the Republic. On the use to be made of the League of Nations (in contrast to the ruderies about it from most British writers who considered it, Crompton included), *Biggles Goes to War*, 252–3, 255.

96. The original, terrestrial 'Mad' Carew may be found in the poem by J. Milton Hayes, 'The Green Eye of the Little Yellow God'. Elias, *The Mine Detector* ([1916]; 'revised edition' 1940). Westerman, *The War – and Alan Carr*, 9–19 chapter 1, 'Six Bells – War'. *At Grips with the Swastika*, 52–6. *When the Allies Swept the Seas* is also set in the Second World War. *In Dangerous Waters* is his Spain book, pro-Franco. *Eagle's Talons* and *Standish Pulls it Off* are Ruritanian. Bruce, *Dimsie Carries On*, 9. Bruce provided a nice gloss on mingling of characters from several series ('How this war does shake everyone together like a kaleidoscope!', p. 95) once they are clear about what war they are in.

97. Orwell, *Complete Works*, XII, 303. Catherall, occasionally writing as 'A. R. Channel', produced at least 100 titles, of which all but ten appeared after the Second World War, and only five in its course.

98. A. J. P. Taylor, *English History 1914–1945*, 469 note. *Biggles Sees it Through*, 11. Channel, *Phantom Patrol*, 253, 64. Orwell regarded the British sympathy for Finland as part of the British cult of the underdog (Orwell, *Complete Works*, XVI, 205). Johns, writing in retrospect and probably before Hitler's attack on the USSR (but not published until August, after it), may have revised proofs after 22 June 1941 when Finland attacked the USSR in collaboration with Nazi Germany, so we encounter Ginger disillusioned:

He had been eager enough to go with the others when the Air Ministry had allowed Biggles to accompany a party of volunteers to help the Finns in their struggle against Soviet aggression, but now that he was there he saw no reason to congratulate himself. They had been in Finland only a week, but as far as he was concerned it was enough. Practically forbidden to fly over Russian territory, their work had been confined to long-distance reconnaissance raids along the frontiers . . . (*Biggles Sees it Through*, 10)

It would be fascinating to know if author and publisher had to make last-minute changes after Finland supported Hitler's Operation Barbarossa; but Oxford University Press destroyed their records in the 1960s, to the shame of its Delegates.

99. The story was renamed, and became the title-story of *William and the Evacuees* (which, like the story, appeared in May 1940). For Churchill, 'William's Midsummer Eve'.

100. *Sea Scouts at Dunkirk*, 12, 79, 199–200, 128. Was this why Greene made the local poacher the only hero in 'The Lieutenant Died Last'?

101. Denis Gifford (ed.), *Comics at War* (1988), 42–3, for Bunter in the Nasti U-boat. The reproduction is given no date for the original, and the anthology is invaluable but irritating for the higgledy-piggledy assemblage and want of provenance. Professor Andrew Hook first called my attention to the significance of text-to-tabloid as a turning-point in cultural retrogression, and as always I am most grateful for his stimulus.

102. Tintin in fact mocked intellectualism and anti-intellectualism: it is a standard gag that Tintin and his Captain cannot stand the magnificent opera-singing of Bianca Castafiore, but they should have solved the mystery of the lost *Castafiore Emerald* (1963) had they thought of Rossini's *La Gazza Ladrone*. 'Curly Wee' also ran in the *Liverpool Echo*: the verse quoted is in the wartime 'Count Curly's Quest', republished in *Curly Wee* (1948), the episodes being abridged and

somewhat rewritten. Ryan successfully reworked the idea of adult vainglory saved by child genius in the tales of Captain Pugwash and his cabin-boy Tom from 1952. The idea of idiotic but adulated adult saved by slighted child assistant seems a purely post-war convention, but it is basic to *Treasure Island*, implicitly, the Squire being impeded by his stupidity, the Captain by his self-righteousness. Reduction to pictures with supportive text removed the respect-abilisation from such situations and left them plain subversive.

103. W. O. Lofts and D. J. Adley, *The World of Frank Richards* (1975), 143. Richards, *Autobiography*, 180–9. Mary Cadogan, *Frank Richards* (1975), 191–208. Jeffrey Richards, *Happiest Days – the Public School in English Fiction* (1988) is invaluable. Orwell, *Complete Works*, XVII, 414–16. D. W. Brogan, *Glasgow Herald*, 30 December 1961 (perhaps the best essay yet written on Richards, by the UK's leading Americanist). *Picture Post*, 11 May 1946. For Haydon, see 'Monty Hayward' in Leslie [Charles Bowyer Yin] Charteris, *Getaway* (1932), retitled *The Saint's Getaway*. I am deeply grateful to Professor Alastair Fowler for his comments on the *Magnet* and its superiority to the subsequent Bunter series.

104. Richards, *Punch*, 9 November 1960. Apart from any influence Vernon-Smith (the eternal rebel against school conformity, masters' regulations and schoolboy conventions) may have had on *1984*, O'Brien may owe something to an editorial 'My Own Page' supposedly by the corrupt bully and prefect Gerald Loder (and in fact probably by William Leslie Catchpole) *Magnet* 1,633 (3 June 1939): Orwell quotes from that issue (Orwell, *Complete Works*, XII, 68), and his view of Loder (ibid., 65) seems based on the Catchpole piece, which Orwell evidently thought to be Richards's once he accepted that Richards wrote all the stories). Orwell's note that Loder is 'given to saying sarcastic things about football and the team spirit' conforms to Catchpole, not Richards. So, a rebel might think that Loder was on his side; but (as the Catchpole self-portrait makes clear) he is not, and really supports the establishment he mocks, chiefly for reasons of personal power.

r 799

" WELCOME, WILKES "

Page 236

Frontispiece

FIGURE 2 The Quisling as schoolmaster (Jeffrey Havilton,
School vs Spy) – see pp. 76 n. 72, 409–10.

2

Rations and Quislings

'You leave this boy alone', said Mrs Bott, drawing William's unwilling head to her breast and impaling it on a diamond brooch. 'He's found me clothes coupongs for me, which is more'n you ever did, and I shall be grateful to him for the rest of me life. . . .'

Then Mrs Bott, still beaming happily, clasping her book of clothes coupons in both hands, rose to make her speech. It was a rambling incoherent speech. No one was quite sure what William was getting his prize for, except that it was for some act of heroism out of the common. One or two had a vague idea that he had saved Mrs Bott's life and was being presented with one of the Humane Society's medals. . . . Actually the prize was a bar of chocolate to which Mrs Bott impulsively added half a crown.

'And I wish there was more boys like you, William', she said earnestly.

Richmal Crompton, 'William Goes Fruit-Picking',
Modern Woman (April 1945),
republished in *William and the Brains Trust*
(April 1945), chapter 12

William had almost given up hope of being allowed to make any appreciable contribution to his country's cause when he heard his family discussing an individual called 'Quisling' who apparently and in a most mysterious fashion existed simultaneously in at least a dozen places.

'I bet there's one of 'em in England', said Robert darkly. 'Getting things ready or thinking he was getting things ready. . . . Gosh! I'd like to get my hands on him.'

'But who is he?' said William.

'Shut up!' said Robert. 'They're jolly well going to put a spoke in his wheel in Turkey. They never expected to find him in Holland or Belgium.'

'Holland or Belgium?' said William. 'Thought you said he was in Holland or Turkey. Thought –'

'Shut up!' said Robert and went on darkly: 'And he's right here in England, too. We'll have to keep our eyes open.'

Crompton, 'William Does His Bit', *Modern Woman* (September 1940)
and *William Does His Bit* (April 1941)

Rationing was probably the most unavoidable symbol of the 1940s to impress itself on the child population of the UK. In its most obvious form it meant scarcity, and perhaps disappearance, of sweets, chocolate, candy and (especially after American soldiers in transit had given them a taste for it) chewing-gum.[1] Its effects would have probably annoyed most children in inverse proportion to their parents: the child might most bitterly resent the loss of sweets and sweet foods, less bitterly the loss of nourishing foods, less bitterly still clothes (clothes obsession by most children, especially males, is well and truly post-war), less bitterly than that – soap. The priorities would vary with genders, classes, regions and ages, but the inverse from child to adult holds good, on most evidence. Far and away the best observer of Home Counties England in the war is Richmal Crompton in her 'William' stories, not least by virtue of her Gibbonian irony; and to her hilarious wisdom we will shortly return. But, like her fellow-authors, her availability to her young readers was under serious threat. When Frank Richards was silenced, innumerable lesser figures likewise saw their outlets and incomes vanish. Scandinavian forests closed, Canadian timber sailed at risk almost anywhere in the Atlantic. Publishers as late as February 1946 were reduced to 10 per cent of the paper they had used in 1939. Much depended on the accident of individual prejudices. A publisher like Wren Howard of Jonathan Cape, who would prefer to publish fiction for children than for adults (if driven to prioritise), meant a fair future for proven successes on his juvenile list such as Arthur Ransome.[2] It may not have been sentiment: Penguin's inauguration of its Puffin series in November 1941 was an investment to ensure that the reading child would mature into the Penguin-reading adult. The initial title, Barbara Euphan Todd's *Worzel Gummidge*, drew on its hardback success from publication in 1936 (although it was far older, having lingered in its author's possession as a reject for many years and been ultimately taken by the popular Catholic doctrinal firm, Burns Oates and Washbourne).[3] The *Wizard of Oz*, as a film reaching the UK in 1939, made scarecrows children-friendly for a much wider potential audience; and Gummidge, while more crotchety than L. Frank Baum's American creation, was firmly, indeed remorselessly, English in his crotchets. The Land Army, now including the elder siblings of many children, made the scarecrow a much more familiar figure; and no doubt, in the view of some of its recruits, many scarecrows were much more human than the farmers. London children as evacuees discovered the countryside with foreboding and trepidation: Worzel Gummidge helped make it theirs.[4]

Scottish publishers seem to have noted and profited by the diminution of juvenile titles in the lists of their London rivals. On the comic front, D. C. Thomson of Dundee stood firm, and its recently launched *Beano* and *Dandy* moved into the vacuum created by the slaughter of boys' weeklies in the Amalgamated Press, as did its comics for older boys *Adventure*, *Hotspur*, *Rover* and *Wizard*. Chambers of Edinburgh, heading its list with the Chalet School books by Elinor M. Brent-Dyer, and Blackie of Glasgow with Angela Brazil and Percy F. Westerman as its flagships, could restore some happiness to tear-stained faces deprived, perhaps, of much else in addition to beloved authors from London houses.[5] In books, as in lives, London took it and its casualties mounted, its publishers of Paternoster Row and Stationers' Hall saw their firms gutted, and its great wholesalers Simpkin, Marshall were bombed with the loss of six million books (Britain would lose 20 million in all throughout the war).[6] Firms running series had a particular incentive to continue an author and his/her favourites; but, for all of its pride of place for Crompton's 'William', George Newnes ended the *Happy* magazine in which he had appeared, keeping alive the ailing patriarch of its stable, the *Strand* (minus its star, P. G. Wodehouse, captured and put into a concentration camp by the Germans when France fell, and later boycotted in the UK for his innocent but idiotic decision to accept a German invitation to broadcast so as to tell his friends and family he was all right).[7] Newnes also maintained Enid Blyton's *Sunny Stories*, although in mid-war the ever-lessening supply of paper reduced it from weekly to fortnightly. Here, the presence of Blyton's husband, Hugh Pollock, in the firm would have been an argument to retain *Sunny Stories* instead of *Happy Mag*, despite the marriage itself later proving a war casualty.[8] Newnes found another outlet for the 'William' stories in *Modern Woman*, with a few going to *Homes & Gardens*. *Happy Mag* ended at the same time as the *Magnet*, May 1940, and William remained unchronicled for a couple of months until Newnes established him in his new home. The evacuation of the series indicated the downgrading of the juvenile market: William survived among features catering for his elder sister's interests (and even his mother's) rather than his, albeit no home or garden would have many hours of peace with William in it, nor any modern woman much sophistication when William let his darts of sarcasm fly.

We will return to the impact of rationing on reading, including the fate of children whom it starved of reading; but we must also face wider meanings. How far did readers find war itself rationed? How did censorship affect what children read? The classic case would be George Orwell's *Animal Farm*, prevented from publication in 1944 in the interest of the war effort by an official of the Ministry of Information (who warned off the contract-flourishing Jonathan Cape) and by T. S. Eliot (who as a right-wing pillar of (recent) Englishness thought it fundamentally anti-establishment and hence no choice for Faber & Faber). Orwell had begun the war by seeing children at risk from right-wing conspiracy; he then assumed that his story for children would be at risk from left-wing conspiracy. What he had only faintly anticipated was conspiracy from the right to safeguard the left. Ironically, both Cape (with its Ransome titles) and Faber (with its large list for young folk headed by Eliot's own comic verse *Old Possum's Book of Practical Cats*) could have given *Animal Farm* natural colleagues. Secker & Warburg, who defied official pressure (and Warburg's wife), were not children's publishers, and so *Animal Farm* was robbed of its appropriate category. Yet its towering strength rests on its being a child's story, one following the convention that prefers animals to human beings to the point of finding betrayal in humanisation. Orwell, about to adopt an infant son, knew from his Swift that satire must win its status as a story if the satire is to succeed, and this story had to be child-captivating. As such, it really works. The child blazes with anger at the unfairness – a crucial basis for juvenile judgement – when Boxer is treacherously taken to the knacker's yard so that the pigs whom he has served so well may get drunk on the proceeds. The adult may know that Boxer is the old Russian proletariat, or the original workers who stormed the Winter Palace, or the soul of the Russian soldiery, and that the pigs are Stalin and his lickspittles and spin-doctors. But the child gets Orwell's moral just as well by knowing none of these things.[9] Boxer lives as a character in his own right, as do Benjamin and Clover, Napoleon and Squealer; and Boxer has no difficulty in joining the child's contemporary heroes produced by Henry Williamson in *Tarka the Otter* and *Salar the Salmon*, by Richmal Crompton in William's Jumble, by Enid Blyton in George's Timmy and Jack's Kiki, by Eric Linklater in the Golden Puma and the Silver Falcon, by the *Dandy* comic's Black Bob, by Tolkien in his Eagles and C. S. Lewis in his Unicorn. None is a fully anthropomorphic figure (granted that Alison Uttley's Sam Pig and Maud Budden's Curly Wee may justly have their following without reproaches deserved by the humanoid pigs of *Animal Farm*). All of them defy humans at various stages: the Puma is killed when killing the Hitler-figure of Linklater's *Wind on the Moon*, but all of the others also show independence of mind, sometimes with mental superiority to their human friends or acquaintances. Raymond Williams seems to have found *Animal Farm* an anti-human book; if so, he was quite right, and so was it.[10]

But was truth rationed elsewhere, and if so how? Let us return to that conversation between Biggles and von Stalhein supposedly in the first days of the war (coinciding with actual British offensives around the Kiel Canal).[11] Johns must have worked on the story almost from the war's outbreak to be ready for serialisation in the *War Thriller* from 9 March 1940: it *is* a fine war thriller, but careful, measured and probably judiciously revised with one eye on the as yet unknown quirks of Second World War censorship, which Johns of all people had reason to fear, all the more because its magazine outlet had an audience mostly from readers of age for armed service. No doubt the report of the RAF raid on 4 September 1939 on the great canal linking the South Baltic with the North Sea influenced Johns's choice of location; it also gave the book drive, so conspicuously lacking elsewhere in the phoney war, and elation, which was rapidly vanishing during the weeks of its serial appearance. But the metaphor implicit in von Stalhein's discovery of the sleeping Biggles spelt itself out with implications for the UK's lack of pre-war preparedness. Johns had given credit for government foresight in which he did not himself believe, when, at the opening of the story and of the war, Colonel Raymond of Air Intelligence tells Biggles, Algy and Ginger:

'I may as well tell you that you were earmarked for this particular job months ago; in fact, it would hardly be an exaggeration to say that this job was specially created for you. . . . Some time ago, perceiving that war might not be averted, we took the precaution of acquiring from one of the [neutral] countries [on the Baltic coast] an uninhabited island so small as to be negligible. . . .'

– whence the secret base. At the end, when after much success it has been lost,

Colonel Raymond smiled knowingly. 'A secret base – yes; but not the only one we possess. We've been busy in the Baltic for some time past. Bergen Ait isn't the only island that threatens Germany. But that's for your private ear – perhaps I shouldn't have told you. . . .' ·

Biggles, facing von Stalhein, reflects more of the real situation on preparedness for war as Johns saw it:

Biggles realized the futility of protest. 'Purely as a matter of detail, how did you find your way here?'

The German held up Biggles's map. 'It was most thoughtful of you to make pencil marks that brought me almost directly to Bergen Ait. An officer of your experience should have known better.'

'You're quite right. I deserve to be shot for such criminal folly', agreed Biggles. . . .

'. . . I have a firing party on parade outside. I presume it will not be necessary for me to use force to induce you to report yourself to them. I will make the necessary introduction before the *unter-offizier* takes charge.'

Biggles rose slowly from the bed. 'You won't object to my having a cigarette?' he asked politely.

'Of course not', replied von Stalhein reproachfully. 'Is there anything else I can do for you – any messages – you know the sort of thing? I hate being dramatic, but at such moments as this it is usual –'

Biggles lighted a cigarette and flicked the dead match away. 'That's very kind of you, von Stalhein', he said coldly. 'I hope to do as much for you one day.'

The German smiled confidently. 'Then you will have to be very quick about it. Shall we go?'

Biggles nodded. 'I suppose we may as well.'

Von Stalhein clicked to attention and bowed as Biggles preceded him through the door to the depot.

A squad of marines, under an N.C.O., was in waiting.

End of chapter; and a tenth of the book elapses before Ginger (who has lost himself on a teenage exploration of the island's interior) puts the firing-party out of action with a machine-gun.[12]

Biggles has faced firing-squads before, though not composed of Germans. Johns, as a First World War pilot, had been captured and apparently was told of his own imminent execution for throwing bombs from his aircraft. His observer, A. E. Amey (remembered as Algy Lacey?), had been killed in the crash, and Johns had recalled the episode for the readers of *Popular Flying*, edited by himself, in June 1936. In 1938 Winston Churchill's volume of speeches came out, warning of Hitler's bellicose intentions, its US title being *While England Slept*. Johns had been vociferous as a journalist in demanding a build-up of air defence, and in 1939 government pressure on the publishers, George Newnes, resulted in his removal from the editorships of *Popular Flying* and *Flying* with effect from

May. Various Biggles books had carried implicit messages on the need for alertness against Germany and Japan, whether directly or allegorically (for example in the Ruritanian *Biggles Goes to War* (1938), serialised in *Modern Boy*, September–December 1937); but, under wartime conditions, any implied criticism of government inadequacy was emphatically rationed. Neither Johns nor Oxford University Press would have wished to attract a vendetta from the Churchill government (vindictive when under artistic threat, real or imagined; witness its fury against the *Daily Mirror* over Zec's cartoon of a wrecked seaman captioned that the petrol price had risen by a penny, or the movie *The Life and Death of Colonel Blimp*, which Churchill may have suspected of implying his own anachronism). It would have been ironic, since Churchill had spoken for the policies with which Johns was broadly in sympathy. But the Churchill government's existence was fortuitous where *Biggles in the Baltic* was concerned: it had been written and serialised during the pre-miership of Johns's enemy, Neville Chamberlain, indicted by Johns for inadequate air strategy, which Chamberlain's men answered by the removal of one enemy – Johns himself. *Biggles in the Baltic* was Johns's first chance to reply to a ruler who muzzled his critics. Secret suppression was the convention at that time – an enraged Churchill might be as bad – and, with war powers, Johns was even more vulnerable to government vengeance. But, like Swift before him and Orwell after him, Johns, when defeated and silenced as a journalist, could turn back to his imaginative resources. And so Biggles slept, to be awakened by von Stalhein.[13]

Biggles in retrospect has been written off as a wooden, textbook hero; and perhaps in his later, formulaic career as an air detective working for Scotland Yard he was. But in the 1930s and 1940s he is far from formulaic, for the very good reason that, like Gulliver, he had several functions to perform and thus became several different people. Johns, in the creation of Biggles in First World War short stories beginning with 'The White Fokker' in 1932, drew on mem-ories of his own and his fellow-officers' experiences, and so Biggles is variously brave, judicious, foolish, frustrated, love-lorn, drunk, re-bellious, childish and, above all, surrounded by comrades who will shortly be dead. These appeared in *The Camels are Coming*; and, while the subsequent stories from the Great War (as it was still commonly called during the Second World War) made Biggles less vulnerable, they compensated by making him more comic. Johns appealed to his schoolboy readers by reminding them – sometimes in prefatory words – how recently Biggles had been among their counterparts of his day. But the first stories had appeared in Johns's own magazine, *Popular Flying*, thus firmly linked to what was otherwise intended for an adult audience. That Biggles, with his love for what turns out to be a German spy ('I will be very kind to you, my Biggles') and subsequent alcoholism ('He's drinking whisky for his breakfast'), was a character with problems that bourgeois children were supposed not to know about.

It may well have been that, in the privations of inter-war depression, many of them knew far too much about parental love affairs and excessive drink, and working-class children might know even more; but Oxford University Press would hardly acknowledge such an audience awareness. The *Modern Boy* and the *Gem* were bought by boys (and girls) of all classes, and it was there that Biggles found his first formally child audience, beginning in January 1933, although the first stories had found book publication by John Hamilton in mid-1932. But Johns's initial presumption of adult readers (to be told the ordeals of the flyers who had fought and died for them) stayed with his early Biggles work as a recurrent ghost. *Biggles Flies Again*, the first collection of post-war Biggles short stories, began in mid-1933 in *Popular Flying*. They are not particularly adult stories, but they have some adult context: 'Three Weeks' involves the marooning of a USSR spy on an island, to be picked up three weeks later when he can no longer affect the issue; and Biggles leaves with him a copy of Elinor Glyn's *Three Weeks*. Glyn was a great sex-symbol of the 1920s; and, even if airmen did not read her, they would probably have known

> Would you like to sin
> With Elinor Glyn
> On a tiger-skin?

Her *Three Weeks* was in fact published first in 1907; but, twenty years after, Glyn's *It* (1927) was the classic identification of sex and personal magnetism, and the clear implication was that the Russian spy would have been left in an agony of frustration, sexual as well as professional. The *Modern Boy* was not expected to be as modern as that, but it no doubt won a guffaw from the average reader of *Popular Flying*. Sex thereafter disappeared from the stories, more or less – in fact, Biggles's ineptitude when confronted by women is an occasional recurrent joke – although, following the Melville convention in Polynesian adventure, the teenage Ginger experiences a camaraderie with faint notes of young love with the Kanaka girl Full Moon, in *Biggles in the South Seas*.[14] But Johns did not ignore the possibility

of fathers and uncles helping themselves to the latest Biggles; and
Penguin Books (rather than reprinting Biggles in their new children's
series, Puffins)[15] brought out *Biggles Flies Again* in the month of the
first Puffins, November 1941. The implication was that this was
adult fare – and, since Lane apparently went searching for a Johns
book in the first months of Penguin in 1936–7, he would not have
been initially ready to take a 'juvenile'. But, by 1941, the children who
had read Biggles in *Modern Boy* in 1933, when thirty of the first
Biggles stories were reprinted,[16] were now in the armed forces, to
which Penguin inside covers told readers to send their books when
read – and in the case of air-force personnel, Biggles had sent some of
them there. Unlike Johns's first Biggles publishers, John Hamilton,
Oxford Univerity Press deliberately aimed at the child market as
defined by 'Mr' and 'Mrs' 'Herbert Strang'; but, without formally
seeking a return to the young adult market, *Biggles in the Baltic* had
first emerged in the adult weekly *War Thriller*. It was intended for
the age-bracket of Biggles when he had first fought, and of his
comrades who were killed: Ginger, having started out in 1935 aged
about 15, was now of an age with the youngest recruits.

How much did children's writers think primarily of the adult
buying the book and reading it over the child's shoulder? It's hard to
be precise: even in comics, there must certainly have been awareness
among those for the youngest that adults would be reading them to
the children. *Tiger Tim's Weekly*, a casualty of the war, must have
been so prepared. Strips with captions in hyphenated syllables ('funny old Stri-py') might pretend direct address to children, but no such
simplification assumed the absence of an adult helper. Magazines
founded in Victorian times, such as *Little Folks*, might presume
independence from a nurse or nanny but were firmly written to
homologate presumed parental prejudices. *The Boy's Own Paper*
showed frequent signs of being written in the expectations of
scrutiny by ministers of religion as well as by God – sometimes
quite a likeable, friendly God, not necessarily on the side of questionable authority, but still God. But the *Gem* and *Magnet* had
definite sights on children first and last, in accordance with Richards's convictions. The D. C. Thomson comics seem to have
followed that example. Their more tabloid (ultimately fully tabloid)
Beano and *Dandy*, born at the end of the 1930s, were definitely non-
parental in aim, as a result of which they were ready for the Second
World War scene, when most parents had no time for supervision.
Comics presuming knowledge of new media, such as *Radio Fun* and
Film Fun, were more likely to assume an adult awareness: radio-

listening and film-watching were often likely to remain supervised, and the comic material had to know that it catered for graduates of a shared experience. (It may be why those comics survived: belief in an adult readership meant that chances of survival were greater, to judge by the drop in publication of children's books.) As regards the books, school stories between hard covers did not buck the public-school ethic, but schoolmasters writing school stories were careful to ensure that portraits of teachers were from a child perspective, albeit a well-informed, imaginative child.[17]

A writer for children also writing for adults, such as Richmal Crompton, might inject slightly acid asides which children might not get, might skip or might elucidate with the aid of an adult (whose appreciative howl of laughter would increase the interest). That was all right: Crompton wanted an adult audience, but, win or lose, she was firmly on William's side against the adults – sometimes ruthlessly so. It's clear that William disposed of some of her private vendettas, including the over-zealous fire officer who annoyed her when she volunteered in the Second World War, and who was savagely reborn as Section Officer Perkins to be humiliated in (and, eponymously, by) 'William – the Fire-Fighter'.[18] Where Crompton's unfulfilled ambition in the adult market injured her matchless achievement with William was when concentration on adult novels evidently impaired her child-market productivity, and William short stories slid from eleven in 1941 to two in 1945.[19] Granted, the wartime William stories showed no diminution in Crompton's very high standards; but Noel Streatfeild's distinguished adult novel *I Ordered a Table for Six* (1942) may partly explain why her output for children in the war years was lower in quality than her norm. Like Crompton, she shone in satire at adult expense, but unlike Crompton she was uneasy in sharing such barbs with children. Neither writer would have dreamed of patronising their child audience, or to have played what Second World War children might have called Quislings, where an author ostensibly on the child's side hints at subliminal conformity to the vigilant, over-watchful adult. The war was a bad time for such authors: it rationed adults.[20] Blyton proved the spirit of that time, taking advantage of the lack of parental involvement to build a children's world whence adults were excluded, and to do so in language excluding adult consumption. Her enchantment immunised countless children from trauma when their homes were bombed, their families scattered and their parents distanced, and her narratives implied that such conditions were natural for thousands who in peacetime would never have known boarding-school, parental divorce or parental death, or other means of child isolation. It was the creative response of a child who had suffered isolation.

Johns came into a different category: he wrote primarily for people who were interested in what he had to tell them of the air and its people. If children were those most interested, he would tell his tales to children. If adults wanted to read him, he was ready for them. In a sense, he was most aware of adult members of his audience when he was on the ground and put in political bits for them. Equally, girls could enjoy Biggles's lack of ease with young women where boys thought it natural but irrelevant.[21] *Biggles in the Baltic* was Johns's first chance to speak at length to the audience he had lost when *Popular Flying* and *Flying* had been taken from him four months before war and ten months before serialisation began in *War Thriller*. Biggles had begun in April 1932 in *Popular Flying*: Biggles could speak for Johns, politically, but only briefly and inferentially. Here, it was his innocent and exhausted frame trapped by Nazi Germany which had to convey his message, much as the early boy pilot had spoken in his lifestyle. Here, Biggles's self-accusation of criminal folly leading to the invasion of his island and destruction of his base had its particular meaning for Johns's old audience, accustomed to his attacks on government folly. Here, too, that audience could enjoy his Swiftian irony in crediting the government with exactly the kind of preparedness he had so often excoriated them for not making. The very fact that he began by having Raymond invoke secrecy, now omnipresent in government-speak, expedited the story while enhancing the irony: the editor of *Popular Flying* had been fired by secret intrigue from a government with little to justify its secrecy (and, if Johns's readers bereft of his editorials lacked a reason for change of editor, they had had ample reasons to deduce it).

> Colonel Raymond pointed to a map of Europe that nearly covered one wall of his office: its varnished surface was decorated with drawing-pins of different colours, each marking a point of strategical importance. 'I need hardly say that what I am going to tell you is in the strictest confidence', he said earnestly. 'One careless word might undo the work of months. . . .'
>
> '. . . We have been preparing this [South Baltic island] depot for some time. The aircraft are, in fact, already there, as well as other equipment likely to be required . . .'

Johns was here positing a reverse operation from the German pre-war penetration of British North Sea defences foretold by Erskine

Childers thirty-six years earlier in *The Riddle of the Sands* (which had previously inspired Johns's *The Black Peril* (1935), where Biggles and Algy – picking up for the first time the working-class nomad Ginger – foil a USSR attempt at air infiltration of the North Sea approaches to Britain: Germany became the putative enemy once more in 1936). Johns, satirically, was now suggesting that Britain had been making similar but even more radical pre-war preparations in 1939. It had its charms. Ostensibly, he was telling his youthful readers that a wise and benevolent government had everything in hand, and had had it there since Munich. Actually, he was telling any well-informed adult who flew the Baltic with Biggles that this is what the government should have been doing and certainly had not. His former readers of *Popular Flying* would add *Biggles in the Baltic*'s camouflaged mockery to what they remembered of its more explosive editorials of past years.

For build-up of morale, the book was in other respects admirable. If Biggles was no longer so comic, Johns had not relinquished his ability for combining fighting and fun. (In *Biggles Goes to War*, he even made diplomacy constructively amusing where most chauvinist writers were merely boisterous at its expense: Biggles briefly became a first-class international diplomat, combining wit with skill.) Biggles, rescued by Algy's torpedo sinking the *Leipzig*, lands to be greeted by the secret Squadron's Cockney cook, murderously swinging a rifle: 'Luv a duck, sir, if it ain't the C.O. . . . What have you been doing, sir, if I may make so free as to ask?' – to which Biggles replies, in the finest music-hall traditions: 'Riding round the front in a hansom cab with Hitler'. This has immediately followed a supposed death-struggle between Biggles and what proves to be Algy, ending in schoolboy recriminations. If Johns knew war flying through the time-lenses of the First World War, he could at least endow its practitioners of Second World War with their precursors' high spirits. By the time of book publication, these were badly needed: events were rationing high spirits fairly drastically. Norway and Denmark were invaded by the Third Reich on 9 April 1940, and Norwegian resistance ended on 10 June. Johns had been all too correct in his belief that the UK had needed a pre-war Scandinavian strategy, and Scandinavia provided the theatre of the next Second World War Biggles novels, published in August 1941.[22]

The theme of secrecy in *Biggles in the Baltic* was sounded in the overture to purpose within the subsequent, Baltic-set chapters. The story turns in part on what might be termed the Looking-Glass war of British and German attempts to capture one another's codes,

Biggles's tiny 'Z Squadron' winning, and thus vital in Biggles's
talk with von Stalhein preliminary to his own jointly anticipated
execution:[23]

> 'Suppose I ask a few questions for a change?' suggested von
> Stalhein. 'Where are your friends?'
>   A ray of hope shot through Biggles's mind, for all the time he had
> been talking, although he had not shown it, one terrible thought
> was uppermost in his mind. It was Roy, in the signals room, whom
> he was thinking about, for on his desk lay the most vital document
> any German agent could hope to secure – the British secret code-
> book. The German code was there, too, but that didn't matter. At
> first he had taken it for granted that Roy had been found, and the
> code-book with him; but now, in view of the German's question, it
> began to look as if this was not so, otherwise von Stalhein would
> have commented on it. One of his few weaknesses was vanity, and
> if he had indeed secured the code-book he could hardly have
> refrained from gloating over it.
>   So Biggles merely effected [sic] a yawn. 'Why, aren't they here?'
> he enquired.
>   Von Stalhein regarded him narrowly. 'No', he snapped, 'they're
> not. But doubtless they will return in due course. I'll wait for them
> – but there is no reason why you should. . . .'

We discover in the next chapter that Roy has escaped, though
initially not far enough. Whatever Johns may have been expecting
or fearing as official reaction to his book, all we know is that he said
he was asked by the Air Ministry to write stories about the Women's
Auxiliary Air Force, and that since the first of these – the first
instalment of *Worrals of the W.A.A.F.* – had begun to appear in the
Girl's Own Paper in October 1940, it was Johns's next substantial
fiction after *Biggles in the Baltic*. The same issue (or its sequel)[24]
carried an article by Johns, headed 'Life in the WAAF'. Readers
might have noted that it said nothing about WAAF personnel
actually flying aircraft, which Worrals does as her main work. What
Johns's serial story was describing was activities of the women's
section of the Air Transport Auxiliary, headed by Pauline Gower
(who wrote mildly feminist air adventures for the *Chatterbox* and
would share honours with Johns as non-fiction columnist for the
Girl's Own Paper), and in which the tragic hero of British female
aeronautics, Amy Johnson, was serving when she died. Johns would
base Worrals (of whom much more later) on Johnson and Gower. But

why should he ascribe their work to the WAAF and why did nobody pull him up? The answer, I suspect, was not carelessness but camouflage. *Biggles in the Baltic* may indeed have invited some official alarm, since the search for enemy codes and the protection of Britain's own were a massive priority and were vital work of the WAAF. Britain had done at home what Biggles had done in the Baltic: it cracked the German code. My conclusion is that Johns was called in, asked not to write about codes again, and was invited to write fiction for girls on what the WAAF was *not* doing as a way of distracting enemy attention from what it actually was doing. (The whole thing would easily have been handled over lunch.) It accounts for the Air Ministry's sudden confidence in Johns as a propagandist when but a few months earlier he had been terminated as a propagandist by (rather than with) extreme prejudice. It explains why codes vanished from Johns's Second World War fiction. It does not mean that he was told much of the WAAF code-breaking, simply that he was told enough to silence him in future. Withdrawal of *Biggles in the Baltic* would naturally have invited attention as to why the Air Ministry feared a child's story; and the Nazis would hardly take long to read that riddle. In any event, Johns made no future contribution to the Looking-Glass war, never again implying (as he had) that the German mirror had been cracked.[25]

   Worrals of the W.A.A.F. did run into censorship trouble, but not in the UK. Eire under de Valera was officially mathematically neutral. In fact, de Valera secretly aided the UK where possible but knew well that, apart from the IRA's alliance with Germany, some of his own party with former IRA affiliation took their Anglophobia to a pro-German level. De Valera isolated key figures by assigning them to tasks of seeming importance but relative insignificance, among them press censorship, placed under Frank Aiken. The *Irish Times*, still Protestant, Unionist and Tory, was firmly pro-UK subject to frequent censorship, and itched for means to ridicule the censors and expose their partiality. R. M. Smyllie, the editor, knew that ridicule reigned supreme in any battle for Irish public opinion, and his staff of satirists were unmatched in the world. Seething at the censors' insistence on seeing proofs of the book-review page in advance the reviews he had the first Worrals book reviewed in terms which led to the review's suppression: the review was submitted for state scrutiny in January 1943, over a year after book publication, which might have suggested an ambush; but humour was in rather short supply among the censors. Smyllie then put in the exact same review with the title *Lotte of the Luftwaffe*, and names altered as needful, Worrals, Frecks

and so on becoming Gretchen, Lilli (though apparently not Marlene)
and so on. This was delivered to the censor in proof among a stack of
innocuous items, and was duly cleared for publication. 'Smyllie then
raised all hell on the grounds that the incident proved Irish censorship was biased in favour of the Germans' and the censors threatened to have the entire paper submitted before publication. If
enforced, this would have meant virtual suppression; and they
did in fact ban or hopelessly mutilate 111 book reviews in the next
two years.[26] But Worrals, from camouflage, had scored a direct hit.

Johns accustomed himself to the Second World War in varying
ways with varying success. His short stories published as *Spitfire
Parade* in August 1941 were intended to cash in on, and celebrate, the
Battle of Britain, as a companion volume in date of publication to the
two other Scandinavian forays, *Biggles Sees it Through* and *Biggles
Defies the Swastika*, while Oxford also simultaneously brought out
The Third Biggles Omnibus comprising *Biggles in the Baltic*, *Biggles
Goes to War* and *Biggles in Spain*, all clearly chosen as titles either
concerned with the Second World War or by now related to it.
Oxford had lost its new editor for children to the war, but it could
still deduce that a market existed among children, many of whom
were probably interested in the war raining down on them, although
it proved too much to expect the university press to move Johns's
payment from fixed sums to a royalty. Oxford's assistant editor,
Frank Eyre, later insisted that 'It wasn't until after the war that their
phenomenal sales began', but the facts belie him. Oxford was not
likely to squander its paper rations on an omnibus volume for an
unsuccessful author for children. In fact, Oxford's parsimony induced Johns, or rather Johns's common-law wife Doris Leigh, to seek
an agent, A. P. Watt, whose advice took the Biggles titles to Hodder &
Stoughton. The Biggles books had traditionally carried colour frontispieces of real artistic merit by Doris's brother Howard Leigh,
usually featuring air drama; Leigh died (of heart failure induced
by cancer) in February 1942.[27]

But, if Oxford did not treat Johns well during the war, he had given
it short measure in *Spitfire Parade*. Its first two stories preceded the
Battle of Britain in conception but had been published, and presumably written, in the early months of the war, and were now
reworked for book publication. But Johns was not at ease with the
changes in aircraft manufacture and pilot speech, and his excess of
knowledge of the First World War, and dearth of knowledge of the
Second World War drove him to cannibalise adventures of Biggles
devised to bring to literary life the air wars of 1917–18 in France. As

his biographers remark, 'One Sopwith Camel plus 200 mph does not really amount to a Spitfire'.[28] Johns acknowledged some contrasts in the wars. Biggles's comrades no longer died in the Second World War, although there was heavy attrition among pilots and personnel whom he encountered outwith his squadrons. (Death is as much a character in *Biggles in the Orient* as in a story by Ambrose Bierce.) The Nazis in general are nastier than the Germans of 1914–18. A few Germans show the chivalry and humour associated with – or imagined for – the air wars a quarter-century earlier,[29] but von Stalhein's emotions degenerate from his inter-war obvious affection for Biggles to a homicidal hatred. In either case, he would be ready to kill him, but before 1939 it would be because he had to, after it because he wanted to. Johns was slow to substitute 'Nazi' for 'German' in alluding to the adversary, but the meaning of Hitler's leadership is clear enough from his texts. He stands somewhere between Gilson, who identified the nature of Nazism above all in its murderous racism, and Westerman, who seemed simply to warm up his First World War Teutonophobia, mentally substituting 'Hitler' for the Kaiser in his diatribes (as Elias literally had done). Johns, like many another, discovered that Nazi evil was even worse than the most vociferous British war propaganda could make it: the most odious Nazis are in fact those encountered in the adventures immediately after the Second World War (apart from von Stalhein, who slowly makes his way towards reconciliation over ten years and ten books). In particular, allusion to or symbol for concentration-camp horrors only became a major theme for Johns in 1949.[30] Another factor was vulnerability: it is important in the use of children's literature for war propaganda that, while the heroes may be wounded, and taken prisoner, the likelihood of death outside combat is much less pronounced when the villains are Nazis, the conditions wartime and the heroes male. The commandos' most frightening experiences with the Nazis in Johns's fiction are when Nazi 'were-wolves' begin post-war murders of what they term British 'war criminals' in *Gimlet Mops Up* (including the use of drag disguise at a fox-hunt, appropriately chapter-titled 'In at the Death').[31] Another interesting result of what came to light after the war's end was the divisions and mutual hostilities between the Nazis themselves: it characterises the finale in *Sergeant Bigglesworth, C.I.D.* (1947), *Biggles' Second Case* (1948) and *Worrals in the Wastelands* (1949). This might seem an obvious end to a criminal conspiracy – and, in these post-war books, much emphasis is laid on the criminal identity of Nazism – but it is continually stressed that Nazis (rather than criminals) 'usually end by shooting each other'. Hugh Trevor-Roper's *The Last Days of Hitler* (1947) probably strengthened that feeling.[32] On the other hand, Johns saw it as 'entirely German . . . lacking any sense of humour' rather than simply Nazi (although Nazism is impossible to reconcile with a sense of humour, as Richards pointed out). Johns was following the First World War tradition that the Germans had no sense of humour and were seriously concerned about the fact, realising that it was losing them the war. Johns also insisted that the Germans lacked imagination, which he evidently felt required a sense of humour. That kind of imagination is certainly a credential for telling or writing stories for children. It also meant that his youthful readers could comfort themselves in their privations with the thought that the people trying to bomb and invade them would never be able to produce Biggles books. It was an exhilarating thought.

It was fed by the humour with which Biggles met his ill-luck, such as in *Biggles Sees it Through* when Algy, Ginger and he discover that none of them has the papers they have just informed Raymond they had obtained and that they will have to retrieve them from a jacket partly buried under an avalanche:[33]

Then suddenly he laughed. 'Forgive me', he implored the Colonel, 'I can't help it. It's the daftest thing I ever did or ever heard of. If you only knew what we went through to get those confounded documents – and now we rush back home and leave them lying in the snow like a lot of waste paper. You must admit it has its funny side.'

The Germans had been translating Biggles before the outbreak of war, however, with or without enquiries as to his creator's Aryan race. So had the Norwegians and Swedes. This helps account for Johns's Scandinavian preoccupation in sending Biggles to war in 1939–40; but, if Norway and Sweden knew about Johns, he seems to have had little sense of them. Like many of his predecessors in juvenile literature, he would often plant his hero in territory unknown to either of them, being able to add to the atlases, histories, dictionaries, news reports, and works by Arthur Mee, his own recollections of air-force gossip. His reading was wide. The author of *Biggles Flies South* knew his Herodotus. The author of *Biggles Flies North* knew his Jack London. He knew the desert from personal experience, as well as from the works of P. C. Wren and the unwanted acquaintance of T. E. Lawrence. Yet his Norway and

Finland never come to life with his flesh-and-blood sense of the places and people of the desert, of Arctic Canada, of India and, above all, of his beloved France. And that last was probably the trouble. Scandinavia in the 1941 books is doing duty for what Johns could not bring himself to describe. Britain congratulated itself on Dunkirk. Johns could not forget what – and who – had been left behind. We get some sense of the horror he was fighting when Biggles meets a (though not the) Norwegian Quisling:[34]

> 'I thought you were a Norwegian.'
>
> 'So I am', was the staggering reply, 'but I've always admired the Nazis – and it was made worth my while to play on their side. There were three of us here in the swim, but none of us guessed that you were in it too.'
>
> At last Biggles understood. Three of the members of the flying club were in German pay, and now that he had arrived on a Nazi motor-cycle they assumed, not unnaturally, that he, too, was in Nazi employ. The knowledge struck him to the very core. Spying was something he could understand; there had always been, and always would be, spies. It was one of the oldest professions in the world [Joshua chapter 2], and was, after all, a part of the un-pleasant business of war. But what he could not understand, and what he could not forgive, was a man playing traitor to his own country. Yet there were three such men here, men who were far worse than spies; they were renegades, traitors in the most despicable sense.

Johns stressed the financial motive – no doubt a factor with Quis-lings in many Nazi conquests – because a youthful audience was hardly ripe for being told that Vidkun Quisling was actually a Norwegian political party leader, intending Norway to become Nazi in its own right, albeit in practice merely a leader of Hitler stooges. Such was Sean Russell, head of the IRA, who died on board a German submarine smuggling him back to Ireland on 14 August 1940, save that he would have called the Nazism he had on offer Republicanism. Johns was trying not to dwell on the French variety of accommodationist, Henri Philippe Pétain, whom with the rest of his fellow-soldiers in 1916 he would have revered as the hero of Verdun, and who was now the signatory of the French dishonour-able peace with Germany and the head of state in the part of his country that he had not signed away. But this was evidently what he had in mind: Pétain became Prime Minister on 16 June, twelve days after the end of the Dunkirk evacuation and six after resistance had formally ceased in Norway.

There were other interpreters of Quisling available for British children, as shown in Crompton's 'William Does His Bit' (*Modern Woman*, October 1940):

> 'This particular man was a Norwegian and helped the Germans to get a footing in his country, and other people in other countries who try to do the same are all called Quisling.'
>
> 'Why?' said William. 'Why can't they call them by their real names?'
>
> 'They don't know what their real names are.'
>
> . . . 'How do they do it? How do they get people to let ole Hitler in?'
>
> Mrs Brown sighed resignedly.
>
> 'I'm not quite sure, dear. I think they sort of make people believe that they'd have no chance of resisting him and so it's best to let him in. They try to frighten people. At least, I think that's it.'
>
> 'Why doesn't the gov'ment lock 'em up?'
>
> 'They don't know who they are.'
>
> 'Thought they knew they were called Grisling.'
>
> 'No, dear, they don't.'
>
> 'I s'pose they *pretend* to be called other things jus' to put the gov'ment right off the scent.'

William then concludes that an ARP exercise rehearsing disaster bulletins is an attempt to create alarm and despondency, and denounces the Supervisor of Marleigh Report Centre to a policeman as

> 'ole Grissel. He's handin' the country over to ole Hitler. I tell you, I've seen him doin' it. He was doin' it all this mornin'. Listen. If you let him go now he'll give the country over to ole Hitler straight away. I tell you I've heard him doin' it – telephonin' people and tellin' 'em that the whole place was blown up jus' to scare 'em. He's got people workin' under him, too, same as he had in Norfolk. They were all telephonin' an' tellin' people the whole place was blown up jus' to scare 'em. . . .'

Although in the process William pulls the Supervisor's moustache as hard as he can to prove he is disguised, 'Mr Balham was an extremely patriotic little man, and he felt that William's zeal, though mistaken, was on the whole commendable. After dismissing the policeman, he had refreshed William with a large currant bun and a glass of lemonade and finally presented him with half a crown.' This is kind enough, but Crompton's target was clearly the excess of patriotic zeal which she saw as understandably omnipresent. She had not dismissed the possibility of spies, and William accidentally catches three – a supposed ornithologist actually sketching aeroplane designs (April 1940), a listener-in to armed-forces café gossip, and the 'old soldier' to whom she passes on the important data (January 1943).[35] Crompton also enjoyed herself caricaturing the simulated exercises which an eager schoolboy might so readily take to be the real thing, and where (she implies) some of the participants also lose contact with the difference between simulation and reality. In so doing, she provided her contemporaries and posterity with some of the clearest evidence we could ask on how events were retailed, confused, discussed and reinterpreted, and what form counter-invasion or air-raid precaution exercises took. Crompton believed in heavy rationing of spy mania, although in her quiet way she knew how to convey what to expect if the invader came and how to act if (not when) he did. Like Blyton, she knew how to convey the economics of courage: a child who feels fear is braver than one who does not, if s/he does not give way to it. But Crompton went farther: William actually captures his last two spies because his fear of them gives him the clue to their guilt. She makes very little fuss about his courage, but he follows them and gets his proof. As for Quisling, Crompton's answer was to laugh him off. Like Johns, her finest message was to trust in the English sense of humour. She could also lay claim to imagination based on experience, as he did: the female spy picking up canteen gossip is a volunteer, as Crompton herself was, in the same role. They evidently agreed with Yeats that all ladders start 'in the foul rag and bone shop' of the writer's heart. Curiously, although Johns lacked her experience, the most effective antagonist for Biggles that he created in the Second World War was also a canteen waiter, a Japanese passing as Burmese. No better elaboration of the ubiquitous slogan 'CARELESS TALK COSTS LIVES' exists in Second World War children's fiction than *Biggles in the Orient*. He may well have got the idea from reading Crompton, from whose Ginger, closest friend of William, Johns had probably taken the name of the boy with whom Biggles's readers were intended to identify. Crompton also won graceful textual homage from Blyton and Brent-Dyer.[36]

This intertextuality was noted by child readers with pleasure long before academics made livings from it. In the Second World War it created resonances of a united front. The fictionists for youth seem to have had broad agreement with one another, and to have made much less of their differences in quality and outlook than subsequent critics and librarians were to do. Controversy among fellow-writers for the young was firmly rationed. Crompton gleefully satirised A. A. Milne's Christopher Robin poems, and M. Pardoe's Bunkle and siblings wondered how fictional counterparts avoided the need to relieve themselves; but those were the limits of censure apart from covert hostile reviewing.[37] Henry Williamson's drift into sympathy for Hitler in the 1930s earned internment for him when the Second World War began, but his *Tarka the Otter* received clear homage in Alison Uttley's Sam Pig tale 'The Boat' and in B.B.'s prizewinning *The Little Grey Men*. Blyton largely excluded war from her wartime fiction, and Johns was largely preoccupied with it, but his remarks against war (such as Biggles's bitter asides in the context of spies) are more drastic than hers. Anger against adult brutality is as strong in Blyton as in Eleanor Graham in 1938, and the resentment against parental folly masquerading as wisdom is common to both in the years of war's advent. Blyton and Noel Streatfeild played simultaneously with themes of ousted rulers in 1939–40. They also had a common interest in themes of escapism and rediscovery of responsibility in the circus. Streatfeild's *The Children of Primrose Lane* mixes William Brown and Ginger by starting with three children called Brown with hair identified as 'ginger', and one of the other families has as its only child an analogy to Crompton's spoiled, lisping, selfish, ruthless Violet Elizabeth Bott, always infuriating William and Ginger quite inescapably.[38]

It's not surprising, therefore, to find Kitty Barne, prizewinning novelist for children, producing in *We'll Meet in England* another Norwegian imbroglio which supplements Johns's *Biggles Defies the Swastika*; although set exactly a year later, it also pays it amusing tribute. Johns's leading strength was to put his readers very firmly on the Norwegian map, as Biggles, pursued by the ever-doomed von Stalhein, hurtles between Oslo, Narvik, Stavanger and other appropriate points. Barne's story of an Anglophone family, whose Norwegian sailor father is away and (as it proves) in the navy of the Norwegian regime in exile, is set initially in 'Holmsund', but where that stands on the Norwegian coast (a dozen or so degrees of latitude in extent) is anyone's guess. It is presumably southern enough to make the sail voyage to England (on which the story climaxes) a shorter and less Arctic affair than Spitzbergen or Trondheim would necessitate, yet it must be northern enough to prevent the Nazi agent in thin disguise from calling up auxiliaries rapidly. Barne's readers learned rather more about Norway than Johns's, although (in another sense) it is also a slightly crash course:[39]

> No helping with the hay this year, hanging it over the fences to dry, fetching it in sledges where it was too steep for wheels. No going up to the *saeter*, the uplands pasture where the cattle spent the summer; no cheese-making there; no St John's Eve feast on mid-summer night when you danced all night and were allowed to drink egg-flip. The picking of bilberries and cowberries would have to be done by someone else and they'd never find her pet places. Other people would be doing all these things while she was – where? Doing what? Who could know?

We'll Meet in England was paperbacked as a Puffin (PS 21) in 1944 and marketed alongside pre-war fiction depicting life in Russia, Sweden and the Netherlands, but it hardly proved its companion status as the Norwegian volume, even as limited by the line of blurb 'Norway under Nazi rule' or 'Norway under the Nazis'. It described an English family somewhat irritated by an inquisitive neighbour considerably less inclined to pull rank or to bully than, say, the District Visitor in Eleanor Graham's pre-war *The Children who Lived in a Barn* (appropriately, she was the editor of Puffin Books who selected Barne). The presence of King Haakon in England permits a Norwegian identity for the boat secretly repaired and destined to bring the two eldest children to freedom – 'their own King Haakon gone over the water, after the Nazis had hunted him like a wild animal half over his kingdom, to England, where they meant to join him' – and when she proves seaworthy Hertha tells her: 'You've got pluck, I can feel you have . . . You stand up to the sea like a proper Norwegian. Haakon's the right name for you.' There are happy allusions to Vikings and their opponents, and the boat is a credit to all concerned, fighting a storm in one of the best ordeals of its kind that modern juvenile fiction has to offer. The tension rising before departure is well managed, especially as the Nazi neighbour suddenly reveals plans to take the older children to a German indoctrination camp: 'In many ways they are well-brought-up young people, but now they need a man, Rudy particularly. They need discipline. They need training. They need the society of girls and boys with a broader, finer, grander outlook – the New Outlook, in fact.' He makes it clear he is conscripting them to be janissaries among 'my first batch of young people . . . drawn from various places in Norway. To Germany. They will go to join their young comrades there to-morrow.' What is never clear is whether Pieters, the Nazi in question, is meant for a follower of the real Quisling or merely a German in fraying Norwegian disguise. The former is probably intended; but Barne, like Johns, Woodcock and others, wanted to make little of collaboration in countries conquered by Hitler.[40] Brent-Dyer, in *The Chalet School in Exile*, had a much harder road to hoe here, given Austria's almost wholehearted acceptance of *Anschluss* in 1938, but in her case also the message was clear. Nazi Europe, apart from Germany itself, was held under duress, and the true feelings of the people were against Hitler. Brent-Dyer even made the case for such sentiment in Germany, accurately but most exceptionally.

We'll Meet in England deserved its high reputation, and its Puffin selection, but it partook of a Dunkirk solution, coming dangerously close to a synthetic happy ending. The children are got away by legerdemain manipulated by an unexplained American with multi-disguise expertise: he is frankly called a Scarlet Pimpernel. They are also aided by a mysterious uncle, who for loquacity would make Calvin Coolidge sound like Mr Chatterbox, and who is very Norwegian with some admirably Peer Gynt ambience. Subsequently, the rest of the family are mysteriously transported to England by these two, justifying the book's title, but making the ordeal of the voyagers in the tiny sailing-craft seem little more than a *rite de passage*: as the English to whom they were fleeing had the habit of asking in these days, was their journey really necessary? It is at least necessary for the grateful reader, thrilled to bits by it, all the more with the vessel's captain, a septuagenarian Cockney no doubt owing something to Arthur Ransome's Peter Duck, but also showing a strong family resemblance to Biggles's Cockney cook in the Baltic. Yet the end turns the English voyagers, like Biggles, Algy and Ginger before them, into symbols of the Dunkirk departure, a defeat which in English eyes became a glorious victory. Our heroes are away and are safe. It becomes too easy to forget about the unfortunate Nazi-ruled Norwegians or French left behind them. Brent-Dyer was not prepared to settle for that easy option, but even her later wartime books made the war-bound continent grow a little dim.

A third book for children concerned with escape from Norway, Percy Woodcock's *War is Declared* (1944), was the work of an experienced yachtsman and hence was more professional than Barnes about the voyage in which the children escape (though both

Barne and Woodcock seem to have made close study of Ransome's
We Didn't Mean to Go to Sea, the classic mix of juvenile inexperience
and realistic sailing). It begins with the outbreak of war on 3
September 1939, and assumes Norwegians to be neutrals, friendly
to the UK and angered by German aggression. But while Woodcock
was firm about whence they were starting – Bergen – he wants them
back at sea as fast as possible, since his book is obsessed by its boys
surviving German torpedo attacks, as his own son had not.[41]

Brent-Dyer looked hard at Quislings in *The Chalet School in Exile*.
Nazi supporters and persecutors of the Jews or spies on the Chalet
girls were all too easy to present, if stronger meat than most juvenile
authors provided. But once the Chalet School has escaped from
Anschluss Austria to Guernsey in the Channel Islands, a new
Quisling is introduced within its ranks: Gertrude Beck, actually
Gertrud Becker. Brent-Dyer rations her disclosures judiciously. Some
suspicion is shown against her, then her mind is gradually opened to
us:

> she almost wished that she had nothing to do but enjoy this
> delightful place. Then she set her lips and squared her shoulders.
> She had been sent here on a mission – a mission for the Führer and
> Greater Germany; she must accomplish it, and not be so selfish as
> to think of her own pleasure. At home, in Germany, she knew that
> her cousins and friends were living only just this side of starva-
> tion, while she was revelling in good food. Until she came here, she
> had not tasted milk for nearly two years. Eggs had been a great
> luxury, and as for the meat dishes which they had six days in the
> week at their mid-day meal, they were a treat which Gertrude
> thought she could not sufficiently enjoy. And there were sweets
> and cakes, too, though not so many as she would have liked.
> Gertrude was frankly greedy about sweet things, probably as the
> result of having been deprived of them for so long.

This was clever enough, as propaganda for British child readers
resenting food rationing: Germany was suffering more, and hence
Britain looked more likely to win. It was turning the arguments from
the German radio programme beamed on Britain, spoken by 'Lord
Haw-Haw', on their heads. He (or they) constantly spoke of British
food and diet privation; Chalet readers could thus send his curses
(though not their chickens) back to roost. D. C. Thomson's *Beano*
comic was making the same point more vulgarly in its strip of the
same year, 1940, 'Addie and Hermy – The Nasty Nazis', where Hitler

and Goering are perpetually hungry and ensnared by foolish attempts to feed themselves. Brent-Dyer was more subtle in propaganda as she continued to disclose Gertrud's mind:

> the friendliness and kindness which were offered her gave her a strange feeling of meanness that she had never known before. It is true that she had been taught that spoiling the enemy was only the right thing to do, especially in wartime. But somehow she couldn't feel about it as she had expected. Still, it was her business to try to find out what it was that these girls had been so nearly caught hiding in the mountains round the Tiern See, and she must do it.

This is a very different matter from the natural way Blyton unexpectedly moves the mind under the reader's scrutiny to a small gypsy or African (or brownie or governess). The reader of *The Chalet School in Exile* has already witnessed a lynch-mob pursuing a Jewish victim later to be murdered offstage, and has accompanied a desperate band of old friends (if the reader is a veteran of the series) pursued by Nazis in their turn, but this assails one with a new violence: we find ourselves in a mind at war with Britain, and, for all the loathing that Brent-Dyer presumes of us towards Nazism, this particular enemy is not repulsive. The Chalet books made much of the school's trilingualism, and Brent-Dyer, without any foolish intrusions like German expletives, makes Gertrud's thoughts a little German in prose style ('that mysterious thing called "cadence" was un-English'). It is one of the most audible voices in the series.

Although Gertrud becomes increasingly sympathetic as a character, Brent-Dyer is coolly analytical as to her success in pumping information. As a new girl, non-English while officially not German, she is accepted by a Form lower than her own as a playmate, and initially merely establishes rapport.

> Then Gertrude, urged thereto by a letter which came from England, but originally came from a much greater distance, began to feel her way. . . .
>
> 'How long have you been here?' she asked Daisy Venables when she caught her alone one day.
>
> 'Oh, not quite two years', said Daisy carelessly.
>
> 'Oh, I did not mean in Guernsey', said Gertrude, laughing, 'but in the Chalet School. It was in Austria-Tyrol, was it not?'
>
> 'Oh yes. Auntie Madge started it there', replied Daisy. 'I didn't know you meant that, Gertrude. I've been four years at school.

Before that, we lived in Australia, in Queensland. But that was when – when Mummy was alive', she added with a gulp.

Gertrude was not interested in the whole of Daisy's past, but the gulp had touched her rather hard little heart. If she *had* a soft spot, it was for her mother . . . So she said in gentler tones than usual, 'It's hard for you, Daisy. . . . I know how I should feel if anything happened to *my* mother.'

Daisy looked up, and met the genuine sympathy in the blue eyes. 'Auntie Jo says it would be wrong to fret and wish her back, for she had such a hard time; . . . sometimes – in bed – it does seem so hard not to have her with us.'

'I know', said Gertrude, still gently, 'But if she had such a hard time, it would be selfish to bring her back here. But I am sorry for you, Daisy. I love my mother, too, so dearly.'

Yes; and if she failed in her mission, trouble might recoil on the head of that beloved mother. Gertrude was old enough to know that the Nazi regime is utterly ruthless. She shivered, though the sun was warm, and paled a little as she thought of it.

Daisy noticed it. 'Are you cold? But you must have *taken* cold if you are. It's almost as hot as summer today.'

'Just a sudden idea that scared me', replied Gertrude with a forced smile. 'Let's talk of something else. It wasn't a nice idea. Tell me about the School when it was in Tyrol. Where was it exactly?'

Brent-Dyer thus shows Gertrude as most dangerous when her own instincts are most sympathetic – and most genuine. It is a stage beyond the argument beloved of reflective spy fiction from John Buchan to Mary Treadgold's *We Couldn't Leave Dinah* (1941), where little Mick is told:

'do not allow yourself to start by thinking "I am going to pretend to be a stable-boy". *Be* a stable-boy. Live yourself in your rôle from the moment I leave you here to-night. Forget that Michael Templeton ever existed. *Be* Petit-Jean. Think like Petit-Jean – even when you are alone. . . .'

Good stuff – but Gertrud succeeds best when she thinks of herself as Gertrud, not Gertrude. Daisy babbles the history out:

'The last term finished in June, when the Nazis ordered the School to close. That was because Auntie Joey and some of the others tried to help poor old Herr Goldmann the jeweller when some little pigs tried to kill him because he was a Jew. They did save him then; but the beasts went back to his house later, and killed him and Frau Goldmann. They shot Vater Johann at the church too, because he helped our girls to escape somehow. Bill was there, too. That's when her hair went white.'

Senior prefects are now suspicious of Gertrud, and one of them sees and stops the conversation. Brent-Dyer did not attempt to diagnose the feelings of a Nazi schoolgirl on hearing of the murder of Jews, but it has to be taken as part of her renewed unease:

> she was again conscious of the queer feeling of shame over the part she was playing. She almost thought that if she had had only herself to consider, she would have dropped it. But there was her mother. Gertrude had a wholesome fear of the Gestapo activities, and she knew that even such an insignificant being as herself was marked by them.

So, what has proved her greatest weapon for her mission is also the likeliest cause of its destruction. Brent-Dyer in early 1940 had more propaganda points to make than superficial anti-Nazism: she also wished to repudiate the root cause of Nazism – national hatred:

> the leaven of the Chalet School atmosphere was working more and more strongly in the German girl. She noted how careful the girls were to speak as kindly as they could about her country. She saw how they did everything in their power for peace, hushing the younger ones when they talked about 'horrid Germans' . . .

That, written by a headmistress and school-owner of those days, would seem to have reported one attempt at rationing of dangerous talk of various kinds. But the bitterness with which her next volume, The Chalet School Goes to It (1941), comments on the suspiciousness of British mainland local authorities, suggests that such a courageous educational principle had to be rationed in its turn. In The Chalet School in Exile, Gertrud hears of her mother's disappearance (to Denmark, as it turns out, whence readers were left to hope she ultimately reached Britain) and determines, expressly contrary to German instructions, to jettison her Chalet schooldays and return to Germany in quest of her parent. She uses 'a Nazi, who was living, quite unsuspected, at Petit Bôt', and leaves a message behind her for the School by which the Catholic Brent-Dyer could again indict Nazism as the enemy of religion:

'I am a Nazi . . . I was sent here to try to find out things about the Germans and Austrians who had been at your School. Now I have heard that my mother has disappeared, and I am going back to Germany to find out what has happened. I haven't done the School any real harm. I could find out so little at first, and later on I didn't try to. You've all been so good to me, I could not. Please forgive me, and oh, pray – for you believe in God and prayer, but I was taught that neither is any use – that my mother may be safe. I am sorry – I am sorry! Gertrud Becker. I have signed my proper name.'

On which Miss Annersley comments: 'Oh, where is that poor, plucky, silly child?', who is in fact torpedoed:

when the war first broke out, she, in common with most other young Nazis, had rejoiced over the exploits of the U-boats! . . . For the first time Gertrude realised what the U-boat campaign really means. She knew now what the people in the *Athenia* [sunk on 4 September 1939, a few weeks previously] must have felt when, without a warning, there came the awful blow which forced them into little ship's boats, and out to the open sea, with the possibility of death by drowning or exposure before them. And she had rejoiced in the loss of the great liner! If ever a girl learned her lesson by bitter experience, Gertrud [sic] Becker was that girl.

Gertrud is rescued by a British vessel:[42]

'I must see your captain. He won't want me aboard his ship when he hears, but I must tell him.' The man stretched out a hand, and felt her head. 'Cool', he remarked *sotto voce*. 'What's worrying you, kiddy?'

'You see', said Gertrude, stumbling a little, 'I'm not English. I'm a German– I *was* a Nazi. You can't want me here when you know that.'

The man grinned cheerfully. 'We don't war with women and kids', he told her. 'As for Nazi, you say "were"?'

'I'm not now – I couldn't be. Not after they torpedoed us like that. Besides, the School made a difference. But I must see your captain and tell him.'

. . . she told her whole story to a big man whose hook nose and black eyebrows meeting above his nose filled her with fear. However, she got through to the end, and then waited to hear the words that would turn her off this haven.

Instead, what happened was that the man stretched out his hand. 'Shake', he said tersely. 'I like pluck.'

To an outsider, this is the Britain who saved us.

But plucky Quislings (as she was, not British Quisling but school Quisling) had to be rationed in their turn. For once, Brent-Dyer had to revise her story in a subsequent volume (as opposed to merely misremembering it). Gertrud returns to the School 'a wiser girl, a nicer girl' in *The Chalet School in Exile*, but *The Chalet School Goes to It* reports her, in the words of the Head, as 'at present in Scotland somewhere' partly because of the continued uncertainty over her mother ('We all know what vengeance the Gestapo take on the friends and relatives of those who fail them'). Brent-Dyer had become fond of the Quisling she had created, but when no longer using her must have recognised how difficult any return would have been, and how hard for trust to be renewed. The Gertrud episode remains unique in the literature, but a comparable case exists in *We Couldn't Leave Dinah* – not in converting a Quisling, but in discovering when Quislings may not be Quislings. Mary Treadgold, first children's editor at Heinemann from 1938, and from 1940 BBC producer and literary editor, had antennae much closer to government preferences than had Brent-Dyer running her Margaret Roper School away in Hereford: Heinemann's managing director, A. S. Frere, worked at the Ministry of Labour (and Evacuation) during the war. Treadgold, writing her first novel between 7 September and 25 November 1940, also set her work in the Channel Islands, but chose an imaginary Clerinel rather than Guernsey. She placed Clerinel north of Brittany and south of Cornwall, distant enough from Jersey and Guernsey to remain immune from their fall on 1 July, only to capitulate to a surprise occupation on 23 September. Mick and Caroline Templeton are accidentally left behind after the headlong exodus when Hitler's intentions suddenly become clear. The story makes very little of collaboration by local residents with the Nazi invaders, though it acknowledges acceptance. But the children realise they must conform to survive, as when they are surprised by a German general's seven- or eight-year-old granddaughter:

But before she could bid a further more enthusiastic farewell to Nannerl, to her intense surprise Nannerl's short legs clicked to attention and an arm shot out in salute. 'Heil Hitler!' The stentorian squeak quite startled a sparrow that had just dug up a worm close by.

'Heil Hitler!' Caroline gravely raised her arm and looked pointedly at Mick. 'Heil Hitler!' said Mick sheepishly.

The representative of the Herrenvolk nodded to each like a benign Sunday school teacher.

Johns got Biggles out of Nazi-ruled Norway without one utterance of the inevitable Nazi greeting: presumably the image of Biggles Heiling Hitler was too blasphemous to contemplate, whatever the necessities. But small children might be allowed to play games, for the most patriotic of reasons. The story turns on games and ritual: the Pony Club's late president had been 14-year-old Mick, and its present president is a slightly older Clerinel boy of comparable gentlemanly social position with French and German parentage, Peter Beaumarchais. The Templetons discover that his father has enabled the Germans to make an easy arrival and capture a crucial tower. Then Peter finds them hiding in a stable loft in the abandoned Templeton home, and Mick erupts:

> there came a bellow from the far corner, and a small stocky figure shot, like a pea from a peashooter, out on to the middle of the floor, where it confronted the intruder with squared fists, wild hair, and a face wild with fury.
>
> 'Get out, you beastly Nazi! Get out, get out! This is our house. Get out, or I'll half kill you!' The floor-boards creaked ominously as he danced up and down with rage.
>
> Peter merely bent a considering gaze upon this pugnacious apparition clad in a camel-hair dressing-gown, and shifted his weight from one foot to the other.
>
> 'D'you want a hiding?' Mick dropped into traditional schoolboy idiom, squaring up to the still figure with a great show of fist and rolled-up sleeves. Caroline continued to sit like an image upon her sack of oats.
>
> 'No, I do not. Don't be an ass, Mick.' The Pony Club President's words dropped like little cold pebbles into the middle of Mick's tempestuous challenge. But his eyes anxiously searched the faces of his former friends. 'I only came to see what I could do to help.'

At the sound of Peter's voice, with its very slight foreign intonation, Caroline's frozen brain began to thaw.

'So that you could run off and tell your Fifth Column father and his fat friend, I suppose? All right. You've seen us now. Run along and say your piece.'

'Mick.' Caroline spoke from her sack of oats. Mick's onslaught and Peter's quiet withholding had given her the time she needed to recover herself. As her brother hurled his taunts a curious peace of mind was settling down upon her. For the moment it didn't seem to matter to Caroline whether Peter came as ally or enemy. She had watched his unmoved face while Mick was storming at him and had seen the flicker of pain in his eyes. She had known for a moment that quite startled her of compassion for somebody who was being badly hurt.

The meeting has been preceded by the sudden revelation of Peter's father's treachery, so that Mick's violence is understandable. The story is thrilling enough – if limited in its revelations of islander or Nazi depravity – but the destruction and rebuilding of confidence among the children is its highest terrain. The Templetons must then accept that Peter's father is being blackmailed by the Nazis by threats over his wife's German relatives (Treadgold may have drawn on Brent-Dyer: *The Chalet School in Exile* was published in mid-April 1940). Peter agrees to stay to lunch, but only when a grudging support for Caroline's invitation is given by Mick – and (convincingly) confidence is restored by eating, followed by fruit-drops. Peter's exposition is managed with a bleak dignity, and a much more explicit indictment of the Munich generation than, say, Johns's genre would allow him:

'We're not Nazis.' The abrupt statement shot out in the middle of an afternoon siesta almost winded Caroline, the idea was so uppermost in her mind. Having got his audience thoroughly awake Peter rattled the fruitdrop round his mouth and continued:

'I know it must look as though we were. But – what do you know of Nazi Germany?'

He shot the query so unexpectedly at Mick that that young man jerked into a sitting posture as though galvanized. Caroline cast frantically about. What did she know about the Third Reich? Heaven knows everybody was always talking about it.

'Jews', said Mick weakly.

'Concentration camps', Caroline backed him up in an effort to sustain the family's reputation for intelligence. Really, Miss Biddle seemed to talk about nothing but Hitler's Germany in the Current Topics class at [Caroline's school in England] St Dorothy's. Caroline racked her brain but nothing more illuminating emerged. Peter was smiling at the contorted expressions on his friends' countenances.

'You are like everybody else', he said, 'nobody knew anything about Germany. Not France nor England nor America nor the Great League of Nations. If they had known – thought a little harder, watched a little closer – there would have been no war.'

It turns out that Peter has for a time been educated in Germany by Nazi relatives of his mother.

'But did you like it?' Caroline sounded quite staggered at the idea that anybody could possibly have been happy living in Germany.

'Yes. I tell you I was happy. And when the Nazis came into power I was still happy. Nobody noticed changes at first. Gradually the little German boys were brought into the Nazi Youth Movements and there seemed to be less time for play. But that was all. Grandmother and the Aunts believed in the Party. They were great admirers of Hitler. I used to hear them talking of the wonderful things he was doing for Germany. And then' – Peter's voice hardened – 'Father left his job in America. He came to fetch me. He had heard things in America, and he knew Germany was now no place for a French child to live. I didn't want to go with him. . . .'

Peter's denial of teenage Nazism convinces partly because of his flat statement of infantile Nazism – and of its consequences.[43]

'You would think, wouldn't you, that it would concern nobody that one small unimportant French boy should leave a vast country like Germany? That the Nazi Party would not interest themselves in what happened to a ten-year-old child? No. I wrote home each week to Grandmother and the Aunts. They answered me each week. Father thinks now that the letters were opened. For five whole years Germany kept track of us as we moved from town to town [in France]. And then quite suddenly she pounced. Two months ago some naturalized Germans' – Peter's voice was stinging with contempt – 'called on Father at La Falaise. They told us a great deal of news about our relatives in Nuremberg, how well they were, how good, how kind they were, what good citizens they were. We were so pleased to meet friends who knew our relations. And they knew my friends too, and brought me messages from them. It seemed such a pleasant meeting. And then just as they were going they told us why they had come. It wasn't to bring us loving greetings and news of our friends. It was to tell us that if we did not do as the Government wished our relatives in Nuremberg, good Nazis though they are, would be arrested and put into a concentration camp.'

This is of course propaganda, but propaganda admitting the child reader to adult argument, all the more by its use of successive images: the happy ignorant child, the wandering child, the child under blackmail. Violet Needham took up the worst Quisling dilemma of all, in *The Stormy Petrel*, blunted by its Ruritanian setting: the child Christopher has to choose between parent and country, deepened by the country being actualised by child friends, and ending in Christopher's death. Brent-Dyer's *The Chalet School in Exile* is more firmly conceived as a novel of ideas, ideas most clearly expressed by conduct. Both novels convey Nazism as a terror regime advancing itself by blackmail of its exiles, even of the refugees in flight from it. Brent-Dyer firmly asserted the Chalet School Peace League in answer to the Nazi war machine, partly by the symbolism of the Nazis trying to obtain the Peace pledge for further blackmail and persecution purposes. She acknowledged the irony of war as the only means of destroying the permanent Nazi threat of war:

> The laughter died out of Jo's face. 'I wish you hadn't to go. I do feel lonely when you're away. And the girls will grow up, and you will miss all the jolly part of their first teeth, and seeing and hearing them begin to walk and talk. How I loathe this horrible war!'
> 'But if it is necessary, Joey? If it's to drive something utterly evil from the world?'

This admits the child to adult conversation in a different way: Joey Bettany, now Maynard, heroine of the Chalet School books and now elfin guardian angel to the school, having become a wife and mother after flight from the Tyrol, talks with her husband, the readers merely eavesdropping on an old friend. But the child reader's occasional 'what will X be like when grown up?' has to be answered here as X facing temporary bereavement – possibly permanent – with a husband taken from her by war. You can't have a happy ending. Don't you know there's a war on?

Treadgold at least offers the happy ending to the extent of getting the Templetons off the island. But Peter has to remain. They have given him one thing: Mick's attempt at code-breaking reveals that Peter's father is in fact the principal British secret agent on the island, which he was concealing from his son just as his son was concealing the Templetons and his support of them from his father. But the supposed Quislings have to remain under the oppressor Nazis, although Templetons and Beaumarchaises foil one invasion attempt against Britain:[44]

> Caroline . . . flung herself into the arms of M. Beaumarchais and planted a large kiss on his moustache. 'Good-bye, good-bye', she said. 'Thank you most awfully for having us, and do take care of yourself and not get caught.' She had forgotten forever how she and Mick had once detested the funny little Frenchman. She crept gingerly into the boat with Mick after her. Commander Seymour took his place and the ratings pushed off.
>   'Good-bye, good-bye.'
>   'Good-bye, Mick. Good-bye, Caroline.'
>   'See you after the war, Peter.'
>   'Good-bye, and good luck.'

It was written within six months of Dunkirk, and it is France rather than Jersey or Guernsey that the Beaumarchaises symbolise. (No doubt Treadgold wanted her readers to believe that stories of collaboration with the Nazis in her native Channel Islands probably really meant conscription and might mean secret pro-British conspiracy.) If the book has confronted the Quisling phenomenon, it has used it as a springboard to celebration of courage, not as a means to expose shame or warn against danger. In her ironic mode, Crompton played a little of the same game in having 'William Does His Bit' reveal a patriot in a suspected Quisling. But in general her message was less romantic and more specific. The Quislings under British noses were simply those who indulged themselves in wartime at the expense of the war-beleaguered community, those who circumvented rationing, self-dependence and 'Dig for Victory':

> 'I've always wanted to live in a big 'ouse with a park an' I'm goin' to live in a big 'ouse with a park. I 'ate allotments. I always 'ave an' I always will. Nasty common crowded-up things! As for vegs., me

an' Bott[y] never 'ave cared for 'em. Rather 'ave somethin' tasty any day. I tell you, it'd fair take my appetite away to see a lot of common people diggin' whenever I looked out of the winder.'

'Of course, if official pressure were brought to bear –' suggested Mr Brown suavely.

Mrs Bott's small eyes gleamed with rage.

'You try what you calls hofficial pressure on me, Mr John Brown', she said, 'an' I cancels hevery single subscription I gives to this 'ere bloomin' village.'

Mr Brown coughed and subsided. The lady had them there and she knew it. Difficult though she was, she contributed generously to the funds of the various local organisations, which would have been hard put to it to carry on without her.

She is brought round owing to William's accidentally leaving an 'UNEXPLODED BOMB' notice temporarily outside her Hall, which she subsequently takes to be a vision warning her of the need for vigilance, and hence allotments ('Well, it's come to a choice of a lot of common people tramplin' about outside our very winders or the whole 'ouse blown up an' I think I've made the right choice').[45]

Mrs Bott, as *nouveau riche*, expresses an old target: the usurper of the squirearchy without the old squire's sense of feudal obligations (if any). In the mood of hostility to the traditional deference culture which swirled around 1940–1, the squire became an obvious suspect in the search for Quislings, and it was sometimes softened by the squire's being a recent arrival, possibly proven a German in disguise. The movie *Went the Day Well* (1942) 'never quite made its mind up how to deal with' Squire Oliver Wilsford, intended to be a German agent but taken by most critics to be a local magnate selling his country for the optimum price, financial or psychological. This verdict, from Penelope Houston's masterly study of the movie, was developed by the surmise that 'because Leslie Banks' bland, tweedy, very English style imposed itself too thoroughly on the character, the film seems to forget just who Wilsford is'. The movie posters listed Banks first among its stars. The movie does make a hero of the lady of the manor (not Wilsford's manor), Mrs Fraser (Marie Lohr), who, having been mildly irritating and patronising, gives her life to save a group of children by getting a live grenade out through a doorway and slamming the door with herself on the wrong side and the children on the right one. It wasn't intentionally a film for children (it seems to have made an art of going beyond its intentions), but it was probably a prime favourite with those children who saw it – for, in the best traditions as defined by André Maurois, it is a child who saves the village from the German troops initially taken for British. Harry Fowler, as the Cockney evacuee George Truscott, plays a role much akin to William, unmasking Nazi harshness in response to his meddling, finding what proves to be Vienna chocolate in a soldier's kit, and finally getting away to another village (although wounded) to raise the alarm, helped to get away by a natural ally of the kind whom William attracts, the local poacher, who is killed in the process.[46]

The Quisling squire also dominated *The Radio Mystery* by John Mowbray, published in autumn 1941 well before the film's inception. Mowbray (who seems to have been Gunby Hadath) had the white colonial schoolboy hero enthralled from the first by 'a real English sportsman!', 'a big man in gaiters and tweeds . . . hearty voice . . . Sir Pascal met him more than half-way with a laugh'. The boy is ultimately cruelly disillusioned when his trust in the Quisling nearly delivers a new secret weapon to Hitler. After the villain is trapped, the Scotland Yard inspector muses:[47]

> 'He subscribed so liberally to the War Loans and so forth, you see, and he went about addressing so many public meetings, and chucking his chest out so much as a tremendous patriot, that in his position he was more or less bound to come into contact with men at the head of affairs.'
>
> 'And all the time he was using those contacts against us!'
>
> 'Yes, I'm afraid that he was', the Inspector admitted.
>
> . . . 'Sir Pascal . . . had been promised the governorship of Great Britain when Hitler had won . . .'

But it was Jeffrey Havilton who saw the deeper motivation for Quislings, stated by what to schoolboys is a greater authority figure than a squire – a schoolmaster – when asked by *his* schoolboy prisoner:

> 'It seems to me a funny thing, sir', he said, 'for an Englishman to spy on his own people.'
>
> 'It isn't funny', said Batty, quietly, 'but it's interesting. I used to think about it a lot at one time, until I had quite made up my mind. You see, Wilkes, your trouble is that you are narrow-minded. Nearly everybody in the world is narrow-minded: it's the result of education and environment. You talk about "Englishmen" and "own people". Now I'm concerned with something

bigger. I am a citizen of the world, and I have managed to shake myself free from petty things like nationality. I look for ideas that hold the promise of good for all men, and I don't mind where those ideas originate. The fact that the idea I am supporting now originated in Germany doesn't upset me in the least, nor does the fact that in the preliminary stages of its development it is accompanied by terror and bloodshed. Later on it will help to mould the whole world and make it better. I am willing to kill and be killed for that idea, I am willing to incur the hatred of Englishmen and my own people, I am willing to lose all the things that I most enjoy in life.'

Fussy saw that there was no point whatever in arguing against such an attitude of mind. It was simply a case of one man's meat being another man's poison. He was sorry for Batty.

And that pity is the supreme moment in the victory of Britain's children in their war against the Nietzschean supermen. But in the day-to-day struggle, Richmal Crompton's supreme indictment is turned against Hubert Lane and his family when, because Hubert has not been made a host in a party for children of men in the armed forces, Mrs Lane determines to upstage it hopelessly by a party for Hubert and his sycophantic friends:[48]

It happened that the Lanes were little troubled by rationing problems. Mr Lane had what his wife sometimes referred to as 'Ways and Means', and sometimes as 'Influence'. Whatever this meant, the fact remained that the Lanes had meat and poultry in abundance, almost as much fat and tea and sugar (even icing sugar) as in prewar days and tinned goods on a wholesale scale without having to consider such details as 'points'. It was common knowledge, of course, that Mrs Lane had 'hoarded' shamelessly from the first whisper of scarcity, but even that did not account for the flourishing state of the Lane larder. Mr Lane generally brought a laden suitcase back with him each evening from town, and Mrs Lane did her bit by going round every shop in Hadley every day and buying up whatever she could find in it. . . .

All Hubert's friends were invited and all Hubert's friends accepted the invitation.

Hubert was not an original child and could think of no other tactics than his familiar ones of shouting out to the prospective guests of the rival party the dainties that were being prepared for his own.

'Jellies and cream!' said William incredulously. 'You can't *get* jellies and you can't get cream.'

'My father can', sniggered Hubert.

'Your father's a black marketeer', said William sternly.

Hubert smiled his sly smile.

'You can't prove it', he said, 'and that's all that matters.'

William, as often, proves an instrument of Nemesis by leading the servicemen's children to the Lanes' house and eating the party meal while the Lanes are away buying last-minute luxury additions. But Crompton's message was clear as mud. There might be community spirit beyond all previous experience, but there was also a plenitude of social Quislings.

As usual, nobody struck home as deeply as Crompton, driving home the point that the black market was alive and well and flourishing among her invulnerable wealthier neighbours. Kitty Barne, in *Three and a Pigeon* (1944), confronted the problem of informing against a neighbour, however obnoxious:

> She wasn't so sure now that she wanted to show up Piggott. She wasn't sure that she liked showing up anybody, whatever they'd done. Had they *got* to? It was different for Ivy and Sandy – they were enjoying it frightfully. . . .
>
> She tackled her father at breakfast.
>
> 'Daddy, if you see someone doing something – stealing or anything like that – should you do anything about it?'
>
> The Doctor abstracted himself from his paper and gave her his complete attention, as was his way.
>
> 'Stealing something of yours? You'd do a lot, I should think.'
>
> 'No, I don't mean something of mine. Just stealing.'
>
> 'Shop-lifting, bag-snatching, pilfering, you mean? Yes, you should – in the general interest. "Stop thief." The hue-and-cry – the ancient duty of the citizen. The citizen makes his own laws through his representatives and it's his duty to uphold them.'
>
> That was one of the nice things about Daddy. He always talked to you as if you were grown up.
>
> 'Oh, I see. Then it's good for people to be shown up.'
>
> 'It's good for the community.'
>
> 'It's not interfering?'
>
> ''Course it's interfering, but some things have got to be interfered with. You been reading the paper?'
>
> 'Yes.'

It was true; she had. And there had been a black market case all down one column.

In the event, the wicked Mr Piggott takes flight after being badly mobbed by the children, including the Belgian refugee he had cruelly exploited ('"I sit on Mr Piggott", he said, still calm. "You take his stick"') and being bitten (by the bombed-out evacuee from London, of course): 'his black London-looking coat covered with gravel, one trouser yellow and and sticky with egg, his head, bald now that his bowler hat was missing, nearly as red as his face, thundery rumblings that might any moment burst into new rage purring out of him'. Margot Pardoe put the black market on a level with treason or espionage with much less secular theology, in *Bunkle Butts In* (1943):

Captain James laughed.

'Yes', he said, 'we got a surprise too! It appears that your friend Mr Bentham took a leaf out of the old smugglers' book and has been using Marsh House as a very convenient depot for illegal trading.'

Bunkle looked deeply disappointed.

'Then he wasn't a fifth-columnist or a spy after all?' he said.

Captain James looked grave.

'Billy', he replied, 'any man who deliberately evades the law and sets out to make a handsome profit out of that evasion in wartime, is as much a fifth-columnist as if he were in direct touch with the enemy.'

Bunkle still looked disappointed.

'I suppose so', he said, 'but I was hoping we were really helping the Services, not just a lot of civilians.'

Captain James threw back his head and laughed aloud.

'There's a compliment!' he said. 'Well, Billy, if it's going to give you so much pleasure I can tell you that you *have* helped the Services, too, for although Mr Bentham was only concerned with illegal trading, his friend in the blue raincoat was using him as a blind, and if he doesn't die in hospital from the crack one of you gave him on the head last night, it's more than probable that he will die later in an even less pleasant manner! I can't tell you more than that at the moment. . . .'

And perhaps just as well.

Maud Budden, poet of Curly Wee and the animals of Fun-and-Feather-Land for the *Liverpool Echo*, the *Birmingham Mail* and the

Irish Independent did not deal in war, and may well have been a pacifist, but she also seemed anxious to make much of the anti-social character of the black market. As with *Bunkle Butts In* (and Blyton's *Five Go to Smuggler's Top*, 1945), there is a sense of real evil in the smugglers, all the more since in peacetime many did not see it as reprehensible. Budden's little delinquent piglet Patrick Porker reverts to virtue when ordered to join the smugglers whom he has discovered, or to be tied to a post and be slowly drowned by the incoming tide. (He is ultimately rescued by a swordfish.) He refuses the last chance of release with a flourish rightly admired by its author:[49]

And then he made what I maintain was quite a witty crack: 'This little pig will never go to markets that are black'.

Notes

1. Juliet Gardiner, *The Children's War* (2005), 120–8, an invaluable companion to our subject; Mike Brown, *A Child's War – Growing up on the Home Front* (2000), 56–61; and works cited in each.
2. Michael S. Howard, *Jonathan Cape, Publisher* (1971), 191–8, 205–6, 222, 239. Hugh Brogan, *The Life of Arthur Ransome* (1984), 364–410. Cape's printings accorded higher numbers of copies to Ransome titles for children as the paper famine worsened, viz. *Secret Water* (published 28 November 1939), 15,000 copies; *The Big Six* (12 November 1940), 12,000; *Missee Lee* (5 December 1941), 20,500; *The Picts and the Martyrs* (28 May 1943), 22,750 – Wayne G. Hammond, *Arthur Ransome – a Bibliography* (2000), 119, 123, 127, 131.
3. Todd followed *Worzel Gummidge* with *Worzel Gummidge Again* (1937) and *More about Worzel Gummidge* (1938), but nine years then elapsed before *Worzel Gummidge and Saucy Nancy* (1947). Todd's husband of eight years, John Graham Bower, died in 1940, and the war years yielded only one Todd title (*The House that Ran Behind* (1943), but she reviewed children's books for *Punch*, identified as B.G.B., whence she began the campaign against Enid Blyton later associated with librarians.
4. For pre-eminent use of the scarecrow in wartime children's fiction, see Crompton, 'William's Midsummer Eve' (*Modern Woman* (July 1941) and *William Carries On*), where Crompton appropriates the device of walking scarecrow (from Todd and Oz) to be employed by William (who is not wholly alien to his scarecrow originals) in order to rescue a friendly Land Girl, Katie, from a plot concocted by Hubert Lane. Fairlie Bruce, *Toby at Tibbs Cross* gives its heroine a wartime job to all intents and purposes that of a Land Girl; but Cadogan and Craig, *Women and Children First*, 225–6, remark on 'indications that Dorita Fairlie Bruce did not really approve of women in uniform', so the arrangement is private. Crompton, who clearly did so approve, sympathises with Land Girl exploitation by male chauvinist farmers. See also Doris M. Pocock, *Laura of the Land* (1946).

5. Brent-Dyer, *The Chalet School in Exile* (1939), *The Chalet School Goes to It* (1941), *The Highland Twins at the Chalet School*, *Lavender Laughs in the Chalet School*, *Gay from China at the Chalet School* (1944), *Jo to the Rescue* (1945). Brazil, *The School on the Moor* (1939), *The New School at Scawdale* (1940), *Five Jolly Schoolgirls* (1941), *The Mystery of the Moated Grange* (1942), *The Secret of the Border Castle* (1943), *The School in the Forest* (1944), *Three Terms at Uplands* (1945). Brent-Dyer survived the war by a quarter-century and fifty more book-titles, but Brazil died after one more book, *The School at the Loch* (1946), her publishers half-expecting subsequent delivery of *The School at the Pearly Gates* (Gillian Freeman, *The Schoolgirl Ethic: The Life and Work of Angela Brazil* (1976), 138). Westerman titles are too numerous to list.

6.   Red roared the fire through the heart of London's City,
        Hurled from the clouds by a brute and savage foe,
        They who their own land robbed of light and learning,
        Kindled the books here, a brand for London's burning,
        Lighted the bonfire of Paternoster Row.
   'Sagittarius' (Olga Katzin), 'London Burning', *New Statesman and Nation* 21 (25 January 1941).

7. The most recent and (in spite of a shower of trivial errors) the best biography is Robert McCrum's (2004). Wodehouse, who won his first mastery in school stories, seems from textual evidence in their writings to have had mutual influence on Richards, and also shaped the work of Havilton, strong and most amusing writers for children. For Orwell's defence of him, see *Collected Works*, XVII, 51–63. Wise, fair and gallant, it makes Orwell's usual self-reproach for love of works dear to him since adolescence, insisting on their being out of date. Wodehouse's *The Code of the Woosters* (1938) was the finest anti-Fascist novel of its day.

8. Stoney, *Blyton*, 62–5, 71–3, 79, 82, 86, 98–9, 101, 110–16, 124–31. (Blyton's debt to her first husband included her expertise in dealing with publishers, from whom she always insisted on clear print and a wide margin: her protectiveness towards the children whom she fascinated was practical as well as imaginative.)

9. Orwell, *Collected Works*, XVI–XVII (well indexed) document the full Odyssey of *Animal Farm*.

10. Henry Williamson's *Tarka the Otter* (1927) won the Hawthornden Prize, *Salar the Salmon* (1935) continuing his success. His First World War experiences blighted his outlook and led him into Fascism, for which he was imprisoned in 1939, a tragedy which still enabled him to write works of hatred for cruelty but which in the Second World War were for adults, notably *The Story of a Norfolk Farm* (1941). The poet George MacBeth, whose father had been killed during Nazi air attacks on Sheffield, was in hospital in late 1944 with rheumatic fever as a 12-year-old, found *Tarka* and *Salar*, and felt that 'The extremes of these creatures' lives felt in harmony with my own': *A Child of the War* (1987), 133. Linklater, *The Wind on the Moon* (1944), won the Carnegie Medal. Black Bob is a Scottish sheepdog (Blyton also produced an exceptionally real if over-episodic *Shadow the Sheep Dog* (1942) worthy of inspiration by Anna Sewell's *Black Beauty*). Tolkien's Eagles save the protagonists from doom in both *The Hobbit* and *The Lord of the Rings*. The Last King of Narnia's best friend is a Unicorn (*The Last Battle*, 1956). Linklater makes the best use of the anthropomorphic problem by having his girl protagonists change into animals, where they discover many other beasts of similar origin. Lewis wins remarkable results by making Jesus Christ a Lion, although this might imply a Swiftian reduction of humanity to lower status, which he carefully avoids. In avoidance of excessive

anthropomorphism, Curly Wee, recovering from 'flu, says: 'I'm well', to which the author adds: 'Pigs never say "I'm cured"'.

11. On 4 September 1939, the RAF raided the entrance to the Kiel Canal and bombed German ships. Biggles began his operations on 10 September.

12. Johns, *Biggles in the Baltic* (1940), 11, 12, 255, 186, 188, 189–90.

13. Berresford Ellis and Williams, *By Jove, Biggles!*, 77, 79, 82–102, 170–5. On allied questions of censorship, see Anthony K. Aldgate and James C. Robertson, *Censorship in Theatre and Cinema* (2005), and, for *Colonel Blimp* – a ludicrously misunderstood work on Churchill's part – see Aldgate and Jeffrey Richards, *Britain Can Take It* (1986), 10, 17, 196, and more specifically their *Best of British: Cinema and Society 1930–1970* (1983), 61–74.

14. For bibliographical detail, Berresford Ellis and Williams, *By Jove, Biggles!*, 273–97, is invaluable and highly reader-friendly, but Marvel M. Wagenaar-Wilm, *Captain W. E. Johns Catalogus* ([1993] 2004), is also essential and tolerably manipulable despite being in Dutch. For Elinor Glyn, *It*, see the collected works of Dorothy Parker. Biggles's lack of ease with women combined with respect for their professional skills is a charming undercurrent for *Biggles & Co.* (1936). In *Biggles in the South Seas* (1940), Biggles refers to Ginger, Shell-Breaker and Full Moon as 'the kids', although Johns actually included a preface pointing out that the two Polynesians 'more than once saved the situation', which (he observed) questioned the author's justification for having Biggles alone in the title while his wisdom as a leader was shown in following advice. As the book's magazine (*Gem*, October–December 1939) and book publication both fell within the war years, Johns could not have found a better symbol for rejection of Nazi racism.

15. The same date for the only Penguin Biggles and the launch of the Puffins pushes coincidence a little beyond the credible: it may be that Eleanor Graham, the Puffin editor, rejected the inclusion of Johns as she rejected Blyton and other popular writers. The story that Lane had looked for an adult title from Johns does not eliminate the possibility that he was also angling for juvenile titles to increase the readership of Puffins. Graham may have set herself against war content for the prose Puffins (it provided some Puffin Picture-Book themes). She was not beyond appeal to popular taste in practice: the second Puffin to appear was *Cornish Adventure* (1937), whose author, Derek McCulloch, was known to all listeners to BBC Children's Hour as their 'Uncle Mac' (whom I remember listing as a child among my uncles when praying). The first Puffin, Barbara Euphan Todd, *Worzel Gummidge*, was also a BBC Children's Hour serial.

16. Including at the end Biggles's love-affair with the spy Marie and his near-suicidal sequel. His bout with alcoholism receives allusion clear enough to old readers in *Biggles in the Orient* (1945), 77:

> 'Frankly, Scrimshaw, we haven't much confidence in fellows who grab a bottle when things get sticky.'
> Scrimshaw flushed scarlet. 'Who said – ?'
> 'I said', broke in Biggles, without raising his voice. 'And what I say I mean. The sooner you understand that the better. Oh, I know you how feel. I've been through it myself, more than once. I was going through it when you wore safety-pins instead of buttons, but I got over it – if I hadn't I shouldn't be here now. . . .'

Scrimshaw never has time to get over it.

17. Stories mostly about schoolmasters, for example Talbot Baines Reed, *The Master of the Shell* (1894; Reed died in 1893), and Wodehouse, *The Little*

Nugget (1913; in serial form it is entirely narrated by a master), had boy audiences in mind, although they are unlikely to disappoint adults. Hugh Walpole, Mr Perrin and Mr Trail (1911), was definitely for an adult audience but was banned by the headmaster of Epsom College (whence Walpole, a former Epsom assistant master, had drawn heavily). The headmaster would thus appear to have complimented him on its likely appeal to schoolboys (Kirkpatrick, Encyclopaedia), but his stories of the schoolboy Jeremy are nominally child-directed and very adult-aware. Havilton and his colleague at Glasgow Academy, Walter Barradell-Smith who wrote as Richard Bird, allow masters to have a sense of humour sometimes, but know how to judge them from a schoolboy standpoint. Havilton's final story, School versus Spy, climaxes impeccably on such a judgement.

18. Mary Cadogan, Richmal Crompton (1986), 115. Crompton had a bad leg, from polio, but was expected when in the Auxiliary Fire Service to jump to her feet to salute the local butcher, who was proving a very officious superior. 'William – the Fire-Fighter' (Modern Woman (September 1940) and William Does His Bit) requires full reading, but a savour of Crompton's revenge may be tasted. William mistakes steam from a kettle for a fire, and squirts a large lady, who blames Section Officer Perkins:

> 'Funny thing to come in here, and get a squirt of water in my face and then look round and find you standing there with your hosepipe. You ought to be ashamed of yourself. A man of your age larking about like a schoolboy! You deserve the sack and I hope you get it.'
> 'Madam', said the Section Officer desperately aware of his firemen sniggering behind him, 'I protest. I got a message that there was a fire here and I came along.'
> 'That's a nice tale', said the woman.

19. The paper shortage worsened as war continued, and Modern Woman may have rationed William's appearances presumably for their tangential relevance. Cadogan notes many as shorter than the book texts (The William Companion [1990], 150–1). Crompton served in the AFS from 1939 to 1943 and also worked in the Toc H canteen for service personnel in Bromley and Keston. The slowing-down to five William stories published in the last two years of the war is still not fully accounted for by such duties.

20. Crompton's last two adult novels written in the war and the ensuing months, Weatherley Parade (1944) and Westover (1946), well merit revival for literary and historical value.

21. Biggles – Air Commodore (1937) has elegantly derisive opening chapters at the expense of politicians and service chiefs desperately trying to solve crises while retaining status and avoiding responsibility.

22. Biggles in the Baltic, 11, 13, 160. Johns published some stories of the secret service, written just before and just after war's declaration in 1939, decrying the want of war readiness in more explicit and more critical language; but they can hardly have reached wide audiences in obscure and dying magazines. Ultimately published in 1950 as Dr Vane Answers the Call, they have been recently republished by the Johns and Blyton scholar Norman Wright (2005), with an introduction by me.

23. Biggles in the Baltic, 188–9.

24. Berresford Ellis and Williams, By Jove, Biggles!, 177 note Johns's columns in the Girl's Own Paper on WAAF matters from October 1941, while Wagenaar-Wilm,

Johns Catalogus, 145 ascribes 'Life in the WAAF' to November 1940. I have used the *Girl's Own Annual* which reprints content of the *Girl's Own Paper* from October 1940 to September 1941, apparently in the form of original serialisation, which suggests October 1940 as date for 'Life in the WAAF' (*Annual*, 25). *Annual* also includes additional matter, including a short novel, instalment-divided school-spy in theme, by 'William Earle' [Johns], 'The Ravensdale Mystery'.

25. Mary Cadogan, *Women with Wings* (1992), is invaluable on the women pilots and on their fictional counterparts. I am deeply grateful to the late Catherine Koe for aiding me with her reminiscences of Pauline Gower, her family and school records.

26. Tony Gray, *Mr Smyllie, Sir* (1991); Dónal Ó Drisceoil, *Censorship in Ireland 1939–1945* (1996).

27. For Johns's wartime relations with Oxford University Press, see Berresford Ellis and Williams, *By Jove, Biggles!*, 181–5. The remaining Biggles titles to be published by Oxford were *Biggles in the Jungle* (May 1942), *Biggles – Charter Pilot* and *Biggles in Borneo* (both July 1943). Only the last was a Second World War narrative; the second was an inter-war series of science-fiction memoirs from Ginger to the other pilots of Biggles's Second World War Squadron 666 (another touch of Johns humour), and the first was also a peacetime adventure which looks like an intended short story perhaps originally for the *Biggles – Charter Pilot* collection (which began appearing in the *Boy's Own Paper* in October 1941 and finished in April 1944). The first Hodder title, *Biggles Sweeps the Desert*, came out in November 1942.

28. Berresford Ellis and Williams, *By Jove, Biggles!*, 182–3. Wagenaar-Wilm, *Johns Catalogus*, 79–80, 136–9.

29. The German officer in charge of the soldiers shepherding Biggles to court-martial on the *Leipzig* in *Biggles in the Baltic*; Schaffer, the pilot for whose Dornier Biggles wrestles in *Biggles Defies the Swastika*; von Zoyton in *Biggles Sweeps the Desert*.

30. There is a curious anticipation of it in *Biggles Hunts Big Game* (1948), where the master forger whom they pursue never comes fully into focus but is killed at the end boasting of his own ill-treatment of prisoners who refused to aid in his forgeries for Hitler: he is a Czech Quisling.

31. In this, I am using recollections of what secretly frightened me as a child: wolf-headed murderers emerging from darkness in *Gimlet Mops Up* did. There was a more intellectual fear in reaction to *Biggles Takes a Holiday* and *Worrals in the Wastelands*, i.e. forcing the mind to accept that people could perpetrate horrors in concentration camps of the kind discussed in the latter, re-enacted in *Biggles Takes a Holiday*. Those two very cleverly stress the charm and diplomacy of the most loathsome horror-perpetrators.

32. Trevor-Roper made much of the Nazi betrayals of one another, and probably overdid it. Their mutual betrayals were less nauseating than their cruelty to others. Nazi brutality is a standard fact of stories set wholly or partly in countries under Nazi control; for example the two Gimlet war novels, and the first five Worrals war stories, but it only becomes horrific in *Worrals Goes East* (1944) – above all because the chief Nazi sadist is a woman.

33. The classic First World War story on German humour is that the German higher command decides the war is being lost because the Germans lack a sense of humour like the British. A captured Bruce Bairnsfather cartoon is therefore reprinted and circulated. It depicts Old Bill sitting in a dug-out with a large hole in its side. A friend shouts 'Wot done that?', to which Old Bill replies 'Mice'.

Under the cartoon, the German higher command writes: 'It was not the mice, it was a shell.' Johns's comment is in *Biggles Sees it Through*, 72, and quotation, ibid., 123. On the German lack of imagination, *Biggles – Secret Agent*, 145.

34. *Biggles Defies the Swastika*, 25–6.
35. *William Does His Bit*, 10–11, 27. The real spies are caught in 'William and the Bird Lover', *Happy Mag*, whose book title was 'William and the Bird Man', *William and the Evacuees*, and 'William and the Tea-Cake', whose title remained unchanged from *Modern Woman* to *William and the Brains Trust* (April 1945).
36. W. B. Yeats, 'The Circus Animals' Desertion'. Crompton derided war-created self-important amateur bureaucrats (or, if in the armed forces, professional), but she made no extension of Quislings or spies in the direction of local pacifists, as in the First World War L. M. Montgomery did in *Rilla of Ingleside*; the leading case of it in Second World War children's literature seems to be Dorita Fairlie Bruce, *Nancy Calls the Tune*.
37. M[argot] Pardoe, *Four Plus Bunkle* (1939), 85. Envy of Blyton certainly animated Alison Uttley, Barbara Euphan Todd and (mildly) Noel Streatfeild, whereas Malcolm Saville, Johns and Crompton seem to have respected her as a hardworking colleague. Blyton died on 28 November 1968; and Crompton, a week or so before her own death on 11 January 1969, had a warning of it and thought: 'Enid Blyton, here I come!' (Cadogan, *Crompton*, 156).
38. 'B.B.' was D. J. Watkins-Pitchford, who illustrated his pseudonymous works under his own name. *The Little Grey Men* won the Carnegie Medal for 1942 when the author was teaching in Rugby School (schoolmasters had particular reason to choose pseudonyms, schoolboys being the world's most ruthless parodists and lampooners). Biggles's views on spying receive classic expression in the outstanding First World War novel, *Biggles Flies East* (1935), and are echoed in *Biggles Defies the Swastika*, 47:

> 'Fate or fortune has put an astounding opportunity in your way. It's a chance that we ought not to lose. With you behind the German lines in Norway, serving as an officer in the Air Force, we should learn every move –'
> 'Oh, no', interrupted Biggles curtly. 'I'm a pilot. I've had quite enough of Secret Service work. ... I'm not a professional spy', protested Biggles vigorously.
> 'My dear Bigglesworth, you yourself have seen what Germany is doing in Norway. There's black treachery for you, if you like. We've got to fight the enemy with his own weapons, if only for the sake of the Norwegians.'
> Thus spoke the Colonel. It was a subtle argument that he put forward, put in such a way that Biggles could hardly refuse.

But it is clear that espionage is by its nature Nazi, and un-British.
39. Barne, *We'll Meet in England* (1942), 131.
40. Ibid., 137.
41. Woodcock's post-war *Escape by Sea* (1948) replays the idea with orphan English twin boys whose uncle is arrested when the Nazis occupy Denmark. In his *Looking Astern* (1950), 170, he wrote of his son and his wife:

> Sam was one of the unlucky ones when the *Barham* was torpedoed and sunk off Sollum. The news was an Admiralty secret, and when, a fortnight later, we had a letter saying he was 'presumed to have lost his life' we were asked to keep it to ourselves. It was a hard blow, made none the easier by this ban

of silence. It proved too much for Ellie, and a week later I was a widower. Life can be very grim and there may be times when nothing seems worth while.

Sam Woodcock was a lieutenant in the Royal Navy. The *Barham* was sunk by U-331 on 25 November 1941: its magazine exploded, 362 of its battleship's crew of 1,359 being killed. The Admiralty announced its loss on 27 January 1942, and a casualty list was published by *The Times* on 23 February 1942 and officially published in April 1942. Sam had been his father's constant sailing companion before the war when he was in his teens.

42. William Joyce, the American-born Irish-reared Black-and-Tan runner and sub-sequent London Fascist leader, tried, convicted and hanged for high treason in 1946, broadcast for the Nazis from early 1940, but although he was known as 'Lord Haw-Haw' the nickname was first given by British listeners to the initial announcer on German wartime broadcasts to the UK from his snobbish voice: probably Norman Baillie-Stewart. On the *Dandy's* food-obsessed Hitler and Goering, see Cadogan and Craig, *Women and Children First*, and for example the *Beano* (21 September 1940), when Hitler invents an aeroplane to suck up Lord Snooty's butter, having none of his own, but is tricked into returning it. Brent-Dyer, *The Chalet School in Exile*, 244–5, 245, 229, 247–8, 249, 251, 255, 257–9, 263, 267–9. Treadgold, *We Couldn't Leave Dinah*, 222.

43. Treadgold, ibid., 184, 111–12, 128–9, 130, 131.

44. Brent-Dyer, *The Chalet School in Exile*, 317. Treadgold, ibid., 269.

45. 'William Helps the Spitfire Fund', *Modern Woman* (March 1941), and *William Does His Bit*, 201).

46. Houston, *Went the Day Well* (1992), 27–9, 59, cast-list ibid., 60–1. Anthony Aldgate and Jeffrey Richards, *Britain Can Take It*, 115–37. James Chapman, *The British at War: Cinema, State and Propaganda 1939–1945* (1998), 226–8; Chapman links this film with *The Foreman Went to France* (1942) as suggesting, 'irresistibly, that the governing classes are not to be trusted'. All commentators rightly note the film's long distance from the original story by Graham Greene, 'The Lieutenant Died Last', *Collier's* (29 June 1940), the first British publication in Greene, *The Last Word and Other Stories* (1991), where the poacher, the only British protagonist, survives after heroically defeating the invaders on his own; but one common factor between play and film is the respect given chiefly to the less respectable locals, and the sense of the squirearchy's putting its own interests before the country's (in the story's case, making more of its grudging forgiveness for the poacher's poaching than for his courage in saving the village and perhaps the country).

47. Mowbray, *Radio Mystery*, 10, 44, 46, 250–1. Mowbray had been identified with Hadath until the British Museum (now Library) Catalogue firmly declared Mowbray the pseudonym of one J. G. H. Vahey, with no additional proof (Kirkpatrick, *Encyclopaedia*, 241–2). But apart from the style similarities, and content comparabilities, and Hadath's maternal grandfather being John Mowbray Pearson, Hadath's *The Fifth Feversham* (1948) refers to characters present in Mowbray's *Feversham's Fag* (1927) and *Feversham's Brother* (1929). It is possible that John Dighton, initial scriptwriter for *Went the Day Well*, read *The Radio Mystery*. His post-war play *The Happiest Days of Your Life* (1947), whose eponymous film (1950) he co-scripted, satirised problems of one school being quartered on another, a frequent Hadath theme. Dighton also scripted Will Hay movies guying school stories (Richards wrote a couple of Will Hay scripts before the war), and, if he read Hadath – as he almost certainly did –

then, like most persons outside the British Museum, he would have read Mowbray as the same source.

48. Havilton, *School versus Spy*, 243. (Wilkes is called 'Fussy' as an abbreviation for 'Adolphus', a common name among the upper middle classes in Victorian days thanks to the German origins of the Royal Family. Havilton made less and less use of Fussy's real first name during the seven books of that series (beginning in 1932). Batty – so nicknamed because of short-sightedness – is actually Mr Manders. Havilton in real life, as the schoolmaster B. G. Aston, was known as 'Baggy', from his initials. The similarity of 'Batty' to 'Baggy' does not denote a self-portrait but a grim irony. Baggy entered the British army having written this last book; Batty is killed in trying to be flown to Germany with the kidnapped Fussy, who is saved.) Crompton, 'Hubert's Party', *Modern Woman* (June 1942) and *William Carries On* (May 1942), 236–7.

49. Barne, *Three and a Pigeon*, 167. M. Pardoe, *Bunkle Butts In*, 232. 'Pat Porker and the Smugglers' is as serialised in the Dublin *Irish Independent* (and presumably contemporaneously in the *Liverpool Echo*) in 1943; Budden's rhymes were very English in manner (and sometimes in rhyme), but the ethos was quietly if firmly anti-war. From this standpoint, disdain for the crimes of smugglers was even more understandable: if war was to exist, the last thing a true pacifist would wish to do would be to condone traffic with the enemy, which smuggling in wartime implies. However propagandistic his purpose, Buchan caught the point perfectly in *Mr Standfast*, as Hannay discovers when encountering a pacifist's loathing for a traitor, and believes Hannay to be that traitor. When the story was reprinted in peacetime in a *Curly Wee* annual, the black-market joke was dropped, presumably on the grounds that it was now archaic. But it retained the smugglers' ethnic identity, which (despite the strip's immensely popular Dublin serialisation) was stage-Irish, smuggler expletives being 'begorra' and 'begum'.

FIGURE 3 Evacuees escaping from evacuation (Norman Dale,
Secret Service) – see pp. 152, 358.

3

Evacuees and Gurus

*'Our schoolgirls (i.e. evacuees) have arrived . . .'. . . . 'I have said that
the children are "nice", and so they are. But modern children are poor
creatures. They keep coming to Maureen and asking, "What shall we
do now?" . . .'*

*'This book is about four children . . . They all had to go away from
London suddenly because of Air Raids, and because Father, who was
in the Army, had gone off to the War and Mother was doing some kind
of war work. They were sent to stay with a kind of relation of Mother's
who was a very old Professor who lived all by himself in the country.'*

C. S. Lewis to his brother Warren, 2 and 18 September 1939,
and draft beginning of story (later *The Lion, the Witch and the
Wardrobe*) late September 1939[?]

*Nobody thought that war, when it came, would first appear as a
gigantic, prolonged, nation-wide children's party. But that is exactly
what 'evacuation' meant, to a large part of the country, those first few
months.*

*The author of this book found himself very suddenly host to seven
small guests from Birkenhead. These are some of the stories he told
them.*

Richard Hughes, Preface to *Don't Blame Me!
and Other Stories* (1940)

*Children, go where I send ye!
How shall I send ye?*

Old Negro carol[1]

Grown-ups might tell children (in prefaces, spoken or written) that it
was like a children's party, especially those grown-ups like Richard
Hughes whose marriage was put under strain by the arrival of
evacuees, and who wanted to conceal the strains from their visitors,
their own children, their spouses and themselves.[2] It is doubtful if
Richard Hughes or anyone else would use such language about the
second and third waves of evacuees, which respectively began with

the Battle of Britain in summer 1940 and with the rocket-bombs in 1944. Evelyn Waugh, with irritating perception, opened his impressionistic portrait of Britain's first ten months of the Second World War with a quotation from a Chinese sage: 'A man getting drunk at a farewell party should strike a musical tone, in order to strengthen his spirit . . . and a drunk military man should order gallons and put out more flags . . .'. But if it was still possible to pretend it was a party in September 1939, what games were the children to play? And when games grew jaded, Hughes might tell them stories, or Lewis begin to write stories about them, or Waugh collect material to defame them. In general, the children began their Aeneids with comics, if they could read, or Blytons, or Cromptons, or even instalments of *War Illustrated*.[3]

If they were allowed. The exile from London, Christopher Leach, recalled what amounted to enslavement at 13 as a child labourer, the wages having to be given to his hostess with half a crown (£0.125) in exchange, and 'a selection of boys' magazines' sent by his mother 'destroyed as not being suitable', with subsequent similar gifts meeting the same fate. After protest, Miss Hattersley ('Sister Hattersley' to her fellow-votaries of 'an obscure sect') told him that as to his 'books. I cannot allow such rubbish in my house – I have the others to consider. All you have to do is to ask your mother not to send them. No, don't interrupt. You are in my house, and you are my responsibility.' But Jim Walker of Belfast was sent to 'the delightful little village of Bushmills, with a good view of the Old Bush distillery, which did not mean as much to me then (11 years old) as it does now . . . My best friend's father was the newsagent, so I got to read all the comics, *Hotspur* etc., before they went on sale.' Village children and 'vacees' mixed 'really well'; and, even when they robbed an orchard and were spotted, the owner turned out to be the Presbyterian minister to whom they were sent for Sunday school, after which 'we only had to go up to his door to get an apple or two'. This is idyllic, and is highly credible as well as creditable to Bushmills. The community sympathy for the 'wee waifs' rings true. And so does the processing of the evacuees 'at a church hall outside Portrush'. The Protestant people were guarding their own. Their support of the UK in the war (unlike neutral Roman Catholic Eire), the knowledge of the IRA alliance with Hitler (and the suspicion that Northern Ireland Catholics supported it), the fears of cultural obliteration in the event of Irish unity, the wilder horror-stories of the Inquisition and the Catholic massacres of Protestants in 1641, were mortar solidifying the Protestant house. Protestant Northern Ireland could not afford the luxury of social conflict, whatever might happen in Britain.[4]

The comics taught evacuees to read, dependent on them as they became with the loss of their city life, friends and family. B. S. Johnson remembered the afternoon when

> I read my first story. It was in one of that kind of comics which contains both picture-strips with speech-balloons as well as stories in words with a title illustration, and I read it out of boredom, in desperation almost, after exhausting all that the picture-strips had to give me. It was a spy story with a boy hero who sent messages across the Channel by means of a petrol-driven and radio-controlled model aeroplane: a highly improbable story, I see now, but that afternoon I read it over and over several times, with infinite pleasure, delighting that now I could read stories.

This was probably the *Dandy* or the *Beano*, which in their early lives were divided between text and strip as described, with several stories, each of about 3,500 close-printed words. When the two comics went over to strips alone, they evidently deprived their child audiences of a valuable step in education (an argument which, to do the Thomsons justice, would probably have had considerable weight with them – but it does not seem to have been made).[5] Admittedly, some kingdoms opened by reading were more inaccessible for imitation than others, even when magic a.k.a. science was not invoked. Bob Holman contrasted the freedom taken by Crompton's William and his friends with his own still parentally-controlled environment:[6]

> They were, of course, not supposed to go out during the black-out, but each parent was ready enough to suppose that his particular son was safe in the house of another parent, and so the Outlaws roamed the countryside unhindered in its thrilling new unlighted condition. They formed bands and tracked each other down. They occasionally leapt out from behind trees to terrify nervous pedestrians, they pushed each other into ditches, they narrowly missed being run over several times a night and had given heart attacks to innumerable motorists.

'I could not understand', Holman recalled, 'how William's parents had let him out during the black-out. But I could not go out and often took comfort in listening to the radio.' The answer is that Holman was thinking of autumn 1944; Crompton was writing in autumn

1939. Experiment became convention, and rules inadequately enforced from their very novelty became second nature in due time. The *Magnet* had shown how, even within boarding-school walls, a similar early freedom could be exploited by the schoolboys of Greyfriars as late as 24 February 1940. But the blackout began to claim its accidental victims, who would ultimately include the second editor of the *Magnet*, Herbert Alan Hinton, killed on New Year's Day 1945.[7] The *Magnet* itself had died just before Dunkirk, which had given an entirely new meaning to 'evacuees'. Had it survived, Richards could hardly have avoided the inclusion of Greyfriars men among the rescuers: his sailor lad, Tom Redwing, would for once have taken the lead in law-breaking, defying any school prohibitions as he embarked for Dunkirk with his father. Redwing's beloved lawless Smithy would have gone with his friend, and it is hard to see the Famous Five staying out of it. Richards's erstwhile stablemate W. E. Johns had seen the point, and, when asked in 1942 to try his hand at commando stories, began with just such a fugitive schoolboy, Nigel Peters, not as crew for *his* father but seeking to rescue him from Dunkirk (Redwing's loss and recovery of his father in the First World War had been crucial to his arrival and survival at Greyfriars). Westerman, with or without some justification in reality, had sent his fictional Sea Scouts into action from his old Portsmouth/Poole haunts, thinly disguised as 'Easthaven', but also brought them back, slightly damaged but good for further usage. Johns marooned Nigel Peters 'on a stricken battlefield with a mob of victorious Nazis', an ugly likelihood for schoolboy rescuers, as indeed is his reaction: 'terror took him by the throat and he ran as he had never run before, not even on the last sports day, when Smith minor had beaten him by a yard in the junior sprint'.[8]

All this might be determinedly realistic (above all in Smith minor defeating his 14-year-old rival), but it is in fact flashback after an introductory tableau enshrining as dizzy a schoolboy fantasy as the *Rover* or *Adventure* at its most wild-eyed could supply. Two commandos operating on a beach near Caen suddenly find themselves confronted by a boy, now aged 16, who informs them that their leader has just walked into a Nazi trap:

> 'I'll give it to you straight. I'm not going to stand here talking any longer – it's too dangerous. There's ten thousand francs waiting for the man who turns me in to the Germans. That's how badly they want me.'
>
> 'For doing what?' asked Copper in a dazed voice.

'Pulling up railway lines, cutting telephone wires, setting fire to dumps – and that sort of thing' was the calm rejoinder. 'It's my guess that you're Gimlet King's outfit. Oh yes, we know all about Gimlet – so do the Nazis. They've got you all taped through their spies, even to your names. You've led them a fine old dance up and down the coast, but if ever they get hold of you they'll skin you alive. With my own ears I heard *Generaloberst* Gunther – he's in charge in this area – promise to drown every Kitten [commando under King] that fell into his hands. That was after you bumped off his garrison in the Luvelle lighthouse. If daylight finds you here you won't have a hope.'

'Cub' Peters had become one of a group of teenage French resistance boys, developed from a clutch of 'waifs and strays' from ruined Dunkirk or other gutted homes now hiding in the woods:

At first they had lived like animals, content to keep out of sight, but as time went on some sort of order had emerged. Louis, who had the instinct of a town rat for danger, by reason of his age became the leader; and food forays, from being haphazard affairs, became cunningly organized pillaging expeditions on the Nazi storehouses. From this, growing bolder, they came to inflicting damage on enemy property whenever and wherever it could be found. Louis had been an apprentice motor mechanic, and it was but a short step from making military vehicles unserviceable to jamming the breechblocks of cannon.

By the end of a year the gang had become a small, well-organized, highly mobile force, intensely loyal, with its spies in every town and village, and its headquarters deep in the Forest of Caen. Lacking imagination, apparently it never occurred to the Nazis that the dirty little ragamuffins who hung about their camps under the pretence of looking for scraps, but really to listen to their conversations, could be the thorns in their sides.

Turning the boy, obvious material for evacuation, into a failed evacuator of the British, and then into a successful irritant to hasten evacuation of the Germans, initially displaced the agenda for commando propaganda in *King of the Commandos*: on first appearance, indeed, the commandos are made almost as ludicrous as the Nazis in face of the apparently invincible infant. It doesn't last: chapter 5 has Gimlet and his men rescuing Louis from the Nazis who are about to flog him:[9]

... another body of troops, six ... By their side, a little apart, marched a sergeant, carrying at the slope a short-handled whip, the several tails of which hung far down his back. In the centre of this imposing procession, looking singularly out of place, a slim youth, his hands in his pockets, walked with jaunty step and defiant air. As the party marched across the square towards the scaffolding the youth began to sing, and the song he sang was the Marseillaise.

'*Stillschweigen!*' roared the sergeant.

The boy continued to sing. Indeed, he sang with greater enthusiasm, whereupon the sergeant broke into the ranks and struck him across the mouth. With blood running down his chin the boy continued to sing. He sang while his shirt was ripped off, and he was tied, spreadeagled, to the tripod.

This recognised one propaganda point: children are more convincing as martyrs than as fighters, especially when the author mingles vibrations of the Crucifixion of Christ, the Children's Crusade and the film *Casablanca* (1942). *King of the Commandos*, published in October (1943), was perfectly timed for its audience to thrill reminiscently to the use of the Marseillaise in *Casablanca* as a symbol of Resistance revived despite quiescent appearances. Johns's affectionate heart no less than his judicious head wanted to insist as passionately as possible on the survival and integrity of French resistance, as much as on the success and continuity of British commando raids. The British might seem to have run from Dunkirk, as Nigel Peters does, but they regroup for devastating results with their invincible French allies, all the more effective because the Nazis despise them. However much Johns might admire Churchill, Louis on his cross silences Churchill's complaints about the Cross of Lorraine. Johns took every opportunity to salute the Free French, which to the ordinary reader meant Charles de Gaulle. Johns's ideas on boy guerrillas may have been wishful thinking for France: did he realise, as the *Rover* did, that they had real-life counterparts in Britain? Children who should have been evacuated were running loose, sometimes at much younger ages than young Peters at Dunkirk. Houses were bombed, and frightened children ran away from them; fathers were at war or otherwise absent from home; mothers disappeared, possibly killed in bomb raids. Waugh may only have produced a cruel absurdist caricature when he depicted in the Connolly children his most memorable characters and incidents in *Put Out More Flags*, but his account of their

'Auntie' was no doubt true of several former guardians of the millions of evacuees:[10]

> To this woman, it seemed, the war had come as a God-given release. She had taken her dependants to the railway station, propelled them into the crowd of milling adolescence, and hastily covered her tracks by decamping from home.

Reading may have restrained many children from theft or vagrancy, but even those who could read found fewer and fewer means. Comics shrank in size, the twenty-eight pages of the *Beano*'s first number (30 July 1938) being reduced to eight by 1940. Libraries were bombed, and waste-paper campaigns put paid to most chances of second-hand acquisition of books or magazines. Boys' underground swapping met more active discouragement, as fears of disease competed with urge for paper salvage. If supervision was much more uncertain, it gave a field day to the busybody, who in default of any more rational guardian was given a free hand, and the comic wearily tolerated by parents became a natural target for the snobbish instincts of new guardians. Was the child free from hair-lice? did it wash the back of its neck? was it free from habits such as nose-picking? were no other faults visible? then to radiate visible virtue confiscate its comic!

Of course, if the child's evacuation meant a long journey, the comic was less likely to win adult reproof, and children bound for America or Australia might be given several: Colin Ryder Richardson remembers the *Beano*, the *Dandy*, the *Mickey Mouse* and *Film Fun*, one of which he was reading on the *City of Benares* taking him to Canada when a torpedo from a submarine struck the port side. Ninety children were on the doomed ship, of whom thirteen survived. Colin and the comics were in his bunk on the starboard side. 'I knew immediately what had happened. I could smell the cordite.' The Hungarian appointed to guard him, Laszlo Raskai, got Colin aboard a lifeboat swinging violently in the gale while 'the liner rolled in the heavy seas'. The boat got clear; Raskai stayed helping others and went down with the ship. The boat, once at sea level, 'filled with water but stayed afloat because of buoyancy air tanks', and got away from the *City of Benares* with great difficulty as all its oars and sails floated away. The ship sank in half an hour; the full moon and the ship's emergency generators made everything visible. Colin, aged 11, was sitting beside an elderly nurse, whom he desperately tried to keep alive, holding her head 'above the waves using my body as support under her whilst still clinging to the seat' as the seas rolled outside and inside the boat. Others heard the boy doing all in his power to keep the nurse in good heart, talking, comforting, encouraging. 'Eventually the old lady died in my arms, but by that time I had no strength to move to let her go because of my stiffness and the cold.' Thirty died in the boat that night, and Colin had to help get the bodies out and make them float away lest they capsize the boat. 'We were all covered in oil.' After twenty hours, when the equinoctial gale quietened, they were picked up by the HMS *Hurricane*; another lifeboat whose crew included six boys had to wait eight days. Colin's gallantry and good spirits made him the mascot or symbol of the will to survive, to his fellow-survivors in the boat. He was the boy hero who led his mates in the fight for survival. Convention expected him to show the stiff upper lip, and he showed it. Internally, he wanted to cry, and knew he must not. The result, as he saw it, was that after return to Britain he 'became shy, sensitive, stoic, basically a depressed loner'. Meanwhile, the *Beano* had its next issue, on 21 September 1940 (the *City of Benares* sank on the 17th): Lord Snooty's magician-like Professor magnified germs to enormity to be dropped on Germany, leading Hitler to write in desperation to Snooty: 'I have had three doses of measles already and mine moustache is coming out in purple spots'. No doubt it gave smiles to many amid the Battle of Britain above and the bombs below. But Colin's days of comics were over. 'My sea experiences made me feel that they were shallow, unimportant, rather than humorous.' The child had survived. His childhood had not. But he never lost his urgency to help others survive. Fifty years later he developed cancer, and developed in reply psychological resources to aid medical treatment, resulting in an exhilarating, shrewd, sensible book, *Mind Over Cancer* (1995). Above all else, children's literature in the Second World War had developed in children the yearning to be heroes: the boy who was a hero wished he had never had to be one – but he remained one, vanquishing his internal anguish which clung to him so long.[11]

The few evacuee stories which featured sea adventure naturally suffer when Colin Ryder Richardson's war becomes a yardstick. In *War is Declared*, Percy Woodcock was desperately fantasising hairsbreadth escapes from torpedoed vessels, with which (in all probability) he had once tried to convince himself and his wife that their son had managed to survive. The relative ease with which its young heroes Pat (evidently his chosen variant for his lost Sam) and Bruce cope with two successive shipwrecks, and two lifeboat voyages (one holding only the two of them), may seem thin when we think of the

City of Benares survivors, but Woodcock compels compassion by
what we know was rooted in his mind whatever his literary exor-
cisms: Lieutenant Samuel Woodcock gone down (or blown up) in
HMS *Barham*, the great battleship, a day's voyage from Alexandria.
Isobel Shead, the Australian writer, began *They Sailed by Night* with
a couple of very realistic family discoveries of their bombed-out
homes, so that torpedoing in the Indian Ocean, life-savings and
rescue after twenty-four hours inevitably seemed routine. The children make rescues but do not assume control, certainly not to Colin
Ryder Richardson's extent, since a boy's mental rescue of the dying
and physical removal of corpses was deemed surplus to child reader
requirements. It is initially set between the sinking of the *City of
Benares* and the stoppage of government-directed emigration, which
does allow mention of real deaths:[12]

> 'Only last week you said you wouldn't risk sending me across the
> sea – what about all those children that were torpedoed on the way
> to Canada by a U-boat?' he eyed her anxiously. 'That's why the
> Government says they're going to stop . . . And you said . . .'
>
> 'Never mind what I said', she interrupted him. 'That was last
> week. I've changed my mind. Last week we didn't think the Jerries
> would be able to get through our defences to bomb London. But
> they have. Hundreds killed last Saturday night in the East End,
> and thousands injured.' She stopped and drew a deep breath.
> 'D'you think I can go on with raids every night and people being
> killed all round us, and not try to get you out of it?'

On the other hand, P. L. Travers, a.k.a. Helen Lyndon Goff, had no
torpedoes in her novel of child evacuees crossing the Atlantic in
August 1940, *I Go by Sea, I Go by Land* (1941), for all her Australian
origin. Travers, the creator of Mary Poppins, needed little training in
the use of English voices, and the narrative is supposedly the diary of
Sabrina Lind (aged 11 ¼). The scribe's cold eye sees much: a bomb-
dodger's belated regret at her own decision to emigrate meets the
purser's refusal to return to port with the pilot, 'And the lady went
away with weeping and nashing [sic] of teeth'. A lower-class evacuee
'has black hair and a very rosie face and never says H if she can help
it' – but, deciding to like her, Sabrina asks 'why should you bother
with Hs anyway?' and is moved at hearing how her new (somewhat
token) friend's father was an engine-driver killed at his work.

   The isolation of the evacuee might induce reading, if it could be
done. Hostile environment drew evacuees closer to the friendship of

books, sometimes with effective precaution against adult realisation
that reading was happening in the bedroom during the hours under
adult curfew. With stockings to be darned, or other routine work, a
kindly father might read stories that girls – or, more precisely, boys –
might like. Mr Reeves, coping with ten children on their farm who
had never seen cows milked, read them what would have been his
own remembered favourites, such as W. H. G. Kingston's *Peter the
Whaler.* Wales had been an early choice for many parents – even
Colin Ryder Richardson found himself near Abergavenny before
Canada was made his destination – and children who did not know
Welsh found themselves (in Welsh-language classes) with extra
leisure for reading (in English). But storytelling, without the cold
constriction of print, must have been a resource for many guardians
of evacuees, temporary and permanent, and it was natural for
Richard Hughes to fight the loneliness of the charges now in his
Snowdon home when as billet-officer he had been unable to place
them in other addresses. Llanfrothen in the heart of Welsh-speaking
Wales on the borders of Carnarvon and Merioneth, awesome in giant
crags and pure streams, daunted the hearts and revived the fears of
the little ones left to the billet-officer while 100 of their Birkenhead
companions had been chosen, as war began. Hughes was English-
born, but convinced of his own Welshness by descent from an
Ancient British chieftain (duly confirmed by the College of Heralds),
although his ancestors' last known Welsh residence had been in
Tudor times. He was an author of genius, as his extraordinary *High
Wind in Jamaica* (1929) had shown. Among its other successes was
its ability to bring children to thinking life in a story for adults: one
child kills, and another is killed, in its course; and, if it has real
pirates, they are left little romanticism outside their own delusions.
By 1939, he had far more practical experience of children, having
three of his own (of whom the three-year-old furiously resented the
evacuees and tried to scare them away by stampeding black heifers
at them). At the end of the day, a circle was formed round the fire by
children and bard (the Welsh might deny his Welshness, but who
were children and Birkenhead babes to object?), and each would
'choose objects to go in the story, thinking very carefully about what
we wanted . . . as soon as he had gone right round the circle he had to
begin'. Hughes's daughter Penelope continued:[13]

> An evacuee once asked for a chamberpot in the story, with great
> daring for those days. Out of that grew the story of the forlorn ill-
> treated wooden doll, who ran away one night downriver, using a

china pot as a boat. . . . The moment in the story when the river carrying the pot reached the open sea, and little waves began to break into it until finally it was so full that it sank, held us riveted.

The story went on with the wooden doll finding she could swim. A merchild met her and befriended her, and the two of them later made their way back up the river to the house from which the doll had run away. After a while the distressed merparents came in search of their lost child. The stormy night, with a merman and huge walruses flopping through the orchard, while rain lashed the windows of the house, was not the expected stuff of bedtime stories. Much later, when I was grown up, I discovered there was another purpose to my father's watery story: that having an orgy of wetness could break the evacuee's bedwetting – and it did. In the book, at the publisher's request, the pot was changed to a china pudding-bowl.

Penelope Hughes tells us her father would have forgotten the stories next day, but that the children were able to recall them for him months later (adults inhibited him, and if any were present 'the stories were never so good'). And the following year he published them as *Don't Blame Me! and Other Stories*, the pusillanimous publisher being Chatto & Windus. They are masterpieces in their own right, but it is possible to see the intention to fight the evacuees' fears with a logic of civil nonsense and realistic magic bereft of any shade of patronising. A story called 'Home' tells of a King and Queen who learn from an enchantment that they will never return to their palace in 'their country of dark forests and steep rocks' but are given the opportunity of entering another land 'of green fields and wide, winding rivers, with blue sky, and white roads, and yellow corn-stacks', and before they do so they leave their royal robes on their horses and don farmers' clothes and advance on foot and finally come to a little farm whose dog greets them and[14]

> There were three little children sitting on the floor in front of the fire, toasting their bare toes; but as the King and Queen came in they jumped up and ran to them.
>
> 'Oh, Daddy!' they said. 'Oh, Mummy! How glad we are you are back!'
>
> The Queen sat down in a big armchair and took one of them on her knee.

'Yes, my dears', she said, 'and we are glad to be back too.'
But at the same time she knew for certain she had never seen them before; and she had not the slightest idea of their names.

The beauty of that is its silent likening of the evacuees' condition in a strange country with three strange children in a family circle claiming their allegiance to that of a King and Queen: if the King and Queen feel at a loss and unable to work out the identities of the children in their new family, why should small evacuees feel embarrassed at being in a similar situation? Hughes went into the Admiralty for the rest of the war, and helped write its history, but what he did in his Welsh farm to console the seven little girls from Birkenhead he may have thought the best war work of all. As he told the American Academy of Arts and Letters thirty years later:[15]

An apparently intelligent man tells you, 'No, I never read *novels*'. He plumes himself on his serious-mindedness: yet isn't this at the very least confessing unwillingness to face facts about his fellow-men – and himself? . . . there is one unpalatable fact which Fiction might *make* him apprehend: the fact that other people are not 'things' but 'persons'. . . .

Maybe that is the supreme lesson he is refusing to learn; and the failure to learn it can prove disastrous. For the absolute solipsist the asylum doors gape. Even the gates of hell: one vast failure to learn it built the gas-ovens. The archetypal non-reader of Fiction was Hitler.

Unhappily for evacuees at the time and since, Fiction has chiefly enshrined them as Waugh victims. *Put Out More Flags* deserves inclusion as children's literature in that it shows the mind of Evelyn Waugh at its most masterfully childish, and the three Connolly children – sex-mad, destructive, imbecilic – as anti-social as their creator. Basil Seal's exploitation of evacuee-billeting to blackmail money from reluctant hosts indicates the possible darker side of the work in other hands than Hughes's. It was an area where corruption might have flourished, and if it had not done so before, it may have burgeoned after a judicious reading of *Put Out More Flags*. The book is evilly perceptive as to evacuee potential in assessing rural society:[16]

'he's your boy, isn't he?' she said, turning to Barbara.
'He's my brother, Doris.'

'Ah', she said, her pig eyes dark with the wisdom of the slums, 'but you fancy him, don't you? I saw.'

Details such as that keep the book off the juvenile list, but Waugh was a ready stage for the enterprising child reader in quest of agreeable emancipation. Elsewhere, his childishness took the form of a petulant patriotism, alternating with an even more petulant Popery. As a Roman Catholic, I take pleasure in contrasting his charity with that of the Anglo-Catholic C. S. Lewis, whose welcome to evacuees from the beginning of the war impressively repaid him in the fullness of time.

One of them opened a wardrobe. The child who did that, Lucy, was not of course a real child, but she owed her existence and its consequence, the Narnia chronicles, to Lewis's hospitality, perhaps even from his desire to develop children's imagination. Up to then, he had sought an adult audience, or as near it as university students may get. Dealing with evacuees trained him to envisage the children for whom he was writing, and the children of whom he would write.

The Lion, the Witch and the Wardrobe (1950) got under way without the Lion: Aslan, Lewis's Christ-figure, 'came bounding into' the book when it was apparently well advanced, without prior warning to Lewis. Hence he had already conceived Narnia as Lucy first saw it, a winter-bound kingdom, a police state, a totalitarian terror-kept rule. The obvious origin for the White Witch is Hitler, the one being whom Lewis was prepared to state was in Hell, Antichrist much as the Witch is anti-Aslan. Aslan's arrival in the story lightens the grim opening: Lewis would seem originally to have cast Witch-ruled Narnia on lines parallel to Hitler's Europe – the host required by law to betray his guest, the removal of dissidents to a condition neither alive nor dead, the discovery of treachery in close kindred. The evacuee children who first prompted the story remain in the opening, whose first words were ultimately 'Once there were four children whose names were Peter, Susan, Edmund and Lucy. This story is about something that happened to them when they were sent away from London during the war because of the air-raids. They were sent to the house of an old Professor . . .'. The war background vanishes, and the war, unmentioned again, is definitely over in later books. But, in the first book, the evacuee status in our world seems related to the children's alien status in the Witch's Narnia. Lewis had little to learn about the literature of the terror state:[17]

Lucy suddenly said: 'I say – where's Edmund?'

There was a dreadful pause, and then everybody began asking 'Who saw him last? How long has he been missing? Is he outside?' and then all rushed to the door and looked out. . . .

'What on earth are we to do, Mr Beaver?' said Peter.

'Do?' said Mr Beaver who was already putting on his snow boots, 'do? We must be off at once. We haven't a moment to spare!'

'We'd better divide into four search parties', said Peter, 'and all go in different directions. Whoever finds him must come back here at once and –'

'Search parties, Son of Adam?' said Mr Beaver; 'what for?'

'Why, to look for Edmund, of course!'

'There is no point in looking for him', said Mr Beaver.

'What do you mean?' said Susan. 'He can't be far away yet. And we've got to find him. What do you mean when you say there's no use looking for him?'

'The reason there's no use looking', said Mr Beaver, 'is that we know already where he's gone!' Everyone stared in amazement. 'Don't you understand?' said Mr Beaver. 'He's gone to *her*, to the White Witch. He has betrayed us all.'

'Oh surely – oh, really!' said Susan, 'he can't have done that.'

'Can't he?' said Mr Beaver looking very hard at the three children, and everything they wanted to say died on their lips for each felt suddenly quite certain inside that this was exactly what Edmund had done.

It is perhaps the most frightening moment in children's war literature.

If the evacuees enabled Lewis to bring children's literature to the sublime, he had given them too secure a life to confront social conflict. It was Enid Blyton who faced that, and its resolution, and she did so by diagnosis of a division of which few English writers were aware: Scots versus English. Scottish nationalism was not very visible to English eyes during the Second World War, making Robert MacIntyre's by-election victory at Motherwell in April 1945 a genuine sensation. Orwell, moving away from his pre-war Scotophobia, made informed comment in his 'Notes on Nationalism' just after it, distinguishing Scottish nationalism from Anglophobia. In this perception, Blyton preceded him in *The Adventurous Four* when the Nazis maroon the children:[18]

Tom was glad to see that neither Jill nor Mary cried. Good! That would show the enemy how brave British [in their case, English] children could be! . . .

Andy shook his fist at the disappearing ship, with the small boat bobbing behind it.

'You think you can beat a Scots boy, but you can't', he cried. 'I'll beat you yet! You and your submarines!'

(Blyton did not aspire to classic status, more especially once she went into high production and her style glutinised; but she had learned her business from the classics and their votaries, and this has a breath of the spirit of the captive Jim Hawkins's defiance of the pirates in *Treasure Island*.) The English bourgeois children have already made friends with the older but scarcely literate Scots (Caithness?) fisherboy by the time The *Adventurous Four* opens. As Mary Pollock, writing approximately at the same date, Blyton explored group conflict in *The Children of Kidillin* (1940) where she discarded possible divisions of class, religion, education and parental income simply to confront mutually hostile Scots and English cousins with one another. They are evacuees – and, in common with Blyton's own divided family, the cousins are unknown to one another ('One's called Tom, and the other's called Sheila. They live in London, but their parents want them to go somewhere safe till the war's over. They're coming tomorrow!'). The conflict is sanitised (for example the Scots boy, Sandy, wears a kilt, eliciting no derisive comment from his English critics, even at the height of mutual recriminations – a somewhat improbable immunity). Blyton was evidently anxious to kill one common English assumption about Scots at the outset: their supposed meanness. Our first sight of Sandy and his sister Jeanie is of their buying 'bulls-eye peppermints' for the expected evacuees. Their major row producing Sandy's 'I wish you'd never come!' is answered by Tom's bitter 'When the war is over we'll go back home. Sandy and Jeanie will be glad to be rid of us then', which actually horrifies Sandy at the thought that he was violating the laws of hospitality:[19]

Sandy wanted to say a lot of things but he couldn't say a word. He was ashamed of himself. After all, his cousins were his guests. How *could* he have said to them that he wished they had never come? What would his mother and father say if they knew? Scottish people were famous for the welcome they gave to friends.

Cousins in Blyton do not assume family loyalty: here, as elsewhere, their friendship actually triumphs over a relationship whose convention is to be unwanted. This follows her own practice, but her instinct may well have been sounder than more pious observers might assume. C. S. Lewis, less pious in this, apparently agreed with her: witness the loathing of his original four for their cousin Eustace in *The Voyage of the* Dawn Treader. Blyton, whose Scots husband had made her an encyclopaedist, would have known the accepted form of patriotic Scottish cults: Agnes Mure Mackenzie's *I Was at Bannockburn* (1939) was one way in which the war of independence was recalled up for a new generation, supposedly conjured up for 'Jean' and 'John' (convalescing from measles in Edinburgh) by a portrait of Sir Walter Scott, with unacknowledged obligations to Kipling's *Puck of Pook's Hill*. Blyton avoided any such issues, centring dispute around accent and language (she may have known of Hugh MacDiarmid's establishment of the modern Scottish nationalist agenda initially on a linguistic basis: *The Golden Treasury of Scottish Poetry*, with his introduction a triumphant clarion call, published by Macmillan in December 1939, and Blyton's most convenient means of attuning herself to Scottish culture).

> Sandy and Jeanie had been showing off to Tom and Sheila. They had taken them for a long walk, up a difficult mountain, where a good deal of rough climbing had to be done. The English children had panted and puffed, and poor Sheila's shoes were no use at all for such walking.
>
> 'Can't we have a rest again?' asked Sheila at last. 'I'm so tired. This is a dreadful place for walking. I'd much rather walk in the park.'
>
> 'In the *park*', said Sandy scornfully. 'What, when there's fine country like this, and soft heather to your feet! And look at the view there – you can see the sea!'

Her work was still scholarly: the dative 'to your feet' was good middle-class Scots.

> The four children sat down. Far away they could see the blue glimmer of the sea, and could hear very faintly the shrill cry of the circling gulls. Tom was so tired that he only gave the view a moment's look, and then lay down on his back. 'Phew, I'm tired!' he said. 'I vote we go back.'

'But we're not yet at the burn we want to show you', said Jeanie. Sheila giggled.

'It does sound so funny for a stream to be called a *burn!*' she said. 'It sounds as if something was on fire – going to see the *burn!*'

'The bur-r-rn, not the *burn*', said Sandy, sounding the R in burn. 'Can't you talk properly?'

'We can talk just as well as *you!*' said Tom, vexed, and then off they went, squabbling again!

Blyton knew how to evangelise nature for children, but, awareness of the aesthetic contrast for the veteran and the neophyte in the remote sound of a gull or sight of the sea, goes farther than the usual pedagogical perception. She also noticed how rapidly the urban sophisticate could be humiliated by country cousinhood.

'There'll be no time to finish the walk if you lie there any longer', said Sandy. 'This is the fourth time we've stopped for you – a lazy lot of folk you Londoners must be.'

'All right. Then we'll *be* lazy!' said Tom angrily. 'You and Jeanie go on, and Sheila and I will stay here till you come back – and you can go and find your wonderful bur-r-r-r-r-rn yourself.'

Partly by compensation, and partly to provide another cause of anger, the English children prove educationally more advanced than their Scots cousins. The convention is repeated, with more justification, in *The Adventurous Four*, where Andy is clearly not from a book culture. But neither are Sandy and Jeanie, with scant respect for the future Davie thesis of the democratic intellect (whatever might be the chances given to that with governess education, as practised in Kidillin). To Blyton, the social periphery had country wisdom, the social core had its books. It is a variant of the imperial veneration for the heroic attainments of the superior native coupled with amusement at his obvious unfitness for white man's education (variously expressed in such works as *Biggles in the South Seas*, the *Beano*'s 'Big Bonehead' and Conan Doyle's *The Lost World*, while being explicitly repudiated in two other stalwarts of the juvenile reading-shelf: John Buchan's *Prester John*, and, oddly enough, the Bosambo stories in Edgar Wallace's 'Sanders of the River' series). Blyton did not mean it racially: George, based on herself, exhibits the same traits in the 'Five' books, which evidently originated as a variation on the Kidillin theme. George conquers her antipathy to her cousins in *Five on a Treasure Island* when they join her in the cult of her forbidden pet, the dog Timmy, and hence become slightly uncertain allies in her war against her father. *The Children of Kidillin* had used the same idea of canine friendships and adult enemies, but with Nazi spies and their dog as the enemy against whom the children unite their forces. (The progress is suggestive.) Blyton, with slightly heavy irony, uses the mutual hostility of the English dog (ecumenically called Paddy) and the Scottish dog Mack to make fun of the children's quarrels (as opposed to making fun of the children). Then the dogs stand firm when the children are threatened by the spies' 'big brute of a dog', after Paddy has been rescued by Sandy from the mountain burn, and Tom makes the *amende honorable*: 'What a day! . . . Quarrels and adventures and dog-fights! Goodness, Scotland is a most exciting place – much better than London, I can tell you!' Despite Blyton's conspiratorial 'you should have seen how pleased Sandy and Jeanie were to hear *that*!', as marking the sealing of concord, her anonymous revisers removed both speech and comment after her death. It might have seemed an absurd capitulation for an evacuee from the Blitz, but she rightly documented the contempt of many evacuees for the premature panic of the 'phoney' war (bowdlerisation of Blyton has in general been a foolish activity). She also noted, as Brent-Dyer had, that there was nothing phoney about the naval war from the very start. Tom identifies the spies' wireless transmitter:[20]

> 'I've seen one before. These men can send out radio messages as well as receive them – and oh, Sandy, that's what they've been doing, the wretches! As soon as they see the steamers pass on the sea in the distance, they send a radio message to some submarine lurking near by, and the submarine torpedoes the steamers!'
>
> 'Oh! So that's why there have been so many steamers sunk round our coast', said Sandy, his eyes flashing in anger. 'The hateful scoundrels! I'm going to smash their set, anyway!'
>
> Before Tom could stop Sandy, the raging boy picked up a stone and smashed it into the centre of the transmitter. 'You won't sink any *more* steamers!' he cried.

That was propaganda by catharsis. It was what child readers would so dearly have wanted to do. Blyton's audience was chiefly English, but at that point they would gladly settle for being Scots. Listeners on the English periphery used to talk back to the wireless, and frequently hurl abuse at Lord Haw-Haw, whose reiteration that the British were starving once led an Ulster Presbyterian grandmother to hurl a sizzling frying-pan into her set, yelling 'Smell that, ye bugger!'[21]

The break-up of Blyton's marriage to the Scottish Major Hugh Pollock ended the signature 'Mary Pollock' and deferred Blyton's subsequent use of a Scottish locale. But an aspirant Scots writer seems to have taken note of her use of Anglo-Scots child tension and furthered it: Ayrshire-born (like Hugh Pollock), Agnes M. R. Dunlop wrote as Elisabeth Kyle, and began her second literary career as a children's author in 1941 with *Visitors from England*. The title seemed intended to cash in on Kitty Barne's Carnegie Medal-winner, *Visitors from London*; but, while the young English duo are clearly evacuees, nothing is made of the war. Matters begin on Blytonian lines of national conflict (' "He's Scots, so he's likely to be an awful tough", Peter said gloomily') with social pretension prematurely held against the English ('La-de-da English with their fine clothes and fine manners. I wouldn't be seen dead with such') and Scots concern for appearances ('they'll see the room in the morning, she told herself as she led Margot past the sitting-room she had scrubbed and polished that morning so as to give them a good impression of Scots house-wifery'). This is scene-setting, less dramatic than Blyton, but picking up as the gradations in Scots society and their consequent rivalries are brought into play. Anglo-Scots prickles are better flaunted when young Scots characters visit Peter and Margot in London, and make rather more of the impact of war, in *The Seven Sapphires* ('No doubt the English are as kind-hearted as anyone else, once you get behind their faces . . .').[22]

The English have a considerable literature for child consumption inducing kindness to animals. In the main, it doesn't seem intended for self-glorification, although irritated dissident Anglophones have implied it – the North American Marshall Saunders's *Beautiful Joe* (1894) included a horrific story of an Englishman (unnamed, and thus permanently identified by nationality) who comes to a very bad end after hideous cruelty to animals, and the Irish Protestant squirearchs Edith Somerville and [Violet] Martin 'Ross' – conscious of standing apart from both English Protestants and Irish Catholics – grimly realise the clash of cultures in *The Silver Fox* (1898), where the English lady weeps for her dead horse, and the Irish peasant girl who has saved her life reminds her that she had shed no tear when the Irish girl's brother had been killed. Anna Sewell's *Black Beauty* (1877) was in fact an attack on ill-treatment of horses; and, being set in England, the ill-treatment is by the English, nor does it mask a means for class hostilities by exhibiting working-class cruelty to beasts (as frequently if incidentally abounded in literature): its human heroes are cabmen and stable-hands. The Second World War was not kind to animals: Shead's *They Sailed by Night* begins with a useless search for a dog killed or stampeded by the bomb which obliterated the family's home and street.[23] Johns in *Spitfire Parade* resurrected a First World War story, greatly improving it as a story at the cost of hard, authentic war-flying in 1918, originally 'The Funk', renamed 'The Coward': initially a cowardly pilot learns courage – indeed foolhardiness – when his pet goldfish is killed by a German pilot; in the rewrite, the coward has a little pig, called Annie.

> Ginger watched him curiously, and with compassion, as he went into the sty and, sitting on the edge of the feeding trough, tweaked the piglet's ear, a demonstration of affection which the animal appeared to appreciate, for it rested its nose on his knee, grunting contentedly. It seemed that Henry had, as he had claimed, a way with animals.

He duly loses his fear and distinguishes himself by crazy courage in an aerial fight over the Thames Estuary (where Amy Johnson was killed), and when he returns with his plane shot to pieces they discover why:

> 'Just after you took off a dive bomber came in low and plastered us. He dropped a stick of bombs, but this was the only one that did any damage.'
>
> 'Damage', grated Henry. 'The swine killed Annie – my little Annie.'
>
> Understanding dawned in Biggles's eyes. 'I see', he said.
>
> 'I went up to avenge her', burst out Henry. 'Revenge! Revenge is sweet. I'll get the hound who killed my little Annie if I have to shoot every Hun out of the sky.'

But Johns evidently could not bring himself to kill the pig as he had once killed the goldfish, and Annie was saved by taking to her heels at the first bomb, duly returned to base by a farmer who found her 'tearing across my land' and identified her by the RAF markings painted on her flanks by Henry's derisive fellow-pilots. It achieved the exceptional balance of satire and pathos available to few, and the odds fall in favour of the absurdly idolised pet in the end:[24] 'Peering through a net in the back of the vehicle, looking very scared and pleased to be home, was Annie'. Johns was asking his readers to keep

their humour as best they could amid the domestic tragedies of the
Blitz, when, like Annie, so many of them had to flee to escape
destruction. But the evacuees could seldom indulge themselves with
pets in the vortex of war. Blyton, whether avowedly setting her
stories in time of war, or inferentially so (inference easily for a war-
surrounded child to make), returned to the theme of outlawed
animals. George is forbidden to have her dog in *Five on a Treasure
Island* (1942). Ownership of pets seems restricted to the wealthy, like
Fatty Trotteville and Lady Candling in *The Mystery of the Disappearing Cat* (1944). The parrot is only permitted in *The Island of
Adventure* (1944) because the harassed, overworked aunt thinks that
it is sympathising with her. Blyton was in fact noting the climate of
the times with the reminiscent grief of a child forbidden to have
animal pets long ago.

But the *Zeitgeist* was also reflected in child minds; and, with the
loss of so much else among the evacuees, few could have the
luxury of keeping pets when human relationships were so shattered. A child allowed to quell its fears by the adoption of a new
pet, as Henry in Biggles's squadron had, was very fortunate. Violet
M. Methley in *Vackies* (1941) has a six-year-old maddening everyone by its devotion to a tortoise, although its determination wins.
P. L. Travers may have been more representative in having Sabrina
coolly telling her readers at the outset how her last days in the
family home saw 'special Treats like . . . killing off Mrs Metcalfe
and Mrs de Quincy, two special hens, to supplement the meat
Ration' (Mary Poppins is a trifle hard-bitten, and Travers may have
reflected the pragmatism of her Irish ancestors on such matters).
But Crompton certainly marked a new departure in animal-loving
in these days when children sang 'Run, Rabbit, Run' with the
sang-froid of a God of Battles indifferently noting the choices of
sacrificial victims. Crompton had let herself go in making William
so devoted an owner of the mongrel Jumble, but any other animal
in her stories has to take its chances where it can find them. Her
Second World War showed William going through toils of intrigue
to save the life of a little female evacuee's pet rabbit: 'They just say
it's war-time and they're only keeping rabbits for food and I must
get used to eating them. They say they've left Ernest as long as
they can and if they leave him any longer he won't be fit to eat.'
Eventually, William manages to get a guarantee from General
Moult that Ernest (whom the general is led to think belongs to
him) is to be given to the little girl and not to be eaten. William
finds her nursing 'a large fluffy Chinchilla rabbit' which her aunt

has just given her. When he produces Ernest and the general's note,[25]

> The little girl stared at Ernest with an expression of contempt that almost rivalled Ernest's own.
> 'Oh, *that* thing', she said. 'Goodness, I'd quite forgotten it! It's just an ordinary table rabbit. Mother!' she called, 'here's this ole rabbit back we lost. Can we have it for supper?'

The little girl is a solitary evacuee, but William is exceptionally sympathetic with evacuees in general from the first. Crompton makes constructive use of native infant envy of coddled evacuees, but William himself is statesmanlike:[26]

> 'We've gotter do something for the evacuees', he said sternly to his Outlaws that evening. 'Nothin's been done for 'em for ever so long.'
> 'They did enough for 'em at Christmas', said Ginger.
> 'Yes, but they wouldn't let us help', complained William. 'Stopped us every time we tried to give 'em a good time. Gave 'em a party an' then wouldn't let 'em have a good time.'
> Their minds went back to the Christmas party given by the residents to the evacuees. It had had the makings of a good party, but, just as the Outlaws were succeeding in working up what seemed to them the right spirit, Authority had stepped in and accused them of 'getting rough'. They had been ignominiously ejected from the Village Hall in the middle of a game invented by William, called Lions and Tigers, in which the evacuees were joining with zest and which had already shown the weak spots in the party clothes hastily put together by kind-hearted but un-skilled residents.
> 'They say that they could hear the noise at the other end of the village', said Mrs Brown sternly to William when the affair had been reported to her.
> 'Well, that only shows they were enjoying themselves', said William. 'You can always hear the noise at the other end of the village if people are enjoying themselves.'

Ultimately (though he has to capture a German spy to do it), William gets control of a cottage and throws a party for the evacuees: 'Sounds of revelry had, indeed, been heard as far off as the next village, and the guests had departed home in that tattered condition that seemed to be the inevitable result of any game organized by the Outlaws'.

But, by this stage, the local children are becoming so resentful that they want to be evacuated in their turn, however uncertain of what the process means:[27]

> 'A whole *tin* of sweets each. It's not fair, it isn't. Puttin' on side an' havin' parties an' eatin' whole *tins* of sweets. It's not fair. We oughter be 'vacuated, too.'
> 'I've been 'vacuated', said a small, foursquare child proudly. 'It made my arm come up somethin' korful.'
> 'Shut up, Georgie Parker', said Arabella. 'It's a different sort of 'vacuated you have done on your arm. It's to stop you turnin' into a cow you have it done on your arm.'

This is in spring 1940. A year later, envy had ripened into hostility, as is shown when a self-created child psychologist appeals in vain to the better nature of the village children (not including William or his Outlaws):

> The speech by which Mrs Dayford urged the little guests to show patriotism and self-sacrifice was lengthy and eloquent.
> 'Remember, dear children', she ended, 'that we are at war. Remember that we must all display the spirit of patriotism and self-control. We must eat, of course, in order to live, but let us show a spirit of service and comradeship this afternoon by eating as little as possible – as *little* as *possible*, dear children, so that what is left may go to the strangers we have welcomed into our midst, the evacuees.'
> She sat down amidst an applause that marked not so much approval of the sentiments she had expressed as relief that the speech was over and that the real business of the day might now begin. As one man, the little guests fell upon the feast outspread before them. The thought that the residue was to go to the evacuees had whetted their appetites. Not one but had suffered at the hands of the evacuees (tough young guys from the East End of London whose methods of warfare were novel and unpleasant) and the thought that their tormentors might profit from their abstinence urged them on to as yet greater feats of gastronomy.

So another busybody bites the Crompton dust. She was particularly alive to power-trippers versus workers, on social projects, and William from time to time proved precisely the parody of the ignorant

busybody her satire required (for example when he begins organis-
ing evacuees).

Norman Dale, possibly inspired by this passage, opened his *Secret
Service* (1943) from the point of view of the London evacuee:

> 'And what part of London do you come from?' 'Hackney, lady', said
> Peter.
>   'Hackney? That's in the East End, isn't it? Of course. . . .'

He is duly challenged to combat, butting and kicking a child-hating
cook when she shakes him violently, and later retaliating on a bigger
boy at a children's party: 'He stopped being a quiet, friendly little boy
and became a tough, wiry little demon, fighting in every way he could
. . . No one had ever taught Peter that it is wrong to kick when you
got into a fight.' For this he is disgraced, and runs away, which
enables his author to pitch him into a good spy thriller. Peter is
evidently Cockney, but Dale spares us the usual embarrassing
middle-class author self-insurance on the snob scale by the use of
Cockney dialect, as though all the English did not have accents of
their own. Yet Peter is clearly akin to the more rural, more middle-
class William, all the more when he links up once more with his best
friend, Ginger. William would certainly have sympathised with
Peter's first reaction to Mrs Chater, the evacuation officer, whose
'Of course' when she identifies Hackney as East End is worthy of a
Crompton character:[28] 'The thing [Peter] had found about living in
the country was that it was full of ladies with bright, beaming smiles
who told you where to go and what to do, and didn't pay attention to
anything you said'.

Essentially, Mrs Dayford and Mrs Chater are anti-gurus. The
classic pattern of fiction for children had always presumed a godlike
figure, perhaps two, from the adult world, godlike above all in the
rarity of its interventions for whatever reason. When the guru
intervenes, the guru listens. Kipling's Kim has his guru, and also
his imperial secret agent. The guru might be from the periphery, even
beyond its racial or colour frontier, as Kim's is, but the secular
authority-figure must be from the metropolis, the core. The author
may introduce itself into the story as guru: P. L. Travers does, as 'Pel',
a supervisory family friend, in *I Go by Sea, I Go by Land*, inviting the
thought that Mary Poppins (revived during the war in *Mary Poppins
Opens the Door*, 1943) is both guru and author, which, if true, seems
too active for a true guru. Evacuees certainly need gurus, all the more
when their situation throws up anti-gurus (from Dale's Mrs Chater to

Waugh's Basil Seal). Lewis, like Hughes, is author and guru outside the story, but relevantly to its making – as 'the Professor' in *The Lion, the Witch and the Wardrobe*, only present outside Narnia (and no longer guru (or, one suspects, Lewis) when he enters it as the boy Digory in *The Magician's Nephew*). Crompton occasionally appears as guru (most notably in 'William and the Four-Forty' (May 1948) as an author rejoicing in the name of Miss Surley). The guru must not be a surrogate mother or father – in *Treasure Island*, replete with father-figures (for the most part very sinister ones such as Billy Bones, Black Dog, Long John Silver and Israel Hands), the guru is Ben Gunn, who may seem contemptible but whose apparent absurdities conceal the clues to quest and/or existence which the hero needs. Enid Blyton may have brought off a guru in Bill Smugs, in *The Island of Adventure* (the child protagonist is usually doubtful as to whether the guru shares its priorities or loyalties, even national ones); but repetition dulls a guru's force, and becoming stepfather to the child(ren) is fatal.

Jesus Christ is of course a guru, all the more because of His most unusual liking for children, perhaps unique in the Bible, apart from the very sad case of Eli (in the story of the infant Samuel). From this, it follows that Lewis's Aslan is a guru in *The Lion, the Witch and the Wardrobe*; but, as my daughter Sara pointed out, Aslan is a much weaker figure in all the other stories (perhaps inevitably, since Jesus Christ does not appear in most of their originals: Shakespeare's *King John* (nephew Arthur), the voyages of Máel Dúin and St Brendan, Genesis 1 and 2 and so on). Tolkien disapproved of the Narnia stories as being allegory and hence unsound ('It really won't do, you know!'); but, while we must respect his insistence that *The Lord of the Rings* (and still more *The Hobbit*) had no such origin, Gandalf – leaving aside *his* sacrifice, suffering and resurrection – is undoubtedly a guru. So is Obi-wan Kenobi in that remarkable amalgam of mythology and science fiction, the first *Star Wars* movie. Lewis experimented with other guru figures, rightly exploring the comic possibilities, resulting in the mouse Reepicheep, the Marsh-wiggle Puddleglum (based on Pascal) and the horse Bree; and, in Uncle Andrew the magician, and the architect of evil the Ape, he showed the anti-guru as contemptible and – in the effects of his meddling – dangerous. The Ape is in fact Antichrist, partly based on Lewis's Belfast boyhood image of Pope Leo XIII, and in Antichrist we certainly find the recipe for anti-guru.[29]

Guru was a crucial category in children's fiction during the war, especially in the evacuee context. Malcolm Saville, taking topography as his starting-point, introduced his story with guru discussion of its location to the neophyte – Bill Ward in *Mystery at Witchend* on the spirit of Shropshire's Long Mynd, Miss Ballinger (who proves to be an anti-guru but plays the guru's topographical knowledge well enough to unsettle the reader's loyalties in *The Gay Dolphin Adventure*, 1945), Alan in *The Secret of Grey Walls* (1947). A Johns story may follow *Kim* in making a guru a non-white (Fee Wong in Biggles in Borneo, Li Chi in *Biggles Delivers the Goods*); or he may be a priest (*Worrals Carries On*, *King of the Commandos* and (in a touching and apparently irrelevant cameo) *Biggles 'Fails to Return'*). The Johns stories imply that the guru's priorities are probably admirable in themselves (save for Li Chi's piracy), but they have to be suspended for the duration of enemy action. Here again, the anti-guru is dangerous: *Worrals Flies Again* (November 1942) stars a nun who proves to be the local Nazi intelligence chief in drag. In the Chalet School series, Joey when married becomes a sort of guru, though a very vulnerable one during the war itself. Richard Hughes naturally was a guru for the real-life evacuees, and the kind above all they needed, but his stories shift very cleverly, and it is well to be very sure of the tale and all its possible interpretations before acknowledging possible gurus.[30]

What with her weekly-and-then-fortnightly *Sunny Stories* and her mind-boggling geometrical progression in productivity, Blyton established herself as guru in its most obvious sense for children, a trusted alternative to parents and other productivity figures. Correspondingly, one of her most interesting services in the war was to distance the protagonists from gurus. The evacuee child had to learn that there was no guru in sight or earshot. Blyton's fisher-boy Andy

> longed desperately for some grown-up who could take command and tell him what would be the best thing to do. But there was no grown-up. This was something he had to decide himself – and he must decide well, because the two girls were in his care.

The last point is as near as Blyton gets to hinting at rape dangers from enemies. There is also one hell of a dilemma in it: to tell the British authorities about the nest of Nazi submarines preying on vessels during the battle of the Atlantic, Andy and Tom have to leave the girls to take their chances on Nazi forbearance. It may well be the most Spartan alternative confronting children in any fiction from the Second World War:[31]

The girls said nothing. They did not like being left alone on the island – and yet they knew Andy was right. Somehow he must get home and tell the people there the secrets they had discovered. The raft would not really take four – and the girls were not strong enough to stand days and nights of tossing about on the sea.

'Well, Andy, it's very important that you should get back and tell the secret of these islands', said Jill at last. 'So, for the sake of our country, Mary and I will stay behind here without any fuss and do the best we can, whilst you and Tom set off for home. But do rescue us as soon as possible!'

Johns suggests a danger of rape unless Gimlet rescues a girl in the French resistance betrayed into Nazi hands.[32] It is what Lewis meant when he said he wrote[33]

'for children' only in the sense that I excluded what I thought they would not like or understand; not in the sense of writing what I intended to be below adult attention. I may of course have been deceived, but the principle at least saves one from being patronizing.

When being taught the ten commandments as a child, I asked what was adultery, and was told that adultery is something only adults do. Lewis took it so far as to exclude one of his original four children, Susan, from ultimate salvation at the end of Narnia (The Last Battle) because she has become interested in feminine frivolities, i.e. the paraphernalia of sexual allurement. In fact, he very much needed that prohibition on sex: The Lion, the Witch and the Wardrobe can only work with an absolute suspension of concerns about sex and paedophilia, since it turns on a faun inviting a little girl to tea while secretly intending to betray her (to the local Hitler, the White Witch – whence all evil flows). Lewis took himself out of his stories – he is clearly 'the Professor' in the various drafts, but if he is anywhere in the Lucy-and-Faun encounter he is Lucy, and in any case the scene derives from Alice's encounter with a much more deer-child Faun in Lewis Carroll's Through the Looking-Glass. But fauns in the sense Lewis was employing are companions to Silenus and similar voluptuaries in Rubens paintings or to Comus and damnable entourage in Milton masque. 'I mean to say: "Nymphs and their Ways, the Love-Life of a Faun"', worried Tolkien. 'Doesn't he know what he's talking about?'[34] Fortunately, he didn't. As to Lewis's intrusion into his story on a guru basis, the Professor's role is too brief, and he could not compete with Aslan, whose entry into the story, unplanned, sidelined the Professor, a character from the earliest drafts. Still less is Lewis a guru in *The Magician's Nephew*, but the Professor when the boy Digory becomes rather good at dealing with his uncle, the anti-guru. His one retention from guru status is his absence of sex-life, despite the charming companion of his childhood, Polly.

In some ways, gurus are listeners rather than lookers: the child, especially the evacuee, has to act and may receive some moral reinforcement when telling the guru. Lewis as the Professor plays that role, and so does Aslan (albeit closer to auricular Confession as a High Anglican sacrament or near-sacrament). So does Hughes's method of storytelling. Blyton's occasional interventions in pauses or finale of her own stories almost seem as though she has been listening to the tale that has unwound, as though she were some sort of medium (and she certainly felt unaware of her own creativity). BBC Children's Hour made the guru a creature of sound, but in part one whose presentation implied his own listening to what he presented.

The BBC Children's Hour 'Uncle Mac' (Derek McCulloch) retired in 1950, and the practice of other uncles on the wireless – such as 'Uncle Jim', who explained fossils and archaeology and early earth history in agreeably thriller-ish school broadcasts – was likewise eroded after that. Most children were probably used to, and sceptical about, adults claiming bogus avuncular status; but Uncle Mac convinced infant listeners during the war that he really was another uncle, who lived exclusively in the wireless and in gramophone records. He had been created long before the war, but his supreme value must have been to the evacuees or other lonely children cut off from any real family of their own for much of the time. His voice made you feel that he at least knew about you, cared about you and wanted you to be happy.[35]

What ultimately replaced gurus was self-reliance, all too easily becoming self-absorption and self-aggrandisement. The Blyton reader found a guru rather than an ultimate Authority in Blyton with her occasional chorus-like interventions, irritating – and distancing – to adults, reassuring to many children. But, as Authority, Blyton must have impinged on some children in her capacity as creator. Her refusal to mention Hitler and the Nazis, even Germany, by name is clearly judicial. Sheila Ray, her finest critic, finds it 'difficult to explain'; I suspect it was a form of bush-telegraph to children that this was the unspeakable. The Nazis' first appearance (by seaplane) in *The Adventurous Four* is almost ceremonially established:[36]

'Let's get up and shout and wave', begged Jill. 'I'm sure they will love to rescue us.'

'Haven't you seen the sign on the wings?' asked Tom, in a curiously angry voice. The girls looked. The sign of the crooked cross was painted on each wing – the sign of the enemy, the foe of half the world.

'Golly!' said Mary, and she drew a deep breath. 'Enemies! Using these islands! Do they belong to them?'

'Of course not', said Andy. 'But they are desolate, and out of the usual ships' course – and they've been noted by the enemy, and he's using them as a kind of base for something – seaplanes perhaps.'

Submarines as well, it proves. This is again grateful homage to *The Riddle of the Sands*. It was also subtle propaganda. *Sunny Stories* began serialisation of *The Adventurous Four* on 6 September 1940. Blyton wrote it, therefore, during the Battle of Britain, when the 'crooked cross' (vaguely equating the swastika with Antichrist) was at war only with the UK, left 'standing alone'. But there were the dominions. And there were the European countries conquered by the Nazis. Metaphor was nothing new to readers of *Sunny Stories*, full of naughty children, symbolising you the reader in your more anti-social moments, who are punished by brownies or elves. She had produced her version of Hitler in one of its short stories, 'The Strange Looking-Glass' (2 February 1940):

There was once a man who was chief of a big country. . . . he had made the people think that he was the most wonderful man in the world.

'I am the great Lord Biff', said the chief, and he dressed himself up in a fine uniform and walked up and down the palace he had built specially for himself, very pleased to see how frightened every one looked.

He gathered around him fierce and cruel men, and they did all he wanted them to do.

'Take my soldiers into the little country of Nearby, and make it mine', he said. So his chief men did so, and the country of Nearby became Lord Biff's.

'Go to the land of Notfaroff, and tell them I am sorry they do not belong to me', said Lord Biff the next year. 'Tell them I will do all I can to make them Biff men.'

So off marched the soldiers again, and although the people of

Notfaroff hated belonging to Lord Biff, they could do nothing else but surrender, for the Biffians were very cruel and strong.

One day a strange prisoner was captured in a cave of a distant land. He was small, and was dressed only in a piece of sackcloth tied round his waist. His hair hung to his shoulders, and his eyes were the strangest that any one had ever seen, for they were large and shone with a queer light.

The man has a looking-glass in which Biff sees a rat where his own face should be (after the man has called him 'Sir Rat').

Lord Biff got such a shock that he went pale. 'Go!' he said to his men. 'Leave me alone with this man.'

Every one went out. Lord Biff stalked up and down in his fine uniform, trying to make the silent stranger think what a wonderful fellow he was.

'Why do you keep me here, Sir Peacock?' asked the prisoner at last. Lord Biff swung round on his heel and glowered. He snatched the looking-glass from his hand and held it up to his face. The beak of a peacock looked back at him. His own face was not there.

'The glass is untrue!' roared Lord Biff. 'I am not a rat. I am not a peacock. I am a man as strong and bold as a lion. I bring peace to the countries round me, and I am as gentle as a lamb to others weaker than myself. This glass should show a lion's brave face, or a lamb's mild head!'

'The glass shows what it sees, Sir Snake', answered the prisoner.

He held up the glass, expecting to see the bold glance of a lion – but instead he saw the forked quivering tongue of a snake, and the flattened head and sly eyes of one of the most poisonous and treacherous snakes in the world.

Biff turns the mirror on 'my wonderful friends', who are successively revealed as 'a slimy worm', 'a poor, stupid sheep', 'a savage wolf', 'a snarling dog', 'a cruel vulture-bird' and 'a sharp-nosed rat', all of whom he then puts to death. He then searches for worthy followers but finds only 'timid mice' or 'silly sheep'.

Then Lord Biff flew into a fury, as he always did when he could not get his own way. 'What sort of a country is this, that there are only sheep and mice in it?' he roared. 'Where are the lion-hearted people gone, where are the clever tigers, the faithful dogs?'

'You sent them away, or had them killed years ago, Lord Biff',
said the prisoner, who was with him still.

'I didn't! I wouldn't do such a thing! I'll have you killed at once
for daring to say such a thing to me, the kindest and most peaceful
man in the world!' yelled Lord Biff.

The stranger took his glass and held it in front of Lord Biff. He
glared at it – and in it he saw the terrible face of a mad dog, with
bared teeth and staring eyes. He snarled angrily, and taking the
mirror, he hurled it to the ground. It smashed into a million pieces.

'It lies!' he said. 'But now it is gone for ever!'

'It cannot lie', said the stranger softly. 'It is the eye of God. It sees
you always as you are, Lord Biff, and you would do well to repent
and do good instead of evil.'

He gathered up the tiny pieces of glass and disappeared through
the door. Lord Biff did not stop him. He sat trembling in his chair,
knowing that he was only a mad dog leading a troop of sheep and
mice. What could save him now? Nothing!

End of story. Blyton's comment in her introductory letter was: 'I
wonder if you will like "The Strange Looking-Glass" story? What
would we see in it if we looked into it ourselves, and saw what we
really are deep inside ourselves?' The 'we' rather than 'you' distinguishes her from Victorian predecessors, but she clearly did not
want hating Hitler to become an excuse for complacency. The basic
joke is appropriately childish – 'Lord Biff' for 'Hitler', 'biff' being the
current playground slang for 'hit' (Shaw in *Geneva* (1938) had made
him 'Battler'). But the conceit is impressive, the mirror-images showing human sentiment changing from minute to minute. And the end,
with a Hitler neither killed nor defeated, but simply alone in his
dreadful self-created solitude, was memorable and reassuring. It was
wholly at variance with the ending with which she normally tied up
her narratives, the good ending happily and the bad on the road to
reform. This icy tableau alone told the children there is a story
behind the story: for once, a parent is to be asked for further
exposition.

Blyton's vision of Hitler went deeper than proclaiming him a
baddy on the hang-the-Kaiser lines of the previous war; but it sought
no pity for him as, very cleverly, Buchan did for a conscience-ravaged
Kaiser in *Greenmantle* (1916) (thus firmly making him chief witness
for his own war-guilt). Equally, the Nazi airmen and/or submarine
sailors in *The Adventurous Four* are not sadists or even bullies
(nor could Blyton easily cope if they were; like the ancient Greek

dramatists, she kept tragic action offstage). They question the captured Tom:

> 'How did you find this cave?' asked the man who spoke English.
> 'By accident', said Tom.
> 'And I suppose you also found our boat by accident, and saw the submarines by accident?' said the man, in a very nasty voice. 'Are you sure there is no one else here with you?'
> 'Quite sure', said Tom. 'Wouldn't you see them in the cave, if there were?'
> 'We shall not take your word for it', said the man, with a horrid laugh. 'We shall search this island and both those next to it – and if we find anyone else, you will be very, very sorry for yourself!'

But when later Tom escapes, and later still all the children are captured, the Nazis still merely threaten, and actually ensure food and shelter. One injures himself with a tin-opener to aid the captured and hungry Tom (Blyton's constantly food-obsessed children must be in part a device to forge another link with a readership under rationing). Even when the Nazis learn of the escape of Andy and Tom, with the consequent possibility of air-sea search for the Nazis' base and, in fact, fatal effects for it in the long run, their worst threat is to the girls:

> I shall order out my seaplanes and they will find those bad boys, and bring them back again. And you will all be made prisoners on another island till we take you far away to our country where you will stay for a long time . . . [and when] we shall have caught the two bad boys[, t]hey will be punished, you may be sure!

It is a convincing portrait of a German officer, but not of a Nazi monster: obviously the children should have been shot at the earliest stage. When, at the end, the Adventurous Four, reunited with the English trio's father in the RAF, hear the guns firing, Father confirms the fate of the Nazis:

> 'It will be the end of those hateful submarines', said his father gravely. 'There will be no more of our ships sunk without warning by *that* nest of submarines! And I rather think that our aeroplanes will drive off any seaplanes round about those islands – those that are not destroyed will fly to their own country in fear! They are no match for our pilots!'

That last was standard comment from the Battle of Britain onwards, more from lay commentators than from former airmen such as Johns.

> The children were silent as they listened to the guns booming far away again. They were all imagining the islands echoing to the terrific sound of gun-fire. Mary began to cry.
>
> Her father put his arm round her. 'Yes, Mary', he said, 'it is something to cry about, to think that we have to fight so much evil and wickedness. It is right against wrong and we have to be strong and courageous when we fight such a powerful and evil enemy as ours. But dry your eyes – you are on the right side and that is something to be proud of!'

Blyton would leave blanks for reader emotion to fill in (including, it has been said, most of her protagonists' characters). But this message is clear enough – as clear as that of the US naval officer at the battle of Santiago, John Woodward Philip: 'Don't cheer, men, those poor devils are dying'. Naturally, Mary's sentiment is not shared by Andy, a frontiersman in the Andrew Jackson tradition: 'Andy came tearing up to the cottage. "I say!" he yelled. "Do you hear the guns? I guess they are waking up the islands! What a shock for the enemy!" ' This is consistent: throughout the story, Andy's leadership is impaired by his humiliation at forgetting an anchor, or seeing the Nazis win. Blyton was quietly challenging male chauvinism, partly in the somewhat confused psyche of George in the 'Five' stories, partly more directly as here. At the moment of truth, when the boys see the submarines lying 'like great grey crocodiles, humped out of the water', the younger boy (and elder brother) thinks of the country, the elder boy of the girls:

> 'Andy', he said. 'We've got to get home and tell what we've seen.'
>
> 'I know', said Andy. 'I'm thinking that too, Tom. And we've got to get the girls off these islands. We are all in danger. If the enemy knew we were spying on them like this I don't know what would happen to us.'
>
> 'I don't care how much danger we're in', said Tom, and he didn't. 'All I know is that we've got to go and tell our people at home about this submarine base. It's got to be cleared away. Andy, it's serious.'
>
> Andy nodded. Both boys seemed to become men at that moment. They looked gravely into each other's eyes and what they saw there pleased them both. Each boy knew that the other would do his best and even more than his best.

It's doubtful if a male writer has managed so masculine a moment so neatly. But it is not at a cost to female dignity, however much Andy feels frontier necessities of assertion. Within a few pages, they have to hide a boat they have stolen from the Nazis:[37]

> 'Just the place', said Andy, pulling into the tiny beach. 'Jump out, girls. Take the food with you. Give a hand with the boat, Tom. We'll run it up the beach and put it right under that dangerous piece of cliff. It will be well hidden there.'
> They put the boat there and looked at it. The end of it jutted out and could be seen. Jill ran to a seaweed-covered rock and pulled off handfuls of the weed.
> 'Let's make the boat into a rock!' she said, with a laugh. 'Cover it with seaweed!'
> 'Jolly good idea!' said Andy. 'I didn't know girls could have such good ideas!'
> 'You wait and see what fine ideas we have!' said Mary.

In the end, Andy learns enough to accept the ugly necessity to leave the girls behind when Tom and he break away on a frail, child-built raft to get the submarine-base information home. Blyton may have to mute the risk to the girls, but it leaves Andy with a male need to exult over the Nazis who had so emasculated his leadership.

Blyton seems to have written little directly about the war after that, until it was over. A flight of Tempests supplies the clue to an insurance swindle in *The Mystery of the Burnt Cottage* (1943). *The Castle of Adventure*, a 1946 publication, seems set in wartime with an unpleasant spy named Mannheim who is described as greatly disliked in his own country (unnamed, again, but clearly Germany: presumably this is to recognise German hostility to the Nazis, one of the few British wartime novels to do so, however covertly).[38] The sequel, *The Valley of Adventure* (1947), plunges into the heart of bomb-devastated Austria, not saying that the Allies had presumably dropped the bombs, but ably bringing out a neglected point – that bombing must have had drastic effects on inter-valley communication in rural European communities, leaving some absolutely isolated. It does assume an anti-Nazi revolt in rural Austria, on Catholic grounds fairly late in the war. Whatever the merits of this thesis (and it may reflect the influence of Brent-Dyer), it is to Blyton's credit that she makes war no mere matter of rejoicings at an Allied victory. Her cosmopolitan credentials are somewhat impaired by the story's assumption that South Americans ('in touch with the old Nazis'), although called Juan, Luis and Pepi, speak English as a first language. Her surprising sureness of foot in Austrian terrain owed much – including, no doubt, the choice of locale of the story – to her Austrian maid (and, quickly enough, family friend) Mary, who was with Blyton from 1939 to 1945.

What Blyton was less prepared to tackle was the spy on the doorstep, with the doubtful exception of the second 'Five' story *Five Go Adventuring Again* (1943). Set in Kirrin Cottage, i.e. somewhere in the Swanage rural seacoast hinterland, it is the second campaign in the war between George and her father, and global conflicts are secondary if indeed present. Uncle Quentin (surname still unknown) gets a tutor for the boys over the Christmas holidays, sets George also under him, and a drama much more intense than its precursor ensues. The other children take to the tutor, whose feud with George sours their Christmas: their Christmas presents (including his to George, unreciprocated) are described and become an acrid, faintly Maupassant, memory hanging over his subsequent apprehension and temporary imprisonment by the children, with a repentant Uncle Quentin's approval. What is not clear is whether the tutor is a Nazi spy or merely a private profiteer in stealing; George at the height of the crisis makes the most formal guess: 'the secret Father has been working on for ages will be used by someone else – for some other country, probably!'[39] Presumably readers were expected to conclude that the tutor was working for the Nazis, and so were the artists secretly in collaboration with him, and it was left to them to work out what luxuries like tutors and artists were doing out of uniform in the otherwise heavily rationed festive season. By keeping it vague, Blyton could sidestep the argument, which in any case only raises its head because she had addressed the war with perception, dignity and, ultimately, compassion. Supposedly more realistic writers like Arthur Ransome made no contribution to Second World War literature at all, his excellent adventure story *Missee Lee* actually opening with its British child protagonists in a very friendly Japanese port before going on to excitement in pirate-haunted but Japanese-free China, regardless of its publication in 1941 a few weeks before Pearl Harbor was bombed, and a few more before Hong Kong and Singapore fell to Japan. And, for those who epitomise Blyton as the self-absorbed middle-class solipsist, contrast her war record with writers such as M. E. Atkinson, whose slightly smug little Lockitts cycle their adventure-hungry way through England's green lanes utterly indifferent either to wartime privations or skyborne death. Atkinson had her formula, and Hitler was not going to hustle her out of it.[40]

Blyton's abdication from war fiction may have had a personal element. Her husband, Major Hugh Pollock, who worked at Newnes,[41] had gone into the Home Guard, with duties taking him away from his family home, and the marriage foundered, apparently with adultery on both sides. Blyton's divorce and second marriage mated her to a surgeon, Kenneth Darrell Waters, who seems to have been much more authoritarian in relation to society (and to his stepdaughters) than was her first husband. He could not possibly be of the professional value to her that Pollock had been, and he probably sought to compensate for this by what he took to be protectiveness, but which bordered on officiousness. Blyton may have been blamed for many of his dictates, which she over-submissively accepted. The war entailed the loss of her first husband – who was deleted from all family contact and was removed from his post at Newnes at what was taken to be Blyton's demand: the war may therefore have become too painful for her to write about, save in an elegiac post-war fashion. But within any such decision there was a deeper matter. Blyton in these years became a best-selling writer as Enid Blyton, although not as Mary Pollock. She reached thousands of children. She seems to have decided to protect them against pollution by war. It had ceased now to be a question of survival. She had done her bit, and so, by participation in her work by reading, had her audience – *Sunny Stories* forged that relationship with hardening steel over the years. She would now give her young readers stories of courage, comradeship, endurance, intelligence, love of animals – but no more war. Baddies might have the occasional gun, but would nonetheless be thwarted by children unarmed and dangerous. The children might even face death, as Philip does in *The Mountain of Adventure* with a fine brave front and a nasty hidden little kernel of fear, and probably does so from yet another closet ex-Nazi, Meyer; but by now any dangers of death will be strictly rationed.[42]

We must not confuse rejection of wartime subjects with some sort of auctorial immunity. Arthur Ransome delivered *The Big Six* to Jonathan Cape for publication in late 1940, only to have his illustrations destroyed during a bomb raid; he did them again, having first been told that their blocks had survived, and then that they hadn't. Eve Garnett's award-winning *The Family from One End Street* had reflected her anger at slum conditions and her admiration for the humour, resilience, and character of slum families: she had forced her novel on an indifferent publishing world in 1936–7, and saw it gain the second Carnegie Medal for children's literature, whence it won its place in the second batch of Puffin Books, reaching its mass market in 1941. But its sequel, left in her father's house, was fire-damaged in that year, presumably during enemy action, and *Further Adventures of the Family from One End Street* did not see publication in part until 1950 and in entirety until 1956. Mabel Esther Allan had her first novel for children accepted before the war and then returned when it broke out; she was bombed out of Liverpool, keeping up her spirits by writing poetry, but did not get the first of her 133 titles in print until 1948. Mary Treadgold wrote *We Couldn't Leave Dinah* in her own air-raid shelter in her back garden during the Blitz, although its replication in its imaginary Clerinel of some of the actual Channel Island war experience (so far as it could then be known) emphatically did not include counterparts of the pre-invasion air raid on Guernsey, killing twenty-nine, or the more extensive Jersey raids, machine-gunning and bombing the inhabitants of St Helier, La Rocq, Greve d'Azette, Fort Regent, Beaumont and St Aubin, all undefended, no doubt as softening-up of the survivors for capitulation to Nazi takeover. Such a story as Susan Cooper's *Dawn of Fear* (1970), climaxing with the death in an air raid of one of the child protagonists, was simply unthinkable.[43] Crompton's Bromley was the victim of very ugly bomb raids with many casualties, but nobody would have guessed it from her hilarious dissection of an air warden and insistence that native families were being turned into evacuees by official incompetence.

> The bomb fell that night. It was literally a bomb. For the first time since the outbreak of war a German bomber, passing over the village, chose, for no conceivable reason, to release part of its load there.
>
> Fortunately, most of it fell in open country and there were no casualties, but one bomb fell in the roadway just outside the Hall, blew up the entrance gates and made a deep crater in the road.
>
> Mr Leicester, complete with overalls and tin hat, was on the spot immediately. It was he who descried, at the bottom of the crater, the smooth rounded surface of a half-buried 'unexploded bomb'.
>
> All through the months of inactivity he had longed for an Occasion to which he could rise, and he rose to this one superbly. The road must be roped off. Traffic must be diverted. All houses in the immediate neighbourhood must be evacuated. But Lilac Cottage was among the houses that Mr Leicester ordered to be evacuated, and at first Mrs Parfitt did not know where to go. Then Miss Milton came to the rescue. Miss Milton was prim and elderly and very very houseproud. She had had several evacuees

billeted on her, but none of them had been able to stay the course and all had departed after a few weeks. So now she had a spare bedroom to offer Mrs Parfitt and Joan. . . .

Crompton was unerring in her detection of the limits to hospitality when classified as 'my war work':

Miss Milton had drawn up an elaborate code of rules. Joan was not to use the front door. She was to take off outdoor shoes immediately on entering the house. She was not to speak at meals. If inadvertently she touched any article of furniture, Miss Milton would leap at it with a duster, lips tightly compressed, in order to rub off any possible finger marks. Miss Milton rested upstairs in her bedroom from lunch-time till tea-time. She was, she said, a 'light sleeper', so Joan had to creep about the house during that time on tiptoe and not raise her voice above a whisper.

After a week of this both Joan and her mother began to look pale and worn . . .

William decides to move the unexploded bomb from outside the Hall gates so that Joan can go home.

The bomb was not as closely guarded as it had been at the beginning. Even the policeman, whose duty it had been to stand by the barrier, was now generally away on other duties. There was very little traffic on that road in any case, and the inhabitants, once passionately interested in the bomb, had become bored by it and looked on it merely as a nuisance. Occasionally Mr Leicester still came to gaze at it tenderly over the barrier, his eyes gleaming with the pride of possession. His bomb, his beloved unexploded bomb. . . . It justified, he felt, his whole career as a warden, gave his life meaning and purpose and inspiration. . . .

William arrives, scrapes away the earth from the bomb, and is then violently denounced by Mr Leicester, when he appears.

William wiped his hands down his trousers.

'I'm all right', he said carelessly. 'I'll fetch my tray thing if it starts explodin'. . . . But, I say, it's a jolly funny bomb. Come down an' have a look at it.'

Mr Leicester's eyes, bulging and bloodshot with emotion, went from William to the bomb . . . and remained fixed on it. William had cleared all the earth and debris away from it, and it lay there – large, round, of a greyish hue. . . .

Suddenly William gave a shout.

'*Gosh*! I know what it is', he said.

In the same moment Mr Leicester knew what it was, too.

It was the stone ball from the top of one of the brick piers that had formed the entrance gates of the Hall. . . .

Mr Leicester inspects it.

'It *is*, isn't it?' said William.

Slowly Mr Leicester turned to him. With an almost superhuman effort he had recovered something of his self-possession, something even of his normal manner. He looked shaken but master of himself.

'No need to – er – go about talking of this, my boy', he said. 'No need to mention it at all. It would, in fact, be very wrong to – go about upsetting people's morale by – er – spreading rumours. There are very serious penalties for spreading rumours. I hope that you will remember that.'

William looked at him in silence for a few moments. He was an intelligent boy and knew all about the process of face-saving. He was quite willing to help Mr Leicester save his face, but he didn't see why he should do it for nothing.

'Then Joan an' her mother can go home to-morrow?' he said.

'Certainly', said Mr Leicester graciously.

His eyes kept returning, as if drawn against his will, to the round smooth object at his feet.

'An' you'll come an' give your cinema show at her party, won't you?' said William with elaborate carelessness.

Mr Leicester fixed a stern eye on him.

'You know quite well that I am not giving any such entertainments during the war', he said.

William gazed dreamily into the distance.

'I thought that if we had the cinema at the party', he said dreamily, 'it'd be easier for me not to spread rumours.'

Mr Leicester gulped and swallowed. He looked long and hard at William. William continued to gaze dreamily into the distance. There was a silence . . . then Mr Leicester yielded to the inevitable. . . .

'Just this once, my boy', he said graciously. 'Just this once. It must never happen again, of course. And I will take for granted that you will not – er – spread rumours.'

'No', promised William, 'I won't spread rumours.'

Mr Leicester next day informs Joan's mother that she may return to her own house. He then accedes to the request for the cinematograph show.[44]

> 'Isn't it kind of him, William?' said Mrs Parfitt. 'Yes', agreed William. 'Jolly kind.'
> 'Er – not at all', murmured Mr Leicester, fixing his eyes on the air just above William's head. 'Not at all. Don't mention it. An exception, of course. . . . Not to be repeated.'
> 'The bomb didn't explode, then?' said Mrs Parfitt. 'I suppose we'd have heard it here if it had done.'
> 'Oh no', said Mr Leicester, repeating the mirthless smile. 'It didn't explode. It was – er – disposed of. The process', he went on hastily, 'needs specialized knowledge, and the details, I am afraid, are too technical for you to understand.'
> Mrs Parfitt looked at him, deeply impressed.
> 'How fortunate we are to have you for our warden', she said.

Crompton was apparently never even considered for the Carnegie Medal. It will therefore never quite win the lustre it should have done. The same is true of the *Times Literary Supplement*, which never reviewed William.

Kitty Barne, a little later, spared self-important wardens in her anxiety to expose Black Marketeers in *Three and a Pigeon* (1944), and unlike Crompton combined evacuation with actual bombing, to the extent of bombing her chosen family on the first page, Chapter 1 being duly entitled 'Our Bomb' and commencing:

> The queer thing about our Bomb, as the Willards always called it, was the way it fell. No one could call it an ordinary bomb, arriving as it did in their safe area unannounced even by the siren's squall. No one saw the aeroplane or heard it, or even dreamt of it. It stayed up in the clouds somewhere and dropped its bomb like a monkey dropping a nut out of a windy October sky, neither knowing nor caring that the town of Willowfield lay below.
> It gave its whistle-crump-thud just as the answer to the sum they had been doing was going up on the board. Tessa Willard was just telling herself ruefully that she'd got it wrong, as usual, when Miss Mills most surprisingly dropped the chalk and cried, 'What's that noise?'
> No one knew. How could they when they'd never heard anything like it before? No one, that is, but Ivy. She shot up her hand at once

with 'That's a bomb, that is', and Tessa felt a glow of pride, for Ivy was their own special evacuee who had been with them since the very beginning of the war. She'd gone home for a week or so after she'd been at Willowfield a year and had her home blown to bits in the Battle of Britain, so naturally she knew all about bombs. She had come back from that holiday brimful of stories that everyone wanted to hear and she told them with a sort of extra life – though she had always been lively enough – that had come from dodging in and out of shelters, sleeping behind the white line on the platform of tube stations, and being, as she called it, not half in the war. No wonder she got her scholarship and sailed into the High School and into Tess's form, six months younger than anyone else there.

Miss Mills believed her.

'It won't do no more. It's gone off', Ivy reassured her. 'My dad says –' but Miss Mills hadn't time to listen to what dad said. They had a shelter, made at great expense; here was a chance to go and sit in it. Would they line up at once.

They are scarcely in the bomb-shelter when the 'All Clear' is sounded, and the teacher returns to the blackboard:

It was a terrible sum about casks of water and casks of porter, and Miss Mills began to work it out on the board. She made a mistake quite early and instead of coming out it grew longer and longer – like the Mouse's tail in *Alice*, Tess thought – and her voice grew more and more languid, like the Dormouse before he went into the teapot. 'If a quarter of water and a quarter of porter –' she dirged, and started on a second board.

'Upset, that's what she is', whispered Ivy. 'That four's got to be a five. Second line, see? The bombs done it. Shall I tell her?' Over questions of tact like that Ivy generally asked Tess's advice.

'No. The bell's going in half a minute.'

Sure enough the bell went and Miss Mills in a flash of energy took a duster and cleaned both boards. 'Now I suppose you'll want to rush off and see where that bomb fell?' she said, brisk once more. 'If it's right in the fields don't forget we're collecting acorns and rose-hips.'

Thus ended the first section, as well as the last lesson. But it turns out that the reports are wrong: the bomb has demolished most of Tess Willard's home. Her brother ascends to what remains of the second floor to get his mice, and, as the remains disintegrate, cannot get down. Ivy, taught by experience, climbs up, gives him a necessary arm to hold, and gets him down. Both Crompton and Barne observe children being much less afraid of the bombs than adults, but the neophyte country children are foolhardy where the Londoners are bombwise. Barne had already won the Carnegie Medal for her *Visitors from London* (1940), a mildly patronising picture of working-class evacuees in general, but she followed what seems too well established a literary genteel convention that the lower classes are always talking. Crompton never suggested that anyone could out-talk William. Both writers, quietly but firmly, showed how illusory was the idea of a 'safe area', or place where evacuees would be sent. Barne shows that an under-celebrated role of evacuees could be to guide their innocent hosts when first under bombardment, and reminds us of the role of Monarchy as the super-ego in whose name and from whose inspiration courage was renewed. The brave, stuttering King, gallantly fighting his disability on the wireless to identify with his subjects, is, above all, the King of the bombed:[45]

> Ivy carried out her picture of the King and Queen in their crowns and propped it up on the remains of the gate, a Union Jack on top. 'That's what we did with our ruins', she said. For once Willowfield was coming up to London. It was all glorious.

The effect of bombs, evacuees, new story outlets in adult papers, and so on, was in any case to make for a more sophisticated child reader. The world was being changed around it, and, if Crompton gave it occasional adult eyes through which to judge and to take appropriate precautions, so much the better. Quite apart from the physical suffering, family bereavement, financial disaster and psychological trauma the bombs entailed, the little personal tragedies of Parfitts without any William to rescue them must have been endless, and familiar to many of Crompton's readers both adult and child. But what was the use of an air-raid shelter (for instance) if one could not get fun out of it?, asked both Crompton and William in somewhat different agendas. There were its own local evacuees, prompted by social considerations, and prompting anti-social ones:

> 'I bet that was a screaming bomb', said William.
> 'It was the twelve-thirty letting off steam', said Mr Brown.
> 'Was it?' said William despondently. 'It's been a rotten raid so far.'

'I wonder if the Bevertons are coming', said Ethel.

'The *who*?' said Mr Brown, looking up from his paper.

Ethel and Mrs Brown exchanged nervous glances.

'Yes, didn't we tell you, dear?' said Mrs Brown. 'The Bevertons asked if they could share our shelter and we didn't like to say "no".'

'Good heavens! They've got one of their own.'

'I know, but they say it's much jollier to be together. They were sharing the Mertons last week, but Bella quarrelled with Dorita so they asked if they could share ours.'

Mr Brown protests unavailingly:

'why intensify the horrors of war by having them in the air raid shelter?'

'Perhaps they won't come, dear', said Mrs Brown soothingly. 'After all, it's some time since the siren went.'

'They always take a long time getting ready', said Ethel.

'Ready? What for?' said Mr Brown.

'For air raid shelters', said Ethel.

'Gosh', said William excitedly. 'I can hear bombs.'

But it was only the Bevertons arriving.

Mrs Beverton was inordinately stout and her daughter was inordinately thin. They were both dressed in the latest in siren suits, and had obviously taken great pains with their make-up and coiffeurs [sic]. Mrs Beverton wore a three-stringed pearl necklace, large jade earrings and four bracelets. She had, moreover, used a new exotic perfume that made William cry out in genuine alarm 'Gas! Where's my gas mask?'

'So sorry we're late', she said gaily as she entered. 'We just had to finish off our new siren suits. We've been working on them all day but they just needed the finishing touches, as it were. I had to get out my jewellery, too. I always like to feel I've got it with me, as it were. Room for a little one?'

She plunged down on to a small camp mattress next Mr Brown, almost blocking him from view.

'Not squashing you, I hope?' she inquired politely.

'Not at all', came the muffled voice of Mr Brown from between her and the wall of the shelter.

The girls discuss knitting:

'Do you like this colour?' said Ethel, holding up the jumper she was working on.

'Marvellous!' said Bella in a deep voice.

'I want to get it finished by to-morrow. I like the yoke effect, don't you?'

'Marvellous!' said Bella on a higher key.

'Did you see the cardigan Dolly Clavis knitted, with a hood? She's going to lend me the pattern. It'll be useful for cold mornings.'

'*Marvellous!*' squeaked Bella ecstatically.

'You'll have a cup of tea, won't you, dear?' said Mrs Brown to her husband.

But Mr Brown wasn't there. At Bella's third '*Marvellous!*' he had crept quietly out of the emergency exit.

As constant readers of *Modern Woman*, would know, clothes rationing had thrown women back on knitting; and, for all their vanity, Ethel and her friends were making a vocation of it. Crompton being Crompton, she had no intention of benignly leaving it at that: Bella had more to do in the story than merely driving Mr Brown out to take refuge among the bombs. Beneath the bomb-shelter amity, bourgeois rivalries had their claws.

'Marvellous' may well have had its vogue among Bromley flappers (as the late teenage women were only just ceasing to be called – the war killed that thirty-year-old label, partly when Ethel and her friends entered its armed forces). Vogue words had been noted by specialists in observation such as A. G. Macdonnell and Agatha Christie depicting flappers of the late 1920s ('subtle', 'wan' and so on, as comments on everything), and wireless no less than talkies gave this or that word its moment of glory; but, as the war hardened, the services imposed their terminology, and older teen-agers surreptitiously borrowed the new language from their pilot-worshipping juniors when not in the forces themselves. If the 'flapper' disappeared, the 'flap' took on a new lease of life, to be bored became to be 'browned off', 'prang' conveyed military de-struction or damage, 'a piece of cake' told of a simple achievement (perhaps scaled down by modesty), an unpleasantly uncertain outlook was 'ropey', and something finalised was 'buttoned up'. The studious could learn the current RAF terms from *Biggles in the Orient* (1944), where Johns, badly in need of them himself, had set out the results of refresher orientation in a preliminary glossary. No doubt many were widely overused and abused; and Bella's

obsession, like those of her flapper precursors, displayed fundamental insecurity. Back at home:

> 'I'm sure it's nice for you to feel that you're helping mother.'
> 'Marvellous!' said Bella in what she imagined to be a tone of
> cutting irony.
> She took the labels down to the morning-room. She was still
> feeling aggrieved by her mother's reference to Ethel Brown. She
> never had been able to understand what people saw in Ethel
> Brown. Personally she thought that Ethel looked a perfect sight in
> the green jumper. She had never liked her hair. Or her voice. Or her
> eyes . . .

This was taking the psychology of the egregious interloper deeper
than Crompton's younger readers might expect – though Crompton
accustomed them to a no-nonsense analysis of adult motivation, for
example the conclusion of this present story when Mr Brown's
annoyance with William over a public disaster evaporates on hearing
that its effect is the refusal of the Bevertons to return to the Brown
air-raid shelter:[46]

> The look of severity faded from Mr Brown's face. As far as a face of
> his particular cast of grimness could be said to shine, it shone.
> 'So – she won't be coming if there's a raid to-night?'
> 'No, dear. But about William –'
> 'Yes, yes' said Mr Brown impatiently. 'The boy obviously meant
> no harm. I can't see what you're making all this fuss about.
> Actually, when you come to think of it, he was trying to help. I
> can't understand why you're so hard on the child.'
> 'But –' began Mrs Brown.
> 'You're quite sure that the Bevertons aren't coming again?'
> 'Quite, dear.'
> An almost seraphic smile spread over Mr Brown's countenance.
> 'How marvellous!' he quoted.

Among other blessings to its readers, the William saga from time to
time offered a useful survival kit in an adult-ruled world, and it made
sense to top it up with particular applications necessitated by the
war, when supervision might be less but tempers were edgier.

But what William had actually done was involuntarily to wreck
Mrs Beverton's Exhibition of relics of captured or crashed German
aircraft and weaponry by innocently substituting for it discarded

scrap iron once belonging to Miss Milton. Bella's alienation had its
nominal use in the story to explain her mislabelling of the substitution ('I recognise every single piece,' said Miss Milton grimly. 'There's
the old fish slice that I threw away because it was too small, and that
you have the impertinence to label as part of a Dornier wing . . .').[47]
We are not told that the Bevertons are evacuees; but they are
evidently neophytes seeking to impress the district by the success
of their championship of the war effort in its village vigour, the
financial returns to go to the Spitfire Fund. Children all across
Britain were running far and wide (and from time to time running
their seniors' patience to its extremities) in order to boost funds for
aircraft for Britain's defence against the bombers; and the Spitfire
had proved the symbol which took the public's heart. Johns perceived as much when he called one revamped First World War story
'Spitfire Parade' (*Air Stories*, March 1940), and he reused the title
(though not the cannibalised story) for his book of stories of Biggles's
squadron, published in August 1941. Michael Paris in his thorough
Warrior Nation feels that, in Crompton's *William and ARP* (1939)
and *William and the Evacuees* (1940), 'preparations to withstand air
attack and the billeting of working-class children from the city . . .
were seen as faintly ridiculous and quite unnecessary activities'.[48]
Since this is how he saw the Crompton message, it is fair to assume
that many wartime readers also saw them this way; but Crompton's
war service as a cripple in the AFS (which she also sent up rotten)
reminds us that for her to make fun of war support work does not
mean that she thought it unnecessary. But Michael Paris's impression is helpful: Crompton's contemporaries may also have read her
meaning as much more destructive than she intended. *Modern
Woman* may have had private (or even official) protests; it may
not have thought of the point itself (after all, it had printed the story
with no obvious sanitary dilution). But its March 1941 number, the
second next, included a sequel to the Beverton débâcle, which would
presumably have been printed for February had Crompton originally
intended it. In any case, William has one of his attacks of conscience,
as usual with cataclysmic results:[49]

> Mrs Beverton's cousin had made £2 6s. 10 ½ d. [slightly more than
> £2.34: characteristically; Crompton could not resist the touch of
> someone having contributed a halfpenny whether in whole or as part
> of their charity] by her collection. Mrs Beverton, though perhaps she
> would not have made quite so much as that, would still have made
> something. . . . William, whose efforts to bring about a successful

conclusion of the war had been unrelaxing if not always fortunate, felt it intolerable that he should have been the means of robbing the Spitfire Fund of a possible £2 6s. 10 ½d. He felt like a boy under a curse. For the first time since the poem had been set as a holiday task by a callous form master, he appreciated the feelings of 'The Ancient Mariner'. . . . But William was not a boy to labour under a sense of guilt without doing something to extirpate it.

If any comment had been made which Crompton received or saw, implying that her satire endangered the intake of the Spitfire Fund, this was her impish *amende honorable*, down to the last ½d. William is successful in fund-raising by softening up Mrs Bott, unintentionally, in accidentally leaving an UNEXPLODED BOMB sign outside her Hall, and gaining £3 from her benevolent rebound when it proves an apparent illusion. And, as John Rowe Townsend pointed out,[50] 'William was promptly adopted by his contemporaries, perhaps because he was the daredevil that every small boy likes to think himself' – and because his daydreams were those of countless other children: Crompton pre-eminently catered to the child's imagination by being able to imagine it – 'always getting into scrapes, and often scoring off the grown-ups' – frequently unwittingly –

> in the process of getting out of them. The William stories offer to young readers a happy blend of identification and condescension; they can at the same time imagine themselves to be William and yet see him from the outside as a small boy doing ridiculous and laughable things. William in fact is a most effective character – though not particularly lifelike, for no real boy could have his mixture of imagination and eloquence with extreme naivety.

So far as he goes, Townsend is impressive: his last comment suggests that, whatever his acquaintance with small boys, he can have known few politicians. But William is not in all respects a single character: just as Crompton kept him at 11 for fifty years while his world changed so drastically around him, she altered some of his traits as it suited the purpose of her story. His intelligence, for instance, is a variable, although his ingenuity is not. In the war stories, he has a covert propaganda function. He is what Britain is fighting *for*; he is also Britain fighting. The symbol of the UK battling on its own in 1940–1 is Low's soldier; it is also Winston Churchill; it is also William Brown. He was always his own person, self-reliant in a hostile adult world with but few and seldom long-lasting allies from it. He always had to be his own guru, and he came into his own as the guru was fading from the youthful literary scene. He never was an evacuee – even if he found himself at one point dragooned into turning his fellow-children from the village into evacuees, much to the fury of their mothers, whose arrival to minister to the little strangers brought them instead face to face with their own. But he flourished amid the bombs on Bromley and the duds in his village, and his role model remained triumphant: so he had to help the Spitfire Fund, not simply subvert it. Crompton succeeded, not by pretending to be on the child's side – she is an adult, writing from an adult's perspective and making adult's points which a child feels adult by sharing – but by fairly clear indications that in child–adult war she would not pretend adults were necessarily moral superiors to children. Hitler was an adult; Churchill with his baby face and lisp, the King with his stutter, the villagers dressed up in their new uniforms and newer duties – all were triumphantly childlike. And William was the best-known child in Second World War fiction.

Yet history insists on exceptions to (nearly) everything, even the popularity of William in children's literature. Betty Blyth, evacuated from the Edward Worledge Central School at St Olaves, Norfolk (housed at the Hospital School since Chamberlain had proclaimed war), complained fifty years later that, when placed at the village school in Radcliffe-on-Trent, Nottinghamshire, 'initially one of our Yarmouth teachers, Mr Sykes, took our class. We didn't learn much as he spent much of the time reading *Just William* books to himself and ignored us.' On the other hand, to explain why a schoolteacher was sent 100 miles to preside over a class while reading William stories to himself rather than to them would seem to require the imagination of a Richmal Crompton, which alas is given to few historians. Or, thinking about the value of her stories as accounts of England in the Second World War, one should say 'to few other historians'.[51]

But inevitably Crompton, trained as a teacher, was still producing her pupils. The most startling case of an evacuee to whom she would prove a guru surfaced in 1941 when Nelson's, still wisely printing in Edinburgh, confronted a book-length manuscript begun when its author was fourteen and taken, partly written, to South Wales when she was removed there on war's outbreak. *The Swish of the Curtain* used its author's memories of amateur dramatics in Colchester, probably sharpened by conclusion and revision in remote exile. Debt to Crompton proclaimed itself in the first pages as the *Swish* children squirmingly responded to the gushing Mrs Porter-Smith, whose 'dear laddy' and head-patting echoed the 'laddies dear' and head-pressing 'against her perfumed, befrilled bosom' of Mrs de Vere Carter who lived to rue the day she conscripted William into the Band of Hope in his very first book, *Just William*. But Pamela Brown's story quickly made its own way, with spirit. Arguments over reduction of size would seem to have delayed publication too late in the Christmas season to gain many reviews apart from the *Times Literary Supplement*, which gave her New Year honours on 27 December:

> For an author only 15 years old [16 now] PAMELA BROWN has extraordinary smoothness and vigour – in fact a reader of 'THE SWISH OF THE CURTAIN' (Nelson 7s. 6d.) would never guess her to be other than a practised grown-up writer. She tells of the doings of seven young amateurs who organize their own dramatic company; she is obviously an eager lover of this sort of thing herself, and if she has managed to get half as much amusement out of it as her characters do, she has done very well.

The pre-war beginning made it a pre-war story (although the children could have been inspired by Stratford Shakespeare throughout the war, as they are in the book, thanks to a somewhat improbable Bishop). The profits sent the author to the Royal Academy of Dramatic Art where she advanced far enough to narrate her book in John Keir Cross's three-instalment BBC version in 1944, for which a sequel, *Maddy Alone*, was commissioned, book (1945) following broadcast. By this stage Pamela Brown was her own guru, and Noel Streatfeild did not look below her own high standards if she picked up a hint or two from the actress-author for her 1944 offering, *Curtain Up*.

Notes

1. Roger Lancelyn Green and Walter Hooper, *C. S. Lewis* ([1974] 1988), 238. The date is conjectural, but follows the authors' juxtaposition of the document-extracts. In this first draft, the central child is again the youngest, but he is male and is called Peter. There are many versions of the carol, but this seems the most appropriate; it is as I have heard it sung, and differs from printed versions I have seen.
2. Richard Perceval Graves, *Richard Hughes* (1994), 277–84. In fact, when the evacuees arrived, Frances Hughes found she was pregnant with their fourth child, to be named Owain. When the evacuees had returned to Birkenhead, Hughes followed the rest of his family to Laugharne, where they were joined by the Dylan Thomases; their late-night conversations there inspired Thomas's *Under Milk Wood*.
3. *Put Out More Flags* (1942), 7. The sage, unidentified, is quoted from Lin Yutang, *The Importance of Living*, a fashionable work among occidentals at this time. John Blowers of Lowestoft, before he was evacuated to Worksop, Nottinghamshire, 'was fourteen in 1940 and old enough to take a keen interest in following the

course of the War. So much so that a highlight of each week was the day when, on my way home from school, I would collect my copy of *War Illustrated*' (Christopher J. Brooks, ed. and comp., *East Coast Evacuees* (2001), 26). *War Illustrated* was a breezy, sinew-stiffening, very well illustrated but judicious account of the war's progress edited by Sir John Hammerton, friend and future biographer of Arthur Mee of the *Children's Encyclopaedia, Children's Newspaper* and a forest of improving titles including *Why We Are at War* (1940). *War Illustrated* had occasional awkward moments, notably when the issue of 31 May 1940 featured in full panoply on its back cover 'Our War Album. – 39. The King of the Belgians. King Leopold III' and the next issue, 7 June 1940, headed Hammerton's editorial 'TREACHERY MOST FOUL: MAY 28, 1940 Belgium's Traitor King as Hitler's Latest Ally'. The dates illustrated the problems of production.

4. Leach, in B. S. Johnson, *The Evacuees* (1968), 170, 172. Walker, in Ben Wicks (ed.), *The Day They Took the Children* ([1989] 1990), 39–40. See also Christopher D. McGimpsey (ed.), *Bombs on Belfast: The Blitz 1941* (1984), which pays due tribute to the Eire fire brigades sent north during the bombing in reply to Northern Ireland's plea. For Belfast Catholic disaffection, see Brian Moore, *The Emperor of Ice-Cream* (1961).

5. B. S. Johnson, *The Evacuees*, 153.

6. Crompton, 'William and the Black-Out' (*Happy Mag*, February 1940) and *William and the Evacuees*, 199. Holman, *The Evacuation* (1995), 61–2.

7. *Magnet* 1,671 'A Black-Out Blunder'. Coker of the Fifth whacks a temporary master (and burglar) Mr Lamb in error for Wingate, Captain of the School, for which Vernon-Smith, also illegally out in the blackout, is almost expelled. On Hinton, see Mary Cadogan, *Frank Richards* (1988), 154–5.

8. Johns, *King of the Commandos* (1943), 18. There was at least one Sea Scout at Dunkirk – the future Captain Gerald Ashcroft, who served as deck-hand under Charles Herbert Lightoller, formerly Second Officer on the *Titanic*, who with his son Roger (later killed on active duty) got 130 men back to Ramsgate from Dunkirk in his 60-foot yacht *Sundowner*, largely by taking evasive action from hostile aircraft on lines he had learned from his son Brian (bomber command, killed on a Wilhelmshaven raid early in the war [Patrick Stenson, '*Lights*': *The Odyssey of C. H. Lightoller* (1984), 300–12]).

9. Johns, *King of the Commandos*, 14, 19–20, 49–50.

10. Waugh, *Put Out More Flags* ([1942] 1943), 67–8. This, the wartime Penguin edition, must have been much the most influential with its sale of thousands of copies, many sent on to the armed forces, as encouraged by the publishers. Waugh seems to have corrected it: his initial plural, 'the Connollies', now became 'Connollys' with no other alteration to them, first introduced as 'one leering, one lowering, and one drooling'. The *Times Literary Supplement* (21 March 1942) feared the work's probable acceptance as contemporary history and savagely termed the Connollys 'loathsome. Indeed, it is these children who yield the most coherent and successful example of his art', although the Irish novelist Kate O'Brien did not find the idea of Basil Seal blackmailing the billeted by assigning and, after payment, removing them to be 'very convincing, nor are the three children credibly written' *Spectator* (3 April 1942). These and other notices may be conveniently found in Martin Stannard (ed.), *Evelyn Waugh – the Critical Heritage* (1984).

11. I am deeply grateful for the historical and moral aid given to me by Colin Ryder Richardson in letting me know of his reading matter and interests in answer (10 June 2005) to my query, also enclosing his press release (10 March 2005) on the sinking of the *City of Benares*, for which see also *News of the World*, 10 July 2005, and Ralph Barker, *Children of the Benares* ([1987] 1990), 88–9, 101–2, 123–7, 145,

160, 165, 224. Falkirk High School [1985] made a useful project of the *City of Benares*, chiefly on the children in the lifeboat for eight days, on whom Elizabeth Hawkins based her inspiring novel *Sea of Peril* (1995). Elspeth Huxley, *Atlantic Ordeal – the Story of Mary Cornish* (1941), 42, shows how a nurse tried to maintain morale of the children in her lifeboat over the eight days by telling them stories of a secret-service-thriller variety based on John Buchan's *The Thirty-Nine Steps* and the 'Bulldog Drummond' books by 'Sapper' (Herman Cyril McNeile). The popular bourgeois suspicion of comics was mildly articulated by M. M. Lewis, Director of the Institute of Education, University of Nottingham, when he addressed the School Library Association on 29 December 1953 on 'Children's Reading and Illiteracy': 'With regard to the reading of comics it is often said that the children who read comics must be the children who do not read other literature. I am afraid that is not true' (p. 5). 'I am afraid' is instructive.
12. Shead, *They Sailed by Night*, 16.
13. Travers, *I Go by Sea, I Go by Land*, 27, 49. Travers insisted that the incidents and characters were true but made no such claim for the diary; she was in any case a fantasist on the details of her own life. She said that she altered personal and place names so as not to give information to the enemy, in which hope she was probably successful. Penelope Hughes, *Richard Hughes* (1984), 6–7.
14. Hughes, *Don't Blame Me!*, 98. 'Home' was not included in the posthumous *The Wonder-Dog: The Collected Children's Stories of Richard Hughes* (1977), the last lines of whose preface he dictated from his death-bed to conclude the part he had already written and whose choice was therefore probably his. 'Home' may have been dropped because of the *Times Literary Supplement*'s belief that it was too mystical for children (14 December 1940). 'The Wishing-Shell' and 'A Box of Matches' were also dropped, also unjustifiably. *The Wonder-Dog* includes the sequel 'Gertrude's Child' to 'The Doll and the Mermaid', which had started as the wooden doll in the chamberpot.
15. Peter Thomas, *Richard Hughes* (1973), in the 'Writers of Wales' series, begins with quotation of these and other passages from the Brashfield Address to the American Academy of Arts and Letters, 1969.
16. *Put Out More Flags* (1943) 75.
17. Lewis, *Of Other Worlds: Essays and Stories* (1966), 42. *The Lion, the Witch and the Wardrobe* (1950), 80–1.
18. Blyton, *The Adventurous Four*, 140.
19. *The Children of Kidillin*, 3, 24, 26.
20. Ibid., 10, 11, 15, 44, 80–1. Violet Methley begins *Great Galleon* (1942) with mutually hostile cousins all the more critical because of their native origins (English v. Australian), the reconciliation hardening their subsequent anti-Nazi operations, as with Blyton (a.k.a. Pollock).
21. The late Rev. William Mahon Barbour of Limavady told me of this, it being his grandmother.
22. Kyle, *Visitors from England* ([1941] 1962), 2, 3–4, 5. Kyle, *The Seven Sapphires* ([1944] 1962), 125.
23. Shead, *They Sailed by Night*, 8–9.
24. Johns, *Spitfire Parade* ([1941] 1960), 124, 131. For the original story, 'The Funk', see *Biggles of the Camel Squadron* (1934), renamed *Biggles of the Fighter Squadron* (1992), chapter 6.
25. *I Go by Sea, I Go by Land*, 4. Crompton, 'A Present for a Little Girl', *Modern Woman* (April 1942) and *William Carries On*, 209, 230, 232.
26. Crompton, 'William and the Bird Man', *Happy Mag* (April 1940) and *William and the Evacuees*, 76–7.

27. Crompton, 'William Takes Charge', *Happy Mag* (May 1940) and *William and the Evacuees*, 13, 13–14.
28. Crompton, 'Claude Finds a Companion', *Modern Woman* (April 1941) and *William Does His Bit*, 235. The Outlaws are not pro-evacuee necessarily (though in general they seem to be, mildly); but three of them are absent, and William is present but in internal disruption, following their making of 'Sardine Toffee'. Norman Dale, *Secret Service* (1943), 9, 28, 8. *Secret Service* proved to be the first of a series of child thrillers about Peter and Ginger, so, like Lewis's Narnia series, Dale's was a long-term effect of the evacuation experience. So were Blyton's Five, Saville's Lone Piners and Kyle's Peter and Margot.
29. 'William and the Four-Forty', *Home Notes* (28 May 1948) and *William – the Bold* (July 1950). 'Bill Smugs' (a.k.a. Bill Cunningham) marries Alison Mannering, mother of Philip and Dinah, at Lucy-Ann Trent's suggestion made at the end of *The Ship of Adventure* (1950), the marriage taking place before the next book, *The Circus of Adventure* (1952). Psychologically the step is interesting, as an indication of Blyton's desire to legitimise the introduction of a stepfather into her family, before the tribunal which she saw as superior to all others: her books and their readers. But the series declined markedly in the latter book and its only sequel. For Eli, see 1 Samuel 3 and 4. On Aslan, Sara Dudley Edwards (C. S. Lewis issue, *Chesterton Review* 17 (1991), 429–35). For Tolkien's response to *The Lion, the Witch and the Wardrobe*, Lancelyn Green and Hooper, *Lewis*, 241. In the Narnia series, Reepicheep comes into his own in *The Voyage of the* Dawn Treader (1952), Puddleglum in *The Silver Chair* (1953), and Bree in *The Horse and His Boy* (1953), while Uncle Andrew pollutes *The Magician's Nephew* (1955), and the Ape (evidently suggested by the Belfastspeak 'Pape') sparks off *The Last Battle* (1956). Similarly, the White Witch is both Hitler and Antichrist. The Roman Catholic Tolkien's dislike of the Narnia series and its allegories may have hardened Lewis in his determination to revive his ancient hostilities against the Pope (or Papes).
30. Hughes, in addition to having written with credible realism of children in *High Wind in Jamaica*, had also written his most successful play *A Comedy of Good and Evil* (first produced in 1924), in which a beautiful child devil entraps the soul of a saintly clergyman but then insists on saving him to her own self-disgust and the scorn of the sanctimonious angel. The *Times Literary Supplement* (14 December 1940) asserted that his 'impish and unmoral humour is found in many of the situations [of *Don't Blame Me!*] and appeals greatly to the primitive instincts of children; it is a quality which the author shares (and particularly is this noticeable in the animal stories) with the earliest writers of folklore'. The point is a good one, if we forget the imbecility of 'the earliest writers of folklore' when first oral narrators is intended – but scholarship of the 1940s had little respect for oral transmission.
31. *Adventurous Four*, 94, 155–6.
32. *King of the Commandos*, 137–8, 154, 156, 161, 167–90. It is the French Canadian Trapper Troublay who makes the issue clear (' "If those swines lay a finger on that girl, one finger only, I'll – I'll –". Something seemed to stick in his throat' (161)).
33. Lewis, 'Sometimes Fairy Stories May Say Best What's to be Said', *New York Times Book Review* (18 November 1956), *Of Other Worlds*, 38.
34. Lancelyn Green and Hooper, *Lewis*, 241. Lucy and the Faun also have antecedents in Alice's relations with the White Rabbit (*Alice's Adventure in Wonderland*) and the White Knight (*Through the Looking-Glass*).
35. Wallace Grevatt, *BBC Children's Hour* (1988), is invaluable but ill-assembled and, alas, unindexed. The element of magic which still clung around wireless in these years, more especially for children unfamiliar with it suddenly encounter-

ing it, increased Uncle Mac's guru potential: the magic, so-called or otherwise, of dramatised John Masefield for children or Kenneth Grahame's *The Wind in the Willows* made McCulloch magic's ultimate arbiter – and, by one single final word, introduced by his decision, he internationalised his audience and taught them never to think of other children as their enemies: 'Goodnight, children – everywhere!' The use of favourite German stories by anti-Nazi writers, such as Erich Kästner's *Emil and the Detectives*, reinforced the point, also one that Brent-Dyer was making.

36. Ray, *The Blyton Phenomenon* (1982), 159. Adventurous Four, 67–8.
37. *Adventurous Four*, 103, 177, 188, 188–9, 189, 80–1, 88–9.
38. *Castle of Adventure*, 237, 303.
39. *Valley of Adventure*, 322. A remarkable touch in this story is the old Austrian woman's affection for Lucy-Ann, whom she identifies with a granddaughter removed and apparently killed by the Nazis (in a concentration camp?):

> 'So like this little girl, with red hair and a sweet face. She lived with us. And one day the enemy came and took her away and we never saw her again. So now my wife sees her little lost one in your sister. You must excuse her, for maybe she really thinks her small Greta has come back.' (p. 248)

Blyton's indirect use of war must have given many readers their first real sense of the impact of Nazism on family life. It's possible that she intended a racial implication, the child's hair deriving from intermarriage of the old couple's own offspring with a gypsy. On her friend/maid Mary, see Stoney, *Blyton*, 121, and Imogen Smallwood, *A Childhood at Green Hedges* (1989), 24–5, 30, 53, 94, 154. *Five Go Adventuring Again* (July 1943), 144–5.

40. Atkinson produced one of these a year throughout the war. As if in compensation for its exclusion, her girls are very violent in their mutual hostilities.
41. For Hugh Pollock, see Stoney, *Blyton*; also George Greenfield, *Enid Blyton* (1998), 57–8.
42. Blyton frequently asserts the fear in the heart of the child heroes. On Kenneth Darrell Waters, Smallwood, *Childhood* is instructive and disturbing.
43. Terence Molloy, *Eve Garnett* (2002), 64–5, 72–3. Hugh Brogan, *Life of Arthur Ransome* (1984), 373–5. Wayne G. Hammond, *Ransome Bibliography*, 123–4. Mabel Esther Allan, *To Be an Author* (1982), 19, 21–3.
44. Crompton, 'William and the Bomb', *Modern Woman* (June 1941), *William Carries On*, 46–7, 48, 52, 54–6, 56–7, 59–60.
45. *Three and a Pigeon*, 7–9, 25.
46. Crompton, 'William – the Salvage Collector', *Modern Woman* (January 1941) and *William Does His Bit*, 167, 168–9, 169–71, 172, 186.
47. Ibid., 184.
48. *Warrior Nation*, 187.
49. Crompton, 'William Helps the Spitfire Fund', *Modern Woman* (March 1941) and *William Does His Bit*, 192.
50. Townsend, *Written for Children* ([1965] 1983), 191.
51. Other reminiscent testimony is less disconcerting. 'The popular books in the library were *Just William* . . .' (Joe Ashton, 'Hitler Did Us a Favour'). 'When I was old enough to belong to the library a new world opened for me. I read my first "William" book and went around for days wearing a bemused grin because I had discovered something wonderful': Leslie Thomas, 'What do Whistles Mean?', in David Childs and Janet Wharton (eds), *Children in War* (1989), 121, 180.

"GET OUT OF THIS AT ONCE!" THUNDERED THE SECTION
OFFICER. "HOW DARE YOU COME IN HERE! DON'T YOU
KNOW THAT YOU'RE TRESPASSING?"

WILLIAM HAD MARCHED HIS BAND UP TO THE END OF THE
LINE, WHERE THEY TOOK THEIR PLACES, STANDING STRAIGHT
TO ATTENTION.

FIGURE 4 Woman's vengeance on wartime patriarchy (Richmal
Crompton, 'William – the Fire-Fighter') – see pp. 90, 123 n. 18.

4

Women and Fathers

'Who cares for you?' said Alice (she had grown to her full size by this time). 'You're nothing but a pack of cards!'

At this the whole pack rose up into the air, and came flying down upon her; she gave a little scream, half of fright and half of anger, and tried to beat them off, and found herself lying on the bank, with her head in the lap of her sister, who was gently brushing away some dead leaves that had fluttered down from the trees upon her face.

Lewis Carroll, *Alice's Adventures in Wonderland* (1865)

Unity or dichotomy? Sequel or innovation? Evolution or revolution? These are the obvious questions facing the historian of literature written during the Second World War in its relationship to that of the First. Paul Fussell has made the grand case for the imagery of the First World War dominating its sequel.[1] Joseph Heller's *Catch-22* (1962), he noted, carries First World War assumptions rather more than those of the Second World War in which it is situated. Charles Schulz's comic strip *Peanuts*, he could have gone on to add, set the air-combat fantasies of the dog Snoopy in the First World War, although the US participation in that war was much shorter than in the Second. Children's literature for young UK subjects read or at least written in the Second World War clearly had its common links with that of the First World War, most obviously in the writers. Angela Brazil, for instance, lived on until 1947, to delight the Second World War readers of *Five Jolly Schoolgirls* (1941) with slightly muted versions of the same values animating *A Patriotic Schoolgirl* (1918). Frank Richards began the Second World War at Greyfriars in the *Magnet* with the expertise of having brought out story after story about the same schoolboys at the same age during the First World War. Percy F. Westerman duly brought out twenty-seven titles from 1939 to 1945 inclusive, most, notably of sea combat, gallantly asserting the valour of heroes comparable to those he had been describing since *A Lad of Grit* (1908).

But there is sharp change, sometimes revolutionary. For one thing, the Second World War produced far more female writers. Men continued to write 'in drag', so to speak, for such weeklies as survived: if L. E. Ransome no longer wrote as 'Hilda Richards', as he had done in the *Schoolfriend* and then the *Schoolgirl* in the 1920s and 1930s, he still pleased readers of the *Girls' Crystal* in the 1940s as 'Ida Melbourne'.[2] But there were far fewer. The drain of men to the war services was more comprehensive, and tapped a wider age-range when the Home Guard is taken into account. Women had become supreme in genre after genre: the detective story, the historical novel, the mushy romance. In children's fiction, no male writer combined a popularity, a fecundity and a quality equal to Richmal Crompton's. Enid Blyton in the course of the war wrote 220 issues of her *Sunny Stories* with its three-story, one-serial-instalment, one-picture-story, Blyton-letter, domestic-pet-letter weekly (later fortnightly) contents, as well as publishing ninety-five books of fiction and fifty-one of non-fiction between 1939 and 1945 (a few of which had appeared serially in *Sunny Stories*). Her achievement is simply heroic, and her purpose in part was certainly to boost morale among the children as well as hooking them on reading. Elinor Brent-Dyer had seven books in the period, Elsie J. Oxenham eleven, Dorita Fairlie Bruce seven, Kitty Barne six, Noel Streatfeild five, and Patricia Lynch – the UK's most widely read contemporary non-British author for children – six. Catherine Christian, Agnes M. Miall, Alison Uttley, Violet M. Methley and many others would produce what in all senses may be called a decent half-dozen or more titles apiece. Despite the gigantic achievement of Bessie Marchant, L. T. Meade and Angela Brazil herself in past times – not to speak of such remoter predecessors as Charlotte M. Yonge and Maria Edgeworth – the seminal female names in children's literature had been North American: Louisa May Alcott, Martha Finley, Susan Coolidge, Kate Douglas Wiggin, Eleanor H. Porter, Laura Ingalls Wilder and, from Canada, L. M. Montgomery. Now, Britain would lead. British writers for children had more urgent things to say than did their American colleagues, once Britain had entered the Second World War, even if, like the Blyton of 1942–5, their method of saying it might not seem too obviously aware of war. For most British writers who mentioned the war at any point, it was invisibly behind them, stiffening their sinews, when not present on their pages. North American writing was necessarily more remote.[3]

So, the status rise of the British female writer for children to international pre-eminence is one definite discontinuity. Yet sometimes the discontinuity or revolution could be present in the writer herself – and here the most startling example to hand is that of the dying Lucy Maud Montgomery, whose *Anne of Green Gables* (1908) had put Prince Edward Island on the literary map, and whose *Rilla of Ingleside* (1921) may well be the best children's novel to emerge from the First World War. She left among her papers when she died in April 1942 a collection of stories 'The Blythes are Quoted', tangentially alluding to Anne Blythe, née Shirley, and her family, and covering a period of some forty years on the island they had made famous. Only the final story is set in the Second World War, when its author was a tragic, lonely figure who had buried one child and seen another go his way in a wretched, self-gratifying, self-destructive existence, while her own husband, a Presbyterian minister, had embittered their married life by his conviction of his own damnation. He would survive his 67-year-old wife by a year.

The last story could have been completed any time between late 1939 and early 1942, but the probability is very early 1940. It did not appear until 1974. But Montgomery may well have intended the entire book for publication in her lifetime. Why should she have withheld such a thing until posterity? Or so one might say on the basis of the first thirteen stories. She might have had more doubts about co-existing with the published text of that final work, 'A Commonplace Woman', which in plot, character and execution eclipses its bedfellows and equals any of her lifetime's short stories, of which some dozen or so reached great heights. 'A Commonplace Woman' is the work of a dying woman (whenever it was written) describing a dying woman; elsewhere in Canada in late 1939 and early 1940, the Governor-General, Lord Tweedsmuir, much enjoyed as a writer by children in his earlier identity as John Buchan, was also dying, and also writing a story about a dying person: *Sick Heart River*. It, too, ranks with the best of its author's work. Buchan died two years before Montgomery. His book's protagonist was a hero of several of his earlier works, Sir Edward Leithen, whose last weeks turned away from his arena of success and sought instead to save endangered lives, boh white and Indian in the Canadian wilds.

Montgomery's last work makes but the briefest mention of Anne, whose creation thirty-odd years earlier had made her creator and their island famous: Anne and her husband stop visits of their grandson Walter to the house of an unsuitable young lady. Walter bears the name of their dead son, his uncle, killed in the First World War, and the text alludes ominously to another grandson now in the Canadian Air Force – among 'several' of the Blythes' grandsons about to take part in the Second World War. We are evidently to assume that Anne will lose some of this generation also, whether or not she lives to discover it. But this is simply the double circle of death surrounding the death central to the main story, which begins brutally enough:

> It had been raining all day, a cold, drizzling rain, but now the night had fallen and the rain had partially eased, though the wind still blew and sighed. The John Anderson family were sitting in the parlour – they still called it that – of the ugly house in the outskirts of Lowbridge, waiting for their Great-aunt Ursula, who was dying in the room overhead, to die and have done with it.
>
> They never would have expressed it like that but each one in his or her secret soul thought it.

We get a view of various persons in the house, including the mercenary doctor in attendance, dismissing the dying body as that of a woman of no importance (Wilde's phrase: was Montgomery, improbably, thinking of it?). And then we enter on the secret soul of the dying woman who, unbeknown to all, proves to have been the mistress and model to a world-famous artist who has made her anonymous hands immortal and, without ever knowing it, made her a mother. She manages to plant the child on a wealthy couple, stays close to her (with no hint of her own motherhood) as a dressmaker, and sees her marry a drunk who proposes to divorce her when her adoptive parents lose their money:

> She was sewing in one of the upstairs rooms of the house the day Geoffrey Boyd came home drunk and whipped Patrick mercilessly in the library, while Isabel crouched on the floor outside the door and moaned in her helpless anguish. The last time Geoffrey had come home drunk he had hung his fox terrier up in the stable and whipped it to death. Would he kill Patrick, too?
>
> When he came out and the sobbing boy ran to his mother, he said to her, 'When I have Patrick all to myself – as I shall have sooner or later, my darling – he shall have a good dose of the whip every day. You have made a baby of him with your coddling. I shall make a man of him. Was your father a minister, do you think?'
>
> Ursula had sewed quietly and steadily through it all. Not a stitch was misplaced. Even Isabel thought her very unfeeling. But when Geoffrey came reeling up the stairs, she was standing at the head, waiting for him. Isabel had taken Patrick to his room. There was nobody about. Her eyes were blazing and her gaunt little form in its plain black gown was quivering.

'Get out of my way, damn you', snarled Geoffrey. 'You have always backed her up.'

'I am her mother', said Ursula, 'and her father was Sir Lawrence Ainsley.'

Geoffrey laughed drunkenly. 'Why not the King of England and be done with it?' he said. 'You the mother of anybody!' He added something too foul to repeat.

Ursula put out both hands, hands still beautiful in spite of everything – the hands Larry had kissed and painted – the hands that had been so much admired in his portrait of an Italian princess.

Ursula gave the unsteady Geoffrey a hard push. She did it quite deliberately, knowing what she meant to do, knowing the probable consequences. She did not care in the least if they hanged her for it. Nothing mattered except saving Isabel and Patrick.

Geoffrey Boyd went backwards down the long staircase and fell on the marble floor at its foot. Ursula looked down at him for a few moments, with a feeling of triumph such as she had never experienced since the day Larry had first told her he loved her.

He is dead all right, the daughter and child are safe, the murder is taken to be an accident. And the old lady's last thoughts:[4]

Yes, they have despised me – the whole Anderson clan have always despised me. But I have lived, oh, I have lived, and they have never lived – at least none of my generation. I have been the one who has lived. I have sinned – so the world would say; I have been a murderess – so the world would say. 'But I have lived!'

She spoke the last words aloud with such force and emphasis that old Maggie McLean awakened and started up in alarm. She was just in time to see poor old Ursula Anderson die. Her eyes lived on for a moment or two after the rest of her died. They were triumphant and young. The old dog lifted his head and gave a melancholy howl.

And that, bar some petty trivialities in the chorus-line of unworthy but superior-minded attendants, is that. The dog's howling in fine banshee fashion is crucial: in one of the more startling blends of paganism and Calvinism to which Montgomery's consciously Scottish genius gave rise, Anne's son Walter is killed in the First World War, and his brother's dog, 3,000 miles away, howls all night. Walter's death is expected by Walter himself and intended for the making of the redeemed post-war world for which the First World War's home fires had optimistically burned. Ursula's death is simply to reaffirm her readiness to risk her life in this world and in the next so that her posterity would be safe. She has nothing of Walter's confidence; yet her own readiness for self-sacrifice has saved its much smaller quota. And she dies proud of her defiance of the laws of man – which possibly also defied those of God, and possibly not. It is the last and strangest war message from the most famous lady of the manse in literary history. Like Ursula, her creator had strayed from predictable paths. If her message is, as it seems, a deliberate sounding of echoes of the First World War in a story opening the Second World War, it also seems to say that, in the first war, men had lives to give, and in the second, women have lives to take.

As early as October 1940, W. E. Johns was publishing Second World War fiction of revolutionary importance, built around his female hero, Worrals. She was certainly no female Biggles. Separated by only a few months, he wrote scenes in which each of them (having been imprisoned) thinks of the eighteenth-century jail-breaker Jack Sheppard, Biggles thus: 'Jack Shepherd [sic] once asserted, and on more than one occasion proved, that neither bolts nor bars will hold a man if he is determined to get out. There's always a way – if you can find it. Let's try.' Worrals's female sidekick, Frecks, remarks as they are nail-filing their way through iron bars while in the hands of Nazi spies: 'You'd have made a good partner for Jack Sheppard [sic]'.

'Not me', declared Worrals emphatically, without pausing in her work. 'I'm afraid I should have hit him on the head with a spanner or something. Every time he got out of jail the fool got drunk and was thrown back in again.'

Since *Biggles Defies the Swastika* was surely written after *Worrals of the W.A.A.F.*, we must assume that poor Biggles was deliberately mired in cliché where Worrals, the revolutionary creation and hence the iconoclastic pragmatist, thought for herself. Biggles after Scandinavia meant chiefly either last war's reworkings, or new adventures from inter-war years, at least until 1943 when he took out new leases of life, partly by opening up quests in the Far East, partly by revisiting Johns's beloved Monaco.[5] Worrals shot her creator W. E. Johns into the front ranks of Second World War radical juvenile fictionists. The *Girl's Own Paper's* first instalment, appearing in October 1940, was hailed by Graham Greene in the *Spectator* as

the spirit of these [comic-book war] heroes . . . best exemplified by
a heroine – Worrals, who shot down the mysterious 'twin-engined
high-wing monoplane with tapered wings, painted grey, with no
markings' in area 21-C-2. Her real name is Pilot-Officer Joan
Worralson, W.A.A.F., and we hear of her first as she sat moody
and bored on an empty oil drum, complaining of the monotony of
life. 'The fact is, Frecks, there is a limit to the number of times one
can take up a light plane and fly it to the same place without
getting bored. . . .' Boredom is never allowed to become a serious
danger to these lone wolves: one cannot picture any of them
ensconced in a Maginot line.

Greene was gathering momentum for his next novel, *The Ministry of
Fear* (1943), perhaps literature's deepest contemporary witness to
wartime London – and its motif of danger and conspiracy in fiction
for children makes its epigraphs (all taken from the nineteenth-
century favourite, Charlotte M. Yonge's *The Little Duke*, 1854)
simplistically presage the crises of identity and survival darkening
the text. 'The Unknown War', as he termed this essay, silently
dissented from Orwell: to Greene, comics brought a more intense
involvement in war for their readers. Both in 'Boys' Weeklies' and
later in 'Raffles and Miss Blandish', Orwell argued that pulp fiction
about war outdrew reports of its realities: Greene seems to have
taken child fictional escapist war literature as committing its readers
to a deeper reality. He also confirmed its alienating effect on children,
much as Blyton was doing in less bellicose fashion, Crompton
recording in William's fantasies of his own war heroism, and so
on. Of the war as described in the comics – in which Worrals,
however dignified by the heavy text of the *Girl's Own Paper*, was
therefore part – Greene summed up:

None of the leaders in this war ever dies, on either side. There are
impossible escapes, impossible rescues, but one impossibility
never happens – neither good nor evil is ever finally beaten. . . .
We are all of us seeing a bit of death these days, but we shall not
see their deaths. They will go on living week after week in the
pages of the *Rover*, the *Skipper*, the *Hotspur*, the *B[oy's] O[wn]
P[aper]*, and the *Girls'* [sic] *Own Paper*; in the brain of the boy
who brings the parcels, of the evacuee child scowling from the
railway compartment on his way to ignominious safety, of the
shelter nuisance of whom we say: 'How can anyone live with a
child like that?' The answer, of course, is that he doesn't, except at

mealtimes, live with us. He has other companions: he is part of a war that will never end.

Graham Greene may thus have proved himself our finest historical witness on *how* British children read in the Second World War. But, for all that he rightly listed – indeed top-listed – Worrals in the *Girl's Own Paper* alongside the *Rover*'s 'Steelfinger Stark, the greatest lock expert in the world, who broke open the headquarters of the German Command in Norway', and so on, Worrals had a message for the post-war world as well as for the fantasy war. Certainly, boys found school improved when taken with doses of Billy the Penman. As Greene records a classroom rebuke for 'an untidy piece of dictation':[6]

'The Headmaster would have got a shock if he had known he was scolding the boy who was known as "Billy the Penman", the handwriting genius of the British Secret Service. This was a secret shared by very few people indeed.' (It was a fine piece of work which enabled Billy the Penman to substitute 500 'lines' – 'I must do my best handwriting' – for the details of a new anti-aircraft gun before the Nazi plane swooped down to hook the package from a clothes-line.)

Worrals was in that company not for adventures going beyond the credible – Johns's matter-of-fact maintenance of comic perception and use of commonplace accidents kept most of his stories just about believable – but for breaking the taboo on female pilots killing opponents in air combat, and doing so in the first instalment of her existence. Johns kept it credible, apart from the detail that WAAF personnel did not fly. Worrals, delivering a fighter aircraft, intercepts a radio message to all aircraft demanding that an un-marked monoplane be stopped 'at all costs', and finds it. Her complaint in the first paragraph – 'Men can go off and fight, but girls – oh, no' – was accurate, but is now about to be archaicised:[7]

Her face, although she did not know it, was like white marble: her lips a thin straight line: her eyes, expressionless. The hand that moved towards the gun control was stone cold. She jerked the handle up. Her thumb found the small round button which, when pressed, would spurt a hail of death. 'I've got to do it', she told herself. Then again, 'I've got to do it. This is war.'

She eased the control column forward and the grey monoplane seemed to float towards her. Her feet adjusted the rudder-bar, bringing the gun sights in line. Nearer and nearer floated the monoplane until it seemed to fill them. It was all quite impersonal. . . .

Almost viciously she jammed down the button. Instantly, little specks of orange flame spurted down from the muzzles of her guns. They ended in gleaming silver lines that leaped across the intervening distance and ended at the starboard engine of the grey monoplane. Black smoke swirled aft. The sickly reek of it, mingled with the biting fumes of cordite, poured into Worrals's lungs. She coughed. When she looked up the monoplane had disappeared.

Death is the best of all equalisers, even if you are administering it. And (like Billy the Penman) it is also a claim for child equality: Worrals is 18, her friend Frecks still 17, both recently schoolgirls. But that had been commonplace for fighter pilots in the First World War, provided they were male. What Johns now had to do was to make the equality, thus demanded in his incredible first installment, become the article of faith binding author, protagonists and readers.

The first thus ended chapter on a note that its author evidently fashioned as lethal, and poetic. The last one concluded with Worrals shot down by her devoted if patronising male admirer, who grabs her after Frecks and she have reeled out of the crashed Rockheed plane:

'Take it easy, kid,' he muttered. 'What's going on here?'

Worrals got unsteadily to her feet. 'Phew!' she gasped. 'I can't tell you all about it now. There are some casualties in that machine – a German air force officer among them. They were making for Germany, but we stopped them. I'd got the controls when you butted in and plastered us with lead.'

She deals equally effectively with her male chauvinist head of station.[8]

'Miss Worralson', he said severely. 'When I restored your leave it did not occur to me that you would have the temerity to overstay it. I trust you have a sound excuse?'

Worrals controlled a desire to go into hysterics. She swallowed. 'I never offer excuses, sir', she said stiffly. 'But if you'll take a look in the cabin of that Rockheed you'll find an explanation. In the pocket of the man on the floor you'll find a chart showing certain bridges in this country which have been mined.'

The C.O. blinked like an owl in sunlight. He walked quickly to the big machine, went into the cabin, and returned looking stupefied.

If men try to shoot you down, you deal with them firmly. Worrals did not actually kill anyone else until *Worrals Goes East*, her fifth adventure, published in 1944. Her homicidal modernity had impressed her first readers, notably Greene; but, whatever the Air Ministry may have hinted to Johns, they had sown the wind and reaped the whirlwind.

As for the WAAF's vital decoding work for which Johns was providing a smokescreen in Worrals, he would write in 1953:[9]

During the war, such a good recruiting medium did Biggles prove that I was invited to find a female counterpart, which explains why that intrepid young woman, Worrals of the W.A.A.F., appeared suddenly in the sky. She undertook some remarkable missions, but none (although for security reasons this couldn't be divulged at the time) more desperate than were actually being made by girls in the same Service. Well has it been said that much that sounds improbable can be true. Truth can sound like fiction and still be true.

On the other hand, truth would not be allowed to sound like fiction which gave any clue to the success of code-breaking. So Worrals remained professionally airborne, although frequently dealing with spies, intelligence-gathering and propaganda warfare. Women who were led to the WAAF by Worrals may have been dismayed by being grounded, but Johns could reasonably claim that the qualities of courage, resource, reliability, imagination, humour and patience – and sense of gender equality – which he had instilled in Worrals and Frecks were those which the code-breakers would need.

Worrals's air career arose from being modelled on two of Johns's airwoman friends of many years' standing, who in war served in the Air Transport Authority, Pauline Gower and Amy Johnson. He had known Amy Johnson first of all after her ill-fated marriage, when she was known in the air world as 'Johnnie' Mollison – an easy evolution to Joan Worralson. Pauline Gower was a fellow-writer, for the *GOP* as well as the *Chatterbox* and other schoolgirl journals.[10] Originals of fictional characters are much exaggerated in importance by commentators, save for deliberate caricature, or life portraiture against fictional context (for example Disraeli putting Gladstone into *Endymion* (1880), which he completed after his final electoral defeat at Gladstone's hands). Conan Doyle, vital influence on so many (Richards, Johns, Brent-Dyer, Blyton, Streatfeild, Saville, Crompton), used several figures from the medical world of his Edinburgh student days (and his father) as models for the first half-dozen pages of his first Sherlock Holmes story, and occasionally looked back to one or other of them for a characteristic or a turn of speech; but, once *A Study in Scarlet* was moving, Holmes established his own personality and conduct. Crompton at least drew on the conduct of her younger brother, Jack Lamburn, when she began her William stories: at 37 he joined the RAF in 1940, rising from Pilot Officer to Flight Lieutenant, and served for a time in Iceland under Air Commodore Cecil George Wigglesworth, believed to be one of Johns's models for Biggles in nomenclature and a little more. Mary Cadogan found this 'intriguing but appropriate'.[11] Biggles adopted a modified version of William in his own Ginger. Biggles must have included some self-portraiture, as did Blyton's George, the most famous of her Five.

Worrals and Frecks changed relatively little in the eleven years, eleven books (six wartime) and three short stories (one wartime) of their career. Frecks, a likeable Watson with Watson's humanity, to modify Worrals's austerity, radiates conventional schoolgirl-story fun and reliability – Richards's tomboy of Cliff House, Clara Trevlyn, was an obvious starting-point. But Worrals made claims on credibility, and needed strong underpinning from female heroes of the air. Particularly in *Worrals of the W.A.A.F.*, she shows some of the temperament, frustration and vulnerability of Amy Johnson, whose death in an ATA crash in the Thames Estuary on 5 January 1941 may have seemed like an ill-fated Worrals-like exploit at that time. Writing after her death, Johns, seeking to modernise a First World War story for *Spitfire Parade*, said of its bellicose new hero: 'Taffy's idea of a direct flight between two points was via the Thames Estuary'.

Worrals almost faints (after crashing the Rockheed), but so, in 1942, does Biggles. Both times, the sky turns black: it was probably a personal reminiscence. But the cool, well-organised, unflappable Worrals of subsequent stories recalls the tone of Pauline Gower's fiction: measured, crisp, delivering necessary detail with no unnecessary poetry. (For example: 'He liked to feel he was a man with real worries. Like most successful businessmen, he got happiness from the delusion'.)[12] She wrote verse, satirical, light-hearted, self-mocking. Not for her such lyrical openings as the Francophile Johns's to *Worrals on the War-Path*:

Deep night lay across the fair land of France, night as black as the
soul of its Nazi conqueror. Only here and there a star gleamed
mistily, wanly, as though afraid of what it might reveal. Everywhere, everything was silent, as if all living creatures were afraid
to breathe lest the sound be heard by the ever-watchful German
masters. Only one thing moved – the Spectre of Fear, and he
stalked triumphant through cottage and château, from the fertile
fields of Flanders to the rocky, sun-washed shores of the Medi-
terranean Sea.

No doubt Pauline Gower would have seen a place for such Churchillian prose, but not in a Gower narrative. The end of that particular
adventure (published in July 1943) seems much more reflective of her
judicious irony:[13]

'Thank goodness', muttered Frecks, with a sigh of relief, 'I shall be
just in time.'
    'In time for what?' asked Worrals.
    'My sweet-ration coupons expire today', explained Frecks. 'I've
been saving them up for a good gorge. An awful thought just
struck me that I'd missed the boat.'
    'Where are your coupons?' asked Worrals.
    'In my tunic pocket.'
    'Where's your tunic?'
    There was a moment's silence. Then Frecks uttered a strangled
cry. When she spoke again her voice was vibrant with chagrin.
'What do you know about that?' she moaned. 'After humping my
uniform in a sack all the way from the Cevennes to the Camargue I
left it in that beastly dungeon. Do you think the food people, in the
circumstances, will issue me with a new lot of coupons?'
    'I should say', answered Worrals evenly, 'it would be easier, and
much quicker, to go back to the Camargue and fetch your uniform.'
    'What a revolting business war is', muttered Frecks, as the
Whitley glided down.

It was an admirable point of audience-identification, Frecks at her
most Watsonian – and the reader coming up from Johns's spell to a
rationed world had the abiding consolation that the magnificent girls
in their flying-machines, however godlike, suffered from the same
privations. The constant Johns reader was invited, sardonically, to
notice the self-parody: the overlooked vital papers of *Biggles Sees it
Through* are superseded by the ration-book. It was a reminder that

Frecks shared the sweetie enthusiasms of readers only a few years her junior, thus bringing the godlike within the child compass. These were ugly times for sweet-eaters. A few months earlier, William had heard a rumour that ' "there's not goin' to be any soon . . . They jus' aren't goin' to *make* 'em soon." "Gosh!" said Ginger. "Fancy havin' to go without *sweets*!" "I say", said William, "why shu'n't we start makin' sweets an' sell 'em to the sweet shops?" ' – the medical effects of the prototypes subsequently precipitating William into being taken for a child of 'gentleness', 'quietness' and 'seriousness' who becomes an exceedingly improving companion to the bullying Claude.[14]

But Johns also knew that he catered for adolescents, and this at least required recognition of sex, however unwelcome an object on the *Girl's Own Paper*'s horizon. Johns had composed occasional airborne romances for his allegedly more adult readers, and manages the love-affair between Ginger and Jeanette Ducoste in *Biggles 'Fails to Return'* with economy, delicacy and charm. True to the spirit of Pauline Gower, however, Worrals treated the subject with realism, irony and, where necessary, pragmatism. Thus she rescues a member of the Free French resistance being held prisoner by the local *gendarmerie* (handled with courtesy by Johns and by Worrals, as cops doing a job albeit for the wrong people – and shot down by Gimlet, an interesting distinction for coming times). The charge is that of murder of a Vichy/Nazi secret agent passing as a *gendarme*, and Worrals initially represents herself to the guard as the prisoner's 'sweetheart':

'But why should Jean kill Duclos?'
'That is what we should like to know.' A look of inspiration flickered in the officer's eyes. 'Perhaps Duclos had been making love to you?' he suggested, his mind running on what, to him, might be a sufficient reason for murder. 'Did Duclos make love to you, mademoiselle?' he challenged, suspiciously.
'Never, monsieur.'
'Ah, well, he might have done', said the officer in a disappointed voice.

This is standard humour of the *Reader's Digest* type on the subject of French sex-obsession; indeed, the episode is introduced by the authorial assurance: 'Worrals understood well the French temperament'. But if we momentarily pardon the absurd convention, the joke is tolerably funny. 'Making love', of course, simply meant 'paying court', not in any sense of consummation. The term is repeated a little later, when Worrals is operating a temporary refuelling-stop in a hidden base for Spitfires en route to besieged Malta:

> At two o'clock precisely the first Spitfire announced its arrival with the curious whistling hum peculiar to the type. The floodlight blazed a trail of radiance along the improvised flarepath and the machine made a safe landing. The pilot was the squadron leader, a veteran night-fighter of about twenty years of age. After the first shock of surprise at finding a girl in charge of operations he made hilarious love to Worrals for ten minutes while the machine was being refuelled.
>
> 'If you don't get out of my way I'll hit you on the head with a rock', threatened Worrals, striving to be serious.
>
> Promising to come back as soon as he had won the war the young man roared away into the night.
>
> 'Nice boy', observed Worrals smiling.

It is an elegant little reminder that the air war was once again appallingly close to a children's war, and thus appropriately commemorated most fully during the war by children's books; it was also a reminder that the girls had to be older than the boys. The obverse side of 'making love' was the more modern meaning of the term, which WAAF personnel sometimes discovered to be followed by unwanted pregnancies. Worrals, of course, did not, as shown by her method in response to her swain rescuing her from France at the end of the operation:[15]

> 'Next time you go off on one of these –'
>
> 'Yes, I know – I can find myself another pilot', murmured Worrals drowsily. 'I seem to have heard you say that before. My! How sick you'd be if I took you at your word.'
>
> 'All right – all right, don't rub it in', rasped Bill. 'The next time I fall in love I'll choose a girl who stays at home and –'
>
> 'Leads a nice, quiet, respectable life, and puts your shoes by the fire to warm, and – here, please look where you're going. If you rock the machine like that Frecks will think we've shed a wing, or something.'
>
> Frecks' face appeared round the bulkhead. 'Say! What goes on?'
>
> 'It's all right', answered Worrals. 'It's only Bill. He usually chooses moments like this to get emotional. Don't take any notice

of him. I'm going to sleep.' She settled down in her seat and closed her eyes.

She duly rescues him come peacetime, from a mess he has landed himself in, in Africa, but firmly declines to marry him, at least until she has stopped appearing in works by W. E. Johns. The sense of revolutionary feminism remained, as for instance in a desert operation (*Worrals Goes East*, 1944):[16]

Worrals laid a hand on Nimrud's arm. 'Listen, O mighty hunter', she said sympathetically. 'This is a war on which rests not only the fate of men, but women. Therefore, it is only right and just that women should do their share.'

'Always the ready answer rises to thy lips, O lady', grunted Nimrud. . . .

'It's queer to think that had it not been for the war, at this moment I should probably be cleaning a typewriter in a dingy office, or perhaps going off to the cinema', mused Frecks.

'Where would you rather be?' inquired Worrals.

'I'd rather be here', asserted Frecks. 'All the same, I don't mind telling you that this ghastly loneliness frightens me nearly to death. But there is a thrill in it.' . . .

'The legs of a man like me were not made for walking', protested Nimrud.

'What were they made for?' inquired Frecks.

'For gripping the flanks of a thoroughbred mare', averred Nimrud earnestly.

'Have you ever wondered what the mare thinks about that?' asked Frecks.

'What does it matter what she thinks?' returned Nimrud wonderingly. 'Once I am astride her, no power under God – to Whom all things are possible – can move me.'

'This should teach you to remember the mare's legs next time you are on her back', remarked Frecks calmly.

There was a short pause. 'Are all *bints* in thy land like thee, *effendim*?' inquired Nimrud curiously.

'Most of them', replied Frecks brightly.

Nimrud thought for a moment. 'It may be that the men have done some evil thing in the past that they should be thus afflicted?' he suggested gravely.

'That may be the answer', agreed Frecks.

The best revolutions are preached by laughter. The best discussions of sex are, too. The parable of the mare is sufficiently graphic.

Johns's feminism came in part from Amy Johnson, Pauline Gower and his other airwomen friends, but much also derived from his common-law wife, Doris Leigh, with whom he lived for over forty years. His original marriage broke down during the First World War, but it was never possible for him to engage in divorce proceedings once he had been launched as a children's writer, and certainly not when the destruction of so many magazine outlets had tied him so inescapably to the publications of the Religious Tract Society (including BOP, GOP and the ensuing books under the imprint of Lutterworth Press). Its people received Doris Leigh as Mrs Johns and would have been outraged should they learn they had been deceived. Blyton could divorce her husband amid the Second World War; Johns could not. The publications, which prevented Doris Leigh from winning the official status she wished, naturally attracted her attention in other ways. She made Johns take an agent, the illustrious A. P. Watt. She saw that, despite all printing restrictions, reprint after reprint of Oxford's Biggles titles was called for. Oxford refused to accept Watt's demand for a royalty, and the last new titles came out from them in 1943. Meanwhile, Hodder & Stoughton published their first Biggles in 1942, having – appropriately – begun their Johns titles with the third Worrals, Worrals Flies Again (famous for the passage when, as a spy in France, she tells the 'idiot' of the château that he is obviously a person of normal intelligence and that his maintenance of a disguise in her presence is clearly a chauvinistic refusal to treat women as reliable; he collapses into cringing agreement). It appeared simultaneously in September 1942 with its immediate predecessor, Worrals Carries On, still handled by Lutterworth Press. Hodder, with wider distribution, published Biggles and Worrals for the rest of the war but relinquished Worrals to Lutterworth after one post-war title. Feminism could sell itself as a necessary item in war equipment, but was less readily convertible for peacetime use.

Sex might be rationed amusingly in juvenile war fiction, but it stood on an ugly cusp. It was agreed that the war made sexual allure more rational. William, notoriously despising his sister's fashion-consciousness in peacetime, is much more respectful of her when she returns from war service wearing her ATS uniform. (The ribald Crompton did not share his reverence: 'Actually, though she would not have admitted it, Ethel had put on weight during her sojourn with the Forces and had tried without success to get into what she dashingly called her "civvies"'.) William also makes friends with a girl in the ATS and sympathises with her difficulty in coping with the famine in cosmetics when her fiancé is due to visit her during a leave:

> 'We're allowed to spend three-and-six a month on the stuff' she said, 'and I got mine right at the beginning of the month and I've finished it all and I've had two of the kids' birthdays this last week and haven't a cent left. And he hasn't seen me for ages, so I don't want to give him too much of a shock. He'll be wondering what came over him to ask me to marry him.'

But what happened when female operatives fell into Nazi hands: what part would sex play then (apart from Worrals's flirtations with the *gendarmerie*)? It was bad enough when their captors were Nazi women:

> One of the girls was fair, with a disfiguring scar on her forehead. . . .
>   'We're ready', said Helen. 'Where is that unnatural beast of a woman they call Hylda? She's worse than any male Nazi.'
>   'As bad as that?' queried Worrals.
>   Helen touched the scar on her face. 'She did that, with a red hot knitting needle, because I tried to protect my father', she said simply.

Frecks falls into Hylda's clutches:[17]

> A printing machine stood on a bench. Hylda went to it and depressed a lever so that the iron presses opened a little way.
>   'Put her hands in there, Ali' she commanded.
>   Frecks made a sudden and desperate attempt to free herself, but she was powerless in the grip of the native, who forced her hands between the metal plates. Hylda pressed gently on the lever. The plates closed, holding her hands fast.
>   'Now, dear English lady', sneered Hylda, 'if you do not answer my questions truthfully, and politely, I am going to crush your hands flat. Where is your friend?'
>   Frecks took a grip on herself. 'Find her, Nazi', she spat through her teeth.
>   Hylda's face paled with passion. 'Have it your own way', she rasped.
>   'No', said a voice close at hand. 'We'll have this my way.'

Worrals. That Frecks is faced with so hideous a fate rather than Worrals increases the vulnerability of the child reader. Worrals's confidence facing extreme risks (Amy Johnson) and firm reliability in command (Pauline Gower) puts her somewhat in the adult bracket, but Frecks is as close to schoolgirlhood as a hero of juvenile fiction can be after graduation. Figures like Biggles's Ginger and the commando 'Cub' Peters are experienced vagrants, however good as targets for boy reader-identification. The Worrals stories are more revolutionary in message than Johns's other work, but are more firmly aimed at middle-class audiences than the tales of male heroes. They even appealed to an old middle-class female tradition, if anything preceding the twentieth century. Bessie Marchant (1862–1941) had enthralled the readers of her near-150 books with the dauntless courage of many an intrepid girl (and, especially when writing as John Comfort, many an intrepid boy). For that matter, Enid Blyton, anti-feminist especially on mothers as career women (despite or because of her own professionalism), nevertheless triumphantly exhibits the tomboys who force the men to acknowledge their superior wisdom, notably in the wartime books *Hurrah for the Circus!* (1939), *Five on a Treasure Island* (1942) and *Five Go Adventuring Again* (1943). (Crompton by contrast is oddly anti-tomboy, Brent-Dyer pro.) What gives the Worrals stories the edge is simply the air dimension. An airborne woman seems to break down all male barriers of self-privilege (to say nothing of inducing ancient fears of airborne witches). But *Worrals Goes East* raised the ugly but obvious point that such power was far from limited to Britain, and that the Nazis might be ready to concede more to women than the UK was. Worrals's victory at the precise moment in question is essential: only a woman can truly vanquish a woman. Male victory there would be psychological bankruptcy; it would also look uncomfortably like British bullying.

But female heroes do face male bullies. How far did Johns allow for the implied threat of rape, in all of his wartime fiction? Naturally, juvenile fiction could not be too explicit about it. C. Bernard Rutley's *Pursued by the Swastika* (1944) has an English girl stealing a German car in occupied France with the comment 'it was either that or throwing up the sponge, and I'd rather end up in a car smash than have those brutes beat me into submission with their awful whips'. Johns is a little more subtle about it, as in Worrals's first adventure, where the chief spy (masquerading as the local Rector) 'smiled faintly, a sardonic smile in which there was little humour. "When you leave here", he said slowly, "it will be to go to a country where they know how to control impetuous young women like yourself".' Her chief adversary (von Brandisch: Johns liked aristocratic villains) is less menacing in that direction, perhaps because of his fondness for reconnaissance in the garments of a nun: his attempt at seduction of Worrals is entirely political (with a shrewd if useless hint that Britain undervalues its female operatives: 'You should belong to the Party. We know how to reward efficiency'). But such circumspection was absent from English working-class circles, at least according to their persevering and sympathetic observer Elinor Mordaunt (who suffered three leg-breaks in researching the war in the East End of London). Nancy, the motherless Cockney in Mordaunt's *Blitz Kids* (1941) sees her father denouncing any question of a boyfriend for the eldest daughter who has so self-sacrificingly taken on the upbringing of the children and cooking for the family:

> 'You men are that overbearing', I said, 'There's our Molly been "moiling and toiling" as the saying goes, for over two years, and no thanks for it. The end of it is, she'll die, like our Mum died, and what will you feel like then, I'd like to know? Worse than a murderer.'
>
> 'Who do you think you're speaking to, Miss?' he said. And I said I know right enough, and was tired of knowing, and tired of the way men went on throwing their weight about, as though they was Lord of Creation, which they wasn't.
>
> He was sitting on a chair in front of the fire, was my Dad, with his feet on the mantelpiece and no shoes on, or there's no knowing what he would have done to me.

And to Nancy Healey it was all part of the same war. Her brothers, apprehended by the River Police for boarding a craft, 'said that they would never have come aboard if it hadn't been for me. Which was true enough, but mean. Just like Adam in the Bible, and Hitler and Mussolini and his lot, who put the blame on everyone but themselves.' But her reaction to a possible husband of her own is to tell his mother how she will ' "let him have more than his share' of the rations after marriage, 'Being a painter and decorator and all that, and needing nourishment as the man of the family'. The mother dismisses such lowering of feminist stakes as unjustified, since the war should be over before the little girl and boy could be married:[18] 'And that there Hitler's gone to the place he ought by rights to be in by now, which is hot, and not mentioned in polite society'.

The feminism of W. E. Johns was revolutionary because, as the
creator of the supremely masculine symbol for the latest public form
of warfare, he would have been vigorously, if vaguely, identified with
male chauvinism in all senses, to the general ear and the allegedly
authoritative literary critics who informed it. Well before Worrals,
Johns was widely read by girls, headed by the fans of Amy Johnson
and the readers of Pauline Gower. In a quiet and unflagged way,
Johns over the years had racked up quite few pungent arguments in
favour of female flyers, even at Biggles's expense ('Biggles shrugged
his shoulders and looked at Ginger helplessly, for the female mentality was one of the things he did not understand'). From his
editorial cockpit in *Popular Flying*, he had proclaimed the future
of women with wings early and exultantly. But it took the war to
liberate his feminism, probably because it took the war to drive it
home to Doris Leigh how male control forced her to live out a lie as to
her marital status. If publishers were going to maul her identity, she
would ensure that they were forced to rethink their own, whether
or not publishers enforcing social conformities and deceits, and
publishers enforcing financial constraints and denials, were the
same publishers. Her intervention in the male literary world seems
to have interlocked with his search for a female hero, and shows the
way in which the war could arouse gender-assertiveness. If serial
publications had not been so drastically eliminated, Johns would
never have been so hopelessly dependent on the embattled Christians in Lutterworth Press and on the *Girl's* and *Boy's Own Paper* –
Doris Leigh and he might still not have married, but she would not
have had it so inescapably driven home that she was male convention's prisoner. Biggles and Worrals would prove on many
occasions that a prisoner's base may prove the ideal pivot whence
to strike for victory.

   Elinor Mordaunt was a feminist well before the Second World War
– about forty years before, in fact, when on her version of events her
husband in Mauritius variously attempted to put her up as a stake at
the card-table and as a slave to sea-captains. Her own antecedents
were squirearchical to the point of aristocracy: her maternal grandfather was one of the Bingham Barons of Clanmorris, in Connaught,
where the Binghams had been landlords and administrators since
the Elizabethan colonisation. The most famous Bingham of the day,
the third Earl of Lucan, was as infamous for his evictions during the
Great Famine as for his instruction to the Light Brigade to charge for
the guns at Balaclava; but Mordaunt remembered her grandmother
Lady Clanmorris 'telling me how, during the terrible famine, it broke

her heart to see good meat fed to the hounds with children starving all around' (the Baron being the Master of the Galway Blazers). Her father was St John Legh Clowes, of Cheltenham (her own name being Evelyn Mary Clowes, and the husband in Mauritius apparently Wiehe); he seems to have shared Irish frames of reference, as she mentions his telling a farmer that she was 'Beef to the heels like a Mullingar heifer', this being in answer to some compliment for her. She had voyaged under sail across the earth's oceans as far as Australia and as late as the 1920s, and had written almost fifty books, but she seems to have found her supreme ideal of human conduct in the courage and cheeriness of the Cockneys under Hitler's bombs. She left a memoir of that sojourn, *Here Too is Valour*, published about the same time – October 1941 – as *Blitz Kids*, some of whose rhetoric and ravages can be sourced from its pages. But the revolutionary impact of the war on her was to make her a novelist for children – once: she died the following June. The mutual sympathy of upper and lower classes, in some circumstances, has had some shrewd observers, Frank Richards among them: it seems clearer among women than among men, and it has a covert, though strong, anti-bourgeois impetus. Sean O'Casey had such a relationship with Lady Gregory, who seems to have been related to Mordaunt. Mordaunt had had to earn her own bread in very reduced circumstances from her days as a single parent in Edwardian Australia, and she knew much of life in primitive conditions. But *Blitz Kids* seems unique as a novel voiced as of the Second World War proletariat, and if her preparation and prejudices affected it, its mastery of Cockney vocabulary is too nice not to reflect authentic feminist rhetoric perhaps induced in part by her own comments to informants.

Dad in *Blitz Kids* is not a bad bloke, even if all too ready to beat the bare backsides of his progeny (offering to do it in a magistrate's court, to the horror of the legal dignitary who has just instructed him to resort to it – but at home, not that Hitler had left them much of a home). Female writers frequently show a genius for apparently benign, but horribly revealing, portraits of fathers uttered by good-natured daughters. Apart from a bout of pneumonia forcing him into hospital, and thus enabling Molly to marry, Dad resides at home, working as a porter in the Billingsgate fish-market. His utter self-absorption does not prevent good-natured affection, and can even compel sympathy, as when his daughter remarks how, at her mother's death, 'You wouldn't think a great big man like Dad, over six feet tall and ever so old, could cry, but he did. He just put his head

down upon the kitchen table and cried and cried and cried.' The
deeper grief is nevertheless shown to be that of the eldest daughter
Molly, who will replace her mother partly because she had looked so
much to her: a neighbour gives her a black dress to wear, but Molly
weeps so much for her mother that she returns from the funeral
without having realised she was wearing it back to front. Similarly, it
is she who is 'half crazy with fear' when three of the younger children
are held prisoner by river crooks: 'Dad was asleep on his iron bed as
usual having said there was no hoping that the Germans or anyone
else would take us off his hands: he only wished they would. Though
that was his fun, for he thought no end of us.'[19] The historian is at a
loss to decide how much of this male chauvinism is based on
Mordaunt's painstaking East End Blitz reportage, and how much
are relics of St John Clowes, of Lord Clanmorris, of Mr Wiehe, late of
Mauritius, or of Mordaunt's second brief husband, R. R. Bowles.

But if Dad is alive and visible throughout *Blitz Kids* (which he
concludes by marrying one of his hospital attendants), he has few
counterparts in middle-class juvenile fiction of the Second World
War. Fathers were a strictly rationed commodity in the reading
created for children. Blyton never fully recovered after being betrayed as a 12-year-old when the father she adored walked out of the
family home to live with his mistress: fathers are few in her fiction,
and good fathers much fewer. This applies less to the very small
number formally set in the war (where fathers in the armed forces are
permitted benevolent last-minute appearances) than to her supposedly escapist literature. Either Father is dead, or else he is dangerously irresponsible and/or as frankly hostile to children as a
pantomime witch. The classic case is 'Uncle Quentin' in the 'Five'
series, beginning in 1942: significantly he is always so styled,
although the leading child character is his daughter George. It takes
six books to civilise him, and in the first three he consistently betrays
his daughter to persons with whom he has the smallest acquaintance. It is admitted that his scientific researches are of some
importance (Blyton hints national importance), which is more than
can be said for Uncle Jocelyn in *The Island of Adventure* (1944), in
which all fathers are dead, one from an aircrash, one unspecified in
cause but improvident in effect.

> 'Uncle Jocelyn is quite impossible. He's always buying old papers
> and books and documents, studying them and filing them. He's
> making it his life-work to work out the history of the part of the
> coast where we live – there were battles there in the old days, and

burnings and killings – all most exciting. He's writing a whole history – but as it seems to take him a year to make certain of a fact or two, he'll have to live to be four or five hundred years old before he gets a quarter of the book done, it seems to me.'

His wife is 'Too hard-worked, no money' and later 'worrying herself to death because she can't pay some bill or other, and Uncle swears he hasn't got the money, and wouldn't give it to her if he had'. Blyton underlines the point by a device necessary to make the aunt accept custody of a parrot, but her way of doing it has side-effects, clearly intended for the watchful child:

'Poor Polly, poor old Polly', said Kiki unexpectedly. Aunt Polly looked at the bird, startled.

'How does it know my name?' she asked in astonishment.

Kiki didn't. It was a name she herself was often called, and she often said 'Poor old Polly!' or 'Poor old Kiki!' She saw that she had made an impression on this sharp-voiced woman, and she repeated the words softly, as if she was about to burst into tears.

'Poor Polly! Dear Polly! Poor, dear old Polly!'

'Well I never!' said Aunt Polly, and looked at the parrot more kindly. Aunt Polly felt ill, tired and harassed, but no-one ever said they were sorry, or seemed to notice it. Now here was a bird pitying her and speaking to her more kindly than anyone had for years! Aunt Polly felt strange about it, but quite pleased.

The children, whom readers are expected to identify with or at least welcome as friends, are in fact shown as unfeeling, however perceptive, in response to this tragic situation. Blyton, like Crompton (and Stevenson before them), was evidently drawing from Mark Twain's *Tom Sawyer* and *Huckleberry Finn* – it helps to account for the curious affection for vagabonds in their writing, much less naïve in Crompton's. Aunt Polly owes a little to Tom Sawyer's Aunt Polly (originally derived from Twain's mother), a much less pathetic figure, but one whose hurt at Tom's unintentional cruelty in letting her think he was dead is echoed by Blyton when the children return from an adventure:[20]

They tied up the boat at last and went up to the house. Aunt Polly met them at the door, in a great state of alarm.

'Wherever have you been? I've been so worried about you. I've been nearly off my head with anxiety. I really feel queer.'

She looked very white and ill. Even as she spoke, she tottered a little, and Philip bounded forward and caught her as she fell.

'Poor Aunt Polly', he said, dragging her indoors as gently as he could and putting her on the sofa. 'We're so sorry we upset you. I'll get some water – no, Dinah, you get some.'

Soon Aunt Polly said she felt a little better, but it was quite plain that she was ill. 'She never could stand any worry of this sort', Dinah said to Lucy-Ann. 'Once when Philip nearly fell down the cliff, she was ill for days. It seems to make her heart bad. I'll get her to bed.'

It is an acceptable gloss on Twain, whose text is much less concerned about the possible effects on Tom Sawyer's Aunt Polly of an actual conviction that the boy has been drowned: Twain has to burke the health issue, so that Tom cannot seem destitute of all decent feeling although deciding to prolong the public belief in his own decease. Blyton is seldom a notable realist, but at this feminist moment she quietly confronts her Master with female realities. The Twain antecedent also accounts for Blyton's use of a black servant as Aunt Polly's only assistance. It is certainly not a racist usage, as we will notice later.

Even sympathetic fathers in Blyton often pose ambiguities. Her first adventure series began in 1938 with *The Secret Island*, in which an orphan of lower social origin rescues and hides on an island three children, ill-treated by an aunt and uncle, with parents supposedly dead having crashed their private plane (built by the father) while on a flight to Australia. We are told little of the circumstances which gave the father's cruel sister power of attorney, but it is clear that the parents have been guilty of gross negligence in leaving their children so much at risk while making so hazardous a journey. They genially repossess their children and adopt the protective Huck Finn figure at the end – and then, in *The Secret Mountain* (1941), two stories later, they disappear from another flight. Blyton evidently assumed the stories would be taken as still happening pre-war, not wanting to age the children; but she and her readers would sense the contrast between children deprived of fathers who are risking their lives on aircraft in the struggle against Nazi Germany, and children whose parents continually lose themselves while out joyriding with scant regard to those children's future. In 1941, Blyton was still writing some fiction with formal relevance to the war.

The more subtle and certainly more sophisticated Eleanor Graham, author of *The Children who Lived in a Barn* (1938) and future founder-editor of Puffin Books, went over very much the same ground as *The Secret Island*. Their publication was so close in time together that neither is a likely plagiarism from the other (Blyton's serialisation in her own weekly magazine *Sunny Stories* before publication gives her the edge in any such dispute). Both employ what Sheila Ray calls in this context the 'Cinderella' theme: all will be well at the close, but in the meantime the originally privileged protagonist(s) is seriously disadvantaged and even more seriously humiliated by powerful though secretly vulnerable authority figures. Both happy endings turn on the long-delayed return of parents immobilised by a plane-crash. Graham's family suffers from a sadistic district visitor, a misanthropic landlord, snobbish local magnates, and above all from the folly of their father, whose utter failure to provide for the children in case of accident lands them into their misfortunes. It is clear also that the Graham father's unfortunate mixture of snobbishness and bohemianism has put his children at the mercy of critics and enemies. Blyton's aircrashed father has equally failed to make anything like a satisfactory relationship with his own sister which would have put the children on a better-protected footing. Graham's work is important for our study, since she would be editor of Puffin stories, Penguin Books' children's reprints beginning in 1941, and her standards and outlook would sway the available paperback choices for juveniles in the last four years of the war. Ironically, she would claim that 'I was, of course, frequently urged to get some Blyton on our list but I never did. It was not intended for that kind of public.' This puts Graham in a somewhat older tradition: that of the fable told by Aesop about the fox whose inability to get a bunch of grapes led him to declare that the grapes were sour. Had a Blyton title been available to Graham, and still more to her overlord, Allen Lane, it would surely have been adopted with rapture at any time during the war years, when Puffin was desperately trying to build itself a reliable readership. Twenty years later, Penguin besought Blyton to appear in court in their defence in the Lady Chatterley trial.[21] The similarities between the two stories show that the two ladies were catering for similar appetites.

The diminishing status of fathers in the juvenile fiction of the Second World War worked its way out in very different directions, as may be seen from the cases of Elinor Brent-Dyer, Carol Forrest and Eric Linklater. Brent-Dyer, a victim like Blyton of a father's abandonment of his family in her infancy, nominally accorded men deferential status; actually, the patriarch in her Chalet School series,

Dr (afterwards Sir) James Russell, is a meddlesome bully who uses his medical status for every kind of tinpot dictatorship. The stories follow the female auctorial convention of the oppressive patriarch's alleged benevolence, but the reader has ample evidence whence to make much harsher judgements. When in *The New House at the Chalet School* (1935) an estranged sister of his is discovered in the last stages of mortal illness, his first – and his repeated – reaction is violently to abuse his sister-in-law for finding her, coupled with the presumably ludicrous demand that she never do any such thing again. The indictment multiplies over many books: in the last Second World War publication, *Gay from China at the Chalet School* (1944), one of his daughters (Sybil) accidentally scalds her younger sister (Josette) and makes it worse by dragging off her garments succes- sively and hence her skin away with her vest (Brent-Dyer intended her readers to learn that lesson for any domestic or war-sent accidents of their own). Josette's life is in danger. Their aunt's comment speaks for itself: 'I think Sybil has had the lesson of her life. I was raging when I heard what she'd done; but no one could keep on, she's such a poor little bundle of misery. Even Jem – and he was wild with her for days – has had to come round and forgive her.'[22] Brent-Dyer, as a devout Catholic, invites the Christian reader to think of the Lord's Prayer, with its promise of salvation dependent on our forgiveness of those who injure us – but a father's refusal to forgive his daughter until she practically becomes another medical case (and this for an accident, however careless) is as ugly a transgression of the prayer as can be imagined. There are other examples of authoritarian, inadequate fathers – would-be iron dis- ciplinarians (or wildly indulgent permissives) abdicating their re- sponsibilities to the Chalet School (the first book even introduces a father whose practice is literally to dump his daughter on the charity of a boarding-school by secretly decamping after her admission, leaving no fixed address). There are some exceptions: the kindly Herr Florian Marani, father of the first head girl when the school was founded in the Austrian Tyrol, ends his days in a Nazi concentration camp after his daughter and her schoolmates are smuggled across the border into Switzerland having tried to prevent the murder of a Jew. Brent-Dyer got them to England, via the war-menaced Channel Islands and some hideous moments in the Channel itself from a U-boat and the bombs and machine-gun bullets of a biplane; but in that book, *The Chalet School Goes to It*, a Colonel Black, the father of six, goes about his security duties at the school so officiously as to be described by Joey Maynard, the heroine of the series, as 'a wretched

Nazi dressed up in our uniform, going round to make people discontented with the Government'. (Joey had met her Nazis, having led the hopeless attempt to save the Jewish goldsmith from a Nazi lynch-mob.)

Guardians are no better. In *The Highland Twins at the Chalet School*, Betty Wynne-Davies is expelled for fooling around with a real Nazi agent ('He bowed to her. "Fräulein", he emphasized the title, "I make you my apologies. Both of us are in hands too powerful for us. Believe me, I would not have told of you if I could have helped it." He turned his head towards the Head. "Gracious lady, this is the *gnädiges Fräulein* who gave me my information. I deeply regret that I must acknowledge it, but so it is." He stepped back as he ended, with another low bow; but Betty was too far gone to see it or to heed its mockery. With a bitter little cry, she threw up her hands, and swayed forwards. The next moment Elizabeth Arnett had sprung forward and caught her. She could not support the dead weight, but she lowered the fainting girl to the floor, while the Colonel and the Chief Constable, thankful to get away, gave a signal, and the prisoner was marched out at once'). Understandably, some discussion takes place about the guardian to whom she is about to be handed over:

> 'Betty is so afraid of her guardian. It isn't as if she had a father and mother to go home to. It would be bad enough then; but she has no one. And Mr Irons is so stern.'
>
> 'Perhaps, knowing Betty's character, he feels that sternness is the best thing for her. He may feel that she needs a very firm hand over her.'
>
> Elizabeth shook her head. 'It isn't that. He just doesn't bother with her. He isn't married, and he doesn't like girls. He sent her to school when she was only five, and she has been at school ever since. . . .'

It is much to Brent-Dyer's credit that this concern is shown *after* the dénouement, when the miscreant would normally be bundled out of the story to sentiments of general satisfaction.[23]

Carol Forrest has been neglected by critics, partly because her works were of half novel length, selling in hard covers from the waning news empire of C. Arthur Pearson for three shillings and sixpence (just over a sixth of £1) in place of the six shillings now asked by Faber & Faber for juvenile titles, or the seven shillings and sixpence by John Lane, which by 1944 would be eight and sixpence.

The House of Simon (1942) sparkles a somewhat starry-eyed devotion to Boy Scouting and Girl Guiding, common in the literature of the previous quarter-century, but it faces the challenges of blitzed London as resolutely as any middle-class narrative without quite catching the voice of the bombed that we get from Mordaunt's Nancy Healey. (Mordaunt, a neophyte in juvenile literature, was unfashionable and therefore authentic in working with first-person narrative, probably with a real informant in mind: it was a popular narrative system before the First World War, her time as a child reader, so that when she embarked on the genre a half-century later, it came naturally to her.) Forrest gets notes of the kind that Mordaunt made into a symphony:

> 'Do raids happen in the daytime, too?' she asked anxiously.
> 'Might 'appen anytime', Mrs Hatchett assured her cheerfully. 'Just about now – round dinner-time's Adolf's usual visiting time.'

The siren, to Forrest's children just arrived in London, is a 'shrill wailing noise like jackals howling' (Nancy Healey, her ear more London and less nice, compared it to 'a cat being run over on tramlines and squelched up'). Their presence is occasioned by their father, who had sent his four children from Portugal when

> the war got worse. Mr Dellacott didn't seem to notice it at first, but just as it was time for the twins to go back to school in England he got one of his rare paternal moments when he developed a sense of responsibility and decided that England was much too dangerous for them, and Portugal too uncomfortable with the influx of refugees. America was the place – and just then, conveniently, Aunt Jennifer wrote that she was going there on business for a year. Almost before they had read the letter, . . . they had said good-bye to Father, who was going to join them later in America, and were on board the *Sea Urchin* under the care of Captain Corrie, who was taking a cargo of sardines and oranges to England.
> . . . What a flap poor Father would be in, if, after all his worry about their safety, he could have known that the *Sea Urchin* had berthed on the very night of the big raid on Dockland [7 September 1940], and that his children had spent the night in Captain Corrie's little house in Bermondsey with the second Fire of London raging not very far away from them!

The Captain, forgetful of their luggage on his ship, dumps them in a
settlement house in use as a 'rest and feeding centre', where they
discover that Aunt Jennifer has sailed for America the previous day,
presumably because their father's burst of paternal responsibility
has stopped short of letting Aunt Jennifer know that her four nieces
and nephews were to join her voyage in the quest for safety (through
the submarine-infested Atlantic). The children, exceptionally well
characterised, organise themselves as best they can (the youngest, a
seven-year-old, being sometimes the most practical, especially in
dealing with his artistic elder sister, who, left to herself, would
wander away from them all: 'all she wanted was to stay there among
all the ruins and the glory and paint and paint and paint'). The
settlement head does what she can ('I've got half an hour to spare
now, if Jerry agrees; but that last bomb was rather uncomfortably
near our shelter and knocked it about too much for us to use it to-
night. I've got to find somewhere to put these people before black-
out, and I must inform the warden. I could send one of the youngsters
from here, but their mothers won't let 'em out of their sight, and my
own staff are too busy patching windows and finding clothes and
bedding for everyone, to be spared . . .'). 'Jerry' quietens down long
enough for the children to be planked on a train to the settlement
head's cousins in Dorking, identified from a sign in the station roof
by Simon, the seven-year-old ('I'd like to see a Fifth Columnist find
his way about this country these days. Not a sign to tell you where
you are!'). But the military have requisitioned the house, and the
cousins have gone north the previous day in response to orders. The
children seek a barn, to be told that all the farmhands are sleeping
in it, while the house is reported full of 'vacuumees'. Eventually,
after what seems an imminent strafing from an unidentifiable plane,
the vicar finds them and sends them to another farm. There they
meet more evacuees and a farmer's wife, and are quizzed by the
farmer:

> 'Now just why d'you think we should do you a favour to get you
> out of this mess when your own silliness got you into it, eh?'
>   Tessa-Jane flushed crimson, and Mathew jumped up in one of
> his white furies to face the big man who stood in the door.
>   'We don't want any favours! We can pay for anything we have!
> And it wasn't our fault anyway – we couldn't stop the beastly war!'
>   'We only came here because Mr Bacon told us to', Tessa said in a
> low cold voice.
>   Katrina saw a twinkle in the farmer's eye.

'I expect you're Mr Jelly, aren't you?' she asked politely.
'I am.'

'Well, don't take any notice of them. It's only 'cos we're all feeling pretty silly that they're in such a rage. Only – well – silly things do happen in a war, don't they? And – we've had about enough of them. You know what it's like! Or maybe those sort of things don't happen to you?'

Forrest knew how to integrate character with ambition, and it impresses rather than surprises when Katrina discovers she wants to be a doctor, and Matthew a farmer, in his case like having met like in Farmer Jelly ('I'm not saying I haven't had problems and I'm not pretending I haven't been a fool, times in my life. Leastways you don't lack spirit the lot of you'). The phenomenon is old: it has been explored by the Greek, medieval and modern dramatists, the last from Shakespeare to Eugene O'Neill and Margaret Collins – the age-old apparent naïveté of the country mockingly confronting the sophisticated vulnerability of the townsfolk. Compton Mackenzie was at that moment fashioning from close observation a Hebridean version in his adult novel of the war, *Keep the Home Guard Turning* (1943), to reach its climax in *Whisky Galore* (1947). Blyton set it sensitively in a rural-Scottish/urban-English wartime confrontation in *The Children of Kidillin*. This is specifically in the evacuee context, where such wartime confrontations must have been edgiest. Malcolm Saville shows gradations of it in the BBC 'Children's Hour' serial subsequently given book form, *Mystery at Witchend*, where the Cockney nephew becomes a farmer while mourning his lost Wool-worth's dime-store, and the ebullient twins learn that a country servant is not servile. Rural–urban unease and hostility in the Second World War usually seem of more importance than class, both in books and real evacuee life, although the rural hosts often took the evacuees to be below their own status, and vice versa. But in Forrest's *The House of Simon* these things are dwarfed by the one not mentioned: the selfishness and incompetence of the father. By the end of the story, he is suddenly discovered to have been living in their neighbourhood for a week ('getting to know my family incog so to speak'), paying court to a local artist while merely hinting in a letter to his children that they might look her up since 'you've chosen to plant yourselves almost on the doorstep of an old friend of your mother's and mine'. Meanwhile, they have established themselves in a house which they have managed with much travail to make habitable and profitable, 'you've chosen to' being as brazen a

construction as ever a father used to dismiss his duties. Yet at their
worst moments they blame the war, not Father. Only when he returns
does something like criticism cross infant lips. Getting Simon to
school had been a major ordeal, in the course of which he nearly died
in a bog while playing truant, and the prodigal parent once restored
undoes the work done in reconciling him after his escape:[24]

> 'Father says I'm not to go to school any more', he said calmly.
>
> 'Then Father will have to explain that to the law of England',
> Mathew said, equally calmly, without looking up from the thumb-
> stick he was cutting.
>
> 'You can't do that', Katrina said. 'You can break the law or keep
> it – you can't explain to it.'
>
> 'Well, silly, I mean the thingummybobs of education, the people
> who've got to see everyone's educated.'

We know very little about what causes particular books to get
written and what alters the writer's intentions en route. But it seems
to be very clear that Eric Linklater wrote his first book for children,
The Wind on the Moon, because, during a brief leave from his duties
as a Major of Royal Engineers in Orkney, he was told to look after a
couple of infant daughters while his wife was nursing their newly
born Magnus. Nature had not seemed to have equipped him readily
for the task, and, in his irritation at the unaccustomed activity, he fell
back on what he could do: he told them a story about two badly
behaved little girls who first grew very fat and then very thin and
then were turned into kangaroos, their father having told them:

> 'There is wind on the moon . . . I don't like the look of it at all.
> When there is wind on the moon, you must be very careful how
> you behave. Because if it is an ill wind, and you behave badly, it
> will blow straight into your heart, and then you will behave badly
> for a long time to come. . . .'

But in fact the warning, like so many other oracular warnings from
Oedipus onwards, causes what it is supposedly seeking to prevent. (I
am assuming that these bits were part of the original story; some
version of them was.) And the story becomes increasingly critical of
the father, all the more when he becomes imprisoned by a Hitler-style
totalitarian regime and proves extremely graceless in response to his
daughters' courageous rescue of him. Linklater was a great man, and
a great writer: his ability to turn his own story against himself gave

further proof of that greatness. It's important that he was a great writer by the time he was forced by the exigencies of war into childminding and hence writing for children. Others have responded in comparable circumstances – the great Gaelic Munster poet Eoghan Ruadh Ó Súilleabháin (Red Owen O'Sullivan) composed the rich tapestry of classical objects of beauty and power, 'Seothó a thoil', when briefly put in charge of one of his own bastards, understandably tearful at sudden dependence on a strange man. Ó Súilleabháin's self-satire adds a delicious comic element to the grandeur of his litany of fabled and mythological jewels, weapons and garments promised to the child in the event of its silence, but it is hardly pointed – and may not be particularly conscious – whereas Linklater's intentions are clear. Like his Master Byron, Linklater as the author of *Juan in America* (1931) and *Magnus Merriman* (1934) knew on what and to whom he was directing his satire, and here, as elsewhere, his targets are unmistakeable – the little girls, their absurd, endlessly informative governess, their community and its social and legal systems, and then, as the story hardens, Hitler – and his victim, the girls' father, the Major. Linklater's children remember him as a severe and intolerant parent; Linklater's book says the same thing, but becomes a storyteller's apology for paternal inadequacy, with delicious self-mockery (for which *Magnus Merriman* had already shown his talent in a younger, literary context):

'Do you remember', said Major Palfrey, 'the night in Midmeddle-cum when I was packing and you climbed the apple-tree and tied bells on the branches? It was just twelve months ago, and the moon – do you remember? – had a stormy ring round it, and I told you that when there was an ill wind blowing on the moon it might blow into your hearts, if you were naughty, and keep you naughty for a year.'

'I suppose we haven't always behaved really well', said Dinah, 'but we have learnt a lot of things that we wouldn't have learned if we had behaved in a perfectly ordinary way.'

'And we have had a lot of fun', said Dorinda.

'And we have rescued you', said Dinah.

'Yes, yes', said Major Palfrey. 'Except for the worry you have caused your poor mother, and the waste of so much time that you might have spent with Miss Serendip [their governess], I find it difficult to blame you.'

'It would be very foolish indeed to blame them for coming to save you from Count Hulagu's dungeon', said Mr Corvo.

'When I was a boy', said Major Palfrey. 'I had to obey my parents in everything.'

'I like to think for myself', said Dinah.

'So do I', said Dorinda. 'Well, sometimes it's a nuisance, of course, but when it isn't a nuisance I do.'

'The moon is quite calm now', said Major Palfrey doubtfully. 'Thinking for yourselves, perhaps, won't always have such unusual results as it has had in the past year.'

This is a gorgeous lampoon of the conventional child morality story. Yet, while deliberately reducing Major Palfrey's basis of morality to superstition as wild as could be imagined (and all delivered with scientific sobriety), Major Linklater knew how and where to draw an air from an old enchanted harp. The moon-wind's intrusion into the girls' hearts derived from the fragment of ice in the heart of Kay in the fairy-story of the Snow-Queen, on which Lewis obviously drew for *The Silver Chair*, as well as for *The Lion, the Witch and the Wardrobe*; and Linklater, like Lewis, translated the story's influence into an image of totalitarianism. In both cases, sweetmeats were symbols of corruption, Lewis using Turkish delight as the White Witch's means of seducing Edmund, Linklater as making his Hitler-figure, Count Hulagu Bloot, a glutton for candy: ' "The Tyrant is very fond of sweets", said Mr Corvo. "He likes to see people being killed, and he likes peppermint creams. He is a strange man." ' Hitler was reputed to share similar tastes. Count Hulagu finds the fugitives on their first escape by tracking down peppermint creams stolen and then spilt by the girls. All of this had its place in the economy of child entertainment: no doubt Lewis found it as useful to make Turkish delight a taboo as Linklater to indict peppermint creams. It is much more satisfactory to have sweetmeats denied for serviceability to Hitler-types than merely to have them denied by rationing. But the loss of the peppermints is made another occasion to show the pompous mistakes of the father:

'The peppermint creams', said Dorinda. 'Where are they?'

'There', said Dinah.

'Who's been eating them? They're nearly all gone.'

'Not I', said Mr Corvo.

'Nor I', said Major Palfrey.

'Oh!' cried Dorinda. 'There's a hole in the bag! I must have been spilling them all the way!'

'That can't be helped now', said Major Palfrey. 'We have things more important than peppermint creams to think about. Mr Corvo, as you know the route, will you be so kind as to lead us?'

'We must go swiftly and quietly', said Mr Corvo. 'Keep close together, make no noise, and be ready for anything!'

He moved towards the door, but before he could reach it, it was thrown violently open and two soldiers came in with rifles pointed. Other soldiers could be seen behind them.

And then a more menacing and fearful figure entered. With a sneer of triumph on his face, Count Hulagu Bloot appeared.

This blundering from a repressive father may owe a little to Blyton. If, in fashioning his story for print, Linklater studied form with *Five Go Adventuring Again*, a popular choice for children in the year preceding *The Wind on the Moon*'s publication, he would have profited by the father's insistence on the excellence of tutors for children as educators, when their real use was that of guardians. But, while Blyton allows her bogus tutor some conventional cramming of Julian, Dick and George, with appropriate attention to Anne, Link-later makes a real governess, Miss Serendip, a crammer far over the frontier of sanity:[25]

'Will you pass me the pepper, Dorinda? Pepper, as I dare say you know, is a spice. There is black pepper, white pepper, and red pepper. Pepper used to be a monopoly of the King of Portugal. Much of it is now grown in Penang. Penang means the Island of Areca Nuts. At one time it was a penal settlement, or prison. The word prison is derived from the word *prehensio*. Our prisons used to be very badly conducted, but gradually reform was introduced. Newgate was a famous old prison, Sing Sing is a well-known modern prison. Thank you, dear. Put the pepper back in its proper place.'

Lucky old pepper! Once returned, it will be the only thing in her discourse in its proper place. The charm of the character is that her endless facts are not only true but in many cases also useful and interesting. But her force-feeding renders them hopelessly counter-productive. The father, of course, is peripheral to this, apart from his self-saving reliance on the tutor to rid himself of his parental obligations; and (as will be noted later) Linklater's chief use of Miss Serendip was to hand governess instruction the neatest needling it had received since Lewis Carroll's Mouse recited the history of post-Conquest Norman settlement as the driest thing it knew in order to dry the animals recently immersed in the pool of Alice's tears. No worthier descendant of the Alice books may be found than *The Wind on the Moon*. Culturally, the British drew on high Victorian military confidence as they faced apparent military obliteration; Linklater instinctively turned to the Victorian genius of child literature as he summoned up enchantment for his daughters and, as it proved, his new child public. But, as a storytelling father, his finest moral service was to apologise for parental shortcomings in so sublime a form.

Blyton was Linklater's inferior in quality, but in quantity she far outran him: the 'Five' stories reached probably her widest book audience, even if Hodder & Stoughton unscrupulously coupled them to memories of the *Magnet* by appropriating the 'Famous Five' *nom de guerre* from the silenced Frank Richards. Uncle Quentin was ultimately allowed to make a real peace with his daughter George in the sixth of the series, *Five on Kirrin Island Again*, and to assume some heroic stature in the process; and Blyton definitely said farewell to them all at its close – prematurely, as her readers, and (no doubt even more vociferously) her publishers, ensured. An apparent father of a rather touching aspirant artist, the 16-year-old Martin, draws his supposed son into conspiracy involving murder and treason in that book; but the boy breaks and confesses at the high point of confrontation. Blyton was accused of not stretching her readers' imaginations. She left plenty of scope to them in her economical portraiture of Martin and his guardian, Curton. By this stage the book has moved into high thriller gear, and nothing more is said on their ugly relationship apart from the timorous Anne subsequently shouting at Curton: 'You're a very wicked man . . . I simply can't *bear* you!' This is important, as a child voice is needed to exorcise the pseudo-father (Julian and Dick having reached for adult cliché in response to Martin's revelations). The dog Timmy, frequently presented by Blyton as more adult in reactions than the children or their parents, 'sniffed round Mr Curton, and then walked away, nose in air, as if to say "What a nasty bit of work"'. Martin gives but one more clue: 'If you can get me away from my guardian – and never let me see him again – I'd be happy'. That bleak hope is our one whiff of a hidden hell.

Blyton was drawing more than a name from Richards, whose school stories frequently featured refugees from the slums, child accomplices in crime, even sympathetic schoolboy crooks. Blyton's success with Martin was achieved by her own circumspection in narrative and her sense of pace in moving characters and readers in the chase; Richards would sometimes explain too much, partly to fill up his 35,000 to 40,000 words. But this economical eradication of a pseudo-father coincides with the redemption of Uncle Quentin, ready to sacrifice his work, and apparently his country, to save his daughter's life:

> As soon as the men were out of earshot, George's father spoke in a low voice.
> 'It's no good. I'll have to let them have my book of notes. I can't risk having you buried down here, George. I don't mind anything for myself – workers of my sort have to be ready to take risks all their lives – but it's different now you're here!'

(But she has given the notes to Timmy, who of course gets them back to safety, so that sacrifice cannot be made.) At the conclusion, Quentin presides over the healing of harms, although Blyton does not disappoint her child audience's yearnings to see adults shown up for childishness ('Her father's face fell at the thought of the men being lost underground. He did so badly want to see their dismayed faces when they arrived at the quarry!').[26] He has a dignified cock-a-doodle of victory, as Sherlock Holmes would term it, when Timmy has finally extricated the miscreants from the rabbit-warren. And he proposes to get Martin into an art-school. He has joined George, Timmy, Julian, Dick and Anne at the close of the book as a hero. But the war years in the 'Five' series had meant war between old and young, when George was embattled but Julian had even greater depths of alienation:

> 'So you only gave me the island when you thought it wasn't worth anything', said George, her face white and angry. 'As soon as it is worth money you take it away again. I think that's horrid. It – it isn't honourable.'
> 'That's enough, Georgina', said her father, angrily. 'Your mother is guided by me. You're only a child. Your mother didn't really mean what she said – it was only to please you. But you know well enough you will share in the money we get and have anything you want.'
> 'I won't touch a penny!' said George, in a low choking voice. 'You'll be sorry you sold it.'
> The girl turned and stumbled out of the room. The others felt very sorry for her. She took things so very seriously. Julian thought she didn't understand grown-ups very well. It wasn't a bit of good fighting grown-ups. They could do exactly as they liked. If they

wanted to take away George's island and castle, they could. If they wanted to sell it, they could!

Five on a Treasure Island (1942), whence the above, takes no formal notice of the war (much more implicit in its sequel). But the analysis of adult power virtually equates it with potential totalitarianism. Admittedly, the story (and the series) begins with the frank statement that the 'Five' are brought together because Julian, Dick and Anne will be paying guests (in all but name) at George's mother's house, Kirrin Cottage:

> 'I had to see Quentin's wife in town the other day, about a business matter – and I don't think things are going too well for them. Fanny said that she would be quite glad if she could hear of one or two people to live with her for a while, to bring a little money in. . . . Fanny is very nice. She would look after them well.'

This wrong-foots George's possessiveness (against which Blyton has made some minor points so far); but it turns out that the 'sale' of the island is a swindle, whence the supposed purchasers will get away with its treasure, and the real owners, whether the nominal owner George, the actual owner Fanny or the managerial owner Quentin, will not realise a penny. The ending is classic:[27]

> Uncle Quentin listened in the utmost amazement. . . .
> 'You've been very clever', he said. 'And very brave too. I'm proud of you. Yes, I'm very proud of you all. No wonder you didn't want me to sell the island, George, when you knew about the ingots! But why didn't you tell me?'
> The four children stared at him and didn't answer. They couldn't very well say, 'Well, firstly, you wouldn't have believed us. Secondly, you are bad-tempered and unjust and we are frightened of you. Thirdly, we didn't trust you enough to do the right thing.'

It was at this point that Blyton laid down her cards before her child audience. She was on their side, however much she might moralise on social grounds. And she would not cover up for parents. She sought to instil a social code – but with it, as befitted a writer of child thrillers, she instilled a secret code. Parents would let her readers down. She could not keep such a message in perpetual semaphore, but it would be a basic convention of her relationship with her readers. Hence her exceptionally strong hold over her child public. And hence, also, the adult fear, and even hatred, of her work, all the greater because the adults could never really face up to the reason why. She was ostensibly condemned for being unrealistic, but she was really condemned for the *realpolitik* of her analysis of the generation struggle, and, of course, for utilising her vast increase of outlets to establish well-padded child sanctuaries against hostile parenthood, more especially hostile fatherhood.

Blyton's divorce and second marriage during the war made for one variation in the anti-paternal warfare. Her second husband, the surgeon Kenneth Darrell Waters, seems to have had a temper as bad as Quentin's, although the marriage was well after she had written *Five on a Treasure Island*. But she made some attempt to sweeten the stepfather image. The fourth of the series, *Five Go to Smuggler's Top* (1945), is a somewhat difficult work whose intentions are mildly problematic. It introduces a family who, like some other one-off intruders in her series, are in some respects more interesting than the regular protagonists. Blyton was experimenting with the detective story at this point, being by now on her third of the *Mystery* series begun in 1943 with *The Mystery of the Burnt Cottage*, and silently drawing constructively, imaginatively and not at all slavishly on Poe, Conan Doyle, Christie and other masters. The stepfather in *Smuggler's Top* is ably set up as a suspect, having the conventional giveaway that his eyes do not smile when his mouth does, and a temper that signals its imminence by the tip of his nose turning white. He has also hired a servant with no prior warning to his household, whose alleged deafness does not prevent his transmission of reports of conversations. And he himself dislikes dogs, which means that Timmy has to be smuggled into Smuggler's Top ('if my stepfather ever finds out we shall probably all get a jolly good thrashing, and you'll be sent home in disgrace'). But at the conclusion he turns out to be innocent of complicity in the nefarious dealings of his servant, endangered and victimised by the real master criminal (who is apparently insane, an interesting but obviously underused device in Blyton), and even reconciled to leaving *his* Gargantuan residence to the satisfaction of his wife. He actually shakes hands with Timmy at the end, having been invited by Timmy to do so, and comments – with some justice – 'Well – he doesn't seem like a *dog!*' And the *envoi* is: 'The children felt sorry about one thing, though – they were sorry that they had thought Mr Lenoir so horrid. He was a queer man in many ways, but he could be kind and jolly too.' His brutality to his stepson is less easily elided, but Blyton managed to convey an attempt on the stepfather's part to compromise in place of prohibition, not simply allowing his smile to fulfil his duties of affection. Much more remarkably, she shows that the rebellious stepson has a real yearning for paternal kindness in one of the most extraordinary scenes in her entire œuvre. Both Uncle Quentin and the boy 'Sooty' Lenoir (obvious schoolboy nickname) are kidnapped, and the boy is left without a light beside the drugged scientist.[28]

From somewhere there sounded the drip-drip-drip of water. After a time Sooty couldn't bear it. He knew it was only drops dripping off the roof of the tunnel in a damp place, but he felt he couldn't bear it. Drip-drip-drip. Drip-drip-drip. If only it would stop!

'I'll have to wake George's father up!' thought the boy desperately. 'I must talk to someone!'

He began to shake the sleeping man, wondering what to call him, for he did not know his surname. [Neither did Blyton.] He couldn't call him 'George's father!' Then he remembered that the others called him Uncle Quentin, and he began yelling the name in the drugged man's ear.

'Uncle Quentin! Uncle Quentin! Wake up! Do wake up! Oh, won't you please wake up!'

Uncle Quentin stirred at last. He opened his eyes in the darkness, and listened to the urgent voice in his ear, feeling faintly puzzled.

'Uncle Quentin! Wake up and speak to me. I'm scared!' said the voice. 'UNCLE QUENTIN!'

The man thought vaguely that it must be Julian or Dick. He put his arm round Sooty and dragged him close to him. 'It's all right. Go to sleep', he said. 'What's the matter, Julian? Or is it Dick? Go to sleep.'

He fell asleep again himself, for he was still half-drugged. But Sooty felt comforted now. He shut his eyes, feeling certain that he couldn't possibly go to sleep. But he did, almost at once!

The passage, if ribaldry be distanced, merits respect. It could never be written for child readers today; paedophile scandals have been too numerous. Indeed, the episode probably inspired the lampoon TV film of 1982–3 which culminates in the Five having Uncle Quentin arrested as a paedophile (from *Five on a Treasure Island* onwards, we are reminded that he 'never had much liking or admiration for any children', clearly including his own daughter, although at the end of that first story he changes his mind about her and her cousins). But what Blyton has succeeded in doing in *Smuggler's Top* is to show how step-parents and stepchildren may both need each other, and yet cannot express an affection waiting to be realised. (Significantly, we never see Sooty and his stepfather reconciled.) More specifically in the war context, Blyton describes how in, say, an air raid, a child may need and find comfort from an otherwise alien source. It leaves the alarming thought that advantage might have been taken of some friendless infants by predators during bomb alerts, and the knowledge that, on the continent, children in concentration camps were vulnerable to abuse of any kind before being killed. Yet the benign encounter deserved its memento, and it is appropriate that Blyton, perhaps the leading innocent of all writers of her time, should have given it to us. It probably comforted many a frightened and lonely child, as so much of her work in the days of the bombs must have done.

Nevertheless, the overall picture of fathers arising from the books written for children during the war is one of inadequacy, if not worse. It is in sharp contrast from the patriarchal, patriotic visions inspired by imperial wars and by the First World War. It coincided with the new feminism of the Second World War, and may have been more durable. We will notice a decided diminuendo in feminism as war gave way to peace, or at least as hot war was followed by Cold War. But paternalism hardly wins much of a post-war fictional revival, especially as women still dominated the juvenile book market and indeed the new world of librarian assertiveness. Even such evangelical publications as the *Eagle* comic, founded in 1950, presumed a fatherless world consoled by so many of its heroes from St Patrick to PC 49. If occasional benign fathers were permitted to return to their children's series from the wars, they found it difficult to maintain personality with benevolence. At best, Father had obtained an armistice.

The one sure means of status-maintenance for Father is to go into the Secret Service, as does Bunkle de Salis's Daddy, the Major (later Colonel and, presumably, ultimately knight-at-arms). The work keeps him away when the plot so requires, but enables him to be *deus ex machina* as needed. In Dorothy Carter's impressively professional series starring the girl pilot Marise Duncan, her father, in whose winged steps she learned to fly, reappears in her various war adventures in impeccable Nazi disguise, whence he certainly succeeds in worsening German–Japanese relations ('We're in this war till it's won, Daddy and me').[29]

William's father, arguably, does not fit in here, since his place remains what it always had been, disapproving of his son, but occasionally finding common ground with him where his own interests are at stake. These personal interests might in the past have concerned the common good, whether improvement in family finances or removal of an uninvited, self-satisfied guest; but they might also be purely selfish. In the war, they may cover questions as fundamental as allotments on Hall grounds or as personal as the gift of a Stilton cheese. The basic assumption remains that what Mr Brown terms principle is largely dictated by his own prejudice, preference or pleasure, and that everyone knows it. Crompton wrote her stories from the first without illusions, and she brought none to her war fiction. William's age remains unaltered, but there is a faint, almost subliminal hint that his father may have been quite like him when young, and that he may grow up with some of his father's sardonic self-interest not wholly destitute of altruism.

The storytellers did not want to face the deaths of children's fathers in the war: the Victorians had met such challenge, indeed if anything obsessively so. But that tide had turned. The closest we get to it is, curiously, in Blyton. The Mannerings, in *The Island of Adventure* (1944), are children of a widowed mother left with little money, which at that date sounds like an unmentioned war death (all we know of the late Mannering is that, like his son, he hated cruelty to animals). Uncle Quentin's 'workers of my sort have to be ready to take risks all their lives' is very much the serving father's sentiment, retrospective since in a post-war story, and its common bond transcending class in 'workers' seems to speak from the *Zeitgeist*, or what it was believed to be. The tensions of a serving father's leave, and the unspoken fears as to whether he would subsequently return, are reflected in Noel Streatfeild's *The Children of Primrose Lane*, all the more commendably in the author's effort to plumb lower-class sentiment (although the children seem too ready, possibly unthinkingly ready, to persist in their adventure which robs them of their farewells to him). W. E. Johns's emblematic Cockney, Tug Carrington, has his own memories of his father:

Algy took Tug by the arm and ushered him out of the room. 'Come into the mess and have a drink', he invited.
'Meaning booze?'
'Not necessarily, but we don't always drink cold water.'
Tug laughed, a short harsh cackle like the sound made by an angry cockerel.

It was so unexpected that Algy started. 'What's the matter?' he asked sharply.

'Matter? Nothing – except if some of the blokes in this war would stop pouring booze down their necks we should get on faster.'

'I take it you have a rooted objection to alcohol?' remarked Algy, for the sake of saying something.

'I have.'

'Why?'

'Because my old man used to flay the hide off me every time he got tight.'

'And how often was that?'

'Every night.'

But, by this stage, the reader of *Spitfire Parade* already knows Air Commodore Raymond's words to Biggles: 'the war is a personal matter with him; his parents were killed in one of the first raids on the East End' (which he follows with 'I doubt if he should have been given a commission, but it's too late to alter that now'). And, when Biggles objects to the first name Tug:[30]

'Is that what they call you at home?'

'It would be if I had a home.'

Biggles tried different tactics. 'I suppose we must blame your father for a name like that', he said cheerfully as he wrote it down.

'You might if he was alive – and if you were looking for trouble. My old man was pretty handy with his dukes.'

From a public-school origin, Nigel ('Cub') Peters lives his two years in the French resistance in a similar spirit of revenge, distasteful as such personal motivation might be to Raymond. At the end of that time, and after his first mission with the commandos, he finds that his father is in fact alive. The end of *Gimlet Goes Again* happens just before he meets his father, who intends him to become an officer and thus separate from his Cockney and French Canadian comrades; they reunite after the war. Blood-feud, however nasty, is a more altruistic motivation than status-recovery: another form of devaluation of Father.

But there must have been many families whose fathers never returned; and they might have gained comfort from a sensitive fiction conveying how others might feel in similar bereavement. The conventions of the day meant that few of them gained it.

Notes

1. Paul Fussell, *The Great War and Modern Memory* (1975). Heller's own Jewish identity of itself questions the Second World War being reduced to War for War's Sake as the First World War had been, and Heller himself deliberately invites the question in making his hero/spokesman Yossarian an Armenian in place of his author's Jewishness. He does history a good turn in reminding it that, for all the considerations of racism, class supremacy and so on as issues distinguishing the later war, the wars have strong comparability as well as contrast. Westerman represents the many Brits who saw the two wars as part of the same British–German conflict, sometimes obsessively, for example having one of his largely indistinguishable protagonists en route to warfare off Zeebrugge muse (in his very early twenties) whether this action resembled action there twenty-two years earlier (*Fighting for Freedom* (1941), 18, 27: same thought, same character, no awareness of duplication, with Haig's backs-to-the-wall order of March 1918 already invoked to compare with British withdrawal from Norway in May 1940, p. 10). Schulz's 'Peanuts' cartoons appeared in daily US newspaper syndication and book collection from 1950 to 2000.

2. L. E. Ransome is noticed in W. O. G. Lofts and D. J. Adley, *The Men Behind Boys' Fiction* (1970), 280–1, and receives a wealth of references in Mary Cadogan and Patricia Craig, *You're a Brick, Angela!: The Girls' Story 1839–1985* ([1976] 1986), noted as one of the writers whose work quickly usurped the identity of 'Hilda Richards' after Charles Hamilton (our Frank Richards) had inaugurated it. But Mary Cadogan, *Women with Wings* (1992), 154 now assigns the identity to Eric Lythe Rosman, presumably for all the work hitherto assigned to Ransome (an index-link to Ransome, p. 29, produces Rosman, so the supersession would seem firm – unless further identities have surfaced in the meantime).

3. Marcus Crouch, *Treasure Seekers and Borrowers* (1962), 88–9 singles out as 'a stronger comment on the war' [than that of any other literary work for children published in the Second World War] *Johnny Tremain* (1944), by the popular American historical novelist Esther Forbes. The book won the premier US award for children's fiction, the Newbery Medal. Its subject is the American Revolution, but Crouch's salutation stressed: 'There was no anachronism in the story, but James Otis, talking to the Boston rebels of 1773, summarized the war aims of 1943 that "we die . . . only that a man may stand up" '. The British readiness in these years to adopt Britain's American foes of 1776 as part of the British heritage is an interesting phenomenon: Orwell, for instance, was convinced that Tom Paine had written much of the Declaration of Independence (Orwell, *Complete Works*, XVII, 238), which helps account for his use of the Declaration as basic to the English ideological inheritance in the appendix on Newspeak in *1984*. Crouch admitted that the first English edition of *Johnny Tremain* 'attracted little attention', only obtaining more attention when republished and redesigned in 1958.

4. Montgomery, *The Road to Yesterday* (1975), 232, 248–9. I am deeply grateful to Professor Mary Rubio and to Dr Jennifer Litster, both of whom have been invaluable to me on Montgomery and much else.

5. *Biggles Defies the Swastika*, 228. *Worrals of the W.A.A.F.* (1941), 151. *Biggles Defies the Swastika* was evidently written before *Biggles Sees it Through* (von Stalhein in the former says that never hitherto has he held Biggles, Algy and Ginger prisoners simultaneously (p. 222), but in the latter, set some weeks earlier, he does (pp. 50–8)); but, whatever the interval between the composition of *Swastika* and its publication date (August 1941), it must have been well after

the first *Girl's Own Paper* appearance of the serialised *Worrals of the W.A.A.F.* in October 1940. Johns might expect those of his girl readers who also read Biggles to pick up the discrepancy; and, given the work's theme of female superiority to male, he did expect it, probably rightly.

6. Greene, 'The Unknown War', *Spectator* (29 November 1940). US editions of *The Ministry of Fear* delete the Yonge epigraphs, or at least some do. Orwell, *Collected Works*, XII, 58, 258, 524; XVI, 351. Mary Cadogan, *Women with Wings* (1992), 161, notes that Johns erroneously made Worrals a Pilot Officer (inapplicable in the non-flying WAAF) but rectified it to 'Flight Officer' between serial and book; her book is invaluable.

7. Johns, *Worrals of the W.A.A.F.*, 28–9.

8. Ibid., 214–15. It is relevant to the 'Fathers' theme in this chapter that Worrals is later described as knowing Squadron-Leader McNavish, her station's CO, 'as well as he knew himself – perhaps better': *Worrals Flies Again* (November 1942), 8.

9. Johns, Foreword, *The First Biggles Omnibus* (1953), 7–8. This was the fourth Biggles omnibus, but the first to consist of Hodder & Stoughton titles, all the Second World War Biggles books appearing under their imprint.

10. Cadogan, *Women with Wings*, 105–20, 165–70, is as always essential; but Michael Fahie's life of his mother, *A Harvest of Memories: The Life of Pauline Gower, M.B.E.* (1995), is an extraordinarily beautiful and instructive work by one of the twin sons after whose birth she died. Pauline Gower lives for me above all in the reminiscences of her schooldays given to me by the late Mrs Catherine Koe. Berresford Ellis and Williams, *By Jove, Biggles!*, 189.

11. Cadogan, *Richmal Crompton* (1986), 115–16.

12. Johns, *Spitfire Parade* ([1941] 1952), 53; *Worrals of the W.A.A.F.*, 213; *Biggles Sweeps the Desert*, 195; Pauline Gower, 'Kites, Worries and Ink', *Girl's Own Annual*, XI, (1939), 349.

13. Johns, *Worrals on the War-Path*, 11, 190–1.

14. Crompton, 'Claude Finds a Companion', *Modern Woman* (April 1941) and *William Does His Bit*, 226, 252. 'the "personal points" system introduced in July 1942 . . . covered sweets and chocolates . . . these points were detachable from the main ration book and were intended as an individual ration rather than going into the household pot like the other foodstuffs. Everyone over six months of age was allowed 8 oz. of chocolate and confectionery every month; the ration went up to 16 oz., and finally settled at 12 oz. for the remainder of the war – indeed until 1953': Juliet Gardiner, *The Children's War* (2005), 121. Johns was not suggesting that women were more infantile than men in addiction to such confectionery; *Biggles in the Orient* (November 1944) turns on Japanese sabotage of pilots by doping them through free issues of chewing-gum and chocolate.

15. *Worrals on the War-Path*, 75, 73, 104, 190.

16. *Worrals Goes East* (June 1944), 115, 128, 160.

17. Crompton, 'Entertainment Provided', *Modern Woman* (May 1943) and 'Youth on the Prow', ibid. (May 1944), both in *William and the Brains Trust* (April 1945), 116, 166. Johns, *Worrals Goes East* 159, 172–3.

18. C[ecil] B[ernard] Rutley, *Pursued by the Swastika*, 217. Johns, *Worrals of the W.A.A.F.*, 71; *Worrals on the War-Path*, 152. For contrasts between UK and Nazi/USSR use of women in the air, see Cadogan, *Women with Wings*, 175–95. Mordaunt, *Blitz Kids*, 101, 81, 107.

19. Ibid., 15, 83. Johns, *Biggles & Co.* (1936), 101. Mordaunt died the next year, on 25 June 1942, possibly as a result of her tough work in the blitzed East End;

she may have been 70 by then (her *Who's Who* entry conceals her date of birth). She sailed for Mauritius in 1897 (it is 'Terracine' in her fiction). Her short stories invite the judgement 'mordant', many of high quality. 'Her secret lay in the intense and vital interest she took in life' (*Times*, 27 June 1942). She was born Evelyn May Clowes and seems to have had three children by Wiehe, two stillborn, the last born in Australia; her autobiography *Sinabada* (1937), 71, 322–3, is of near-Trappist taciturnity on her marriages (the second 'really in love [with] . . . a man several years older than myself, but it began and ended in tragedy', probably in the early 1930s). She travelled the world for the London *Daily News* in 1923. *Here Too is Valour* has remarkable judgements:

> Many of the people in London *dare* not part with their children . . . For them it would mean the beginning of the end, the breaking-up of the family; the husband staying out at nights rather than coming home.
> . . . it strikes me that the children in London are thoroughly enjoying the war, that nothing, apart from loneliness, the lack of familiar friends, will break the spirit of the average Cockney youngster. (pp. 48–9)

20. Blyton, *Island of Adventure*, 19, 23, 39, 236. Kiki the parrot had a real antecedent, belonging to Blyton's aunt, using self-referential 'Polly': 'Well, as you can see, it wasn't surprising that I found Kiki turning up in a book. I was pleased, and I know you are too' (Blyton, *The Story of My Life* [1952], 112–13). The detachment from her own writing process is characteristic; in fact, Kiki begins the book and series.

21. Sheila Ray, *The Blyton Phenomenon*, 153, 30, 75. Eleanor Graham, 'The Bumpus Years', *Signal* 9 (1970), 97–108, 'The Puffin Years', *Signal* 12 (1973), 115–22. Graham coexisted with Blyton titles when part-time editor of Methuen's children's books until she joined Puffin in 1941. The first real attack on Blyton, arising from what seems primarily to have been professional envy, came from Barbara Euphan Todd, author of *Wurzel Gummidge*, who under the initials B.E.B. (her married name was Bower) contributed to the widely read, fairly Philistine *Punch* ('Our Booking-Office (*By Mr Punch's Staff of Learned Clerks*)'). Despite or (probably) because of Kiki's kinship to Gummidge in the part-intelligibility of the non-human, *The Island of Adventure* was reported 'colourless and full of machine-made characters' (*Punch*, 6 December 1944), and of *Five Go to Smuggler's Top* 'it is often hard to know which to like less – the pert children or the bickering parents or the host who threatens to poison a visiting dog. True, they are only "people in books", but these can and should set certain standards' (*Punch*, 5 December 1945). The criterion is meaningless – it outlaws *Vanity Fair* and *Put Out More Flags*, for instance – but dentists' waiting-room periodicals of unknown authorship can become *vox populi* where professional judgements gain more rigorous scrutiny. For Blyton to Penguin on *Lady Chatterley's Lover*, 20 August 1960, see Steve Hare, *Penguin Portrait* (1995), 243–4:

> I cannot IMAGINE why Penguin Books Ltd have put my name on their *Lady Chatterley's Lover* list. (Can you? After all, I'm only a children's writer – whose opinions surely would not weigh with the adult public! Don't you think there is something slightly comic about E.B. declaring that *L. C. Lover* is a fit and proper book for everyone's reading?)
> I'd love to help Penguin Books Ltd. – they are doing a fine job with their

publications – but I don't see how I can. For one thing I haven't read the book – and for another thing my husband said NO at once. The thought of me standing up in Court solemnly advocating a book 'like that' (his words, not mine – I feel he must have read the book!) made his hair stand on end. . . .

22. Josephine Maynard to Miss 'Bill' Wilson, n.d., *Gay from China at the Chalet School* (1944), 107.
23. Brent-Dyer, *The Chalet School Goes to It* (1942), 156. Brent-Dyer, *The Highland Twins at the Chalet School* (1943), 265–6, 268. With some artistry, Brent-Dyer keeps Betty out of focus for part of the time of her treason, and the result is a chillingly convincing study in the trivialities which make Quislings.
24. Forrest, *The House of Simon* (September 1942), 19, 12–13, 27, 31, 46, 132, 112, 134. The dry allusions to 'Jerry', observed at the time as akin to but displacing the usual weather topic, reached their apogee from persons advertising their bombed premises. Basil Woon, *Hell Came to London* (1941), 171–3, quotes:

> A very old-established and sedate firm of drapers and dressmakers . . .:
> WE DEEPLY REGRET THE INCONVENIENCE WHICH MAY BE CAUSED TO OUR CUSTOMERS BY DAMAGE DUE TO ENEMY ACTION AND WILL REOPEN AS SOON AS ADJOINING PREMISES CAN BE PRE-PARED.
> Inside a police cordon there stands a venerable wine shop, apparently undamaged. It is closed, however, and the explanation is in the window:
> TIME BOMB, GENTLEMEN, PLEASE!
> Many of the smaller shops have huge signs in their shattered window-fronts bearing the single word:
> BLAST!

In those days this word used as an expletive constituted bad language, whence the pleasure of being legally improper.

> In a motor-dealer's showrooms all the glass is out and a smart limousine is on its side, but otherwise undamaged. Bright and early they affixed a sign:

> PLEASE NOTE BLAST-PROOF QUALITIES OF OUR CARS.
> At Tottenham Court Road:
>

> BOMBED out
> BLASTED out
> But
> NOT
> SOLD OUT!
>
> . . . in a side street a sign on a building almost totally destroyed reads:
> WE WERE GOING TO BUILD A NEW BUILDING ANYWAY – THIS SAVES US £11,000 FOR DEMOLITION. – THANKS, GOERING!

This sort of thing was obvious reading for children and fitted in with the pastiches in their comics as well as the ironies of Crompton and the sardonic resignation of Johns.

25. Linklater, *Wind on the Moon* (1944), 1, 351–2, 299, 310–11, 9.
26. Blyton, *Five on Kirrin Island Again* ([1947] 1991), 136–7, 140, 151, 49, 126, 152.
27. Blyton, *Five on a Treasure Island* (1942), 108, 8, 182–3.
28. Blyton, *Five Go to Smuggler's Top* ([1945] 1974), 155–6.

29. Dorothy Carter, *Marise Flies South* (1944), 217. Cadogan, *Women with Wings*, 130–5, 159–60, 165, 191–3 is an excellent account of Carter, save that Cadogan was unable to trace her identity beyond flying credentials. The index to *Girl's Own Annual* vol. 60 accidentally credits Carter with the authorship of 'A Daughter of the Snows', actually signed by Eileen Marsh (who also gets a credit in the index). Marsh, mentioned in her own right by Cadogan (pp. 118–19), writes in a style of similar simplicity to Carter, with very similar characters (enterprising daughter, quiet mother occasionally capable of tough stuff, exemplar father) if somewhat looser use of flying expertise. Google identifies Marsh as Dorothy Eileen Marsh Heming (1900–48); Marsh also used Carter for a heroine's last name. Carter had no books after 1948.

30. Johns, *Spitfire Parade*, 31, 11, 29.

LETTY BUTTED THE CAPTAIN WITH JOYFUL ZEST.

FIGURE 5 War of liberation (Richmal Crompton, 'Mrs Bott's Birthday Present') – see pp. 380–1.

5

Officials and Genteel-men

'That's a great deal to make one word mean', Alice said in a thoughtful tone.

'When I make a word do a lot of work like that', said Humpty Dumpty, 'I always pay it extra.'

'Oh!' said Alice. She was too much puzzled to make any other remark.

'Ah, you should see 'em come round me of a Saturday night', Humpty Dumpty went on, wagging his head gravely from side to side, 'for to get their wages, you know'.

(Alice didn't venture to ask what he paid them with; and so you see I ca'n't tell you.)

Lewis Carroll, *Through the Looking-Glass and What Alice Found There* (1872)

The periodisation of Britain in the Second World War works out roughly as: phoney war; Battle of Britain; Blitz; Barbarossa (Hitler's code-name for his campaign against the USSR); American entry; synchronisation; peace. These roughly coincide with the volume-titles of Churchill's memoirs, 'The Gathering Storm' covering the phoney war, which culminates in the Nazi conquests of Denmark, Norway, the Netherlands, Belgium and France. Waugh's title, *Put Out More Flags* eloquently captures the false bravado, culminating in the 'putting out' of more flags in the sense of candles being put out, concluding in what Waugh called the 'Churchill Renaissance', when only one national flag was still flying in Europe against Nazism – the Union Jack. Churchill's 'Their Finest Hour' would cover both the Battle of Britain and the Blitz; Tug Carrington, hero pilot of one, orphan of the other, symbolises both. It also covers something repulsive to both Waugh and Churchill: social revolution, not of course intended in government action, but in the consequent social upheavals and the bitter reappraisals of the ten or twenty years of previous British history, the time of blood-feud for Tug Carrington and Nigel Peters, a demand for a war of revenge but carried out with lower-class or under-class priorities in the minds of many of the hardest fighters. With it fell Brideshead; Waugh's *Brideshead*

Revisited unintentionally argued that the 'Churchill Renaissance', for all of its shrewd (and moving) utilisation of traditional English identity, with upper-class values in middle-class hymns, had (like many another Renaissance) brought to birth the new as well as reviving the old, and that crass egalitarianism and/or Philistinism, darkly identified with the (apparently blameless) Hooper of the novel's prologue, displaced a beautiful aristocratic culture to which even God appeared to offer special terms of salvation. (After all, Waugh's people were not aristocrats but publishers, and Lord March-main's salvation suggests an exceptionally favourable contract, with the Roman Catholic Church as literary agent.) But Brideshead fell, revisitable only for war's necessities and with Hooper's unctuous patronage on what his rising order had despoiled. Waugh made it a tragedy; Enid Blyton declared it an urgent necessity: her two leading novels published near the same time as *Brideshead Revisited*, *The Island of Adventure* and *Five Go to Smuggler's Top*, have as happy endings the abandonment of the ancient stronghold, worshipped for its antiquity and labyrinths by its male owner, enslaving his wife to whom its doom means freedom. Blyton is icily clear that the silver lining to the destructiveness by some Hitler-surrogate is that the tyrannical great house must fall. Her language is exceptionally brutal:

> 'What is going to happen to your Aunt Polly and Uncle Jocelyn?' asked Jack. 'I'm sorry for your aunt – she oughtn't to live in this ruined old house, slaving away, looking after your uncle, being lonely and miserable and ill. But I suppose your uncle will never leave Craggy-Tops?'
>
> 'Well he's got to now – and do you know why?' said Dinah. 'It's because the well-water is salt. The sea did go into it, entering from the old passage down there – so it's undrinkable. It would cost too much to put the well right, so poor old Uncle had to choose between staying at Craggy-Tops and dying of thirst, or leaving it and going somewhere else.'
>
> Everyone laughed. 'Well, Jo-Jo did some good after all when he flooded the mines', said Philip. 'It has forced Uncle Jocelyn to make up his mind to move – and Aunt Polly will be able to get the little cottage she has always wanted, and live there in peace, instead of this great ruin . . .'

And, more mildly, but firmly:[1]

> 'Do you know we're leaving Smuggler's Top?' said Sooty. 'Mother was so terribly upset when I disappeared, that [step-]Father

promised her he'd sell the place and leave Castaway, if I came back
safe and sound. Mother's thrilled.'

'So am I', said [his step-sister] Marybelle. 'I don't like Smuggler's
Top – it's so queer and secret and lonely!'

The fall of the great house becomes a compensation for wartime
bereavement, or deprivation of necessities, in fact. *Brideshead Revisited* was published after *The Island of Adventure*; but, if Blyton
did react against the snobbish cult of English Gothic, she could have
found enough of it to annoy her in Waugh's *A Handful of Dust* (1934).
Blyton's was fundamentally the housewife's reaction to pretension –
and who is going to keep it clean? – but, as Vo Nguyen Giap would
point out when leading the Viet Minh against the French a few years
later, the housewife is the most important person in a guerrilla
revolution.

Blyton and Waugh wrote these books well after the Blitz (though
not, we must remember, after the German rocket 'flying bomb' attacks
on England in summer 1944, in some respects more horrific still). The
'revolutionary phase' of the war was over, or had at least adjusted
itself into convention; but Blyton and Waugh gave their adversary
witness to its implications. Fiction took its time to deliver, especially
as novel: Crompton as short-story writer was much closer to contemporary record. No doubt alliance with Russia seemed vaguely
revolutionary, even in Churchill's hilarious version of sponsorship
('if Hitler invaded Hell I would make at least a favourable reference to
the Devil in the House of Commons'), but it was chiefly the writers on
the right, such as Waugh, who saw it as a cutting edge of Revolution.
Left-wingers had not forgotten the Nazi–Soviet pact: they accepted the
Soviet Union in comradeship, but no longer in adulation.

Many of the most revolutionary elements in British popular culture
in 1940 had little if any identification with the USSR at all, at least
until the Grand Alliance was born in 1941–2. A characteristic
manifestation of the *Zeitgeist* emerged in the wartime comics from
the intransigent enemy of the trades unions, D. C. Thomson of
Dundee. The old school story for boys was doomed, subverted before
the war as it had been by its most popular and most remarkable
veteran, Frank Richards.[2] Gunby Hadath and a few others did what
they could with war themes such as schools fighting the bombs, or
schools making the best of evacuee schools quartered on them, or
schools losing pupils as adults in armed forces or quests for
sanctuary moved their families away from catchment areas.[3] But
the youthful proletariat no longer seemed invited to join in the

public-school cult in any of its inter-war versions, from Greyfriars School to Bendover College. If you wanted Gunby Hadath's *Grim and Gay* running in the *Boy's Own Paper* from October 1941, you paid your eightpence which last year had been sixpence and which next year would raise to ninepence; Hadath's title was Churchillian and his bombs tolerably plentiful, but any previous lower-class audience was written off. They found their fodder for twopence throughout the war in *Adventure, Rover, Skipper, Wizard* and *Hotspur*, where as early as February 1940 the tumbrils were beginning to roll. The *Hotspur*, the most socially upmarket, was certainly anticipating a Churchill Renaissance by appeals to a sublime imperial past, 'The School of No Surrender' bidding defiance not to Nazis in Europe but to sepoys at Lucknow. Its 'Reckless Men' of 'Q' Squadron dutifully lined up Spitfires against Messerschmitts. Looking forward to 9939, 'The Last Rocket to Venus' featured embattled evacuees from an uninhabitable Earth (possibly with faint thoughts of preparing readers for evacuation to North America). By contrast, 'Deadshot Dickon's School for Snipers' took what would prove an unduly optimistic look at the Western Front. But its perennial public school, Red Circle, was forced to cope with 200 evacuees planted on it from 'the industrial town of Ironmoor', defying its snobbish boys and masters and defending elderly imported temporary teachers from persecution:[4]

> At first Eggy and his pals had been as anxious as anyone else to get rid of the unwanted new master and then, quite by accident, Eggy had discovered something which had given him a terrific shock.
>
> He had seen a telegram to Mr Sloop which told him that his son, a flying-officer in the RAF, was missing, believed killed in action.
>
> 'It might have been his only son', Eggy had said. 'The chances are that he used to support his father. Without a job, Mr Sloop would have an awful time.'
>
> Eggy had told his special pals and they had wondered whether they should tell the other fellows what they had discovered, but they decided against doing so.
>
> 'Most of these chaps have never been poor', said Eggy. 'They wouldn't understand what unemployment means. They would probably still go on trying to get Mr Sloop the sack.'

This was in its way also a child of Richards, like almost all other school fiction. The *Magnet* author had played revolutionary notes in the name of service *esprit de corps* during the First World War, even having a soldier flogging a snobbish baronet.[5] Richards had made many a grim struggle for individual scholarship boys against snobs. Even the *Hotspur* passage above is followed by a hasty 'Eggy was actually very wrong in thinking that about the ordinary Red Circle boys', much as Harry Wharton and Co. would repent of a rag against the French master on hearing that M. Charpentier was in financial trouble through support for poverty-stricken relatives.[6] But the cutting edge of class conflict is clear enough. The poor boys from the town are right; the well-to-do school regulars are in the wrong. The usual (although not invariable) Greyfriars assumption was that school spirit would soften the neophyte and make him welcome, however unpleasant some of his encounters. For the *Hotspur* in 1940, the school spirit was simply anti-social, and the voice of the urban proletariat was the true one.[7]

But the school spirit was taking much worse punishment, quite literally, in other columns of the paper. Following the recent success of Agatha Christie in *Ten Little Niggers* (1939),[8] 'The Schoolboy Who Condemns' featured eleven headmasters lured to a ducal castle on Dartmoor whence they cannot escape or find the persecutor who flogs them, imprisons them, threatens them with Poe-style deaths and so on, all for crimes they have committed against their pupils, or even defended as educational policy, for example:

> They cowered against the wall. They were afraid to stay in any one place for long, lest a trap-door should open under their feet, or some horror descend from the ceiling. Their nerves were on edge all the time. Vane was nearly gibbering.
>
> For more than an hour they remained in that horrible chamber, and then from one of the walls came a hollow voice.
>
> 'Professor Vane, you once said at a school-teachers' conference that the only way to rule boys was to rule them by fear. How do you like being afraid?'
>
> The Professor shrieked:
>
> 'Let me out! Let me out of here, I beg you. I've changed my views, honestly I have. I'll never say anything like that again. Mercy!'

Or again:

> For about ten seconds Eccles lay there wondering what had happened to the bed-clothes, and then a powerful hand came out of the darkness and gripped him by the hair. A deft twist, and he was turned over on his stomach.

It was all done so suddenly that Dr Eccles had no time to struggle. A gasp escaped him, and then somewhere in the air above him he heard a swishing sound.

The next moment a pliable cane lashed down across his pyjamas. Swish! Swish! Swish!

With the full strength of a powerful arm the cane was wielded, and at the third cut Dr Eccles struggled and yelled at the top of his voice. The room rang with his cries.

Pinned in that helpless position, he found it difficult to turn, and meantime the cane worked fast. He must have received fully a dozen strokes when he was released as suddenly as he had been seized, and lay there sobbing with pain and rage.

The evacuee and her or his comic, the air-raid-shelter child and hers or his, are among the most poignant visions that the historian receives from this time. The reading of the comic (girls do not seem to have liked the word) could become a milestone in memory as strong as the impressions and opinions it might form. But the disruptions of the lives of those for whom the comic catered had begun with the outbreak of war, and the *Hotspur* at least seemed to pick that up. If change so big swept through Britain with the Battle of Britain and the Blitz – with its Finest Hour – that it partook of phenomena of revolution, the process was an earlier one for many children. Fathers torn away from them, then mothers, then homes – even then in some cases by bombs as well as by evacuation – revolution had happened in their lives. The *Hotspur*'s violation of the taboo on violence to the headmaster symbolised it. This was a very different matter from a crooked headmaster of a crooked school such as Squeers runs in Dickens's *Nicholas Nickleby*; and from portraits such as Richards developed with additional refinements over the years, of misfits who should never have been form-masters (such as Selby of St Jim's, or Hacker of Greyfriars); and from elegant etchings of magisterial inadequacy drawn with the professional touch of a schoolmaster of Glasgow Academy writing as Richard Bird or as Jeffrey Havilton. Only a bogus or crook headmaster (occasionally intruded into one of Richards's schools by the folly of the governors) was subject to possible brutality to his person; an ordinary master, however customarily respected and feared, might occasionally be deluged in soot or even ambushed and whacked, with consequent hell to pay, but the suggestion of violence to the Head won reactions from even his most rebellious boys, somewhat akin to Cavaliers' sentiments on the sacred majesty of kings. (That kind of sentiment is conspicuously

absent from the post-Second World War Richards stories: Divine
Right of Heads seems an apparent casualty of the war.) The *Hotspur*
story is not treating of vengeance on a crook or bogus Head: these are
not simply Heads, but Heads of their profession, heard with respect
and publicity (however ill-judged) at major professional conferences,
not only – as was traditional – 'Dr', but even the very unusual
'Professor'. The *Hotspur* tyrants-turned-victims do not seem to have
enjoyed the clerical status of public-school headmasters – fortunately since, to devout High Anglicans or Roman Catholics, the
person of a priest was actually sacred (and no doubt this in part
accounts for the Divine Right of Heads). But during the wars the
clerical status of non-Roman Catholic headmasters was less emphasised, and in the stories tends to disappear. It is impossible to imagine
Dr Arnold of Rugby other than as a clergyman. It is impossible to
imagine a headmaster in most *Beano* or *Dandy* stories actually being
one. Yet the violence of the act of describing the violence to the
headmasters has a slight whiff of anti-clericalism. Many revolutions
do begin with particular violence towards the established clergy. The
fall of the high priesthood is implicit in the overthrow of the *ancien
régime*. As Orwell would put it in *Animal Farm*:

> Moses, the tame raven . . . was a spy and a tale-bearer, but he was
> also a clever talker. He claimed to know of the existence of a
> mysterious country called Sugarcandy Mountain, to which all
> animals went when they died. . . .
>   [When the animals revolted] Mrs Jones . . . hurriedly flung a few
> possessions into a carpet bag, and slipped out of the farm by
> another way. Moses sprang off his perch and flapped after her,
> croaking loudly.

Similarly, the erosion of the revolution is symbolised by the return of
Moses:[9]

> A thing that was difficult to determine was the attitude of the pigs
> towards Moses. They all declared contemptuously that his stories
> about Sugarcandy Mountain were lies, and yet they allowed him to
> remain on the farm, not working, with an allowance of a gill of beer
> a day.

And, at the end of the war, the old headmaster might be subtly new
panoply as the school story entered its Indian summer before rekind-
ling its autumn fires with the new schoolboy heroes of Anthony

Buckeridge – Rex Milligan and Jennings (and Darbishire). A. Harcourt Burrage introduced a headmaster in *Odds Against* (1947), chiefly concerned about his own powers as a painter which he uses to honour boys of courage and merit. Gunby Hadath's *The March of Time* (1946) sought gallantly if unskilfully to address the archaism or relevance of the public school, but at least did so with a 'brand-new Head', a 'very young man, with deeply-set eyes and clean-shaven'.[10] Red Circle school using characters closely resembling Richards's prototypes exploited his Greyfriars boxer turned sports master, Larry Lascelles, when at the *Hotspur*'s foundation it was established with Dixie Dale, another sportsman, as a housemaster, and after the war he was its Head.[11]

One of the most distinguished of all post-war school stories was the novelist L. A. G. Strong's *Sink or Swim* (1945), with a superb character as Head, in holy orders, but universally known as 'The Boss', ruthless, charismatic, entertaining and childlike. A devoted friend confides (somewhat improbably) to the school captain:

'He's been the same ever since I've known him. He's never grown up. Don't let that blind you to his great qualities, though.'
'No fear of that, sir.'
'He is a great man – in some ways. Only he takes a very simple view of life. It's all in black and white. There are no half shades.'
'I know, sir. And –'
'Yes?'
'I was going to say, that even then it depends very often on the way he's feeling at the time.'
As the words left his mouth, Terry wondered if he had gone too far. But Mr Stoddert merely nodded.
'Yes', he said. 'It's an unfortunate trait in a public figure. It causes a good deal of misunderstanding.'
'That's just it, sir. People think he's inconsistent. Or even that he's a hypocrite.'
'I've told him so, before now.'
'Have you really, sir? Whatever did he say?'
'Oh, stormed and bellowed and paced up and down the room. But he saw the point, as soon as he'd calmed down. He's very fair-minded, really.'

This was obviously in the final phase of Britain's war, the stuff of Churchill's 'Triumph and Tragedy', all the more since the Rev. Athelstan Gray is elsewhere credited with 'an actor's voice' which he

used . . . quite shamelessly in the pulpit, with the result that he was
the most sought-after preacher in that part of England . . . With all
his natural gifts went an impulsiveness which his many critics
called irresponsible, and a trick of suddenly and violently speaking
his mind which meant that at any moment the congregation might
be electrified . . . He achieved publicity by his very nature.[12]

It could well have been a portrait of Churchill himself, particularly
for his ability to contain revolution by exuding a whiff of it. But the
revolution was definitely over in 1945, ready as Churchill was to seek
electoral capital by denouncing it. As Harry Hopkins would put it in
his *The New Look*, Britain turned to Marks and Spencer, not Marx
and Engels. But even a common identity in consumerism harked back
to the days of common destiny and briefly dissolved – or partly
dissolved – class barriers, when Blyton's little bourgeois adventurers
worshipped their fisher-boy leader (its links to the pre-war *Secret
Island* do not fully apply here – the lower-class orphan Jack leads the
once and future bourgeois Arnolds, but at that point their social
status, as unpaid domestic drudges, is even lower than his). Mordaunt pursued the Blitz among bombed-out slum-dwellers to act as
her models for fictional lower-class kids. Streatfeild painstakingly
got herself into workers' homes to populate her imagined Primrose
Lane. At this stage, it was identification, not patronising; indeed, the
most unflattering working-class child portrait in *The Children of
Primrose Lane* seems partly based on the author herself.[13] Barrie in
The Admirable Crichton (1902) had shown how crisis could dissolve
class barriers, ruthlessly restored when normality returned; Blyton's
Andy is somewhat Crichtonian, and like Crichton he is unlikely to
maintain his ascendancy when the children leave the milieu where he
has shown himself the natural master. He is too devoted to his father,
too seaborne and too Scottish to be redeemed by a warm-hearted
bourgeois adoption, as the rediscovered parent Arnolds adopt Jack,
and as Barney will rediscover his father in *The Rubadub Mystery*
(1952). Hence Andy as a leader who will remain in his own lower class
typifies the war *Zeitgeist* at revolutionary flashpoint, but cannot
travel beyond it. The sequel, though a post-war publication (1947,
serialised from March 1946),[14] is firmly set a year after the destruction
of enemy submarines, which are mentioned as though the enemy was
still an existing, if a more remote, phenomenon; and the bourgeois
three only have maternal supervision, the father's absence unexplained but to be taken as still in the RAF whether living or dead.[15]

   Eric Linklater's 'The Art of Adventure', his Rectorial Address at the University of Aberdeen on 26 October 1946, saw the end of the war as synonymous with the reimposition of order, after a wartime where revolution had to be nourished, at least as adventure, even when order was asserting itself: 'Never before had this country been so closely regimented, yet never had it more needed lonely adventurers; and never had it found so many'. Linklater, like Sir Walter Scott, was best as a historian when not formally writing history (where his own work was largely potboiler romantic). He had an ear for the historical dimension of a question which (again like Scott) he periodised in generations. It was in part Linklater's romanticism to see the revolutionary element as resurrecting long-buried historical national marks (and myths); Churchill instinctively shared that outlook (or inlook), and as war leader could be at his most stirring – and thus cliché-breaking, rule-questioning, humdrum-smashing revolutionary – when inhaling and expectorating historical atmosphere. Thus Linklater:[16]

> The late war, indeed, was a new encyclopaedia of adventure, of individual and small adventure, and that was a strange unlikely characteristic of a struggle waged with conscript forces, with more massive armament, with a more ponderous deliberation of policy than ever before; but because our battle-lines were so long – straddling three continents, the seas between and the sky above – and because with insufficient strength we had to engage a more numerous enemy as best we could, until our potent allies were ready to attack, we were often compelled to use, as well as our known divisions in the field, a hidden reserve. A reserve that neither our friends nor our foes believed in, that we ourselves had almost forgotten. A reserve that we had inherited – it was a fortune indeed – from our ancestors the Scottish soldiers of fortune and the Elizabethan voyagers. And with this heritage of audacity in their souls, with this ancestral complement of self-reliance, our soldiers and sailors and airmen set out on their forays to wound and perplex the enemies whom we could not, as yet, challenge to decisive battle.

Linklater's adventure amounted to celebration of people being forced to make decisions themselves, alone or in small groups and then fragments of those groups, sometimes in defiance of existing known commands (the Nelson eye), sometimes in furtherance of them by hitherto unimagined means. His little girls acting in defiance of their father to help him regain his freedom in *The Wind on the Moon* are a perfect example of it.

Shaw in reviewing a dramatised version of Anthony Hope's *The Prisoner of Zenda* (*Saturday Review*, 11 January 1896), ridiculed the English at their high peak of imperial complacency:[17]

> The notion that in England every futile, harum-scarum, good-naturedly selfish Johnny is a hero who only needs opportunity to display the noblest qualities, and have his hand kissed by veterans and high-souled ladies, is as popular, because as widely flattering, as that other idea that our yachts constitute a reserve fleet, and our shopmen a reserve army which in case of invasion would rush from behind the counter to hurl the foe back in confusion from the soil of England. It is, of course, pleasant to think that valuable qualities are dirt cheap in our own country; but I, unluckily, am constitutionally sceptical as to the heroism of people who never do anything heroic.

Fifty years later – more exactly, forty-five – a much diminished England, isolated, humiliated, sent scuttling from the continent of Europe in a disaster whose full horror was only averted by the inexplicable delay of the victors, proved that the little petty-bourgeois pleasure-boats and fisher-boys' small craft (Blyton's Andy and Richards's Tom Redwing) might be pathetic replacements for the yachts of the late Victorian plutocrats (a yacht of old-style plutocratic dimensions in British juvenile fiction of the late 1930s was usually American),[18] but that perhaps they did help constitute a reserve fleet at Dunkirk. And the shopmen became a regular army in the Home Guard while their errand-boys and petty pilferers went into the firing-line. No doubt many encountered no greater heroic moment than they had before it; but the expectation of meeting the firing-line on one's roof or one's head gave an incentive to revolution. And it was Shaw himself (after the appropriate obstetrical interval of nine months) who made the great definition of revolution in *The Devil's Disciple* that it makes people discover they are someone other than whom they had believed themselves to be – the reprobate learns that he is a natural clergyman, the clergyman learns that he is a natural general.

Much of the heroics, as Crompton reminded everyone, were the result of luck, coincidence, folly, illusion – but they were still adventures, and in children's hands or books they still had the revolutionary ideal of children overcoming or surpassing grown-ups. William captured three spies in twenty-four wartime stories, which was probably a realistic statistic; but (as a rule to the deep regret of his seniors) he remained perpetually on the alert, poised for adventure, awaiting his revolutionary moment. Conspicuously, Linklater did *not* invoke the awesome power of Victorian Britain and Empire: he talked of lone Scots adventurers and small English privateers, from days when Scotland and England were small, weak, peripheral countries sometimes no more than French or Spanish satellites. Grandiose neo-Elizabethan panoply in the 1950s might assume first-class power status for the Tudor monarchy. Linklater knew better. Children and childlike combatants could 'wound and perplex'; children's fiction above all else celebrated the trick, the subterfuge, the deceit of seemingly innocuous infants bringing destruction on their opponents. From translating Homer in the public schools to the retelling of *Odyssey* by Andrew Lang or Roger Lancelyn Green (or Enid Blyton); from Brer Rabbit retold by Joel Chandler Harris (or Enid Blyton); from the various legends of Merlin retold by Tennyson or Sir James Knowles or T. H. White (or Enid Blyton); from the deeds of Loki retold by (among others) Enid Blyton – the trickster is a perpetual object of fascination for the young. He brings heroics with the compass of possibility of a child. He is weak, but he can outwit the strong. Most of the William stories turn on tricks, all the better because the audience cannot be sure that William will win. The Billy Bunter stories are even more dependent on such a point, with the difference that, while William is heroic, if frequently absurd, Bunter is anti-heroic, William likeable, Bunter dislikeable, both facets of the sometimes benevolent, sometimes malignant Odysseus, Brer Rabbit, Merlin, Loki, Fionn Mac Cumhaill (as in Ossianic legend though not as in *Ossian*) or Gwydion (as in the *Mabinogion*). But the whole character of Second World War fiction had to posit such roles for children (even Waugh's Connollys seem ultimately to be shrewd tricksters rather than simple delinquents). Johns's Worrals and Frecks are women, fighting their corners against British men as well as German Nazis; but they are also girls, a year or two from being children, playing tricks that children in a crisis could play. Their planes are important, their wit and resource much more so: above all, they shine in the art of pretended foolishness and (less pretended) vulnerability, and do it better than men, who are less able to discard self-importance. Johns's commandos are introduced as tough guys who are hopelessly outclassed by a parcel of cunning teenagers, however much control they regain later: 'wound and perplex' might be the Grey Fleas' motto.

The famous sneer of the librarian Eileen Colwell in reviewing Blyton's *The Sea of Adventure* in 1948 – 'But what hope has a band of desperate men against four children?' – misses the point completely while hitting the nail on the head. Blyton was of course still creating in terms of Second World War presumptions, and a Britain in arms against Nazis at the height of their power had to believe the apparently absurd dream. Thanks to Blyton, children during the Blitz were given the greater will. The surviving wartime atmosphere of *The Sea of Adventure* (for all of its nominally post-war status) is maintained by the enemy's aeroplanes, seaplanes, guns, parachutes, secret bases, midnight raids and the facts that they are referred to as 'the enemy', that they are not defeated at the end – we are simply assured that they will be – and that much of the terror felt by underground resistance in Nazi-occupied territory chills once again when the children hide during enemy sojourn on Puffin Island, and are even threatened by watchers outside their home. And implicit in the whole idea of this and the variety of other child interventions into wartime conflict is the strength of what seems beneath contempt. Several writers for children were to attempt variants of the theme throughout the Second World War, but its sublime assertion was being worked out during the war by J. R. R. Tolkien in *The Lord of the Rings*. While the forces of Sauron rain death from the skies over Gondor, the centre of enemy power collapses very suddenly because two small hobbits have worked their way almost entirely unnoticed through the defences of Mordor and reached Mount Doom.

Linklater worried about the post-war fetish of security, understandable in the age of nuclear terror, understandable also as war receded and austerity was expected to unbend (although sweets would be rationed until 1953):[19]

> Security is indeed our contemporary Mecca, and our politicians, our economists, and social prophets all look towards it, and plan their itinerary. . . . I would not suggest that you take Lady Macbeth for your exemplar in life, but it is worth your while, perhaps, to observe that in her opinion 'Security is mortals' chiefest enemy'; and another Elizabethan, a doughty shipmate of Sir Walter Raleigh called Lawrence Keymis, held the same belief. 'To kiss security', he wrote, 'is the plain highway to a fearful downfall.' So, then, if security is your chosen objective, I suggest that you approach it warily, and not without proper reconnaissance; for it may be an ambush.

It was in fact an ambush in active preparation during the war itself, as far as children's literature was concerned.

To return to our periodisation: once Britain had had its finest hour and was encumbered as well as emancipated by what Churchill called 'The Grand Alliance' (the USSR and the USA having been provided to the UK as such by the folly of Hitler's war declarations), British culture began to redevelop security-consciousness. It was now the Americans and the Russians whose susceptibilities had to be protected where once it had been the Germans. Curiously enough, T. S. Eliot was the most eminent voice in restraint of undesirable children's literature in American as well as Russian contexts in 1944. As the author of *Old Possum's Book of Practical Cats* (1939), he had the best of credentials as an open critic of books for the young; but his was a more soft-footed path. Perhaps he had been frank enough in his last cat-portrait, 'Cat Morgan introduces himself'. It is supposedly spoken by the cat of Faber & Faber whereof he was poetry director, but on suitable occasions Eliot could style himself Cat Morgan, who 'once was a Pirate what sailed the 'igh seas, but now, 'as retired as a com-mission-aire'. His avant-garde days were well behind him, and his right-wing politics had also become more circumspect.

Three months after Eliot's veto for *Animal Farm*, he was speaking on 9 October 1944 as president of the British section of 'Books Across the Sea' in the Waldorf Hotel, where he evangelised the forthcoming exhibitions of British books for children in New York, and American ones in London. His sense of cultural control was so strong that he actually began by seriously discussing though ultimately dismissing a view that no more children's books should be published:[20] 'People sometimes ask me why there should be any new children's books when there are so many established children's classics'. One wonders, bemusedly, who, if anyone, produced this startling piece of totalitarian Philistinism, and why they should have taken it to be appropriate conversation to hold with Eliot. Its argument was not likely to have appealed to Hitler, Stalin or Mussolini (though its implicit ruthless authoritarianism would have); they encouraged children's literature of the more nauseating exemplary-young-party-comrade variety. Orwell was to do savage hatchet-work on the species in *1984*, where Winston Smith invents the edifying life of Comrade Ogilvy:[21]

At the age of three Comrade Ogilvy had refused all toys except a drum, a sub-machine gun, and a model helicopter. At six – a year early, by a special relaxation of the rules – he had joined the Spies; at nine he had been a troop leader. At eleven he had denounced his uncle to the Thought Police after overhearing a conversation which appeared to him to have criminal tendencies. At seventeen he had been a district organizer of the Junior Anti-Sex League. At nineteen he had designed a hand-grenade which had been adopted by the Ministry of Peace and which, at its first trial, had killed thirty-one Eurasian prisoners in one burst. . . .

(This was the irreverent outgrowth of Orwell's gloomy reflections in 'Boys' Weeklies' on the unlikelihood of providing appropriate left-wing literature for children.) Eliot's supposed interlocutors recall a different tradition, better known in his native Missouri. H. L. Mencken, reporting Biblical fundamentalism in the adjoining state of Tennessee in 1925, attended a revival meeting in the hills where[22]

> there arose out of the darkness a woman with her hair pulled back into a little tight knot. She . . . was denouncing the reading of books. Some wandering book agent, it appeared, had come to her cabin and tried to sell her a specimen of his wares. She refused to touch it. Why, indeed, read a book? If what was in it was true, then everything in it was already in the Bible. If it was false, then reading it would imperil the soul.

Sympathy with such logic the author of *Old Possum's Book of Practical Cats* would naturally have disclaimed, but that he wanted his New York audience to savour its British equivalent is instructive. The invention of imaginary extremists against whom to take a seemingly moderate position is an old device; whether or not Eliot had heard such opinions in 1944 England, it strengthened the impression that some form of cultural convention needed to be imposed. One opposed prohibition of new literature for children; one therefore strongly urged the fostering of high standards. One sounded firm:[23]

> children, as much as anybody else, need contemporary books as well as classics; and particularly is this so in the case of English and American children reading books from the other country. The early impressions children get of another country are very largely from the books they read for pleasure. The notions that English children form of the life of American children, and *vice versa*, are the foundation for the ideas which they will have later. To concern ourselves with children's books, therefore, is simply to plan a long way ahead.

The chimera of a future with no books published for children had its own relevance to Eliot, in any case (as well as to his employers, Faber & Faber, with their long 'juvenile' list). The Exhibition of American Books for children, at Chaucer House, Malet Street, London, was opened in Eliot's presence on 13 November 1944 (to last one week), by Sir Ernest Barker, the great political scientist and philosopher of liberalism, who remembered the three American books which most affected his own childhood – Hawthorne's *Tanglewood Tales*, Cooper's *The Last of the Mohicans* and Mark Twain's '*Tom Sawyer* – or still more, perhaps, *Huckleberry Finn*'. This change of three to four was no doubt gratifying to a Missourian; but Eliot hardly wished to be thought of as Missourian, primarily, and if Missourian hardly yearning for the uncouth Missouri of the 1840s when Mark Twain (then still Sam Clemens) witnessed what became the raw material of his books. One very clear fact to Americans listening to remarks made in Britain in the early 1940s on US literature was that the nineteenth century had made a great impression, and the twentieth century very little. Orwell's fine essay 'Riding Down from Bangor' some months later unintentionally made the same point: for all of its gospel of progress and modernisation, the USA that had taken firm root in the British child mind was the lost world of Leatherstocking, of Tom and Huck, of Alcott's March sisters, of John Habberton's *Helen's Babies* and, as Ernest Barker said, of old stories retold by American masters.[24] Barker, whose son Nicolas would be the major British historian of typography of his time, noted the sharp contrast between British and American book production, which might account for the difficulty that British booksellers reported in selling American books: 'American books come to us with a type, an amount of paper, and a spelling which are all unusual, and similarly with the books that go to the United States'.[25] He was almost certainly right: book-buying children were often conservative, although comic-buying children might be much more ready to welcome the exciting presentation of Superman and his terrestrial rivals if their comics were picture-comics rather than word-comics. A print-dominated child had only recently established its authority over the printed word and resented its newly mastered spelling having its conventions challenged in more expensive and exotic print. A picture-dominated child was interested in looking at new kinds of picture.

What neither Barker nor Eliot mentioned, though what many of their audience may have thought, was that the child of 1944 was conversant and sometimes all too familiar with British comics which weekly produced their versions of America, a place excitingly and timelessly dominated by cowboys, 'Red Indians', gangsters and some very peculiar forms of education. Your favourite frontiersman might be pursued by Injun hordes in one series and find himself at ferocious war with Nazis in the next. Most of the authors of these products in D. C. Thomson's *Adventure* were British and are unlikely to have visited the United States. Some wrote blatantly and happily in the same Scottish strain as Barrie's pirates and Indians in Peter Pan's Never-Never-Land, though others had got up their history of the American west with great industry and, sometimes, insight. Medicine-men played around with the supernatural, though their western enchantments might be rivalled – in the same area – by Chinese disseminators of invisibility and Viking horns inducing berserk consequences for the mildest imbiber. Some were intentionally quite funny, such as the saga of 'Mild Bill' the cousin of 'Wild Bill' (Hickok, presumably), who accomplished deeds of daring-do with the crook of an umbrella. There was little actual anti-Americanism (since Richards had retired from publication with his repulsive capitalist schoolboy Fisher T. Fish), but it made for a far more unreal view of the USA than readers of the new Puffin storybooks could acquire for ninepence about Sweden, the Netherlands or even Russia.[26]

Barker, the embodiment of British liberal instincts at their least aggressive, told his audience that cultural ambassadorship was probably 'best when uncalculated, as with the book which came across like light seed on the wind, settled, and germinated'. He cited Whitman's poems and Herman Melville's *Moby-Dick*. Eliot, as an American, a publisher and a conservative, remained severely author-itarian: 'we believe that the books that children read for pleasure have an important relation to their education, and that the education of children has an important relation to the future maintenance and development of Anglo-American relations'. Children's pleasure was therefore a serious matter. In so saying, he echoed sentiments in inchoate circulation. Children were certainly interested in Ameri-cans, having learned to chew gum from many a GI and profited by their easy generosity. This sometimes went to extreme results, as when sweet rations and GI departures meant that gum fell into short supply, so that when a whale was washed up on the coast of north Wales the children endeavoured to extract portions of its carcass in the belief the blubber made chewing-gum. They also saw Americans literally giving their lives to save British families, such as the crew of the American USAF plane who deliberately crashed in Escott Park, in Sheffield, rather than endanger housing areas by landing on them when the aircraft was doomed.[27] In his October speech, Eliot had made clear his association's purpose to promote better understanding between the English-speaking peoples through books:[28]

> The American and British sections together hope to co-operate in establishing relations with groups of people among our allies and to help those which are temporarily famished even of books in their own languages and to establish exchanges.

This was eminently, and even movingly, praiseworthy but carried with it a role for British culture-custodians which would supervise, judge and maybe even grade what children were reading and how far it might be trusted to further British images in America and British–American interests across the world. It symbolises the move away from freedom of writing for children in the heady days of Blitz and after; as Waugh would put it entitling the books in his future trilogy, *Men at Arms* was succeeded by *Officers and Gentlemen*. Values, style, taste, social attitudes, characters with whom to identify – were to receive closer scrutiny from official eyes: the two exhibitions were putting British culture for children on parade on an official basis. (Ernest Barker was speaking for the former freedom of discovery, Eliot for its future control.) One ominous note had been struck, and Eliot must have sensed its irony. On view at the meeting on 9 October was the 2,000th book sent by the United States to Britain as an 'ambassador' in the Books Across the Sea project: it was an inscribed copy of Dixon Wecter's *When Johnny Comes Marching Home*, a study of American soldiers' return to their families and residences after various wars. Eliot was now an expatriate, dressed more English than the English; but he certainly did not want to see a return to American isolation. Americans had to be convinced that contemporary British culture, above all the culture of the future Britons, was worth remaining in Europe to further and defend. And if British children's literature was not of a standard that Eliot thought appropriate, so much the worse for the future. The natural puritanical instincts of librarians could now take more formal shape: it was no longer 'go out and see what the children are doing and tell them not to do it', but it could be 'see what they are reading and make sure they ought to be reading it'.[29]

British – or rather, English – standards of quality in children's literature had had one yardstick well established, the Library Association Carnegie Medal founded in 1936; but the war had put it at some disadvantage. For one thing, the Medal had its own problems as to what and who it was for, and who was to decide to whom it was to be awarded, and on what principles and how firmly phrased. It originally established itself as 'for the best book for children published in the British Empire' in 1936.[30] Descriptions were loose, and the Association decided by 1941 that it no longer meant the best book; to do so risked libel actions, especially in a year in which no award was made. The 'British Empire' became 'England'. Given Andrew Carnegie's Scottish birth and identity (other than in his American industrial, plutocratic and philanthropic capacities), the terms were either mad or bad: supposedly, the Association was honouring Carnegie's memory, and was clearly doing so with a view to attracting interest and support from the many trustees and funds established under Carnegie's estate, and yet its elimination of Scots as well as Welsh and Northern Irish was either bigoted or parochial or both. The Association may not in fact have meant to exclude them: in these years, better-class persons spoke of 'England' when they meant 'Britain' or 'the United Kingdom', an affectation of ignorance having long been an emblem of the aristocracy, the judiciary and the intellectual. The Liberal and Socialist historians R. C. K. Ensor and A. J. P. Taylor entitled their excellent Oxford histories of the British Isles in the late nineteenth and early twentieth centuries *England* and *English History* respectively, and in the late 1950s Nancy Mitford explained that such a usage (or should it be 'an usage'?) marked one as 'U' rather than 'non-U'. In part, the usage 'England' was a sudden substitute for 'the Empire' from 1940 in many more places than the Carnegie Medal. The old joke, that when Stanley Baldwin's wife sought instruction before her marriage on what to do when Baldwin wished to exercise his conjugal privilege she was told 'shut your eyes and think of the Empire', was now rendered 'Lie back and think of England'. The patriotic song 'There'll always be an England' replaced imperial rallying-cries. But it was 'England', not 'Britain'.[31] It was not until Eric Linklater, Welsh-born Scottish nationalist parliamentary candidate and Orcadian resident, became a prime candidate for the Medal for 1944 that the terms were finally changed to read:[32]

The Library Association Carnegie Medal will be awarded for an outstanding book for children by a British subject domiciled in the United Kingdom (Great Britain and Northern Ireland), published in Great Britain during the year, which is considered worthy of the award.

Chief librarians, in consultation with their children's librarians, are asked to submit a preliminary list of not more than six titles, from which the Committee will make a final selection. The award is open to works of non-fiction as well as fiction and the choice should be based upon a consideration of all the following points:

Fiction: (1) Plot; (ii) Style; (iii) Characterization; (iv) Format (including production and illustrations, if any).

Non-Fiction: (i) Accuracy; (ii) Method of Presentation; (iii) Style; (iv) Format, etc.

These lists should reach the Secretary of the Library Association, Chaucer House, Malet Place, London, W.C.1, not later than the 28th February, 1945, giving author and title and including only books within the terms of the award and published during the year 1944.

The particulars for 1943 had specified 'an English author, published in England', and for the first time no award was made that year: a major writer having entered the lists for 1944, in Linklater's case, it was clear that the Association would be on the dilemma-horns of the English question (viz. What is 'England'?) if they did not hastily house-clean. An award for Linklater (almost certainly 1944's best choice) could leave the Medal open to legal action from any publisher who correctly pointed out that Linklater was ineligible under the old rules. House-cleaning had also taken place in other directions. The first award had been announced in the *Library Association Record* for 1937 by the editor, R. D. Hilton Smith, F.L.A., in an effusive editorial bearing the genial comment:[33]

> The intention is not merely to memorialise Andrew Carnegie; it is hoped that any author who is awarded this medal will thereby receive a hallmark of excellence which will have considerable publicity value and will encourage the publication of better children's books. It is not to be assumed that we think that such writers as Walter de la Mare, Arthur Ransome, [Erich] Kästner, Rose Fyleman, and several others who may be named, are not writers of the highest class for children; we need more such authors, and many more books.

The nominating body was vaguely described as 'the Children's librarians from many important libraries', and the decision was to be made by 'the subcommittee charged with this matter'. However blind the horse in question, it knew a nod and a wink, especially since it had given them: Hilton Smith was one of the four judges. The first Medal went to Arthur Ransome for *Pigeon Post.* Ransome's inventive genius might well divide his admirers into different categories — sailing enthusiasts, students of child character, English landscape-lovers and (for the work which made his series take off, *Peter Duck*) zealots for a modern *Treasure Island* — but few would rate *Pigeon Post* supreme for any of these. De la Mare, most delicate and elusive of children's fictionists, had nothing new that year, nor would have in prose again, so that hint had to await Faber's publication of his purely retrospective *Collected Stories for Children*, which was duly given the Medal for 1947. It was essentially marking his lifetime's achievement, just as Ransome's was for his series. Both were great writers, but the awards strayed far from encouragement of new talent or even best or outstanding book of the year. Edward Ardizzone, later the great war artist, had a strong claim in 1936 for his *Little Tim and the Brave Sea-Captain*, so ably mingling text, artwork, character and epic story. Another original newcomer was Barbara Euphan Todd's *Worzel Gummidge*. As for the other names touted, the German Kästner was ineligible, and clearly a blind. Fyleman had an élite vogue, but by now at least her publications were too slight for even the most partial judgement which could sustain scrutiny.

The children's librarians were evidently aggrieved at this stitch-up (not that anyone should have grudged Ransome his prize), and formed their own Association in 1937, which would protest against the 1938 Medal going to Noel Streatfeild's *The Circus is Coming*, more especially because only two members of the subcommittee had bothered to be present to make the choice. The protest was officially ignored; but one candidate preferred by the Children's Librarian Association, Streatfeild's cousin-in-law Kitty Barne, was given the Medal for 1940 when her *Visitors from London* made itself topical by treating of evacuees. The subcommittee was a little jumpy by this point: it had tried to avoid giving any award for 1939 and was told by the Library Association executive committee that it was to choose Eleanor Doorly's *The Radium Woman*, a life of Madame Marie Curie, dead as recently as 1934, and as a Polish-born French scientist a nice blend of wartime alliance and technical aspiration. The war continued to dominate selection the next year, with Mary Treadgold's Channel Island thriller *We Couldn't Leave Dinah*. The Library Assocation was also running into problems about its criteria. The early vagueness was offset by very firm justification of the Ransome award after it had been made:[34]

> The Committee of selection were actuated by one or two principles which we believe to be of importance in the consideration of

children's books for such an award. In the first place it had to be a book for 'children', and what was taken to be the normal average reading age for children was that into which the book was expected to fall; that is to say, it was to be a book for a child somewhere between the ages of nine and twelve, but need not be absolutely within these age limits. Its appeal was to be universal, and therefore it was to be a book which appealed to both sexes equally, so far as any book could. It is possible that the greatest books for children do possess this equal appeal. In literary form it should be in the best English; its story should follow the line of the possible, if not the probable; its characters should be alive, its situations credible, and its tone in keeping with the generally accepted standards of good behaviour and right thinking. On the physical side, the book should be well bound, the type perfectly legible, the paper of good quality, and the binding and decoration adequate.

Such conditions ruled out J. R. R. Tolkien's *The Hobbit* from the following year's entry, it being neither possible nor probable; and Bilbo Baggins in fact departs from the standards of good behaviour and right thinking generally accepted among hobbits in order to follow Gandalf and the dwarves. But the conditions were evidently incompatible with the Second World War. Barne and Treadgold had written convincing war adventures. Then the 1942 award went to a fine entry, *The Little Grey Men*, written and illustrated by 'B.B.' (D. J. Watkins-Pitchford); but its protagonists were gnomes. Crouch's account of the Carnegie Medal, *Chosen for Children* (1957), was defensive on the issue:

> He chose to write about gnomes, but [it] is not a fantasy. It is a consistent picture of the natural world. There is no magic in it. Even the destruction of Giant Grum (the gamekeeper) is accomplished not by the intervention of Pan but by the application of a piece of sportsman's lore.[35]

'Lore' is right: it gave its young readers sound instruction in committing a neat and almost undetectable murder, by shoving leaves up a gun-barrel. Its ruthlessness was no doubt one result of the war climate, increasing public tolerance of what authors might say and children read. Pan (who tells the gnomes how to do the job) is of course as much fantasy as he was in Kenneth Grahame's *The Wind in the Willows*, albeit as homicidal as he was in Saki's 'The Music on the Hill'. Two years later, Linklater certainly confronted Hitler (as Hulagu Bloot) but had previously turned his heroines into kangaroos, which took credibility and possibility even farther than hobbits and gnomes. The conceivable had been stretched beyond all previous children's experience, and the Library Association responded by welcoming fantasy.

But was War still Art? In 1943 and 1945, the wartime years of no Medal, leading candidates were war-related fiction, and this may have been their doom. It is also possible that the overworked librarians did not get enough time from their other duties; with premises endangered by bombing, and personnel reduced by armed or civilian services recruitment, 1943 could simply have been one task too many, what with the number to be read, the notices to scan, the correspondence to be mounted. The Linklater entry for 1944 was unavoidable – no adult novelist of such stature had hitherto come under the Medal's terms (once 'England' had been dropped); and, with exhibitions and donations of children's literature crossing the Atlantic both ways to the applause of T. S. Eliot and Professor Sir Ernest Barker, this was no time to repeat 'Prize withheld as no book considered suitable'. But 1945 was another matter. No further books across the sea could be conscripted; massive post-war reappraisal and redevelopment filled librarians' in-trays and cups. Nevertheless, there were strong candidates each year, and their omission may have been due to more than overworked staff. Was nothing suitable? Children clearly felt much was, as sales of Johns, Blyton, Crompton and Westerman leaped upwards, and the BBC beamed its discovery of remarkable new figures such as Malcolm Saville, whose *Mystery at Witchend* received the signal tribute of wireless broadcast alongside publication in 1943.

Saville's case certainly pinpoints some crisis in the status of children's fiction in Second World War Britain. Victor Watson, in an appreciative analysis of his work in *Reading Series Fiction* (2000), remarks that he 'started off as "his own man" and was obliged to turn into a Blyton'.[36] So did Blyton, whose pioneer work in the late 1930s was of high quality, and whose translation into a triumphant machine in the 1940s led to critics' losing sight of her best work. But Saville differed from Blyton, Brent-Dyer, Crompton, Richards, Johns and other great mass-producers in opening his authorial career in 1943 with his best book. Ironically, the Carnegie Medal winner of 1941, Treadgold, had done just that, not that anyone save possibly herself realised it at the time; but her titles would never come anywhere near Saville's eighty. The classic case is the great Edgar

Wallace, whose ocean of books contained many of distinction, but who never produced anything to equal his eldest literary child, *The Four Just Men*.

Ransome's fans will include those to make such a case for *Swallows and Amazons*, but his mass readership seems definitely to have preferred *Peter Duck*: does one want them with or without villains? Saville has a slight comparable conflict with the villainless second story, *Seven White Gates* (1944). But what keeps *Mystery at Witchend* firmly in the lead is its use of the war, a much more unreal, though important, background force in *Seven White Gates*. *Mystery at Witchend* comes close to being the outstanding novel of children in the Second World War, all the more because it enchanted so many of them during it, first by wireless and then in print. It was clearly intended to alert children to the dangers of Nazi penetration in the countryside, to alert them even more to loving that countryside, to preach its glories to town children by means of assuring town children how much they would enjoy making it theirs, to delight in Shropshire topography with a precision, fervour and confidence harking back to Stevenson's *Kidnapped*, to think about one another's characters and how best to learn the subtleties of adolescent diplomacy, and to celebrate the Home Guard as human but heroic. As such, it had blended beautifully with the spirit of BBC Children's Hour and 'Uncle Mac'. It is just possible that one strike against *Mystery at Witchend* in the eyes of the Carnegie adjudicators (if their eyes were open to anything at all in 1943) was that very airwave success. It may have been obscurely linked to serialisation in comics (would the Carnegie Medal judges have thought kindly of serialisation in *Sunny Stories* or the *Boy's* – or *Girl's* – *Own Paper*, or *Happy Mag* or *Modern Woman*?). Since wireless reached a mass audience, it was by definition vulgar (especially as the favourite programme of the war years, *It's That Man Again* (*ITMA*), was most emphatically vulgar).

Mystery at Witchend was one of the clearest cases of a book between the bombs: Saville wrote it while functioning as an ARP watchman at nights. After a professional life in publishing, at Oxford (at 19), Cassell, the Amalgamated Press (1922–36) and Newnes (initially 1936–41), he had ample precedents to study, notably Richards, Crompton and Blyton. But he wrote *Mystery at Witchend* when his wife, two sons and two daughters had been sent to the Shropshire the Savilles had come to know in 1940. Its first line, 'They changed trains at Shrewsbury', opens discovery for the young Mortons, disappearance for the author. Its cool, intimate, humorous prose covers a father's fears that children sent to safety from the bombs could face dangers from sabotage and espionage. He sent them every chapter for comment.

Mystery at Witchend could have been termed 'improbable' – but so, by the standards of the pre-war Carnegie Medallists, were all British children's experiences from the start of the Second World War. It climaxed on the very late discovery that Nazi agents had penetrated into Shropshire whence they were to blow up all nearby reservoirs, actually succeeding in the case of the smallest and nearest at hand, in a scene of some considerable power. The children are 15-year-old David Morton, his nine-year-old twin sister and brother Mary and Dickie, and their friends Peter (Petronella) Sterling and Tom Ingles; the Home Guard is aided by Bill Ward, a sailor on leave whose father is its local captain:

David was now on the rock with Peter and shouting, 'Higher, Tom! Higher! It's coming now!' There were confused shoutings also from the men on the hill-tops, and some with very grim faces were sliding down to meet them.

'Let the pony go, Ward', one called. 'She'll look after herself.'

Then strong arms hoisted the twins on to broad shoulders, and another gave a helping hand to Tom, and all climbed till they were as high as the rock on which Peter and David were standing, and the rushing noise became a mighty roar. They were all looking now at the spot where the steep valley was made narrower by the jutting rock.

'Jiminy!' breathed Tom. 'Great Jiminy Cricket! The reservoir's gone!'

And even as he spoke the earth shook again, and the rock was hidden in a cloud of spray. They had a dim vision of Peter and David clinging together, and then a colossal wave of grey-brown water swung round the corner in a mad, whirling, tearing roar of fury. The first wave was crowned with bushes and trees and planks, and swept majestically down the valley. Actually they were standing well above its highest level, but if they hadn't climbed quickly they would all have been swept away in the flood.

'Gosh!' said Mary thoughtfully. 'Just like the children of Israel.'

'No', said Dickie. 'I know what you mean, but it's old Pharaoh in the Red Sea.'

The last is a nice touch: the children's brush with death gives them a faint breath, *Titanic*-style, of momentarily being nearer, my God, to

Thee, but they translate the Divine proximity into a cheerful argument about Biblical stories. The progress of the ruined reservoir may derive in part from Macaulay's 'Horatius' when the Tiber carries away the fallen bridge, but the spectacle seems a sufficiently effective guess as to the fate of some British landscapes had such a Nazi campaign made its mark. When the reservoir-keeper's daughter sees the result –

> in one place the pipes themselves had been torn up and the broken ends were sticking up grotesquely from a welter of mud and debris.
>
> Peter forced back a sob. Lovely Hatchholt! The valley in which she had known every stick and stone – every sheep track, every rabbit-hole, every nest – nothing now but a muddy, smelly waste.
>
> The others seemed to understand, for they didn't say anything to her when they caught her up. Even Dickie and Mary were awed into silence.

Saville could write. It's particularly notable because of the relative absence of such scenes from Second World War fact and fiction, the country escaping most of the urban horrors, and what it did sustain receiving little report. The book itself is arched all too symmetrically, having begun with the arrival of the Mortons at Shrewsbury in flight from destruction ('We had bombs in London'). And Saville has been subtly invoking rural literary images, hinting of potential danger from mysterious strangers but playing with carefully planted local superstition to convey menace when the actual danger is almost entirely from human agents. The children are not so much the discoverers as the occasion of spy-discovery (much as the realistic Crompton's William is), chiefly because the twins get lost on the mountain and have heard why the Devil's Chair on the Stiperstones is sometimes invisible:[37]

> Something had happened to the weather. A damp, cold wind touched them gently, and as they looked round, bewildered, the outline of the rolling hilltop wavered and grew indistinct.
>
> Dickie turned back the way they had come, and slowly pointed across the valley to the Stiperstones. The hills were there, but looked different. Softer.
>
> 'Mary', he whispered. 'Look! The Chair's not there. It's gone. It's like Bill said, Mary. He's in his chair . . .'
>
> And the mist came rolling silently across the valley as if a giant was blowing great balls of soft white cotton wool.

Reworked as dialogue alone, that made a memorable end to the second of four wireless instalments. Listeners and readers would hark back to Bill Ward's talk with the twins on the train at the start of the story, when many would have felt that the children would ultimately experience the Devil in his chair. In retrospect, it would seem a metaphor for the Nazis gaining a base on the Shropshire hills, as well as a neat device to drive the twins back to the spy haven they have just left. But the Devil on his chair actually contrasts with the Nazis in being openly frightening: Saville presented Second World War children's fiction with a real psychological challenge – likeable spies. Only Brent-Dyer's relatively innocent and cruelly blackmailed Gertrud comes into that category – the Nazi general's spoiled but endearingly lonely granddaughter in Treadgold's Channel Island is not a spy. Blyton's *The Island of Adventure* (1944) was a story of forgers rather than spies (although Johns, post-war, made much of Nazi uses for forgery). The *Times Literary Supplement* took it for a spy story, however; and while this, no doubt, was shoddy reviewing – all too frequent a fate for children's books in leading literary journals whence librarians formed opinions – the error is probably instructive. Blyton's withdrawal from direct war fiction after her divorce from Major Pollock certainly resulted in metaphor, conscious or unconscious. Jo-Jo, the black servant, is in fact a spy, and an extremely intelligent one, whether in Nazi or ordinary crook ranks; he is unpleasant to the children, specifically (as is ultimately discovered) to keep them from finding out his forger colleagues on the island. Blyton smoothly gives us the clue to this in detective-story concealment:

> What fun they would have had if he had been jolly and good-tempered! They could have gone fishing and sailing in his boat. They could have fished properly with him. They could have gone out in the car and picnicked.
>
> 'But all because he's so daft and bad-tempered we can't do any of those things', said Lucy-Ann. 'Why, we might even have tried to sail out to the Isle of Gloom to see if there were many birds there, as Jack so badly wants to do, if only Jo-Jo had been nice.'

Before the story ends, the boys at least find varieties of unpleasantness when 'a different Jo-Jo altogether' condemns them to death in 'horribly polite tones'.[38] In less strategic hands, the usual Nazi/crook is simply made nasty to keep him a hate-object for patriotic purposes. Even the sophisticated Crompton does not want to risk a sympathetic enemy agent:

The man was sitting at the writing-table at work on a complicated diagram. He swung round as the door opened and something flashed into his face that made William – he didn't know why – want to turn and run for his life. It vanished so quickly that William thought he must have imagined it, and the face beneath the blue glasses became once more bland and expressionless.

Crompton, writing for publication in April 1940, wanted to convey with characteristic economy the Nazi as creator of fear. Her story is, as always, a comedy – Wing-Commander Glover, who corners the fake ornithologist spy, is a deliciously observed monocled snob – but her readers were to know the enemy. In another lightning glimpse of the menace beneath the spy's mask, the bird man appears at William's home, having come 'to invite William up to the cottage and there to find out by fair means or foul what had happened to his diagram'.[39] The reflective child would find much to chill her or him in that 'foul'. The murderous spy on one's family doorstep is a real nightmare, all the stronger because not laboured.

Gunby Hadath had (for him) an almost poetic moment of comparable discovery, amid his normal diet of wholesome school stodge:[40]

The bright beam stripped the German of that mask of hearty youthfulness which he and his companion had worn at their tea. The corners of his eyes were too puckered for youth. The skin of his face was too weathered, his cheeks were too pinched. His close-cropped hair was devoid of all colour or sheen. No youth was he, though in years little more than a boy. Here was one of these young men, as the Swinger sensed gradually, who had been caught up in their Leader's evil machine which had ground the very breath of youthfulness out of them. Here was a young man who had never enjoyed any boyhood.

Maud Budden, a few years later, would make the same comment even more poetically on a Scrooge-like character asked to entertain a child:[41]

But all the stories Geoffrey knows are tales of stocks and shares.
He's never heard of Goldilocks who visited the bears.
Snow White and all the Seven Dwarfs mean nothing at all to him.
He's never heard of Anderson, nor yet the Brothers Grimm.

These things go even farther than Graham Greene in discovering what is meant by a 'lost childhood'. In their different ways, Noel

Streatfeild, her cousin-in-law Kitty Barne, and Mary Treadgold used the same idea in characterising Nazi youth camps. Streatfeild, in *The House in Cornwall* (1940), used the vehicle of a Ruritanian dictator concealed in England by the traitor uncle of the customary clutch of resourceful children:[42]

'I'm sorry to interrupt this interesting dissertation, nephew', Uncle Murdock broke in, 'but Doctor Manoff has finished. Kindly stand.'
    Sorrel, who had noticed how much John was hating Manoff, gave him a pleading look, for he was still sitting. At her glance he got leisurely to his feet. Manoff had been standing at his place until they were all up. When at last John was upright he moved towards the door; but behind John's chair he stopped. He breathed through his nose as if he were a dragon who could puff out fire. His voice came in a growl.
    'Murdock. This boy must be taught.'

Saville alone presented a character conforming to child stereo-types of air-force hero. The twins discover a fighter pilot, so named and so chapter-headed, who – while no Biggles – could apparently have fulfilled a bit-part in Biggles's Squadron and spoken a chorus-line in the Mess, or who might have befriended William near Marleigh Aerodrome. If no Biggles, he is no odious hero akin to Glover, and plays along charmingly when they insist he is their prisoner because he has found their secret club headquarters. Yet, at that moment of discovery, Saville (like Blyton later) reveals as a means of concealing:

Suddenly Mary felt the tears sting her eyes – their wonderful work of yesterday for nothing, because somebody had discovered their secret!
    'What shall we do, Dickie?'
    'It's our camp, isn't it? We found it. You found it – you and Peter. We've had a noath [an oath] about it and we're in charge now, aren't we? It's an enemy in there, isn't it? We'll go and kill him and tell the others after. . . . We'll do it by ourselves just like we always do . . . Come on, Mary!'
    And so Richard the Lion Heart went into battle, and within two minutes had led his gallant army through the gorse tunnel into the camp. The enemy showed as much surprise as the attackers, and both stared dumbfounded at the other. The twins had not had time to imagine what sort of an enemy they were going to find, but they

would never have guessed that he would be young, with laughing brown eyes, and in Air Force uniform with two rings on his blue sleeve, and with wings on his breast. He was sitting on the grass at the foot of the tree with a suit-case and a raincoat beside him and looking at them in the friendliest way.

Pope uses the device in *The Rape of the Lock*. The mock-heroic can convey respect for what in its small compass may be heroic. Dickie is a slightly silly and very innocent nine-year-old, and yet he has become Richard the Lion Heart in miniature because of what we do not know – that the enemy whom it seems anti-climactic, indeed idiotic, to have taken for an enemy is in fact a terrible one. But John Davies, as he calls himself (the Nazi spies who have landed by parachute take Welsh names) is kind to the children to the end, so much so that Dickie cannot bring himself to think him wholly an enemy when all is known and Peter's father's reservoir is in ruins:

> 'Gosh, Dickie!' Mary said with a sigh. 'An' John Davies too, I s'pose. But I can't really and truly believe he was as bad as the others, can you?'
>
> ' 'Course he wasn't', said Dickie. 'He was decent to us. He was all right' . . . then he suddenly turned to the Captain. 'But he *can't* have been a spy. He knew all about Spitfires and Hurricanes, and he was in AIR FORCE UNIFORM.'
>
> 'I'm sorry, Dickie, but he was one of the worst. I think we shall find that he'd been in England for a long time before the war – probably a schoolmaster – and it's quite easy for them to get a British uniform. They could either get one from a prisoner of war or make them. Lots of spies come in uniform. . . .'
>
> 'Well, anyhow', Dickie muttered, 'I think he was one of the best. He was a decent sort of spy. . . .'

It touches the edge of one of worst moments of childhood, captured by Graham Greene in 'The Basement Room' (1930), later screened by Carol Reed on a title classifying its genre – *The Fallen Idol* (1948). The experience as used in children's fiction was normally given far more limelight, and usually involved barriers of age and/or class and/or experience, but seldom of gender. Richards employed it ably. J. I. M. Stewart, writing as Michael Innes, handled it with deep sympathy in *The Journeying Boy* (1949), where Humphrey, the eponymous hero, discovers that the cousin he believes to have risked his life to save him is in fact proposing to kidnap him; J. K. Rowling ingeniously added the barrier of time in *Harry Potter and the Chamber of Secrets*, where Harry Potter is betrayed by the narrator of a cherished book – as though Biggles had sold his reader into slavery or William made fun of us to Hubert Lane. (The latter somehow seems the worse of the two; the former might be a ploy to deceive the real enemy.) Dickie's youth, and the clear indication that while stronger he is less intelligent than his twin sister Mary, add a further dimension, one which again invites respect for Rowling's use of betrayal by beloved fiction: Dickie is at the age when action heroes may be allowed ethical ambiguity. We may be on the side of pirates or outlaws or gangsters (hence *William the Outlaw* (1927) and *William the Pirate* (1932) and *William the Gangster* (1934)), however respectable our families, if only we are young enough. A centenary play performed in 1994 at Stevenson's old school, Edinburgh Academy, showed him as a pre-teen schoolboy dreaming of an embryo Long John Silver, and dreaming that *he is on Silver's side*. The Second World War left no place for those sentiments, and Dickie has to be gently but firmly robbed of his illusion. His next speech provokes a roar of laughter, but is elegiac for his dream ('"I say", Dickie broke in, "spies are awful liars, aren't they"').

As a wireless serial on 'Children's Hour', this must have been deeply emotive and highly self-identificatory. Even when Dickie came charging in to confront the all-too-friendly enemy, his battle-cry 'Come on, Mary!' must have elicited child listener memories of 'Come on, Margaret!' with which on Sunday 13 October 1940 on Children's Hour, Princess (later Queen) Elizabeth closed her first broadcast made at the age of 14 for her fellow-evacuees, her sister joining her to recite their final good wish in unison: it had been less than three years earlier. The serialisation would have slowly developed the audience's doubts about 'Fighter Pilot John Davies' until next instalment when the twins, now in the hands of Davies's supposed aunt, see him again in her house with a parachutist with a twisted ankle whom they had also discovered, supposedly another British officer:

At the top of the stairs they turned to the right down a dark passage and then to the right again, and came to an open door. Mrs Thurston reached across to close the door, but the twins were close enough to see everything. The room was brightly lit with a lamp. On a bed at the side of the shuttered window was lying the English officer. He was in his shirt-sleeves, with his bandaged ankle stretched out in front of him, but his sound leg was resting on the floor. Seated in a chair at side of the bed was another man, who looked up sharply at the sound of their steps. The twins recognized him instantly as John Davies, although he had a different, slightly startled look on his face. They had been looking at a piece of paper which was resting on his knee, but just as the twins smiled at him and were ready to speak, Mrs Thurston closed the door quickly and urged them forward.

Mrs Thurston then puts them into a bedroom into which they realise they have been locked:

'We're real prisoners this time', she said. 'This is our biggest adventure, Dickie. . . . Did you see John?'
    He nodded.
    'Did you see that paper?'
    He nodded again.
    'What did you think it was, Dickie? The paper, I mean.'
    He sat on the bed and slipped his shoes off without untying the laces.
    'Like a drawing . . . or a map.'
    'And there was something else, Dickie. Did you notice what I noticed? Did you hear?'
    He looked puzzled for a moment.
    'Wasn't anything to hear, was there?' Then they stared at each other without speaking, and Dickie's second shoe dropped to the floor.
    'Of course', he went on. 'Of course there was something to hear. They were talking all the time . . .'
    "'Course they were', said Mary slowly. 'But they weren't talking English.'

End of chapter, change of location in wireless instalment. Saville, certainly at this opening of his literary career (in his early forties), was a highly allusive writer, and his child audience would in many cases have known Peter Pan's 'to die would be an awfully big adventure'. That the twins are in mortal danger becomes evident when their brother and Tom's uncle Alf Ingles of the Home Guard come in search of them and Mrs Thurston denies that they are there (Ingles and David then double back and rescue them from the bedroom). The story is not a violent one, apart from the reservoir deluge, but its quiet tone and slow pace of revelation is much more frightening than violence would be. The lonely rural retreat proves a front line.

Mystery at Witchend may well have been the most widespread diffusion of a domestic, rural story for children of the immediacy of war. Its fine characterisation (the romance of David and Peter is delicately and almost invisibly permitted its growth) and its celebration of the Anglo–Welsh frontier compel respect, and the present reader should now be able to judge its stylistic merit. It is probably the most distinguished outgrowth of the war as children's war fiction; Saville's major rivals for wide audiences were all series writers of pre-war reputations. Linklater's first book for children was a war product, but its war content is limited to a disguised Hitler oppressing a Ruritania. *We Couldn't Leave Dinah* seems its only real rival as a first book born and inspired by the war, and it is hard to see either outdoing the other. Both were later to weaken their characters by subjecting them to sequels attempting to take post-war status with little ageing, but that lay hidden from Carnegie judges' eyes. Probability had necessarily vanished from the Carnegie criteria, but its ghost could take little exception to Saville's use of real country for an imaginary invasion where Treadgold imagined the terrain while symbolising the real Nazi conquest. Saville had the advantage in peopling his landscape; Treadgold had five or six memorable figures, but Saville had more sensitive psychological explorations, several *rites de passage* being observable even among adults – notably Peter's fussy, old-maidish and ultimately self-reproachful father. Crompton is unmatched in deflation of adult pomposity, but Saville succeeded in making Mr Sterling a figure of dignity and decency in all of his absurdity. Above all, Sterling has to do the hard work of showing how the finest of human impulses prove to be security disasters, as he recalls his hospitality to a saboteur:[43]

> 'He *was* smart and I was slow', he said. 'Reckon I've been a foolish old man all along over this business. I've always tried not to believe the worst, but I was all wrong this time. I trusted the fellow and now I've failed in my trust', he finished almost in a whisper.
>   Peter dropped what she was doing and went over to him. 'Nonsense, Daddy. He made a fool of us both. They made fools of us all. I told you how nice and helpful and friendly he was on the hill. . . . Don't you worry, darling.'

The convention that children prove heroes is fundamental to children's literature, especially in wartime – and the equalisation of duties, disappearance of servants and destruction of houses naturally deepened the meaning of this. But while *Mystery at Witchend* begins with the characteristic instruction of temporary status of child–adult relations declared by David's father on going into the armed forces ('Take care of Mummy for me, old chap'), it ends with the affirmation that child care of parents may be an endless process. Evacuee relationships are usually temporary; it is the locals who are real. Treadgold perhaps makes something of the same point, as Mick and Caroline escape to freedom and Peter and his father remain on the Nazi-ruled island.

Saville and Treadgold were both publishers' employees inspired (presumably in both cases) by the inadequacy of some of the authors they handled, and both had BBC experience and public-relations knowledge. To have missed *Mystery at Witchend* cannot have been an easy task for even the most overworked adjudicator. Allowance having been made for personal prejudice (Graham Greene was denied the Nobel Prize because an adjudicator disapproved of his relations with a colleague's wife), there remains the likelihood of the war having become an inappropriate subject in culture-dictators' eyes. This would certainly account for the coldness and/or condescension to actual war fiction for children by reviewers, as well as by librarians. Other candidates for the Carnegie Medal in 1943 were that year's Biggles, Worrals and Gimlet volumes, of which *Biggles 'Fails to Return'* had quite exceptional quality as the haunting story of what proves an unnecessary mission to war-silenced Monaco, with a charming and delicate boy–girl wartime romance, a shrewdly worked-out series of cross-purposes, a grimly honest confrontation of higher-command doctrines of expendability, and some elegant development of comedy thriller. *Worrals on the War-Path* was too obviously dependent on its predecessor volume, *Worrals Flies Again*, for its chief German and French as well as British characters. [Gimlet] *King of the Commandos* had atmosphere and pace; unfortunately, it also had the snobbish and humourless Gimlet. There was no William book for the first year since 1922: Crompton's war work and disability were beginning to slow her down at the age of 52. Blyton had a warless (or nearly warless) series of detective stories commencing with *The Mystery of the Burnt Cottage*, with one good character, the pompous, clever, boastful Fatty, an English Hercule Poirot always being deflated by his fellow-children; but, while a good whodunit, it was weaker than other stories of that year and other Blytons of past and future years. Orwell's remark in 'Raffles and Miss Blandish' (1944) about the 'boredom of being bombed'[44] may not be true of the 1940 to which it alluded, but may reflect much of the 1943/4 when it was conceived and written.

Back in 1940, on 14 March, the *Listener* – and hence the BBC staff and interested circles – asked 'What Should We Tell Our Children?' via an essay from the 50-year-old Scots writer Willa Muir, Socialist, feminist, libertarian. A long-time victim of censorship (she had been fired from teaching in London when she married the 'atheist' poet and critic Edwin Muir in 1919, and wrote *Mrs Grundy in Scotland* (1937)), Willa Muir was anxious to be realistic, even if it was middle-class (and non-evacuee) realism:

> When a child's sugar is rationed, when he [her only child was a boy] is fitted for a gas-mask, he is already *in* the war, just as we all are. This war is not confined to the fighting forces: it has long ago reached the Home Front. So we can't keep our children out of war, much as we should like to.

She touched a crucial nerve, and probably a representative one. The Spartan mother, hungrily thinking of her offspring as cannon-fodder, may have been a myth of 1914, but she was certainly the myth as good as the mile when it came to public symbols. (For that matter, Patrick Pearse, from an anti-British perspective, wrote a poem 'The Mother' expressing comparable sentiments, while also prophesying his own mother's refusal to grudge the lives of her sons (duly shot for their part in the Easter Rising of 1916).) Willa Muir's conviction that people would like to keep their children out of the Second World War seems vindicated by most of the war literature. Orwell in *Tribune* on 4 August 1944 produced the somewhat perverse paradox that[45]

> you do less harm by dropping bombs on people than by calling them 'Huns'. Obviously one does not want to inflict death and wounds if it can be avoided, but I cannot feel that mere killing is all-important. We shall all be dead in less than a hundred years, and most of us by the sordid horror known as 'natural death'. The truly evil thing is to act in such a way that peaceful life becomes impossible. War damages the fabric of civilization not by the destruction it causes (the net effect of a war may even be to increase the productive capacity of the world as a whole), nor even by the slaughter of human beings, but by stimulating hatred and dishonesty. By shooting at your enemy you are not in the deepest sense wronging him. But by hating him, by inventing lies about him and bringing children up to believe them, by clamouring for unjust peace terms which make further wars inevitable, you are striking not at one perishable generation, but at humanity itself.

Much critical comment on what to tell the children or have them read was conditioned by the previous World War. Hence Orwell's hostility to the word 'Hun' as in 'Hating the Hun'. We have noted that adverse comment on the enemy from sources supposedly reflecting or aimed at the lower classes usually attacked Hitler (any comparison between whom and Attila the Hun was probably most unfair to Attila). The middle classes are quoted as preferring to call the enemy 'Jerry', which in fact was a term for a chamberpot, satirically abbreviating 'Jeroboam', which held six bottles of wine or four of champagne. The same cultured scatology associated Churchill's famous V-sign with obscene violation of enemy private parts. It is difficult to see adverse effects of any of this; but in any case the popular image of Nazi Germany became much more horrific when full facts on the Holocaust emerged, and this was reflected in much children's literature from Blyton to Johns, or, to put it differently, from the implicit to the explicit. But the omnipresence of rationing, of 'don't you know there's a war on?', of 'careless talk costs lives' or its dreadful male chauvinist elaboration 'Be Like Dad and Keep Mum', seem much more frequent in common speech, although the belligerent might tell William when he enquired about lemons: 'Lemons? It's a shame, an outrage, a crying scandal. Hitler shall pay for this.'[46]

In 1942, *Biggles Sweeps the Desert* (partly reflecting its part-recycling from his First World War stories) contrasted the Germany of the First World War with the new Nazi variety. This was not inconsistent with the chivalry of First World War air-combat mythology (and in some respects, fact), widely though the Hun had been formally hated on the home front. In fact, the First World War had not always been so nice, especially for Johns himself, when captured and told he would be shot, to avoid which proceeding he escaped. He did not blame German pilots for hostility, since he had been on an illegal bombing mission, the like of which could have taken its toll among their people. What follows is thus a public rebuke to the new Germany, a covert settlement of accounts with the old, and a grace note of sympathy with soldiers whose relatives were the victims of air war, such as Tug:

'Do you speak English?' inquired Biggles, in a friendly tone of voice.

The Nazi's right hand flew up. 'Heil Hitler!' he snapped.

Biggles nodded. 'Yes, we know all about that', he said quietly. 'Try forgetting it for a little while.'

The German drew himself up stiffly. 'I understand I am a prisoner', he said in fairly good English.

'That's something, at any rate', murmured Ginger.

Biggles ignored the German's rudeness. 'I invite you to give me your parole while you are here; we would rather treat you as a guest than a prisoner.'

'I prefer to be a prisoner', was the haughty reply.

'How about trying to be a gentleman for a change?' suggested Henry Harcourt.

'I'd knock his perishing block off', growled Tug Carrington.

'Will you fellows please leave the talking to me?' said Biggles, coldly. Then, to the prisoner, 'Years ago, officers in the air services – and that includes your fellows as well as ours – when we weren't fighting, managed to forget our quarrels. It made things more pleasant. I'm not asking for an indefinite parole – merely for while you are here with us.'

'Things are different now', returned the German, with a sneer.

'Yes, so it seems', replied Biggles, a trifle sadly.

The Nazi breaks his parole and steals an aircraft, in which he is shot down and killed 'by a stroke of ironic justice, by his own command-ing officer, von Zoyton', whom Biggles then captures. A sandstorm enables him to escape, Biggles radios the Nazis to tell them where their CO is roughly located, and von Zoyton, on return to his oasis, radios Biggles the location of some very necessary water supplies. They continue hostilities to an inevitable end with a very First World War duel, which von Zoyton survives to take service with an ugly bunch of ex-Nazi crooks in the first post-war Biggles adventure. Even then, Biggles is rather pleased at his final escape, having sent most of his associates to Kingdom Come:[47] 'He wasn't a bad chap at heart. Probably it all came from getting mixed up with the wrong crowd when he was a kid. His mother should have warned him.' The Spartan mother is thus firmly fixed on the Nazi side, and more appropriate offspring for her occur in the next three books (von Zoyton never reappears). But, during the war itself, Johns's real indictment of Nazism began with the Gimlet books of 1943–4. Orwell noted British public opinion seemingly caring very little about the war against Japan; Tolkien was critical of it, Ransome practically opened Missee Lee (November 1941) on a Friends-of-Japan recruit-ment. Johns was savagely anti-Japanese, varying villains between open brutality, veneer of courtesy and absolute treachery. Little exists in anti-Italian vein among the children's books, bar the Beano's 'Musso the Wop He's a Big-a-da Flop', and an Italian Prefect of the Special Police on the Riviera who sentences female relatives of

Free Frenchmen to be shot in *Biggles 'Fails to Return'* (where, however, his only appearance is a knock-on part, being hit on the head with a revolver by Algy almost on sight). Yet the Italians may well have been the ethnic group suffering most persecution in Britain during the war, especially at the hands of children. Data are too small to make much of, but the popular image would suggest that the Italians were presented in children's literature as easier targets than the Germans or Japanese. On the other hand, there were visibly much more of them, since British Japanese were few in number, and most German families (including the Windsors and Mountbattens) had judiciously Anglified some years before.[48] Austrians were handled much more gently than was altogether logical. Apart from the kindly fellow-Catholic Brent-Dyer, Mark Strangeways's *The Secret Base* (1944) posits a schoolboys-cum-uncle-and-yachting-crew *ad hoc* force who discover themselves at war with a secret German base in a remote Pacific isle on 3 September 1939, and in mid-combat the intrepid Cockney Man Friday recruits an Austrian from the Nazi forces:[49]

'This', said Albert, 'is Fritz. 'E feels that 'e doesn't want to stay with Jerry any longer.'

Fritz, who spoke English well, came forward hesitatingly.

'I am an Austrian', he said slowly, and waited, as if that explained everything.

'' E means', put in Alfred, 'that 'e ain't a German, and that 'e doesn't like the Germans. That so, isn't it, Fritz?'

The Austrian nodded violently. He was having some difficulty in putting his thoughts into words, but at last they came.

'Austria is not Germany', he said. 'Perhaps you think that we wanted the Nazis to take us over? But you are wrong. We hate the Nazis, and if we had been allowed to we would have fought them. Austria is not Germany, I tell you. They killed my brother, and they would have killed me, but I pretended to be a Nazi. I thought to live to fight another day. You see?'

'You mean that you've always been against the Nazis', said George, 'and have been waiting to get your own back!'

The man nodded eagerly.

'Yes, yes. But more than get my own back, as you call it. I mean to fight for Austria. My country is an ally of yours, only perhaps you do not understand that yet.'

This was probably written in 1944. Over two years later, Blyton's sympathetic portrayal of Austrian survivors of allied bombing in *The*

Valley of Adventure harmonised with the same theme. Hitler's own Austrian origin gained no mention in any of these.

But all of these were international attitudes. however varied. Crompton, needless to say, enjoyed herself with some of the variants:[50]

> 'Ladies and gentlemen', shouted William, 'the first item is a dog race between Jumble an' Hans. Jumble's my dog, an' Hans is Ginger's aunt's dog that we've borrowed for the race. He looks a German dog, but he's not a Nazi one. He's same as a refugee. You know, the ones that come over in rowing boats . . .'
>
> 'He couldn't row a boat', objected the girl with red hair. 'He couldn't *possibly* row a boat. Not a dog. Well, have you ever *seen* a dog rowing a boat?'
>
> 'I never said he rowed a boat.'
>
> 'You did.'
>
> 'I didn't.'
>
> 'You did.'
>
> 'I didn't. I only said he was *same* as the people that came over in rowing boats.'
>
> 'How can he be the same? He's a *dog*.'
>
> 'Oh, shut up! . . .'

And Crompton was not going to join any chorus of sentimentality on this or any other score. Linked to this story is another, with peripheral characters common to both: the second features a supposed refugee who proves to be a spy.

Willa Muir's idealism of 1940 was not ill-served by any of this, and much of it fitted in with her explanation of the war:

> what does it mean to a child if you talk to him about 'our country' and 'other countries'? Children interpret what they don't know in terms of what they know already. A child's idea of the country he lives in derives from what he knows of his home, his school, his home-town, the places he has been to on holiday.

A reservation comes in here: the seaside disappeared for most children from 1940 to 1945, apart from indigenous inhabitants and a Blytonian Scotland. Beaches were mined. Child awareness able to reach back to pre-war seashore must have had to come to terms with a vaguely shrunken country, and hence a diminished self, in ways not fully realised when Muir wrote.[51] 'For him, his country is an extension of life as he knows it, an extension of himself. What he thinks other countries are like, unless he has been abroad, I really don't know . . .' Apart from their imaginary cowboy America, self-mockingly absurd in the *Dandy*'s Desperate Dan but serious enough – and sometimes Nazi-invaded – in the columns of the *Adventure*,[52] the British child's literary imagination was chiefly fed international perspective through historical narrative (usually chauvinist, unless England is at the mercy of a Scottish writer). Brent-Dyer was firmly internationalist European, and the *Magnet* and *Gem* boasted school-boy excursions to China, India, Polynesia, Brazil, the USA, Canada, France, Spain, Egypt, Kenya, the Congo, the Sahara and so on, while Biggles had flown all over the globe. It was not always condescend-ing – Richards and Johns respected Chinese culture in a bluff, civil tourist way – although home was quite definitely best. William, much more obviously a symbol of the English child in wartime, had never gone abroad (apart from Ireland early in 1922, still thought of as part of the UK); he repeatedly says he does not want to visit foreign countries, although he makes friends with French, Lithua-nian and Icelandic children. Linklater's Miss Serendip wearies any child with foreign parts. Blyton disliked foreign travel, and the most her fictional children get is a Greek island cruise in *The Ship of Adventure* (1950) or a happy holiday in Ruritania. Almost all of them identify foreign lands with their historical past, taking much more pleasure in it than the present – a fairly characteristic tourist response – and, in Richards's case at least, the children actually if not formally enter an earlier time in many of their adventures. Johns, of all people, made history come alive to meet Biggles, on a few occasions, the most successful being the haunting prelude of the boy in Cambyses's Persian Army inaugurating *Biggles Flies South* (1938). Ransome's *Peter Duck* and *Missee Lee* are excellent voyages to the Caribbean and to the China seas respectively but are obviously set long before their dates of publication. Girl's school and other stories in general seemed more internationally minded than boys, whence the confidence with which Barne, Treadgold, Olive Dougan, Agnes M. Miall and others were able to move their heroines around Nazi Europe. (Worrals is obviously much more at home in France than either Biggles or Gimlet though not, of course, than 'Cub' Peters when we first meet him.) Muir continued:

> I suspect that he thinks of relations between countries as if they were relations between children, between boys at his own school, say, and boys at another school, or between a bigger boy and a

smaller boy. So it follows that children even as young as five years old should appreciate the argument that small countries must not be bullied by big ones . . . it is something any child can understand.[53]

That is also Biggles's case for supporting the smaller country in *Biggles Goes to War* and, much more muted, for volunteering for duty in Finland against the USSR in *Biggles Sees it Through*. That was the explanation given for British support of Belgium in 1914 and of Poland in 1939. But this moralism had its dangers, such as Crompton had identified as long ago as 1930 when Ginger's Cousin Percy had invaded the world of William and his Outlaws:[54]

the Outlaws listened to 'entertaining stories' of Cousin Percy's manly boyhood, till, as William said, 'I feel the only thing I want to do is go an' sneak on someone or bully someone.'

If anything, children's fiction in the Second World War backed away from anything like Cousin Percy. Blyton stayed carefully away from paragons; and, while her *Sunny Stories* fiction (apart from serials) was highly moralistic, she let her adventurers rip with occasional gangings-up on infant Percys.[55] The anti-adult strain was too strong to admit much on adults' valuation. Surviving school stories still worried about bullying (rightly), but the ethos of most of the authors seemed one of accepting children's creation of their world and letting them get on with it, coupled with the implication that they knew adults' business better than adults themselves did. Apart from Gimlet, no bully is a hero, and the authors debate how far bullies may prove cowards – sometimes, dismayingly, they do not. Richards's imbecilic, self-worshipping Coker was hilarious as a bully, and heart-warming as a hero; his Loder was a nastier, more traditional case, whereas his covert imitator, Edwy Searles Brooks, had a hero, Handforth, who sought to combine bully and hero, not very convincingly. Second World War fiction had no place for that, but Blyton's pompous, wealthy, boastful Fatty made a splendid slightly tarnished hero, all the more by striking a Holmes–Watson alliance with the other outsider in the group, the little girl Bets.[56]

An unexpected third is later added to them in the shape of the clearly proletarian Ern, nephew of the hated policeman Goon, and the victim of *his* bullying, while the other children in the 'Mystery' series become mere shadows. Bullying in fact became much more obviously identified with adults – Piggott,[57] Goon, Mrs Bott or some other. Saville in his sequel to *Mystery at Witchend, Seven White Gates* (1944), produced a portrait of a self-tortured bully in Peter's Uncle Micah, with the twins acting as liberators (clever, since in their half-fantasy life they had previously made a touching stand against Nazi bullying whereas here they charmed and diagnosed the bully's underlying problem). Crompton did not make William a psychologist, except for purely tactical purposes; but, in an interesting wartime feminist development, she brought William's friend Joan to suss out the vain Mrs Bott and her connection with a crook and fraud.[58] But, in general, Crompton's formula was one of William's resolution of adult problems being largely involuntary. Blyton assumed that at least some of her child adventurers were responsible, more so than adults, but she reached a unique point when Lucy-Ann and Philip tell Bill and Mrs Mannering that they ought to get married (induced partly by Blyton's need to sanitise a stepfather, partly in recognition of war's revolutionary effects). Johns accepts child leadership when Cub begins commando adventures by teaching the commandos what is what in their present operation, and Ginger (still the child-identification point) bullies his superiors, Algy and Bertie, into illegal descent on the Air Commodore to discover why Biggles has failed to return. Brent-Dyer's Chalet School nominally repels any question of child leadership, but under wartime conditions it becomes caught in an impossible situation with a temporary headmistress, solved when a schoolgirl sees that her judgement is wiser than her superiors' and thus cuts the Gordian knot.[59] (It is covered up, but that is what happens.) If the trend was to show paternal inadequacy, it was also very definitely towards child responsibility.

How far was fiction falsification? Muir addressed the question carefully in the real-life context:

'We do not tell them things that make them feel panicky or scare their imaginations. For instance, we do not tell them atrocity stories. That is an absolute rule, I should say, for children of twelve and under.'

Thus Muir at the war's beginning, thinking of widely manufactured atrocity stories of the First World War. The Second World War might not change that law in its course, though events would reveal bombing horrors to children. But were they to be kept from news of the Holocaust? Or how were they to be told? These questions lay before a war-weary information dissemination squad – parents, teachers, guardians, librarians, writers – in 1945 and beyond. In the event, the best telling would be done by a child from the dead, Anne Frank, whose diary was published in 1947.

Muir, the protective bourgeois (if bohemian) mother, insisted: 'We do not tell them that they are going to be killed or hurt, either in the black-out or by a bomb'. A working-class mother or elder sister as described by Elinor Mordaunt with food to get, space to make, men to manage, kids to mind, had no such luxury: they had to be told that if they ran loose during the blackout they might get hurt, since otherwise they certainly might get hurt. The misery of home-loss in evacuation meant that they had to be told about bombs. Muir saw that as met by 'we tell them they are going into safety'. The young grew up more quickly in the East End than in the West, but the young grew up more quickly in September 1940 than in March. Muir, most instructively, drew a hard line between fiction and reality; she refused to believe that the imaginative child might people reality with nightmares from its books:[60]

> I should never let children believe that they are surrounded on all sides by sinister spies, not even if they happen to look on spy-hunting as a pleasurable adventure. A spy-hunt on the cinema screen, or in a book, is one thing, but in real life is quite another. Every child must feel that he can go out of his home into the street with positive confidence, that he is not dodging enemies all the time. It is our job to assure children that life can be carried on, war or no war, and that it *is* going to be carried on.

The innocence of the last two sentences is heart-rending, but the notion of effects of spy fiction on children is almost certainly mistaken. Muir was probably thinking of her own sufferings from spies in 1919 who lost her her job, or spies since that time who gossiped venomously at her expense. Crompton had shown for years how her characters (not simply William, but men and women more than twice his age) acted out their favourite film and film-star fantasies, and that boys like William, too active for much reading, became highly credulous about what they read or heard. Blyton had one character in *The Sea of Adventure* denounce its cast of children for supposedly acting out the part of William![61] By the time such infant students of the spy genre had really got going, it was not they, but their unfortunate adult neighbours, who could no longer enter the street 'with positive confidence' but found themselves 'dodging enemies', small enemies but very determined. Even Biggles nearly shot an innocent pilot as a spy in *Spitfire Parade* (rewarmed from the First World War, but a useful reminder to youthful readers to curb their pursuit of suspects).[62]

Metropolitan reviewers for children echoed Willa Muir's strong liberalism as to wartime effects. Lorna Lewis, later to write good work for children on job-holding under Blitzkrieg conditions, *Tea and Hot Bombs* (1943), began her *Time and Tide* wrap-up on 20 April 1940 by saluting the war as a further incentive to juvenile reading:

> The addition of Hitler and German measles to other non-central European pests is likely to make the Easter holidays rather more complicated than usual this year. A newly published batch of books for boys and girls is therefore doubly welcome.

None of that batch was war-conscious, and much of what would follow them was frankly escapist; but, as Rupert Hart-Davis remarked in reviewing crime fiction in the *Spectator* (19 July 1940), 'no one can escape the wrath to come, but if any members of the garrison can spend an occasional hour in Cloud Cuckoo Land, they may well add to their own value at the barricades'. By the time Lorna Lewis, most industrious of fiction-reviewers for children, reported to *Time and Tide* on the autumn books (26 October 1940), the wrath had arrived:

> To turn from Bombs to Books is the right kind of evolution. On this occasion it is also a statement of fact, for these juveniles were lately rescued from a partially bombed-out flat. Indeed, even as I refer to their pages, small clouds of sticky concrete dust and other souvenirs of my late home fly from them. The rescuer's task has been a happy one, for the general standard of this batch is high. There is much to recommend to the younger habitues of shelters and to those more fortunate above-ground dwellers.

'More fortunate': she evidently wasn't thinking of evacuees, which is instructive as to social assumptions on who read what and who reviewed for whom. Middle-class children migrating in parental or avuncular care were all evacuees, but seem to have been socially invisible to contemporary observers. And working-class children were assumed not to be readers (though not by everyone: Streatfeild had a working-class girl in *The Children of Primrose Lane* (1941) neatly detect a German spy by showing that he lived in German syntax). Lewis still had no war interest to report beyond noting that the British publication of Helen Dacre Boylston's latest instalment in her series on nursing in the USA, *Sue Barton, Senior Nurse*, 'seems a useful book for girls in their 'teens, especially at this moment when nurses are badly needed'. But it altered the usual sound-bite for future blurbs: C. Fox Smith's *The Ship Aground* was 'a really first-class pirate story which kept me enthralled one evening in spite of Goering's activities overhead'.

The first signs of control over the children's books being called for emerged from L. A. G. Strong, recently much lauded by John Betjeman, George Orwell and others for his foray into school stories with *Wrong Foot Foremost*, which opened wartime novels of different schools forced to merge (a theme later mined endlessly by Gunby Hadath). Strong's writing was elegant, as always, and his plot reminiscent of early Wodehouse school fiction, especially as to boxing (with a wayward, irrepressibly heroic guardian crying out for treatment by the later Wodehouse). On 6 December 1940, he told *Spectator* readers:

> The children's book business remains a muddle. Last spring, through the enterprise of one individual, a meeting was convened at which publishers, children's librarians, authors, teachers, and reviewers were given a long-needed chance to pool their understanding. The really valuable contributions came from the librarians, who substantiated what some of us have been saying for years: namely, that apart from books for very young children, there is no system and precious little sense. Publishers are working in darkness, undecided whether they are aiming at the grown-up who buys the book or the child who reads it, knowing little of children and what they like, and, in common with the majority of authors, ludicrously underestimating the child's intelligence at any age between eight and seventeen. They were splendid women, those librarians. They spoke vigorously, from the heart. One of our most experienced reviewers confirmed every word that they said, and the teachers weighed in, too.

The gathering has not been identified, but Strong's evidence gives us the fact that at last such a thing had happened, and that an early effect of the war was that women were its driving force. Control was on its way. It followed rapidly on the first revolt of children's librarians on the vague and hence exclusive system of judging the Carnegie Medal, and on their formation of their own organisation. The links with publishers (now beginning to develop children's departments to the level of specialist heads) and booksellers (ditto) also meant personnel migrating from one to another, most notably when Eleanor Graham, author of *The Children who Lived in a Barn*, and *Sunday Times* book-reviewer for children until the war, who had looked after the children's department in Bumpus, the booksellers, became editor of Puffin Story Books for Penguin in 1941 at the behest of Allen Lane, its founder and ruling genius since 1936. Penguin had succeeded where so many attempts at paperback had failed after some years' existence. Graham had left-wing credentials – *The Children who Lived in a Barn* seeks sympathy by dealing with bourgeois children in suddenly reduced and apparently orphaned circumstances, but is a searing indictment of the cruelty of class and its charity bureaucrats and benefactors. She clearly disliked war fiction. Since war fiction reached mass child readership through the comics, Johns's works and so on, a class divide began to emerge: war was vulgar (which, as Wilde had pointed out, was a good way to undercut its appeal). Lane, having reprinted *Biggles Flies Again*, and Penguin, which had profited by war's advent, had no reason to share these views, but they accepted them. War, in Orwell's *1984* word, was 'prolefeed'.

This was not happening on the adult front, where regiments of half-fiction, half-fact, part-memoir and part-propaganda made their mildly lucrative way through the book market, give or take bombing disasters to bookshops and libraries. In part, the awareness of how much Muir's decent totems and taboos had been violated by war realities made for an unspecified search to rebuild gentility: war and its effects had aged countless children, horribly, but the petty bourgeoisie should have defences built for the future, or at least their defences should not be undermined from within. Underneath the social anger of *The Children who Lived in a Barn* is the resentment that, if such things had to happen to children, it was even more reprehensible that they happened to middle-class children (who in happer circumstances constituted the bulk of the book-buying classes, especially in Bumpus). A literary 'not before the children' philosophy even divided the adult from child fiction of such a writer as Linklater. Almost by title definition, such works as *Juan in America* and *Ripeness is All* had an earthiness transcending class boundaries, where *The Wind on the Moon* spoke the language of gentility, however absurd its governess and repulsive its Count (perhaps a faint Draculan earthiness trembled audibly if not visibly in his rank). Graham would be styled – perhaps self-styled – for Penguin's Silver Jubilee souvenir:[63]

> Her great desire, pursued with a constancy which may owe something to her Scottish blood, has always been to find books which show how life is really lived, and so help children to increase what by nature they lack – sheer experience of life.

This was uttered in the quieter world of 1959/1960. In the Second World War children might justly ask to be released, however briefly, from the amount of sheer experience of life which dogged them so ruthlessly. If they had more to learn about how life is really lived – and they knew a lot more about it than most of their successors in 1959/60 – they needed no instruction at all in how death is really died. Graham's vague devotion to realism chimes in partly with the Arthur Ransome cult – which by the Second World War had become Oxbridged Chinese pirates from long ago, and fears that the formidable aunt might realise that friends of her nieces were camping in the neighbourhood. *Missee Lee* and *The Picts and the Martyrs* sold, with special status from Cape and its unscrupulous public-relations department, but they had long outgrown the real-life children of their origin, much as they were far from the war against Japan, and the Britain of the evacuees. Ironically, Graham's repulsive district visitors in her own fiction had all too much resemblance to certain evacuation officials of the Second World War, as Noel Streatfeild would later demonstrate in her post-war retrospective *When the Siren Wailed*. But Graham gave the first Puffins little of that.

Graham was appointed in 1941. She had been preceded by the launch of Puffin Picture Books in 1940 under Noel Carrington, with whom Lane had treated before the war for such a series. Carrington's interests ran strongly to Nature, as did those of many standard writers for children.[64] Lane was still cashing in on the war. Of the first four titles, three were on war on land, on sea and in the air, respectively. But the fourth was James Gardner's *On the Farm*, appropriate since the war sent far more youngsters back to the land than the most heartfelt agrarian crusade of the inter-war years had ever drummed up; and it was the only one still in print in 1944. The eighth Puffin Picture Book, Roland Davies's *Great Deeds of the War*, was particularly strong in war spirit, 'if your turn comes' being clearly spelt out amid the gallant deeds of Captain Warburton-Lee at the Narvik Fjord on 10 April 1940, the destruction of the *Graf Spee* in December 1939, or the heroism of Irish Staff Nurse Patricia Marmion in carrying patients to safety from a bombed hospital. (Marmion's nationality was important: as Churchill noted, the neutral Irish produced plenty of volunteers, while it was the Irish in the UK who posed occasional problems in commitment.) A few months later, there appeared the star Puffin Picture Book to date, *The Battle of Britain*, by the novelist David Garnett and the all-purpose James Gardner (PP 21) 'Based by permission on the Air Ministry Official Account of Great Days of 1940'. But it too was gone by 1944 along with the other war titles. The ethos of Penguin marked its change in its retrospect of 1960 by the embarrassed note amid its general self-congratulation:

> **December 1940** As yet there had been no books for children. Now in their turn came the first PUFFIN PICTURE BOOKS – another series that was to enjoy great success for many years. The fact that the first three books in the series bore the titles *War on Land*, *War at Sea*, and *War in the Air* – a little violent, we might feel today, for the opening of a children's series – will perhaps seem more natural when we remember the time when they were published.

And, after a run through the disasters out of sequence ('the fall of Holland, Belgium, France, Denmark, and Norway, the fall of Chamberlain, and the beginning of the Blitz'), it happily drew attention to *On the Farm*: the absence of the two items most likely to have dictated both the war titles and their sale – Dunkirk and the Battle of Britain – is significant ('when we remember' that 1959/60 followed – or rather, sought to escape from – Suez, Hungary and so on). Graham's first five Puffin Story Books could hardly have been more assertive in their exclusion of war: Barbara Euphan Todd's *Worzel Gummidge*, Derek McCulloch's *Cornish Adventure* (pointedly noted on its cover as by 'Uncle Mac' of the BBC Children's Hour), Mrs (Mary Louisa) Molesworth's *The Cuckoo Clock* (first edition 1877), Herbert Best's *Garram the Hunter* (Nigerian hill tribes) and Will James's story of a cowboy's horse *Smoky* (the only survivor to 1944, although *Gummidge* would return, with sequels). Only two titles appeared in 1942, Eleanor Doorly's *The Insect Man* (about some improbable children learning about the life of Henri Fabre), and Eve Garnett's *The Family from One End Street*, honestly working-class in preoccupation, safely middle-class in tone. 1943 brought Doorly's life of Louis Pasteur (somewhat over-fictionalised), Graham's own version of Henning Haslund's *Tents in Mongolia* and Rutherford Montgomery's tale of Canadian wildlife, *Carajou*. Fortunately for Puffin, that marked the end of the dull Penguin-style covers, an appropriately illustrated set appearing in 1944 on Vitaly Bianchi's *Mourzouk* (a Russian lynx), John Budden's *Jungle John* (in the 'Indian Jungle'), Magdalen King-Hall's *Jehan of the Ready Fists* (imaginary squire for Richard I), Dhan Gopal Mukerji's pigeon story *Gay-Neck*, and J. B. S. Haldane's *My Friend Mr Leakey*. War in these, where it existed at all, was firmly far away and/or long ago (Coeur de Lion provided quite a bit of it, very well done). The authors were not isolationists or anchorites: Haldane was a prominent

Communist, as he announced in his biographical note, thereby shocking children unable to believe that such a beautiful and good book
featuring a likeable archangel (Raphael) could have been written by a
Communist (inaccurately diabolised in another favourite fantasy
story of the day, C. S. Lewis's *Out of the Silent Planet*). Haldane's
note contained Puffin Story Books' only formal allusion to Second
World War published during it:

> He hasn't felt like writing stories for children since about 1933,
> when Hitler got power in Germany, and the world became a nastier
> place. But he hopes the world will get nicer again after we have won
> the war; and then perhaps he will feel like writing more stories.

But alas he didn't. And after a time, he didn't feel like being a
Communist any more, either. Like other authors, he had made his
point: Hitler was a death of children's literature, as well as of children.

Haldane's presence affirms the left slant, though its most conspicuous note in his book was the benevolent egalitarianism, and
charming but covert propaganda points such as a girl having her
name changed from Victoria to 'Irene, which means Peace', and a boy
having his changed from Augustus to Tom. (Augustus, in addition to
its imperialism, was synonymous with snobbish or upper-class
names (actually derived from German princely use); and the RAF
used 'Gussie' to mean an ineffectual aristocrat or snob.) But he also
stood for the internationalism which was Graham's great service to
the series and to the children emerging from the Second World War:
James, Montgomery and Bianchi took matters little farther than the
cowboy and world wildlife interests long established among children
from Fenimore Cooper and Sir Charles G. D. Roberts to the *Adventure* comic and (in its day for it) the *Gem* or the *Magnet*. But John
Budden and Mukerji (from two different viewpoints on India) meant
more serious commitment, as did such discoveries of the Europe now
being liberated, even in forty-year-old works like Nine van Hichtum's
Afke's Ten, a vivid picture of family life in the Dutch Frisian Islands,
seen successively from the viewpoints of most of the children
occasionally as duets but as a rule individually, ending with their
parents. The last chapters feature a brief return of the brother in
national army service, whose irony might have struck older readers,
given what little chance his successors had to play a significant part
when the Nazis invaded in May 1940; but, within a few months of
Puffin publication, he simply corresponded to most British boys
of his own age in post-war call-up. Marjorie Fischer's *Palaces on*

Monday, first published in 1937, gave a red-starry-eyed view of the USSR seen through a deeply sympathetic American lens; no doubt it was appropriate for the wartime alliance in 1944. Annette Turngren's *Flaxen Braids* recruited enthusiastic readers of an apparently authentic account of a Swedish family migrating northwards in the late 1930s: it was an exciting, emotional rural Sweden, very different from the sophisticated Stockholm. Norway was represented by Kitty Barne with *We'll Meet in England*, presumably permitted by peacetime publication in 1945. Robert Gibbings revived interest in the South Seas (much cherished by pre-war story-readers of Richards and Johns) by means of *Coconut Island*. The thrill of Graham's 1945 booklist, over fifty years later, is still triumphant: it was a liberation in its own right, a declaration that the siege of the British Isles had been raised. It corresponded to post-war growth in the adult world from the United Nations to the Edinburgh Festival, and it leaves its own questions as to what happened to that new European sense for British children.

Puffin Story Books were now ninepence (approximately £0.04 in modern currency), rising to a shilling by late 1945. The volumes on sale in the Sexton Blake Library (one of the few series surviving under Amalgamated Press auspices after the slaughter of summer 1940) were by now sevenpence (slightly over £0.03). Despite Blake's assistant Tinker having started out at the age of his early teenage readers some four decades previously, the years had taken their toll: Tinker, with whom the reader was supposed to identify, was now a lad of over 20. The series had eased towards the girl-conscious older schoolboy, apprentice or armed-forces conscript. By the destruction of the *Magnet*, the *Gem* and their spin-off *Schoolboy's Own Library* (fourpence halfpenny (£0.02) at the date of demise in summer 1940), the Amalgamated Press had opened a real gulf between the middle-class and working-class child reader. Graham might claim to bridge that with *The Family from One End Street*, probably her best seller of all her choices in her first years as Puffin editor, and in one way she had: middle-class children read it in shoals with affection, if probably also with condescension. It had been a slightly revolutionary item during its earliest days, as publisher after publisher turned it down only to see it win the second Carnegie Medal under the imprint of the modest Frederick Muller in 1937. It opened up an unknown world to many readers, though one which many more had discovered in more accurate detail from the Blitz and the evacuees. But it could not take the place of the utopian Greyfriars, where the master hand of Richards held his readers from all classes in thrall. That Greyfriars still survived in the *Knockout* comic in the shape of a mentally subnormal comic strip deepened the divide. Where any child may have travelled effortlessly from the Greyfriars Famous Five to Afke's Ten, these were now different worlds. Any sort of serialisation seemed to savour of comic-book status, and with it an intolerable intellectual slumming. Blyton was suspect by issuing her *Sunny Stories*. Crompton brought magazine William stories out subsequently as books. Even Graham's exploitation of Uncle Mac with her second Puffin Story Book was forgotten, while serialisation in Children's Hour apparently de-intellectualised Saville. Newnes published all three of them (though not everything from all three of them), and its magazine-linked traditions and output did not help its status with the Carnegie Medal or with Eleanor Graham (Newnes may in any case have felt too competitive for a deal with Puffin). Saville was a Newnes editor.

Graham laid down certain ideals in the *Listener* before the war was three months old. Her observation was acute and useful:[65]

> Figures still show that as a nation we are hardly book-conscious for our children. It is not a question of price or income, for toys cost far more and the cinemas are always full. It really seems as though the average person looks on books for children as rubbish – or at least, great waste of time.

She testified to the growth of juvenile sections of public libraries, and to the demand by children for reliable factual matter. This last was one reason for the rise in *Biggles* readers: you might not discover many Norwegians in *Biggles Defies the Swastika*, but you discovered a great deal about Norway during the actual Narvik expedition; you thought of Shropshire as a familiar landscape after *Mystery at Witchend* and *Seven White Gates*; at least you apprehended (without necessarily identifying) the frontiers of Swanage and the realities of Beaconsfield from Blyton. But Graham hardly wanted to bag those quarries. In fact, she was at cross-purposes:[66]

> It was in America that the craze started for stories with an 'other land' background and some of their best have proved successful over here. We have had them with scenes laid in China, Hungary, Russia, France, Norway and so on. . . .
>   With girls, this carefully concocted story proved highly satisfactory, but it was interesting that boys did not respond as well, though some really excellent books were devised for them, books

that were well written, had a good plot and gave lively descriptions
of country or native life. Yet they never had the whole-hearted
popularity of, say, a Westerman or a Biggles. It seems that boys
want action all the time, violent action, and can't be bothered with
character building or descriptions.

As Sherlock Holmes would put it, her example was an unfortunate
one for her argument. Such Johns stories as *Biggles in the South Seas*
or *Biggles 'Fails to Return'* did delicate work in character development when Ginger becomes a kindred spirit of the Polynesian girl
Full Moon or falls in love with the Monégasque Jeanette Ducoste,
neither type of relationship having existed for him before; so did
such earlier works set in the First World War as *The Camels are
Coming* and *Biggles Flies East* in deepening and strengthening
Biggles himself. All of these and most of the rest of Johns's books
in the 1930s and 1940s had good plots, and gave lively descriptions of
country or native life, albeit the natives in *Biggles Flies East* seemed
to spend most of their time in justifiable resentment at perpetual
exploitation by either the Germans or the British. The Second World
War stories continued to do memorable work in plot, description and
character: *Biggles in the Orient*, for instance, returns very seriously to
alcohol as a theme in squadron disintegration. The pilot Scrimshaw
becomes alcoholic and paranoid, and finally commits suicide in
action (kamikaze-style, showing Japanese victory over his mind),
and the sergeant Gray is accused unjustly of drinking and killed
before he can clear himself. All the Worrals stories are far in advance
of their time in gender assertiveness. What these things prove is not
that Johns's works were inferior to 'really excellent books . . . devised
for boys . . . well written' and so on, but that Graham had read little
or no Johns and felt no obligation to do so before rating him so far
below the good. It was this kind of condemnation without consultation which would characterise the forming of cultural authoritarianism during the war. On girls' stories, Graham seems to have done it
again, in finding that stories of life abroad replaced the school story:
the Chalet School combined both, in location and in much of its
personnel. It also satirised them: *Lavender Laughs in the Chalet
School* (1943) makes fun of the kind of girl around whom series of
foreign locations are dreamed up, arguing (as Crompton had done in
attacking A. A. Milne)[67] that the writer's child is both easily spoiled
and easily dehumanised. And then Brent-Dyer shows where such
series may have quality when the coddled Lavender proves to have
made one real friendship on her travels – a friendship across the

colour line. Alas, it was the last real instance of international quality for a Chalet School book; that hallmark of the series did not survive the war.

At the war's end, no less than at the war's beginning, Eleanor Graham took stock of 'Children's Books in Britain To-day', this time for *British Book News 1945*, and found her subject's 'world' to be[68]

a lively, changing place where the old standards are being challenged and new are emerging. The false will, we hope, drop away leaving behind all that is best and true, worthy of development and just exploitation. . . . we have begun to plan with greater sense of responsibility, not only books children will enjoy but those which will help to fill that background of general knowledge which cannot be achieved wholly at school, however excellent the teaching.

This may have sounded a little strange in the ears of those who had so recently 'filled that background of general knowledge' which could be 'achieved wholly at school', now finding it and themselves targets in the latest phase of history. In fact, Graham was contrasting her present day with twenty years earlier, the same retrospective sweep she had given herself in 1939. But where in 1939 she had concluded:[69]

Progress has been marked, and it looked before the outbreak of war as though rewards were at hand for years of enterprise and effort. Whether the war will really obstruct the good work which has started, we have yet to discover. Perhaps, with the wide redistribution of the nation's children and some reconsideration of their needs, it will actually stimulate it.

– in 1945 she made no formal attempt to answer her questions of 1939. Informally, she had answered it in more than one way. In 1939, 'we' was a partly passive entity, having 'yet to discover'. In 1945, 'we' had 'begun to plan'. The writer was no longer a mere reporter or reviewer: she was a cultural architect for 'the nation's children' and was proclaiming as much. She was careful to conceal her chief credential: her c.v. at close of text called her 'bookseller, publisher, and author . . . also a critic of children's literature', but neither text nor c.v. mentioned that she was the editor of the war's most significant contribution to British publishing, Puffin Story Books, bringing works of unquestionable quality within the reach of children with shillings, where the texts otherwise cost six times that sum. Nor did she mention the war's most significant contribution to British authorship, the rise and rise of Enid Blyton (nine titles in 1939, nineteen in 1945, and geometric progression in sales figures). She certainly did mention, and even price, the first publication of Puffins present or future, citing their original publishers only.[70] Her avoidance of authors never to be Puffins made for somewhat selective encomia. Ransome, for instance, was commended in the Edinburgh-born Graham's most regal manner (conferring on him, so to speak, the second star on the right and straight on till Morningside):[71] 'Ransome has shown us how important early responsibility and achievement are in the development of the good citizen'. What she deserved for that was Crompton's William turning his most unanswerable logic: 'I've shown 'em how import'nt early resp – what you said – an' achievin' are in developin' the good citizen too. I've invented Sardine Toffee or' (for he was fundamentally a truthful boy) 'pretty nearly, anyway. That'll give the good citizen a whole stomachful of development.' Crompton's deflation of post-war youth-cultural architecture was pitiless.[72]

Graham's only recognition of Second World War fiction involving war was Barne's *Three and a Pigeon*, which, with her *May We Keep Dogs?*, 'incorporated sound and useful information' (presumably about the pigeon, rather than about the war). The war itself, she felt,[73]

> has inevitably slowed down active progress in some directions, but children continue to read. It may be hoped, therefore, that when normal production is again possible, we shall go ahead with added purpose and an even clearer insight into the stages of development from infancy to maturity which alone will assure progress on the right lines.

Perhaps Graham did herself less than justice. She had, like Blyton, emerged from the war with an achievement on which to build, and a territory over which to mount guard. To see the spirit which won them for her, we have to turn back to her manifesto at war's beginning. As it happened, she spoke eloquently for Blyton, for Johns, for Ransome – we may pay her the supreme compliment and say even for Crompton, to whom a manifesto was normally a mere target. In 1939, Graham was still speaking as an author:[74]

> We don't give children books to dull their minds and quell their activities. We recognise them as human beings much like ourselves. They want books for relaxation and diversion – books for hobbies, books to satisfy questioning minds, books to stimulate.

From this, we can see why Graham's Puffin Story Books were to prove one of the greatest series for children in human history, and why they never quite lost the faint touch of ill-informed patronising. It symbolised the British achievement in the Second World War rather neatly.

Notes

1. *The Island of Adventure*, 325–6; *Five Go to Smuggler's Top*, 184. Waugh added an ironic preface in 1959 on the unforeseen revival of the English country house.

2. Richards's part in subverting the school story is at its most obvious in the scripts on Bendover College that he wrote for Will Hay, vanquishing all adversaries as the lovable ignorant schoolmaster – the curriculum, from being arid instruction at Greyfriars, became benevolent Squeers, inviting similar questions as to the depth of Dickensian satire to reach subversion (*Pilot*, 13 February 1937 to 19 March 1938, logically finding its fruition in Second World War Will Hay school-story movies such as *The Ghost of St Michael's* (Ealing, 1941: script by Angus Macphail and John Dighton but firmly on the lines Richards and Hay had established). The parodies nominally by Dicky Nugent and actually by George Richmond Samways and successors from the 1920s (Dr Birchemall and St Sam's), very frequent in the *Magnet*, comparably attacked both the fictional genre and the boarding-school ethos. Richards's very last *Gem* and *Magnet* school story series (autumn–winter 1939 and winter-spring 1939–40 respectively) put highly malevolent crooks in charge of St Jim's and Greyfriars forms (the *Magnet*, 9 December 1939 to 23 March 1940, was followed by the holiday series featuring Soames and the Nazi spy Braun, and the first instalment of a new school series, but the last complete series kept the Remove at the mercy of a sadistic criminal).

3. This contrasts with the healthy survival of the girls' school stories via Brent-Dyer, Brazil, Blyton, the *Girls' Crystal* and so on. See Cadogan and Craig, *Women and Children First*, and Rosemary Auchmuty, *A World of Girls* (1992) and *A World of Women* (1999), the last of which by definition points to the fundamental difference that the girls'-school series traditionally presumed that their characters would grow up, where the boys' from Richards and Crompton onwards did not. Brent-Dyer might retard the clocks but not stop them. Dorita Fairlie Bruce in the Second World War put her leading characters into young womanhood. Johns's awareness of the girls' school in Worrals's recent past enabled him to produce a tolerably successful school story for *GOA* as by William Earle, 'The Ravensdale Mystery' (vol. 62, 1940–1) in which the French mistress turns out to be a German spy, – as Biggles's French inamorata had proved to be, long, long ago. Various other Second World War stories of women in the services or the Land Army are clearly and consciously post-school where few male service stories are, no doubt from the omnipresence of killing (apart from schoolboys caught up in the war like Cub Peters). Crompton satirised the post-school element of the image of female armed services when (entirely for altruistic motives) William convinces an elderly schoolmaster that Ethel in her ATS uniform is actually a retarded schoolgirl dressing up ('Entertainment Provided', *Modern Woman* (May 1943) and *William and the Brains Trust*). Hadath did look at the school misfit in *The Swinger* (1942), which crowns his

inevitable from-blackguard-to-hero progress by graduating him into the RAF, in its way a Sherlock Holmes solution ('The Three Students', 'The Sussex Vampire').

4. All this material comes from the *Hotspur*, February 1940.

5. *Magnet* 522 (February 1918).

6. *Magnet* 950–1 (April–May 1926).

7. Even here, the *Hotspur* followed Richards's pioneer work. Richards would have St Jim's reform Talbot (*Gem* 334–41, June–July 1914) from cracksmanship, and Greyfriars reform various other attractive boy crooks – for example, Lancaster (*Magnet* 1,209–19, March–May 1931), Flip (1,247–54, January–February 1932), Valentine Compton (1,499–509, November 1936 to January 1937) and Skip (1,545–55, October–December 1937)) – but lower-class scholarship boys such as Linley, Penfold and Redwing bring the school round to their ethics, not vice versa, the school being at fault in its snobbishness (Mr Quelch is pointedly anti-snob, partly because the lower-class boys have a love of learning seldom in evidence among middle- and upper-class boys).

8. *Ten Little Niggers*, whose American title was later sanitised as *And Then There Were None* (and, less successfully, as *Ten Little Indians*), assumes nine murderers isolated on an island, with each being murdered by the tenth prisoner.

9. Orwell, *Animal Farm* ([1945] 1975), 17, 19, 100. Specifically, Moses suggests Rasputin, whose powers of survival were almost but not quite as impressive. But the story's effectiveness partly depends on suggestion rather than identi-fication of real antecedents (Major for Marx, Napoleon for Stalin, Snowball for Trotsky – but where is Lenin, without whom it is difficult to envisage the Russian Revolution? Yet *Animal Farm* works without him). Moses from Ras-putin I owe to Mr Keith Mears; many thanks for much else also.

10. Hadath, *The March of Time – a story of school life in war time* (1946) implies a wartime setting not evident in the text, but its stress on the need for public schools to win American respect is probably mid-1940s, certainly not inter-war. Page 18 introduces Mr Ormond, the brand-new Head.

11. The *Hotspur* began on 2 September 1933, last of the Thomson non-tabloid comics to be founded, also the first with a permanent set of characters, clearly in a policy to pick up readers from the *Gem* (now reworking twenty-odd-year-old stories) and the *Magnet* (beginning to decline from 200,000) – a policy which seems to have taken five years to hatch (W. O. G. Lofts and D. J. Adley, *The World of Frank Richards* (1975), 87). No doubt 'Red' Circle followed 'Grey'friars; but the Calvinist Thomsons drew the line at a designation drawn from such Papist exemplars as friars, and someone remembered the Sherlock Holmes story 'The Red Circle', thus using a major Greyfriars source.

12. *Sink or Swim* (1945), 131–2, 63.

13. Millie Evans. She also owes much to Crompton's Violet Elizabeth Bott, pluto-cratic child of lower-class Cockney *nouveaux riches*, corresponding to William's lower-class behaviour in recoil from middle-class parents. It is Millie who gets her picture in the paper at the end. Her father is a warden, which suggests that Streatfeild may have been as irritated by war-created lower-class new officials as Crompton.

14. *The Adventurous Four Again*.

15. When met in the first instalment of *The Adventurous Four* (*Sunny Stories*, 6 September 1940), Andy is 14, just left school, very much a mark of working-class status. His father owns a sailing-boat with cabin as well as a little boat; and, while that is wrecked, the government compensates by the reward of another at

the end (nominally for Andy). Boat-owners after Dunkirk were heroic figures, regardless of their class, and Blyton must have written this less than three months after it. The story with its images of young children and working-class fishing-folk using frail boats to check Nazi armed forces was evidently prompted by Dunkirk.

16. Linklater, 'The Art of Adventure', in *The Art of Adventure* ([1947] 1948), 278, 277–8.

17. [George] Bernard Shaw, *Our Theatre in the Nineties* ([1932] 1954), II, 8–9.

18. Hiram K. Soss, the stage American but benevolent millionaire in R. J. MacGregor, *The Young Detectives* (1934) and *The Secret of Dead Man's Cove* (1937) is a good case in point. Biggles has unpleasant encounters with Americans in early peace-time adventures (*The Cruise of the* Condor (1933), *Biggles Flies West* (1937), *Biggles Flies North* (1939)), some of them with yachts, but Johns's crook hero acquires an American father-in-law-cum-yacht in *Steeley Flies Again* (1936) and duly reforms.

19. Linklater, *The Art of Adventure*, 278–9. The passage has every relevance to the world of today. It also reminds us that the *mentalité* associated with the aftermath of the mass murders of 11 September 2001 is less new than we think.

20. [London] *Times*, 10 October 1944. In these days, *The Times* preferred to report speeches in *oratio obliqua* whence I have translated Eliot here and (together with Sir Ernest Barker) below.

21. Orwell, *1984* ed. Bernard Crick (1984), 196.

22. Mencken, 'The Hills of Zion', in Alistair Cooke (ed.), *The Vintage Mencken* (1955), 153. In its original form, the piece was drafted in April 1925.

23. *Times*, 10 October 1944.

24. Orwell, *Tribune*, 22 November 1946, Orwell, *Collected Works*, XVIII, 493–7. The essay is one of the most stimulating pieces ever written about children's literature, and very useful for us in charting the kind of reprints that British publishers produced in the late 1940s when paper controls relaxed. Orwell probably saw the report; was he covertly sympathising with Barker?

25. *Times*, 14 November 1944.

26. British and Irish writers of North American stories with little or no personal acquaintance with America had been building up an impressive readership for a century or more, and by the Second World War such British popular writers as Peter Cheyney and James Hadley Chase (whose real name was René Brabazon Raymond) were widely taken to be American.

27. *Times*, 14 November 1944. I am obliged to my former student Mr Luke Meadows and to his father for the whale, and to a Sheffield taxi-driver for the crashed plane.

28. *Times*, 10 October 1944; *TLS*, 18 November 1944.

29. Notwithstanding Eliot's hostility to *Animal Farm* (its message then not seeming to the national purposes of Eliot's two fatherlands as he saw them), Eliot and the Exhibition clearly meant to ensure a future of British–American child reading without common cause and idealism being shared with the USSR – which the *Rover* had celebrated in 1942–3 with its heady cults of Russian commandos fighting in Romania, or which the *Boy's Own Paper*, equally stern in its publishers' religious and political conservatism, extolled praising egalitarian-ism in USSR fighting ranks: 'In the Red Army canteens, officers and men dine together, and at the theatre and cinema the high ranks have no special claim on the best seats' ('Red Army in Action', *BOP* (August 1943), 4). Dorothy Carter, *Comrades of the Air* (1942), gave Marise friends among the Russian pilots and made the most of Russian use of women pilots (a circumstance missed by

non-readers of Carter until the world heard of Valentina Tereshkova as the sixth Russian cosmonaut, circling the planet in 1963). There was some disagreement on such questions among would-be cultural dictators: Eleanor Graham encountered hostility to publishing the fairy-stories of J. B. S. Haldane, *My Friend Mr Leakey*, as a Puffin, and possibly to the very pro-USSR Fischer, *Palaces on Monday*.

30. *Library Association Record* 39 (4th ser., vol. 4, January 1937), 1.

31. Ibid., 43 (4th ser., vol. 8, January 1941), 8.

32. *Library Association Record* 47 (4th ser., vol. 12, January 1945), 2. This in fact followed a bitter letter from Eileen Colwell, then Children's Librarian, Hendon, and Honorary Secretary of the Association of Children's Librarians (ibid., 46 (4th ser., vol. 11, January 1944), 14–15), stating that the Medal Committee had only nine members, only one of whom was a children's librarian, and the original committee had none. She pointed out that the American Newbery Medal drew on twenty-two librarians for children. She demanded a return to the 'outstanding book of the year'. Fifty titles had been nominated by librarians in 1940 and 1941. This was because selections of six had been asked for, most children's books were published late (for the Christmas trade) and 'many Children's Librarians have not yet learnt how to read critically' (a process whose nature and timing she somewhat wisely ignored). The Carnegie Medal subcommittee had met seven times, six with only a third of its members present, with letter-votes being accepted. As of now, the award got no publicity. 'Having attained its rightful status, the Library Association Carnegie Medal can influence the standard of children's literature enormously and give all concerned with the making of children's books a much needed encouragement and inspiration.' She too simply spoke of 'England', even when contrasting with the USA.

33. See n. 30.

34. *Library Association Record* 39 (4th ser., vol. 4, May 1937), 218.

35. Crouch, *Chosen for Children*, 30. The deaths of the father and son of John Sholto Douglas (eighth Marquess of Queensberry (1844–1900), best remembered for his destruction of Oscar Wilde) may respond to reconsideration in the light of this intelligence.

36. Watson, *Reading Series Fiction*, 102.

37. Saville, *Mystery at Witchend* (1943), 216–18, 222, 116.

38. Blyton, *The Island of Adventure*, 64, 304.

39. Crompton, 'William and the Bird Lover', *Happy Mag* (April 1940) and (as 'William and the Bird Man') *William and the Evacuees*, 73.

40. Hadath, *The Swinger*, 221.

41. Ultimately republished as 'The Mean Pig and the Kitten', *Curly Wee* [annual], c. 1949.

42. Streatfeild, *The House in Cornwall* ([1940] 1974), 41.

43. Saville, *Mystery at Witchend*, 99, 239–40, 240, 157, 158, 242–3.

44. Orwell, *Collected Works*, XVI. 351.

45. Orwell, *Collected Works*, XVI, 317. This comes close to a secular theology for the Lord's Prayer, much to its credit. It may be more relevant for our generation, with its xenophobic media, than for the British who had endured the Blitz.

46. Crompton, 'Too Many Cooks', *Modern Woman* (May 1941) and *William Carries On*, 20.

47. Johns, *Biggles Sweeps the Desert*, 69–70, 88; *Sergeant Bigglesworth, C.I.D.* (August 1947), 188.

48. I am obliged to Professor Richard Demarco for his impressive reminiscences of childhood in Scotland during the war years.

49. Strangeways, *The Secret Base* ([1944]), 110–11.

50. Crompton, 'William's War-Time Fun Fair', *Homes and Gardens* (June 1943, but probably written six or seven months earlier, to judge from internal evidence) and *William and the Brains Trust*, 71.

51. Crompton, 'William and the Tea-Cake', *Modern Woman* (January 1943) and *William and the Brains Trust*. The *TLS* (20 November 1943), in an otherwise favourable review of F. O. H. Nash, *Lucy of the Sea Rangers* ([1943]), complained about 'the mysterious refugee-spy family which is distressingly inevitable by now'; but the son is subsequently adopted by kindly English people, 'and in his new home he grew and flourished, becoming in time a cheerful, happy boy' (p. 196). Gwendoline Courtney, *The Denehurst Secret Service* ([1940] 2005), similarly turns on a refugee being liberated from spying 'relations', with variants. Olive C. Dougan, *The Schoolgirl Refugee* (1940), has comparable devices, again seeking sympathy for the youthful victim of the spies. In general, the hate-objects seem to be naturalised Teutons, as in the First World War, with actual refugees receiving less hostile treatment, especially with provable Jewish family links. Muir, *Listener* 23 (14 March 1940).

52. As noted by Graham Greene, the comics flung superheroes into the Second World War, and enlisted old stalwarts with happy indifference to supposed times of original series-dating, something which indeed Richards had pioneered without excuses of a World War to keep up with. Cowboy stories in particular presumed a late nineteenth-century dating, but *Adventure* and others conscripted the best gunmen on their books on the apparent principle of 'Have Gun, will Time-Travel' – for example, 'They Branded Solo Solomon', Nazi nasties having marked the Wild West hero with a swastika (*Adventure*, 8 February 1941). The underlying message was that the USA (in the form that British comic-readers knew best) was neutral but increasingly on Britain's side, with entry in support of Britain inevitable (Desperate Dan in the *Dandy* in Dudley D. Watkins's inspired hands being the most ingenious of all pro-British neutrals).

53. Muir, *Listener*, 23 (14 March 1940).

54. Crompton, 'William and the Clever Cousin', *Happy Mag* (December 1930) and (as 'The Outlaws and Cousin Percy') *William's Crowded Hours* (June 1931), 86–7, 89.

55. For example, Cecil Dearlove in *Five Go Off to Camp*.

56. *The Mystery of the Burnt Cottage* (1943), *The Mystery of the Disappearing Cat* (1944), *The Mystery of the Secret Room* (1945) and *The Mystery of the Spiteful Letters* (1946), followed by eleven more, annually until 1955, the rest less regularly until 1961.

57. In Kitty Barne, *Three and a Pigeon*.

58. Crompton, 'Joan to the Rescue', *Modern Woman* (June 1941) and *William Carries On*, 100–11. (William had been accused of stealing Mrs Bott's diamond brooch, which Joan revealed to have been appropriated by Mrs Bott's resident fortune-teller.)

59. Blyton, *The Ship of Adventure*, 327. Johns, *Biggles 'Fails to Return'*, chapter 1 (that he also falls in love in the story mixes child responsibility with *rite de passage*, sensibly enough; but he never returns to his previous significance as a mover and shaper of events, however much we still see things through his eyes in most of the subsequent books). Brent-Dyer, *Gay from China at the Chalet School*.

60. Muir, *Listener*, 14 March 1940.

61. Horace Tipperlong, whom the children mistakenly take for a crook on the ground, that no real ornithologist could be so pretentious while also being so ignorant – but he was (*Sea of Adventure*, 212).

62. Johns, 'The Flying Spy', *Spitfire Parade*, from 'Suspicions' and 'Off and Away!', *Biggles in France* (1935).

63. *Penguins Progress 1935–1960* (1960), 'published on the occasion of the Silver Jubilee of Penguin Books'. It made it clear that the success of Penguin was owed in part to well-established heads of department developing their policies over the years, in contrast to the wild swings of power and command afflicting British publishers in recent times.

64. *Enid Blyton's Book of the Year* ([1941]) is a highly resourceful month-by-month revelation of seasonal change through uses of verse, plays, songs and serial story (of four children's discoveries of Nature), relieved by Brer Rabbit anecdotes. It must have been a godsend to evacuees trying to make sense of the country. So must *Round the Year with Enid Blyton* and a variety of other works – for example, *Birds of Our Gardens* (1940) and *Enid Blyton's Nature Readers* bks 1–3 (1945) as well as fictions with nature-study intent (*The Children of Willow Farm* (1942), *At Appletree Farm* (1944) and so on). To these, one would add *Shadow the Sheep Dog* (1942), which, while a good episodic story in its own right, silently feeds much nature data to the reader. Johns wrote a column 'The Passing Show' for Newnes's monthly magazine *My Garden* from 1937 to the end of 1944. Saville's *Country Scrap Book* (1944) and *Open-Air Scrap Book* (1945) no doubt owed something to what the author learned of his children's discoveries of Shropshire, fully to be enshrined in *Jane's Country Year* (1946). The rural themes must have been reassuring to the displaced urbanites, and thus strengthened their reliance on Blyton in particular. Johns even brought the rural element into the Battle of Britain in *Spitfire Parade*, what with Angus's encounter with the bull and Henry's romance with the pig. Crompton shifted William's milieu to her needs between rural and urban values, but William must have taught a lot of children what *not* to do in the country.

65. Graham, 'Twenty Years of Children's Books', *Listener* (30 November 1939), [Children's Books] Supplement III.

66. Ibid.

67. Crompton, 'William's Busy Fortnight', *Happy Mag* (June 1931) and (as 'Aunt Arabelle in Charge') *William the Pirate* (May 1932).

68. *British Book News – a Selection of Books Published in Britain 1945* ([1947]), 19. The next essay, Noel Carrington's 'Children's Books by Auto-Lithography', did mention in his ensuing c.v. that he was the editor 'of the PUFFIN PICTURE BOOKS' (ibid., 28–9).

69. *Listener*, 22 (30 November 1939), Supplement III.

70. With the slightly odd exception of Vitaly Bianchi's story of a lynx, *Mourzguk*, translated from the Russian and credited to Allen & Unwin, price three shillings, and Penguin Books Ltd at one shilling (no mention of Puffins).

71. *British Book News 1945*, 20.

72. Crompton, 'Youth on the Prow', *Modern Woman* (May 1944) and *William and the Brains Trust* (April 1945), unmentioned in Graham's survey for 1945.

73. *British Book News 1945*, 26.

74. *Listener*, 22 (30 November 1939), Supplement III. The *Listener* reported (12 January 1939) that a survey responded to by 800 child readers in Bethnal Green (London) placed Crompton's William as the readers' first choice, followed by Dickens's *Oliver Twist*, J. M. Barrie's *Peter Pan* [and *Wendy*, presumably], Mark Twain's *Tom Sawyer* and R. M. Ballantyne's *The Coral Island*. This would have been primarily working-class readers.

Part Two

Lessons which May have been Learned

" He was not conscious whilst he lay with his head on my knee."

FIGURE 6 The priest and the assassin's child (Violet Needham,
The Stormy Petrel) – see pp. 75–6 n. 71, 113.

6

God's Things and Others'

*'Render therefore to Caesar the things which are Caesar's; and unto
God the things that are God's.'*
Jesus Christ, quoted in Matthew 22:21

Some years ago, our History Society at the University of Edinburgh,
having been revived under the leadership of a mature student,
Mohammed Hameed, invited a survivor of Auschwitz, Dachau and
Belsen (now a lector in a Glasgow synagogue) to give an account of
his experiences. He spoke quietly, but with horrific effect, in an
excellent lecture towards the end of which he told how, when the
American troops drove in through the gates, he and his fellow-
prisoners were lying on the ground, physically capable of lifting their
heads but no longer of standing or even sitting beyond the use of
elbows. He took questions, one of which asked where God was while
he was going through his sufferings. He smiled like a man who has
had an unexpectedly easy question. 'God?' he said. 'Where was God?
Lying on the ground beside me in Belsen.' As he concluded, Mohammed embraced him, and the rest of us gave him a standing
ovation; I suppose it was the best lecture we had ever heard or were
likely ever to hear.

We do not think generally of God as vulnerable; yet Christianity as
well as its parent, Judaism, turns on such a belief. When throughout
the centuries humans persecuted one another in God's name, it was
God whom they persecuted. Nietzsche's equation of Judaism and
Christianity as comparably weak is perfectly correct: his Nazi disciples had the strength he demanded. We know very little of how
children really look at religion: they may tell parents what they think
the parents want to hear, or may defy parents in terms they think will
impress, but neither may be a true index to what relation they
acquire with God in their own minds. A child as disgusted with
hypocrisy and false ostentation, in the spirit of the disgust that
Christ expressed for such conduct, may sound to an intrusive adult
like a sceptic where its belief may be far deeper than the adult's.

Shaw provides such a figure in the title-role of *The Devil's Disciple*. A child grown into an adult is not a reliable guide to its child reactions: it is too anxious to talk in the terms of an adult, or to think in them. But we can say one thing with confidence about children: they are weak, physically. A vulnerable God, in a manger or on a cross, makes sense to them.

Adults writing books sought to put thoughts in the minds of British children during the Second World War; but what thoughts they may have put into children's minds is a very different matter. We see the process of inculcation; we cannot judge that of reception. We can say that the war brought increased public expressions of Christian belief by children's authors, and that these were not necessarily a product of obvious markets or public demand or publishers' prejudices. The evidence suggests that it was the wish of writers themselves (it certainly is not likely to have come from their literary agents). Stock critics were uneasy with it when the war broke out. One such instance was Joyce Lankester Brisley, author of the Milly-Molly-Mandy series (about a child described by commentators as the reader's 'better self': as Wilde noted, 'the highest, as the lowest form of criticism is a mode of autobiography'). Brisley in 1940 produced *My Bible-Book*, a succinct and interesting retelling of many episodes from the Bible, from 'the story of the first man and woman' to 'Paul Ship-wrecked'. A previously Christianised child, accepting anything which had been already told to it from the Bible, might be taken aback at Brisley's clear classification of episodes before Abraham as 'the oldest stories', with Adam and Eve told separately in two mutually contradictory versions as in Genesis 1 and 2 (simultaneous gender creation versus Eve being drawn from Adam's rib). The telling was interesting and easily assimilable (it is not Brisley's fault that one reader confused 'conversion' and 'conversation'). Lorna Lewis wondered whether 'this fashion for telling Bible stories in plain prose to quite oldish children [is] really good? . . . sometimes I feel that Elijah and Daniel and Ruth and Naomi are better tackled in their original lovely and dramatic wording by anyone over ten . . .'.[1] But such books sold, and may have brought many children along the only road to the Bible they would get. Lewis's war work among the less reading classes should have made her more sensitive to wider social needs.

The popular children's writers of the day testified to their Christian origins in startling profusion. Jesus's life was retold by Blyton (1943), Malcolm Saville (1958) and Eleanor Graham (1959). Blyton

(1942) and Derek McCulloch ('Uncle Mac') produced versions of Bunyan's *The Pilgrim's Progress*. Theodora Wilson Wilson (1938), G. B. Harrison (1940) and Blyton (1944) rivalled Brisley as storytellers from the Bible. Dudley D. Watkins, master artist of the *Dandy* and *Beano* and creator of Desperate Dan, Lord Snooty, Oor Wullie and the Broons, yearned all his life to illustrate a Bible. Streatfeild and Crompton were the daughters of clergymen, which they utilised for information rather than approbation on clerical discourse and conduct. Johns actually had Biggles say the Lord's Prayer 'with the salt wind ruffling his hair and the gulls mewing a melancholy requiem' over 'two sailors who had gone down to the sea in a ship, never to return' – a very deliberate borrowing from Masefield, for Norwegian victims of a U-boat still making war after Germany's surrender (*Biggles' Second Case*). Frank Richards, who shared the others' religious sentiments, would not have approved of that. Thinking back on his 1940 controversy with Orwell, he wrote in 1945:[2]

In all the long *Magnet* series, said George, there was no mention of God. This complaint was a little perplexing for I have gathered from Mr Orwell's works that personally he has no use whatever for a Deity: though I hope I do him wrong. But surely it should be clear, even to George, that a work of light fiction is not one into which sacred subjects should be introduced. Religion, in a work of fiction, is out of place: either it looks like humbug, or it makes the rest of the story seem silly. Especially in boys' stories should it be avoided.

It was a Victorian custom to put pills in the jam to make the boy feel sick. All the more because I am a religious man, I carefully avoided putting religion into a boys' story. How well I remember my own feelings of utter distaste when I came upon it in the *BOP*, and in Kingston and Ballantyne, and other boys' writers of that distant day. It was a matter that I took seriously even in boyhood: and I disliked to see it mixed up with football and cricket and practical jokes. I could never get the impression that the writer was sincere: such a subject, in a boys' book, can only be dragged in. One may pray oneself, and have a deep conviction that one's prayers have been answered: but to make a fictitious character do so with a like result seems to me utterly irreverent. Fiction is always dangerously near the edge of lying: and in such a case it goes over the edge.

It has always been one of my ambitions to write a book on

religion: but if I ever do so, certainly it will not begin with 'I say, you fellows', or be published in weekly numbers.

Thus Richards reflected the *Zeitgeist* – not that of the Edwardians, as Orwell insisted, but that of the 1920s and 1930s, where God survived as an option. Richards was armed against that *Zeitgeist's* readiness to charge religious hypocrisy. Nevertheless, he made an exception to his rule. He was not prepared to let his story-villains (or at least his English ones) die with an implication of imminence of eternal damnation. He produced a repentance on the threshold of death more than once, the classic case being the 'Ravenspur Grange' series in mid-1929, when a mass murderer who has already accounted for two detective inspectors, other human obstacles, and very nearly Harry Wharton and the rest of the Famous Five, commits suicide but is persuaded to express sorrow for his crimes before he expires.[3] Similarly, when the Second World War was doing its worst, God was recruited by other authors. The *Times Literary Supplement* even devoted a review article in 1944 to children's 'Tales of Religion'. The Roman Catholic publishers Sheed & Ward were to the fore with *Gay Legends of the Saints* (including a cow called Pansy) and a presumably more austere life of St Benedict:[4] 'It was in 547 that the Saint died on Monte Cassino, having founded numerous monastic houses and foretold the destruction that would more than once overwhelm the one where he reigned as Abbot'. Whether the *Times Literary Supplement* intended this as Divine authorisation for the Allied bombing of Monte Cassino (which was certainly justified by very little else), or as a muted reproof, is unclear; possibly it merely found it amusing. Hardy perennials in pious child literature joyfully took on a new lease of life in fresh reprints. Messrs Pickering & Inglis, the evangelical publishers, ran quite a list of school stories for boys and girls, headed by C. Serjeant's *The Hero of St Basil's* in attractive covers (albeit flaunting ornate school steps) and conforming to the war-economy standards, with nothing to show that C. was for Constancia and that the work had originally appeared in 1906 as *His Captain*, retitled in 1932. It was an edifying story of a schoolboy's devotion to Christ (His Captain) which enables him not only to rescue the school bully from a fire ('Then, very quietly, Jack spoke to his Captain. "Please, Captain", he said, "this is a real S.O.S. this time. Please bring Thompson to his senses and give him courage to do as I tell him. For Thine own Name's sake. Amen" ') but also to convert him, and, by dint of his own subsequent near-fatal injuries, convert his own mother as well ('She went to a great many parties, dances, and "shows"").[5] But the publishing tactics hinted more at the wisdom of the serpent than the innocence of the dove, as did the retitling of other ancient items in the firm's booklist.

The changing times were reflected in other traditionally Christian outlets. Talbot Baines Reed still reappeared with his cheerful muscular Christianity unimpaired in *The Adventures of a Three-Guinea Watch*, still ticking its message away as vigorously as ever for all of its sixty-odd years (modern schoolboys no less than ancient might particularly appreciate its warning that hard work *can* kill an overzealous student), but its parent magazine the *Boy's Own Paper* now came formally from the Lutterworth Press rather than the Religious Tract Society, and seemed more preoccupied with war than with God. The atomic bomb ultimately made it think a bit, editorialising (presumably from Leonard Halls, who served from 1942 to 1946) in October 1945:[6]

I venture the view that the use of this terrible invention will be justified only if it induces the world at last to solve its problems without resorting to war. All *your* hopes, as well as mine, centre on that – on the hope of living free from the fear of murderous extinction, whether instant or gradual.

In the business of turning that hope into reality each of us can play a part: by the honesty and decency with which we treat each other, by our loyalty to the best that we know, and by refusing to agree to the doing of those things which we know to be wrong – in such small yet all-important ways even *we* can help to banish from our world '*the terror by night . . . the arrow that flieth by day*'.

Psalm 91, of course, promises that God will deliver us from these things; but the *BOP* seemed to leave it up to ourselves, especially those of the age-group for which it still issued its truncated size ($7\frac{1}{2}'' \times 5''$ from March 1942, having begun the war at $11'' \times 8''$) and paper-restricted circulation.

The *BOP*'s most celebrated contributor in these years, W. E. Johns, nevertheless brought in God much more than ever before, if not in the evangelical Protestant form to which the magazine had given so much. France had been Johns's great love other than Britain, from the time of his First World War service, and during the Second World War he brought out six France-related novels, time and again introducing Roman Catholic clergy as symbols of hope. *Worrals Carries On*, serialised in the *Girl's Own Paper* from October 1941, had Worrals, unexpectedly landed in France, stumble over twelve British army fugitives from Dunkirk 'collected by the good padre, Father Giraldus' (the introduction is made by 'Captain Charles . . . not . . . an official British agent . . . an English author': Captain Charles is self-styled – so was Captain Johns). *Biggles 'Fails to Return'* has Bertie thrown over a cliff (by an unwitting collaborator of Biggles) and tended by a Monégasque woman who assumes that he did not fall fatally into the gorge because 'Doubtless, the good Sainte Dévote saved you'. Ste Dévote was believed to have been martyred in Corsica in AD 303; and her feast, 27 January, is a holiday in Monaco, believed to be the day on which Christians secretly reburied her body. The woman tells Bertie to light a candle or two in 'our little church of Ste Dévote'; and in fact he goes to

> where the little church faced across the harbour. A black-robed priest was just opening the doors.
>
> '*Mon père*' said Bertie, taking a hundred-franc note from his pocket, 'this morning I had a fall on the *escalier* above, and nearly lost my life. It is my desire to buy two large candles as a thankoffering.'
>
> The priest smiled. 'Come in, my son. You look pale. Are you hurt?'
>
> 'Not much', answered Bertie.
>
> 'Nevertheless, perhaps a small glass of cordial would help to restore the life which our Sainte Dévote undoubtedly saved.'
>
> 'I think that would be a very good idea, father', agreed Bertie, who was more shaken than he was prepared to admit.

And that is all. The priest plays no other part in the story, and the entire quotation is completely irrelevant to the plot. If Johns had been the author that Eleanor Graham said he was, such a passage would be impossible. In fact, much of his memorable quality in his best work turns on apparent irrelevance, evidently released to catch a whiff of local atmosphere. In a Catholic writer, the reader would take it as part of his kit, save that a Catholic writer would not present peasants and priests ascribing divine intervention to saints – at least not without some reminder that strict Catholic theology limits the effectiveness of Mary and the saints to aid in seeking God's mercy. Johns seems to have made the gesture to symbolise the true spirit of Monaco – and behind it, France – saving the life of British agents and thus at least spiritually lending aid to the British cause. The chapter is entitled 'Good Samaritans' in what seems more accurate use than the term generally gets, since in Jesus' parable the Good Samaritan is from a people, and subscribes to a religious faith, alien to the hearers of the story. This is not 'God is on our side' so much as 'their God is on our side'.[7]

A couple of months later, *King of the Commandos* introduced yet another priest who proves a wholehearted collaborator with the British, having first rumbled their disguises. That, unlike the Ste Dévote episode, is standard stuff for British propaganda in children's books. But it carries one nuance of a more revolutionary character. Johns in his more traditional moments was a latter-day imperialist – as in *Biggles in Africa* (1936), or *Biggles Air Commodore* (1937) – although under the threat of Japanese pseudo-liberationist tactics he became much more little-England, as in *Biggles in the Orient*. A deep, though neglected, theme in the study of British imperial literature is its anti-clericalism. The witchdoctor is the root of native disaffection, or the Mad Mullah, or the prophet Greenmantle – or the Irish priest. Orwell, half-rebellious in his recollection of his Burmese days as an imperial policeman, acknowledged that,[8] with part of his mind, 'I thought that the greatest joy in the world would be to drive a bayonet into a Buddhist priest's guts'. This seems to have been a product of the English state, whose Church is headed by its monarch; the Scots, the Irish and the Welsh for varying reasons do not derive from it, and where they do it is their Englishness coming out. The idea of religious dedication capable of resisting the power of the state seems not only wrong in classic English imperial theory, but vaguely blasphemous, possibly recalling the one time England saw that happen, and the King was killed. Hence the bitterness with which English commentators on the Irish question spoke of the disruptive and even incendiary nature of certain Irish Catholic clerics. Given the persecution to which the English had subjected so much of the Irish Catholic priesthood down the centuries, resentment against Irish Catholic clerical power seems hardly reasonable, but it is logical: what should be mutually supporting origins of authority, church and state, are here mutually hostile; and clergy, in the English polity spiritual defenders of the state, were in the Irish tradition its opponents and subversives. What Johns celebrates in *King of the Commandos* is precisely such a Roman Catholic clergy, but subversive of German rule, not of British. Father Edwinus gives Gimlet lists of German personnel and French prisoners in the local chateau (whose chapel, to the priest's anger, the Nazis have turned into the prison dormitory):

Gimlet opened his notebook and jotted down the names as the priest dictated them.

'This information is of the greatest importance, father', he said, as he closed the book. 'If I get back, your co-operation shall be made known to the leaders of the liberation, when it comes.'

'I ask no thanks', said the *curé* simply. 'What I do is no more than any true Frenchman would do for our beloved France. Is it possible that your Government can help these unfortunates, *monsieur*? Retribution when the Nazis are driven out will be of no comfort to them if they are already dead, as it seems likely they will be.'

'Something shall be done', replied Gimlet firmly. 'How did you learn all this?'

'That is a question I prefer not to answer', returned Father Edwinus. 'I have sources of information. Does it matter where it comes from?'

'Not in the least', answered Gimlet.

Gimlet's ease in talking to the priest may come in part from the Catholic Simon Lord Lovat, Scots commando leader on whom Gimlet is said to have been modelled (but who certainly did not share his snobbery, want of humour or bad manners). But the allusion to the priest's 'sources' again harks back to the bogeys in the British imperial bonnet, that Catholic priests have diabolical powers by means of the confessional. Edwinus does not mean that he violates the secrecy of the confessional, presumably, but that after the act of confessing sins, sympathetic persons confide useful details of Nazi rule of which the priest might be able to make use. Theologically, the priest might believe that, if a person in confession admits to collaboration, however limited, with a regime as anti-Christian as the Nazis, the penitent should make the best possible efforts to subvert it consistent with personal safety or the safety of members of the family. (A Catholic confessing to theft is expected to make any possible restitution in order to be forgiven.) And, for this chapter-title also, Johns seems to be making a statement of *double entendre*. It is 'The Man of God'. A couple of chapters later, Gimlet tells the priest:

'for the next few minutes the work will be better suited for soldiers than for priests – you understand?'

'I comprehend perfectly, *monsieur*', said Father Edwinus quietly. 'I understand also that this is total war, and that the

Nazis started it. . . . What those who were here before me [in the Franco-Prussian war] could do, so I, under God's blessing, can also do. Proceed, my son, and take no account of me.'

This, for all of the priest's historicism, is not intended as First World War stuff, with angels at Mons and bishops blessing Big Berthas. This is the culture of a defeated country, with God as the last refuge. Gimlet is in a highly apocalyptic mood when he settles accounts a little later, wiping out a German officer and then turning on a French spy:[9]

'No!' gasped the man. 'No! In God's name!' His terror was pathetic, but it made no impression on the man who confronted him.

'So you call on God?' sneered Gimlet. 'Were you thinking of God when you betrayed a girl who has more courage in one finger than you have in the whole of your vile body? Yet you would have sent her to her death for a handful of Nazi-tarnished francs. You *Judas*. Now go and spend them in hell!'

Brent-Dyer, as the leading Catholic writer for children published during the war (Tolkien was writing but not publishing), gave testimony to Catholic priesthood in *The Chalet School in Exile* (1940), where some Chalet School girls' intervention to save a Jew menaced by a mob necessitates their rescue by a priest: the Jew, his wife and the priest are killed later in the day, offstage. Brent-Dyer had by then published thirteen previous Chalet School novels, set in the Austrian Tyrol, apparently based on a brief visit there in the early 1920s, and on another in 1930 to see the Passion Play at Oberammergau (remembered for a vivid description in *The Chalet School and Jo*). The Oberammergau experience apparently decided Brent-Dyer on conversion to Roman Catholicism. She remained a vigorously ecumenical writer, unique in her time, and many of her heroines remain Anglicans (including the headmistress Miss Annersley, despite her nickname 'the Abbess'). But because Catholic Austria, and Catholic Bavaria which she had visited for Oberammergau, were respectively Hitler's birthplace and Nazism's, Brent-Dyer was at pains to stress Nazism's intrinsic anti-Catholicism. The priest knows that in saving the girls he seals his own fate:

The others followed pell-mell, and helped to drag them in almost before the mob had realised what was happening. When they did, wild yells of fury rose.

'Quick!' gasped the priest, 'Help me bar the door!'

Jo and the American girls helped him, and they slammed it shut just in time. The foremost hooligans were already flinging themselves at it with howls of rage as they saw their new quarry vanish. It was an easy matter to fling over the great iron bars and turn the heavy key. They were safe for the moment.

But it was only for the moment, and no one knew this better than Vater Johann.

He gets the girls away through a secret passage.

'Down there!' he said, pointing. 'Then straight on till you come out on the mountain-side. I must go back and remove the Blessed Sacrament, and put it to safety. Hasten!'

The urgency with which he spoke put wings to their feet. One by one they entered, and went down the stairs. As Joey's black head, looking wilder than ever before, disappeared, he slammed the trap to, with a fervent blessing on them, and went back into the church to remove its greatest treasure, the Blessed Sacrament, to a place of safety from the disappointed fury of the mob, for well he knew that once they broke in, he need expect no mercy.

It's important that we actually see events for a few sentences through the eyes of the doomed priest – a consideration in third-person narrative to which children are frequently more alive than are professional critics – so that reader-identification can be strengthened. This is the last we see of him, and six pages later we learn that ' "They shot Vater Johann . . . He saved the Blessed Sacrament, so he is quite happy." . . . "if he had lived, it would mean prison for helping you to escape. He prefers death to a Nazi gaol." '[10]

Brent-Dyer was right about Nazi mobs and Nazi anti-Catholicism. Austrian Catholic clerical resistance on behalf of protectors of Jews was probably rare enough, and Nazi arrests of Austrian Catholic clergy even rarer at that point. Brent-Dyer mentioned Nazi closure of Catholic schools after *Anschluss*; and the pattern of Nazi mob action followed by Nazi official measures as she describes them was characteristic (the girls flee from the mob, but they must then be smuggled into Switzerland or be imprisoned by the government). The issue of the Blessed Sacrament is probably the only point in the whole Chalet School saga when Brent-Dyer left her Protestant readers to flounder by themselves. This is a coded message to a Catholic audience: Nazism is the enemy of Catholicism at its doctrinal heart.

The Catholic doctrine of transubstantiation meant that what the priest was saving from the mob was God Himself in the form of a large white host, probably in a monstrance for veneration. The unconsecrated hosts – unleavened bread – were of no consequence, but Catholic readers would also presume the existence of a chalice (ciborium) to hold a reserve supply of consecrated hosts for distribution at subsequent Communion should there be more communicants than hosts consecrated at the Mass itself. Brent-Dyer does not say how the Sacrament (whether one host or many) was 'saved'; non-Catholic children would not understand, Catholic children would not need to be told. He would have eaten them. The book was published in early 1940, and there was no cause to assume any British Catholic sentiment in favour of Hitler which could be inimical to the war effort. But Brent-Dyer, with a far better European sense than most of her fellow-writers, for all of the brevity of her European visits, knew that widespread Catholic opinion in the British Isles had supported Franco, that considerable numbers had thought well of Mussolini and that some portion of these might at least think well of Hitler's anti-Communism (a constituency which must have been disillusioned as badly as much of the left over the Nazi–Soviet pact). Brent-Dyer presumably knew that she had a definite following among Catholic parents, much encouraged to have their children read Catholic authors. (Clerics, especially nuns, would have had far more effect on Catholic children's reading habits than would librarians, however militant, on children in general.) Any pro-Hitler sentiment among Irish readers or Italian-descended children in Britain should be dealt a mortal blow by that sequence. She also knew that in Ireland itself, north and south, Anglophobia was frequently obsessive among Catholics, and no doubt realised that it could lead to some support for Hitler. She ensured that children who read it would know the truth: that Hitler was Antichrist.

Brent-Dyer was also determined that the God whom she extolled would not be identified with a vengeful God. Hence in the same book, immediately after *Anschluss*, she had the girls, who were about to be disrupted by Nazi demands for the withdrawal of their German and Austrian members, sign a Peace League:[11]

We, the girls of the Chalet School, hereby vow ourselves members of the Chalet School ['Peace' in later texts] League. We swear faithfully to do all we can to promote peace between all* our countries. We will not believe any lies spoken about evil doings, but we will try to get others to work for peace as we do. We will

not betray this League to any enemy, whatever may happen to us.
If it is possible, we will meet at least once a year. And we will
always remember that though we belong to different lands, we are
members of the Chalet School League of Peace.

(*The second 'all' disappeared from later texts, possibly in a mis-
print.) The paper becomes of major importance in *The Chalet School
in Exile*, where it is pursued by Nazi agents to discover which
subjects of the Reich have signed it. But it is reasserted in *The
Chalet School Goes to It* (1941), when the School, now fled from
Guernsey, reopens in Wales; and Miss Annersley closes her speech
on it:

> As things are, we can do very little for those of its members who
> are still in enemy country. But remember, they are Chalet School
> girls, who have been trained in the same ideals as you have. God
> alone knows what these girls may be suffering now, and there is
> only one thing we can do to help them. Let us all do it with all our
> might. We mean to gain the victory; for, make no mistake, this evil
> thing called Nazi-ism that has reared its head above the world like
> a venomous snake must perish as all evil must. There are many in
> Germany, more in Austria, who hate it as we do. Theirs may be a
> martyrdom which, in God's great mercy, *we* may be spared. I hope
> we are. But those who belong to our League are part of us, even
> though we cannot communicate with them at present. . . .

So they devise a prayer asking God to watch over all members of the
Peace League, help them to live up to its ideals and to use it when
Peace comes. It plays little part after Peace, but there were no Chalet
School books between 1944 and 1949. Miss Annersley's conclusion –
'this is the least we owe to those German and Austrian members who
are "carrying on" amid such terrible doings as we read of, and we
must pay our debt faithfully. Let us pray' – must be unique in the
Second World War literature for children.[12]

If the Peace League was courageous for its author no less than for
its votaries, she showed awareness of it in the anger with which
Lavender Leigh, niece of a best-selling author for children, responds
to its pledge: 'There had been a moment's silence . . . Then a small
clear voice was heard to remark, 'But that's saying we'll be decent to
the Germans! I call it most unpat–' upon which a Chalet stalwart
shoves a hand over her mouth ('You were going to say our vow was
unpatriotic, weren't you? It isn't . . . it's the truest patriotism and real

Christianity'). The best-selling aunt has previously explained to Miss
Wilson (who had led the fugitive schoolgirls from the Nazi mob):

> 'I think it so *necessary* for a child's tastes to be moulded in the
> right direction from the very first. I have always tried to keep ugly
> things from her. I have never even allowed her to listen-in to the
> war news. I do feel that we should try to keep our children as free
> from all horrors as possible, don't you, Miss Wilson?'
>   'The little ones – yes', said Miss Wilson. 'But I also feel that
> when children reach the teens, at any rate, they ought to know
> something of the evils we are fighting against – something of what
> other children, no older than they, are enduring in the occupied
> countries. After all, it will be, in great measure, the boys and girls
> who are now in their early teens who will have to rebuild life, once
> the war is over. . . . it doesn't do to wrap children up in too much
> cotton-wool. It may have answered in our mothers' day, when a girl
> was, in the main, expected to stay at home until she married, and
> went to a home of her own. But these children will have to go out
> and face the world . . . they must learn something of what war in
> these days of mechanism can mean, so that they can build and
> work to prevent its ever happening again. Or, if that be too high an
> ideal – and it certainly is Utopian – at any rate so that they can
> prevent its ever becoming so gigantic.'
>   Miss Leigh stared at her as if she were talking some strange,
> new language. 'But – that is a terrible view to take of life!' she cried.
> 'As for facing the world, I hope my little Lavender will not have to
> do that. . . .'

It is not clear whether Brent-Dyer had a target in mind (she had Miss
Annersley express admiration for Crompton in an earlier work, so
adoption of Crompton's method in demolition of A. A. Milne might
have tempted her) or whether she was simply dissecting a trend
visible among her fellow-writers for children during the war. Any-
how, Miss Wilson gets a last word – an ominous one for our own
times:[13]

> 'Did *you* expect ever to serve in the army? Yet it has come. No, Miss
> Leigh; make no mistake! From the time they are old enough to
> understand what starvation and terrorism mean, our children
> must be taught about them, so that they can see to it that *their*
> children shall not go through what so many of the children of the
> present day are going through!'

The linking of starvation to terrorism was particularly perceptive, as is the reminder that those who cause starvation also practise terrorism.

Miss Wilson's irritation was all the greater because the Chalet School had had its risks with bombing, and had duly prayed (hardly the rebuttal to make to a prospective pupil's guardian, perhaps, and it was not made). *The Chalet School Goes to It* has its noises of Newport and Cardiff bombing-raids audible to the school; and Beth Chester, frightened that the noise would endanger her mother, who is still making a bad recovery from childbirth, confides to her friend Daisy:[14]

> 'Don't worry, Beth; God will look after your Mummy. We'll ask Him, shall we, us four?'
>
> 'Yes; it's the best thing to do', agreed Robin. 'Let's say our prayers for a minute or two. 'Then I expect the Abbess will be down and want us to have sing-song or something.'
>
> So the four girls closed their eyes, and prayed silently but fervently for those they loved, as well as for Mrs Chester. All around the room other people were doing the same, for that last crash had been unpleasantly near, and many of them were wondering just how near the next would be.

With due honour to Frank Richards's principles, one can see how this can have comforted readers also under bombardment. The open stress on the greatest dangers of bombing (apart from death or personal physical injury) being to expectant or recent mothers was proof of the new world which Brent-Dyer was so conscious the Second World War was bringing. It was part of what girls must become accustomed to, regardless of its revolutionary status as a girls' school-story topic. Beth has in fact resented apparent slighting by her mother to fulfil needs of the other siblings, and her anxiety and potential grief are naturally greater. Brent-Dyer was showing how normal child resentment of parents should take account of the possibility of losing them to war attrition, with the thought that death could remove a parent whose child last looked on it in anger. Christian prayer restores perspective, demanding as it does our forgiveness of others.

On the other hand, Brent-Dyer recognised feelings of vengeance, lightening the subject by its translation to an anachronistic Highland (actually Island) context. *The Highland Twins at the Chalet School* is very much a Second World War novel: the 11-year-old twins never

previously away from their remote Scottish island encounter a
bombing-raid on their train south, glass showering their carriage.
The children tell some blood-curdlers on vengeance by their
McDonald kinsmen on Campbells; and, when a U-boat guns
down their brother Hugh and fellow-survivors of their sunken
destroyer,

> Archie McDonald, filled with the fire that had inflamed his young
> ancestor three centuries before, showed such reckless daring
> during the night raids over Germany, that he was later awarded
> the Distinguished Flying Cross, when all he was thinking about
> was revenge for the cowardly slaying of his brother.

Johns had played that card earlier – indeed, twice earlier, as its
Second World War text was cannibalised, but in *Spitfire Parade* the
story turned on the coward Henry Harcourt's vengeance for the
supposed death of his pet pig from a German bomb. Brent-Dyer
took it seriously in trying to come to terms with her perception of
a Highland *mentalité* conceived somewhere between Macaulay's
History and the more scholarly contributions to the *Adventure* or
some comparable comic. Brent-Dyer's Christian morality reprehended such sentiments (at least from girls; most of Brent-Dyer's
men are past praying for), but she fell for another facet. Flora was the
vengeful twin; Fiona was the 'fey' one. The Catholic Brent-Dyer was
on very shaky ground here. Fiona sees Hugh's death through having
'the second sight', vividly and ably described. Then Dr Jack Bettany
is lost at sea, the Admiralty send out an intimation of his suspected
death, the perennial heroine (now his wife Jo) goes into a depression,
Fiona offers to search for him with the second sight, and Jo provides
her with his rosary beads by which to do it. Inevitably, it is thus
discovered he is still alive, and he returns home at the end of the
book. But in so pedagogic a work, this was a dangerous concession
to the popular Protestant view of Catholicism's entwinement with
superstition. Traditionally, Catholic practices have often been
grafted on pagan ones: the choice of mid-December, a light festival
amid universal darkness, for the birthday assigned to Jesus is the
most famous instance of it. But, however frequent such an imposition, to invoke it remains bad – and indeed dangerous – doctrine.
Miss Wilson, a Catholic, declares very strongly against it, but the
happy outcome forgets her warning. 'I don't like it, Hilda. It's
meddling with powers best left alone.' And it is Protestants who
determine on use of the second sight. Jo recovers so well that she

can once more write the school play in which an old gaffer in a smock-frock laments the loss of the old Christmas: 'Ah, Christmas ain't wot it was in my time. Us didn't stay abed then; us got hup and went 'ear Parson preach, and sing the Christmas 'ymns', to be answered with: 'Oh, we've finished with all that, grandpa. 'Itler 'as seen to that'. Hitler has destroyed Christmas, unless we let it return.

That was a shrewd indictment; but Brent-Dyer had also involuntarily testified to a renewal of superstition during the war.[15] Little of it surfaces in children's fiction; but the revival of the Christian God was shadowed by the return of more uncertain pagan predecessors. Ginger tells a ghost story to the Biggles Squadron Mess which proves to be about talking ravens, but a post-war Worrals novel turned on ill-luck dictated by opals.[16] Crompton ridiculed ghost appearance with delicious satire but, after the war, began to involve herself in psychic phenomena, again, like Brent-Dyer, giving her belief frontiers with Christianity. The contemplation of much evil at work had its impact on the creative generation writing for the young, and people began to augment the protective Christian shield. Thrillers for readers allegedly in the adult bracket were being discharged for a mass readership by Dennis Wheatley as he had his heroes mix traditional Christianity and white magic in opposition to Hitler's supposed black magicians.[17]

Throughout the war, the great Catholic novel was in preparation by an author for children, Professor J. R. R. Tolkien. It, too, played with various forms of magic in the person of the white magician Gandalf. But *The Lord of the Rings* was primarily concerned with very fundamental Christian doctrine. Tolkien denied its being an allegory, which his friend Lewis would create on Christ's Crucifixion in *The Lion, the Witch and the Wardrobe*. *The Lord of the Rings* seems something allied but opposite: a parable. It also reflects the atmosphere in which it was written: the Battle of Gondor is obviously charged by the Battle of Britain. More exactly, Tolkien called it the Siege of Gondor; and it was essentially a Siege of Britain too. It was a siege broken by battles and individual engagements, and as death came down on Britain from the skies – what Edith Sitwell called 'The Terrible Rain':[18]

And yet – who dreamed that Christ had died in vain?
He walks again on the Seas of Blood, He comes in the terrible Rain.

As Naomi Mitchison saw, it was like the fearful parts of old fairy-stories come back, and Tolkien alone found the epic language to translate it into a new story:[19]

> The great shadow descended like a falling cloud. And behold! it was a winged creature: if bird, then greater than all other birds, and it was naked, and neither quill nor feather did it bear, and its vast pinions were as webs of hide between horned fingers; and it stank. A creature of an older world maybe it was, whose kind, lingering in forgotten mountains cold beneath the Moon, outstayed their day, and in hideous eyrie bred this last untimely brood, apt to evil. And the Dark Lord took it, and nursed it with fell meats, until it grew beyond the measure of all other things that fly; and he gave it to his servant to be his steed. Down, down it came, and then, folding its fingered webs, it gave a croaking cry, and settled upon the body of Snowmane, digging in its claws, stooping its long naked neck.
>
> Upon it sat a shape, black-mantled, huge and threatening. A crown of steel he bore, but between rim and robe naught was there to see, save only a deadly gleam of eyes: the Lord of the Nazgûl. To the air he had returned, summoning his steed ere the darkness failed, and now he was come again, bringing ruin, turning hope to despair, and victory to death. A great black mace he wielded.

And thus was Nibelungenlied personified in the Blitzkrieg, with the kinsfolk Wagner and Nietzsche grooms of the stable. And between the dying Theoden King and his doom from the skies stood only the little hobbit Meriadoc 'on all fours like a dazed beast, and such a horror was on him that he was blind and sick' yet hearing one more voice of resistance:

> 'Begone, foul dwimmerlaik, lord of carrion! Leave the dead in peace!'
>
> A cold voice answered: 'Come not between the Nazgûl and his prey! Or he will not slay thee in thy turn. He will bear thee away to the houses of lamentation, beyond all darkness, where thy flesh shall be devoured, and thy shrivelled mind be left naked to the Lidless Eye.'
>
> A sword rang as it was drawn. 'Do what you will; but I will hinder it, if I may'.
>
> 'Hinder me? Thou fool. No living man may hinder me!'
>
> Then Merry heard of all sounds in that hour the strangest. It

seemed that Dernhelm laughed, and the clear voice was like the ring of steel. 'But no living man am I! You look upon a woman. Eowyn I am, Eomund's daughter. You stand between me and my lord and kin. Begone, if you be not deathless! For living or dark undead, I will smite you, if you touch him.'

Tolkien had seen what Johns had diagnosed: the women would be the backbone of the struggle when the men had gone beyond their wits' end, after the men had forbidden the women from war beyond elementary support. Tolkien had always felt *Macbeth*'s false security ill-answered: it was not Macduff who could have shown himself no man of woman born, but Lady Macduff. But Tolkien told his epic in its own terms, informed by what England had suffered and resisted while he was writing, but working his own parable. The eagles bring safety to the defenders of Gondor and the penetrators of Mordor in the end, as the Royal Air Force against all hope cleared their country's skies. But it is only the two little hobbits Frodo and Samwise, and their self-accursed shadow Gollum, who can end the Lord of the Rings and his rule. Like small commandos – like Cub, in fact – they make their way into Mordor and up Mount Doom, and there Frodo fails in his quest, unable to resist the temptation of becoming a Lord wielding power akin to that of the enemy he has sought to destroy. Hitler cannot be vanquished by becoming another Hitler; Satan is not cast out by Beelzebub. Biggles knows he does not vindicate his cause against the Nazis if he acts like a Nazi. But, because Frodo has spared his enemy Gollum, that enemy now intervenes to save him from himself, bites off the finger with the Ring and falls to his death. Tolkien would say that the story was to illustrate the words of the Lord's Prayer:

> Forgive us our trespasses as we forgive those who trespass
> against us;
> And lead us not into temptation, But deliver us from evil.

If the horrors of the Second World War did yet further violence to a vulnerable God, Tolkien shows us that its corollary was won by vulnerable heroes, whose clemency rather than arrogance would be their salvation. The nuclear bomb was no such clemency. And the perfect hero was no such victor. He was highly representative in this: Second World War heroes had to be human.

Equally, their God had to be human. Malcolm Saville would write a fervent life of Christ, *King of Kings*, but his fiction demanded a God to love who would liberate, not simply require. *Seven White Gates* (1944), his second novel (about the same children, also serialised by BBC Children's Hour on the wireless), placed Peter in some bewilderment at the farm of her Uncle Micah, a formidable depressive:

> Peter sat down thankfully. But only for a moment. A glance like black lightning from the head of the table brought her to her feet again for grace. And what a grace! So different from the simple, sincere 'Lord, Bless this Food . . .' of Hatchholt, for this was a personal appeal for mercy and light from Uncle Micah to his Maker.

Significantly, Uncle Micah is put on the road to recovery by the arrival of the Morton twins, who lack the disadvantage of adults' sophistication and Peter's growing maturity, and thus cut the Gordian knot by simple affection:[20]

> Mary said suddenly: 'I'm not going, I want to talk to Uncle Micah. I like him, and I think he wants cheering up', and she gave him the dazzling smile that was usually more than enough for most strangers.
> [Peter] . . . gasped to see Uncle Micah appear with a twin holding each hand. Although they could not hear what was being said, it seemed that an animated conversation was in progress. Any conversation in which the twins took part was likely to be lively, as she knew, but she was surprised to see Uncle Micah pat Dickie on the head and then grimace behind his beard.
> 'Look at him, David! When he does that, he's smiling. He is, really! I saw him do it once before. . . .'

The story naturally entails the twins bringing about the recovery of Uncle Micah, partly by accident, but what is crucial is their logic which gets them to the heart of his tragedy at once, and answer it by ignoring it without entry into complex unexplained psychological reasons which have divided him and his lost son. The Blytonian children-solve-the-mystery is applied to a family crisis by Saville, showing how some problems are those which *only* children can solve. Blyton grasped the formula that children want to triumph where adults have failed; and for much of the time Saville might seem content with that. But here he showed children what they could do by directness and love, unencumbered by adult obfuscation. It reflected the times in its relative indifference to good behaviour.

The Victorian moral precepts accounting for success were hilariously subverted by the verse for children by Hilaire Belloc, appropriately collected and widely distributed at the world war with a message summed up in the Introduction to *Cautionary Tales* when asked whether its satirical tales were true:[21]

> And is it True? It is not True,
> And if it were it wouldn't do,
> For people such as me and you
> Who pretty nearly all day long
> Are doing something rather wrong.
> Because if things were really so,
> You would have perished long ago,
> And I would not have lived to write
> The noble lines that meet your sight,
> Nor B.T.B. survived to draw
> The nicest things you ever saw.

And in the war itself, bombs did not wait on table manners or discriminate between the prig and the pirate. What Saville did realise in *Seven White Gates* was Jesus' teaching of the need to be as children in order to lead. It may have been the ethos of many of the other writers, but seldom as successfully as here.

The war and its impact on Britain, specifically the United States Army, is pivotal to *Seven White Gates*, but its relevance to the main theme of love and reconciliation is metaphorical. The place of God in war fiction is in general much more debatable, once we escape from the old Adam who firmly enlisted God for military purposes. A satirical Irish novel of these years, Mervyn Wall's *The Unfortunate Fursey* (1946), much enjoyed by children for its ribald anti-clericalism, featured Irish bishops in the Dark Ages hurling maledictions against the forces of enemy Irish kingdoms, whose bishops would eagerly reciprocate.[22] Wall would here have targeted the world at war in 1939–45 no less than ancient Ireland, and particularly his own religion: undoubtedly the Roman Catholic Church had many bishops on different sides praying for victory. Pope Benedict XV had denounced the First World War and a few Catholics went to jail in obedience to his opposition to armed service; Pope Benedict XVI would choose his name in order to pledge himself to the cause of peace. But the Second World War lay uncondemned, with subsequent doubts as to the Vatican's loyalties. The Blitzkrieg campaign, the Battle of Britain and the Blitz on Britain made it the hardest war for pacifists to condemn, as it remained when news of the Holocaust began to emerge. The phoney war of 1939 and early 1940 had certainly seemed a natural war for pacifists to reject, and pacifism raised ugly questions about Allied bombing of civilians after the outcry against German civilian bombing. These were not moral questions easily raised in children's fiction, especially since neither publishers nor the civil authorities would encourage the raising of them. In general, writers for children might seem naturally hostile to wars likely to devour the small readers either in their infancy by bombs or in adult youth by battle; alternatively, there were the many writers for children who seemed to see themselves as cultural paediatricians developing their charges for war service and sacrifice. Westerman was obviously a case of the latter. But Johns is described by his biographers for the years that gave birth to Biggles as 'The Militant Pacifist'. Crompton mockingly regarded war as human nature, using William's exploitation of the peace movement with which to rearm his bankrupt followers with weapons confiscated from his enemies in the name of peace.[23] Blyton showed real horror of war: Mary's tears for the slaughtered German sailors at the end of *The Adventurous Four* would seem to have been shed on behalf of her creator. Streatfeild, Saville and other writers involved in support for the civilian population under bombing clearly preferred to think of Britain as victim rather than avenger. The Rev. W. Awdry began his stories of Thomas the Tank Engine during a war in which he and his pregnant wife were left destitute after a bellicose vicar had fired him from his curacy for his principles. His own convictions did not visibly appear in his little books, but his case concentrates the issue. How could war be condoned by the God whose personal appearance on earth brought His own martyrdom, His rejection of armed struggle in His defence, and His instruction to turn the other cheek when struck – the God who would inspire the cause of passive resistance as invoked by the Rev. Martin Luther King ten years after Hiroshima?

Easily, for many writers. The understanding and sympathy shown for pacifists in the First World War by John Buchan when making a pacifist a hero on the British side in the war, in *Mr Standfast*, was brilliant propaganda but was also capable of acknowledging, if rejecting, the pacifist case, and of not denying its integrity: one of the great passages in the book is the utter scorn with which the pacifist Wake lashes Richard Hannay for his assumption that pacifism means support for the enemy.[24] The dying Buchan in Canada devoted some of his last literary hours, as the Second World War began, to celebration of the principle of saving lives rather than destroying them, whence *Sick Heart River*: the hand that made Wake, now dead, fashioned in kindred artifice for Leithen, now dying. The Second World War brought no such diversion of God from war, especially in a religious context. Pacifists were presented as more loathsome figures than Nazi agents: Gwendoline Courtney is kind to the German girl blackmailed into Nazi espionage in *The Denehurst Secret Service*, and wastes little time in denunciation of the alleged uncle and aunt who manipulate her; but its pacifist schoolmistress is demonised, shows to be sadistic and repressive in her attempts to discourage the war spirit in her charges, and ultimately forced to resign her post. By contrast, the traitor school-master in Havilton's *School versus Spy*, although a murderer and kidnapper under our eyes, is given a bleak dignity in the death he so clearly deserves. As for religion, Dorita Fairlie Bruce's *Nancy Calls the Tune* planks her long-time schoolgirl hero, now grown up, at the organ in a rural Scots kirk; but, when the minister's brother proves to be a pacifist, he is described as disgracing his family in terms which would be severe had he become a male prostitute, for which his 'rather effeminate features' and 'lock of long black hair' seem to equip him. Nancy concludes that if he took a peace mission to France, as he hopes to do, 'Goebbels would have him broadcasting for them from comfortable quarters in some hotel de luxe'. The diagnosis of his condition by his brother the minister is self-reproachful:

'I've slipped up badly where Gordon's concerned', he told her in the same gloomy tone, 'though I can't think how it happened. I wish to heaven I could! and then I might stand a chance of putting things right!'

'I can tell you', replied Nancy crisply, 'you've spoilt him out-rageously – but it's too late to remedy that now. The only way is to be really obdurate for once and get him clear of Easterbraes. I am not thinking of him altogether, I'm afraid', with a little deprecating laugh, 'I'm not actually thinking of him at all! You have taught me, during the last few months while I have been working for you, to put the church before most things; if the minister's brother is caught by the military police lurking in the organ-loft to escape service, it will do more harm to the South Kirk than a stick of incendiaries through the roof. For any sort of scandal to touch a church –'

Reader, she married him, or at least was set so to do when Fairlie Bruce took permanent leave of her at the story's end ('him' being minister, not pacifist); and Fairlie Bruce deserves credit for showing how a girl who has not yet admitted her marital ambitions to herself is already thinking from the vantage-point of her future occupation. She also conveys the weakness of the Church of Scotland's peculiar strength: it is a state church, but it has had a long, vigorous, courageous voluntary tradition and is more sensitive than the Church of England to congregational opinion ('There is not a family in it but has sons and daughters serving in the Forces, and they can hardly help being scornful of conduct such as Gordon Macrae's'). Simultaneously, it has an established church's instinctive sense of duty to the state, although a Calvinist established church knows itself to be the state's superior (as in recent years the Church of Scotland has dramatically showed on the Scottish constitution). Fairlie Bruce herself spent her first ten years in Scotland but the next fifty in England; *Nancy Calls the Tune* was an earnest of her future return to Scotland (she came back after her father's death, in 1949). Hence she would naturally think in terms of what some might call a supportive, others a subservient, church, in matters of state.

The extraordinary thing is that at no point is there the faintest suggestion that the pacifist might be interpreting the scriptures more correctly than the minister, or indeed, despite his brother's vocation or his own indiscreet enthusiasm for singing in church, that he could be influenced by any religious sentiment. L. M. Montgomery, writing as a Presbyterian minister's wife rather than writing about a Presbyterian minister's future wife, took the same attitude in *Rilla of Ingleside* to pacifism in the First World War: it was contemptible and irrelevant to religion. Fairlie Bruce redeems the pacifist ('I always believed there must be some decency hidden away in you somewhere, seeing you came of good stock') when he breaks his leg saving the victims of an air raid:

> 'I saw hell let loose last night in Eastport', he answered simply, 'and it knocked all the nonsense clean out of me. None of my fine theories of universal brotherhood could stand up to those kids dead and dying in that orphanage they bombed. And they knew it was an orphanage, damn them! . . . you bet their spies kept them well informed . . .'

There is no thought that comparable actions by Allied air strikes might strengthen a pacifist case ('Goering won't leave many young pacifists in this country by the time he has finished – or has been finished himself'); and the minister can now pop the question ('When

I ask a girl to marry me I like to be able to look her in the face, with no shadow of disgrace in my family background – and now, thank God, I can').[25]

If Dorita Fairlie Bruce could identify pacifism with disgrace to the Church of Scotland and delight for the Devil, what of the Devil himself? Never had an enemy of Britain better deserved the identification than Hitler, for all of the freedom with which children's writers in the past had assigned diabolic status to Joan of Arc (after all, more children may have read William Shakespeare down the centuries than anyone else has), Philip II of Spain, Louis XIV of France, Napoleon, the Nana Sahib or Kaiser Wilhelm II. And Hitler seems to have held a derisive place in British conversation far more than any of his hated precursors. He invited it, in part because, however analogous to the Prince of Darkness, he differed from those precursors in having no princely status. He was the Austrian paperhanger, he was Schickelgruber, he was the man who couldn't grow a full moustache, he was the ranting Führer whose insistence on everyone saying 'Heil Hitler!' so easily invited Hell Hitler. The British looked at him with hatred but fought him with contempt. But if he was as bad as or worse than the Devil, he was never taken to be superhuman; he was not Victoria's grandson, like the Kaiser, he was not a possible evil spirit, like the Nana Sahib, he was not Napoleonic, for all of the horrific sudden success of the Blitzkrieg of April–June 1940. Nobody memorably enshrined him in a romance for adults or children, as Buchan did with such propagandistic genius in the guilt-ridden, nightmare-haunted Kaiser Wilhelm in *Greenmantle* (1916). Blyton produced her Biff, Linklater his Bloot, and as each heaped their noble scorn their instinctive weapon was caricature. Artists had anticipated them. David Low drooped the moustache, jowled the cheeks, inflated the backside. Even official leaflets exploited it: the drawing warning parents against bringing evacuated children back to their London homes showed a shadowy, obscene, smirking Hitler tempting a British mother to bring them back, with the hint that he would force her into prostitution for his enrichment if he could. Churchill's rhetoric proclaimed the caricature war, and its frequently childlike appeal harmonised with the comics, where alone Hitler became a regular literary feature. Dudley D. Watkins and the Thomson comics made Hitler the greatest butt of all, whining for food, snivelling because the British cannot see how great he is, dropping propaganda leaflets whose consumption enables Snooty's goat to win first prize, kicking himself when he hears of it ('Ach! take that Adolf! Der Dangsniggled Lord Snooty has fooled me again!'), painting signs on his palace to avert bombs ('NOTICE TO R. A. F. THIS IS HITLER'S PALACE – PLEASE DON'T DROP ANY BOMBS ON ME – HITLER'). The fear that under-11s would be traumatised by talk of war was answered by imprisoning the enemy images in a theatre of the absurd. Napoleon thought that the retreat from Moscow brought him from the sublime to the ridiculous; the children's Hitler in Second World War Britain never got beyond the ridiculous. Hitler's spies might inspire fear in the pages of Crompton, or Havilton, or Saville – Saville, like Lewis, made the most terrifying figures women, harking back to the old witch/stepmother tradition which Lewis would consciously invoke. But, in general, Nazis, and especially Hitler, are contemptible to the point of banality.

Brent-Dyer was perhaps the only the Second World War writer for children whose religion was transformed by her books (as opposed to Tolkien and Lewis, whose books would be transformed by their religions); and her books, through the voice of a German girl, declared Nazism

'of the devil – come from Hell. The world can never be right until it is gone, and the men who made it are gone also. . . . I tell you that nothing you have heard – *nothing!* – can ever show you how terrible it is. One must live with it to learn that . . .

'the Nazis . . . take the children from their parents when they are yet too young to know, and teach them their own wicked thoughts. . . . once every good German *Mädchen* hoped the day would come when she, too, would have babies. *I* hoped it might never come, for *my* children would be taken from me, and taught things I hate and know to be evil!'

Noel Streatfeild made two attempts at Nazi-style villains. *The House in Cornwall* (1940) and *The Children of Primrose Lane* (1941) are both condemned by aficionados, though they passed muster at the time, when children were glad of a good story; the usual dreadful desire to pigeonhole writers wants to have Streatfeild as the author of *Ballet Shoes* and *Tennis Shoes*. Perhaps *The House in Cornwall* might have won better fanfare had it been called *Hitler's Shoes*, since its best work is in the depiction of a dictator incognito and his slavish English hosts who are holding a Ruritanian boy-king prisoner. The children in both books are interesting, but unduly functional on fairy-story principles in which the talents and traits pay off somewhat contractually; in *My Friend Mr Leakey*, J. B. S. Haldane brought that to a fine art in modern terms by having a joker brother, a chemist brother and a wireless brother, each successively trying to kill large quantities of rats. *Primrose Lane* is the better sociology, with its vision of three working-class families playing in an empty house; but their German spy proves a bore as well as a boor. He is gentility itself compared to *The House in Cornwall*'s Dr Manoff:[26]

> He was enormous, with a great bullet head that was permanently pushed forward. He had a bulbous mouth which was the more noticeable as every time he wanted to point a remark he passed his tongue over his lips, with the result that they glistened with saliva.
>
> He wore a magnificent uniform which accentuated the height of the man and the breadth of his shoulders. The queer thing about him, which struck you at once, was his arms. They were set rather forward, and were of incredible length, hanging practically to his knees.
>
> Manoff moved without one glance at anybody to his chair and sat down. He unfolded his napkin and tucked one end of it into his collar. Then he gave a supercilious glance at Uncle Murdock. He spoke in guttural English.
>
> 'Sit.'
>
> Uncle Murdock sat down with a look of ecstasy. It was as if that one word from Manoff was a pearl. He looked at the family.
>
> 'Sit.'

It was a nice way of showing how dictators regard their flatterers and subjects. But anything closer to Hitler was hard to create for serious consumption by children. Books that took refuge in metaphor, preferably light-hearted, were best. Katharine Tozer's series about the little elephant Mumfie – now real, now a toy, now a dream – brought its idea of fantasy to bear on Hitler, with the result that *Mumfie Marches On* (1942) concludes with the capture of Hitler. As in the Thomson comics, he is greedy and hungry, and is thus literally trapped:

> In the shadowy hedge there moved another shadow. Something was coming down the road. In absolute silence they watched as the dark shape moved along the hedge. It crouched, moving on all fours, half concealed by shadows. Suddenly it stopped: sniffed the air, and with a furtive look from side to side scuttled rat-like out into the road.
>
> The moonlight shone full upon the peaked cap, the grimy mackintosh and the high boots.

'Stuck!' said the Führer.

He sniffed rapturously and began to nose along the road, going faster and faster as the delicious smell of the cream-puff wafted towards him. He approached and then stopped, his head darting this way and that like a hunted animal. Then with a sudden spurt he loped forward to the spot where the bait lay so invitingly. He thrust forward his nose and his mouth under the little black moustache gaped open. . . . there was a horrid 'snap', a flumping sound, and then silence.

The silence was shattered by a series of guttural cries, turning to shrieks as the Leader of all the Germans danced madly in the road, clawing at the sharp end of his nose which was caught firmly in the vice-like grip of the rat-trap.

The Führer danced and shouted, blinded by the cream which had burst all over his face, getting in his eyes and his hair and his ears.

'Here goes', said Jelly.

He flicked with his wrist, and a long coil of rope spun out and descended neatly over the wildly gyrating figure. Jelly pulled the rope tight, feeding it out to the others who clung to it behind him.

'Heave-ho, me 'earties', sang Jelly.

He gave a jerk, toppling over the dancing clown and hauling him over the ground towards them.

It took a matter of seconds to tie up the prisoner, who still screamed in the most ear-splitting manner.

'Shut up', said Jelly. 'We are not the Reichstag.'

He took the yellow duster from his hat, and lifting the rat-trap, crammed the rag into the Führer's open mouth.

'Shan't be able to use that again', he said regretfully. 'Now — what do we do with 'im?'

'Let's drag him into the Lodge and lock him up there', suggested Selina. 'Then Mumfie can ring through to the P.M. and have him fetched away. I would not have him in the house for anything', she said. 'We shall have to spring clean the Lodge as it is.'

'Yes', agreed Mumfie. 'He *is* offensive. Ivan was perfectly right.'

Jelly is a one-legged sailor. Ivan is a Cossack, but a symbol of alliance with the USSR, which may explain why this book was dropped from the lists of Mumfie titles included in their many reprints after the war. (Tozer herself died in childbirth in 1943.) Otherwise he was a fairly traditional skit on Russian literature ('He went about feeling sad and enjoying himself very much in the process'), but one readily extolling the military virtues of General Semyon Timoshenko, USSR commander in the Ukraine in autumn 1941 but diminished from his Soviet heroic status after the publication of *Mumfie Marches On* (though presumably not connected with it). Ivan is less a propaganda figure for the USSR than an affectionate portrait of an ally, poking fun at its self-congratulation. The hero-worship of live objects goes very largely to Winston Churchill, who makes a charming and suitably charismatic appearance, and one of whose cigar-ends Mumfie steals as a present for his bosom friend the Scarecrow. At one point, having to leave Mumfie on his own in 10 Downing Street, he lends him 'a rather used-looking copy' of *Alice in Wonderland* and 'went from the room with his quiet, purposeful tread. "Like a bulldog", thought Mumfie. "Only not a bouncy one".' Churchill is duly apprised by Mumfie of the success of the strategy to capture Hitler as previously determined between them. Mumfie reports to his troops:

> 'I spoke to him myself', he said proudly. 'I woke him up. He is most tremendously excited.'
> 'What did he say?' they choroused.
> 'Well, the line wasn't very good – but it *sounded* like "Whoopee!" He is sending a car for the prisoner at once. Do you think it will be a Black Maria?' he asked hopefully.

Churchill and Hitler became obvious child hero and villain, the big, fat, smiling, cherubic, siren-suited, cigar-wielding word-champer against the small, thin, snarling, diabolic, uniform-strutting, arm-jerking hate-screamer. Dudley D. Watkins used it to some effect. But Tozer picked out one Churchillian quality very accurately – his unorthodox readiness to listen to new ideas and circumvent red tape.[27]

> 'Red Tape' said Ivan. 'It doesn't make any difference whom you ask – you'll come up against Red Tape all the same. Yards and yards of it.'
> 'What is Red Tape?', asked Mumfie curiously.
> 'Red Tape? It's a system you have in this country for tying up Officials. They're all tied up in it – it is supposed, I believe, to keep them together.'
> 'Oh dear. Is *everybody* tied up?'
> 'He isn't', said Ivan in a voice of undisguised admiration, pointing to a portrait which hung in a place of honour over Mumfie's bed.

This was Mumfie's favourite picture and he was very proud of it. Mumfie stared at the portrait. He felt an idea coming into his head.

With what results, we know. It was, of course, true, as Squadron-Leader the Duke of Hamilton had found out the previous May, 1941, when after Rudolf Hess's parachute-landing in Scotland the Duke had to reveal what he alone knew, Hess's identity, and he was told it would take him two weeks to get an appointment with the Foreign Office's permanent under-secretary Sir Alexander Cadogan, whereas Churchill, to whom he appealed in despair, saw him that night. And certainly Mumfie's capture of Hitler in Britain owed something to the acquisition of Hess.

Crompton, in her sardonic sophisticated manner, played readily enough with Churchill as an involuntary accomplice to William, making him a sort of super-William (and no bad description either) – but she made extraordinary use of Hess. She would not have William capture Hitler à la Mumfie or Snooty; but she had him believe that Hubert Lane's cousin had done, on the strength of the Lanes entertaining an army friend who looked like him. William then decoys the supposed Hitler to have him recaptured by his brother Robert, who is briefly on leave from the armed forces. The necessary William–Hitler dialogue to lead Hitler into William's trap certainly met what Hannah Arendt would call the banality of evil halfway:[28]

'I don't s'pose you know England very well, do you?'

Lieutenant Orford ignored this remark and they walked on in silence for some moments. Then William said casually:

'I expect you liked it in Germany, di'n't you?'

'Liked what?' said Lieutenant Orford shortly.

'Well, you know, liked it', said William vaguely, and added after a short pause: 'What d'you think of Hess?'

'I don't think about him at all', said Lieutenant Orford.

Again conversation flagged. William led his companion over a stile and across the field, breaking the silence finally with: 'I expect they're wonderin' what's happened to you over there.'

'Who?' snapped Lieutenant Orford, 'and over what?'

William sighed. The illustrious captive was evidently determined not to give himself away. Probably he'd made a 'cross my throat' promise not to.

'Oh well', he said, 'I suppose you don't want people to know about it.'

As comment on British reaction to the capture of Hess and subsequent mystery, it isn't bad. The Hitler idea hardly works (would a serving officer be allowed to cultivate moustache and forelock to look like Hitler?), but it does testify to the isolation in which British small-town life found itself two years after the war had started. The story is unreal, but so now was the situation, Battle of Britain over, Blitz over, rocket-bombs as yet unknown, Russia as main war theatre. It was at that time Monica Dickens asked another nurse in their hospital 'what she would talk about when a German officer swaggered through the glass doors to take over the ward. "I'd ask him if he'd had his bowels open", she said, and laughed coarsely.'[29]

This raises the question of British isolation; and, as the child survivors of the war would go on to watch the disintegration of the British Empire, the acceptance of status as the USA's leading satellite, and the uncertain but increasing integration in the European community, the question is not simply academic. Firstly, the Empire. School stories had made much of it in terms of personnel, beginning with – and often going no farther than – the stock Scottish, Welsh and Irish children. Both St Jim's and Greyfriars had begun with an eye to British Isles readers, much more so in the former (where the Captain of the School, Kildare, is Irish though not obviously so, and was later purloined by P. G. Wodehouse, who greatly improved him as Adair in *Mike*). Either the Irish boys or their Irishness faded out after the 1920s, as did William's Irish relatives. The Catholic Brent-Dyer made slightly more of the Irish; and, if the quick-tempered Deira O'Hagen merited her parody in *The Terror of St Trinian's* as Deirdre O'Hooligan, then she, the homeless waif Biddy O'Ryan and the snobbish O'Haras were tolerably convincing portraits.[30] But Irish neutrality necessarily dampened celebration of Irish characters. Had the Irish not been neutral, Britain's situation would have been far worse, since Hitler could certainly have effected a quick landing, made maximum use of IRA Quislings, and caught the larger island in a pincer movement. But nobody was ready to admit that. Equally, the Irish secretly aided the Allies, especially on questions such as dousing the lights on Channel ports when requested, repatriating captured Allied personnel and so on, but strictly on the understanding that no word of it was to be let out. Officially, therefore, Eire was wholly unhelpful to the British war effort, and British commentators might well feel deeply hostile to it. The IRA had let off bombs in Coventry, much milder than the hell Hitler would rain on it, but nasty enough. This produced varying reactions in adult fiction. There was the deeply generous Agatha

Christie analysing IRA sentiment in *N or M?* (in which the heroine, a
British secret agent, cannot bring herself to read the last letter of an
executed IRA man to his wife – although, immediately, after the war
Christie's *Taken at the Flood* has an Irish (Protestant) murderer who
has fought for Britain in the war itself, Christie never missing a
chance to fool Constant Reader). There was the deeply ungenerous
Nicholas Monsarrat injecting dark comments on the effects of Irish
lights in Atlantic ports to his narrative in *The Cruel Sea*. Most British
writers for children fought shy of it. Johns, haunted by the First
World War with its Irish air aces such as Major 'Mick' Mannock, VC,
had Biggles born into a Squadron where his closest mate is the Irish
Mahoney; the best he could do in resurrecting stories of them for
Spitfire Parade was to have an Irish American in the Second World
War Squadron, a New York cop originally from Cactusville, Texas (a
town elsewhere famous as the home of the *Dandy*'s Desperate Dan).
The Irish interested Johns, partly because of T. E. Lawrence: he liked
them, and thought they were liars.[31]

The most unsympathetic use of the Irish is in Margot Pardoe's
Bunkle Began It (1942), where an Irish farmer, Flanagan, in the
British Home Guard, proves to be a collaborator with the Nazis and
therefore anxious to murder the children's father, Major de Salis. He
is dramatic in appearance and damnable in vocabulary:

a lean, red-faced man, with dark hair and very blue eyes . . .
    'What the blankety blank are we all here for, then?' he asked
angrily. 'And why the blankety blank, blank, couldn't somebody
have let me know? . . .
    '. . . And what the blankety blank, blank, are we all doing
mucking about here?'
    'Steady on, Flanagan . . . That sort of language don't get a man
nowhere. . . .'

He passes the Major on the road on his bicycle:

Major de Salis paused.
    'Now I wonder', he thought. 'Flanagan? . . . he's got a bit of a
brogue too. So he may not have lived over here for so very long. He
wasn't happy in his mind either, wasn't Mr Flanagan. I don't know.
I just don't know.'

Then de Salis is shot at and takes refuge in heather and scrub oak.

'Quick work, Flanagan', he said to himself. 'You saw a chance of cover for the sound of your rifle and took it. A stray shot *could* have reached me from the others [on Home Guard manoeuvres] and, if I'd been found dead, everyone would have assumed that it was a case of ball instead of blank, just as I did before I began to think. Well, now we know how Schultz got his Home Guard uniform. Funny devils, these Southern Irish. Rather have the Hun trample them and us underfoot than help us by raising a finger to keep them out and Flanagan even ready to open the gate to them. Or do they really think that if we are beaten Ireland will be allowed to go her own sweet way? I wonder how long he's been over here?'

This is fairly adult stuff for a child's book, and one noted for its convention that the hero is the youngest child of a family: Bunkle is a rather more cultured version of William. A father in the Secret Service might be allowed to steal a little of the limelight; but this looks like a Message, and one carefully refusing to distinguish between the neutral Irish and the IRA assassins. Flanagan was so stock an Irish name that Noël Coward deliberately overused it in *Nude with Violin* so as to produce an anguished demand from one of his characters as to whether there was not left at least *one* Irishman named O'Reilly? This particular Flanagan keeps firing, and the reader actually sees some of the action through his eyes: 'were he himself to fire from anywhere nearer the village there was always the chance that he might be seen in the act; and he knew that it was now more than ever important that no one else should suspect him in even the slightest degree' – which certainly suggests over-optimism as Irish. Then he reports back to his Hun at the gate:

His reception by the German was anything but cordial.
'You *would* miss, you fool!' said Schultz, angrily. 'That's the Irish all over. Talk, talk, talk, and no use in action. And for what reason is the exercise cancelled?'
'I don't know', said Flanagan sulkily.
'Nor, I suppose, did you even bother to try to find out. All you can do is to make a mess of one job and then come bleating to me about the other.'
'All right', said Flanagan angrily. 'If that's how you feel you can work on your own now. I'm through!'
He found himself looking down the barrel of a revolver.
'Oh no, you *aren't* through my friend', said the German. 'There

are many ways in which you can be of use to me yet. Besides we don't know for certain that our plans are necessarily impossible of execution just because some parts of them have not worked out exactly as we had hoped. Come, let us put our heads together and see what we can do.'

So, while the two enemies of Britain re-made their plans, the dark crept swiftly over moor and valley. . .

This may be promising, as heads together with one of them looking down the barrel of a revolver should be. But it rather fizzles out, especially for the baddies, Schultz saving himself

'from the firing squad by meeting a bullet from one of the cordon of soldiers I'd ['I' being Major Benson] thrown round farther away, which was just what I'd hoped would happen.'

'You mean he's dead!' said Jill in rather a faint voice.

'Yes, he's dead all right.'

'Good egg!' said Bunkle. 'Can I have the marmalade, please? *Then* what happened?' he asked, when his mouth was comfortably full again.

(Bunkle also owes some antecedents to Billy Bunter.)

'I was forgetting about Flanagan', said Robin. 'What's happened to him?'

'Nothing has happened yet', replied his father, 'because so far as yesterday and last night are concerned we haven't got a shred of confirmatory evidence against the man. I'm as certain as I can be that it was Flanagan who fired at me and I should think it's more than likely that it was he who slashed Willis's tyres, but neither of us actually saw him do either. However, we've put the authorities on to him and he'll be pretty carefully watched from now on.'

'But supposing he goes on trying to have pot-shots at *you*, Daddy?' asked Bunkle.

'Well, that's very unlikely', said his father. 'And he won't have much chance in the meantime because I've got to go back to Town to-day.'

It is quite unusual to leave a villain at large (unless required for sequel, which this one was not). The whole episode is really a parental intrusion into a child's story, Bunkle going on to unmask another villain disguised as an old lady . . . whom he had disliked from the first ('I just feel she's somehow wrong. It was the feel of her hands when she caught hold of me that time, I think'). The Flanagan episode is chiefly justified by Jill's 'I sometimes think that Daddy must have been awfully like Bunkle when he was little', thus giving Major de Salis child benefit, so to say. But the lesson is clear: the Irish have been Britain's enemies and still are, but so far they have got away with it. And all 'Southern Irish' are the same. The Bunkle series, it should be stressed, is an attractive and even realistic one.[32]

The converse applies to the work of Marjorie Dixon (not Irish, apparently), and briefly to that of Patricia Lynch (very Irish). Lynch, whether in Irish or English publication, was quite a favourite with British readers and reviewers, so much so that her name was put forward by indignant librarians for children alongside Kitty Barne's as alternatives when the Carnegie Medal subcommittee so cavalierly made its recommendation for Streatfeild in 1938 with only two of its members present. By any reasonable standard, Lynch was ineligible as an Irish resident and citizen (although born while Ireland formed part of the UK). But her stories of Irish peasant, animal and occasionally supernatural life travelled well – indeed often concerned travelling people, common to both islands, as British children's writers from Richards to Saville could bear witness. Why in 1942 she suddenly produced *Fiddler's Quest*, breaking with her habitual methods by injecting themes of Irish armed struggle against the UK, is uncertain. The story (maintaining her excellent quality) may have been written before Hitler's attack on Russia, during which time persons most sympathetic to the USSR devalued the struggle against Nazi Germany. R. M. Fox, Lynch's husband, was a vigorous literary exponent of the Irish Socialist Republican tradition in the early twentieth century. It might seem ludicrous for a writer of Lynch's stature to start prating about Irish struggles for freedom of twenty years before, when her British publishers (Dent) and audience were struggling for freedom against a far viler enemy. But a greater writer with politics now akin to those of R. M. Fox, Sean O'Casey, wrote *Purple Dust* on the joyous assumption that Britain was finished, as a contribution to the Nazi–Soviet Pact era.[33] Neither Lynch nor Dixon produced anything so contemptible as this – but to publish Anglophobe Irish nationalist fiction for British children at a time when Britain's back was to the wall invited comment as acid as that of Margot Pardoe. They do not seem to have received it. Dixon, the more vehement of the two, seems chiefly Norfolk in affiliation; she may have had Irish ancestry or affections which suddenly demanded their tribute. In her case, the first story is too socially pretentious, not to say squirearchical, to warrant assumptions of left-wing psychology. *The King of the Fiddles* (1941), the milder of the two, is apparently set in 1932 (though it requires an attentive child to work that out, on information supplied more than halfway through). The second book, *Runaway Boy* (1942), may have been written before the other, and both may have antedated the war – if they did not, their production at this moment appears grossly insensitive – but Faber & Faber were apparently ready to welcome them, whatever their reservations some months later about *Animal Farm*. *The King of the Fiddles* introduces its theme of revenge for land-confiscation over 300 years earlier:

'It goes back to the end of the sixteenth century', said Uncle Conor. 'The house was built where the valley opens on to the lough, with the hills of Clare sloping up on each side and behind – the hills into which my ancestors and Shawn's vanished when the English drove them out.'

Jan's eyes flashed. 'I'm glad the Spencers were burnt out', she said. 'I'm glad they had to go back to England.'

'Yes', Shawn meditated, 'but it was a pity about the house.'

It perpetually beats the drum of Irish virtue against English corruption:[34] 'Maybe, if we came back later, you'd show my cousins how an Irish jig should be danced, Tim, for it's from England they come, where folks have forgotten what good dancing is'. *Runaway Boy* is set in 1920 about the quest of the eight-year-old Shawn to find his father, whom readers of *The King of the Fiddles* will know is dead. It picks its way through Irish dialect varying between cod-Paddy, Synge-song and occasional authenticity with flashes of the lyrical. It was marketed as for children of 8 to 12; Janet Adam Smith in the *Spectator* politely opined that 'the book's delicately evoked atmosphere, and moderately complex plot, would only be fully appreciated by rather older children (10–15)'. And perhaps they might need to be even older still, insofar as we can now judge what they were allowed to know about in the Britain, and still more (or rather less) in the Ireland, of 1942. The first sentence is:

Sometimes Shawn and his father left their home in the hills whose windows looked down over the Aughnavangh demesne, and went to live at Illaunroe, the house on the island in Connemara that had been built by a poet's father.

It would be a very advanced child indeed who could identify that poet.

> Then Shawn, who believed there were many things he ought yet to know, asked Desmond what had happened to that other poet, whose father had built their house, and why he didn't want to turn the three of them out and come and live in it himself.
>
> 'He'll never want to do that', Desmond said, 'for, do you see, he's gone.'
>
> 'Gone?' Shawn wanted to know. 'Gone where?'
>
> Desmond looked away over the Twelve Pins, the twelve mountains that stood up, some near, some far, in all their ranging blues.
>
> 'The English', said Desmond, 'put him in prison, and after all the years of his imprisonment were over, he lived for a time longer, out of England, and now he's gone.' He continued to look at the faraway hills so that to his son, following his gaze, it was over those same blue hills that the poet seemed to have travelled. Then suddenly fear took Shawn, for he set a high value by Desmond.
>
> 'But Father', he said, 'you are a poet too. If the English were to hear of it, they'd maybe come after you as well and carry you away over the mountains and shut you up in a prison. Are you not afeard to write poetry so?'

We do not know if anyone recognised the poet as Oscar Wilde; Illaunroe was not much remembered in his connection until the *Letters* were published by Rupert Hart-Davis (1962), although perhaps coincidentally T. G. Wilson's life of Wilde's father Sir William, *Victorian Doctor*, was also published in 1942. But the spectacle of the boy fearing that the English would imprison his father for the same reason they had imprisoned Wilde seems the most *outré* infant nightmare recorded in Second World War juvenile fiction. In fact, 'the English', i.e. the Black and Tans, arrive when Desmond O'Halloran has left his son with a maidservant. Shawn tells the 'very young officer with a scared look in his eyes' that his father has gone to his Uncle Conor, and the officer tells him: 'you'd best not expect him back just yet'. When the Black and Tans have gone, Shawn repeats this to the maid Clare, who, 'throwing her apron over her head, burst into a loud fit of weeping'. Shawn looks for his father for the rest of the book, and, in its last lines, having just met Uncle Conor, is told by him:[35] '"He's dead" . . . Then Shawn knew that all along he had understood. It was only that no one would tell him.' Apparently, Shawn never realises he was responsible for his father's death; and Dixon may have been thinking of Wilde's line in *The Ballad of Reading Gaol* that all men kill the thing they love. Wilde or no Wilde, it is intended that the reader will know that Shawn's beloved father has been killed by the English. Critical comment was more than generous from the embattled British. Frances Bird in the *New Statesman and Nation* (12 December 1942) had a slightly acid tinge in her encomia:

> It has a good picaresque story, and if any child (8 to 12) does not object to the wicked English playing the part of villains, nor to the sad ending, nor to the everlasting Irishisms and Celtic legend — och, wirra, then it's himself will be after enjoying the book entirely.

But Janet Adam Smith (*Spectator*, 27 November 1942) was even prepared to find the Anglophobia to the book's credit:

> The scene is the West of Ireland in the Troubles; and Miss Dixon's handling of the way the battles, burnings and killings impinge on the boy's consciousness, makes this probably the best book on the list [of a dozen or so for review]. These happenings in Ireland twenty years or so ago are about the only mention of war in the whole bundle.

For once the critics seem to deserve higher honours than the author, even if they, too, did not fully understand her work.

But if the British were prepared to continue liking Ireland, however rough their reputations at Irish hands, they faced a different problem in celebrating a total British identity. Shakespeare's *Henry V* includes representative Welsh, Scots and Irish soldiers in Henry's invading troops against France – and, with quite unbelievable tactlessness, the British persisted in trying to show their identification with France by reviving the play on the BBC after France had fallen, and on film in Laurence Olivier's production as France was about to be liberated. W. E. Johns clearly had the spirit of *Henry V* in mind when refashioning First World War stories about Biggles himself into portraits of Angus Mackail and Taffy Hughes in action. Neither was particularly impressive, nor were they likely to be from such origins, stock Jock/Taffy tourist trappings on the early, neurotic, impulsive English Biggles. Johns seems to have been all too aware of the synthetic – in every sense

Jerry-built – character architecture he used here: Mackail means 'son of the kail' (or cabbage), i.e. offspring of the Kailyard school flourishing its sentimentalities and artificialities in the face of the London book-buyer when Johns was growing up. Johns knew his Scotland and could draw a Scot when he liked – Worrals's ferociously male chauvinist Commanding Officer McNavish is real, assuming his own artificialities of manner of which Johns was so conscious in higher ranks. His name hints at knavery in its creation; but men in the Worrals books, like those in Scott's *The Heart of Midlothian*, are present for ridicule, and McNavish's Scottishness is probably homage to Johns's ultimate master. Mackail and Hughes go their way with an occasional grace note to remind us of their function to show Scotland and Wales present and correct. The link with *Henry V* is occasionally asserted without being over-slavish: *Biggles in the Orient* is content to leave Mackail as 'twelve stone of brawn and brain, with heather in his brogue and an old regimental glengarry on his head', but Hughes's 'paternal ancestor may have been one of those Welsh knifemen that helped the Black Prince to make a name for valour'[36] (which seems to imply that Princes of Wales get ahead by exploiting the Welsh). But that's it. That particular book has some fine portraits of different airmen – Johnny Crisp, Scrimshaw and Sergeant Gray from the doomed 818 Squadron at Dum Dum, the South African Bargent (well named) and the near-suicidal Squadron-Leader Frayle in Jangpur – but (once again, apart from Tug Carrington) not those on the chorus-line of Biggles's Squadron 666 (whose number again asserts Johns's impish humour). Johns liked Scotland; it forms a haunting background to two immediately post-war Gimlet stories, but the native figures are more inanimate than the landscape, which – with Gimlet around – is shrewd of them.[37]

Blyton, as we noted, had some sense of an English question in Scotland, and seriously proposed a Scots cult figure for participants and readers in *The Adventurous Four*'s Andy (whose rough workaday clothes won Scots reader-imitation). But Brent-Dyer seems to have been more alert than she to the possibility of actual disaffection in Wales and Scotland, both cases involving English (or British) commandeering of what Welsh and Scots saw as their own private preserve. The Chalet School takes over Plas Howell, in 'Armishire' (Gwent, anyway), while the owner, the Rev. Ernest Howell, is a navy chaplain; and, as part of the bargain, it is required to accept his stepsister as a 13-year-old pupil. This creates a delicate situation since potentially the girl, bitterly resentful of the school's intrusion, might behave so badly as to require expulsion and thereby oblige the school to expel itself. She is reconciled to it, but conceals her knowledge of an unknown passage in which she and two friends discover poachers whose lights breach the blackout and cause a security crisis. Thus begins the school's return to Britain in *The Chalet School Goes to It*; the next book, *The Highland Twins at the Chalet School*, has an island requisitioned by the armed services whence the owners are expelled for the duration of the war, the small twins going to the Chalet School, where they are left in possession of a chart showing secret conduits in their island which would greatly benefit interested and intrusive spies. All of this seems based on reality. The British government did take over Scottish islands, one of which is still uninhabited due to the presence of anthrax spores in the soil following chemical experiments. There were Scottish and Welsh resentments against such sequestration of property and land. And there were attempts by the Nazis to reach dissident Welsh and Scots nationalists, with whom it was hoped links would be established after the model of the Abwehr–IRA alliance. It resulted in amusing Welsh stories, such as an earnest Nazi spy having penetrated to a Welsh village, sizzling in summer sun, under instructions to find one M. Jones and give the password. He finds M. Jones. To lead up to the password, the spy comes in on the cold, causing M. Jones to tell him he is out of his mind, can he not see the steam practically rising from the pavements? The spy desperately persists, adding the password 'Swansea Harbour is frozen over'. 'Ach, it is Jones the spy you want, in Number 7.'

British authors seem to have assumed that the authorities would fear some possible danger from German links with Celtic nationalism, locking the stable door after the Dublin Easter Rising had stolen that particular horse during the previous war. In fact, while English commentators such as Orwell bracketed Welsh, Scottish and Irish nationalism, partly because their votaries occasionally made nice fraternal noises at one another, there was very little co-operation between them, and only the remotest isolated figures showed sympathy with Nazism outside of the IRA. The SNP were obdurately opposed to violence: Scotland would not drink from Ireland's poisoned chalice. The Welsh were only prepared to defend violence against property, not against persons. It would seem that, in their different ways, Blyton, Johns and Brent-Dyer saw a danger of English fears needing to be shown baseless. Daisy Venables of the Chalet School calls the Welsh poachers 'Unpatriotic pigs . . . showing lights for their horrid salmon-poaching, and they might have brought the

Jerries on us and we'd be bombed'. But, when the odious Colonel
Black denounces the little girls:

> he could tell them that they had probably been helping the enemy,
> for it was all very well to tell three foolish children a whole pack of
> lies; but who knew what the men had really been up to? Spies they
> almost certainly were – h'rrumph!
>
> At this soothing statement Gwensi's hot temper flared up.
> 'Indeed and to goodness then, but they would not tell *me* lies!'
> she flared out, rather more Welsh than usual. 'And you are a liar
> yourself to say so!'
>
> More fireworks, once the Colonel had recovered from the shock
> of being bearded like this by a small girl! He was not surprised that
> the war had broken out! When silly babies could speak like this to
> their elders and betters – h'rrumph! – no less was to be expected!
>
> He was interrupted by Miss Annersley, who said sternly,
> 'Gwensi! You forget yourself! Apologise to Colonel Black at once
> for your rudeness! I am ashamed of you!'
>
> 'I *won't* apologise!' cried Gwensi, stamping her foot. 'I won't – I
> *won't!* He's only an Englishman – what does he know about us?
> Owen Owens would never lie to me!'

Miss Annersley's diplomacy soothes the Colonel; but he has been
demonised throughout the story, so that, in the sudden assertion of
anti-German but also anti-English Welsh nationalism, the reader is
emotionally on the Welsh side, however much agreeing that it was
right to send Gwensi to bed, nominally to pacify Black, actually so
that the little girls will get some sleep. The Highland twins prove
equally patriotic, but very defensive against attempts to discover
their hidden secrets (rightly, because there is a spy trying to steal
them, who allies with one of their school enemies, who gets someone
to write a letter in Gaelic to them). Symbolically and openly, Brent-
Dyer is contemptuous of notions of Celts as security risks, but shows
how they can be alienated. In Saville, the Welsh names taken by
German spies (Evans, John Davies) convey a hint that there may be a
Welsh security risk. Blyton did not pursue Wales until the post-war
Mountain of Adventure, but apart from cod-Welsh English (which
Kiki the parrot rightly imitates) Blyton was sensitive enough to
realise that the language was an issue, and Jack actually tries to
learn some Welsh. Brent-Dyer had Welsh spoken freely between
Gwensi and the poachers. Her twins follow Gwensi in defensiveness
about the home that the war forces them to give up:

'I ton't see why we must give up Erisay to anyone', put in Flora. 'It wass *ours* – it iss Archie's. Why should we have to go away from it? It iss preaking our hearts: we will all pe –'

'Flora – Flora! You must speak better!' cried Shiena in dismay. 'You can do it, for I haf heard you. Why must you be so bad?'

'I'm a Highlanter. I want to show these people I am Highlant', returned Flora stubbornly.

It was perceptive enough of Brent-Dyer. Some twenty-five years later, Scottish nationalism would flare up on the issue of evicting island inhabitants to set up a rocket range, and in 1970 the Western Isles defeated a long-standing Labour MP with the SNP Mayor of Stornoway, Donald Stewart. (Indeed, the SNP did elect an MP for Motherwell in 1945, but not on that issue.)

Kailyard still had its following up to the Second World War, after which it still persisted in Scotland in the columns of the Dundee *Sunday Post*, a journal of vast circulation issued by D. C. Thomson, of *Dandy* and *Hotspur* celebrity. The cloying cutesiness of such a national self-presentation at times seemed a national Gethsemane to readers of dignity, the traitor kissing the Scotland it betrayed into humiliation and public derision. Tom Nairn would say in 1967 that Scotland would not be free until the last Church of Scotland minister had been strangled with the last copy of the *Sunday Post*; and while he later changed his mind about the Church of Scotland (for its heroic part in winning Scotland a Parliament again), he never altered his view of the *Sunday Post*. Yet its famous cartoon child, 'Oor Wullie', was not particularly Scots, apart from his dialect, accent and expletives ('Crivvens!', balanced by his seniors with 'Michty me!'). He was in fact the creation of the English artist Dudley D. Watkins in 1936, a year before he invented Desperate Dan to inaugurate the *Dandy*. 'Oor Wullie' was a younger, Scotticised and proletarianised William, some of whose adventures and conventions were taken over for specific episodes: Crompton had endowed William with a debased speech of his own which contrasted forcibly with that of his bourgeois seniors while not – except at very self-conscious and unreal moments – drawing from the working class, and the linguistic variations may have induced Watkins to create his own version, with common speech for children and adults. If Watkins took William's name for his eponymous child hero, he appropriated that of William's family, the Browns, for his other strip launched in the *Post* in 1936, 'The Broons' – also to become a Scottish favourite. 'The Broons', like the Browns, went into the services and did their bit in various ways; but the strip was largely successful in appealing to adults as well as children, probably more so than any other of its kind in Britain (other than the sexually alluring 'Jane' in the *Daily Mirror*). 'Oor Wullie' tired of the war long before the Broons, or William Brown, although he was to give it a grand finale when his vow to celebrate its end by telling his school Head to go and boil *his* head, and hitting PC Murdoch's helmet with a half-brick (as used in Charles Kingsley's *The Water-Babies*), was vitiated by the headmaster's 'Well, William! The war's over! Shake hands!' and Murdoch's similar (though Scottified) gesture followed by 'Wullie, ye're a wee imp! But a wish I had a laddie like ye!'[38]

A comic strip could afford such sentiment – a fine one, symbolising more wars ending than that against Hitler – but the books could not. A comparable exploit for William turns on Violet Elizabeth's treachery apparently to him, actually to Hubert Lane, and in its conclusion William is triumphant but alienated, rejected by the girls with whom he has made common cause during the war, and indifferent about it.[39] Blyton's junior detectives make no peace with their enemy policeman, Mr Goon – not that they gave conspicuous notice to the war. 'Oor Wullie' celebrated the war's outbreak with industrious but unsuccessful attempts to participate in the armed forces, more crudely than William's efforts. But one curious strip (*Post*, 12 May 1940), as the war grew dark, caught something very unusual in child literary fare – the boy who identified with Hitler. It may also have been borrowed from William, who, in one ill-conceived moment ('William and the Nasties', June 1934), had briefly sought to drive a Jewish sweet-shopkeeper from the village, and who later ('What's in a Name?', August 1937) played with being a 'Green Shirt' dictator. This was well and truly pre-war in the William saga; but Wullie, after the manner of Tom Sawyer, tries to recruit volunteers whom he will then get to 'Dig for Victory' in the back garden, where his parents have told him to work himself. One recruit announces himself a Nazi ('I'm no' gaun tae join yer army – I think Hitler's a great man'), whereupon Wullie and Fat Bob reduce him to crawling away on his hands and knees. Their last choice is a conscientious objector (CO), and here the treatment is less predictable:

'I dinna believe in fechtin' – I widna harm a fly.'
   'Weel, if ye saw a German attackin' yer puir auld gran'maw – what wid ye do?'
   'Nothing! She can tak' care o' hersel' – she's dead!'

This was a straight parody of First World War (and perhaps Second World War) tribunal questioning of conscientious objectors, with the joke startlingly on the CO's side. Wullie and Bob tell the boy very much what COs were told:

> 'We'll let ye aff the army so long as ye tak up agricultural work!'
> 'O.K. then!'
> 'Noo we'll awa wi' oor army – one conchie – tae dig up the back garden! – an' keep yer gun on him, Bob!'

But Bob is called in to his tea by his mother, whereupon the conchie, finding himself alone with Oor Wullie, takes the spade and hits him over the head with it, and Wullie muses after his retreating form: 'Jings! Some conchie that! – Widna hurt a fly, eh?' And in a final strip, looking very much like a patriotic poster of the British workman, Wullie digs ferociously: 'Ah weel, tae pot wi' them! I'll dig for victory masel!' The propaganda intent of the end is obvious, but the message as to the CO is more opaque, beyond the clear implication that conchies make good fighters when threatened themselves. Scotland had many agricultural workers drawn from COs and later from Italian prisoners, as the most remarkable Scottish short-story writer of the time, Fred Urquhart, depicted so memorably from his own experience as a CO. He was also an outstanding writer about, though not for, children. Once again, the lesson seems to be one of war-committed Scots, in general, but aware of greater complexity to their own national identity.[40]

But if English identity for children sometimes recognised a Scottish or Welsh frontier, and was often though not always curiously tolerant of the vagaries of an Irish one, what had become of the super-ego, the Empire? Essentially, it had disappeared. Imperial fiction was still throwing out – or throwing up – wretched little degenerate descendants of Kipling in the children's annuals as late as the outbreak of war, but the Empire vanished from war literature save for anachronistic productions still ladling out pre-war mixtures usually very watered.

The Commonwealth did not. The war could loom large in children's stories from across the Empire, provided that citizens of its countries were accepted as equals; and their loyalty be not taken for granted. L. M. Montgomery, for all of her First World War fever and fervour, had taught that lesson for Canada in *Rilla of Ingleside*. Australia took the lead in the Second World War, with no writer of Montgomery's stature, but with an impressive stable. Viola M.

Methley may have symbolised the Australian message best when in *Great Galleon* (1942) she engagingly played the obvious card of cousinly rivalry, English boy against Australian girl:

> 'Isn't it a bit of a sell, don't you think, to expect another boy and find that it turns out to be just a girl?'
> 'We're quits there! Anyway, girls are as good as boys down under.'
> 'Pity you didn't stay in Australia, then!'
> 'Too true! And I would have if I'd known what snobs you were at home, trying to make me feel like dirt, when I'm as good as you and the same family, too' . . .

She saves his life, and they duly bag their Nazi spies and soldiers 'for England', i.e. altruistic aid by Australia (as by Canada).[41]

The most distinguished imperial anachronism was no doubt Ransome's *Missee Lee* (1941), whose Japanese opening is equally ironically offset by its confident allusions to Hong Kong and Singapore. Although the story is off the imperial beaten track (as all good imperial stories are), the knowledge that security awaits the travellers in those interesting ports underlies the most hazardous of South-East Asian adventures up to 1940. The fall of Singapore bred a morale collapse through children's fiction.

The Empire played little part in the William stories, but it was comfortably present at the back of those written in the 1920s: William used an imperial hero to justify his own Conservative candidacy for Prime Minister ('William, Prime Minister' June 1929). Ten years later, it survived purely as a basis for satire ('William and the Man from Africa', July 1939). An insurance agent from Bulawayo, whom William assumes to be a hero defying the denizens of the jungle, is a guest of his cousin Mr Brown, and William mistakes as heroic memoirs what are really overheard fragments of insurance chatter ('I've probably taken more of that risk than anyone else in Africa' . . . 'I admit it's dangerous but I've managed to get through all right so far' . . . 'Invasion, civil war, rebellions, revolution, insurrection, military and usurped power'). The story turns on the difficulties and triumphs in the way of this imperial hero maintaining the heroic reputation he never knows he has. He cannot be called a fraud, since he has not the faintest notion of the status the Outlaws assign him. He avenges a robbery by some toughs through getting a boxer into disguise as himself, who then puts six assailants to flight under the admiring gaze of hidden

Outlaws and their schoolboy enemies. If any symbolism was intentionally present, it was of an Empire still successfully living on its presumed former glory with the assistance of unknown mercenaries. In the ensuing war years, Crompton assigned no role to the Empire at all.

The Empire had had its days in school fiction with varying success: in general, Australian boys made a strong impact, also Canadians, Indians most of all. Canadian writers had won audiences for over half a century with tales of wildlife: H. Mortimer Batten, who had reminisced about Canadian wildlife from his days as a forest ranger in the pre-First World War *Little Folks*, found a new mass readership for his tales of wild fox and wolf, *Red Ruff* and *Starlight*, reprinted as Puffins just after the Second World War. Indians alone broke the image of Empire as a white man's club, initially through the cricket hero of his generation, Ranjitsinhji Vibhaji, Maharaja jam sehab of Nawanagar, whence Frank Richards in 1908 derived his schoolboy demon bowler Hurree Jamset Ram Singh, nabob of Bhanipur, most intelligent, if least articulate, of the Greyfriars Famous Five. But alongside such attempts at exotic imperial incursions into school life were the Americans, essentially their successful rivals. The Empire was dying, the Americans were arriving, and the Second World War was to make it decisive. The *Hotspur* comic met the falling and rising contingents from overseas by assigning separate houses for their Fourth Forms at Red Circle, with the initial provision of Canadians sharing with Americans in Transatlantic House, whose nickname, Yank House, justly prophesied small future for its inhabitants from north of the 49th parallel. Yank House was headed by Cyrus Judd, later by Spike Dewey; Conk (Colonial) House by Kit Delaney and Punja Singh. A little innocently, the *Hotspur* assumed close friendships between American and Canadian, Australian and Indian, neither alliance being at all likely in the 1930s and 1940s. Richards was very hostile to the USA, pointedly exposing its segregationist practice despite its democratic theory, listing as its national disasters the Chicago Fire, the San Francisco earthquake and the Declaration of Independence, and producing in Fisher T. Fish and his father a wholly repellent duo obsessed by money-making. The contrast with his imperial creations was extreme. Yet his Canadians, in common with those of many British writers, seemed almost indistinguishable from Americans apart from a British linkage often very remote. Richards would not have approved; but, in the early years of the war, Canadian material (notably by H. Mortimer Batten) was being used by BBC Children's Hour and elsewhere partly to open up an American sense and look forward to American intervention in the war. So, too, was the use of much American children's fiction in reprint and for broadcast purposes: not only Twain and Alcott, but also Susan Coolidge's *What Katy Did* series. Eleanor Graham got a US Western into her first batch of Puffins in November 1941, Will James's *Smoky* (first published in 1926), uniting the appeal of the vanished American cowboy to the English love of quadrupeds.[42]

The most remarkable come-hither for the USA (already well established in British popular culture through such characters as Mickey Mouse and Popeye, whom Orwell was happily classifying as English) was in Dudley Watkins's creation Desperate Dan. There seems to have been a vague British benevolence towards American gangsters. Cowboy heroes were often ambiguous, at least (like Richards's Rio Kid) firmly separating law and ethics: it was partly Robin Hood up to date. Richards was much more kindly disposed towards some American gangsters than to Fisher T. Fish and sire, especially when the gunman Poker Pike is temporarily domiciled at Greyfriars to protect an American millionaire's child and in various contretemps wins a reluctant respect from both boys and masters.[43] British writers, like James Hadley Chase, and Irish writers, not all like Peter Cheyney, were making careers of writing imitation gangster fiction. Comics went in for cowboy/gangster thrillers with no such elegant objectivity as purred through the prose of Richards. Watkins's genius was required to make the full transition: Desperate Dan and his Cactusville became an adjunct of D. C. Thomson's Britain, and as such produced the most cunning courtship of the USA in juvenile literature. On 12 October 1940, the *Dandy* featured Dan as a swimmer being bombed by a Nazi aircraft whose pilot takes him to be a camouflaged plane; the bomb bounces back ('Der Wow! I am being blown up by mine own bomb!'). Dan, to avoid further damage to his swimsuit, paints the Stars and Stripes on his chest to show his neutrality; but it washes off, and when a Heinkel is about to bomb him he irritably inhales, thus bringing it down. Then he sews the Stars and Stripes on his chest, but enough of it is torn off by a rock to make it look like a swastika; he is fired on by a British submarine and is obliged to jump on the torpedo and guide it back to shore. Finally, Dan has sheriffs' stars and bars of iron nailed to his chest, and then accepts $50.00 to join the British navy with duties as a minesweeper, making the last words of that week's strip:

British Captain: That iron on Dan's chest is attracting all the magnetic mines in the sea! And he's so tough they don't even hurt him!

Desperate Dan [floating supine with mines blowing apart as they strike him]: Ha! Ha! This is better than being neutral!!

On 18 January 1941 he had become a chimney sweep and was sweeping Nazi planes out of the sky ('Der Wow! Der new kind of der antiaircraft shell! Oh der my!') and chucking them into the Cactusville garbage-truck, again supposedly by accident. By 29 November 1941, he was blowing Nazi aircraft out of the sky while trying to blow barrage balloons back to their moorings; he is in the RAF at the time, possibly as a non-combatant. Quite apart for its ability to recruit American Tough, link up dubious American morality with the British war effort, and construe American neutrality as covert support for the UK, the magnetic-mine fantasy must have been a fine morale-booster when that weapon was dismaying Britain. Desperate Dan was probably also stepping-stoned via Canada: the name presumably derives from Dangerous Dan McGrew, who, like his namesake, was the work of an Englishman who matured in Scotland – in McGrew's case Robert Service.

Brent-Dyer made little of the Empire, but American girls had been prominent from the second Chalet School book: the seventh Head Girl is American (after two Austrian and four English), and two Americans figure prominently in protest against the persecution of the Jews in *The Chalet School in Exile,* one of them in fact so thunderous in her rage that 'Before her flood of [American] language, the young ruffians fell back a moment, and Miss Wilson took advantage of it to drag . . . Herr Goldmann into the Gasthaus'. Like Watkins, Brent-Dyer was recruiting the neutral Americans. Cornelia Flower has in fact had a stormy induction (in *The Head-Girl of the Chalet School*), but in the revived school in Guernsey and Wales she is the most visible link among the pupils with former years (apart from Maria Marani, whose father is dying in a concentration camp). Brent-Dyer's Americans may be in danger of being spoiled brats (as at first Cornelia certainly is) and are usually children of somewhat ostentatious wealth, but they duly embrace the English tone and multilingual speech of the school. There is the faintest anticipation of overpaid and over here (though not, of course, over-sexed: just as well, since Cornelia was briefly held prisoner by a lunatic). But Brent-Dyer had met the American challenge long before the war, and thus warmed an old goodwill in her welcome for potential American involvement.

Perhaps the most remarkable use of the Americans in Second World War literature for children is Malcolm Saville's *Seven White Gates*, where the Morton twins are lost in a strange cave, and once again encounter a stranger in uniform (as they did in *Mystery at Witchend* to find that he proved to be a spy):

> Dickie was more outspoken. . . . 'But you'll 'scuse us asking, but we don't know who you are. An' what are *you* doing here, anyway? . . . Maybe we don't trust you. . . .'
>
> 'You're wearing uniform', Mary broke in suddenly, 'but you're not English.'
>
> 'You talk like the pictures', Dickie said thoughtfully, and then laughed. 'Gosh! I know what you are! You're an American soldier – you're a Yankee Doodle.'
>
> 'You've said it, kiddo. I'm the U.S. Army, but there's just a few more of us here as well. . . . Come and meet the other half.'

It usefully reminds us that the Americans were a welcome invasion, but in many ways – particularly to children evacuated from London – were unknowns. Saville has deeper symbolism ahead. First, there are the twins' private reactions to the Americans: 'They're sort of crinkly and ugly, but I like them', and recognition of the language barrier: 'Funny how you Yankee Doodles can't speak English like us'. Then they meet a US army officer and, after further struggles with the effects of rock-falls and unwisely reused cable-cars, get back to their people with him, having realised that he is the long-lost son Charles who had quarrelled with Uncle Micah and emigrated. The drama in the story is the self-tortured father, striding through the night in isolated anguish and stifling himself in his punitive religion. We never discover the nature of the quarrel; and it is ended in the atmosphere of dotty, half-forgotten children's fantasies embedding strangely perceptive pity for the old man and confidence in the dramatising of his recovery of his son. The self-satire is crucial. It is a hackneyed drama, although economically worked, as it has to be. Charles injures himself in aiding the twins, and so is wounded at the moment of reconciliation:[44]

> Then Mary took charge.
>
> 'Your brokenhearted father is waiting for you over there, Uncle Charles. I promised you. We promised you, I mean, didn't we? I asked him to say his heart's desire and he was too shy to say it was you, but I know you are. Can you get there with a stick? He

promised to wait there till someone took the hankie off his eyes. He looks lonely, doesn't he?'

'So do you, Uncle Charles', said Dickie suddenly as he looked up at him.

The big man laughed shakily. 'Maybe I am! Wait here, all of you. I'll manage with this stick', and he hobbled over towards the hawthorn.

'Don't watch them, you beasts!' Mary cried, and turned her back.

It is a very pretty little allegory, however much of it might be perceived by its audience; it was perhaps enough to Saville's purpose if it radiated the goodwill, the sense of reconciliation and the mingling of comedy and tragedy. Micah is the UK, Charles is the USA, the unknown quarrel is the American Revolution, the injury during the process of return is Pearl Harbor, Micah's isolation and agonised night patrolling is the UK's lonely suffering from Dunkirk to Pearl Harbor, Charles's answer to Dickie is the USA's discovery of the folly of its own isolationism, the Seven White Gates of Micah's farm are the Saxon heptarchy in the whiteness of the white Saxon dragon which Merlin revealed to Vortigern as it fought against the red dragon of Wales. Even the terrific but apparently unnecessary cable-car ride taken by Micah's niece Peter, Cockney Tom and little dog Macbeth which so risks their lives and those of the twins must have symbolised the uncertainty of the air war: would human mastery of air travel mean Britain's salvation or her doom? Rock-falls and resultant entrapment stood for bombed Britain. Like its predecessor, Seven White Gates must have made for intensely dramatic wireless, and the symbolism may have done its work the stronger, subconsciously, as the ear alone filled the imagination of the child listeners.[45]

W. E. Johns might be expected above all children's writers to speak for Empire; and to an extent, during the Second World War, he did. What is curious is that, in the preceding decade, his imperial brief was much more doubtful, and the sudden intrusion of the imperial theme into his wartime fiction carried its own somewhat grim implications. The motif of American intrusion and displacement of Empire is minor but noteworthy. The Empire flickered into momentary relevance for Biggles in a story probably – and regret-tably – influenced by the Mau Mau terrorism inducing explosively hostile reactions to African nationalism (Biggles and the Black Raider, 1953); it featured chauvinistically in a post-war Gimlet novel or two, and questioningly in three post-war Worrals stories. But

Johns was not an active writer in the 1920s, when aerial support of imperial repression was notable. His work in the 1930s had been much more concerned with European security, and his novels proclaimed as much. Only three pre-war novels have imperial relevance – *Biggles in Africa* (1936), *Biggles Air Commodore* (1937) and *Biggles Flies North* (1939). In the first and last, Biggles falls foul of the imperial authorities: he is arrested for murder in *Biggles in Africa* and in *Biggles Flies North*, and his opinion of the officials making the arrests is not high. *Biggles Air Commodore* involves imperial interests, but Biggles's service is largely outside imperial lands. If there is a moral from these, it is that the aircraft was hopelessly underused in imperial policing, and that the Empire was stretched beyond the resources it allowed itself.

But once the war was on, and Biggles had formed his squadron resulting in distinguished but largely unspecified success during the Battle of Britain, Johns profited by his unease in writing Second World War male flying stories to reconsider the Empire. In the 1930s, Johns seems to have regarded the Empire as a necessary but somewhat distasteful obligation, whose purposes are policing largely for capitalist purposes. As child educator, Johns's view of capitalism was fairly low: in *Biggles & Co.* (1936), Stella Carstairs, the daughter of a finance capitalist, tells Biggles:

> 'Large sums of money are at stake between men who are utterly unscrupulous, men of a type you may never have met, and would not understand if you did. They're – pagans. Twentieth-century infidels who worship the golden calf with such fervour that life, death, and suffering mean nothing to them.'

As usual with Johns, the woman (when heard at all) is the realist. *Biggles in Africa*, while a quest for a missing airman, eventuates in the capture of drug-runners, on which Biggles bluntly tells the po-faced Collison who has arrested him: 'As long as I get young Marton and my Dragon they can go on growing *hashish*, and eating it if they like, until they're blue in the face. That's not my affair . . .' He proposes an alliance, which is accepted: 'I'll take Marton and you can have the *hashish* crowd'. His attitude seems not so much racist as (however curious in an airman) Little England. Drug-running does not affect England (apart from nasty Society parties he wouldn't go to and may not even know about). In the Second World War, *Biggles in the Orient* gives drugs an air relevance. Post-war society (as pointed out in *Another Job for Biggles*, 1951) gives drug-running a

British relevance. But, with the war on, the Empire matters more. Not much is done to recruit Empire representatives for the Biggles team (the Squadron gets a French Canadian in 'The Arrival of Angus', but they lose him quickly, and his appearance was in reality due to a Frenchman's role in the original, First World War, story). An Australian drops into the Mess in *Biggles – Charter Pilot*, thus prompting an Australian story (a horrific description of the destruction of a stock-breeders' village when the water dries up, with the last words of the dying preserved by the speech of ravens thereafter taken to be ghosts). Biggles briefly befriends a white South African, Bargent, in *Biggles in the Orient* – belligerent, courageous and rather asinine (he bets Biggles 100 cigarettes they will not return from their mission, without realising he cannot collect if he wins). Gimlet's Commando foursome includes a French Canadian with extensive Indian experience in his days as a frontier trapper, and a taciturn enthusiasm for sadism in questioning prisoners. But while turning out a series of peacetime adventure reminiscences by Ginger to the Squadron between Second World War operations, Johns (probably finding one of them swelling beyond its limits) wrote *Biggles in the Jungle*, in which Biggles briefly assists Carruthers, the acting Governor of British Honduras, to suppress a slave colony, or rather makes him do it. In the early stages, Biggles makes the case for a benevolent empire, concerned with native protection:

'Why did they shoot you?' asked Biggles.

'Becos I ran away. I can't stand dem whips no longer, so one night me and some frens, we run, think mebbe we get back ter Belize. Bogat and his gang shot at us – mebbe dey t'ink if we get back to Belize we say what's going on. De udders all get killed or else caught. I get shot too, but I run till I can't run no longer.'

'Are these friends of yours who were shot – were they all chicle-hunters from Belize?'

'Sure dey were.'

Biggles looked at the others. 'This is a nice thing', he muttered savagely. 'These fellows were British subjects – or at least under British protection. It seems to me that it's high time this self-appointed King of the Forest was shot out of his throne. . . .'

But Algy's reaction is to assume that Carruthers will try to prevent them from following it up, so Ginger proposes that only one of them should go back to Belize to inform him. As it turns out, Carruthers accepts their proposal to investigate, but everything is known to his head clerk, who is in the pay of the slave-owner. It is accepted that local imperial rule falls short of the ideal ('I'm afraid we poor blighters who get stuck in the tropics get a bit slack'). There is then some hard financial bargaining for Biggles's involvement, Carruthers brightly offering wages of three shillings a day (£0.15), which Biggles answers by demanding a bonus from the money saved by capture of the slave-owner, who has been stealing state produce by kidnapping its workers, Carruthers turning that into a reward from the funds to be captured from the loot of the King of the Forest, if captured. This time, Carruthers's hope that 'if the affair was brought to a successful conclusion no doubt the finance people at home would refund your out-of-pocket expenses' gets a derisive 'I shouldn't call that an opportunity to be jumped at' from Biggles. The Empire is still a capitalist service, to be dealt with accordingly; but Biggles's anger against enslavement, and the physical presence of the black man whom they rescue, deepens the meaning of Empire. 'Dusky', as they call him from inability to master his name, is a real, if rather servile, figure (servility making sense in a world where life is cheap when guns abound). Johns had grown interested in cultural trade between whites and non-whites; extraneous to the main action, Biggles saves Dusky, who has been mesmerised by an anaconda.

> He knew it was useless to argue with the old man, for nothing would shake his inherent conviction that he had been bewitched. Indeed, Biggles, to his annoyance, had an uneasy feeling that there might be something in the superstition after all, for he himself had been conscious of a sensation for which he could not account.

The post-war *Worrals Down Under* shows Worrals (and more particularly Frecks) infected by superstitions of an Australian black man whose life they save. *Biggles in Borneo* (1943) leaves Tug Carrington temporarily disabled from trying to teach boxing to a friendly head-hunter. A slightly imitative successor, *Biggles Delivers the Goods* (1946), features another friendly native, this time a one-eyed Malayan pirate, who likes going to the cinema when in port. But his favourite actor is Donald Duck ('very clever, wise guy'), which (save in Orwell's logic) shifts us back to the United States. Whether he knew it or not, Johns had testified to the future of South-East Asia being primarily American when not Asian.[46]

The final benevolent glow of Empire in *Biggles in the Jungle* (published in May 1942) was probably a fast reaction to the Atlantic Charter (23 August 1941) followed by American entry into the war

(8 December), since the implication of these things was US supervision of a post-war world where Empire must give way to self-
government. Hence Biggles recruits a poor black companion. The
British Empire has to be shown as pioneer in asserting the four
freedoms. It was still a long way from Richards's enthusiasm for
Indian–white schoolboy camaraderie and, in one torrid series in
summer 1931, the passionate mutual devotion of the great Kenyan
hunter Kikolobo and the Bounder of Greyfriars Herbert Vernon-
Smith, perpetually saving one another's lives and taking vengeance
on one another's enemies. Johns gets a flicker of this in describing the
relationship of Suba the head-hunter and Biggles's Borneo cicerone,
Captain Rex Larrymore (whose name and short stature may indicate
a kindlier use of T. E. Lawrence than the earlier introduction of von
Stalhein). The various inter-racial brotherhoods have a logical antecedent in Huckleberry Finn and the growth of his love for the
runaway slave Jim, and Jim's reciprocation. (But Richards would
have acidly remarked that he had not stinted inter-racial friendship
and he had not required instructions from a still segregated USA to
get him to do it.)

Biggles had made little enough of Americans before the Atlantic
Charter; afterwards, his allusions to them in the Second World
War are respectful but not wildly flattering. *Biggles in the Jungle*
produces a US millionaire's errant son, cast adrift in the jungle on
a treasure-hunt by fellow-American crooked companions, his disappearance irritating Carruthers because his father is 'kicking up
a nice row' about it, his reappearance coinciding with Algy's and
Ginger's capture by Indians and then by the slave-drivers:

> 'Here comes the Tiger', murmured Algy presently.
> 'I'll tear the stripes off his hide one day', grated Eddie. 'They
> can't do this to me.'
> 'It seems as though they're doing it', grunted Algy.
> Ginger went on working. There was no alternative, for he had no
> wish to feel the whip across his shoulders.

Johns, like Richards, may have been repelled by American emphasis
on its democratic mission while segregation endured: certainly, the
enslaved American white boy is matched by his crooked ex-partners,
whose enlistment of the slave force in their treasure-hunt leads to
rough handling when the slaves revolt.

Five or six brawny natives, fleeter of foot than the rest, overtook

the two white men, Warren and Schmitt, at the head of the
stairway. The hunted men screamed as hands fell on them and
pulled them down. Carruthers, seeing what was likely to happen,
shouted, but he might as well have saved his breath. For a moment
there was a knot of struggling figures. Then they separated, and
the two white men, clutching at the air, swung out over the awful
void. Then they disappeared from sight, their screams growing
fainter as they plunged to destruction.

The principle of Americans victimised by non-whites is reasserted in
Biggles in Borneo, when the Squadron rescues two US airmen 'who
had been shot down on a reconnaisance flight. They had tried to
escape, and in doing so had struck a Japanese soldier. For this, on
being recaptured, they had been brutally flogged', which leaves them,
medically speaking, 'in a bad way'. They 'trembled with impotent
fury when they spoke of [the Japanese commandant of their prison
camp] and his barbaric behaviour towards his helpless prisoners. It
was this man who had caused them to be flogged.'[47]
  But whatever the hidden ironies in exposing American characters
to unpleasant reversals of their national practice, as opposed to their
international theory, the Empire itself seems to confess its bankruptcy in the best of all the Biggles books on the war against Japan,
Biggles in the Orient. Johns naturally wished to declare Japan the
enemy of the Asian peoples, with Britain as their protector. This
might seem to work out well enough with the Chinese, then under
Japanese oppression, and shown by Johns as agents of resistance
whether capitalists (Fee and Ah Wong in *Biggles in Borneo*) or
pirates (Li Chi in *Biggles Delivers the Goods*); there might seem
some analogy with French hostility to German rule. Such nuclei spun
interesting nebulae, forming the mildly comic figure of Ayert and the
wholly tragic one of Kayan:

> Fee Wong turned. 'He say Japanese are crossing river now', he
> said.
>   A strange look came into Biggles's eyes. 'By thunder!' he cried. 'If
> that dam were to burst it would let loose a million tons of water
> and hundreds of tons of timber. The bridge would be swept away
> like a scrap of tissue paper – and so would the barges.'
>   It is unlikely that Kayan the Malay understood these words, but
> he had heard what the coolie had reported, and he was not a
> timber foreman for nothing; it may be supposed that he under-
> stood even better than Biggles what would happen if the dam

burst. His face split in a dreadful smile, showing crimson betelnut-stained teeth. Then, before the others realised his intention, and certainly before they could stop him, he had dashed down to the river. In his hand he carried a heavy crowbar that he had used during the night to move the logs. Using this as a balancing pole, he started across the dam, leaping from log to log with the agility of long experience. It was obvious what he intended to do.

Biggles shouted, but the native took no notice, even if he heard, which is unlikely.

'If that dam bursts he'll be ground to pulp!' cried Algy in a strangled voice.

'He knows', said Fee Wong calmly. 'The Japanese have killed his wife and children, so he no longer has love of life. He prefers revenge. Kayan is a Malay.'

When Kayan was about midstream he chose a spot, drove in the iron bar and heaved. Those on the bank could only watch help-lessly. No one spoke. No one moved. It was one of those moments when time seems to stand still. Ginger saw the log on which Kayan was standing begin to move. The Malay threw all his weight on the bar. The log swung out. Then, with a roar like a high-explosive bomb bursting on a concrete road, the dam fell, and the next instant a thousand tons of logs, impelled by a mighty tidal wave, were hurtling pell mell down the stream. For a brief moment Kayan stood poised on a log. He flung the bar away, and stood with his arms outstretched like a bronze statue in an attitude of triumph. Then he disappeared from sight amongst the grinding timbers, and the flood of yellow, foam-flecked water.

Ginger drew a deep breath and moistened his lips. 'I shall see that sight for as long as I live', he said in a hard thin voice.

And Ginger is the reader-identification figure once more. But Malay or not, Ayert and Kayan were in Chinese service, and the Chinese would have their own post-war agenda beyond the British imperial line.

Biggles in the Orient is set in Britain's own India, and here it becomes clear that Japanese propaganda of liberation of non-whites from British rule has turned the local native population into one almighty security risk. The liberationist propaganda is not men-tioned; but the book is utterly distrustful of non-white natives from start to finish. There is a suicide here, but of a Japanese spy, in some ways even more disturbing than Kayan's in *Biggles in Borneo*. Biggles has discovered that planes are crashing because pilots are sampling chewing-gum or chocolate in the air, not knowing that it has been treated with dope (opium, charas or some other). He deduces that the agent planting the tainted confectionery is a Mess waiter:

> Presently Lal Din came, beaming as usual. 'Cigarettes?' said he, looking round the room.
>
> Biggles, from the easy chair in which he was seated, put up a hand. 'Over here.'
>
> Still beaming, Lal Din approached, and handed over the cigarettes. He was turning away when Biggles called him back.
>
> 'By the way, Lal Din', he said, 'do you like chocolate?'
>
> The Oriental did not start. His walk seemed to freeze to a standstill. He looked back over his shoulder – still beaming.
>
> Biggles tossed a bar of chocolate on a small table in front of him. 'Try that', he suggested.
>
> Lal Din did not move. His broad smile became fixed, the humour gone out of it. The atmosphere in the room was electric.
>
> 'What's the matter?' said Biggles evenly. 'Don't you like chocolate?'
>
> Very slowly the steward reached out and picked up the bar. 'Me eat after work', he said.
>
> 'Eat it now', ordered Biggles. He spoke quietly, but there was an edge on his voice.
>
> The steward did not move. His eyes were fixed on Biggles's face, as if he would read what was going on behind the impassive countenance.
>
> 'Eat it', snapped Biggles.
>
> Very slowly the steward looked round the circle of faces. Then, like an automaton actuated by a hidden spring, he moved. He streaked to the far side of the room, and as he ran he drew from somewhere a small narrow-bladed knife. In front of the fireplace he dropped on his knees.
>
> Biggles was on his feet. 'Stop him!' he shouted.
>
> But he was too late. With a calm, but swift deliberation that was horrible to watch, the steward drove the blade into his side, and dragged it across his stomach. Gasping, he fell forward on his face.

The conclusion explains that a leading local capitalist was masterminding the sabotage campaign, relying on a high position in the event of a Japanese victory. But the whole book testifies to absolute white insecurity against hidden terrorism with little or no means of testing local reliability. Just as the Indian Mutiny revealed that years and decades of white control had taught nothing about native alienation, *Biggles in the Orient* tells the same story almost ninety years later. All Biggles can do in clearing the case up is to show how isolated a white man seems confronting the entire Orient, British subjects, Japanese forces and intermediate ambiguities. 'This saboteur, whoever he is, is as cunning as only an Oriental can be.' Or, later: ' "What beats me is, how you got on the trail of the thing", said Frayle in a voice of wonder. "It was so simple, yet so subtle –" "The Oriental mind works on those lines. I've been in the East before", murmured Biggles as he stood up.'[48]

He had won a battle, in a fine, heroic struggle. But, in doing so, he symbolised the loss of an Empire.

Notes

1. Lorna Lewis, *Time and Tide*, vol. 21 (14 December 1940).
2. Frank Richards, 'Work. 3. Boys' Writer', in Leonard Russell (ed.), *Saturday Book 5* (1945), 83–4. See also Orwell's truly affectionate review, *Manchester Evening News*, 6 December 1945, Orwell, *Complete Works*, XVII, 414–16.
3. *Magnet*, 1,125 (September 1929). The body-count was very high by Greyfriars standards: Richards was responding to editorial pressure to include a dash of Edgar Wallace.
4. *Times Literary Supplement*, 11 November 1944.
5. Serjeant, *The Hero of St Basil's*, 53, 7. For a ferocious diatribe at its expense, see Robert J. Kirkpatrick (ed.), *Encyclopaedia of Boys' School Stories*, 294–5, whose question as to how it passed muster so far removed from its creation is partly answered by the hero's father having been killed 'quite early in the war' (presumably originally in the Boer War, but clearly a movable conflict). I find it better fun than he or its author does, and grant it some inspiring as well as mawkish moments; but it rather goes to prove Richards's argument about religiosity in fiction. For a realistic discussion of religion in 1910–16 public school while actually written in the shadow of the Second World War, see Bruce Marshall, *George Brown's Schooldays* (1946), officially an adult work but one which would have been recognisable to modern schoolboys despite the author's perhaps ironic statement that matters were said to have improved – the story's religious boy is victimised to a point of near-suicide whence he is saved by an agnostic. Marshall was one of Britain's leading Roman Catholic novelists at this time.
6. *Boy's Own Paper*, vol. 68 (October 1945), 5.
7. Johns, *Worrals Carries On* (October 1942), 71; *Biggles 'Fails to Return'*, 86–7.
8. Orwell, 'Shooting an Elephant', *New Writing*, 2 (August 1936), Orwell, *Complete Works*, X, 502.
9. Johns, *King of the Commandos*, 126–7, 146–7, 167–8.
10. Brent-Dyer, *The Chalet School in Exile*, 123, 124, 130–1.
11. Ibid., 57.
12. *The Chalet School Goes to It*, 105–7.

13. *Lavender Laughs in the Chalet School*, 66, 67, 26–7, 28.
14. *The Chalet School Goes to It*, 194–5.
15. *The Highland Twins at the Chalet School* (1942), 221, 244, 284–5.
16. Johns, *Biggles – Charter Pilot* (1943), 99–108; *Worrals Down Under* (1948). Both of these stories had previously appeared in the *BOP.* and *GOP* respectively. *Biggles Flies West* (1937) had turned on a doubloon formally cursed in the seventeenth century in part under our scrutiny. If these things can be granted logic, that has it; the opals don't.
17. Wheatley was more a childish author than a children's one, and thus lies outside our scope; but some of our child readers would certainly have picked up his work. The most obvious text seems his *Strange Conflict* ([1941]). Maurice Richardson described Wheatley's style as like that of a dormitory storyteller after 'lights out!'
18. From Sitwell, 'The Shadow of Cain', quoted in Brian Gardner (ed.), *The Terrible Rain – The War Poets 1939–1945* ([1966] 1977), 198.
19. J. R. R. Tolkien, *The Return of the King*, in *The Lord of the Rings* ([1954–5] 1995), 822, 822–3.
20. Saville, *Seven White Gates* (1944), 57, 125, 128.
21. Belloc, *Cautionary Verses* (1940), 3. The verses were 'Introduction' to the first of the several books as printed *Cautionary Tales for Children* (1908). The oldest item was *The Bad Child's Book of Beasts* (1896), and the most recent were *New Cautionary Tales* (1930) and *Ladies and Gentlemen* (1932). B.T.B. was Lord Basil Blackwood, who was killed in the First World War. Nicholas Bentley illustrated the later works. Belloc survived the Second World War; but this was his last book, and *The Bad Child's Book of Beasts* his first, with about 100 titles separating them.
22. Wall, *Unfortunate Fursey*, 180.
23. Berresford Ellis and Williams, *By Jove, Biggles!*, chapter 11, with several editorial pronouncements by Johns supporting the chapter's thesis as stated in its title. Crompton's satire on disarmament was 'William the Gangster', *Happy Mag* (October 1933), and *William the Gangster* (June 1934). It may have implied that the newly elected Nazi regime would take advantage of international disarmament to rearm at the world's expense.
24. Buchan, *Mr Standfast* (1919, but written in the belief that its first readers would still be at war), 119–23, and, for Wake's heroic death, 340, 346–8, 355–9.
25. Fairlie Bruce, *Nancy Calls the Tune* (1944), 111, 119, 124–5, 160, 186, 187, 185, 191. Rosemary Auchmuty, *A World of Women* (1999), sparkles with perception on Fairlie Bruce's and Brent-Dyer's schoolgirls grown up.
26. Brent-Dyer, *The Highland Twins at the Chalet School*, 113–14. House in Cornwall, 34–7.
27. Katherine Tozer, *Mumfie Marches On* (1942), 166–8, 4, 72, 169, 54–5. The book was suggested by the government according to Peter Daniel Harrison, *Katherine Tozer* (1998), n.p.
28. Crompton, 'Reluctant Hero', *Modern Woman* (September 1941) and (as 'Reluctant Heroes') *William Carries On*, 128. James Douglas-Hamilton, *Motive for a Mission*, 197, puts the Hess mission in both British and German perspective. I am obliged to Lord James and his father the Duke for their generosity in additional explanation.
29. Monica Dickens, *One Pair of Feet* ([1942]), 38: another of those books which had many readers just above child level, and is excellent social history.
30. Wodehouse, *Mike* (1909), only casually mentions Adair's Irishness towards the end, with an air of its having been established from the outset: a natural result of

taking over the character. Adair is one of the very few substantial and likeable characters in Wodehouse who is never comic. Brent-Dyer, *The Head-Girl of the Chalet School* (1928), *The Chalet School and Jo* (1931) and *The New House at the Chalet School* (1935) give suitable introductions to the Mlles O'Hagen, O'Hara and O'Ryan (though the latter appears in several titles). Timothy Shy, a.k.a. D. B. Wyndham Lewis (not to be confused with the much more serious novelist P. Wyndham Lewis, as he frequently is), wrote *The Terror of St Trinian's* (1952) in collaboration with the artist Ronald Searle. They may have had effects on the girls' school story comparable to that which Richards and the iconoclasm of the late 1930s and early 1940s had on the boys'.

31. Christie, *N or M?* ([1942] 1964), 87. (The executed Irish patriot is described as having been a follower of Roger Casement, and shot as a traitor, which would make him IRB or Clan-na-Gael, the IRA only becoming an official if underground name in 1920; but Christie means IRA. Perhaps he might have been an Irish prisoner-of-war in Limburg who accepted the German offer to Casement to fight for Germany; none were shot, so far as is known.) Christie, *Taken at the Flood* (1948), 20, 37, 38, 42–3, 181–90. Both books are very well-observed pictures of rural England during the Second World War and after, respectively. Johns's view of the Irish as liars was stated in a charming letter to me, and was not intended to be hostile: he was a good enough liar himself when he wanted to be.

32. Pardoe, *Bunkle Began It*, 136–7, 138, 140, 144–5, 145–6, 169, 170, 162. Coward, *Nude with Violin*, III, i.

33. It is fair to say that Professor David Krause, the charming and erudite editor and biographer of O'Casey, vehemently disputes this thesis, but it is consistent with O'Casey's denunciation of 'the civilization that could let Joyce die in poverty, crown with a D.Litt. a thing like Wodehouse, deserves fire and brimstone from Heaven, and it is getting it' (O'Casey to Gabriel Fallen, 29 March 1941). O'Casey had been living in England (a thing Joyce never did) for ten years when he wrote this, and would remain there until he died in 1964.

34. Dixon, *The King of the Fiddles*, 105–6, 146.

35. Dixon, *Runaway Boy*, 7, 8, 200. Dixon continued her Irish preoccupations in post-war novels (two), less politically.

36. Johns, *Biggles in the Orient* (November 1944), 10.

37. *Gimlet Comes Home* (1946), and *Gimlet's Oriental Quest* (1948).

38. *The Chalet School Goes to It*, 204–5. *The Highland Twins at the Chalet School*, 22. Dundee *Sunday Post*, 13 May 1945, in *The Broons and Oor Wullie 1939–1945* (1997), 140.

39. Crompton, 'The Pageant', *Modern Woman* (May 1946) and *William – the Bold* (July 1950). The admirable Cadogan, *The William Companion*, 150–1, points out that the *Modern Woman* text was frequently shorter than the book, but that this, the last story it printed, was in fuller text in the magazine (note by David Schutte). The anthology *William at War* (1995), selected and edited by Crompton's niece Richmal C. Ashbee, restores the full text, which partly turns on the polar opposition of Churchill and Hitler, but fooling Hubert Lane into thinking that he is portraying Churchill, and is in fact to be presented as Goering, Bertie Franks thinking himself Anthony Eden is Hitler, Claude Bellew is Goebbels thinking himself to be Montgomery. Ashbee points out that the interval between magazine and book publication led to the doggerel on the Nazis' names being dropped, a remarkable and probably accurate comment on the speed with which the very vivid villains faded after their deaths.

40. *The Broons and Oor Wullie 1939–1945*, 140. Fred Urquhart, 'English Lessons', in

his *Selected Stories* (1946); also his 'The Prisoners' in his *The Year of the Short Corn* (1949) and subsequent collections. I am most grateful to Urquhart's literary executor and biographer Dr Colin Affleck for assistance on this and so much else.

41. Methley, *Great Galleon* (1942), 11. The initial antipathy is exacerbated by the cousins having the same name, Evelyn Royle. Eponymity was less successful in the first marriage of Evelyn Waugh; but surely Methley, however anti-snob, cannot have been alluding to that! Apart from P. L. Travers and I. A. Shead (the latter setting her[?] evacuee story mostly in Australia), we should also note Elinor Mordaunt, whose Australian days were Edwardian, but with powerful effects on her writing.

42. 'There is a nice story of someone taking a blue pencil to *Smoky* and setting out to translate it into good English. For years and years no one in Penguins – except perhaps Allen Lane and myself – realized the reputation it had, and how justly. It has won prizes galore in America through the years. But the general staff at Penguins considered it a mere cowboy yarn and a blot on the list' (Graham, 'The Puffin Years', *Signal* 12 (September 1973), 117–18). It is worth remembering the context in which Graham sought to maintain gentility: her more extreme genteel critics apparently had no idea that she would be fighting to establish a market for Puffins among young persons supremely proficient in western dialect as written if not as spoken.

43. *Magnet* 1,468, 1,471–8 (April–June 1936) constituted a fascinating series of psychological studies. The idea of gangsters becoming part of a stately mansion and so on has been employed by many writers from Wodehouse down (arguably it goes back to Euripides' *Alcestis*, with the drunken Heracles in the gunman's role). But Richards made a remarkable figure of Poker Pike, who would as readily have taken on assassin's and kidnapper's work if hired but whose professionalism in guarding the spoiled son of the millionaire mixes a stoicism with a genuine sympathy for the weak: hence he too obeys the principle of reverence for the Head. Equally, the means by which the schoolmasters find themselves growing in affection for the gunman is well developed and elegantly drawn out. And since it becomes clear that the gunman is fundamentally a sportsman, above all one extraordinarily tolerant of schoolboy horseplay, he wins the hearts of the boys inside and outside the story.

44. Saville, *Seven White Gates*, 193, 195, 196, 227–8.

45. Saville's two wartime books in that 'Lone Pine' series must have had a more representative quality from their being launched nearly simultaneously with their own broadcasting, in ways hard for the reader dependent solely on print fully to grasp. It is too easy in reading to think of the children from London as very similar in voices. They would have some resonance with classics of children's literature from Children's Hour use of well-known voices. Thus David Morton was played by Charles Hawtrey (who played the Children's Hour detective Norman Bones, whose cases had been running since 17 July 1943, a few weeks before the four-part *Mystery at Witchend* began on 8 October 1943, a week after its first copies went on sale). Tom Ingles was played by Harry Fowler, who had graduated to film and radio stardom from newspaper-selling on the London streets; he would star in the immediately post-war movie in which masses of Cockney boys round up a gang of crooks, *Hue and Cry* (1946), with Alastair Sim in a cameo part of an author of boys' weekly comic instalments on a detective like Sexton Blake, the author himself forcibly suggesting Frank Richards. Dickie Morton was played by Peter Mullins, who played the boy David Copperfield in 1944, when *Seven White Gates* was also broadcast and

published. Mark O'Hanlon, *Beyond the Lone Pine: a Biography of Malcolm Saville* (2001), 36–7. Wallace Grevatt, *BBC Children's Hour* (1988), 92–4.

46. Johns, *Biggles in Spain*, 255–6, 101, 38; *Biggles & Co.*, 26; *Biggles in Africa*, 233–4; *Biggles in the Jungle*, 31, 40–1, 122; *Biggles Delivers the Goods* (April 1946), 50.

47. Johns, *Biggles in the Jungle*, 14, 130, 178; *Biggles in Borneo* ([July 1943] 1944), 43, 42.

48. Johns, *Biggles in Borneo*, 126–7; *Biggles in the Orient*. Something of the same message of an Empire's death may be found in *Biggles Delivers the Goods*, in the character and fate of Major Marling, who has gone native in anger against his ostracism by his fellow-British for marrying an Asian princess, lives among 'his people' on the Burmese mainland near the Mergui archipelago, is convinced he can deal with the Japanese but is overwhelmed by them, and at the end of the story has a very uncertain lease of life, while his son (the royal wife being now dead) goes with Marling's reluctant permission back to Britain. Johns's coda on Marling was strangely present-tensed: 'Major Marling was still at Shansie when the squadron left Elephant Island, and there, presumably, he remains, the white father of his people' (*Biggles Delivers the Goods*, 181).

FIGURE 7 Nazism faces the enemy (cover withdrawn later
in the war) – see p. 103.
Reproduced by permission of Girls Gone By Publishers http://www.ggbp.co.uk

7

Identity, Authority and Imagination

'I know you have some queer friends scattered up and down the globe –'
  'While men are decent to me I try to be decent to them, regardless of race, colour, politics, creed, or anything else', asserted Biggles curtly. 'I've travelled a bit, and taking the world by and large, it's my experience that with a few exceptions there's nothing wrong with the people on it, if only they were left alone to live as they want to live.'
  'All right – all right', said the Air Commodore soothingly . . .
                                  W. E. Johns, *Biggles Delivers the Goods*

What did the writers tell the children the war had done to them? Implicitly, they told them it had cut them off from their Empire, leaving it to them to deduce that they had lost it. Nobody wrote for them from Canada the way L. M. Montgomery had written, giving tiny Prince Edward Island the resonance of enormous Canada, yet making faraway seem home partly by valorising her remote Scottish origins. Australian works invited interest, but not identification such as Montgomery's *Anne of Green Gables* had won.[1] If a transoceanic writer was to win allegiance from British children after 1945, it would almost certainly be an American. In the wake of the 1944 Exhibition, US titles for children found British imprints, notably that year's Caldecott Medallist Robert McCloskey's *Make Way for Ducklings* (1944), mixing advanced American illustrative technique with a beautiful simplicity of story about a family of ducks whose progress through the city of Boston was kept safe from harm by Michael, an obviously Irish American policeman, and his colleagues. American books could easily outshine British in presentational skills, but the appeal would be endangered by the ostentation. The British struggle and self-sacrifice were not always the easiest background against which to accommodate the flamboyant American deliverer: Cinderella may have found the Prince's wealth a trifle irritating with its eternal contrast to the poverty she knew – nice to share but uneasy for one's self-respect. The genius of *Make Way for Ducklings* was that it showed the old American rural values surviving in the apparent heartlessness of urban traffic. It was an assurance that the America which had won the hearts of Orwell and countless other Europeans through the March sisters and Huck Finn might still be found alive and honoured in the most ruthlessly modern surroundings. (In fact, the story's wonder owes much to other antiquities – marks of colonial Boston, and folkways of rural Ireland – but if a child reader had some knowledge of either or both, they could be easily welcomed and taken in one's stride; and, for the many British who had none, the Ducklings still bask in more superficial appreciation.) Reviewers beamed with approval, apart from the *Times Literary Supplement*, whose defensive chauvinism on 18 November 1944 took refuge in insisting that such things sometimes happen 'in London near St James's Park – the holding-up of the traffic by a policeman to allow a family of ducks to cross the road' and thus questioned its originality. The claim makes little sense for Second World War London, especially since the route in question was notoriously made their own by senior civil servants going to club lunches; but it prefigured post-war prickles against Americanisation.

Once the Americans had done the work for which the British had wooed them in the long first years of the war, British adults were inclined to sheer away from them. For all of the enthusiasm brought by T. S. Eliot and Ernest Barker to the exchanges of children's books in 1944, the USA slid well down most publishers' agenda in the early post-war years.[2] Eleanor Graham was ready to let Puffin readers' imaginations gallop through twentieth-century Dutch, Swedish, Indian, Mongolian, African, Russian, Norwegian, Polynesian or Australian landscapes, but American interest was initially confined to Americans abroad or in previous centuries.[3]

Austerity Britain after the war hardly wanted its children's eyes fixed on the wealthy and luxuriant USA. (But British children remembered. 'Any gum, chum?' became a nostalgic battle-cry.) Ginger's affectations of American slang vanished from the Biggles saga after the war: indeed, the first Biggles book set after the war featured a highly unpleasant American gangster, of German origin but pointedly American speech and greed.[4] Blyton had made little use of America, and her one notable post-war American character was a deferential, persecuted American black paratrooper (possibly reflective of some Britons' preference for black American GIs over white).[5] Saville had made Americans welcome, but Charles came home and his American army comrades vanished. Brent-Dyer's diminished into insignificance in post-war stories. Richards's return to writing, now in book form, revived Fisher T. Fish, as capitalist and as self-centred as ever.[6] Comics acknowledged the demand for American cowboy and gangster stories still, and the *Hotspur* even added a fresh generation of Yanks to the permanent heroes of Yank House. But youngsters now wanted American comics, and Superman and Batman entered the field in their eponymous journals. The post-war generation gap was to be most strongly marked by the youthful preference for, and adult withdrawal from, American inspiration. The writers could not help but follow the adult lead: they knew American produce was inimical to their own traditions, even though they might normally side with children against adults, and thus be roundly denounced or cold-shouldered by adult librarians and critics. British and Irish parents and journalists became concerned in the 1950s by the campaign against US horror comics, but if anything that enhanced the American appeal to their juniors, especially when British adult journalism indicted *MAD* magazine for being insufficiently respectful to the British monarchy.[7]

If British writing for children lost hold of the Empire, and lost ground to the United States, how fared its European identity? Some European writing had made its impact on British children before the war, notably Erich Kästner's *Emil and the Detectives* (1929, Englished 1931). He presented an ordinary child caught up as victim in a story of crime, mystery and quest, and won many British disciples. It played the Dr Watson trick, of showing events through the eyes of a natural person with whom the reader could identify. The 'detectives' with their different skills, leaderly, intellectual and so forth, are found by Emil: imitators such as Blyton (in her *Mystery of . . .* series) or Ransome are over-preoccupied with their gangs of children, with the odd result that the identification-figure may have been originally intended as an infant or an eccentric. (Richards might avoid this with a story seen through a new boy's eyes.) Blyton, as has been unkindly remarked by Margery Fisher, cast many of her children only in outline, thus assisting reader-identification; but the child cannot easily identify with Philip's enchantment of animals or Fatty's wealth or George's ownership of an island, however ardently desirable. Series principle militates against the charm and thrill of the child discovery of other children's talents, power and superiority to adulthood. The Blyton reader – and the Ransome reader – know that the series children outsmart adults. Crompton, who may have influenced Kästner, scored by keeping William's success doubtful until a story's conclusion (the supposed capture of Hitler leaves him outsmarted by his usual dupe, Hubert Lane, and reduced to exchanging end-of-story gripes with the cat, which is equally annoyed by its wartime rationing). The Second World War made for more dependence by British children upon gangs for social life, the normal family unit being greatly reduced in efficacy. The influence of *Emil and the Detectives* and of British orphaned children in the Second World War produced the Ealing movie *Hue and Cry* (1946), with its masterpiece mob of boy detectives who momentarily take over the BBC news summary. The pre-Nazi German world actually possessed some of the frightening anarchy to be found in Second World War Britain, from a child's standpoint. Where children were regimented – as with the evacuees – children in stories might run away from what they considered intolerable, and take refuge in gangs (for example in Norman Dale's *Secret Service*, 1943). Kästner's first Emil book appeared in yet another English edition in 1940 – in Nazi Europe, his books were all banned and burned by Nazi order – but his popularity may have suffered, most unfairly, in the understandably anti-German atmosphere of the Second World War, however strong his influence; his British sales quickly picked up after the war's end. His *Lottie and Lise* (1949, Englished 1951) took up a theme that would grow increasingly more relevant to the post-war British child: picking up the pieces after a parental divorce.

Inevitably, one effect of the war had to be strong Germanophobia, often not wise enough to limit itself to Naziphobia. Brent-Dyer's first post-war Chalet School book, *Three Go to the Chalet School* (1949), grapples courageously with this. The diminutive Verity-Ann, brought up by her late grandparents, defies all authority with a devastating silvery courtesy. Inevitably, it ends in confrontation, when she refuses to sing a Bach Christmas carol ('The music is by a German. I do not approve of *any* Germans')[8] and they are only rescued from a total impasse by the return of her father from presumed death (in South America, not Germany). Brent-Dyer was faithfully recording post-war anger, but in most cases there were no missing-presumed-dead fathers to return and so persuade obdurate loved ones to see reason. Those who did make such returns might well deepen hatreds. And Germanophobia unobtrusively spread xenophobia, give or take the Americans and their gum.

Distrust of Europe grew alongside a new English chauvinism. It was natural that BBC Children's Hour and allied programmes had made much of classic English encounters with European enemies (without harking back to the oldest Arthurian adventures where the English were the European enemies – Arthur was usually served up in Normanised versions). The exceptional wartime conditions of teaching could add to this, Brent-Dyer and Crompton facing the phenomenon from impressively different standpoints. Brent-Dyer in *Gay from China at the Chalet School* (1944) showed how the wartime dearth of teachers could resurrect impressive-looking drop-outs of earlier years. Several senior teachers suffer injuries in a coach accident. A temporary Head is appointed; girl readers would have appreciated being treated as adults in Brent-Dyer's frank discussion of Miss Bubb's determination to chisel a permanency out of her situation. Miss Bubb's regime is clearly a de-Europeanisation (significantly highlighted by her intention to end separate Assembly for the Catholics). It is also a reassertion of the more status-conscious barriers between staff and pupils of earlier decades. The story develops into a duel between headmistress and one girl in particular, and gains in character interest but loses its European relevance (as the school itself increasingly does). Crompton shows how the same want of teaching staff with which Miss Bubb attempts to blackmail the school's owner could transform the lives of schoolchildren benevolently; like Brent-Dyer, Crompton was a teacher:[9]

> The younger masters at William's school had vanished gradually with the course of the war, to be replaced by older men emerging often from the retirement of years. The new Maths master was half blind, and the new French master was more than half deaf, and the new Latin master so stiff with rheumatism that he could only walk with a stick. All three were such easy game that it was hardly worth trying to rag them.
>
> The new history master, however, Mr Polliter, was a very different proposition. He was old, like the rest, and, like the rest, he had retired from teaching many years before, but, unlike the rest, he was a distinguished scholar, who had the knack of making his subject interesting both to the expert and the lay mind. He was the author of several 'best selling' biographies and a popular broadcaster on historical subjects. William, of course, did not know this. All he knew was that a subject that had consisted formerly of dates and maps and genealogical tables and wholly uninteresting facts, had suddenly become alive and exciting – even more exciting than the Wild West stories with which he beguiled his leisure hours.
>
> . . . Week after week, William came home with fresh news of the Napoleonic wars – news that was obviously more real and exciting to him than the news that appeared in the daily papers.

As so often with Crompton, the light it throws on the mood of the times is both unusual and fascinating. She was writing of a moment (early 1943) when the war had dulled, with Russia and America now in it, but D-day followed by the V-bombs more than a year away. The cultivation of morale by charismatic light on the English past could diminish the present conflict (their finest hour though it had been) into subordination to glories long ago. It was timely, in its way. The entry of America into the war meant the end of Britain's solitary triumph, and inspiration from the past was easing its way into dependence on the past. Mr Polliter is a wonderful creation in reminding teachers on any level that their first duty is to win enthusiasm from their students. But he is also a harbinger of future difficulties for the English in readjusting themselves to a Europe where they ought not be either lonely or leaders. Recall of the Napoleonic wars enabled them to relive their prowess as both. Inter-war Europe had had sufficient individual countries imposing leadership or splendidly isolating themselves.

Alongside the uneasy client status of the Free French in Britain, French books made their wartime way into the hands of British children. Some of them were dreadful. There was a hideous series *Les Malheurs de Sophie* (1859), exhumed and translated for pre-war, wartime and post-war audiences: its author, Sophie Rostopchine, Comtesse de Ségur (1799–1874), was an immigrant to France, having been born the daughter to the Russian soldier-statesman Count Fyodor Rostopchin, which may partly account for the savagery with which the infant Sophie in the story is continually disciplined for her own and her readers' good. De Ségur had been a pillar of the French Right, and literally beat home the continual lesson that the child would be spoiled if the rod were spared. It must have been sick enough medicine for all child sado-masochism, and in bomb-battered Britain will have added appreciably to the anti-European sentiments of its readers. Four volumes were published from 1936 to 1944 inclusive, translated by Honor and Edgar Skinner. Fortunately, a very different product of the French aristocracy, Antoine de Saint Exupéry (1900–44), wrote his *Le Petit Prince* the year before he disappeared in a reconnaissance flight for the American forces based in North Africa. It may not have been entirely new to the British or Irish child readers; it seems a natural progression from Oscar Wilde's 'The Happy Prince', now becoming increasingly available to them. *Le Petit Prince* (Englished 1943 [USA] and 1944 [UK]) is very consciously written from the same empathy for children and self-distance from grown-ups. This even dominated the dedication, to Léon Werth, a left-wing Jew suffering in France:

TO LÉON WERTH

I ask the indulgence of the children who may read this book for dedicating it to a grown-up. I have a serious reason: he is the best friend I have in the world. I have another reason: this grown-up understands everything, even books about children. I have a third reason: he lives in France where he is hungry and cold. He needs cheering up. If all these reasons are not enough, I will dedicate the book to the child from whom this grown-up grew. All grown-ups were once children – although few of them remember it. And so I correct my dedication:

TO LÉON WERTH WHEN HE WAS A LITTLE BOY

There is another little boy to be considered, the one from whom the person grew up who wrote the story. It has been remarked that the story tells of a very lonely person in the little prince and hence a comparably lonely one in the author. But the author in the story is not lonely when he is with the little prince. The little prince at one point remarks:[10] 'Only the children know what they are looking for . . . They waste their time over a rag doll and it becomes very important to them; and if anybody takes it away from them, they cry . . .', and a railway switchman replies to him that they are lucky. The little prince came from an asteroid and supposedly returned to it after allowing himself to be bitten by a snake, but to the eyes of grown-ups he died. A few months after writing Le Petit Prince, Antoine de Saint-Exupéry vanished somewhere in the skies over the southernmost part of his native France, according to radar, because he was shot down by a German aircraft or died for some other reason. I think he found the little prince again. Anyone who objects to my thinking it may classify my observation as postmodernism.

It would have been a good idea for the children who read Le Petit Prince or its English version in 1944–5 to think that being European was a good idea since people from there wrote books like that. But there is no longer any writing books like that, and maybe Saint-Exupéry died (or found the little prince again) to make sure it was no longer necessary to write books like that.

The book in translation with its drawings by the author went through eight editions in twenty-one years, six of them in the last twelve of those years. It appeared in Britain before it could appear in France, which reminds us of Free France's ghostly existence in

Britain. That was the most important reason for Britain's realising it was European. But the war ended, and people forgot they had also been trustees for other people – especially when many of the other people were dead. Subsequent history has dissolved that Anglo–French mutual identification: de Gaulle's presidential insistence that the UK was an American catspaw, and Britain's and the USA's inability to understand the independence of French nationalism, have been read backwards to assume similar dominant attitudes during the war. But in fact identification was much closer, for all of the prima-donna sound-biting at one another's expense by the ruling few: witness the US and UK support of French reoccupation of Vietnam in 1945–6, for which thousands would die during the next thirty years. Winston Churchill proclaimed the Battle of Britain as continuation of the Battle of France. W. E. Johns, who loosely agreed with many of his views, mourned the sufferings of the French in book after book. In fact, the whole tone of Johns's Second World War fiction makes France as beloved as England by every form of symbolism that could reach a child. Johns was not normally as sensitive an artist as Brent-Dyer or Treadgold: he lived in a time when male writers of tough stories were expected to keep stiff upper lips. But he makes his readers mourn locality after locality in France – northern France and Paris were no doubt obvious enough, but Worrals operated as far as the Cévennes, the Rhone and the Camargue, Gimlet reached Sarthe, Biggles Monaco and the Riviera. Worrals directs admiring French allies, from café, church and family and domesticity in general, Cub is second-in-command of a French teenage guerrilla band, Ginger has a touching romance with a girl while Bertie is rediscovered by his former mechanic and his wife: the French people in fact play a more profound personal part in the stories than the British. Johns's cannibalisation of First World War stories of air confict in France no doubt deepened the identification: France had been his theatre of war, however far over the globe he hurled Biggles. But his closest point to his fellow-pilot Saint-Exupéry was a strange love-story told by Biggles in *Spitfire Parade* recalled from the Battle of France (where we are told that Biggles, Algy and Ginger served, but which Johns seems to have found too painful to write stories about). It is the only Biggles story (since Biggles's own romance with his nice First World War spy) to be solely about love, and it may be so because of something Johns urgently wanted to say, metaphorically, about his lost France. A young pilot crashes in the grounds of a French chateau, falls in love with the comtesse's daughter who nurses him, leaves because he believes it would be dishonourable to remain, and flees (still badly disabled) to a hospital, whither the girl follows to be killed en route by a German bomb, though surviving long enough for a message: 'Tell him', she said, looking at the sky, 'that I shall be waiting for him, up there'. It's possible that the boy's reactions to the French girl's death express Johns's own feelings on France's capitulation on 22 June 1940: 'Tony said not a word, but there's no doubt something in him died at that moment'. Biggles tersely finishes what he knows:[11]

> 'He used to come back with his machine shot to rags. The truth of the matter was, I have no doubt, he was looking for Old Man Death, and he didn't care who knew it. He was wounded, and went to hospital, but even then he couldn't die. When he came out he was posted to you, Wilks. From what I hear, he's still crazy, roaring about in the blue – looking for her. He's been looking for her for six months -'
> 'Yes', put in Wilks, 'he has. And now, at last, he's found her.'
> Biggles started. 'What do you mean?' he cried sharply.
> Wilks stared into the fire. 'He and I ran into a bunch of Messerschmitts this afternoon. We got three of them. Then they got him – in flames. He jumped clear, from twenty thousand – without a parachute.'

Curiously enough, there was a persistent rumour that Saint-Exupéry was also shot down by a Messerschmitt; V. S. Pritchett takes it as a fact in his *New Statesman and Nation* critical essay of 3 May 1952. There seems no firm basis for it, but Johns's brief story strangely anticipates the quest for the little prince and the fate of his historian.

Johns had an even stranger anticipation in the case of the Francophone Belgian Georges Remi, who drew the strip cartoon 'Tintin' as 'Hergé' (i.e. his initials reversed, R. G.). Tintin began his conquest of Britain and Ireland only in 1951 (though no doubt instalments in French had made their way across in the 1930s and 1940s) – his adventure 'King Ottokar's Sceptre' ran in the *Eagle* comic in 1951. Its teenage reporter hero's superiority to adult friends and enemies harmonised with the 'Harris Tweed' strips from John Ryan, equally insistent on teenage valour and resource in contrast to adult imbecility. From Tintin's early involvement with the imbecile Sûreté detectives Dupond and Dupont (to be known when the English translation began in 1951 as Thomson and Thompson), Ryan, a Catholic, may even have got the idea of asinine detective and genius boy: Tintin had first appeared in a Catholic Belgian paper.

Tintin from the 1950s would appear in British publication where locale, histories and loyalties were made firmly English. Another reason for including him here is to get a sense of the fate of children's literature had the Nazis conquered Britain. And Tintin seems to have been in a number of ways a child of British standard fare for children, including Richards and Johns, and possibly Crompton. Its beginnings had more in common with George Orwell's fears of the effect of British comics than with their actual consequences. Remi was born in 1907, in Brussels. The boy thus knew the horrors of a country at the heart of a world war, from 7 to 11 years of age. He would have heard of the patriot King, Albert, who rallied resistance to the invading Germans, and the patriot Prince, the future Leopold III, who took time off from his Eton schooldays to serve in the Belgian Army. Leopold may even have helped inspire the many English school stories where young heroes doubled service to the Allied cause with fulfilment of educational obligations: he was certainly their nearest real-life equivalent. The strong-arm methods of the early Tintin may reflect a child's unfulfilled yearnings to avenge the indignities suffered by his elders under German occupation – and also, it may be, under British condescension, for Britain was not popular in inter-war Belgium. Certainly, young Remi was left with a great hatred of war, and of the men who brought it about: this coheres with his detestation of gun-runners, Japanese, Germans and arms manufacturers before the Second World War, but it could also induce the thought that a war over in two-and-a-half weeks was preferable to a war devastating your country over four years.

In 1929, the 22-year-old Remi was on the staff of a clerical-Fascist Brussels newspaper, *La Vingtième Siècle*: the editor, the Abbé Norbert Wallez, was a priest who kept on his desk a signed photograph of Mussolini flourishing its thanks for his services to the cause of Fascism. Wallez was probably no more anti-democratic than a number of Catholic political parties in Europe such as Dollfuss's followers in Austria, or the CEDA in Spain (although he was to the right of the Catholic party in Belgium): these people settled for democracy rather than totalitarianism in most circumstances but preferring dictatorships like Salazar's in Portugal to anything that might encourage Communism. Wallez's paper's staff in 1929 also included Remi's near-coeval, Léon Degrelle, future leader of the Rexists, the small Walloon (Francophone) Fascist party which would welcome Nazi conquest in 1940. Degrelle was but one polar extreme in the Belgian Catholic response to the Nazi invasion; another would be the resistance leader Walthère Dewé, who ran an air-wireless-telephone operation, 'a particularly ardent Catholic patriot' as M. R. D. Foot would point out, resisting the Nazis 'quite as much for religious as for patriotic motives; knew and welcomed the dangers of his work; and expected the martyrdom he received on 14 January 1944'.[12] Most of Belgian Catholicism would have lain between these two, neutral, silent, unaligned.

Hergé's Tintin strips before the war had little of the viciousness to be found in French right-wing clericalist comics such as Le Pèlerin. Hergé's villains might be big-nosed financiers, notably Tintin's arch-adversary Roberto Rastopopoulos, but he was Greek and in fact modelled on a Greek American tycoon, where Le Pèlerin would have had him clearly as a Jew. Tintin's first foreign adventure was a supposed journalistic investigation of the USSR for the paper in which he appeared, Le Petit Vingtième, a children's newspaper in the Abbé Wallez's organisation. Pictures and text were crude, absurd in Tintin's virtual invincibility, and excessive in violence (Tintin's included). It showed charm, skill and humour. Its vigorous anti-Communist evangelism did nothing to delay the literally breakneck pace. Its most obvious literary ancestor was Cervantes's Don Quixote, whose ironies it should have applied to its own conspiracy-consciousness, and which maintained its capacity to laugh at itself; this it shared with some of the best British writers for children and others, notably Scott, Dickens, Stevenson, Conan Doyle, Richards and Johns. Tintin would even be described as Don Quixote by enemies in an adventure some years later, and his Sancho Panza was his mongrel Milou,[13] whose comments delight the reader while remaining incomprehensible to the other characters (save occasionally Tintin). The post-war American strip Peanuts developed its own form of this through the dog Snoopy, but Blyton's Kiki has the variation of intelligible but hilariously irrelevant speech. The story's thesis was that the USSR rulers were defrauding the people, much as the pigs would do in Animal Farm. It was much more ignorant than Hergé would show himself in Tintin's later globetrottings, notably the Chinese adventure The Blue Lotus: Tintin's USSR in 1929 seems to have had Lenin alive, Trotsky in the ascendant, Stalin as third man. It was rude about gullible British Communists, but even ruder about the Germans, presented as stupid bullies. After Hitler's rise to power, Hergé would make much of German villains, until Belgium's capitulation. Tintin's second adventure, Tintin au Congo[14] (1930), presented 'our' Congolese natives as adult-size children, guarded by kindly old Catholic missionaries: Tintin at one point teaches actual Congolese children that 'our country' is Belgium, integrationist if insensitive. It was a start, however limited, for his subsequent internationalism which the Belgian no less than the British Empire fostered and frustrated simultaneously. *Tintin au Congo* explains a good deal about Belgium's responsibility for the tragedy of 1960 following withdrawal: it justified Belgian hostility to any thought of Congolese self-government.

Tintin became strongly anti-racist after Remi's emotional involvement with the Chinese youth Chang Chong Jen and Tintin's comparable love for Chang in *The Blue Lotus*, which he began in 1934; it would be reprised in a story of emotional power and beauty, *Tintin au Tibet* (begun in 1958). The USA had been handled roughly in the strip from 1931 (*Tintin in America*) on grounds of corruption, gangsterism and so on. Towards Britain, Hergé was more ambiguous. Britain in some ways had taught him his trade: he was studying the *Rainbow* comic as a boy in the First World War, and evidently stayed close to British examplars as a writer and artist for children. Tintin's many intricate adventures give strong indications of the author's familiarity with the Amalgamated Press *Magnet*, *Gem*, *Modern Boy* and so on: for instance *Les Cigares du Pharaon*, begun in December 1932, seems prompted by the Greyfriars adventures in Egypt (*Magnets* 1,277–84, July–September 1931) including kidnappings amid ancient Egyptian phenomena, the villain being a Greek and so on. Hergé's growing use of aeroplanes with increasing awareness of their possibilities reflects the boys' weeklies, notably in the work of Johns, George E. Rochester and Hedley O'Mant, all with war flying experience. A British locale for a story, *L'Île Noire* (begun in April 1937), was partly prompted by the Loch Ness Monster (a mid-1930s press topic as sardonically acknowledged by Crompton, 'William and the Monster', *Happy Mag* (April 1934) and *William the Detective* (July 1935)). The first appearance of *Le Sceptre d'Ottokar* (begun in August 1938) showed obvious influences of George V's Silver Jubilee, Edward VIII's abdication and George VI's Coronation, not to speak of the Bayeux Tapestry; and the *Modern Boy* from 25 September to 4 December 1937 ran *Biggles Goes to War*, essentially with the same background of an aggressive power menacing a smaller country in which our heroes find themselves up against trusted high officials secretly intending to sell out for plum jobs in the intended conquest. In both cases, the aggressive power was clearly a metaphor for Germany, although the local agent in *Ottokar* is specifically named Müsstler, pointedly composed of Muss[olini] and Hi[t]tler. *Biggles Goes to War* also involves the clever theft of a German-built enemy plane in the story, much as *Ottokar* would in its turn. The country under threat in *Ottokar* is inspired by Poland and was probably meant to be read as such. Poland's right-wing clerical-Fascist regime under Colonel Beck would have appealed to Hergé's editor. But Hergé's imaginary Syldavia is a monarchy, which Poland no longer was; the history of that monarchy is drawn primarily from Poland, but its present King, Muskar XII, was probably based on Leopold III of Belgium. Hergé depicts Muskar as a man of innocence, honour and courage, ready to take necessary but hateful decisions against his will. In what was to follow for Belgium, he seems to have identified himself as the King's man.

Belgium was neutral until invaded by Germany on 10 May 1940. Hergé, in the Belgian Army from September 1939, sent his copy to *Le Petit Vingtième* for his new serial, the first version of *Tintin au Pays de l'Or Noir*, which would be discontinued and greatly changed when resumed in 1950, and further changed for the final version in 1971. The first text is said to have been anti-Nazi, with the German villain of *L'Île Noire*, and also seems to have been anti-war, Tintin denouncing war's approach with philosophic passion. Hergé was on sick leave when Belgium was invaded. On 28 May 1940, Leopold III, having declared that he as King controlled the army, capitulated, with disastrous results for the armies of Britain and France, his allies of less than three weeks' standing. The Belgian government had never accepted Leopold's belief as to his control of the army, nor did it accept the capitulation. The government was a coalition under Hubert Pierlot (Catholic) and Paul Henri Spaak (Socialist). The Liberal Minister for Finance, Camille Gutt, had gone to London on 27 May to negotiate financial arrangements. After the armistice of 28 May, Leopold declared himself a prisoner in his own country. Pierlot and Spaak fled to France and reached Vichy and thence Spain, but were imprisoned until October in Barcelona by Franco's pro-Nazi brother-in-law Serrano Suñer, after which they escaped to London, where Gutt had been established since August. The Belgian government from October thus had a constitutional legitimacy which de Gaulle, for instance, lacked; but the Minister for Finance and the Minister for the Colonies, Joseph de Vleeschauwer van Braekel, were more questionable in acting on their own before the arrival in London of Pierlot and Spaak. Among other matters, they arranged for the freezing of Belgian assets in the UK and the USA, and placed the Congo, and its high uranium and other mineral wealth, at UK and US disposal (the USA had commenced its nuclear programme in September 1939 and was hindered by the loss of Norway's heavy water). The Nazis therefore had a need to discredit the exile Belgian government and its British links: public opinion was encouraged to be anti-British. Wallez's papers were closed down. Hergé had refused to work for Degrelle, now a vehement supporter of the Nazis, but took up ground between Degrelle and Pierlot, where he might believe the King stood, and where Raymond de Becker, the editor of the Belgian national Francophone evening paper *Le Soir*, certainly stood. De Becker, like Spaak, had been for neutrality, but Spaak's had been pro-Allied where de Becker's had been pro-German. De Becker saw his stance as pragmatic, and his current policy was to try to help Belgium return to self-sufficiency while accepting Nazi supervision. De Becker was of a distinguished Catholic family; he was also a future Belgian gay liberationist – two loyalties which he may have thought to have common ground with fringes of Nazism but which would find themselves intrinsically at enmity with it. *Le Soir* was heavily manipulated by the Nazi military regime run from Brussels while also controlling north-eastern France. De Becker was quite serious in attempting to win as much editorial independence as he could; did he also realise that homosexuals in Hitler's Europe would be destined for eradication by mass murder? Did he realise the more visible certainty of such a fate for the Jews? And how vulnerable was Hergé, married, but famous for a comic strip in which male mutual affection was supreme and women were largely absurd or irrelevant? In any event, Hergé went to work on *Le Soir* with de Becker, a juvenile supplement housing Tintin until September 1941, after which the comic strip was printed in the main paper among major 'news' stories. *Le Soir*'s circulation was about 300,000.

The first adventure to appear under the Nazis was *Le Crabe aux Pinces d'Or*, with Tintin embattled against drug-runners. It began on 17 October 1940, when the Blitz on London was at its worst, but the British were also bombing – Amsterdam, Rotterdam, Flushing on 6 October, extensive raids on Germany over the 20th and after. Like many another Francophone, Hergé admired and learned from British culture while not much liking the British: *L'Île Noire*, for instance, had portrayed the Scots as hospitable but boastful and cowardly. *Le Crabe aux Pinces d'Or* introduced two British sailors, presumably reminding readers that Britain had once claimed to rule the waves. Allan Thompson (reduced to Allan when Tintin was Englished, since Dupond and Dupont when English were Thomson and Thompson) is mate of a drug-running ship: he is brutal, sadistic, homicidal, avaricious, ready to exploit the peoples of the earth to his advantage, treacherous and falsely flattering. His nominal superior is a miserable, whining, incompetent drunk, ignorant of what the mate was doing and slavishly dependent on him: Captain Haddock. The name may have derived from Albert Haddock, the embodiment of English-ness in the *Punch* series by A. P. Herbert collected as *Uncommon Law*; Hergé's wife named Haddock 'a sad, English fish'. Belgian (and watchful German) readers may have been expected to see Allan as a Churchill type, Haddock a Chamberlain type: bully and weakling. Allan's Britain is clearly utterly selfish, savage and dishonest. Haddock (in this story only) is incapable of command, and, when rescued by Tintin, perpetually endangers them both. Drunk, he tries to take control, sets fire to their lifeboat to get warm while inside it, knocks out Tintin thus crashing the plane he has commandeered for them, imagines Tintin is a bottle of champagne and tries to strangle him to open it while dying of thirst in the desert – all readable as British attempts at leadership risking Belgium's existence for sodden dreams by deluded wrecks. Even when sober and benevolent, the English captain aborts a rescue bid by Tintin after his own capture by Allan: he insists on shaking hands in classic English congratula-tion, which obstructs Tintin's line of fire. He is given the coda, that of fainting during a broadcast of his own when given water, his talk topic being Drink, the sailor's worst enemy. Churchill, not Cham-berlain, was famous for wireless broadcasts, and for drink; but, by the time the story ended its serial run, Chamberlain had long been dead, and the readers would be more aware of Haddock as a disastrous Englishman in command than of any particular comman-der. Certainly, the thought of Churchill fainting when accidentally given a glass of water during a broadcast might occur even to a friendly caricaturist as an obvious joke.

The Tintin adventure which followed, in *Le Soir* amid the Nazified news from October 1941, reflects more editorial manipulation in the Nazi interest than any other. De Becker may well have been the least pro-Nazi of the several collaborationist groups – certainly less than Degrelle and his Rexists, or the Flemish Fascist party, or his arch-rival Paul Colin, the journalist whom Resistance assassins would one day kill – and de Becker would ultimately resign with bitter denunciation of the Nazis, for which he was deported and was lucky to remain alive. What he probably sought was a Belgium gaining the status of Franco's Spain (for whose triumph Belgian right-wing Catholics had prayed from 1936 to 1939). Meanwhile, he had to run *Le Soir* according to short-term Nazi demands; and, if he was fool enough to think that this would evolve towards Spanish-style autonomy, the initially benign Nazi supervision would let him do so while convenient. De Becker and the Nazis knew that *Le Soir* was the most visible Belgium spokesman on a day-to-day basis; his very dreams of independence tightened controls of his own making. As for Hergé, the D. C. Thomson comics of Dundee reflected war pressure across the North Sea at this moment with much the same urgency. Fare for children and adults was integrated in *Le Soir* much as the *Sunday Post* mingled the news and Oor Wullie. Both comic-strip heroes were at this point national symbols, Wullie as Scotland indomitable amid Nazi *blitzkrieg* (under British rule and English cartography), Tintin as brave Belgium in a dangerous world (under Nazi rule and servile editorship). Both newspapers were populist, with deeper cultural roots shared with their readers than even the London *Daily Express* could claim. And the two boys, Tintin and Oor Wullie, were genuine symbols of courage, however tragic Tintin's enlistment in a Nazi popular front, as would happen for this new adventure, *L'Étoile Mystérieuse*, and never thereafter.

The Nazis are not visible in the story: occupation in late 1941 was not ostentatiously officious, and Tintin could promenade through a warless Brussels. If symbolically Tintin recalls Oor Wullie, Milou reflects the more English antecedent – his fellow-mongrel Jumble, inseparable from Crompton's William since his first appearance in *Home* magazine in June 1919. The story itself would carry for Tintin's new, adult audience as well as his enlarged child public the initial reassurance that Tintin was in his Brussels and all was Right with the world. The initial story plot would play with pleasantly sophisticated mockery towards the same conclusion. Earth is threatened by annihilation, as Belgium had been by the war. A star is approaching and the astronomers announce imminent collision, while a lunatic appears and reappears proclaiming the end of the world. But the astronomers' predictions are inaccurate (to their professional fury and chagrin), and the lunatic is taken back to the asylum. All most amusing, and quite a comfortable way in which to recall 1940. Then the side-effect emerges: a meteorite has fallen in the Arctic Ocean carrying a valuable new scientific element; and this, the only significant result of the star-that-wasn't-the-end-of-the-world, must be rescued for Belgium and international science, the team to obtain it coming from Belgium, Switzerland, Sweden, Spain, Portugal – and Germany.[15] (All the neutral countries were in some danger of Nazi conquest, and were exceedingly circumspect.) But the expedition is threatened by sabotage from rivals in a ship bearing the name of the American Arctic explorer *Peary*, carrying the US flag. This is masterminded by an obvious, odious Jewish financier, Blumenstein. In addition, a frame, discarded from the strip after serial publication, showed two Jews exulting at the news of the end of the world, whence they expected to make money. Hergé would seem to have put in that utterly irrelevant as well as repulsive interpolation for reasons extraneous to the needs of the work; his irrelevant jokes are usually much more protracted, and their logic given contextual substance. This particular joke of Jews trying to make money from stellar impact (or Nazi conquest) is as dotty as de Becker trying to gain independence from the Nazis by subservience to their more repulsive desiderata – which would indicate that it came from de Becker, possibly after a Nazi hint that an anti-Jewish joke would not come amiss in the popular serial. Hergé dropped the item with such alacrity from later editions that it seems possible he disapproved of it from the first.[16] Blumenstein is another matter, and is not redeemed by the later change of his name to Bohlwinkel (apparently in the belief that the latter was not a Jewish name). But the later emendation does suggest one thing: the name had not been chosen to vilify Jews, in which case Hergé would have known what was a Jewish name and what was not. It was chosen to vilify a specific Jew. The target is obvious: the man who had linked Congo minerals including uranium to the United States with British assistance by utilising his international financial links, many of them with fellow-Jews such as Roosevelt's Secretary to the Treasury, Henry Morgenthau. The man who had become the Belgian government in London when his King was held prisoner by the Nazis and his Prime Minister and Foreign Secretary by Spain. The man who in all the cabinet had been most critical of the King and least ready to give him credit from the moment the German invasion began and the King proclaimed his control of the army. The man who had been secretary to the Belgian delegation at the Reparations Commissions 1919–20, chief secretary to the Minister for Finance 1920–4, Minister for Finance 1934–5, and from 1939; and who after the war would be first managing director of the International Monetary Fund 1946–51, after playing a major part at the United Nations Monetary and Financial Conference at Bretton Woods, New Hampshire in July 1944 – Camille Gutt.

Since Camille Gutt's actions may have been critical in keeping Congo uranium out of the hands of Mussolini and therefore of Hitler, we may all owe him our lives or our freedom. He had been quicker off the mark than either the Nazis or their Belgian friends. Degrelle may have been sidelined by the victorious Nazis, but he was intelligent as well as charismatic, and he offered his Rexists to 'liberate' the Congo from British and American control in February 1941. It was too late. Privately, de Becker might not have been enthusiastic about

Degrelle's recapture of the Congo, had the Nazis allowed it and the Italians enabled it; but, once shelved, it supplied material for a pro-Nazi attack on the Belgian cabinet, more especially on Gutt. Naturally, Hergé could never afterwards acknowledge Gutt as the target in mind in the demonisation of Blumenstein/Bohlwinkel, innocent of anti-Jewish intent though he insisted he was. At the time, many if not most of the readers of *Le Soir* would have added up the international Jewish 'financier', his American links and his zeal to acquire the rare wealth of what would otherwise be Belgian (or Belgian-and-friends') territory. Gutt's career in Belgian and international finance was perfectly open, and his place in the cabinet – in August 1940 almost the only active place – well known. Hergé had a personal motive – retaliation for Gutt's hostility to Leopold III, a sensible hostility from any anti-Nazi standpoint, but a kind of treason to a romantic Belgian royalist, not to speak of a romantic supporter of Muskar XII in Syldavia.

The Iceland episode in *L'Étoile* would have given a clear signal to readers as to the code in the plot. Blumenstein instructs the sole oil supplier to Iceland, Golden Oil, owned by himself, to deny sales to Tintin's colleagues. This is a direct allusion to Britain's tenure of Iceland after the German occupation of Denmark from April 1940, and its sequel, the American intervention at Britain's request, from June 1941, opening up the Battle of the Atlantic in that theatre. (By late December, with the USA in the World War since 8–11 December, American occupation of Iceland was official.) In passing, British popular awareness of Iceland hardly extended to children's literature or anywhere else much in public prints; but Crompton introduced an exceptionally lovable little girl from Iceland into the William saga as early as January 1940: the war had cut her off from her home during a holiday in England. Crompton's eyes were always sharp, and would seem to have anticipated the exigencies of British war policy, perhaps in the light of information from her brother Jack, who was a Flying Officer in the RAF serving there for a time. Tintin's ship succeeds in refuelling in another ploy previously used in *Biggles Goes to War* (a former comrade in arms). Biggles learns that the proposed landing-field en route to his beleaguered Ruritania ('Maltovia') has been trapped, and falls back on his emergency system – 'I sent a cable to Jerry Banham, at Weisheim. He used to be in 40 Squadron, you remember: he's the Shell Company's agent in this part of the world now. I asked him to bring a load of petrol along this road to-night . . .' – and it is duly delivered with characteristic British phlegm:[17] 'What do you think you're trying to do – get me the sack?'

In *L'Étoile*, Captain Haddock, Tintin's ship's captain (under illusory hope of his detoxication), recognises a fellow-captain in Iceland with whom apparently Masonic exchanges of handclasping and code-word-shouting result in his transmission of fuel, just bought by him, into Haddock's craft. Both men are English, and the evident English and American control of Icelandic shipping is dealt with as a fact of life. Freemasonry was a great clerical-Fascist bugbear, also hated and outlawed by Hitler and Franco; many Belgian Catholic readers would probably expect English deals to have Masonic underpinning or overlay. Beating the enemy by mastery of his code outweighed the crime of Masonic aid, however much de Becker and Hergé, as Catholic products, might deplore the Freemasons (whose ritual in this version is in any case sufficiently ludicrous).

Involuntary British aid came to the author as well as to his heroes. Tintin is forced to parachute on to the meteorite to claim it for the international philanthropic scientific expedition in which he has sailed (viz. Germany, Belgium and benevolent neutrals). He does so from a German seaplane, the Arado 193, a firm statement as to the real leaders of the expedition. The *Boy's Own Paper* for October 1941 carried a story by Johns supposedly recounted by Ginger to Biggles's Squadron, in which Biggles, Algy and himself accompany a slightly crazy scientist named Augustus Duck to investigate an island suddenly discovered in the Atlantic. The island anticipates Tintin's meteorite in that it proves to be sinking first slowly, then rapidly. In each case, the inhabitants are ordinary creatures grown to enormous size (the *BOP*'s fine picture of Biggles facing a gigantic crab would naturally have interested the recent creator of *Le Crabe aux Pinces d'Or*). Given Hergé's apparent inspiration from previous Johns fiction, it looks as though he or perhaps his major adviser on Tintin at this point, Jacques van Melkebeke, had seen the *Boy's Own Paper* for October 1941. There was certainly a vast market in illicit journalism in Belgium at this time, running to 300 papers. *Le Soir*, as an official Nazi organ, may have been able to tap contraband items in government hands, especially if *L'Étoile* had Nazi approval for its covert propaganda content – which it would have had so that de Becker could protect himself and ingratiate himself with the masters whose grip he thought he would thereby lessen. The neutral countries whose scientific luminaries supposedly appear in the story, Sweden, Switzerland, Portugal and Spain – or the one not mentioned, Eire – may have supplied means of watching British literary products for children. Certainly, the *BOP*, as both religious in origin and semi-official in manner (though not in status), was the periodical most likely to fall into the hands of de Becker, van Melkebeke or Hergé. The touch of official status on its own part, with the hint that there was more than fiction in the story, had been a convention of the Tintin strip since the long-ago voyage to Russia; and the end of L'Étoile carried the ominous threat that Blumenstein/Bohlwinkel, the leader of the saboteurs, would soon be 'unmasked and punished' – unmasked as Gutt, since otherwise the word is meaningless.[18]

The entry of the USA into the war diminished Tintin's propaganda value. The Nazis realised that the USA could look attractive in however hostile a treatment, and thus had banned Tintin en Amérique and, while they were at it, the British-based L'Île Noire. Hergé, clearly to his satisfaction, was allowed drift back to fantasy. The Nazis may have insisted that Haddock, if retained, was not to be British: so he became the inheritor of a French ancestor's booty under the patronage of Louis XIV. The post-war English version assumes that all the characters are English, unless otherwise required by the plot, and thus an English Haddock has an ancestor ennobled by Charles II. But readers of Le Crabe and L'Étoile must often have noticed the vanishing of their Haddock's Englishness, and would have known why. Haddock was still alcoholic but now comically rather than tragically; and Tintin's growing affection for him, and patience with him, deepens the boy hero's humanity and authority.[19] Once again, there is a peculiar link with the Johns series of Ginger's science-fiction reminiscences ultimately collected as Biggles – Charter Pilot (July 1943); once again, an adventure appears in the BOP on the eve of Hergé's new serial in Le Soir. This time it was set in Australia and entitled 'The ghosts of Cow Creek' (book-titled 'The Adventure of the Haunted Creek'). It turns on ravens having learned human speech, and having survived as the last inhabitants of a town bereft of water, and thus taken to be ghosts. The series is usually taken to be one of Johns's weakest works in his vintage years 1935–50, but this story is memorable because the ravens, if no longer frightening when identified, still carry the sounds of settlers dying of thirst. Ginger first hears them like this:[20]

> The others had been gone about an hour, and I was sitting staring into the fire, when just behind me an anguished voice said, quietly but distinctly, 'They're all dead.'
>   I didn't move. I couldn't. I was petrified. I felt the hair curling on my head. I just sat, stiff and tense. Then another voice said, some way off this time, 'Water – water – water'. This was followed by a

peal of hysterical laughter right over my head. I looked up, but there wasn't a thing in sight, except the stars.

Le Secret de la Licorne (begun on 11 June 1942) and its sequel Le Trésor de Rackham le Rouge (begun on 19 February 1943) ultimately bring Haddock and friends to the island once inhabited by his marooned ancestor, where they hear an apparent ghost shouting 'Que Le GRRRAND CRRIC MA CRRRROQUE!' (probably meaning 'Squander my rich Rotgut!', but in the English version 'RRRATION MY RRRUM!'). It proves to be parrots (after Haddock, like Biggles, decides to try conclusions with the ghosts by means of a gun). It turns the Johns tragedy into comedy, since the thirst that the Haddock family fears will kill them is not a want of water.

After the war, mutual exchanges of influence between the British writers for children and Hergé resumed their normal course, all the more when Tintin proved, via translations, to be assimilable in his turn to other cultures. But his Communist enemies did not forgive or forget, however many others were ignorant of his 1929 Soviet studies. After Belgian liberation in early September 1944, a conquest even more rapid than that by the Nazis in May 1940, a work was circulated entitled Tintin au Pays des Nazis, whose title betrayed its vengeful Communist origin: the Communists had little patriotic achievement of which to boast during the days of the Nazi–Soviet pact, and hence their search for alternative scapegoats in 1944–5 was industrious. Hergé was silenced, and Georges Remi was jailed in September 1944, with Tintin only able to resume his current quest (for the Incas) in September 1946, at which point the script became much less racist. Unlike Tintin, Georges Remi had not been a hero. But how many creators of heroic children, in comparable circumstances, would have lived up to their creations? And how many of us who are their historians?

In spite of – and no doubt because of – exposure to literature of heroic English men and boys, Hergé's hostility to the British and the Americans may have been the most genuine of the various postures he had been obliged to take up for Le Soir. But his material had proved stronger than he, shown during the war in Captain Haddock's metamorphosis from a cringing drunk to a hypocritical drunk and thence a heroic drunk. If he started as a satire on Chamberlain and developed into a version of Churchill, it was a Churchill increasingly lovable and courageous. Once Englished, Haddock might even be taken as a complimentary form of English national identity; and Hergé apparently came to prefer him to Tintin. Arguably, Haddock reasserted his original Englishness, now no longer ignominious. If he retained Churchillian overtones (he really cannot be thought to have undertones), they were now patriarchal where once they were poltroonish. He still had to be guided by his wise young friend, with Belgium – or perhaps western Europe – restraining rash Britain much as the UK saw itself restraining the rash USA. Haddock in the English versions of the 1950s and 1960s even became a means by which outmoded and discredited English authority could return, in children's literature the crusty squire (usually though not always disguising the drunken sailor) being a welcome replacement for the smoother squire whose place was his base to welcome Hitler, like Sir Pascal Lanch in Mowbray's *The Radio Mystery*:[21]

> 'This is the German High Command calling. The German High Command calling. The German High Command calling Sir Pascal Lanch. The High Command calling Sir Pascal Lanch. STAND BY. STAND BY.' . . .
>
> 'Instructions to Sir Pascal Lanch are to stand by. Sir Pascal Lanch to stand by for the next full moon with a high tide. Then to have all in readiness . . . I will repeat that . . . Stand by for the next full moon and have all in readiness to assist according to plan. ACCORDING TO PLAN. Message ends.'

If Haddock had also acquired a heart of gold behind a firecracker temper, England could be grateful for the belated compliment.[22]

Haddock's place in remodelling English or British national character as expressed by Authority had one formidable origin in art for children. Edward Ardizzone, born in Haiphong of French origin, came to Britain at the age of five in 1905, and became a British subject in 1921. His first book, *Little Tim and the Brave Sea Captain* (1936), makes Tim a stowaway (for adventure) confronted by the captain, whose stern integrity rebukes him and makes him work his passage. But when disaster overtakes the ship, and only the Captain and Tim are left on board, they form a splendid partnership, with the severity now showing the heroic stature it feeds:

> 'Hullo, my lad', said the Captain. 'Come, stop crying and be a brave boy. We are bound for Davey Jones's locker, and tears won't help us now.'
>
> So Tim dried his eyes and tried not to be too frightened. He felt he would not mind going anywhere with the Captain, even to Davey Jones's locker.

They stood hand in hand waiting for the end.

Just as they were about to sink beneath the waves Tim gave a great cry. 'We're saved. We're saved.'

He had seen the lifeboat coming to rescue them.

The contrast with the Haddock of *Le Crabe*, the human wreck whom Tintin must sustain and survive four years later, could not be more marked, yet the similarity of situation is so clear that Hergé was surely inspired by Ardizzone's triumphant success in the same text-and-pictures work as himself. It is noteworthy that when Tintin was translated into German his name became 'Tim'. One obvious ancestor of both was Stevenson's *Treasure Island*, where again common interests war with mutual suspicion. Stevenson's Captain Smollett is not the only Captain with whom Jim Hawkins must deal: he stands, Right but Repulsive, defying his opponent 'Captain' Silver, wrong, murderous, treacherous, yet attractive to Hawkins and the reader even to the end when they know him so well. Captain Smollett never takes to Jim Hawkins, although Hawkins's vagaries ultimately save his life; 'Captain' Silver never loses his affection for Jim Hawkins, although remaining perfectly ready to cut his throat. Ardizzone's Captain makes the leap impossible for Smollett, and is clearly fond of Tim when the story ends; and Haddock by the end of his first story has the early stages of his subsequent lifelong comradeship with Tintin. Perhaps his drunken readiness to murder or imperil Tintin in their first adventure – and once or twice later – may reflect subconscious Silver threads in his ever-widening heart of gold.

Ardizzone's intentions are the clearest as between Stevenson, Hergé and himself. None were English, all were inventing Englands. Ardizzone's Little Tim is somewhat autobiographical, displaying boyhood memories of Ipswich. As a child evidently yearning for acceptance as British (to judge by the speed with which he sought citizenship when of age to do so), his ideal of the Britannia who he wanted to rule him was the Captain. This, to be sure, was the Captain maritime, supreme arbiter of his vessel when at sea, sworn – and swearing (within the confines of publishers for children) – representative of King and God. Something of this divine majesty crossed the ethical divide: a pirate captain also radiates Authority, in a rather more modern form in that he is electable and deposable. He might be mad, obsessed, comic, tragic, Ahab, Hook, Flint, maimed, haunted or dead, but he was Authority, in a form more absolute than any vested in a single figure on land. A Headmaster was constrained by governors and parents or guardians. A Captain while at sea had to fear only the elements, or disease, or actual physical hostility from a mutinous crew or a bellicose ship – until the twentieth century threatened him from above and below, by submarine and by aircraft, at first physically and perilously, later economically and fatally. The Second World War was the doom of naval hegemony less in itself than by virtue of its place in time. Brent-Dyer captured it perfectly as Jo of the Chalet School and her friends and baby triplets suffered from their vulnerability to plane and U-boat when crossing from Guernsey to England in spring 1940.[23] Within a few weeks of that imaginary escape from the doomed Channel Islands, the last and perhaps the greatest moment of Captains as Kings came when the innumerable masters of their tiny craft saved the army trapped at Dunkirk. Appropriately, Ardizzone's love for his adopted Britain suspended his books for children in the war – but it was for service in the Royal Artillery and then as one of the leading war artists.

The author is in literature the supreme Authority. Enid Blyton brought this to a fine art, notably in the weekly, then fortnightly, wartime diet in her *Sunny Stories*: what later commentators would call her 'Nannie' persona, but what in her case was a figure even more archaic to most minds, a governess, although a governess with fine scientific instincts of child control.[24] The wartime child's dependence on Blyton completed for many of her readers what the selfishness and complacency of earlier generations of comfortably financed parents had begun, and what the exigencies of working-class families had counterpointed – dumping childrearing on Nannies, governesses and, in less affluent cases, the poor relation or eldest female child. Christopher Robin Milne in *Enchanted Places* bitterly recalled his father's poem of the child whose mother mysteriously disappeared when she went down to the end of the town without *him*, and reflected that in his own case the loss of a Nannie would have been far more disastrous than that of either parent. An author has less authority when doubling as a parent.

But the traditional author often sought Authority as Captain. Stevenson's first readers of *Treasure Island* were told by *Young Folks* that its author was Captain George North. No doubt the enormous success of the early Victorian Frederick Marryat, as authentic a Captain as ever avasted or belayed, induced the myriad imaginary captains to follow. But they remained naval: army captains were figures of far less temporal or spiritual significance, and the appearance of such a captain in peacetime usually meant fraud or even murder in the pages of Edgar Wallace or Frank Richards.[25] The Royal Flying Corps took its titles from the army, whence Major James

Bigglesworth (promoted just before the end of the war). 'Captain' W. E. Johns was a second lieutenant when the First World War ended, and left the RAF in 1927 as a Flying Officer. His captaincy, like Stevenson's a publisher's promotion (in all senses), recalled the traditional naval authority. In establishing an ideal of authority, he inhabited that naval captaincy: Biggles at his best is lord of his own demesne with higher authority remote, and, as a rule, inadequate. At one point in his last-ever war novel, *Biggles Delivers the Goods* (April 1946), Johns had Biggles and his allies capture a 1,000-ton coastal supply vessel, greatly expediting the delivery of rubber hidden from the Japanese with which they had been charged, to have their own Authority, Air Commodore Raymond, tell them smugly:[26]

> 'You've done well. Getting hold of the *Sumatran* wasn't on the schedule and the Admiralty were inclined to be a bit uppish at first about airmen playing at sailors, but I smoothed things over by pointing out that it had saved you a lot of work. . . .'

The author seems to give himself a self-mocking grin.

What Authority, other than themselves, could Johns and his fellow-authors for children offer? From the first, Crompton had sent up Authority rotten, whether as parents, teachers or vicars (as the daughter of the Rev. E. J. S. Lamburn she cut her anti-clerical teeth even earlier than did the minister's wife L. M. Montgomery). From time to time, she even introduced an otherwise unnamed figure 'Authority', as at the time when William uses a charitable bazaar to sell his sister's discarded collection of photographs from passionately autographed ex-boyfriends: 'Authority of course had never given its photograph to Ethel. It had contented itself with finding occasion for conversation with her and lending her the novels of Dickens and Sir Walter Scott.' Authority disappeared from the books by wartime, its country presumably having need of it elsewhere. But various figures made attempts to succeed it in themselves. Youth needed Authority: the Nazis had been early in the field with that principle, as Streatfeild, Barne and Treadgold had grimly noted and as news stories printed alongside Tintin in *Le Soir* continued to testify. Crompton sourly observed in early 1944 that 'the Youth Movement idea'. . . was sweeping England', and she savagely indicted its votaries:

> The Vicar, who disliked youth in any form . . . agreed . . . that youth in war-time, deprived in so many cases of parental control, needed discipline and restraint.

'My Movement', [Mrs Sedley-Mortimer] wrote, 'is not for entertainment, but for inculcating the virtues of industry, obedience
and self-control. . . . Mine has a higher function. It aims at training
the character.'

Crompton is not specific about Nazi-style discipline here save in the
ruthlessness of recruitment and membership maintenance. She
singled out for prime ridicule its puritanism; evidently she saw in
it the ancestor of what Orwell's 1984 would feature as the Junior
Anti-Sex League (in reality no ancestor, but the same phenomenon
from the same time). She also dissected its representative evangelist:

Her chief characteristic was a capacity for talking incessantly
without need of encouragement or response from her hearers, and
she prided herself, rightly, on never being at a loss for a word. She
said that from her earliest youth she had felt that her great gifts
should be put at the service of her fellow creatures, and so she had
put them at the service of her fellow creatures. Whether her fellow
creatures appreciated them or not was a matter of indifference to
her. She knew what was good for people, and she gave it them
unstintingly, whether they wanted it or not.

Crompton seems also to have diagnosed that the new freedom
taken by women during the war was already under threat by
repressive agents for the restoration of conformity and subordination. The attack on cosmetics was one feature of this. It's impressive
that Crompton, aged 53 when writing, lashed out against the killjoys
trying to reduce the younger women doing their bit in the war to
menial drabs. She makes no bones that girls have more fun when
cosmetics enhance their attractions, and that they deserve it: Mrs
Sedley-Mortimer is made to look like a drunken lunatic in her
attempts to caricature beautification, and serve her right. The new
Authority over Youth is shown by Crompton to consist of 'frumps'
mobilised by what are essentially Fascists. She saw the same thing in
mid-1942 in the airs which the new military gave themselves,
especially while firmly based at home:

Captain Fortescue had taken half an hour posing himself for the
first snapshot and was still not quite satisfied with the result.
    'Stand just there with the camera', he barked to the sergeant,
who was almost worn out by the nervous strain of the proceedings.
'No, not there . . . *there* . . . and when I say "three" pull the trigger

down. . . . Stand a little more to the left . . . now a little to the right. . . . Wait a minute. . . . Come and take my place and I'll make sure it's all right. . . . Yes, that's all right. . . . Now change places. . . . No, it's not quite right. . . . Take a step forward. . . . Now you're too near. . . . Take a step backwards. . . . Wait a minute . . . I think I'll have my other cap on. . . . Fetch it from the tent. . . . Now we're all right. . . . No, one minute . . . I'll have my field glasses in my hand. . . . Fetch my field glasses. . . . Now we're ready. . . . No, you're not quite in the right position . . . a little to the left . . . now a little forward. . . . No, backwards and to the right. . . . One minute . . . I'll have my gloves. . . . Fetch my gloves. . . . No, on second thoughts, I won't have them. . . . Take them back. . . . Hurry, hurry, hurry. . . . Don't take all day about it, man. . . . Now, are we ready? . . . Ready, steady. . . . One, two, th –'

The 'three' ended in a high-pitched squeal of terror. Letty [Farmer Jenks's goat] . . . had romped out of Mrs Bott's garden . . . across two fields, through another hedge, and into the field used for the camp, where, attracted by the back view of the gallant captain, she had butted into it with joyful zest. . . . the snap, as a snap, was a complete success. It showed the captain prostrate on the ground, his face distorted by terror, and Letty standing proudly over him, her front paws on his chest, his cap worn rakishly over one ear. . . .

Crompton had taken her degree in classics, and had taught the subject at Bromley from 1917 until invalided by polio in 1925. She did full justice to the traditions established by Aristophanes in *Lysistrata* and still more by Plautus in *Miles Gloriosus*. She had diagnosed the new Authority with her customary precision.

Modern Woman printed in February 1941 her story about the Outlaws' attempt to capture what they thought was a German parachutist who turns out to be a RAF variety-show guest artist, to the mixed annoyance and relief of the army major and the local constable whom the boys have called in:

[They] went off, leaving parachutist and Outlaws alone.
'Well, we *thought* you were one', said William in a small voice.
The parachutist looked down at the four dejected faces.
'I say', he said suddenly, 'how would you like to come to the aerodrome with me and see the show?'
The four dejected faces beamed, sparkled, radiated.
'*Oh!*' gasped William. '*Could* we?'

The *deus ex machina* – or, in the present case, *machinis* – is the more potent because Crompton here seeks to induce a reaction otherwise rarely prompted by her for the Outlaws: pity. They have, after all, been brave as well as wrong, and they have been trying to defend their besieged country. And so they deserve the final liberation to Olympus reserved for the greatest classical hero-victims such as Heracles:

> The Outlaws sat in a crowded hall surrounded by a god-like company of men in Air Force blue – men who sailed the skies and brought down German bombers as regularly and unconcernedly as you and I have marmalade for breakfast.

(In the event, marmalade would shortly be much less regular and invite much more concern; but if Crompton was being ironic, it was very gentle irony.)[27]

> That in itself would have provided one of the greatest thrills of the Outlaws' lives. But, added to this, the god-like beings were jovial and friendly. They teased Ginger about the colour of his hair. They called William Old Bill. They gave them humbugs and peardrops. . . .
> It was the happiest day of their lives.

Authority was reborn from the air. It was the oldest source of Authority in folk-legend, much of it retold by a variety of modern writers. Elijah in his fiery chariot, Jesus ascending from Mount Olivet, reaffirmed that celestial home of Authority. Tolkien's eagles delivering Bilbo, Gandalf, Pippin, Frodo and Samwise link ancient mythology and Judaeo–Christian tradition with the air-pilot saviours of Britain (Bilbo's experience preceded the Second World War, being in *The Hobbit*, but Pippin specifically reinvokes that event in what he takes to be his own death at the end of the fifth book of *The Lord of the Rings*). But Tolkien also links us to the fairy world, and the judgemental fairy had been going great guns at least since the *Iolanthe* of Gilbert and Sullivan gave her a new, if parodic, lease of life still under great demand during the Second World War. A little more traditionally, Carlo Collodi's *Pinocchio* revived the principle in the same decade as that in which *Iolanthe* was born, the 1880s; and the watchful fairy, while less regal than the Gilbert variety, carried her judicial powers successfully to the Disney film in 1939, thus ushering in Second World War cinema for British children. (Under

Disney, she had become a Blue Fairy, an adjective which must have provided some silent amusement to ribald *British* fathers enforcedly watching alongside their entranced children.)

Blyton's *Sunny Stories* and short-story collections saturated the British infant reading public with the judgemental fairy. Blyton shrewdly varied the formula between fairies of obvious integrity and fairies of narrowly self-centred interests nevertheless proving suitable Nemeses. Some fairies were also allowed to be naughty in child-fashion, a wise evasion of too much fiction directly reproving children: naughty fairies would also receive correction from fairy Authority. But the fairies in Blyton usually work as tricksters, often not regarded until the effects of their judicial enchantments become felt, frequently absurd in appearance or merely amusing. It accords with her own judicial moments: she was pre-eminently the author as accomplice, and hence made real Authority an accomplice as well. Her most obvious Authority figures among the children (much more real Authority within themselves and in social judgements than are her adults) can be forceful, but are frequently proved wrong. Sometimes this is covert feminism: the little girl is right, the big boy is wrong (whether or not the big boy is a physical or moral bully). Sometimes it is the great fairy-tale rule that small is beautiful, small is powerful, small is more intelligent – Odysseus will triumph over hostile elements and gods. (The classicist Crompton, more subtly and satirically, is very frequently at work on the same premise, whether with William's struggles against the world or with Violet Elizabeth's ensnarings of William. She is less intrusive an author/Authority than Blyton, but her voice is very audible, the friendly but not uncritical voice of Athena contemplating Odysseus.)

Blyton, having seriously analysed her fairy-story Hitler, was on the lookout for Hitleresque traits in children to be isolated, diagnosed, denounced and (if possible supernaturally) punished. The self-assertive leader may or may not be allowed remain in status – he is more likely to be permitted to do so when he is of lower class than the others, but with special skills and rather older age ('Smuggler Ben', Andy, Jack of *The Secret Island*, Barney of *The Rockingdown Mystery*) – but he will be 'taken down a peg or two' (as will William) by being proved wrong when at his most authoritative. Blyton played this cleverly enough with her Five. The initial convention is that the authoritative, responsible Julian is proved wrong, and the wayward, self-centred, unreasonable George is proved right; but, from time to time later when George asserts her vaunted maleness in authoritarianism, she also is proved wrong. Like Johns, Blyton made one or two of her strongest realisations of the meaning of Fascist Authority after the war, and hence after the worst revelations of Nazism's work: in the post-war Secret Seven series, the leader Peter grows increasingly authoritarian until in *Shock for the Secret Seven* (1961) his rule is successfully defied, while in its sequel the little girl whom the group have excluded proves to be the victor. In *The Mystery of the Burnt Cottage* series, Larry is displaced from leadership in the third book, Fatty (his supplanter) is frequently deflated for his pomposity, and Pip is invariably proved a fool in his contempt for his little sister Bets. In *The Island of Adventure* series, Kiki the parrot is a perpetual demolition of all Authority by repeating and muddling its clichés. This last case identifies anti-Authority with a winged being, and in doing so vindicates good (i.e. child) as against bad (i.e. false adult) Authority. Much more powerfully, *The Castle of Adventure* pits eagles in combat against German spies. But Blyton was too much a product of the Second World War to be entirely at ease with the idea of salvation from the air: *The Mountain of Adventure* turns on false rule of the air by a mad King of the Mountain, whose pretend Authority is executed by Germans and Japanese, so as to realise conquest of the air by personal flying. Her older air-beings, the fairies, were ambiguous in their own morality, or at least frequently unreliable (however useful in their effects on children); and the deepening war did nothing to make Authority from the air more reassuring. This may also explain why C. S. Lewis never took his allegories of Jesus Christ so far as Olivet: Digory, initially a self-portrait as the Professor, is allowed to fly on the Pegasus for which all children yearn, but the lion Aslan never flies (although he is clearly master of the air). At the end of *The Lion, the Witch and the Wardrobe*, the story first drafted in the war, Aslan has no Ascension but simply slips away.

The mingling of Authority, air, war and the supernatural won its most striking expression from Roald Dahl in his only Second World War book, *The Gremlins* (US edition 1943, UK 1944). Dahl's first book, it was never reprinted, and poses its own textual problems. The central human figure, a pilot named Gus, becomes 'Barry' at one point. The book was got up as a Walt Disney 'book of the film', which it was, but Disney's feet grew cold and the film was never completed. War-related topics diminished in interest for the US public in 1943, according to polls. The fallibility of psephology would proclaim itself five years later by predicting Harry Truman's defeat in the Presidential election of 1948, but in 1943 Disney was impressed by the finding. British writers and publishers for children seem to show similar withdrawal symptoms at that time, as was indeed shown by the *Observer's* acid comment when Disney was still vigorously Gremlinising in autumn 1942:[28]

> It will seem strange indeed to the future historians who, unravelling the tale of our troubled times, discover that in the critical year 1942, a distinguished American travelled 5000 miles in order to make a film about elves.

For these were not elves, although they bore at least studio kinship to the seven dwarfs (or, as Tolkien would insist, dwarves). Disney's *Snow White* had conquered the western world in 1937. The gremlins were small beings who bored holes in planes' wings, penetrated their magnetos, and generally caused incessant and unforeseen damage to aircraft. They seem to have been originated to soothe ill-feeling between pilots and ground staff as to who was responsible for little, though possibly fatal, mishaps. Their filmic origin probably lay in Dahl's air crash in the Libyan desert, when his inexperience at the controls of a Gloster Gladiator nearly cost him his life on 19 September 1940. ('Don't blame yourself: blame the Gremlins!') He redeemed himself as a fighter pilot (Hurricane) for 80 Squadron, shooting down at least five enemy aircraft; but secondment as UK air attaché in Washington DC gave him the contacts for US publication and ultimately the Disney link. Like much of Dahl's work, it is heavily derivative, even in its iconoclasm. The Gremlins are gratifyingly human in their vanity and touchiness; among Snow White's dwarves, the one real success as a psychological study was the comparably prima-donna Grumpy (actually a more complex and ultimately more heroic figure than any of Dahl's Gremlins). There is charm in the Gremlins' revenge on persons denying their existence, by upsetting their beer and so on. It turns out that their hatred of aeroplanes arises from a factory being built over their own rural dwellings: simultaneously with Dahl's scripting and Disney's quest, D. J. Watkins-Pitchford ('B.B.') was also recruiting gnomes in *The Little Grey Men* (1942) for celebration of the environment, and the renewed literary courtship of the British Isles countryside – of the England they wanted to be always – brought its Malcolm Savilles and 'Romanys' to BBC Children's Hour when so much of the landscape faced new threats as well as old. Dahl invested his Gremlins with an anger at environmental destruction much more intense than the norm; and his plot, having begun with a sympathetic and semi-autobiographical standpoint for Gus, showed his conversion to the

Gremlins whence he recruits them to RAF support. They trick the medical authorities to get him passed as fit for air combat once more. The final cry 'love them, fear them, respect them' carries an even greater shock. We might not be surprised to discover God in the Disney machine, but few would expect to find Him in the Dahl one. Yet Dahl was a product of Repton public school under (in rather too many senses) the rule of the future Archbishop of Canterbury, Geoffrey Fisher. The Gremlin anger at desecration of their temples, and the Gremlin punishment of those denying their existence, are the attributes of the Old Testament God whom Fisher seems to have impressed on his pupils as ferociously as possible. And the Gremlins, however theophanous, anticipate Dahl's persecuted but ultimately vindicated future child heroes, notably an even more improbable aeronaut, James, flying the Atlantic on his giant peach. Dahl's Authority proves to be the child, more radically than occurs with most authors outside the comics. And Dahl's numerous obligations probably extended to the comics. In his original draft (until excluded at the instance of Disney's curiously Teutonymous lawyer Gunther Lessing), Dahl had Hitler complaining that the Gremlins were being given credit for Luftwaffe successes, an engagingly postmodernist joke but one familiar to *Beano* and *Dandy* readers accustomed to very similar causes of Führer grief at the accomplishments of the comics' own characters.

The Gremlins, like the Little Prince, were born as a work of art from a pilot coming to terms with the crash in the desert that nearly cost his life. Another crash victim, the more matter-of-fact Johns, limited his sense of desert magic to sky, sand and mirage, although he too knew how to play with the makings of the praeternatural. In the Second World War novel *Biggles Sweeps the Desert*, Ginger foolishly leaves his aircraft without taking his water-bottle for what he imagined was a moment when grounded in the desert, and then cannot find it:

> He walked along, muttering. The rocks became monsters, marching beside him. He shouted to scare them away, but they took no notice. He saw Biggles sitting on one, but when he got to it it was only another rock. Beyond, he saw a line of blue water, with with little flecks of white light dancing on it. It was so blue that it dazzled him. Shouting, he ran towards it, but it was always the same distance away, and it took his reeling brain some little time to realise that it was not there. He began to laugh. What did it matter which way he went? All ways were the same in this cauldron.

More monsters were coming towards him. He rushed at them and beat at them with his fists. He saw blood on his knuckles, but felt no pain. The sky turned red. Everything turned red. The sand seemed to be laughing at him. He hated it, and in his rage he knelt down and thumped it. It only laughed all the louder. The voice sounded very real. He tried to shout, but he could only croak.

The passage is in part an affirmation of Authority. Biggles has told the Squadron not to stir without a water-bottle; Ginger has disobeyed his order, pays for it, and is rebuked at his rescue. The desert rock turning into a monster, then Biggles, then again a monster, is a neat turn of childhood fears and their relation to sins against Authority. Ginger is the child reader in the story (he has read about Biggles and Algy when he meets them in *The Black Peril*; he cites Johns's magazine *Popular Flying* (where Biggles was first published) in *Biggles Flies South*). In the Second World War itself, Johns may have captured something of the fairy-story terror element in the Blitz, noted in Naomi Mitchison's poem, and related it to child suspicion that the sufferings induced by bombing, bereavement and evacuation were in some way just retribution for some otherwise unpunished solecisms committed by the child itself. Biggles is suitably paternal when he rescues Ginger:

Opening his eyes, he found himself gazing into the concerned face of his leader.
'All right, take it easy', said Biggles.
'You were – just about – in time', gasped Ginger.
'And you, my lad, have had better luck than you deserve'. Compassion faded suddenly from Biggles' face. 'I seem to remember making an order about all ranks carrying water-bottles', he said in a voice as brittle as cracking ice. 'If we were within striking distance of a service depot I'd put you under close arrest for breaking orders. As it is, if you feel able to move, we'd better see about getting out of this sun-smitten dustbin. It will be dark before we get back as it is.'
Ginger staggered to his feet. 'Sorry, sir', he said contritely.

But the reader knows perfectly well that Biggles would do nothing of the kind. His real role is to revive the delirious Ginger with water (portrayed on the book-jacket), and in any case his initial briefing has already stated who the real Authority is:[29] 'If you break that order, any of you, you won't have to answer to me; as sure as fate the sun will turn on you and shrivel you up like an autumn leaf'. Johns had already confronted bogus and real Authority in his best sortie into historical fiction, a boy's impression of the fate of the Persian Great King Cambyses's army in the same Libyan desert in 525 BC, a prelude (and a tragic echo) in *Biggles Flies South*. The piece is in two parts: 'I. "The King has Spoken."' 'II. The Desert Answers.'

The theme of real Authority (Nature) versus unreal (human) was formally asserted in *Biggles Hits the Trail* (1935), when Ginger won his flying credentials and Biggles told him:[30]

> 'Never forget the fact that you are only allowed to visit the world above your earthtied fellows on sufferance. By your art – call it a trick if you like – you have learned to overcome a great natural force – gravity; and you cannot flout Nature with impunity. Treat Nature with respect and she will tolerate you, even encourage you; but treat her with contempt, and your days are numbered . . .'

The irony of petty-minded Authority on the ground lording over high-flying pilots no doubt did much to deepen the natural rebel instincts of Dahl and Saint-Exupéry. It made W. E. Johns a rebel for life. First World War songs summed up the army's feelings clearly enough:

> Forward, Joe Soap's A-a-a-rmy, marching without fear,
> With our brave com-ma-a-ander ten miles in the rear.

But the Royal Flying Corps might be worse off, when, like Johns, they were ordered to throw bombs from aircraft, thus risking being court-martialled and shot as terrorists by the Germans if captured. Johns suffered such a fate, bar the shooting. Its effects were to leave a consistent strain in his writing against the invulnerable Authority who had thrown him and countless other pilots to their possible doom. As late as 1960, Biggles explains to his subordinates while on a murky mission in the heart of Africa:[31]

> 'Actually, I foresaw this situation; but the chief [Raymond] was chary of giving me firm orders to act on my own account. That, of course, is what he, or the Colonial Office, would like me to do, because then, if there was serious trouble, they could disclaim any responsibility. In other words, if things went wrong, we should be left to take the rap.'

This is consistent with Johns's fiction for boys from the first. On 4 March 1933, the *Gem* commenced (alongside the current instalment of Tom Merry and Co. of St Jim's) *The Spyflyers*, Johns's first novel and only non-Biggles book of the First World War. The theme of spies turning up in the higher ranks of both German and British armies was old enough, George E. Rochester, for instance, running *The Black Hawk* in the *Magnet* early in 1929, in which the young hero, fleeing from execution as a spy by orders of a British court-martial, finds his chief accuser, a British colonel, to be in reality a high-ranking German officer who then has him sentenced to execution as a spy by orders of a German court-martial. (He survives, to receive the VC.)[32] But what was new about the Johns story was that the British Major Trevor, who proves to be a German spy, is the Intelligence Officer at whose instructions the intrepid heroes undertake their near-suicidal missions behind German lines. In all the literature of resentment by First World War soldier-writers, few indictments can equal this. The young heroes finally overhear their superior officer telling his German colleagues of his success in manipulating them:

'I think I started a good scheme when I got them flying over in that Hannoverana; they little knew I was making carrier pigeons of them. I had a slot put inside the fuselage and von Henkel or Hartzmann just collected my messages while they were drinking beer in the mess. Simple, wasn't it? There they were, working hard to find out who was carrying the information which they themselves were carrying. I flatter myself that they'd hardly be likely to suspect themselves!'

Virtue wins, although Trevor survives to be demoted by the Germans. The novel does little with character (Norman Wright estimates it to be of earlier date than Biggles, resurrected when Biggles had won book publication for *The Camels are Coming*),[33] and we never learn why Trevor betrays. But he is a traitor rather than a spy.

Johns produced a different and more unanswerable indictment of First World War Authority almost three years later via his airborne Robin Hood, Steeley, in *Sky High*.

'He gave up a lucrative job to become a Tommy when the great call went out for men. He died at Cambrai. His widow, the mother of three gallant sons [also killed in action], is still alive, dragging out her last years in the dismal conditions that the miserable pittance of a Tommy's pension only permits. She has lost everything, even her home had to go; it was sold to pay the household bills when her husband was killed. Yet all around her thousands of people who had never lifted a finger to save their country live in luxury. Is *that* fair?'

This was not peculiar to Johns: Leslie Charteris, whose Saint stories were Steeley's stable-companions in the *Thriller*, made similar charges, with or without justification for his own Robin Hoods. Richards used it in the *Magnet* to explain how gallant soldiers ended up as burglars. It supplied the basis for the bonus marches on Washington dispersed by General Douglas MacArthur on the orders of President Herbert Hoover. It gave a rationale for Hitler's rhetoric. But Johns was probably its supreme exponent in air literature. A variant occurs in another rebellious novel of his, *The Unknown Quantity* (1940), whose heroes murder miscreants rather than robbing them, or smuggling, like Steeley. One of them[34]

> had been court-martialled and reprimanded for dangerous flying at home, and awarded the Distinguished Flying Cross for the same thing on active service. A marked lack of respect for senior officers, amounting almost to irresponsibility, had retarded his promotion.

The *Rover* comic would ultimately produce a proletarian version of this tribune in *Sergeant Braddock, V.C.*, although in his case the joystick was frequently indistinguishable from the slapstick.[35]

From the first, Biggles is potential victim and exploited saviour of the Higher Command, as he all too well recognises. In a First World War dogfight, for instance:[36]

> his lips set in a thin line as his eyes fell on ten more machines roaring down on their left flank. Seven or eight more were coming down on the opposite side. The sky was raining Huns!
>
> He crouched a little lower in the cockpit, curled his lips back from his teeth in a mirthless grin, and shifted his grin on the control-stick so that his thumb rested on the gun-button. In that brief moment before the clash he felt a pang of bitterness against the Higher Command that had sent them, like sheep, to be slaughtered.

The First World War stories also carry an element of almost Roman imperial jocularity as men are half-cozened, half-bullied into mortal peril. This accorded with the disenchantment of so much literary reappraisal of the conflict, but when Biggles takes on peacetime missions much of the same mixture is evident. In *Biggles & Co.* (1936), he investigates air-linked gold robberies carried out in the interest of Nazi Germany, and discovers that the man who has hired him is an agent for the Germans, though at bottom out for himself. In *Biggles Air Commodore* (1937), he runs into the self-protective principle on the highest level when the Japanese (not named) are discovered to be sinking British ships from a secret base, and the Foreign Secretary considers the matter and buck-passes to the head of Admiralty Intelligence, who promptly reciprocates.

But how much of this remains in the Second World War? Far too much. Biggles's demand for rank (in *Biggles Air Commodore*) both in the navy and in the air force if he is to dispose of the enemy, was Johns's assertion of the inherent mortal peril in which the UK in 1936 lay because service jealousy made real cooperation between navy and RAF near-impossible. Johns proved a true prophet. Navy defensiveness and resentment against rising air power, and air favour for Bomber Command over Coastal Command, played their ugly part in the loss of 3,000 UK vessels over 1941–2 in the continuing Battle of the Atlantic. And what did Johns offer as real Authority in its place, other than Nature? Colonel Raymond of Air Intelligence and Scotland Yard in the pre-war books became Air Commodore Raymond; and, once Johns got up to date with Second World War RAF slang, perhaps in part through the useful pamphlet '*It's A Piece of Cake!*', he happily opened *Biggles in the Orient* with Ginger using the prevalent abbreviation 'Air Commode'. This, however, disappeared, probably at the publishers' insistence: lavatories remained largely unspoken. (Hence also, presumably, avoidance of the collective noun for Wing Commanders: 'a flush of WCs'.) Authority in the story quickly becomes something very different from the bleatings of the Higher Command: the tragedy of the pilots crashing because of a secret weapon is met most forcefully, if not always most wisely, by their own *esprit de corps*. Survivors are in fact riddled with guilt at their failure to be killed, which has nothing at all to do with Higher Command sentiment. Much of this is of course based on Johns's reactions to First World War conditions, but here he frankly faces up to it, by Biggles's readiness to cite his one-time alcoholism as a warning to the new generation. The Squadron becomes the Authority, and as such is entitled to make its demands on newcomers, not as a Club, but as survivors making demands on other survivors.[37]

Inevitably, Biggles himself becomes identified with Authority, and with Authority as National Character, in the stories, but its effect is very different from the Authority against which Johns revolted. Biggles gains loyalty, so much so that his regular squadron members refuse or avoid promotion to stay with him, but it is the kind of loyalty (whether primarily to him or to the squadron) which is both hostile and suspicious towards the Higher Command. Ginger leads his seniors, Squadron Leader Algy Lacey and Flight Lieutenant Bertie Lissie, into open defiance of the Air Commodore when he tries to sidestep Biggles's 'failure to return' from an unknown mission. Tug Carrington in the very last Second World War novel makes it clear that he regards the Higher Command as having left the Squadron to face a massive Japanese attack without even permission for self-defence; it had merely chosen sadistically to leave the Squadron guessing and did in fact use the opportunity, though more to obliterate Japanese vessels and soldiers than to protect the airmen. Ginger is also ready to move Algy into defiance of Biggles where he feels Biggles's own survival is in danger and being ignored by him. This assumes much more egalitarian relations than ranks imply, most of all between the former peacetime trio, but in general across the Squadron. Johns's reader-awareness in fact introduced youths of near-schoolboy status – Ginger, Cub, Steeley's Brian Ballantyne – in circumstances where their first action is to save the great leader (Ginger asked to help Biggles escape from Russian spies, Cub telling Copper and Trapper of Gimlet's capture in a Nazi trap, Brian informing Steeley that the police are about to arrest him and on what evidence). The war stories give less opportunity of doing this: the one where it conspicuously seems to happen, *Biggles 'Fails to Return'*, reveals an unnecessary rescue attempt, Biggles and the Sicilian princess having managed their escape preparations very well themselves; but a great principle has been established in the friends making their desperate attempt to save the leader whom the Higher Command has decided is expendable. This is very good war-story realism: soldier expendability was not so blatant a Higher Command philosophy in the Second World War as in the First World War, but it was certainly present.

Biggles's anxiety as regards the Squadron, and above all Algy and Ginger, dominates the Second World War stories. If he is Authority, it is Authority concerned to preserve rather than expend human lives:[38]

The thought of Algy a prisoner in enemy hands affected him far more than he was prepared to reveal to the others. Probably they felt the same. While he did not allow himself to dwell upon the possibility of Algy or Ginger becoming a casualty there was always a fear of it lurking in the background of his mind. If one of them went it would make a difference. The others would go on and the war would go on but things would not be the same. In war, duty, as defined by the High Command, made no allowance for personal feelings: they were supposed not to exist; and the British fighting forces in their many wars had established a sort of tradition in this respect. However a man might feel it was considered weak to let others see any sort of emotion. The whole thing was of course a pose. Everyone who had fought an action knew it – commanding officers more than anyone, although the rank and file did not always realise it; did not suspect that behind the dispassionate voice giving orders that would send men to their deaths, a man's heart was being mauled. Perhaps it was a good thing. If men were going to break down every time a comrade failed to return the will to win would soon break down. After it was all over – well, a man might let himself go. Alexander the Great had shut himself up in his tent for three days. Julius Caesar . . . Mark Antony . . . they had broken down and wept, and they were soldiers. Wellington had been unable to restrain his tears after Waterloo – and his troops called him the Iron Duke. Thus pondered Biggles, with gnawing anxiety in his heart, but with hardly a word of reference to Algy on his lips. His job was to get rubber, not indulge in private enterprises to satisfy personal feelings. Nevertheless, he mused, without comradeship a war would be hard to fight, and while he was not prepared to jeopardise his mission to save anyone, least of all himself, he was not prepared to let Algy go without making a desperate effort to save him.

This was not published until April 1946, possibly delayed for reasons of paper shortage, but it was probably composed when the war's end was at least in sight, if not fact, and Johns probably intended it as a guarded farewell to war fiction. It had to leave some content for decoding. Alexander the Great, Julius Caesar, Mark Antony and the Duke of Wellington were all commanders in the field. Johns is not alluding to chairborne commands. Biggles is to revive the Wellington spirit (and the English usurpation of the Greco–Roman tradition). The national ethos must be Authority sharing the privations of those whom it directs.

But the other requirement was humour. This most readily took the form of joshing, sometimes with schoolboy high spirits; indeed, Johns rightly posited the principle of a schoolboy (though certainly not simply a public-schoolboy) air force. It knew that it needed the humour to meet death, a salutary lesson for the surviving boy pilots of the First World War to teach the children in the Second World War; the firing-line had changed. In their Libyan desert war, Biggles finds Ginger, whom he thought had been killed in air combat, while Ginger has then shot down a Messerschmitt in fact flown by Biggles:

> 'Great Heavens!' breathed a voice.
>
> Ginger stared at the face of the man who stood bending over him. It was Biggles. His eyes were round with wonder and his expression one of utter disbelief.
>
> 'Ginger!' he stammered. 'I thought . . . I thought – you were dead', he gulped. . . .
>
> 'Where have you been since I shot you down?' asked Ginger.
>
> 'So you've discovered it was me you chose for a target?' returned Biggles, coldly. 'If you want to know, I've been frizzling on the crown of a palm. . . . I could have been outside the oasis by now, but it struck me that while I was here I might as well try to collect General Demaurice. I was lying here when you kindly trod on my face. . . .'

This is partly English – and teenage boy – avoidance of emotional expression, but giving it some release in what seems real bereavement. The English were not exceptional in such behaviour, but they liked to imagine that they were. (A fine American instance of it is the film Grease, in which 1950s teenage boys have an impulsive moment of affectionate embrace, and then hastily start combing their hair as though that was what they intended to do in the first place.) But Johns was really grappling with vital questions such as protection of one's family as perhaps a greater obligation than protection of one's country, friendship and comradeship testing the rigid limits of command Authority, love restrained from destructiveness by laughter. Biggles is cool enough in telling the other pilots of it afterwards:

> 'We had a beautiful wrestle there, all to ourselves. I got the best of it, and was pulling a bunch of stinking rags off my Arab to make a gag when I saw the uniform underneath. And there, as large as life, was Ginger, looking scared stiff, with his face all covered with sand. It takes a lot to shake me, but I don't mind admitting that when I saw Ginger's face I nearly passed out. I don't believe in

ghosts, but I thought I'd grabbed one. Naturally, I thought it was Ginger in the Spit that crashed – we all did. But for a ghost this one seemed pretty solid. Moreover, it spluttered.'

'You nearly choked me', said Ginger indignantly, amid more titters of mirth.

'You don't know how right you are', replied Biggles warmly. 'I was feeling sort of peeved at the time.'

The Squadron all know that Ginger has been living with Biggles, as unofficial ward, for several years, and had known what was not said during the time Biggles thought Ginger had been killed; the relief shining through the whole passage is Authority deserving its place by proving its humanity. But it immediately follows a characteristic assertion of Authority in the terms Johns thought proper:

'Our jolly little plan seems to have come unstuck this time', murmured Bertie.

'You mean *my* plan', answered Biggles. 'I get the credit when things go right, so I'll take the kicks when they go wrong. This time it didn't work out. Plans don't always work out, you know. If mine never went wrong I shouldn't be a man, I'd be a magician; and, moreover, I should have won the war long ago. . . .'

Johns tried to address the question in *Biggles Takes a Holiday* (1949), his retrospective confrontation of the Second World War horrors unknown at the time. Von Stalhein, appropriately, discusses Biggles's success as team Authority, speaking to Stitzen who is nominally his own leader:

'They work as a team; and they've been working together for so long that each seems to know by a sort of telepathy when another is in trouble. One never seems to get them together. Get one, and the others come after him. To give the devil his due they make a formidable combination. I once tried to organise a task force on the same lines, but it didn't work.'

'Why not?'

'Because I found it impossible to eradicate certain factors inseparable from human nature, factors which Bigglesworth appears to have overcome.'

'Such as?'

'Oh – selfishness, jealousy, a tendency on the part of some, to use the British army idiom, to dodge the column. You can't rule

those things out by any method that I know of. You'd have to find
the men in which they simply do not occur.'

'Leadership, Erich. Leadership. That's the answer. Find me this
man Bigglesworth and I'll soon cope with the rest.'

Stitzen exemplifies his concept of leadership by hanging himself
with the cord of his pyjamas after Biggles finds him and arrests him:

> Before taking this final step he had set fire to his room, presumably
> in the hope of destroying the bungalow and all that it contained,
> including the records of his own damning experiments. He may
> have overlooked the fact that his fellow-conspirators were con-
> fined in the same building, or he may have determined that they
> should die with him. That would never now be known.

The indifference and the mass murder amount to the same thing,
both typifying Nazi leadership. Other post-war Johns books tell the
same message of self-destruction, with mutual betrayal and blood-
lust intoxication as its hallmarks. The only acceptable Authority is
one that works to create and maintain life.

The Worrals books make the same point, but more sharply, women
being at the cutting edge of male Authority. Worrals becomes
Authoritarian when men have to be taught their place. The idiot
of the chateau, on one of Worrals's wartime missions to France, is
making coffee in the kitchen:[39]

> There were four cups on the table. He smiled sheepishly when he
> saw them, but went on with what he was doing.
> 'You're up early, Lucien?' said Worrals sharply.
> Lucien chuckled, and put on his insane grin. He did not answer
> the question.
> 'For whom are you making coffee?' asked Worrals.
> Lucien indicated himself and the girls. 'What about the other
> cup?' went on Worrals relentlessly.
> Lucien hesitated. It was only momentary, but it was not lost on
> Worrals. 'For my mother', he said.
> 'Lucien, you're lying', grated Worrals.
> The customary idiotic smile came on again.
> 'And take that silly grin off your face', snapped Worrals. 'You
> can't fool me any longer. We're all sitting in the crater of a volcano;
> it's likely to blow up at any moment, and you know it. If we're to
> get out of this thing alive it's time we got together and pooled our

resources. And don't leave things like this lying about to let the world know you've been to England.' Worrals held out the stub of the cigarette that she had picked up in the cellar.

Lucien's face was a study. The foolishness went out of it in a flash. Expressions of alarm, annoyance and, finally, humour, chased each other across his mobile features. At the finish it was a serious, keen-eyed, good-looking young man who stood by the table, one hand resting on it.

Johns may have known J. M. Barrie's *What Every Woman Knows*, which ends its message of female superior (if concealed) authority with Maggie's cry to her husband: 'Laugh, John, laugh. Look at me; see how easy it is', followed by stage directions for him to succeed in doing so, with the final authorial 'He is saved'. The true British message of Authority turned on the gospel of Wodehouse, for all that Britain in the Second World War understandably but unjustly rejected Wodehouse himself. Life is affirmed through laughter.

This was crucial to Churchill's wartime leadership, and he knew it. A Prime Minister with an umbrella does not realise he is funny; a Prime Minister in a boiler suit knows he is. So does a Prime Minister who watches the Marx Brothers, or a Prime Minister making vulgar V-signs at the enemy and pretending it is simply a Victory code. Importantly, it is also childish humour. Churchill could play readily enough with the adult humour of cumbersome House of Commons parody, but his wartime image made him a child accomplice. Appropriately, he becomes such in his major invasion of a story for children: a William story, naturally. Hubert Lane has stolen a digging-fork from a Land Girl to get her wages stopped by Farmer Jenks; William sneaks out of bed on Midsummer Eve (1941) to terrorise Hubert into giving it up, pretending to be a murderous scarecrow come to life to avenge its theft:

> Fortunately for William, it happened that an eminent politician with a particularly resonant voice was speaking on the wireless that evening, and hid their son's bleatings and burrowings from parental ears downstairs. In a few seconds Hubert had returned to his bedroom and pulled back the curtain. The scarecrow had advanced almost to the front door. Glancing up from beneath the shadow of the hat, William saw Hubert's face like the face of a panic-stricken sheep at the window. Then the window was flung up and the fork came out, missing William's head by a fraction of an inch.

> ... Fate was kind to William, and all the people who might
> have confronted him on his adventurous career were sitting by
> their wireless fervently drinking in the words of the eminent
> politician. ...
>
> As he crept across the hall and up the stairs, the voice of the
> eminent politician was up-raised stentoriously in his peroration,
> drowning even the creaking of the middle stair and William's
> sudden stumble on reaching the landing.

As it happens, we can be very precise in contextualising this. The
allusion is to Churchill's radio broadcast, not of 23 but of 22 June
1941, and would have been read as such by its initial purchasers in
Modern Woman for July 1941. Crompton must have written the story
at high speed to reach the magazine deadline. Hitler had invaded the
USSR earlier that day. Churchill told the BBC listeners (putatively
including Mr and Mrs Brown, and Mr and Mrs Lane):[40]

> No one has been a more consistent opponent of Communism than I
> have for the last 25 years. I will unsay no word that I have spoken
> about it, but all that fades away before the spectacle that is now
> unfolding. The past, with its crimes, its follies, and its tragedies,
> flashes away. I see the Russian soldiers standing on the threshold
> of their native land, guarding the fields that their fathers have
> tilled from time immemorial. Any man or state who fights on
> against Nazidom will have our aid. Any man or state who marches
> with Hitler is our foe.

We can see the allusion to tillers of the land working itself out in
Crompton's creative mind as William's championship of the Land
Girl. The feminist Crompton rose to the wartime role of women
(including herself) by giving William friendships in a segment of
population hitherto at natural hostility to him: girls of the age of his
sister. (They are also closer to the working class; but William himself
is no snob, although living in a snobbish world.) Whether she wrote
with awareness of the massive participation of Russian women in
jobs hitherto male is uncertain; she may have. (In any case, it greatly
increased from the advent of the German surprise attack.) The idea of
supernatural threat from a walking scarecrow no doubt derives from
M. R. James's 'Oh, Whistle, and I'll Come to You, My Lad', principally
concerned with bedclothes on an empty bed in a double-bedded room
coming to life and attempting to kill the spectator, but concluding
with the words: 'the spectacle of a scarecrow in a field late on a

winter afternoon has cost him more than one sleepless night'. William in fact throws a stone at the scarecrow before becoming inspired to utilise it, and the Colonel in the James story tells a boy frightened of a sinister waving from a window by a figure that 'warn't a right thing – not to say not a right person': 'Another time, like a brave English boy, you just throw a stone . . .'.[41] But the main point is that William, who does not believe in fairies, makes use of them and their alleged folklore to defeat Hubert, who does. Churchill's declaration of support for Russia while proclaiming his lifelong hostility to Communism, struck listeners forcibly. Orwell applauded its common sense and noted widespread Tory sympathy for the USSR in the coming struggle. Crompton seemed in tune with Churchill's private 'if Hitler invaded Hell I would make at least a favourable reference to the Devil in the House of Commons': invoking fairies and Worzel Gummidge was the equivalent from William and his creator. Crompton had produced many a childlike jeer at the Soviet Union: the Russian Revolution had variously induced William to Sovietise his brother's possessions, involuntarily assist a burglar whom he thought was rescuing a princess, and win social status for his brother by passing him off at a cricket week as a fugitive Romanov.[42] She probably had seen little to choose between National Socialism and the Bolshevik variety. But now here was Churchill making the despised Communists his means of thwarting Hitler: at last the long isolation of the UK was over. William and the Outlaws are given an agonised time of frustration as they seek the missing fork:

> The Outlaws would have abandoned the search as hopeless if it had not been for William. William was definitely of the bulldog type. Having once taken hold, he didn't let go. . . .
>   'No', he said firmly, 'we're goin' to do it. We *said* we'd do it an' we're *goin'* to do it. . . .'

('We shall not flag or fail. We shall go on to the end. We shall fight in France, we shall fight on the seas and oceans . . .'.) And then the thing in which William does not believe becomes the means of his victory. He even makes his non-belief in it achieve his result, by selling the avenging scarecrow thesis to Hubert, much as Orwell saw Churchill's use of his anti-Communism to win credibility ('His hostile references to Communism were entirely right and simply emphasised the fact that this offer of help was sincere'):[43]

'Midsummer Eve's to-day, isn't it?'

'I know', agreed Hubert, lulled into a sense of false security and sucking his humbug openly. There was a triumphant swagger in his walk. He had, he considered, scored off the Outlaws at last. The fork was safely hidden in the box-room behind a pile of trunks, and the Outlaws had in any case no proof that it was he who had taken it. . . .

'All sorts of funny tales about it', [William] said. 'Animals talkin' an' people gettin' their wishes an' such like.'

'I know', said Hubert earnestly. 'They're true, too, but they don't happen till midnight an' we're in bed by then, so we can't see it.'

'That one about scarecrows is s'posed to happen earlier, you know', said William.

'Scarecrows?' said Hubert with interest. 'I never heard one about scarecrows.'

'Oh, there's nothin' in those ole tales', said William contemptuously. 'I don't believe any of 'em.'

'No, but what's the one about scarecrows?' demanded Hubert, taking another humbug out of his pocket and slipping it into his mouth. 'I never heard one about scarecrows.'

'Well, you bet there's nothin' in it.'

'No, but what is it?' demanded Hubert, his curiosity whetted beyond endurance. 'What *is* it?'

'Dunno if I remember it right', said William, 'but they're s'posed to come alive jus' after dark an' come to anyone what's stole anythin' out of their fields durin' the year an' get it back off them.'

Hubert paled.

'G-g-get it back off them?' he stammered.

'Yes', said William carelessly. 'They leave the person what stole it in a jolly nasty mess, too. They've got the strength of ten men when they come alive, scarecrows have. Well, I know I wouldn't like to be knocked about by a scarecrow come alive with the strength of ten men.'

'The s-s-s-strength of ten men?'

'Yes, or it might've been twenty.'

'I don't believe it', said Hubert, but looking like a boy in the grip of a nightmare.

'I don't either', agreed William. 'I don't believe a word of any of those soppy ole fairy tales. It wouldn't come to me, anyway, 'cause I've not stolen anything off a field. An' you haven't either, have you?'

'N-n-no', said Hubert hastily. 'No, 'course I've not. '*Course* I've not.'

'I think those ole tales are all silly', said William scornfully. 'People must've been bats to believe in 'em. We've got a bit more sense now. 'Bout half-past ten the scarecrows are s'posed to come alive. Never heard of anything so cracked, did you? Well, here's your house, Hubert. . . . Nearly tea time, isn't it? I'll be gettin' on home.'

Crompton's creative mind racing into production under the impact of the Churchill speech would have responded to her Bromley towns-folk's shop-counter or armed forces canteen chit-chat the following day (the actual Midsummer Eve). Orwell captured some of his own neighbourhood's equivalent in his diary. People who had long doubted USSR claims would be hoping against hope that there was something in them. Orwell quoted a wholesale grocer in the Home Guard: 'Damn it, there's two hundred bloody millions of them',[44] and no doubt he had his Bromley equivalent if perhaps not so appropriately wholesale. It is echoed by William's 'knocked about . . . strength of ten men . . . or it might've been twenty'.

Churchill therefore was a comic, heroic, cunning Authority, rightly seizing the unexpected opportunity, giving William his alibi and just for once also giving William his identity. Crompton might well signal the event of the speech in such mock-mythical terms: as A. J. P. Taylor would put it, it 'settled the fate of the world for many years to come',[45] and it is only right that the first of its achievements should be to humiliate the greedy, lying and predatory Hubert, and to liberate the oppressed (though high-spirited) Land Girl. The super-natural in its bogus scarecrow epiphany is also Authority, of course: here, too, was a neat parable. If Hitler is only going to yield what he has stolen by fear of imaginary terrors (Bolshevik power, Eastern strength), let us make sure he believes in them. Churchill was not a frequent intruder in children's fiction from other hands (probably he would have been delighted to know he had had a brief meta-morphosis as William); but towards the end of the war a character was drawn somewhat on his contours, by (of all people) a pacifist clergyman. The great cult of aircraft spun many literary side-effects, but does not seem to have included the personification of aeroplanes while the Second World War raged. If anyone did produce the adventures of Sidney the Spitfire and Horace the Hurricane, it has not, fortunately, come to the notice of this historian ('"Johann Junker will need some new wing-tips before he can have another piece of cake", smiled Sidney satirically'); it is hard to see how it could be done, given the short life of the aircraft, the incessant injuries and the obvious physical analogies to the action of dropping bombs – as children would have rapidly pointed out. But a more peaceful form of transport lent itself to development. *The Three Railway Engines* by the Rev. Wilbert Awdry met its juvenile public in 1945, to be followed by *Thomas the Tank Engine* the following year.

Awdry's pacifism ironically illustrates the rejection of violence implicit in the choice and the ensuing cult. The aeroplane might be the transport of the future, its making offered more appeal to the inventive child, its development might be crucial to the future battles. But the train, especially in Awdry's hands, won affection and identification. Dahl's lost Gremlins might have induced greater affection for the plane, had they hit the screen; but the book of the film-that-never-was makes the Gremlins the objects of reader, and hence viewer, affection, and not the planes which have a thankless time of it, what with Gremlin-drilled holes in wings and outright crashes. Dahl might have moved on to anthropomorphic aeroplanes had his career as a novelist for children not been put into cold storage; that he did produce a flying peach when he returned to juvenile fiction twenty years later would indicate as much. But, however tempting a Dahl-versus-Awdry battle for vehicular pre-eminence might seem (who better to give the lofty Dahl his comeuppance than a pacifist parson?, or who better to offset the worship of order and reliability in Awdry than the anarchistic ex-pilot?),[46] the victory of the train was what happened and may well have been inevitable. During the Spanish Civil War, when European children first experienced civilian bombing, André Malraux noted that recipients of toys collected in the Madrid bullring stayed away from the toy aeroplanes, which remained untouched when the children withdrew. Boys had taken dolls rather than touch the aeroplanes. Their juniors in 1940 seem not to have shared the little Spaniards' horror: the European child had learned to think of bombs from the heavens as a fact of life, not simply a nightmare. Older children would speak to younger ones with the condescending knowledgeability that forbade enquiry, let alone surprise or shock – and as Crompton's William shows, collections of parts of crashed German planes were set on foot by children and exhibited by adults. William enjoyed designing aircraft so invincible that he maintained Hitler was trying to bomb him personally to prevent its realisation ('It's a troop-carryin' aeroplane, an' it's goin' to go six hundred miles an hour an' it's goin' to be camouflaged so's to look like a cloud in the sky an' like a barn when it comes down so's the troops can hide in it').[47] Biggles took off into the best-seller lists as never before. But the Malraux note was relevant.

No doubt time was also relevant. William was perfecting his aerial contrivance against Hitler in January 1941. By 1942, soldiers seem to have replaced airmen as foci of emulation in Crompton's stories, no doubt reflecting talk about troops being needed to repel invaders or troops preparing for European and African combat. By the end of 1943, William was trying to sell his soldiers, with the authorial reflection that 'the craze had been comparatively short-lived': Crompton was a present-giving aunt (honorary and otherwise) reporting current trends. Aircraft are back in prominence after D-Day, but in the context of heroes being decorated after unknown achievements: the Squadron Leader pretends that his is for rescuing a general's pet monkey from the Germans, which sounds like a story invented for a less air-combat-conscious generation. (William in late 1944 is still eleven, but now reflects different contemporaries from the Battle of Britain's child observers.) The Squadron Leader holds his Authority as a soldier, rather than as an airman. Trains would also increase in interest when travel through Britain was unrestricted, and peace began to look more interesting – though not more abundant – than the increasingly remote war. But the train had been quietly building up its following over the years. Puffins and others brought out their train books; and the new sizes, large and small, to which war had driven the publishers, harmonised with the sense of difference. A train, after all, was familiar as an object while being formidable for an occasion: trains had been there to watch, but evacuees had taken them, soldiers had disappeared in them, and, as the Chalet School girls sometimes learned, aeroplanes could threaten them. Trains held excitement in which children might sometimes participate, as they could not do in aircraft. And the trains could be celebrated in song, with a music to their wheels such as nobody could ever claim for the aeroplane. Poets had realised that quite early: W. H. Auden in his 'Night Mail' for John Grierson's pre-war Post Office film, Eliot for 'Skimbleshanks: The Railway Cat'.[48]

The first children's train-book of the war, Julian Tuwim's *Locomotive* (1939), was adapted by Bernard Gutteridge and William J. Peace from the original Polish, for Tuwim was a Pole and, as he proudly proclaimed during the war, a Jew; his illustrators, Jan Lewitt and George Him, were Polish artists in England:[49]

Can I mount the slope by the dusky pinewood?
I think I can, I think I can!
I thought I could, I thought I could!
Through the fields and cuttings, unseen it tears,
Just as a toy train runs under chairs.
And still the wheels sing with their clashing rhyme,
I've got to be there in time, in time,
I've got to be there in time!

These were essentially hymns to bigness (brought within reach by Eliot through valorising the cat). But Lewitt and Him found an outlet for their talents in the celebration of a train of smallness when they illustrated Diana Ross's *The Little Red Engine Gets a Name* (1942). It coincided with what seems a trend towards identification of Britishness with the beauty of the little. Germany had become Goliath; Britain, slingshots and all, had been David. (Children's Hour broadcast that story in early wartime.) The Germans were to be shown as lacking the British spirit, the greater moral fibre, the sense of righteous cause. Once the Russians and Americans had entered the war, the British were more inclined to present their air power as big, the better to assert their place as one of the Big Three – so the cult of the small sought other outlets (one of which would have been Dahl's Gremlins, had they ever got off the ground). Ross's Little Red Engine was despised and belittled by the Big main-line engines, but came the day when, in good fairy-story triad, the Big Black Engine ('Pride of the North') ran into a snowdrift and the Big Green Engine ('Beauty of the South') ran into a tree on the line and was derailed, and the Little Red (hitherto nameless) Engine pulled the King on his journey home ('I'm a main line train and I'm carrying the King WHOOOEEEOOOOOO', and Lewitt and Him made a magnificent smoke lettering for the engine's whistle-and-blow). So the King gave him the name 'Royal Red – By Special Appointment' and made him a Main Line Engine.[50]

The Rev. Wilbert Awdry took up many of these themes, but was careful not to fall into Ross's assumption that the reward of smallness is bigness. *Thomas the Tank Engine*, second of the books, became the great favourite; and the eponymous hero, having made a fool of himself on the main line, wins his ultimate just award by being given his own branch line. Moreover, his Authority was not the remote King but the tangible Fat Director, whose Authority is offset by giving orders in whose exhausting fulfilment he cannot participate for medical reasons, or having a goat eat his top hat for his tea, or in joining Thomas's Fireman and Driver in fishing in Thomas's tank (briefly piscoferous): a figure of Churchillian comedy and humanity as well as Authority. His transformation to the Fat Controller was one of the most intelligent observations on the birth of the welfare state by an author for children.[51] Awdry represented it as beneficial that Director became Controller on the ground that he knew the needs of the engines; but, for good or ill, the welfare state was shaped by company directors becoming state controllers. The Churchillian outline and formal attire (not that Churchill would have wanted to wear a top hat to talk to railway engines) had its own irony. Churchill's war had been heroic; but its opponents for reasons of conscience could often be heroes themselves, and their heroism went all too easily unrecognised. Awdry as a curate was bullied, abused and finally deprived of his job by his Rector for his refusal to become an army chaplain; the local bishop (Ernest Neville Lovett of Salisbury) refused to license him when he was offered a new curacy; and when finally the sympathetic Bishop Ernest William Barnes of Birmingham offered him a place, he was denied the right to preach a farewell sermon in the parish he was leaving by the Rector ejecting him, along with his wife and two-month-old son. Awdry painted his small-is-beautiful world with a sense of justice and injustice. The engines were very consciously and lovably humanised. 'This world is God's world', Awdry told his biographer Brian Sibley. 'He makes the rules. We have free choice, we can obey Him or disobey Him; but we cannot choose to disobey Him and live happily our way. If we disobey, we bring trouble on ourselves and other people.' He also told Sibley that he wanted his epitaph to say: 'He helped people to see God in the ordinary things of life, and he made children laugh'.[52]

The God of Whom Awdry spoke might reply, in the words of Psalm 148:22: 'The stone which the builders refused is become the head stone of the corner'. The man whose Church and nation in arms stood against him made the clearest case for Divine authority of all our writers for children. Nor was it a case dependent on belief in Awdry's God, still less in Awdry's Christian sect. To put it another way, people convinced that they did not believe in God could enunciate such an ethic substituting the state, or the law, or the King, or what they wanted. God at the official centre of human Authority was endangered by humans usurping his Authority and claiming to act in His name; a God rejoicing in human freedom to do what is right could be a God worshipped under another name, all the more if the worshippers were convinced that their godliness was Godless. So

Awdry was simultaneously the most revolutionary and the most traditional of our authors. Apart from his personal courage, his most revolutionary aspect was to link God with laughter. But it was much more representative of writers for children than was his pacifism. If God were gone – especially the horrible God of Kipling's 'Baa, Baa, Black Sheep', who took his pleasure counting the strokes of a cane – where would the child look for Authority in the world of the Second World War? The modern state had offered its many substitute icons, but Authority was ultimately at its most powerful in facing the child, and now the child saw its symbols of Authority crumble before its eyes, sometimes beginning with its most obvious physical sense of a stable Authority – its house. Palaces and parliaments were shattered by bombs: perhaps their meaning became much more real and more welcome, as the then Queen said of the bombing of Buckingham Palace that now she could look the East End in the face, or when Churchill in Parliament was transformed into Churchill on the wireless, inspirational sound in place of unreadable print. Theirs was thus a more real Authority, but a less visible Authority. The one story for older children to make Churchill a character, and – as use of real persons in writing for children demands – a real character enacting some great event of history, was playing with fairies and ghosts, mockingly, but firmly, and with that half-spiritual quality of his place as a child's hero. He became what Britain had not had for nearly a quarter of a millennium – a hero king. The last hero king had been William III. It is no disrespect to the memory of the undoubtedly heroic George VI to put it like that: George VI's heroism was a much more modern one than Churchill's, and as such its greatest heroism was in private and probably in mind. But attempts to bring him on stage in children's literature could not be more than cardboard, and too easily were even less. Percy F. Westerman ended his *Fighting for Freedom* (1941), set in the weeks before and after Dunkirk, with decorations for some of his heroes:[53] 'A few minutes later, without being announced, and in quite an informal manner, His Majesty entered the room, followed by a court official carrying a cushion and another with a sheet of paper'. The minds of older readers in so many instances would automatically switch back to memories of the popular song by a writer whose film *In Which We Serve* (1942) was as simplistic a tribute to naval war heroes as any by Westerman but who swam far deeper in the springs of humour, Noël Coward. Recent school study of British kings made it all too easy to recall 'The Stately Homes of England', written as recently as 1938:[54]

Tho' the pipes that supply the bathroom burst
And the lavat'ry makes you fear the worst
It was used by Charles the First
Quite informally
And later by George the Fourth
On a journey North . . .

Could some horrid Gremlin have foisted this on the innocent Muse of Percy F. Westerman?

So, if Churchill was a hero king, why was he defeated in 1945 by the votes of many recent readers of children's comics and story-books? A hero king has nothing to do with parliaments unless like Charles I he wars with them, or, like Cromwell, he closes them down. Churchill was heading a party which when elected had hated him and which during the war was eclipsed by him. The waning of reader interest in the war would have distanced his admirers: he was a great man in war, but the sooner war was over the better, and heroes put back into history where they belonged. Churchill had in fact asserted the Authority of the past for British identity: this had worked, and now the past had to return to itself, and he with it. Roosevelt's death – much more remotely and less personally – must have had a comparable finality. The visible Americans in battle-dress had become much less numerous in the UK since D-Day.

What was of course omnipresent during the war was new and frequently irritating local symbolism of Authority, ruthlessly dissected by Crompton, attacked in the shape of Goon the local police-man by Blyton,[55] and in the case of the Home Guard made slightly absurd and then unexpectedly heroic by Saville (in *Mystery at Witchend*). Brent-Dyer had lashed their petty tyranny in *The Chalet School Goes to It* but acknowledged in *The Highland Twins at the Chalet School* that with real spies around they had their uses. Brent-Dyer had also raised the ugly question of how far such brief Authority might come to resemble the horrific regime they were fighting. With normal sources of Authority – parental, magisterial, neighbourhood often gone, even for good – where was it to be found? Blyton herself became one answer, as she threw the protection of her prose around her votaries. Brent-Dyer provided another, by a highly peace-directed God. Both of those were traditional – Blyton was merely a modern application of the authority of the storyteller, and the historian. Implicit in wartime fiction for children was the assumption that their duty might lie in resisting authority, becoming their own authority, denying the compromises that adult authority had made or insisting on compromises that adults had rejected, the last unusual in fiction for children, but possible especially where a child may conclude that a perceived enemy or outlaw could be an ally. (J. K. Rowling has played cleverly with this last, and Lewis uses it in The Silver Chair when the name of Aslan forces the children to do the reverse of what they had agreed to do, and take what had seemed false commands to be true.) Flouting authority in the cause of a higher good is almost always attractive to child readers, and a nice balance is achievable between the responsible youth such as Blyton's Julian and his irresponsible but frequently wiser cousin George, or between the normally orthodox Harry Wharton and the instinctive rebel Herbert Vernon-Smith. Crompton's William establishes his own authority, which becomes the ultimate condition of most child heroes distanced from adults. The child working for anti-Authority or false Authority in an Oliver Twist situation offers nice psychological studies from a Frank Richards devising St Jim's cracksman Talbot or boy criminals Lancaster, Compton, Skip and Flip of Greyfriars – most interesting in Talbot, whose false Authority is simply his dead father. Tintin, if we put L'Étoile Mystérieuse in its contemporary context, might seems a fine example of this, with the author, no less than his hero, led astray by false logic and false gods. Yet Hergé had arrived at L'Étoile by devotion to the two most traditional Conservative totems, Church and King, the latter by thought processes perfectly in key with the British Tory. Percy F. Westerman's bitter rage (in mid-story) against 'Leopold, son of a lion-hearted king' for having 'surrendered to the enemy with totally unexpected suddenness'[56] documented the petard that hoist his logic. If the memory of Albert I invited devotion instead of reserving the lion's share of praise for his suffering people, the penalty would be paid for putting trust in princes. The same monarchical principle would insist on the leader's always receiving blind obedience. Johns wrote more wisely when he would have Ginger deliberately disobey Biggles's orders in the interest of Biggles himself: during the Second World War, he flatly puts the authority of his will above Biggles's in Biggles in Borneo, and above Raymond's in Biggles 'Fails to Return', which Johns makes clear involves conduct in defiance of armed-services regulations. Ginger's arguments are perfectly reasonable, in human terms, and could have had him court-martialled or even shot, in war terms. Comparably, J. K. Rowling posits Harry Potter's defiance of the edict of Albus Dumbledore, who then finds Harry's action natural, justifiable and sometimes laudable.

The classic wartime crisis is when the child realises that the official Authority is in fact false and destructive of what the child knows it stands for. The classic case of it is in the ancient Roman tale of the schoolmaster of Falerii who sought to sell his pupils to the Roman general Camillus, at that time leading the Romans against the town. That tale has the Roman general tell the schoolboys to beat their master back to their town so that all ends happily save for the master. Jeffrey Havilton was making his own version of that in *School versus Spy* when Mr Manders ('Batty'), having defended his treason to his pupil 'Fussy' Wilkes, shoots a college servant 'Toodles' who had been blackmailing him (' "Perhaps", he said to Fussy, "that will help you to make up your mind" '), kidnaps the boy and rows him to where a German seaplane will pick them up:

> 'I dare say', said Batty, reading his thoughts, 'that you could tip the boat up if you tried, Wilkes. But it would be a poor return for all the trouble I've had with you to-night. You can't possibly realize what a job it was to get you from the cave up to the road. It's a lucky thing you're thin, though even so I thought we were stuck for good two or three times. Still, you could upset the boat. And what good would that do? I am certainly a better swimmer than you. I should drown you and then right the boat and proceed on my way.'
>
> The thought had been in Fussy's mind. He abandoned it.
>
> 'Or you could try rushing me', said Batty. 'But, honestly, do you think you're up to it yet? I know you're tough, but you were *very* sick [in reaction to the murder he has witnessed], weren't you?'
>
> Fussy abandoned that thought, too.
>
> 'Or you could shout', said Batty. 'But we're three hundred yards from shore and it's a dark night. Still, you could shout. I shall then throw you overboard, hit you on the head with an oar, and row on.'

The supreme horror is in the didactic quality, the schoolmaster still teaching the witness to his murder and treason, and prepared to do so right to the point when he murders his pupil, if he has to. He is clear that he does not want to murder Wilkes as he murdered Toodles, which he had prefaced by 'He's due at five and it's just about that now. When he does come you'll realize that Toodles doesn't present quite the same problem as you do. I quite like *you*, Wilkes. I don't like Toodles at all.' But, if he must:[57]

> Fussy gloated in the stern and made up his mind to dive into the water as soon as the right moment came.
>
> Batty read his intention with uncanny accuracy.

'I shall shoot you as soon as you stand up, Wilkes', he said.
'Please yourself. The choice is still open to you. Drown with a
bullet in you or come aboard and take your chance of getting safe
to Germany.'

While he was speaking the right moment came and passed. The
boat drew close up under the seaplane.

'After you, Wilkes', said Batty.

Fussy climbed aboard.

In the end, Batty's death from the machine-gun bullet fired from a
pursuing aircraft takes the role of a *deus ex machina*, as, if alive, he
would no doubt have pointed out to Wilkes. Wilkes has been
hatching desperate tactics, now unnecessary. But, at the end, we
are simply left with the worthlessness of force as an argument, that
for all of his intellectual resources the teacher who depends on force
has abdicated his Authority. Quite apart from the Nemesis of the
machine-gun bullet, Batty is dead, dead by his own new order which
otherwise simply demolished the remains of his old.

Notes

1. Apart from P. L. Travers's Mary Poppins; but few identified her with Australia
   (and she may owe more to the Ireland of Yeats's friend George Russell, 'AE', on
   whose *Irish Statesman* Travers had worked). The familiarity which British
   children would have found for themselves in Montgomery is explained in great
   part by Dr Jennifer Litster's doctoral dissertation (University of Edinburgh,
   2003), 'The Scottish Context of L. M. Montgomery'.
2. Hutchinson's were a striking exception, especially in 'Hutchinson's War Adventure Series', selling at six shillings (£0.30) per book. In particular, they ran
   the Dave Dawson books by the English-American R. Sidney Bowen, in which the
   American Dawson and his English 'pal' Freddy Farmer zoom in and out of
   various superheroic adventures decidedly lacking Johns's ability to keep his
   story possible if not plausible. They were in the RAF in most of the books with
   English publication (six by 1946) but, when Dawson was shifted to the war
   against Japan, Hutchinson's declined the later titles. What English youth made
   of him would be worth knowing. The Battle of Britain and the Blitz must have
   made air combat with Biggles real enough, but Johns never implied that British
   success in air warfare was inevitable, as was basic to Sidney Bowen. *Dave
   Dawson on Convoy Patrol* ([1943]) opens, for instance:

   > Wave after wave of German bnmbers roared in over the city from every
   > possible direction, dumped their tons of life-blasting missiles, and then went
   > streaking away towards safety with British searchlights, anti-aircraft shells,
   > and night-flying Spitfires and Hurricanes hot on their tails. Some made it, but
   > some others were caught by the two-fisted hard-fighting boys of the RAF, and
   > once caught the Nazis didn't stand a chance against such flying skill, daring
   > and perfect marksmanship. (p. 1)

The mortal wound to its own credibility is dealt at the end of the page where it emerges that our heroes are billeted in the Savoy Hotel. The book's end is worthy of its beginning, with 'Air Marshal Manners' telling Dawson and Farmer: 'England will never forget what you two have done today. Not only England, but the entire civilized world.' (pp. 7, 152). The Johns finale is exemplified by *Biggles Sweeps the Desert*, when a Group Captain, who has looked into the Squadron's oasis to fuss, is told that they have disposed of the enemy and destroyed *his* oasis and would the Group Captain stay to dinner? 'The Group Captain looked round the ring of weary, grimy, sun-tanned faces. "The honour's mine", he said.' (p. 208).

3. Graham did open with a little American rough by including Rutherford Montgomery's *Carajou* ([1937] 1943) as her eleventh Puffin, being an enthralling if brutal story of a wolverine's battle against an Amerindian and his friend, a great bear (the wolverine is ultimately killed by eating a porcupine). But her edition made no allusion to Montgomery's having two other titles appearing in London the same year, *Thumbs Up!* (on airborne US Marines at war from Pearl Harbor) and *Hurricane Yank* (a more realistic version of US pilots in the RAF than Dave Dawson), both in Hutchinson's War Adventure Series.

4. Max Grindler, otherwise known as The Pike, in *Sergeant Bigglesworth, C.I.D.* Similarly, Gimlet's first post-war adventures, *Gimlet Comes Home* (1946), pitches him against an American gangster, rather disturbingly bearing President Franklin Delano Roosevelt's mother's name, [Slim] Delano, though he shows no sign of kinship to her high-society clan.

5. *The Mountain of Adventure*: he is pursued by Alsatian dogs, and in fact Blyton was probably relying on reader association with Harriet Beecher Stowe's *Uncle Tom's Cabin*, then on sale in British children's series – the book's hard cover shows an Alsatian forcing the runaway up a tree. During the war, one innkeeper put up a notice reading: 'NO AMERICANS EXCEPT NEGROES AND GENERAL EISENHOWER'.

6. *Billy Bunter of Greyfriars School* (1947) netted Richards over £1,000, his new publisher Charles Skilton having persuaded him to accept royalties instead of the £1.50 per thousand words that Richards assumed he would be given. Skilton's honourable conduct should be less surprising on the part of a publisher than it is. Fish did not play a big part in this story, but his being sold stolen goods by Bunter results in his being 'ragged' with the clear implication that capitalism is dishonest. The *Hotspur* had by now introduced a character like Fish into Red Circle but made him a London 'spiv': the moral was less anti-American but just as anti-capitalist.

7. Oddly enough, *MAD* was not making an anti-monarchical point but merely reflecting on what versions of well-known US comic strips might be like in other countries, and used the Royal Family for a British form of the Irish American 'Life with Father', in which the Duke of Edinburgh played Jiggs and the Queen Maggie. The British were abnormally sensitive on monarchy in the late 1950s.

8. Brent-Dyer, *Three Go to the Chalet School* (1949), 87–8, 240. Margery Fisher, *Who's Who in Children's Books* (1975), 107–9: good book, though weak on Blyton.

9. Crompton, 'Entertainment Provided', *Modern Woman* (May 1943), and *William and the Brains Trust*, 107–8.

10. Antoine de Saint-Exupéry, *Le Petit Prince* ([1945] 1958), ed. A. Shuffrey, including a brief life, 75. It was illustrated by the author, translated by Katherine Woods, published USA 1943, UK 1944. It is the most translated work in French, having eighty foreign editions (Stacy Schiff, *Saint-Exupéry*

(1994), 400). P. L. Travers reviewed it ecstatically in the New York *Herald-Tribune* (11 April 1943), remarking that 'all fairy-tales are portents' – subsequently relevant to the fate of Saint-Exupéry. The *Times Literary Supplement* ignored it until 1962.

11. Johns, *Spitfire Parade*, 165–6. Johns evidently imagined the events from his own First World War experience – Dunkirk is unmentioned but must have happened in mid-story, in the Second World War context.

12. M. R. D. Foot, *Resistance* (1976), 254–5.

13. The post-war English version would render Milou as Snowy; post-war British wireless had a long-running sequence of thrillers whose hero Dick Barton, Special Agent, had a sidekick, Snowy White.

14. The strips, still black and white, were now book-published after press serialization; but the initial newspaper instalment is, exceptionally, the date specified here unless otherwise stated.

15. The English text, translated post-war, substitutes Munich for Jena as the German university, and Paris for Fribourg thus making the Swiss scientist French, so that commentators have assumed that conquered lands as well as neutrals were involved, apart from Belgium and Germany. De Becker, however absurdly, was firmly peddling the notion of a Belgian–German 'special relationship'.

16. Benoît Peeters's invaluable *Hergé Fils de Tintin* (2002), 175, gives ugly examples of de Becker's anti-Jewish material in *Le Soir*, October–November 1940, and cites Hergé to Madame B., 17 March 1954, ibid., 196, pointing out that extermination camps were not dreamed of when he created *L'Étoile* in 1941, otherwise he would not have made his financier Jewish.

17. Johns, *Biggles Goes to War*, 38–9.

18. I have been unable to see the first version of *L'Étoile Mysterieuse* as it appeared in *Le Soir*, but sufficient deductions as to its main points of difference from later versions may be made from secondary literature. The post-war revision deleted the US base of Blumenstein/Bohlwinkel operations and substituted the imaginary São Rico, but the French text conveys the spirit of the original in ways its English form, *The Shooting Star*, does not: '*démasqués et punis*' becomes 'be brought to justice'.

19. Since most readers of the present book will be more familiar with the Anglophone text than with the French original, the latter version runs thus: Haddock descends from François de Hadoque, Capitaine de la Marine du Roy, endowed at Versailles by Louis XIV with the Chateau de Moulinsart on 15 June 1684. Louis held some fortresses in what is now Belgium under the Peace of Nijmegen (1678) and had seized more, and the Nazis ruled Belgium and north-western France in a military unit which this reaffirms by historical antecedent. It also shows Tintin and friends perfectly happy to take pride in a grant of a castle from a foreign potentate ruling through military incursion of questionable legitimacy. The English version of 1959 made Charles II endow 'Marlinspike' (with bad dating), a benevolence from that king of the kind he was best known for giving to recipients of even more questionable legitimacy. The pirate Red Rackham was always English and stays English.

20. *Biggles – Charter Pilot*, 103.

21. Mowbray, *The Radio Mystery*, 231.

22. I have pieced together the story of Hergé and the Nazi occupation from several sources, the most comprehensive of which is Peeters, *Hergé*, though I am also obliged to his *Tintin and the World of Hergé*, trans. Michael Farr (1989), 69–71, 86–90, and Farr's own *Tintin: the Complete Companion* (2001); and, for a more

critical view, Jean-Marc and Randy Lofficier, *The Pocket Essential Tintin* (2002), 48–62. Harry Thompson, *Tintin* (1991), 90–6, 106–10 is still useful. *Archives Hergé* 4 (1980) has early texts of *L'Île, Ottokar* and *Crabe*, but I was unable to find any such publication for *L'Étoile*. Otherwise I have used Martin Conway, *Collaboration in Belgium* (1993) – authoritative, chiefly focused on Degrelle; Foot, *Resistance* – masterly, most helpful for comparative data and at times deeply moving; Naval Intelligence Division, *Belgium B.R.* 521 (February 1944), which, rather to its own surprise, one suspects, has useful information; and Hervé Hanquin, *Dictionnaire d'Histoire de Belgique* (1988), intentionally helpful. Spaak's memoirs mislead if not watched carefully. I found some wheat in the chaff of apologetics for Leopold III. Camille Gutt and the Congo uranium are my own contribution to the debate on *L'Étoile* – and something to intertextualise *Tintin* with children's literature in Britain. Camille Gutt, *La Belgique en Carrefour 1940–1944* (1971), has a wonderful sense of humour and gives very vivid accounts of conversations in May 1940 with memorable snapshots later, briefly acknowledging his role in accessing Congo uranium and gold to the USA. The Lofficiers make much of *L'Étoile's* debts to Jules Verne's posthumous (and apparently unrevised) *The Case of the Golden Meteor* (trans. Frederick Lawton, 1908), which partly turns on gold on a meteorite flooding the market, a danger alleviated when it is pushed off Greenland into the sea. Other similarities are much less striking than those with Johns; for example, the rival scientists in Verne are two amateur astronomers having a feud which ends when one saves the other's life. Jan van Welkenhuyzen, *Quand les chemins se separent* (1988), is a useful narrative of King against cabinet in 1940.

23. Brent-Dyer, *The Chalet School Goes to It*, 28–43. I would be the last person to claim expertise in air-naval warfare; but, because her characters are more vivid than theirs, I found her account more memorable than more professional variations on the theme in the works of Percy F. Westerman and Rowland Walker.

24. Professor Aubrey Manning, discussing Anthony Trollope's mode of addressing characters and audience in his early work, wondered who else used such methods. This is in fact what Enid Blyton does, in what has been foolishly dismissed as a Nannie method. E. Nesbit does it also, notably in the very moving last lines of *The Railway Children*. Blyton probably got it from her, but there are indications that she had read *Barchester Towers* to her advantage. Carlyle does it, notably in *The French Revolution*, probably inspiring Trollope's use of it.

25. For example, Captain Monty Newton in Wallace, *The Three Just Men* (1926). Richards, *Magnets* 1,059–67 (June–July 1928) and 1,631–42 (May–July 1939) exhibit a couple of choice specimens, sadistic as well as swindlers.

26. *Biggles Delivers the Goods*, 176.

27. Crompton, 'William and the Wonderful Tramp', *Happy Mag* (February 1931) and (as 'The Outlaws and the Tramp') *William's Crowded Hours*, 191–2; 'Youth at the Prow', *Modern Woman* (May 1944) and (as 'Youth on the Prow') *William and the Brains Trust*, 162, 173; 'Mrs Bott's Birthday Present', *Modern Woman* (August 1942) and *William and the Brains Trust*, 45–6; 'The Outlaws and the Parachutist', *Modern Woman* (February 1941), *William Does His Bit*, 162.

28. Quoted (no date), Jeremy Treglown, *Roald Dahl* ([1994] 1995), 60.

29. *Biggles Sweeps the Desert*, 42, 43, 15.

30. *Biggles Hits the Trail*, 10.

31. *Biggles and the Leopards of Zinn*, 89. The foreword and book are strongly critical of imperialism.

32. This is to suggest Rochester as a source for Johns, assuming that Johns was

studying form for boys' stories as early as 1929 – he had already tried his hand an adult thriller, *Mossyface* (1922) – but *The Black Hawk* only obtained book publication in 1936 and then by John Hamilton, with whom Johns had already published ten titles including *The Spyflyers* (1933).

33. *The Spyflyers* ([1993] 2002), 135–6, and 12 (introduction by Jennifer Schofield (= Piers Williams, co-biographer of Johns)), quoting Norman Wright.

34. *Sky High* ([February 1936] June 1951 'completely revised and reset', but on a rapid collation I find no changes), 40–1. *The Unknown Quantity*, 29.

35. George Bourne, *I Flew with Braddock* ([1959]), is a rarity among Thomson products, a book from a comic serial (another being *Morgyn the Mighty* from the *Beano*'s 'strongest man in the world'); but the initial stories appeared long before it, the supposed date of first adventure being 25 May 1940. It is a glorious iconoclastic series of pratfalls for snobbish officers – and a fairly ruthless indictment of the prevalence of incompetent privilege in the British armed forces in the Second World War. Where the officer class made much of nicknames without comment on them (it is Tug Carrington, the Cockney, who is called on to explain what is in fact his first name), Braddock is, as always, confrontational even on his own surname: 'Braddock – rhymes with haddock'. The indications are that Braddock was inspired by Tug's debut in *Spitfire Parade*.

36. Johns, 'The Great Arena', *Biggles of the Camel* [recent edns 'Fighter'] *Squadron* ([1934] 1992), 141–2; *Biggles Air Commodore* (May 1937), 33–4, 44, 46.

37. Johns, *Biggles in the Orient*, 11, 77–8; *The Camels are Coming*, 245.

38. Johns, *Biggles Delivers the Goods*, 129–30.

39. Johns, *Biggles Sweeps the Desert*, 106, 107 (General Demaurice is Free French, hence a rescue priority since the Nazis will kill or torture him when he is flown to Germany), 120, 117; *Biggles Takes a Holiday*, 128, 190; *Worrals Flies Again* (November 1942), 130–1.

40. Crompton, 'William's Midsummer Eve', *Modern Woman* (July 1941), and *William Carries On*, 80–1. Churchill, BBC Broadcast, 22 June 1941, quoted in *Chambers Dictionary of Quotations* (1996), 264.

41. James, 'Oh, Whistle, and I'll Come to You, My Lad', *Collected Ghost Stories of M. R. James* ([1931] 1964), 150, 142. Crompton, like Conan Doyle, could write amusing tales making fun of beliefs in ghosts, while holding spiritualistic interests (Cadogan, *Crompton*, 19–22, pointing to her book of chilling tales *Mist and Other Stories*, 1928). In any case, Crompton read James, being a professional writer studying ghost stories from the English Master.

42. Crompton, 'The Weak Spot', *Home Magazine* (June 1921) and *William the Fourth* (April 1924); 'The Mysterious Stranger', *Happy Mag* (September 1925) and *William the Conqueror* (March 1926); 'William and the Russian Prince', *Happy Mag* (August 1933) and *William the Gangster* (July 1935).

43. Crompton, *William Carries On*, 70, 75–8. Orwell, War-time Diary, 23 June 1941, *Complete Works*, XII, 517.

44. Orwell, ibid., 517.

45. Taylor, *English History 1914–1945* (1965), 529.

46. Treglown, *Roald Dahl*, 247, describes an interview duel which became good-natured between Dahl and Brian Sibley, later Awdry's biographer. Page 248 mentions Dahl's dissent from a Tory Party panel whose majority would exclude Enid Blyton 'from a list of approved texts', Dahl backing Blyton books 'because children liked them'.

47. Crompton, 'William the Salvage Collector', *Modern Woman* (January 1941) and *William Does His Bit*, 165; 'Soldiers for Sale', *Modern Woman* (February 1944) and *William and the Brains Trust*, 142.

48. Auden, 'Night Mail', in film *Night Mail* (1936), and Auden, *Collected Shorter Poems 1927–1957* ([1966] 1975), 83–4. For Eliot, see *Old Possum's Book of Practical Cats* (1939).
49. Tuwim, *Locomotive*, [18].
50. Ross, *The Little Red Engine Gets a Name*, [20], [32].
51. Awdry, *James the Red Engine* (1947), 3.
52. Sibley, *The Thomas the Tank Engine Man* (1995), 331.
53. Westerman, *Fighting for Freedom*, 315.
54. Quoted in A. Norman Jeffares and Martin Gray (eds), *Collins Dictionary of Quotations* (1995), 185.
55. Lexicographers inform us that by 1943, when Blyton introduced Mr Goon as the stupid, bullying village policeman in *The Mystery of the Burnt Cottage*, the word was of American origin and was known to be either a stupid individual or a hired thug. It is doubtful if an unkinder epithet for a policeman has been invented. She also popularised 'Plod' in several of her fairy-stories culminating in the Noddy series, which in the fullness of time gave birth to Arthur Daley's 'Interplod' when confronted by international police cooperation in the TV serial *Minder*.
56. Westerman, *Fighting for Freedom*, 54, 135.
57. Havilton, *School versus Spy*, 248–9, 245–6, 250.

FIGURE 8 Worrals, understanding the French temperament
(Capt. W. E. Johns, *Worrals on the War-Path*) – see p. 195.

8

Gender

*'My sight is failing', she said finally. 'Even when I was young I could
not have read what was written there. But it appears to me that that
wall looks different. Are the Seven Commandments the same as they
used to be, Benjamin?'*

*For once Benjamin consented to break his rule, and he read out to
her what was written on the wall. There was nothing there now
except a single Commandment. It ran:*
        ALL ANIMALS ARE EQUAL
        BUT SOME ANIMALS ARE MORE
        EQUAL THAN OTHERS
               George Orwell, *Animal Farm*

'The nineteenth-century dislike of Realism is the rage of Caliban
seeing his own face in a glass.

The nineteenth-century dislike of Romanticism is the rage of
Caliban not seeing his own face in a glass.' Thus Wilde, replying
to hostile critics of his *The Picture of Dorian Gray* in the 'Preface' for
it which he published in the *Fortnightly Review* for March 1891.

It erases his critics, but, as he intended, it also erases most
criticisms to have emanated from his century, for the obvious reason
that most criticism of anything is a repetition or contradiction of
what somebody else has said, sufficiently memorably about something else.

The foregoing is a case in point.

The twentieth-century Reactionary dislike of Gender, Class and
Race as yardsticks of Second World War stories for children is the
rage of Caliban discovering that someone can enjoy a story he likes
more fully than he can.

The twentieth-century Revolutionary dislike of Second World War
stories for children by yardsticks of Gender, Class and Race is the
rage of Caliban discovering that someone can enjoy a story he is
afraid to like.

It is to the Second World War that we owe our urgency in
consideration of Gender, Class, and Race. From the standpoint of

the British child, the war was initially portrayed as class liberation, was then imagined as gender liberation, and was finally discovered to be about race liberation. The last discovery was made by most authors for children well after the Second World War, although one or two, like J. R. R. Tolkien and Frank Richards, straddled the period in that perception. In accordance with Wilde, in 'The Critic as Artist', the best criticism on the matter was made in the fiction of the better writers: Richmal Crompton in what became self-criticism, Joan Lingard in what included autobiographical criticism, J. K. Rowling in what rose to theological criticism. Our authors were above all not reducible to simple formulae. The war had its ebb and flow, its ideological cross-currents, its alliances and estrangements, its arrivals and departures. For many writers for children, it began with the unwelcome discovery that they disliked Neville Chamberlain, and it ended with the even less welcome discovery that they did not dislike Clement Attlee. Many of them may have been very annoyed both at liking and at disliking Winston Churchill. The Bolshevik of yesterday is the elegist for Munich. The feminist of today silently blackballs tomorrow's female candidates. The white racial xenophobe of next year prefers black barbarism to white civilisation.

In all of these things, the little we know is dwarfed by the much we do not even perceive. Such questions were hard enough while people were open in expression of bigotry; now that they have been forced into hypocrisy, the historian must work harder. And there was plenty to lie about during the Second World War, at all times.

We may begin with Gender, although initially from an unusual angle. Bestiality has made few literary friends for itself (apart from André Gide). It is much more relevant to children in early puberty than people care to acknowledge: certainly, many boys in Europe and America – and probably across the world in general – obtained some of their initial sexual experience from close encounters with animals. Television, sex-talk and the erosion of individual isolation have probably cut down the relative incidence of bestiality in early male puberty; the speculation may offer some comfort to latter-day puritans (but not too much: the Bible belt would also have been the bestiality belt, and its constituents would certainly have overlapped). Sex-awareness from the study of animal behaviour left the rural child much more sophisticated than its urban counterpart in point of knowledge before personal experiment. Children read many stories of animals, gaining valuable zoological detail from the informed narratives of Henry Williamson, for one, on salmon and otter. But, in actual gender relationship, the classic romance for twentieth-century British children was provided by a farmer, Beatrix Potter, in *The Tale of Pigling Bland* (1913). Naturally, it avoids naturalism; it is, in fact, a thriller, and one of the best ever written, recognising that love is the best pivot of adventure and not a mere accessory, cheapened into sex-chatter, Bond-style. So far from concluding in porcine copulation, Pigling Bland and his rescued beloved, Pigwig, have their last sentence in verse. It may be allowed transposition into love-ballad. But its theme is the rescue of pigs from pork-butchery, and it is their mutual love that ennobles him and saves her. Potter's most successful contemporaries (notably Kenneth Grahame) and successors (notably Alison Uttley) had a comparable though not similar charm, but their more humanised animals depend very little upon gender relationships within their own species. (Otters procreate in both.) The Uncle Remus stories, whether as redacted by Joel Chandler Harris directly across the racial dividing-line in Georgia or as reworked by Enid Blyton, occasionally allowed for marital status for Brer Bear or some other less central character, but otherwise Blyton seems to have made little use of birds and bees doing it.

But it is Blyton who poses the most curious phenomenon in gender relationships. Child love of individual animals – or for that matter toys, or even imaginary fairies or other non-existent companions – can act as a substitute for, or stepping-stone to, emotional involvement with another child, especially in the early teens. The most extreme case in Blyton's fiction is that of George's dog Timmy, whose anthropomorphic status is asserted by his being the Fifth of the Five. Significantly, Julian assumes before meeting him that Timmy violates a possible class taboo:[1]

'I say, George – what about a bathe?'

'I must go and get Timothy first', said George. She got up.

'Who's Timothy?' said Dick.

'Can you keep a secret?' asked George. 'Nobody must know at home.'

'Well, go on, what's the secret?' asked Julian. 'You can tell us. We're not sneaks.'

'Timothy is my very greatest friend', said George. 'I couldn't do without him. But Mother and Father don't like him, so I have to keep him in secret. I'll go and fetch him.'

She ran off up the cliff path. The others watched her go. They thought she was the queerest girl they had ever known.

'Who in the world can Timothy be?' wondered Julian. 'Some fisher-boy, I suppose, that George's parents don't approve of.'

Present-day comment might raise its coarse eyebrows over George being suspected of having 'to keep' a fisher-boy 'in secret', but at various times several standard child heroes hide secret protégés or protégées: William does, and so do a group of Chalet School girls. Blyton's Find-Outers keep Fatty's Buster within a more formal canine status by adding 'and Dog' to their chosen self-baptism. Buster, intentionally or otherwise, does his bit by digging up the occasional clue, and he probably began as a satire on Sexton Blake's blood-hound. Buster, like Kiki the parrot, plays the pivotal role in getting the children acquainted: it is in fact a reasonable convention in several Blyton series that the animal creates friendships among mutually suspicious or hostile children. But Blyton drew a conscious distinction between animals on the human frontier such as (in their different ways) Buster and Timmy, and animals based on actual models, notably the parrot Kiki, and the chaos-making dog Loony in *The Rockingdown Mystery* (1949) and sequels. Loony is well ob-served, and highly credible, and hence shows the contrast between his highly real self and the somewhat contrived Timmy and Buster. Kiki's gender is of some importance: from time to time she flirts with Jack, or is jealous of his attention going elsewhere, or responds sexily to his ruffling of her feathers. But his enthusiasm for birds is the mainspring of their relationship, leading to his tutor's conclusion:[2]

> 'If I grew feathers, he would probably do everything I told him', thought Mr Roy. 'I never knew anyone so mad on birds before. I believe he knows the eggs of every bird in the world. He's got good brains, but he won't use them for anything that he's not really interested in.'

(The brief glimpse of the teacher's mind gives a hint about Blyton in her teaching days.)

The most startling exhibition of animals in the gender context occurs in *Hurrah for the Circus!*, published just after the war's outbreak. The human side of the story is triangular, and is itself much more gender-conscious than Blyton would later permit herself. Jimmy and Lotta are unrelated but friendly children attached to Mr Galliano's Circus. They are simply good companions until Jimmy makes friends with the boy attendant on the tigers, Fric, and Lotta grows jealous, not realising that neither Fric nor Jimmy like one another but that Jimmy must cultivate Fric to gain access to the tigers. What follows is partly cat-conversation (pioneered by R. M. Ballantyne in *The Coral Island*). But there is more to it:

The two tigers in the first cage sniffed and growled a little. Then Queenie, one of the two tigers, lifted her head high and sniffed harder. Yes, this was the boy who so often came outside the cage and talked to her in that lovely, gentle voice. This boy had no whip, no iron bar. This boy had a voice that was gentle like the leaves, not fierce and harsh and frightening.

Jimmy stood inside the tigers' cage, his heart thumping against his side. He was not afraid. Jimmy had never in his life been afraid of any animal, and he never would be. But he was excited, and he felt sure that the tigers would hear his heart thumping and wonder what it was. He put his hand over his heart to hide the thumping.

Queenie began to purr. She left her corner and silently slunk over to Jimmy. She put her great head down beside his right arm. Jimmy spoke to her in his special animal-voice, strong, and low, and gentle.

'Old Queenie', he said. 'Old Queenie, you beauty. You great, green-eyed, graceful tiger. You love me, don't you? And I love you. I love your grand head and your slanting eyes, your fine whiskers and your slinky body.'

Ultimately, Jimmy has to pay court to Queenie and Ruby in front of a number of circus-folk when a monkey is trapped in the tigers' cage:[3]

Jimmy still stood at the back of the tigers' cage. He did not even stretch out his hand, but his gentle voice went on and on, talking to the two tigers whilst they watched him.

'Don't you want your head to be rubbed, Queenie? Don't you want your ears stroked, Ruby? Then come to me.'

All the other tigers in the farther cages had stopped pacing round and round as soon as they heard Queenie purring. Basuka, hearing Jimmy's voice, began to purr too. All the tigers gradually became quieter. And still Jimmy's low voice went on and on and on. It seemed to Lotta that it had some sort of magic in it. Every one had to listen. Every one seemed to feel that they too wanted to go to Jimmy and be stroked. It was very strange.

W. W. Robson noted of Arthur Conan Doyle's 'The Brazilian Cat': 'the horrific creature is markedly feminine, contributing a strange erotic undercurrent'.[4] Blyton by nature and by necessity labours it, and the great feline menace is present only in potential, but she seems to have realised a comparable implication. She wrote only one other book about Jimmy (the very Italian Mr Galliano was probably dropped after 1942 as a wartime consideration, most likely on the advice of Kenneth Waters, her new husband). She would endow *The Island of Adventure*'s Philip Mannering with some of Jimmy's animal magnetism, expressed less verbally. It was founded on the rule of never showing fear to an animal, but Blyton insisted on love as no less vital than the absence of fear. She was also a pioneer in distinguishing between circus and non-circus animals. Jimmy refuses a place as a tiger-boy on the grounds that tigers 'are not the right kind of animals for tricks. They don't enjoy them. I only like teaching animals that love to learn.' And he is hostile to a money-making motive – performance has to be vocational, for man and beast alike. His love for the tigers is love for love's sake.

Philip in *The Island of Adventure* is merely animal-centred as a foil to the ornithologist Jack, but its spy-hunting sequel, *The Castle of Adventure*, introduces a startling variation. A little 'gypsy' girl follows the group, fascinated initially by Kiki (reasonably enough) and then by Philip. She is necessary to get them into the mysterious castle, and later in finding a way out of it. There is clearly social condescension here, and Tassie does not gain the deference for her undoubted woodlore and folk-wisdom that gypsies receive in Saville's tales. But the most alarming point is her being 'more like a very intelligent animal than a little girl' only partly domesticable (she is persuaded to have a bath, and is pleased by the gift of shoes but wears them around her neck).[5] Blyton in her innocence would not have seen the predatory sexual implications of such powers of fascination; in fact, they have some common ground with Bond's seduction of Honeychile Ryder in Ian Fleming's *Dr No*, if less embarrassingly childish. Propriety prevented the removal of Tassie's (and, later, Jack's) clothes for under-earth burrowing after Philip's pet fox-cub to get in and out of the castle, although it would have been necessary. Whatever the class, and even race, elements here, Blyton's sexual detail is advanced no farther than the tiger-cage. Waters or someone else may have advised Blyton that she was on what could prove a volcano slope; for the future, Philip's pets are non-human, including a slow-worm, a mountain-kid, a lizard and two puffins (most of them female). They are all abominated by his sister Dinah, who enjoys a condition of perpetual bickering with him. Blyton as 'governess' in *Sunny Stories* might deplore sibling hostility, but as adventure-novelist she took it to be a natural condition. It is not homicidal ('Dinah was scared. She had certainly meant to give Philip a hard blow – but she hadn't meant him to disappear off the face of the earth. She gave a yell. "Philip! Are you hiding? Come out, idiot!'' '). But Blyton does manage to convey Philip's chemistry for repulsion as well as attraction, especially to German spies:[6]

'Now – you tell us everything!' said Scar-Neck, and his voice was suddenly very ugly and threatening.

Philip said nothing, but stared defiantly at the man. Scar-Neck lost his temper, raised his fist, and gave Philip such a blow on the side of the head that the boy fell off his chair. He picked himself up.

. . . Philip's left ear glow[ed] bright scarlet, and beg[a]n to swell.

'Now will you talk?' said Scar-Neck, his voice growing thick with rage. The others looked on, saying nothing.

Still Philip said nothing. . . . Then . . . the man took out a revolver and laid it on the table beside him.

'We have ways of making sulky boys talk', he said, and his eyes gleamed with rage.

Philip didn't like the look of the shining weapon. He blinked a little, and then stared at Scar-Neck again. But still he said nothing.

He is rescued when Scar-Neck is about to try conclusions with a rope. It is another German in a later adventure who answers his 'insolent' conduct by conscripting him for lethal experiment.

The general role of animals in the gender context is asserted, consciously or otherwise, by the innumerable pony books of the time, and since. Mary Treadgold specifically asserts the pony fixation of Caroline in We Couldn't Leave Dinah to be a proof of immaturity, in this instance a wish to escape a world dissolving into war, in most stories to postpone acknowledgement of sex. The same imagery touches Saville's Mystery at Witchend. The isolation of the Long Mynd has prevented the pony-riding Petronella ('Peter') Sterling from knowing other children, and Saville moves delicately through her initial encounters with the Mortons. Initially, albeit briefly, she falls foul of the twins by unintentional patronising at the expense of the nine-year-old Dickie's masculinity while rescuing him from a bog:

'When I say heave', said the girl, 'we all pull, and the little boy must move his left foot just a step towards us. Now HEAVE!'

And they heaved to such purpose that there was a loud and succulent 'plop' as an indignant Richard shot out of the mud and landed on his face at his rescuers' feet.

'You do look comic', laughed the girl as Dickie scrambled up. 'If you could only see yourself! And I bet you smell like anything!'

But Richard couldn't see the joke. He didn't like being laughed at. He went very red, and although he wouldn't have admitted it for anything, he was very near tears and had to turn his back for a moment. But Mary knew how he was feeling. In a flash she was at his side and facing the stranger.

'Just you BE QUIET', she raged. 'You'd look funny, too, if you'd fallen in there. P'raps you will some day. And he doesn't smell . . . and if he did just a bit . . . well, we like it. And if you don't like it I'll jump in, too, and then we'll *both* smell . . .'

Peter extricates herself from this as rapidly as she gets Dickie out of the bog, but when thrown together with David alone she proves as sensitive. It begins well enough by her trying him out on the pony:[7]

once on he felt strangely insecure – Peter looked as if she were part of the horse, but he felt as if he didn't belong to anything, particularly when Sally began to move. Peter was saying something about toes up and knees in, and showing him how to hold the reins in a special way, and everything seemed to be happening at once.

'Don't look so unhappy', she laughed at him. 'And don't be so stiff and uncomfortable', and she led Sally into a trot. This was terrible! He was bouncing up and down in a maddening, uncontrolled, and rather painful manner. But somehow he stuck on and after a little while began to have some conception of what was expected of him, and when his mistress [sic] told him that he had had enough for his first lesson he was almost sorry to dismount.

'Well done, David! That wasn't too bad for a start. I'll soon make a horseman out of you. Do you know that riding is the most wonderful thing in the world? You can't imagine what it's like to fly along the top of the mountain even on little Sally.'

The Amazon initiation may have had less challenging antecedents, such as Biggles's comparable lesson for Ginger in an escape from the Nazi oasis in *Biggles Sweeps the Desert*:

Said Biggles in a curious voice: 'Ginger, have you ever ridden on a camel?'

'Come to think of it, I don't think I have' answered Ginger. 'Why?'

'Because', returned Biggles, 'I'm afraid you are going to have a perfectly beastly time.'

Ginger started. 'Doing what?'

'Having your first lesson.'

'What's wrong with a camel?'

'Quite a lot of things', murmured Biggles. 'To start with, he is usually as bad-tempered as he is ugly. His breath stinks like nothing on earth, and if he doesn't like you he may spit in your eye a slimy lump of green cud. Riding a camel is like sitting on a broomstick in a choppy sea.'

'Why are you telling me this?' inquired Ginger, in a startled voice.

'Because this seems to be where we go riding on a camel in the desert – or rather, on two camels.'

Curiously enough, Ginger only comes to enjoy the experience when they gallop: 'he could have laughed with relief. There was no more jolting. It was like skimming through the air in a glider.'[8] Both his and David's experiences could be termed rides of passage, although Ginger has by now had many varieties of these. But where Johns's intentions are comic (other than being statutorily pacemaking and patriotic), Saville has work to do in gender perception. David is taken away after lunch by Peter's father to explain the work of the reservoir. The story requires this, as the Nazis will later destroy it, and the Second World War child reader has to learn, however painlessly, how dangerous the threat to Britain's water-supply could prove to be. But it is made the occasion for a flare-up of jealousy from Peter. If her pony has reinforced her superiority, her father (hitherto very much the only man in her life) leaves her vulnerable to his unanticipated bonding with his own gender. David's masculinity and Mr Sterling's femininity exacerbate the situation ('Mr Sterling . . . would not permit Peter to put the crockery away. He had a special place for everything, and did not trust even his daughter to deputise for him').

All of this cleverly reworks the conventions: girl mastery of environment, boy ineptitude as cavalier, male rule in the kitchen, but Saville acknowledges that in an adventure story cross-gender mutual discovery best expresses itself in athletic contest: the Atalanta pattern. Blyton initially projected something of the same in George's superiority as seafarer over Julian and Dick; but the Five, being cousins (well, four of them anyway), do not prefigure future sexual union, and Blyton, perhaps having been a forceful tomboy as a child, restricts her meagre hints of future love (if any) for charismatic boy and feminine little girl (Fatty and Bets, Philip and Lucy-

Ann). Saville's use of the Atalanta theme is to reverse it: in the original, the runner Atalanta is cheated of her victory and thus forced to accept a husband, while in *Mystery at Witchend* the converse is true. When David has been released from service as Mr Sterling's reservoir dog, he finds that Peter, like himself, has changed into swimming costume but is 'in a fury':

> She jumped in surprise and then would have slipped into the water if he hadn't grabbed her arm. She wriggled fiercely and turned on him in a fury. 'Let me go, you beast.'
>
> But the imperturbable David was also annoyed so he held on. 'Don't be a silly ass, Peter', he said. 'What's it all about?'
>
> She actually gulped and there were tears in her eyes as she said in a shaky voice, 'Fancy asking *me* what it's all about! There's nothing about! I can swim here if I want to, I suppose. I thought I was going swimming with you, but I made a mistake. You'd rather go messing about with old sluices and wheels and things. You'd better go and find Daddy and he'll lend you the key and you can spend the rest of the day there. . . . I only hope the others come soon . . .' and she wriggled free and slipped into the water.
>
> Without quite realizing it, David did the right thing. He stood up, breathed deep, and dived – down, down into the clear green depths. He opened his eyes and looked up through the water. Just ahead and above him he could see Peter swimming away. He kicked hard and came up to the surface. He shook the water out of his hair and puffed. 'Oh, Peter', he said, 'this is grand. That's the best dive I've ever had. What a wonderful place this is. Let's race to the other end.'
>
> She looked at him over her shoulder, grinned sheepishly, and said, 'Right. Go!'
>
> Peter swam very well indeed, but David was better. He had been well taught and he really loved the water, but he did the second wise thing he'd done in three minutes. He let Peter win.

This is very much the junior version of adult fictions valorising love-drama while ominously conscious of its being but an interval in the national struggle for survival. Terence Rattigan's RAF play *Flare Path*, running in London for eighteen months from 13 August 1942, set the contours ably. Johns so far varied the normal austerity of his Biggles stories by having Ginger develop a love-interest in *Biggles 'Fails to Return'*, but it naturally is subordinated (and subsequently eliminated) by wartime duties. Children in the Second World War heard or watched the first stirrings of young love for David and Peter, while urgently conscious that the previous instalment or chapter had closed on the twins, surrounded by probable German spies and themselves isolated on a mist-bound mountain. Within a few paragraphs, David and Peter are secretly observing the mysterious Mrs Thurston photographing the reservoir. Within a few chapters, they are clinging together to save their lives from the flood following the blowing-up of the reservoir by the spy who then hijacks Peter's pony Sally. The fate of pony, reservoir, landscape and self-esteem of her father constitute a rite of passage for Peter of a far more shattering kind than the petulance of young adult tiffs, which in retrospect have become a lost peace.

This is to contextualise the war origins of the Lone Pine series, of which Victor Watson, here writing as witness, observed:[9]

> There is in Saville's work a strong hint of sexuality that in the 1940s and 50s was not to be found in any other fiction. To a generation of boys attending for the most part single-sex schools (I cannot speak for the girl readers), Saville's novels were highly gendered. They communicated a strong sense of 'girlhood' rather than girlishness, and at the same time managed somehow to suggest that girls were both different and interesting, and that companionship with them was exciting and full of possibilities. . . . Saville's suggestion that sexuality and friendship might be closely allied was a responsible one – and this was as far as any writer could go.

It remains, for all of its high quality, a primarily though not exclusively male perspective. Without direct authorial intrusiveness, it is not hard to see David's offstage Daddy giving 'old chap' an approving nod. Johns makes us question Victor Watson's claim of uniqueness, and perhaps here as elsewhere brings us closer to a female view. When Ginger determines to rescue his beloved Jeanette's imprisoned brother:[10]

> Ginger turned to Jeanette and took her hands. '*Au revoir*, Jeanette', he said softly.
>   'You will come back, monsieur?' she whispered.
>   'Not all the Axis armies shall keep me from you', swore Ginger, and moved by an impulse he kissed her on the forehead.
>   Jeanette broke away and ran into the house.

Ginger turned to her mother. 'Have I done wrong?' he asked in a hurt voice.

Madame smiled a knowing smile. 'I ran away from my husband just so', she answered. 'Women are like that', she added vaguely. 'I'll take care of her. Go with God, monsieur. We shall pray for you.'

Ginger raised his beret. 'Thank you, madame. *Au revoir*.'

He turned to the donkey, who was watching these proceedings with big brown eyes. 'Come on, Lucille', he said. 'Let's go.'

Holding the reins, followed by Lucille, he set off down the narrow street.

Saville was inaugurating a relationship to be shaped over the next near-forty years; Johns would terminate this one after the book had ended. Ginger was too useful a reader-link to be sacrificed. But he was never the same man afterwards, almost as though he never forgave his author for the unending conscription.

Boy–girl romance, of a vastly different standard from Saville and Johns, saturated the *Girl's Crystal* in the 1940s through the pens of 'Hazel Armitage', 'Heather Granger', 'Anne Gilmore' and other pseudonyms of John Wheway, as well as of other 'ladies' of more uncertain provenance but similar gender. What they lacked in subtlety they sought to compensate by firm identification with female leadership or at least resource. 'Daphne Grayson' (Cecil Graveley) kept the male and female 'Merrymakers' (whether in Brazil, on board school-ship, or elsewhere) under the command of Sally Warner, whose nomenclatural affinities with Harry Wharton were no accident: apart from the gender change, the whole idea had come from the series built by Richards (as Owen Conquest) around Jack Drake in the school-ship *Benbow* for the *Greyfriars Herald* in 1919–21, and reprinted with little amendment in the *Gem*, 1938–9. Wheway and other scribes assigned to Cliff House stories by 'Hilda Richards', after their removal from Frank Richards himself in 1919, followed his mixture of infusion of schoolboys into schoolgirls' stories; but Frank Richards had kept what he saw as the true Cliff House School under frequent call in the Greyfriars saga. Here he maintained for over thirty years the principle of female superiority in the person of Marjorie Hazeldene. She began as the victim of an obscure gypsy robbery, but quickly blossomed into the object of many characters' affection, ardent or Platonic as the case might be. Her devotees are headed by Bob Cherry, to whose Orlando she has the courage, leadership and independence of Rosalind, the altruism and gentleness of Celia. Her friend Clara Trevlyn has more of Rosalind's banter and boyishness, although like Rosalind she is also prone to swoon in a crisis. Marjorie is consistently recognised as superior to all males in intelligence, good nature and common sense, and is formally treated as such by Bob's father Major Cherry, her own grandfather General Hazeldene, Mr Quelch, Dr Locke, Harry Wharton and of course Bob himself. Her wretched, self-obsessed male chauvinist brother is rescued time and again because of the respect in which she is held even by nuts as hard as Herbert Vernon-Smith, who knows her to dislike him and who yet will do her good turns whose origin she is never to know. Hazel himself is the only character immune to her charms, despises her good nature, prates about female stupidity, and runs whining to her whenever he is in difficulties: theirs is in fact an Ibsen relationship, save that Marjorie never slams the door on him.

Richards firmly continued his feminist saga in her honour when writing his post-war books. Indeed, she facilitated the economies thrust on him. She talks Harry Wharton out of his self-destructive sulks and feuds against his friends in *Bunter Does His Best* (1954), where previous performances of that kind lacking her aid took him ten and twelve issues of the *Magnet* (1924–5, 1932). Richards's supplanters and imitators in schoolgirl fiction had a credible model: Marjorie succeeds in the very difficult feat of being wise, good, amusing and likeable. Richards might derisively answer Orwell's 'Sex is completely taboo' with hilarious remarks about people desirous of raising sex questions with schoolchildren being sufferers 'from disordered digestions', to climax on 'If Mr Orwell supposes that the average Sixth-form boy cuddles a parlourmaid as often as he handles a cricket-bat, Mr Orwell is in error'. But he knew his own business much more profoundly than he would cheapen himself by admitting in his own defence. He provided brief but besotted entanglements for Wingate, Captain of Greyfriars, and Darrell, second prefect at St Jim's, with admirable actresses somewhat older than themselves. (Crompton landed William in one such adoration across the footlights, handling the age difference much more acidly.) 'Kissing, for instance, would be regarded as "soppy" ', said Orwell; in fact, both the word and the attitude are truer of William. Richards deals with it in a story when Bob Cherry has just been rescued from a hideous death in the desert and is brought back to Marjorie and Clara at their oasis:[11]

Slowly the effect of his terrible experience was wearing off – slowly he was putting behind him the remembrance of his wild

Mazeppa-ride in the scorching desert. His rugged face lighted up as Marjorie ran to meet him.

. . . Marjorie pressed Bob's rough hand softly, and almost kissed him in her joy at seeing him alive and well. Miss Clara quite kissed him, on both cheeks, turning Bob's sunburned face crimson.

'It's ripping to see you again, old bean', said Miss Clara. 'Just topping, old bean, what?'

Bob chuckled.

What Richards is saying is that Bob will receive a kiss from Marjorie one day, and it will be the sweeter for awaiting its hour. The tomboyish Clara is faster with her kisses, but they mean much less. The reader assumes that Bob is slightly more in love with Marjorie than she with him, but she has a very good friendship with him, and will probably accept a proposal from him at the appropriate time if only because she would not want to disappoint him. He will be a devoted, lovable and limited husband; she will be a very wise wife. Richards showed himself an economist in the tradition of Jane Austen when it came to kisses. His citation of Byron's *Mazeppa* assumed potential *Magnet* audience interest in romantic poetry, to be prompted by the allusion if not already present. Among other forms of instruction, it has much to say of the language of love in sign and silence:

> Who listens once will listen twice;
> Her heart, be sure, is not of ice . . .

Mazeppa was in fact bound naked to a spirited horse by an indignant husband, while Bob Cherry's comparable pilgrimage on a racing camel was clothed, although supine rather than prone. The sheik thus ordaining his death sought revenge on his father for political rather than erotic differences, although at an earlier stage he had buried Marjorie and Clara up to their necks in sand with a view to luncheon arrangements for hyenas. Marjorie met the danger with her customary quiet courage, more resolutely than Clara. She was in any case of considerable athletic prowess, at one point riding a bicycle a considerable distance with no obvious exhaustion from Billy Bunter's passenger status in the front basket. Richards occasionally returned to the contrast between Bob's great hand and her diminutive one, as they approached one another; but they would have been appropriate partners in muscular development.

Marjorie Hazeldene certainly did not resemble the swashbuckling hockey-knocker or intrepid explorer with trusty elephant-gun to whom Wodehouse occasionally linked a shrinking but enraptured male. But she – and Worrals after her – are in the tradition of John Buchan's diminutive but formidable ladies, headed by Mary, the future Lady Hannay, who turns out to be Richard Hannay's superior secret-service officer in *Mr Standfast*. She is duly domesticated after the First World War, but staggers her husband by taking ruthless charge of his post-war mission at the climax of *The Three Hostages*. Unlike Worrals, she does not thrive on taking men down several pegs in conversation; she is content to do it in action. But in any case her post-war life is laid out on opulent landed social lines. The starving ex-soldier of the inter-war years was male; Johns described the ex-soldier after 1945, female. The *Girls' Crystal* heroines were often moneyed, job-fulfilled or lucky. Worrals herself has advantageous family connections, and hence can afford to wear her feminism with force: she thinks of starting an airline in Australia, which is hardly a dream on the breadline. But Johns frankly begins her first post-war novel, *Worrals in the Wilds*, by affirming her representative situation:

> As Worrals put it, visibility, as far as the immediate future was concerned, was zero. In short, they were in much the same position as a million other girls, when peace had cut short their military careers – the only careers they had ever known – leaving them standing on the threshold of an unknown world called civil life.

Biggles promptly gets a job in the police (admittedly at a far lower rank than Raymond would offer him in his years as an inter-war adventurer). Worrals in her first post-war adventure finds herself a fugitive from the police (' "He was sore. No man likes being fooled by a girl." "Why a girl, in particular?" demanded Worrals hotly. "Shardwell fooled him – I suppose he didn't mind being fooled by a man?" '). The two books were published in 1947 within three months of one another (August (for *Sergeant Bigglesworth, C.I.D.*) and November); the contrast is unavoidable. Within a year, Johns was digging deeper into the fate of the post-war unemployed air-woman. Janet Marlow ('the girl who got the George Cross for keeping the station 'phones going that night at Hendon when we were blitzed') has emigrated to Australia, where she tells Worrals she has been 'a bit browned-off lately':[12] "You needn't tell us", answered Worrals. "You're not browned off. You're half-starved, my lady – that's what's wrong with you. Forgive my being blunt, but that happens to be my unfortunate nature . . ." '.

Blyton, of all people, actually anticipated that problem in her well-researched *The Christmas Book* (1944), where it is discussed by Santa Claus (who explains he is a saint – Nicholas 'Not that I feel like one, really. I don't believe saints do, you know'). He retells the old story of how he saved three girls from prostitution by secretly throwing three purses of money to them, whence Christmas gifts in later times. Blyton did not, of course, use the word 'prostitution' (which her average reader would not have known, whether or not it knew the meaning of 'slut', 'trollop' or 'whore'). But one wonders whether the book's first readers in 1944 would have accepted, or been intended to accept, Santa Claus's assumption that comparable conditions did not exist today:[13]

> The three girls used to talk of what they would do when they were married. Their father was so poor that they had few clothes, not enough to eat, and very few good times. It would be nice to marry, and have a home of their own, and husbands who could give them what they wanted. . . .
>
> But, in those days, nobody wanted to marry girls without any money. Only those girls whose fathers could give them plenty of money were likely to make good marriages. . . .
>
> Their father grew so poor that he thought he would have to sell his daughters. The girls cried bitterly when they heard this. What a disgrace to be sold. What a miserable life they had to look forward to. . . .
>
> Their father was overjoyed when he saw so much money. 'Now I shall not have to sell you', he said. 'You can marry good men, and lead happy lives of your own.'

We cannot judge how far this is tongue-in-cheek (although Blyton humanised Santa Claus better than most have done; as with Lewis's Aslan later, it is the youngest girl who establishes the strongest links with him). Blyton grew up in days when poor Irish children were being sold by their own parents into slavery for the terms of their early adolescence, and her Irish links may have told her of it. Certainly, she wrote strongly against female careers as destructive of family life, whether or not she realised that in some ways her own could be. But she was writing at the point when girls were having to choose between what often proved two forms of servitude: dependence on husbands or on jobs, either of them possibly productive of severe disillusion.

Marriage to a husband of genuine chivalry was another problem:

his chivalry was a pleasant way to dispose of rivalry. He might genuinely prefer the smaller income to avoid the imputation of inability to provide for his wife. (Equally, he might be ready to augment his own finances by putting her to work.) Worrals conspicuously refuses the hand of the boyfriend whom she had enjoyed keeping in his subordinate place throughout the war. Initially, she simply puts him aside with a view to possible later consideration when he decides to go to remoter parts of South Africa:

> Would Worrals like to come along – as Mrs Bill Ashton, of course?
> Worrals said quite definitely that she would not. The war was only just over, and she wanted to get her breath before rushing half-way round the world, with or without a husband. . . . She was very fond of Bill, and all that, but she wasn't quite crazy – and after all, they still had the best part of their lives in front of them.

But, after having rescued him from what amounts to imprisonment in a semi-permanent coma (reminiscent of what Gerda rescues Kay from in the fairy-story 'The Snow Queen'), Worrals rejects him firmly once more, this time on the grounds that it is best for him, which she knows better than he does:[14]

> 'You've got plenty to do without getting involved in housekeeping complications', she told Bill. 'One thing at a time is an old, but sound policy. . . . When you've got things going, and the tin shanty at Magube is replaced with accommodation slightly less primitive – well, maybe Frecks and I will waffle along and spend our holidays with you. But don't get lost again, because as a pastime, looking for a lost plane in Africa is altogether too strenuous for my delicate constitution.'

This story, *Worrals in the Wilds*, ran in the *Girl's Own Paper* from November 1945, but its stable was beginning to lock its door against the Amazon strain of wartime years. Johns had his personal reasons for Worrals's stance, and he found more. His own marriage had been premature, and had thereby subsequently condemned the woman of his real but non-legal second marriage to a lifetime of false identity. Amy Johnson's marriage had been a disaster. Pauline Gower's, after the war, proved happy, but was quickly ended by death in childbirth in spring 1947.

The *Girl's Own Paper* ran the next Worrals story, *Worrals Down Under*, in 1946–7, but in 1948 it became *Heiress*, a would-be adult journal where Johns had no place (it folded in 1956). Meanwhile, Johns's own feminism was eroding, though for what seem different reasons. Firstly, there was Hanna Reitsch. Hitler preached the role of women in domestic life for the betterment of the Aryan race in its Teutonic epiphany, but he had spectacular exceptions at his court, the most illustrious being the film-maker Leni Riefenstahl and the test-pilot Hanna Reitsch. While nominally a civilian, Reitsch won from Hitler the Iron Cross Second Class in 1941 (for perfecting a cable-cutter to enable the Nazis to bomb London with less danger from barrage balloons) and from Goering a special Luftwaffe Gold Medal. After her recovery from a crash when testing a new rocket-plane, Hitler upped her Iron Cross to a First Class, in February 1944. This had its uses to advocates of women's place in air power, like Johns, but its demonic implications revived fairy-story horrors of flying witch-queens, however subliminated. Fairy-stories are never far below the surface of an intelligent writer's imagination, anyway, especially one thinking of a child audience. Early in 1944, Johns finished *Worrals Goes East*, which introduced Nazi female pilots (as well as giving Worrals herself her first kill since her first book). As a writer for the *Girl's Own Paper*, Johns brooded over the implications of the airwoman's life, and in the early 1950s even introduced a surviving crypto-Nazi female test-pilot, based on Reitsch, who attempts to murder Biggles to avenge her brother (a wartime victim in air combat): the story has a mordant humour arising out of its Riefenstahl angle, as the confrontation is set up by an unscrupulous film-maker (male) to make a better film. The Nazi aviatrices in *Worrals Goes East* are Greta (found dead in her crashed plane before the story's action begins) and Hylda: the names encircle 'Hanna'. Hylda on acquaintance proves no female von Zoyton: she leaves an asp, of the variety fatal to Cleopatra, in Worrals's bed, and she later proposes to torture Frecks.

Worrals Goes East was written a year before the Allies reached Belsen and discovered to what its prisoners had been subjected by Irma Grese. But Johns in one of his retrospective confrontations with the concentration-camp murderers, resurrected Irma Grese (although referring to the real one's execution) under the name of Anna Shultz, presumably in error for 'Schulz' but with 'Anna' intentional enough. By this stage, Reitsch had had her alleged memoirs published in the London *News Chronicle* (28, 29 and 31 December 1945), during her fifteen-month imprisonment by the Americans, and had been denounced by Hugh Trevor-Roper in *The Last Days of Hitler* in the excellent schoolboy vituperation of that entertaining post-mortem.

('An ardent Nazi, she had long worshipped at the shrine of Adolf Hitler; in him, she says, she recognised the true quintessence of German honour, whatever that may mean.') Johns knew a great deal more about women than did Trevor-Roper, to judge by their publications, and he is unlikely to have been impressed by Trevor-Roper's confident diagnoses ('There is a somewhat incomplete type of woman whose personal affections are (as the psychologists say) sublimated into abstract terms. When such a woman loves or hates, the object of her love or hatred appears to her not as a human being, but as the visible embodiment of some abstract quality'). But Johns did know how to write a rattling good yarn – and so, when he was not talking nonsense about things he knew nothing about, did Trevor-Roper. The audience which had cut its teeth on Biggles in the early 1940s could go on without fear of disappointment to *The Last Days of Hitler*, paperbacked in the later 1940s: the publishers, Pan, were making quite a corner in Second World War material where claims of authenticity were firmly bannered to succeed the Johns fictions which had developed schoolboy appetites. In fact, the Pan prevalence may have accounted for the failure of Johns and other hardback-book writers for children to produce many retrospective adventures of Second World War, as they had for the First World War. (The comics continued to produce retrospectives, all the more as they subsided into tabloids, but these would have been less competitive with Trevor-Roper's market.) Johns is most unlikely to have missed Trevor-Roper's best-seller, and would have been greatly interested by its account of Field-Marshal Ritter von Greim (supposedly Reitsch's lover) being 'piloted' by Reitsch, who was then 'stuffed into the tail'[15] of the helicopter to accompany him to the Hitler bunker. When Johns got round to writing *Worrals in the Wastelands* (whose action is set in summer 1946), he used the principle of pilot love and excessive passengers by having his Grese figure, Shultz, escape in an aircraft through the love borne for her by its pilot. In fact, the rumour persisted that Reitsch had performed this service for Hitler, who seems to have won her love in one form or another. The extra passenger and the competition for Reitsch's affections reappear in the Shultz story when, on arrival at their destination in Canada, a stowaway emerges from the back of the Focke-Wulf (Reitsch's Bunker transport had also been a Focke-Wulf): this turns out to be Shultz's actual husband, Doctor Wolfe, whom she had had appointed medical officer at the Sternberg Internment Camp for women, where he and she had then carried out tortures and experiments. Shultz is not a pilot, and the Nazi

Hauptmann Otto Rumey whom she fools and murders is handled with sympathy when his fate is known:

> 'I never thought the day would come when I would feel sorry for a Nazi, but I could weep for the wretched Rumey', said Frecks. 'If ever a man had a dirty deal from a woman, he certainly did.'
>
> 'Save your tears for the living', advised Worrals grimly. 'This game is only half played-out. I wouldn't like to think what Shultz would do to us, if we fell into her claws.'

The story itself may well be Johns's finest post-war performance (which puts it above some 100 titles). It is almost unique in his fiction for children in its sexual preoccupation. To that extent it was in keeping with the post-war direction for fiction for girls (though not for boys: William, closer than ever during the war to his long-term sweetheart, Joan, loses all interest in her from 1950). It recalls the work of Johns's master, Conan Doyle, in showing how detective adventure uncovers profound tragedy for which Holmes and Watson, or their successors, can do nothing save pick up the pieces. Johns's stories up to this point had excelled in comedy: it was often comedy of terrors, but comedy nonetheless. Perhaps *Biggles Flies North* (May 1939) alone had been a sombre note unrelieved. If so, it was echoed but surpassed here. The far northern Canadian terrain of both, the sense of wilderness savagery harmonising with human brutality, showed how well Johns had studied his Jack London, even his Robert Service, to which he would probably now have added his John Buchan of *Sick Heart River* (1941). Even the animals, normally productive of some of the funniest moments in the stories, are Johns's Canadian messengers of death, and that only. Worrals and Frecks make excellent companions for themselves and the reader, but even their mutual banter and the preliminary and otherwise attendant feminism are greatly muted. Where there are any light moments, they are bitter Maupassant mirth. At one point, Frecks finds herself invited to tea by Shultz and Wolfe, whom she has just met, and whom she must affect to treat as total strangers of whom she knows nothing; this ends with her necessarily frank statement that she is returning to her plane, but she must conceal its whereabouts from Wolfe, who wants to escort her to it:

> 'I insist', said Wolfe.
>
> 'Doctor Wolfe, I take that to be a challenge to my ability to take care of myself', declared Frecks, half jokingly but with a touch of asperity. 'The age of helpless damsels has passed.'
>
> Shultz laughed. Frecks winced, for it was not a pretty sound.

Feminism, satirically used, gets Frecks out of the trap this time, and thus its value is once again reaffirmed. But the larger meaning of Shultz's laughter is ominous. Shultz above all is the devastating proof that the age of helpless damsels has passed. The armed airwoman (for, though Shultz is no pilot, she knows how to make pilots subject to her will) has become a Frankenstein monster, an Icarus falling on her own kind. At the same time, she is ruthlessly independent. The story presumes three men in love with her, all of whom she is ready to marry or murder as it suits her: with quite imaginative irony, we have to recognise that the two dedicated Nazis Rumey and Hanstadt, still committed to the cause and bent upon reviving Nazism, are morally far superior to the two – Shultz and Wolfe – who have nothing but contempt for such surviving loyalty. We are even to assume that the murdered Rumey really was genuine in disbelieving stories about death-camps. And finally, his avenger Lowenhardt, who denounces Shultz and sets off her flight into the arms of the bear she had previously wounded, is movingly bonded to his dead Hauptmann. As he says when Worrals and Frecks ask what happened to Rumey's body:

'I bury it under many stones so that the bears and foxes do not eat it. He was my officer. We are together for a long time.'

And there is no question of Shultz's personal affections being 'subliminated into abstract terms'. She wants to enjoy the flesh of men by loving, and, when no longer useful or desirable, by killing. By now, the prospect of murder is clearly a pleasure for her contemplation and, where possible, realisation. It will not be sated by retirement to South America to listen to a crowd of has-beens tell one another how they are going to restore the Third Reich. She wants other worlds to gratify her, worlds where she can spin fresh webs and glut herself with their victims. And at the end, when the bear has settled accounts with her, and her murder of Rumey has been made known to his friend and rival, the Nazi U-boat Commander Hanstadt, we hear the final note of the enchantment still haunting the disillusion:[16] 'Worrals . . . turned to Hanstadt. "What are you going to do?" "Never mind me", answered Hanstadt in a dull voice.' Whatever about his audience, Johns had not forgotten that Nazism owed part of its origins to German romanticism including Goethe and the sorrows of young Werther. At least he would have known Thackeray's ribald version of it.

The last Worrals book was a miserable performance by contrast with this, and with the rest of the series. *Worrals Investigates* (1950) as a story fizzles out, apparently because of the failure of Johns's feminism which it records. It is in fact an anti-feminist mission, in which Worrals and Frecks discover a mad millionairess, aided by three brutal female lieutenants (all apparently English), who have declared a man-hating regime on a UK-owned South Sea Island unimaginatively called 'Outside', and have more or less enslaved a group of subordinate women, brown and white. In fairness to Johns, there is a good deal of indignation in the story about white exploitation of Polynesians in present and past, and the class exploitation among the whites is also underscored, credibly. The uneasy aspect is the incidental implications. The real villain is a woman doctor. Granted that Johns's anti-Nazi stories after the war frequently included experimentalist torturers with medical degrees, this still seems a little gratuitous. The main message of the story is given when one of the regime's fugitives explains the millionairess's origins and opinions, as a rich, spoiled brat rejected by the man she loved, whence she sought female rule. And when the issue is joined between Worrals and the mad queen, there is some nasty woman-against-woman hand-to-hand stuff, with Worrals avenging brutality against one of her black allies. It is good to see Johns and Worrals firmly enlisted in the cause of right against white, where Johns's track record in times past was sometimes questionable. But male authorship of female combat, even when as slight and fleeting as here, is somewhat nauseating, and in other hands is the stuff of which pornography is made (and, in the case of Ian Fleming's *From Russia with Love*, pornography's little brother James Bond).[17]

Johns's biographers are right to deny that the book throws Johns's feminist record into question. But its existence at the end of the Worrals saga suggests that the crusade had finished sourly. To answer, as they do, 'The reason why Johns dropped Worrals was because the demand for Biggles had become overwhelming' is to lose perspective:[18] Johns kept the 'Gimlet' series going until 1954, and they were clearly inferior to almost every 'Worrals' in audience and in quality. It may have been that *Worrals Investigates* was the product of gloomy months: *Biggles Gets His Men* and *Gimlet Bores In*, also products of 1950, have many sour notes. In those books, for the first time, the Cold War gripped Johns, and its frustrations and paranoias were not easy to handle. But it is hard to resist the conclusion that, after a hard struggle with post-war anti-feminist reaction and the old Adam within himself, Johns had succumbed to the times. Even in his Biggles short stories in these months, selfish and predatory (if highly accomplished) female crooks raise their elegant heads.

But Worrals had been given her contribution to his post-war collection *Comrades in Arms*, 'On the Home Front', where her introduction in a wartime setting showed her Johns's ideal, if unreal, revenge for her gender as well as for himself on the Higher Command:[19]

'You know why I've come down, sir?' said Worrals.

'Yes, you've come to talk to that girl who's got a bee in her bonnet.'

A little frown creased Worrals's forehead.

'I've been sent to interview Aircraftwoman Day', she replied a trifle stiffly. 'I'll form my own opinion about this alleged bee in a bonnet when I've heard what she has to say.'

The C.O. shrugged. 'You're not proposing to question the verdict of a coroner's jury, I imagine?' said he, drily.

'I most certainly shall, if I find grounds to warrant it', returned Worrals calmly.

'It is my opinion that this girl's friend, Doris Marchant, drowned herself, and apparently the coroner thought so too, since he returned a verdict of "found drowned"', replied the wing commander.

'I'll reserve my opinion until I've spoken to Aircraftwoman Day', answered Worrals evenly. 'I'm told she's here.'

'I'll have her brought in.' The C.O. touched a bell.

'I'd rather talk to her alone if you don't mind, sir', requested Worrals.

The wing commander smiled wearily. 'Going to turn me out of my own office, eh?'

'Not at all, sir – if you can find other accommmodation for us', said Worrals. 'I prefer to see the girl alone. She may speak with more confidence if there isn't a man present.'

And it was that increase in the confidence of woman's voice – and the resultant increase in truth and efficiency which it engendered – which made Worrals so necessary and so enjoyable. Johns showed feminism as not only essential but also entertaining. If he ultimately faltered, he had done outstanding service to the cause.

Woman's future depended on command, and may have depended on it much more once women were perceived in power, however limited that power. Women had commanded a great deal from unassailable vantage-points – those of Jane Austen's Lady Catherine de Bourgh or of Oscar Wilde's Lady Bracknell. It was when they competed for power-posts hitherto sacrosanct to the male (doctor, voter, lawyer) that matriarchies became called into question, and, by granting menial status in the name of job equality, men could regroup and fortify new power enclaves. Worrals claimed air power (including combat power) on levels never conceded in practice. Pauline Gower, commander in the Air Transport Auxiliary (and hence with flying responsibilities never conceded to the actual WAAF), similarly yearned for real command. One such expression of it was her 'Dogs of War' (*Girl's Own Paper*, vol. 63 (November 1941), published alongside the second instalment of *Worrals Carries On*. This takes the Johns girl-pilot-upstages-male-Higher-Command one stage further, by telling the story of a crack female counterspy through the somewhat bemused male eyes of a Squadron Leader. Gower's Roman Catholicism may have led her to read Irish books; at all events, the Dickensian-named Squadron Leader Winger may owe something to the Irish female writers Somerville and Ross, whose *Irish RM* resembles Winger as a likeable, ineffectual authority bearing witness to his own inadequacy. Winger becomes suspicious of Sadie Blunt, 'a true gipsy type' who rescues a pilot from a crashed plane after which the private papers he was carrying have disappeared. Ultimately, she proves to be Secret Service Agent 'F.4', who uses him to foil a plot to run rabid dogs into Britain and demoralise the population with a rabies scare. She rescues him, binds up his wounds, and lives up to her own name:[20]

> 'We have been after Bevis and his fellow Fifth-Columnists for some time now', said the girl, gently adjusting the makeshift bandage. 'I was given the job of getting to know him – you didn't make it particularly easy.'
>
> She looked at Winger humorously, and then continued: 'I found out, quite by accident, about those plans he had stolen . . . My particular job was to trail Bevis, but it was rather beastly when I found that my shot had killed him', she finished rather unsteadily.

Gower, like Johns (and like Conan Doyle in his feminist medical fiction), saw the supreme wisdom of insisting that the successful female aspirant for male power must have a sense of humour. It was vital to offset the inevitable frustration for the character, it could be guaranteed to rub salt in the wounds of the vanquished male, and it would delight the readers. The child thrill of seeing adults vanquished was redoubled by the victorious child (or anyway recent ex-child) being female. Modern feminist dislike of the word 'girl' misses the point here: the appeal of Worrals and of Sadie Blunt lay partly in their being girls as well as women, just as Biggles's Ginger, Gimlet's Cub, and so on, reached their audiences by being boys (Ginger seems to have been 'little more than a lad' for thirty-five years, and at the end of his career is credibly undertaking detective duty in drag as a girl princess).

Johns and Gower had realised that female authority was most likely to be achieved when it could plead security and secrecy. It also enabled Worrals and Sadie to kill their men, however much they might dislike it. After the war, their employment was at best free-lance, as a rule accidental. *Chatterbox*, for which Gower did post-war work, featured a long story in its *Annual* for 1948, 'The Gay Company' by Edgar Garrett. It has the standard device of suspect proving to be detective (Richards had made hilarious schoolroom drama of it in the 'Courtfield Cracksman' series), but here she is a woman, and so annoyed are the girls in the story by the boys' suspecting her that they keep the boys (tied up by the baddies) in bonds until the secret agent has clinched the case:[21]

> 'Everything is all right!' she declared brightly. Then she saw that the boys were still bound and her eyes widened. A smile flickered about her lips as Lydia repeated frankly the story John had told.
> 'Well, I can't say that I blame them suspecting me', she chuckled. 'Indeed, they ought to be congratulated on their vigilance! And now let's untie them to show there's no ill-feeling!'

After she has explained all, she politely repeats:

> 'I'm sorry you suspected me, but I must say you had every reason to!'
> 'Rot!' Peggy Ann declared stoutly. 'They should have taken us into their confidence. We would have *known* you weren't a crook!'

This is what the American matriarch Mammy Yokum in *Li'l Abner* would have called a 'double whammy'. 'The Mushroom', as the children called her, is 50, is chestnut-and-grey-haired (with bun), and likes 'to burst into deep-throated song'. Michael Innes (otherwise the English-literature scholar J. I. M. Stewart) introduced a comparable if much more artistic creation in *The Journeying Boy* (1949), a work *about* a schoolboy more than *for* one, but its wit and zest should have won most readers of 12 and beyond. Miss Margaret Liberty is introduced as an elderly lady reading a Secret Service novel:[22]

'And quite a lot of it takes place in a *train*.'

'I should have thought the Secret Service a bit out of date too.' The bearded man spoke in an appropriately rumbling voice. 'The sort of thing that is exciting in time of war.'

'But I assure you that it is always going on!' And the elderly lady nodded with surprising emphasis. 'I have been told so by persons who are *most* well-informed. Only this April I met an extremely interesting woman at Bournemouth who had good reason to believe that an intimate friend of her brother's was nothing less than a special agent of the Government! I confess that it is since that meeting that I have been inclined to read novels of this sort.'

As disguise, this is the best thing of its kind since Chesterton's *The Man Who Was Thursday*. (The bearded man is the most dangerous enemy agent.) But the incongruity sanitises it, and the age factor removes it from the competitive sphere. Miss Liberty makes but one appearance in the Innes canon, and presumably takes her place alongside the other incongruous but not innocuous spinsters who confuted their juniors under the auspices of Agatha Christie and Patricia Wentworth. Worrals and Sadie had no successors. There were even signs of Frecks, hitherto guardian of the duo's resistance to marriage, salivating at the end of *Worrals Investigates* at the proximity of 'a big sandy-whiskered Scot named Donald MacDougal . . . There's another white man, so don't get jealous. He's the super-cargo – but not a patch on Donald.' Admittedly, she was entitled to let herself go after pursuit by the extreme feminists: 'I had to swim out to the machine with the doctor taking pot-shots at me from the reef. A man-hater above and maneaters below'.[23] Within five years, Secret Service Woman was to be put in her place: in James Bond's sleeping-quarters.

The bitterness of *Worrals Investigates* may be fundamentally anti-lesbian, but if so feminism in general was its casualty no less than lesbianism. (Worrals and Frecks might no longer seem so innocent to their author.) Johns was in any case very cautious in lesbian implications, whereas few of his readers were left in much doubt as to the sex-life of Anna Shultz, of which torture formed an obvious part. Even her laughter while murdering has its sexual ring. Homo-sexual love in general was a Second World War casualty of chil-dren's fiction. Its disappearance would probably have happened without the war. It had flourished in Victorian fiction for children, incisively in girls' stories, often mawkishly in boys'. Louisa Alcott handled male love with strength and realism in *Little Men* (1871), where Dan's falsely taking the blame for the vulnerable Nat is likened to, and even chapter-titled, 'Damon and Pythias'; it co-exists confidently with Nat's love for Daisy, and with little Ted's love for Dan. The book was still widely read in mid-twentieth-century Britain: George Orwell loved it so much that his review of its film (*Time and Tide*, 10 May 1941) signed off savagely: 'In short, if you either haven't read *Little Men* or don't mind seeing the friends of your childhood murdered, this is a good film'.[24] Twain's *Huckleberry Finn* (1884) and Stevenson's *Kidnapped* (1886) (its first disciple) are masterpieces in that regard, both turning on love's triumph over mutual cultural antipathy. This included racial barriers in both books: Scots Lowland–Highland mutual distrust and hatred could easily rival American black–white. School stories naturally produced various versions of 'crush', whether reciprocated or abominated by the recipient, from Susan Coolidge's *What Katy Did at School* (1874) to Brent-Dyer's *The School at the Chalet* (1925). They carried their own ambiguity: an unwanted obsession, obviously rejected by the author, may mask a much deeper friendship. Respectable disdain for the pursuit of boys may be another safe haven for female mutual love. Katy and her friends form the Society for the Suppression of Unladylike Conduct, which proves an excellent arena for the uninhibited Rose Red to luxuriate in her affection for Katy and Clover.

Boys' school stories were less sure of themselves. Talbot Baines Reed captured junior-school idolisation of a rebel prefect in *Tom, Dick and Harry* (1894) but left it oddly uncertain as to whether the prefect is a treacherous, self-satisfied swine or whether the narrator deserves what he gets; possibly both. E. T. Raymond produced a saccharine concoction of coeval schoolboy romance in his best-seller *Tell England* (1922); since he subsequently stated that he had no realisation of the work's homoerotic saturation, it remains unclear what England was to be told. Alec Waugh's *The Loom of Youth* (1917) was all too clear as to what it was telling England, and hence from the 1920s boarding-school romance became much more circumscribed. His brother Evelyn, while writing of nominally more adult characters, also brought homosexuality well within witty literary fishnets. The result was that it was no longer possible for innocent observers or closet gays to let the love that dare not speak its name assume any alias it liked for the purpose. Possibly the last of the old heart-cries from the closet were Hugh Walpole's *Jeremy and Hamlet* (1923) short stories (a few of which were set at school) and the loosely structured novel that formed its less satisfactory sequel, *Jeremy at Crale* (1927), all of them reissued in omnibus with the first, *Jeremy*

(1919), at the beginning of the Second World War. Walpole managed the boy's home life better, and its place as the stories' beginning was an important exception to most school stories of the time, where home was essentially a minor tangent. But he addressed serious questions such as the strains of enforced guardianship when teachers thrust younger boys on older, and even the sexual excitement of public punishment of elder boys witnessed by younger.[25] The balance of quality within the stories (possibly unintentionally) revealed the parochial shallowness of the boarding-school by contrast with the rich, if faded, tapestry of the cathedral town. But the restricted reality of school fiction gave a hothouse character to what discussions of gender it could permit, especially under the direction of Richards, who knew perfectly well what he was doing. Orwell's assertion of sex as taboo in the Richards stories was frivolously knocked aside by Richards in his reply, but Richards was very careful to ignore Orwell's words after 'taboo': 'especially in the form in which it actually arises at public schools'.

The Gem and the Magnet differed markedly as to gender. The Gem had its charming romances – Figgins's love for Gussie's cousin Ethel, and Gussie's inability to realise the fact – but its schoolboys operated in groups of three or four, possibly by executive decision at its foundation. The closest it seems to have got to homosexual love was between the cracksman schoolboy Talbot and his redemptive force, Tom Merry: they weep at parting, and publicly declare mutual admiration in fine Victorian fashion. But Merry remains anchored between the much less attractive Manners and Lowther, the prig and the practical joker, and Talbot was given a private romance with another cracksman's daughter, now turned school nurse. Greyfriars began its saga on Harry Wharton's first steps away from spoiled brat when Frank Nugent and he save one another's lives. Richards explained after the Magnet had been terminated, in 1940, that Wharton had been based on a teenage friend who broke with him for some reason unstated by Richards; they were about 16. That dual memory, the close friendship, the bitter parting, gave Wharton's character a vitality throughout the Magnet's life: his moodiness, his capacity for taking offence, his arrogance, his contempt, his pride, his self-destructiveness are worked through the series alongside his better traits with infinite variations. But Nugent, whom Richards intended as a self-portrait, is much less memorable; his occasional breaks with Wharton are well managed, as are his feminine epiphanies (he makes a foray in drag for a joke in an early number, and is usually the heroine in school theatricals). When Wharton's life is

in danger or his fate unknown, Nugent's face will be the whitest; at
the close of the last full *Magnet* series on 11 May 1940, Wharton's
reappearance having been missing makes Nugent catch 'his chum
by the arm'. Nugent is, in fact, a male wife, more loving than
loved, content to support, repaid by adequate but not comparable
returns. (In 1912, Nugent's parents briefly separated.)

   Greyfriars has many other partnerships: for instance, the zealous
but not very bright athlete Hobson of the Shell, devoted to his long-
haired avant-garde musician friend Claude Hoskins, to avenge
whose wrongs he is ready to risk, apparently even to demand,
expulsion. There is a suggestion that the wayward dandy Hilton
of the Fifth, good-natured but easily corrupted by his repulsive friend
Steve Price, is gay: he is certainly effeminate in a way that Nugent
and Hoskins are not. On the other hand, Richards is quite ruthless in
depiction of mercenary relationships such as that of the assertive,
idiotic Coker of the Fifth, whose long-suffering friends Potter and
Green are purely interested in what loot they can get out of him; but
Coker will never allow himself to see their indifference to him save
for the briefest of periods. Friendships across wealth lines are
frequently matters of tortured integrity. When the scholarship-
holder Dick Penfold discovers that his father the local cobbler has
been ruined in a stock-exchange swindle, his bosom friend the Jew
Monty Newland has to pretend a coolness with him so that Penfold
will not realise that Newland has got *his* father to buy up the shares
and thus restore the lost Penfold fortunes. The greatest of all the
passionate school friendships, Vernon-Smith and Redwing, are the
sons of a millionaire and a sailor, respectively, and Redwing even
throws over a scholarship on hearing that it had been endowed by
Vernon-Smith's father. That connection began in 1918 with Vernon-
Smith saved from death in a doomed skiff by an unknown boy on a
cliff who risks his life to rescue him, and twenty years later he is still
saving him, one way or another. On the eve of war, Smithy is
imprisoned and a double substituted, and Redwing finds him,
alerted by the fact that he himself no longer feels the same kinship
to the boy in Greyfriars. The literary convention that a true wife
knows her husband in any disguise is inverted here: Redwing does
not at first realise that the double is not Smithy, but he does realise
he no longer loves him. And when he finds Smithy, and is imprisoned
with him, he is offered his freedom. Smithy's retort, before Redwing
can answer, strikes the note whose converse Orwell would make the
climax in *1984*:[26]

'What are you going to offer Redwing to let his pal down?' asked the Bounder bitterly. 'You are a fool, with all your cunning! You could offer him the whole world and it would make no difference.' Redwing laughed.

'You can bank on that, Smithy', he said. 'You may as well save your breath, Captain Vernon. If you unlocked that door now, I would not go without Smithy.'

If it be remarked that Orwell denied such friendship, he was speaking in sexual terms, whose existence in the story is purely inferential. Admittedly, the last Bounder story in the *Magnet*, finished on 23 March 1940, concludes with his reinstatement after expulsion, he having rescued Mr Quelch from imprisonment at the hands of a burglar whose appointment as Quelch's substitute has resulted in Smithy's disgrace:

'If I may stay, sir, I can turn in with Redwing!' said the Bounder meekly. 'Reddy will be glad to see me, sir!'
'Very well', said the Head.

And back to the dormitory he comes, a little more Bounderish:[27]

'Come back!' repeated Redwing.
'Just exactly that! Can you make room for a fellow in your bed, Reddy – too bad to root them out to make up a bed for me at this time of night – half-past one in the morning! It's all right, you old fathead – the Head knows I'm here – special permission to stay from the Big Beak –'

And so we leave him to his happy ending, in bed with Redwing. (The next series was a vacation one, featuring Bunter, Wibley, the Famous Five and a Nazi spy and murder plot, and thence after but one more item the *Magnet* was cut off.) We cannot say if Orwell ever saw that episode, although with controversy over his 'Boys' Weeklies' essay impending he may well have thought it sensible to keep in touch. Julia in *1984* betrays the fidelity inescapable for Redwing, and Winston Smith at his last gasp rats when Vernon-Smith never would. Richards had proclaimed the ideal in the *Magnets* that Orwell had seen. *1984* had to show such an ideal among the last remnants of humanity. It is certainly Vernon-Smith's redemption.

If Redwing is the Bounder's redeemer, the Jack Drake series begun the year after Redwing's debut gives Rodney a similar role saving

Drake, and their names seem akin to that role. The tradition of homosexual affection inducing reform, or its converse, was a staple of Victorian school stories: Reed uses it in *The Adventures of a Three-Guinea Watch* (1881) (and does *not* use it in *Tom, Dick and Harry*). On the whole, it tended to avoid the fagging system, although Meredith Fletcher cleverly introduced mutual jealousy of fags over favourite status among fagmasters in her *Iredale Minor* (1910). But one obvious result from the fag system was the great detectives' adoption of teenage boys, originally from the criminal or street-Arab worlds, later from public-school boys migrating in or out of the system. Ferrers Locke picked up Drake from Greyfriars; Nelson Lee took Nipper to St Frank's. Neither survived the Amalgamated Press massacres of 1940. Sexton Blake continued in one format or another until around 1970 with his Tinker grown to vigorously heterosexual young manhood. A comic or two kept its house 'tec supplied with reader-identification boy sidekick to the early 1950s: Dixon Hawke with his Tommy Burke in the *Adventure*, Colwyn Dane with his Slick Chester in the *Champion*, as well as their Nemesis, Harris Tweed and his Boy in the *Eagle*. But publishers and editors were probably becoming uneasy. The war increased frankness of speech on subjects hitherto taboo (or tabu, as Richards gently corrected Orwell). Middle-aged bachelors sharing lodgings with bright young male teenagers were standard fare through the 1930s, but after the war too many people knew too much and were much more ready to say it. The early 1950s brought Tory-government homophobic persecution, with wide publicity in place of pre-war discretion; and, with Angus Wilson's *Hemlock and After* (1952), the explicitly homosexual English novel entered high literature (Proust and Mann had taken the French and Germans there somewhat earlier). It betokened a farewell to innocence; how innocent the actual writers had been we will never know. Frank Richards, post-war, gave an occasional reminiscent glimpse of Redwing's loving anxiety for the Bounder, and the Bounder's re-affirmation of their partnership, but the books made Bunter hog the show. W. E. Johns kept Ginger as his best identification-figure, but broadened the regular cast of characters to include the comic Bertie and diffuse the boy-man element dominating the saga from 1935 to 1943. Blyton's fondness for the word 'queer' ultimately led to many substitutions of alternatives by her publishers, probably without her knowledge: for instance, the initial conclusion of her cousins in *Five on a Treasure Island* that George was 'the queerest girl they had ever known' became 'the most peculiar girl' and so on in later paperback editions.

The common frontiers between series juvenile fiction and weekly fortnightly comics – notably Blyton's *Sunny Stories* and the *Knock-out* mutation of a tabloid Billy Bunter – made publishers aware not only of their exotic rivals being imported from the USA but also of backlash against those rivals. Britain in the 1940s began to take heavy bombardment from superheroes in particular. Superman by Jerome Siegel and Joe Shuster, launched in 1938, and Batman by Bob Kane, in 1939, made their way across the Atlantic in their own individual comic books and in various syndicated strips, even if their female counterpart, Wonder Woman, begun by William Moulton Marston in 1942, did not. Wonder Woman seems to have been an early case of gender-conscience at work: Marston was a psychologist revolted by the male chauvinism of the superhero cult. But in its own way it suffered the penalty of the didacticism that impaired so much Victorian popular juvenile fiction. The British child book-readers may have been ready to accept Johns's Worrals and Blyton's George, wonder women in their own way but not absolutely impossible ones; but the British child comic-reader got some vigorous visibility from firmly feminist figures such as Pansy Potter ('The Strong Man's Daughter') and Ding-Dong Belle (the woman sheriff who locked up all the male sheriffs when they barred her from their congress), both in the *Beano* from D. C. Thomson of Dundee. The latter may have lacked likelihood, but they were comic. Superman had some comic appeal, induced by his disguise as the timid Clark Kent and by his enthral-ment to the domineering Lois Lane; and so had Batman, notably through the fantastic villains he encountered. Both had certain British origins: if Superman's ancestors included Perseus (and Nietzsche), they also ranked with Springheeled Jack of Victorian penny-dreadful fame, and with the fairy-tale traditions which also eventuated in Blyton's benevolent Mr Pink-Whistle and airborne Wishing-Chair. Batman was more obviously British in ambience, even running to a Wodehousian butler and aunt, but his supreme Englishness lay in his adoption of Robin, dressed as fantastically as himself on the job but otherwise living with him in 'stately Wayne Manor' as Dick Grayson to his Bruce Wayne.

Superman was in fact denounced as early as 1940 (Sterling North, Chicago *Daily News*, 8 May) for taking the law into his own hands in the traditions of Judge Lynch, the Ku Klux Klan and so on, if with more acceptable victims. Batman worked more closely with lawmen (lacking superpowers to tempt him otherwise), even if his restraint for want of sufficient legal authorisation induces an occasional 'Holy search warrant!' from his less legalistic sidekick. Superman's extra-legal methods reflected British as well as American popular cults: Edgar Wallace's Four Just Men, Ripper, Jack o' Judgment, Green Archer, and so on, and so on, Sapper's Bulldog Drummond, Leslie Charteris's Saint, Agatha Christie's avengers of the Armstrong child victim in *Murder on the Orient Express*, and Johns's Gimlet in his commando operations are cases in point. Frontier justice prided itself on comparable ethics whether in the remoter corners of British Empire or American west, i.e. the law unless it proved less serviceable than the alternative. Batman's domestic arrangements, as we have noted, were even more English in personnel, if not in technology. Hence, when Dr Fredric Wertham's diatribe against the influence of comics, *Seduction of the Innocent* (1954), denounced Batman and Robin as 'like a wish dream of two homosexuals living together',[28] their British counterparts disappeared or became markedly heterosexual. It was in the USA that the more rational response emerged: a hilariously camp TV series followed by *MAD* magazine's conclusion that Batman was gay while Robin was straight; but these were in the liberationist '60s, not the conformist '50s. As for Superman, enlisted during the war against the USA's enemies, George Perry and Alan Aldridge saw him standing 'as a symbol of a new patriotic faith – the hero supplanting the gangster of the previous generation'.[29] Charteris's Saint and, briefly, Johns's Steeley had made such a transition, to the point of joining government services (US and UK respectively). Superman was a less technologically challenged commando, and as such ancestor of the film forms of James Bond.

In general, print had offered some refuge in subtlety for homosexual themes in child literature, from James's *The Turn of the Screw* to Richards's Bounder serials. Comics left little room for subtlety, and much more obvious space for coarse innuendo among readers. Lesbianism had not been criminalised in the UK; but, as male homosexuality became more visible as well as more vulnerable, female homosexuality was put at more literary risk. Hence male writers of girls' fiction became more sensitive. Worrals and Frecks went into permanent retirement. The post-war *Girls' Crystal* and the *School Friend* (founded in 1950) feminised their heroines and their plots; female sidekicks were reduced to walk-on parts (when not the Secret Enemy to be Unmasked in the Last Instalment). Males were in more continual focus (although sometimes not until quite late in stories of career relevance). Mary Cadogan and Patricia Craig deduce a clear degeneration from 'Girl Sleuth to Brainless Beauty'.[30] Girl sleuths require girl Watsons: the *Girls' Crystal* ran a male detective, Noel Raymond, whose male author even wrote under a male pseudonym and whose Watson was his niece. Johns in 1940–1 knew better when, in a *Girl's Own Paper* serial, he produced a schoolgirl discovering herself to be a sleuth whose Watson is initially a hostile contemporary, as was the original Watson in the first Sherlock Holmes story.[31]

Fiction of the 1940s in girls' weeklies frequently posited initial boy–girl hostility – indeed, a conventional device is boy-vetoes-girl-adventure, girl-defies-boy, EITHER girl-proves-right OR boy-proves-right, but all's-well-that-ends-well. But mutual hostilities giving way to girl alliance under pressure of war is much less usual. The Johns schoolgirl serial, 'The Ravensdale Mystery', is a spy thriller (including a German spy disguised as a French mistress, an ominous piece of symbolism). Its modern editors Peter Berresford Ellis and Norman Wright justly see in its Joan Scott an anticipation of Worrals (although both seem twins, conceived simultaneously), but the initially overbearing Hon. Diana Morley is very different from Frecks. Readers of Worrals might quite well deduce that in Worrals's days as Head Girl, Frecks may have been a cynical, somewhat lackadaisical, mildly hedonistic rebel. Her affectation of nihilism in perpetual quest of nourishment balances Worrals's slight excess of worth, but they have long ago got over any initial antipathies. Biggles similarly requires foils and successively gets them in the initial frivolity and subsequent pessimism of the superficially cynical Algy, then in the adventure-hunger and impulsive enthusiasm of Ginger, and finally in the light-hearted patter with bursts of inspiration whether dotty or divine from Bertie. Gimlet needs foils – preferably without a button – but his arrogance prevents his having any, although in practice the independence of his followers in action constitute foils without words. But Worrals and Frecks are not mere foils, and Worrals's choice of Frecks rather than Bill Ashton at both the beginning and the end of *Worrals in the Wilds* is not simply a rejection of matrimony. The same seems true of other female friendships in the WAAF, notably Aircraftwomen Day and Marchant in 'On the Home Front', where the intimacy is crucial to Marchant's death being murder rather than suicide.

The Worrals–Frecks partnership is the closest duet of any two characters in Johns's serial fiction, and probably owed something to that of Johns himself and his common-law wife Doris Leigh (who by all accounts resembled Worrals in her leadership, judgement and low opinion of male authority). This does credit to Johns, whose imagination was greater and poetry larger than has been realised. But female homosexual regard was naturally better managed by female hands; male equivalents were less certain. Elinor M. Brent-Dyer, whose gender preferences seem to have been towards her own sex, showed subtlety, strength and skill on the theme in her wartime fiction. In a magnificent Cadogan–Craig pun, they 'will stand up to the usual cannons of school-story criticism'.[32] Three cases may be noted. The first, in *The Highland Twins at the Chalet School*, involves an expulsion whose occasion, however, is in spite of an intimate female friendship, not because of it. School series tradition-ally required expulsions – or their self-inflicted equivalent, confes-sion of guilt and (or in) running away – and even more the threat of expulsion against virtuous innocents. Thomas Hughes had his Flash-man (with tumultuous literary effects in the ensuing century). Louisa M. Alcott in *Little Men* had the thieving boy capitalist Jack Ford. Frank Richards expelled many boys in the earlier days of Greyfriars and St Jim's, although they trickled down to a very few in the *Magnet's* last decade; as his character-drawing strengthened, he worked with just expulsions for heroic figures (Wharton, Vernon-Smith, Wibley) and the anti-heroic Bunter, whose sentences have to be rescinded on *deus ex machina* terms (usually saving someone from drowning, or trapping a pardon from the headmaster by a clever trick with frequent antecedents in folk tradition). Brent-Dyer pre-ferred to expose the near-expellee to some frightful entrapment in a flooded landscape, or up an ice-bound mountain, or from an escaped lunatic (Jungian rather than Freudian), after which the miscreant is hospitalised and reforms. But this formula was ultimately bound to exhaust itself and its readers as well as its victims, hence the expulsion of Thekla von Stift in *The Chalet School and the Lintons* (1934): Thekla had arrived in its predecessor *The Exploits of the Chalet Girls* (1933), sent by her father to avoid her contamination by the Nazi doctrines attracting her brother. Brent-Dyer uses the stan-dard device of expulsion as the only possible penalty for conspiracy to have someone else expelled, but in that case she seems to have had comparable Nazi activity in mind: the Nazi-created Reichstag fire of February 1933 which Hitler used as the excuse to frame the Com-munists, suspending civil liberties, press freedom and so on. There is also a hint of Thekla's venom stemming from rejection by Joyce Linton: Brent-Dyer may or may not have picked up the gossip that Hitler's homophobe policy, beginning with the execution of Ernst Roehm in June 1934, had replaced one of indulgence towards homosexual recruitment under Roehm. Brent-Dyer, committed to a schoolgirl series in central Europe of which she had little personal experience, necessarily had to keep herself exceptionally well informed on continental developments. Once in Britain at war, priorities changed. Betty Wynne-Davies is expelled for giving information to the Nazis potentially detrimental to the war effort, opening up the Western Isles and British war-weapon experiment to Nazi penetration. Brent-Dyer may have been responding to wartime pressure over her savage caricature of Colonel Black and his security obsessions in *The Chalet School Goes to It*. If such pressures came from her Edinburgh publishers, Chambers, she may also have learned from them about security-consciousness over the Western Isles. But *The Chalet School Goes to It*, while ruthlessly exposing the colonel as a pompous, idiotic male in contemptible contrast to all of the women and most of the girls, prepares the ground for some disastrous sequel for Betty Wynne-Davies by charting the stages of her quarrel and break-up from her long-time friend and fellow-conspirator in mischief, Elizabeth Arnett. It begins with Betty's jealousy at Elizabeth's affection for Gillian Linton (now returned as a schoolmistress), a self-conscious echo of Thekla's break-up with Gillian's spoiled younger sister Joyce, and it notes that the effect is to isolate Betty. The main point is the educator's one that highly anti-authoritarian girls of 14 may rapidly develop into strong upholders of authority within a year or so. Elizabeth and Betty as anti-authority leaders have been respectively foremost in thought and action. The break, and its consequent defections, leave Betty bereft both of her followers and of her mental guide, and the psychological demoralisation leaves her open for moral seduction by a Nazi agent. It was a shrewd analysis of what prompts alienation. Brent-Dyer managed the plot adroitly, keeping very different issues in the foreground for the most part, such as Jo's presumed loss of her husband in combat, hence the spy's suborning of Betty's allegiance is told retrospectively and in summary:

> he had questioned her very cautiously, and Betty, unguarded in the hatred she felt for the twins, had told him more than she had realised at the moment. When he began to ask her plainer questions, she had tried to draw back, but he told her brutally that she had already given away enough to be of great help to him, and if she did not tell what he wanted to know, he would find ways and means of letting her head mistress know how much she had already told.

We are not told how he has been captured, but he identifies Betty. She duly faints and is caught by Elizabeth, who tells her when she comes to: 'I know I'm to blame as much as you, if not more. I should have stuck to you. It's my fault as much as yours.' The inadequate substitute with whom Betty has consoled herself, a foolish girl, Florence Williams, known as 'Floppy Bill', refuses categorically to speak to her again even when the Head asks her to say goodbye:[33]

'Thank you, Miss Annersley, but I'd rather not. I never want to see her again.'

'Florence', said the Head gently, 'I know you have had a shock; but how much better are you than Betty that you should judge her so hardly? . . . Betty has never done *you* any harm, and you have been close friends this past eighteen months. Do you think you have any right to try to push her further down than she already is?'

But Floppy Bill stuck to her guns. 'I'd rather not, Miss Annersley.'

Miss Annersley gave it up after that. But it was with a stern face that she told Betty that her erstwhile friend would not come. Betty said nothing. Perhaps she had expected this. But her lips quivered, and the Head went away sadly. She left the School an hour later, when the Sixth were all in the Sixth formroom, and when Monica said in subdued tones, 'There goes Betty', Floppy Bill turned her back on the window, and went on talking hockey feverishly with Hilda Hope.

The second episode apparently had its origins in Brent-Dyer's becoming headmistress to the daughters of the exiled Haile Selassie of Ethiopia. It had an element of nature imitating art, since, like many another school-story writer, Brent-Dyer had introduced a Ruritanian princess, Elisaveta of 'Belsornia', in *The Princess of the Chalet School* (1927); and, possibly with her new charges in mind, Brent-Dyer had the princess return to the Chalet environs in *The Chalet School Goes to It* with the Nazis controlling her country. Like most school stories, the Chalet series had only included white girls, and Brent-Dyer evidently felt that she should rectify this. It had come from her own war situation, and she seems to have felt that it affirmed a vital element in British war aims. So *Lavender Laughs in the Chalet School* introduced a new girl – Lilamani from Kashmir. Brent-Dyer's anxiety not to fall into the pattern of racial stereotypes, made all too much of a fine art by Richards, eliminated much distinction from her schoolmates. Her surname, normally the means by which the school's nationalities are flagged, is set aside: 'no one in the school could ever remember Lilamani's surname, let alone pronounce it, and they all avoided it with one accord'. The lead-up is hardly promising. A few hours before Lilamani arrives (and it may be no more than coincidence), Lavender, reformed from early rebellion, resolves to 'work like a nigger' – no doubt an accurate schoolgirl line of that class and time, but hardly tactful. A few pages later, Bride Bettany (Jo's niece) announces the arrival of a new girl ('"there must be something *awfully* funny about her!" . . . Steve . . . only laughed and said "Wait and see!"'). Then (with real, or rather Brent-Dyer, coincidence) a request for information about Indian geography (from Bride, whose own family is Indian-based) puts Lavender remembering her time in Kashmir, where she met 'the little Lilamani, with her silky dark hair, and big, dark eyes set in a little face as fair-skinned as her own . . . soft laughter and musical voice.' So she greets her with delight when she proves to be the new girl. Lilamani has been trapped in France, but gets out from the Riviera, with very little clothing. Lavender insists on dividing her own:

> Lilamani possessed all the pride of her race, and it was only with great difficulty that Lavender coaxed her into agreeing; but after expending all her eloquence, and finally resorting to tears as Lilamani persisted, the elder child at last got her way. Lilamani would take the frocks as 'a love gift', and Lavender promised she would not do such a thing again.

Brent-Dyer got her audience thinking from the Kashmiri nine-year-old standpoint, especially when the child's mother's health is about to collapse:

> Jo knew from her husband that it was very unlikely that the Kashmiri woman would live to see Easter. If that happened, then Lilamani would be very lonely, for it was impossible to get her back to her own people in India. She must stay where she was, and that would be among aliens.

Lavender gets Lilamani invited to Jo's for half-term, Miss Annersley describing it as a request that 'she might share her bed'. When Lilamani's mother does die, and she returns after the needful absence,[34]

> Lilamani looked up at her with mournful dark eyes. 'I have no mother now, Lavender. And everyone is far away.'
>   Lavender bent and kissed her again. 'I know. You're just like me

now – no; not quite. You've got your father in Kashmir, and I haven't any – only Auntie Sylvia. But she's been ever so good to me, and everyone here will be good to you. And when the Head told me about – about your – mother, she said it was so much better for her, 'cos she'll never be ill any more and she has been ill such a long time now. But you won't be lonely, old thing, 'cos we'll all try to make up to you, and you'll go back home some day when old Hitler is beaten. Look, dear! Bride asked Matey if she could change cubicles so that you could be next to me. If – if it gets very bad at night, you just whisper my name, and I'll come beside you for a bit.'

This was not what Matron had intended when she had agreed to Bride's unselfish proposition to change her own cubicle with its big window for Lilamani's which had none; and Lavender would be breaking a very strict rule and liable to all kinds of unpleasant penalties if she were caught, but the idea helped the child a little. Thereafter, for the next three nights, Lavender, when the lights had been switched off, and everyone had settled down to sleep, crept under her own curtain into Lilamani's cubicle and sat on the side of the bed, petting her until she drowsed off into a quiet sleep. On the third night, she was caught by the Head, who, while understanding, told her it must not go on, as she was missing her own slumbers as well as breaking rules. But by that time, school-life was helping the little Kashmiri as even life with Jo had not done, and Lavender was given permission to go in to tuck her up before lights-out if she did not linger. But even so, it was a sad end of term for Lilamani.

Brent-Dyer was enough of a Victorian to regard death as an unwelcome but appropriate intervention in stories for children from time to time, and such a passage as this bravely faces the banality of all verbal consolation and the reinforcement of physical, especially where smaller children are concerned. Modern wisdom would probably outlaw it. Miss Annersley's objection to Lavender's conduct is limited to concern about Lavender's own health – the rule is clearly not important at such a time – and the assumption is that death is best fought by the expression of love. It's also important that Lilamani's loneliness is made much worse by the war, and that in that sense war work demands rule-breaking. Brent-Dyer did not intend to allow Miss Annersley to intervene until the third night, when the first – worst – grief had spent itself. This is documentation for what had to happen during bereavement in wartime, whether from death in combat, at sea or in the Blitz.

The next book, *Gay from China at the Chalet School*, retained the theme of death, love and rule-breaking, although its title is deceptive as regards any continuation of multi-ethnic enrolment. The war has receded, albeit danger from bombing-raids still lurks, especially at night-time, and the famine in teachers has landed the Chalet School with its tyrant headmistress against whom Gay Lambert rebels, running away to see a relative bound for China. This is secretly welcome, since it proves the ultimate cause of Miss Bubb's departure, and it is publicly reprehended, partly because Gay's Odyssey concludes with infecting the school with German measles ('Jolly unpatriotic of her! . . . If she wanted any sort of measles, what's the matter with English ones?' – to which the doctor retorts with thanks that it isn't 'English ones'). But all of this is to provide a context for another death of a mother-figure, and another loving friend who helps the bereaved girl to survive her loss. The teacher's encouragement of such aid is asserted by the hard-bitten Matron:[35]

'Sleep well', she said in the crisp tones that yet held so much kindliness. 'Be brave, little girl. You've a good deal left.'
  Jacynth's lips quivered. 'I know that. But – but – it's a bit lonely.'
  'Yes; I know. But it might be worse. You have Gay, and though she is one of the biggest imps that ever helped to turn my hair grey, she's a good child in some ways. Now go to sleep; and if you want me, call me.'

Eventually they vote Gay winner of the Margot Venables Prize as having done more than anyone else to help others, this being specifically for having aided Jacynth, and specifically not for having brought German measles; her having got rid of the headmistress is unmentioned, but is clearly a factor, especially in the unanimity of the entire staff in support of the students' choice. The circumstances thus harden the need to honour the love of two girls for one another and make it the official basis of the prize. Brent-Dyer continued to talk sensibly about such questions, notably in *Tom Tackles the Chalet School* (1956, but set, written and serialised ten years earlier): here, a girl who wants to be a boy gets a crush on a senior, tortures herself with notions of betrayal, and eventually clears it up without realising that it declares her affections. The effect is to surprise the senior girl that anyone could feel like that about her, but shows her the need for extreme care ('When she could get into such a state over a stupid thing like that row over talking, I should think I could very easily upset her for keeps').[36] Many child readers would agree from their own experience.

Lavender and Lilamani are brought on stage with their friendship already formed although not yet tested: the cosmopolitan traveller Lavender in the course of her selfish, spoiled life has found one friend, romanticised by the short time and faraway place of their friendship. But while Lavender's bestseller-brat performance shows little sign of whatever had made that friendship in the early part of the book (Lilamani appears only in the last third), there is no sign of condescension in their relationship (and with inspiration from an emperor's daughters there was not likely to be). The *Girls' Crystal* for 4 November 1944 opened with a startlingly affectionate but definitely class-conscious transracial partnership of two girls facing Japanese invasion ('Audrey Nicholls', 'Alone Against the Invaders'). This was in the traditions of female lower-class worship for same-sex employer, as nauseatingly established in Baroness Orczy, *Lady Molly of Scotland Yard* (1912), while Craig and Cadogan found in *Schoolgirls' Own* (Gertrude Nelson [i.e. John W. Bobin], 'The Ivory Seekers') for 1921 'Topsy', a 'Kaffir' girl who 'came near to worshipping her young mistress' (English, naturally).[37] Male schoolboy fiction sometimes included stories whose heroes were black chieftains needing to prove themselves by various Herculean tasks to establish their titles, and Rider Haggard's *King Solomon's Mines* firmly established the tradition of the godlike black servant who proves to be a king. Richards's 1931 series in Kenya and the Congo where a heroic and proud Kikuyu is rescued from a lion by the Bounder, each of them thereafter in love with the other, has no condescension, each recognising the other as equal – indeed, each hailing the other as master. 'Alone Against the Invaders' is in that tradition: the Kanaka Daranee 'the little copper-skinned native girl' is, like the Bounder's Kikuyu, right where the white protagonist is wrong on dangers of the locality (in this case the likelihood of a Japanese invasion). In the same tradition, neither exceeds the other either in courage or in resource. But the element of condescension is present in the *Girls' Crystal*, where Richards repudiates it (by identifying it with Bunter). Perhaps it is more muted by the end, having begun:

'Daranee, you dream too many dreams and think too many thoughts', Madge Bryant smiled fondly. 'Of course the Japs will never come to the Isle of Orchids. What next will you get into that funny dark head of yours?'

But Daranee . . . still shook her head. Her oval face was anxious as she stared away across the blue Pacific, her full red lips drooping with doubt. And those lovely black eyes of hers were misty with troubled affection as she regarded her white mistress.

Smiling, Madge stretched out a sun-bronzed arm to ruffle the closely cropped black curls of the little native girl's head as she squatted faithfully at her feet on the veranda of the bamboo-built bungalow which overlooked the sea. But still Daranee's thoughtful expression remained.

'I know. I warn', she said. 'I tell you these things, missy, out of my love for you. Soon the Japanese soldiers come to Orchid Isle.'

Daranee is much quicker off the mark in adapting herself to the invasion and safeguarding the McGuffin, a secret invention of Madge's father. Madge, to do her justice, gives primary credit to Daranee when Daddy gets home and polishes off the Japanese with the aid of Australian marines – to whose country they will then retreat, fading out on:

'Daranee', a quiet voice put in behind her, 'also go back – with you, missy . . . Daranee never leave you, ever.'

'I won't let you, Daranee', Madge said softly.

It is a classic romantic ending, though usually for separate sexes.

Tomboys do not necessarily prefer their own sex, any more than female pilots and aircraftwomen are tomboys. Brent-Dyer's Tom never marries and becomes a missionary in the East End, but Blyton's George is uninterested in other girls although Blyton, her own model for George, wrote affectionately about feminine, insecure little schoolgirls. George became a sex-object for some real-life adolescent boys reaching puberty, much as James Bond in *Goldfinger* conquers a man-hater; but Blyton never takes her beyond demands for sex equality. As for the Madge–Daranee syndrome, it had counterparts, but its most startling cousin is in Tolkien's *The Lord of the Rings*. Tolkien celebrated mutual male love crossing racial barriers by the growth of affection between Legolas of the Elves and Gimli the Dwarf. He seems to have had Jews in mind when first developing the dwarves in *The Hobbit*, and gave them Jewish sense of adventure, Jewish love of music, Jewish delight in parties, Jewish sanctity of traditional quest, Jewish financial acumen, Jewish no-madic traditions, Jewish warmth in comradeship, Jewish suspicion of betrayal by gentiles. Bilbo's redemption from his dull, smug, complacent life by the dwarves is an eloquent metaphor for the impoverishment of western society without Jews. Tolkien denied allegory; but Jews seem to have enabled him to make dwarves.

Legolas and Gimli were his reply to Gentile anti-Semitism and Jewish exclusiveness.[38] He defended inter-racial marriage in the love of Aragorn and Arwen despite its cutting her off from her own folk; and Tolkien shows that in such situations one cultural representative may prove more selfish than the other – the human Aragorn chooses a comfortable death, leaving his elf-widow to her lonely habitation of the sacrifice she has made in marrying him. But the love-story on which the heart of The Lord of the Rings turns is that of Frodo and Samwise, master and servant, both hobbits; and, as with Madge and Daranee, it is the servant, in the end, who proves the vital figure in bringing success to their cause. The Girls' Crystal was anxious (in this, one of its few war stories published in the later Second World War) to preach the comforting propaganda of natives loving British in answer to Japanese claims of anti-imperialistic liberation. Tolkien, intransigent anti-Nazi, was horrified at the use of atomic energy against the Japanese. He had not meant the Ring to allegorise the atomic bomb, but the urgency of his story in showing the need to renounce the Ring and its power, and Frodo's inability to destroy it as possession of it deepens its hold over him, reflect the reactions of a witness to the victorious USA's inability to deny itself the use of its new weapon. In the end, Frodo triumphs through the resolute insistence of Sam on putting Frodo's best necessities first, and through the survival of Gollum because of Frodo's forgiveness. But the USA had not forgiven its enemies, and its failure to do so imprisoned itself and the world in a ring of nuclear terror. At bottom, the annihilations of Hiroshima and Nagasaki arose from the conviction that the Pearl Harbor attack had placed the Japanese out of conventional human assumptions. There remained the further question as to whether their non-white status required a punishment that would not have been allotted to whites, even Nazi whites. So brooded Tolkien in his anger against the way the war was ended in East Asia.[39]

Notes

1. Five on a Treasure Island (1942), 28, 30.
2. The Island of Adventure, 14.
3. Hurrah for the Circus! ([1939] 1974), 42, 60, 67.
4. Robson, Introduction to Arthur Conan Doyle, The Hound of the Baskervilles (1993), xvi.
5. The Castle of Adventure, 35. Blyton introduces a comparable character Jo into Five Fall into Adventure (1950), reappearing in two later 'Five' books. She likes

(rather than loves) Dick – and dislikes George, whom she resembles, with due class-differentiation – but Dick has no animal magnetism and little character, and Jo simply feels he is kinder to her in the first instance than the others are.

6. *The Island of Adventure*, 66; *The Castle of Adventure*, 271, 273.
7. *Mystery at Witchend*, 43, 123 (and below) 128, 130.
8. *Biggles Sweeps the Desert*, 175–6, 178.
9. Victor Watson, *Reading Series Fiction* (2000), 104, 109.
10. Johns, *Biggles 'Fails to Return'*, 122–4.
11. Richards, Reply to Orwell, in Orwell, *Complete Works*, XII, 80–1; Orwell, 'Boys' Weeklies', ibid., 61. *Magnet* 869 (October 1924). The relevant William story is 'William and the Princess Goldilocks', *Happy Mag* (Christmas 1931) and *William the Pirate*.
12. Johns, *Worrals in the Wilds* ([1947] 1950), 11; *Worrals Down Under* (1948), 7, 9.
13. Blyton, *The Christmas Book*, 158, 161, 162, 164, 166.
14. Johns, *Worrals in the Wilds*, 14, 192.
15. Trevor-Roper, *The Last Days of Hitler* (1947), 161, 163. Its Pan paperback edition was published in 1952.
16. Johns, *Worrals in the Wastelands* (1949), 85–6, 125, 70–1, 209–10. Mary Cadogan, *Women with Wings* says little of this book but is invaluable on its background, as she is for so much else.
17. Johns, *Worrals Investigates* (1950), 95–7.
18. Berresford Ellis and Williams, *By Jove, Biggles!*, 190. The general discussion of the book, citing hostile criticism, precedes this on pp. 188–90, rightly condemning the notion that the book's anti-feminism was representative of the Worrals series but too defensive of the book itself. But their defensiveness is better than the critics' moronic inability to see the feminism of the other ten Worrals titles.
19. Johns, 'On the Home Front', *Comrades in Arms* (August 1947), 64. Berresford Ellis and Williams, *By Jove, Biggles!*, 279, believe it 'obvious' that it had been previously published, presumably in a wartime magazine publication; and their opinion is authoritative.
20. Gower, 'Dogs of War', *Girl's Own Paper*, vol. 63 (November 1941).
21. Garrett, 'The Gay Company', *Chatterbox* (1948). In view of the male identities of 'Gail Western' (C. Eaton Fearne), 'Ida Melbourne' (Eric Rosman), 'Enid Boyten' (Horace Boyten), 'Renee Frazer' (Ronald Fleming), 'Daphne Grayson' (G. C. Graveley), 'Hazel Armitage' (John Wheway) and the other girl authors of the *Girls' Crystal*, it seems only fair to posit a female reality behind 'Edgar Garrett'.
22. Innes, *The Journeying Boy* [1949], in *The Second Michael Innes Omnibus* (1961), 51.
23. Johns, *Worrals Investigates*, 164.
24. Orwell, 'Film Review', *Time and Tide* (10 May 1941), Orwell, *Complete Works*, XII, 494.
25. Walpole, 'Young Baltimore' and 'The Runaways', *Jeremy and Hamlet*.
26. *Magnet* 1,641 (4 July 1939),
27. *Magnet* 1,675 (23 March 1940).
28. Fredric Wertham, *Seduction of the Innocent*, 190.
29. Perry and Aldridge, *The Penguin Book of Comics* ([1967] 1975), 166.
30. Mary Cadogan and Patricia Craig, *You're a Brick, Angela!: the Girls' Story 1839–1985* ([1976] 1985), chapter 17. See also their *Women and Children First: The Fiction of Two World Wars*.
31. William Earle, *The Ravensdale Mystery*, *Girl's Own Annual*, vol. 62. First published in a book, Norman Wright (ed.) *Steeley and the Missing Page and Other Stories* (2000), 136–87.

32. *You're a Brick, Angela!*, 204. These authors in general seem unduly censorious of the series; but we are in accord on the high quality of its Second World War volumes. To speak of the 'sentimentalities' of the Chalet School Peace League is to deliver judgement outside of historical context – the theme was a very brave one for wartime fiction.

33. *The Highland Twins at the Chalet School*, 262–3, 266, 272–3.

34. *Lavender Laughs in the Chalet School*, 220, 196, 201, 211–12, 242, 244–5, 238, 271–2.

35. *Gay from China at the Chalet School*, 196–7, 223.

36. *Tom Tackles the Chalet School* (1955), 108; *Second Chalet Book for Girls* (1948), 148–9.

37. Cadogan and Craig, *You're a Brick, Angela!*, 259.

38. The recent trilogy of movies making up *The Lord of the Rings* featured an outstanding performance of Legolas by Orlando Bloom, if anything improving on a somewhat shadowy character in the novel – shadowy apart from his relationship with Gimli, the one casualty in the film's Legolas. The problem was evidently that of very different sizes, which the reader hardly thinks about unless told to, but the viewer cannot avoid. Also, the film's Gimli was played very much for laughs, whereas Tolkien's dwarves were figures of dignity.

39. Tolkien to his son Christopher, 29 May 1945 and 9 August 1945, *Letters*, 115, 116.

THE
CHALET SCHOOL
GOES TO IT

ELINOR M. BRENT-DYER

FIGURE 9 Gardener (Welsh) teaching dark Gwensi and English friends (wartime horticulture gives authority to workers) – see pp. 330–1.
Reproduced by permission of Girls Gone By Publishers http://www.ggbp.co.uk

9

Class

Workmen can, and often do, get on quite well without authors; but no author could continue to exist without the workmen. They are not only the backbone of the nation: they are the nation: all other classes being merely trimmings.
　　　　Frank Richards, Reply to George Orwell, Horizon, May 1940

Tolkien's beautiful story of Frodo and how his servant Samwise preserved him was based on the most painful of British obsessions: class. It is really more English than British, but the Britain of 1939–45 was still ready to let England call the tune, apart from the addition of a verse or two in picturesque dialect. Tolkien had not in fact intended much of a part for Sam; the character took matters into its own hands, as characters do. It responded to what was happening in the Britain around its creation: a still respectful working and lower middle class was making the important decisions while its social superiors were being photographed with the right people and making the fine speeches.

Frodo and Sam stand in the tradition which Orwell described in *Horizon* for September 1941:[1]

The Don Quixote – Sancho Panza combination . . . the ancient dualism of body and soul in fiction form . . . comes up again and again, in endless variations, Bouvard and Pécuchet, Jeeves and Wooster, Bloom and Dedalus, Holmes and Watson . . . the two principles, noble folly and base wisdom, exist side by side in nearly every human being.

Tolkien had known Spanish from his youth; it was the only Romance language he loved for its own sake.[2] *Don Quixote* is an obvious source for his tales of the hobbits. In *The Hobbit*, he had already created the Sancho figure in Bilbo and given a touch of Quixote to Gandalf. Bilbo is on the edge of *The Lord of the Rings*, but he remains pleasantly earthy and uncomprehending in contrast to the over-perceptive, scholarly and sensitive Frodo. Sam may be earthy, and – as the similarity of names indicates – his devotion to Frodo is not incompatible with the character of Sancho. But he is even more idealistic about Frodo than is Frodo about the quest, and it is his determination fixed on tangible sights which will carry them when Frodo's fails. Tolkien by a flick of his finger could summon up a world closed to Orwell: that of medieval Catholicism and its chivalric culture. If Frodo is knight, Samwise is squire. It is the direct origin of Quixote and Sancho, which alternately mocks and follows it. But although Samwise will be Frodo's heir, and seven times Mayor of the Hobbits' Shire, he would not aspire to knighthood if knighthood equates him with Frodo. There is a blazing pride in his insistence on his servitude. The squire status of the much more schoolboy-like figures of Merry and Pippin (very St Jim's and Greyfriars – Tom Merry and Bob Cherry?) respectively serving the heroic Theoden King of Rohan, and the suicidal Denethor Steward of Gondor, assumes ultimate knightly rank: witness their tombs on either side of the King of Gondor. Sam makes no such claims on nobility. He may win bourgeois honours, wealth and property, but to the very end his Frodo is 'Mr Frodo' or 'Master', whom he loves more than himself or anyone else, and may kiss, clothe, arm and defend, but to whom he will always defer. Yet that deference will include defiance where Frodo's safety is at stake:[3]

> 'But I am going to Mordor.'
> 'I know that well enough, Mr Frodo. Of course you are. And I'm coming with you.'
> 'Now, Sam', said Frodo, 'don't hinder me! The others will be coming back at any minute. If they catch me here, I shall have to argue and explain, and I shall never have the heart or the chance to get off. But I must go at once. It's the only way.'
> 'Of course it is', answered Sam. 'But not alone. I'm coming too, or neither of us isn't going. I'll knock holes in all the boats first.'
> Frodo actually laughed. A sudden warmth and gladness touched his heart.

Sam's proud service partly derives from army batmen in the First World War. Dorothy Sayers (in detective stories read by older children between the wars) rather unsuccessfully attempted its realisation in the relationship between Lord Peter Wimsey and his former batman, now valet (not made more credible by the name Bunter). Tolkien had served in the First World War; Sayers hadn't.

The principle draws heavily on the master–servant tradition going back to Dionysus and Xanthus in Aristophanes' *The Frogs* (an obvious origin of Don Quixote and Sancho, even in names). Increasingly, the servant showed himself more intelligent than the master (especially when, like Beaumarchais's Figaro, he had already established himself in another identity) and sounder in judgement on the master's needs, Wodehouse's Jeeves and Wooster being the classic realisation (again, a source of delight for many children). The use of squire–knight relations in children's fiction increasingly allowed for that, especially with the convention in all children's fiction that the child had in some way to save the situation where the adults had failed, or were absent or inadequate. Scott's influence on subsequent fiction made for some perpetuation of the impressive but inadequate hero king Richard in *Ivanhoe* and *The Talisman*, leaving Magdalen King-Hall and others free to tell the story from the Squire's point of view (*Jehan of the Ready Fists*, 1937; Puffin 1946). It implied a little more than being Tinker to Sexton Blake or Tommy Burke to Dixon Hawke, something closer to John Ryan's 'Boy' serving and saving Harris Tweed in the post-war *Eagle*. Usually, the assumption is that such figures are of a lower class than the hero they serve, albeit originally the squire was of the knight's rank and frequently (as in Chaucer's *Canterbury Tales*) his son. Geoffrey Trease complained that King-Hall, Carola Oman (*Ferry the Fearless*) and so on 'feel more at home behind castle-walls' (in medieval times of trouble, who wouldn't, once they or their people controlled it?).[4] Conan Doyle's *The White Company* and *Sir Nigel* had given body and atmosphere to the tradition in general, and particularly underlined the frequent poverty of the squire. It played into the general British cult of aristocracy (much shared by the Irish, when not shooting the aristocrats). It did not assume aristocratic virtue, and frequently (again harking back to Scott) made great play with aristocratic badness and evil use of social position (Frank Richards's Ponsonby is the classic inter-war example). But aristocratic manners, nomenclature and style were present for emulation, partly as a means of moralising to children from something more secure than the doubtful charisma of the bourgeoisie. So Brent-Dyer eased girls with 'de' and 'von' in their names into two early Chalet stories (before reaching the heights with the third, *The Princess of the Chalet School*), while being savage enough about snobbery. So Richards took trouble to portray the likeable if somewhat asinine Lord Mauleverer and Hon. Arthur Augustus D'Arcy as anti-snobbish.

But the frank and proud servitude in class as well as in status characterising Sam perpetuates an ideal irreplaceably vanishing throughout the Second World War. The 'Bunkle' series of Margot Mary Pardoe had its delicate intimations of aristocracy, Bunkle's family being 'de Salis', and their French friend in the post-war *Bunkle Went for Six* 'de Ferier du Cros'. Their speech is very firmly what Nancy Mitford would shortly afterwards require as evidence of upper-class status, from 'writing-paper' to 'pudding' (Sayers, if not Mitford, might have shuddered at the author's ''Varsity men' for 'undergraduates'). Yet, as early as 1943, Mrs de Salis remarks: 'When this war ends, I don't think any of us are going to be able to go back to the sort of life we used to lead' (*Bunkle Butts In*), and in *Bunkle Went for Six* she tells young de Ferier du Cros, about to become their house guest:[5] 'That's the worst of the hugger-mugger way we all live in England these days. With no servants to keep us in order, we're forgetting how to behave to our guests.' The apology we know of course to be 'in the way of pleasantness' (as Judge Jeffreys used to put it): the reader is to envy the French youth for the privilege of the de Salis company (and, not necessarily for reasons of hospitality, Bunkle's is worth having). Male and female servants are nevertheless gone. One of the very few books for boys in the Second World War to preserve the batman myth, Major J. T. Gorman's *Jack Frere of the Paratroops* [1943], was the work for a professional literary hierophant of the British monarchy. It's not a bad story, borrowing the Spy-pretending-to-be-Quisling-broadcaster from Graham Greene; but the batman portions are ludicrous in their servility. ('Richards felt rather as a faithful dog must when unable to let his master know of his presence, or his longing to help and save him, if only he could, from any danger or any enemies' – the author imagined himself to privilege the batman by raising his servant status as high as the canine.)[6] The faithful batman in First World War literature worked, if lightly played. It is simply an embarrassing anachronism in the Second World War; or a dream of lost rule. Monica Dickens's *Joy and Josephine* (1943), much read by schoolgirls, featured the master's disintegration into the meaningless, while his male servant's increasing reality is the last image the protagonist sees of that world.

When the war was over, many women were persuaded on sexist grounds, amid employment famines, to lose much of the emancipation they had earned so gallantly during the fighting; but maids did not return to the households they once had served, apart from a thin trickle. Children's writers might occasionally cater to nostalgia with fanciful portraits of the old reliable. Richmal Crompton's short stories had measured the servant shrinkage during the war itself; but the first post-war William story *Just William's Luck* – the only William novel – derived from a film which invented a new character, Emily, in place of the succession of Brown maids over the past quarter-century, and assigned a lifetime's devotion to her. But if Crompton did so, it was with her usual breaks from standard literary convention:[7]

> 'If I've said it once I've said it a hundred times', said Mr Brown. 'I *must* have breakfast at eight sharp. Can't anyone keep to a schedule in this house? You know perfectly well that if I miss that fast train I have to stop at ten stations on the way to town and –'
>
> Quite suddenly the Browns became too much for Emily. This happened on an average once every three months. She would endure them – and in her heart of hearts adore them – for weeks on end, and then quite suddenly they would become too much for her. Her face worked in an alarming fashion, like something set in motion by a complicated piece of clockwork, and a sound issued like the whirling of rusty wheels.
>
> 'All right', she said in a choking voice. 'I've slaved for you ever since Mr Robert was a baby, but if I don't suit –'
>
> Mr Brown laid down the shoe and shaving cream on the bottom step and raised his hands in a gesture that expressed sympathy, reassurance and surrender.

Crompton's William stories had to create and to reinvent an environment for an 11-year-old from 1919 to 1969, but alone among them *Just William's Luck* could go into considerable detail. A few of its episodes were cannibalised from earlier stories, with some sub-plotting reworked from at least twenty years previously. The convention of the old faithful, blunt-spoken family retainer, frequently a Nannie or with Nannie-ing experience, flourished in inter-war fiction, partly because in reality the domestic-service market was already turning against the employer. But it was inescapable from the 1940s that the end of domestic servants as household members of middle-class families was at hand. The inability of the Browns to retain the same servant(s), to judge from the stories of the 1920s and 1930s, was more representative than *Just William's Luck*'s solitary epiphany of Emily. Yet it did show a revolution: that entire first chapter is written from the standpoint of Emily (apart from a few opening paragraphs through the eyes of the glazier who walks out with her), and is more in sympathy with her than with anyone else in the house (William then being out of the house, but in any case held by his creator more in affection than sympathy). Such a vantage-point is not entirely new in children's literature: L. M. Montgomery's great First World War novel, *Rilla of Ingleside* (1921), has a maid-servant, Susan, as the author's most obvious – if least diplomatic – voice. But Susan is subjected to eternal condescension from her employers, especially from the paterfamilias Dr Gilbert Blythe, attempting to demonstrate his intellectual superiority by 'teasing' her with all the security of a spoiled brat in a wealthy household. He knows she will not leave. Mr Brown after the Second World War has no such assurance, long though Emily's service may have been. Hence he is required to observe certain forms of deference, notably to check himself from foul language in her presence, as he would from any female of his own status. (There was nothing new about Crompton's printing 'bad language' as those early days knew it: as early as 1927, William lured a nauseatingly perfect child, performing King John emerging from the Wash, to call for his servants Dam and Blarst.)[8] Mr Brown polishes his own shoes (with shaving cream in this case, owing to one of William's interventions). He retreats to the kitchen as an appropriate haven, in place of the Victorian convention that he was not supposed to know of its existence, and the inter-war assumption that he would virtually never be found in it. And, for all the length of Emily's service, the adult Browns do not know whom she sees on her afternoons off, although she does tell William – in this matter like other children of his status. Children were in some respects on the servant side of the class divide, especially since the servants often gave them more parenting than they received from their father and mother. The vanishing servant was yet another cause of children's reduction to self-dependence in the Second World War and after.

Frank Richards, resuming Greyfriars in book form from 1947, had little incentive or eyesight to research changes in boarding-school life, but his post-war stories show younger female domestic staff than hitherto (apart from the St Jim's infirmary nurse Marie, whose exceptional employment arose from her cracksman paternity):[9]

> Mr Quelch, being a mere man, did not perhaps realise that house-maids, as well as schoolmasters, had much to do! Probably he had never reflected that Mrs Kebble's staff had their work mapped out, and that to run things smoothly, jobs had to be done at the scheduled times. What was merely an irritating, deafening noise

to Mr Quelch, was to Mary a job of work that had to be done, and that she wanted to get done, and done with.

The trouble is caused by Mary needing to run a Hoover over Mr Quelch's study. Greyfriars might have avoided curricular, dietary and dormitory modernisation over the previous forty years, but it had to acknowledge one revolution. If domestic servants were to be maintained, they had to be given labour-saving devices when the war was over. During the war itself, the Chalet School had felt the pinch on maids no less than on mistresses:[10]

> Miss Wilson sighed inwardly. Gwladys never would have suitable manners for a parlour-maid; but they were lucky to have anyone at all these days. A club foot and short sight had prevented her from being in any of the Women's Services. Their bright, pretty little Guernsiaises maids who had come with them when the school had evacuated from Guernsey had gone long since. Michelle and Rhoda were in the W.A.A.F., and Annette and Olivette had joined the W.R.N.S.; while Dulcie was driving a motor-lorry.

Brent-Dyer's wartime experience as a headmistress makes this information a primary source report, firmly blue-pencilling the mistake that is made in viewing armed-forces recruitment purely from a middle-class perspective. Saville's evacuee children have to learn to cope with rural domestic service of a more authoritarian kind than might be expected in London's teenage labour market, and its protected status had to be asserted from the first:[11]

> Mrs Braid did not seem a friendly sort of person, and once snapped at Richard for getting in the way. Mary answered back indignantly for her twin – they often did this for each other – and so surprised was the housekeeper that she dropped a heavy suit-case.
> 'It wasn't *his* fault', said Mary. 'Can't you see he was only trying to help. We always help. We're jolly useful at helping, and maybe you'll be sorry for speaking to us like that . . .'
> 'Mary', said Mother, in her special, quiet voice, 'go into the other room with Dickie and Macbeth and stay there until you are called. You can be thinking of how you will apologise to Mrs Braid.'

Instead, of course, they think of what they will call her behind her back (viz. 'S.L.' for 'Sparrow's Legs'). The housekeeper resolves the problem by meeting their conscripted apologies with a smile which makes her look 'Not a bit "witchy" and almost nice', and 'rather awkwardly she put a hand on each twin's shoulder'. She plays a very minor part in the spy story that follows, but significantly is an honoured guest at the final party hosted by the children and dissecting the adventure.

Geoffrey Trease, in his over-valued *Tales out of School* (1948), lists Saville along with M. E. Atkinson and 'David Severn (David Storr Unwin, son of Stanley Unwin, the publisher) as 'outstanding exponents of the holiday theme',[12] if below Ransome in quality. But Saville's is firmly, reassuringly yet unflinchingly, a war book; in the wartime context, Ransome, Atkinson and Severn were sheer escapism, the latter two nowhere more so than with their servants. The war does not exist, and, by the look of some of the servants, neither did its precursor. In Severn's *Waggon for Five* (1944), the heroes are conscripted, but only as substitutes for unavoidable absentees in a local cricket match, whose tea is served by the butler from the local stately home, He proves gratifyingly impressed by the visitors' caravan:[13]

> 'I am aware, sir, that it is not customary for men of my profession . . .' He hesitated: his face suddenly half-mischievous, half-ashamed . . . the glance of a boy who is being naughty and who knows it. 'All the same, sir, in spite of myself . . .' He was breathing deeply, gazing . . . at the shining paintwork of the waggon. 'I must admit to feeling drawn, very drawn, if you understand me.' He paused dramatically and gulped. 'The lure of the highway . . . the roving life, sir!'

This falls far short of the enchanted gardens of Wodehouse's Blandings Castle (now, through their author's misfortunes, closed for the duration of the war to many patriotic Britons), and it does little for the young readers' perceptions of the existing war or the ensuing peace. But it has some charm, even some integrity of its own. The war is equally remote from the adventurous Lockett romances of M. E. Atkinson, exhuming the snobbish tradition of lampooning servants' insistence on spinning out messages for 'the gentry'. The device of lengthy and confused rendition of a message increasing reader tension is an old one: Wodehouse frequently brings it to his finest of arts by having Lord Emsworth absent-mindedly deconstruct his news before the anguished bewilderment of its wretched recipients; and, in 'Bunter's Easter Trip' (*Magnet*, April–May 1939), Bunter keeps on confusing his belated revelation of Smithy's kidnapping with demands for sugar while Tom Redwing is tortured with anxiety for the fate of his beloved Bounder. Atkinson was openly anti-lower-class (Wodehouse's chief misinformant is an earl, while Bunter, whom Redwing has just saved from death, keeps reassuring Redwing of Redwing's utter social inferiority beneath himself). Developments in Atkinson's *The Nest of the Scarecrow* (1944) are held up while the tavern maidservant, thanklessly bullied by the upper-middle-class children, makes a good story, exhibiting the education she has so pointlessly received:

> Rosie, enjoying the drama of the situation, waited a full ten seconds before delivering the final sentence of the message. It had come back to her, but she was not going to put the two before her out of their agony until so minded. Rosie's village school education, moreover, had given to her, among other less useful accomplishments, a peculiar capacity for parrot-like repetition of anything once committed to memory. The actual sense of the matter did not interest her, but she could repeat, word for word, a positive anthology of verse as well as certain Collects for the day, hymns and psalms.

She does it all in Mummerset. As reader-training in class prejudice goes, this is fairly impressive. We are invited to sneer at the much more hard-working girl, her education and even her grasp of religious beliefs, while admiring the utterly self-centred groups of privileged factionists dominating the story. The escapist feature plays its important part in this. The absence of war encouraged the readers to think of its being of little concern to them or their world. The story concludes with a shipwreck whose most notable result seems to be the bourgeois children's chagrin at having missed the sight of the crew being actually rescued. The working class exist not only to serve their betters but also to entertain them, even while their own lives are being saved. On the other hand, the young Locketts are suitably deferential where duty dictates. The predecessor volume, *The Monster of Widgeon Weir* (1943), brings them into association with admiring children who have read the earlier books about them, and who then prove to be the children 'of a real Countess':[14]

> 'And to think how we've been about with them! There was that visit to the entertainment, too! And we never knew!' Jane was telling herself that she would never now feel quite the same about

her grand friends. . . . [yet Evelyn's] mother might be a Countess,
but it didn't seem to alter her at all, even when you *knew*.

The series was within a countess's purse, volumes fetching the
highest prices of the day, 7s. 6d. in 1943, a shilling more in 1944.
It would have made a dent in Rosie's wages, but the Lockett stories
were definitely above her station.

Enid Blyton was inevitably the most disparate commentator on the
servant question, on which her contradictory signals are as instructive as ever. She was the creator of a series based on a servant, Mary
Mouse, whose advent transformed Blyton's career. Her marriage to
Hugh Alexander Pollock was disintegrating, yet Pollock, then on
wartime leave from Newnes, was her initial link with her major
publishers. And her work for Newnes had gone beyond being a
story-writer. She adapted old stories and foreign authors for them,
she wrote factual passages in encyclopediae, fact-books, knowledge-
books and nature-books for them, she edited and wrote the text of
Sunny Stories for them. In her early, less book-starred years, she may
have done important but anonymous work easily fed in through
Pollock and now forgotten. Thus she knew a great deal more about
books and their possibilities than most authors.

Ernest A. Roker was the Midlands manager for Hodder & Stoughton,
whom he had served since 1904. John Attenborough, the firm's
historian, singled him out for 'authority, daring, and a readiness
for experiment'. He had built up sales of Hodder's yellow-backs,
working not only with formal booksellers but also with the chemists
Boots, with major libraries and with wholesalers. He knew that
Blyton was rapidly becoming the most productive writer for children
in the country. He knew how to talk to best-selling authors: he had
gone to the Riviera to deal with such Hodder giants as Baroness
Orczy and E. Phillips Oppenheim. He had new ideas on books in his
time: he inaugurated British crossword-puzzle books in 1925, with
great success. When his chief unwisely bought *The Boot and Shoe
Trade Journal*, Roker had tried to give its anaemic sales a transfusion
by a great Shoe and Leather Exhibition in Leicester. He saved a series
of children's books from utter lack of booksellers' interest by
exploiting a phonograph record donated with each volume and
selling them to record wholesalers. He had done deals with Boots
marketing illustrated classics for children. He was put in charge of
Brockhampton Press, founded in 1938 to get rid of theological titles
accumulating at headquarters with little return, and was advised
that business might be transferred to him in larger degree since

Leicester was considered likely to be bomb-free. He wanted to blossom out as a publisher for children, so Percy Hodder-Williams told him in 1940 that he could, provided it did not cut into Hodder's own paper allocation. He worked with colour printers and concluded that their paper offcuts could be bought cheaply and used for large print-runs of series for children. He was in fact seeking to claw back to book-publishing some of the market which had vanished into comic-strips and their papers. He saw Blyton, apparently in London, and suggested a book, hand-size, reutilising *Picture Post*'s previously scrapped offcuts. And Blyton, now well embarked on series about children at school, in adventure, in circus, in wishing-chair and in faraway tree, and on series about elves, brownies, fairies, pixies and so on, suggested a mouse. Being Blyton, the first outline stories followed in a few days. There would be a line of text, under a picture (originally uncredited) by Olive F. Openshaw. Blyton had obtained good results from mixing story-beings; to children and pixies, and children and animals, she now mixed mouse with toy dolls. Blyton had experimented with new designs of storybook to meet paper-rationing, and would make other attempts, but this was by far the most successful.[15] Soon the series was selling at 200,000 per shilling volume, four pictures across two facing pages, each page less than $6'' \times 3''$, whose economical captions gave mild pace with mutual aid of text, picture and book-design.[16] Margery Fisher, usually one of Blyton's more acid critics, was impressed by the design: 'The miniature pictures, neat, two-coloured and unassuming, lent a certain charm to the character of Mary'. Blyton was naturally pleased at the outcome of her association with the serious-minded and distribution-obsessed Ernest Roker, and was ready to listen when he suggested that she meet with his Mr Hodder-Williams. The result was Hodder's publication of *Happy Story Book*, which gave her another outlet, and *Five on a Treasure Island*, which gave her the most successful series of her lifetime. Or at least the most successful after Mary Mouse. The mix of the dog and the children indeed followed the Mary Mouse principle; Blyton does not overdo it, but from time to time the reader sees events from the dog Timmy's point of view.

Mary Mouse is a maid, and the story is told from her standpoint, although from time to time we get it from that of one of her charges. She is defender and symbol of the classic servant tradition. At first she becomes a maid on what seems a volunteer basis, but the first sequel firmly opened on a note of her getting 'good wages'. There seems more of a flicker of tongue-in-cheek than in normal Blyton, especially in the opening of *Mary Mouse and the Doll's House*, where

Mary's tidiness is deemed unnatural by her parents and siblings, thus implying intentionally or otherwise that a good maid is a social misfit by origin. Blyton's 'Green Hedges' (according to Blyton herself) had occasional mice, and the thought that they might help out in the wartime labour shortage may have conceived Mary Mouse (with a faint authorial grin). The idea derives from a combination of old fairy-stories, the Elves and the Shoemaker, the Bears and Goldilocks. The Doll family are out when Mary discovers their house after exile from her native mousehole, and they return to find home decidedly sweeter after a thorough cleaning; they also find Mary asleep on a bed. Mary Mouse is an asylum-seeker, or refugee, topically for Blyton as well as for her audience: in summer 1939, she welcomed into her own home an Austrian refugee, Mary [presumably Maria or Marie] Engler, who remained with them until summer 1945. (Blyton was ready to welcome Engler's parents as well, but the war put paid to that.) This makes the Mary Mouse series the best-selling treatment of the refugee theme known to literature. Her employer, Sailor Doll, may have been a concession to wartime, but neither he nor his wife shone in domestic management, which in all its branches was taken over by Mary. He was, however, capable of imitating a dog when Mary was in danger of being eaten by a kitten; it harmonised with the current theme of new skills shown by the armed forces when domestic Britain was under attack. *Gone With the Wind*, a roaring cinema triumph at the box-office of 1940–1, might have prompted a little of Mary Mouse's character and situation, the role model here being supplied by the Oscar-winning black actress Hattie McDaniel, playing Mammy. Mary brings up the doll children much more thoroughly than their parents do (including occasional spankings, a topic with which Blyton, like many English writers for children of the day, was mildly obsessed). Since the convention of the story established itself with a refugee from a mousehole finding a dolls' house up some stairs in an attic, Margery Fisher regretted later introductions of 'policemen, donkeys and even elephants with a bland indifference to any problems of scale';[17] but here Blyton showed more knowledge of her child audience than did her critic. The whole essence of a doll's house, as Ibsen bitterly pointed out, is existence in make-believe. Macaulay, thinking of his little sisters, wrote in his essay on Dryden:[18]

> All deficiencies are supplied by the susceptibility of those to whom they are addressed. We all know what pleasure a wooden doll, which may be bought for sixpence, will afford to a little girl. She

will require no other company. She will nurse it, dress it, and talk to it all day. No grown-up takes half so much delight in one of the incomparable babies of Chantrey.

Hence the episodes entering imaginary streets, or involving transport to a remote seaside, its donkey and elephant as essential to the story as to an American Presidential election. So the garden came to require a gardener and obtained the services, after unsatisfactory precursors, of a suitable recruit in Whiskers, 'a handsome young mouse'. He duly fell off a ladder while harvesting apples, and was of course rescued by Mary: 'She was so kind to him. She put him in her own little bed', and she slept in a kitchen chair. 'And when he was better, he took Mary Mouse's hands, and said, "You are so kind and sweet, Mary Mouse. Please marry me."' Initially, Mary Mouse demurred; she could not leave the doll children. But all ended happily when the dolls gave their cellar to the mice as a mousehole.[19] In a subsequent book, *Mary Mouse and her Family*, the doll children are behaving badly on Mary's day off when she enters from the cellar and invites them to see her new babies, five in number, born yesterday. The implication is that she coped with giving birth to quintuplets and performing her ordinary work of a day. No domestic servant, slave or free, showed more zeal.

Blyton's various residences at Beckenham, Bourne End and Beaconsfield are most obviously reflected in the Five Find-Outers and Dog 'Mystery' series, set in 'Peterswood'. Although begun (for Methuen) in 1943, they probably reflect the pre-war profusion of domestic staff, especially in households where crimes take place, but in sympathy with maids they show more of a wartime pragmatism: they also show wartime victimisation of employers, as well as pre-war vulnerability of employees. Blyton's would-be detectives analyse the servant personnel a little clinically, but in striking contrast to anti-servant sentiment in adult detective fiction of the 1930s and 1940s. Blyton's Peterswood in part reflects social standards observed by her as early as her Edwardian childhood, but its attitudes to servants are firmly based in the Second World War, although there are more servants around than the war would have sanctioned. People with incomes and pretension live in houses with several servants, but there is little of the former deference to the squire and his relations: Mr Hick, owner of the burnt cottage, and Lady Candling, owner of the disappearing cat, are merely respected as persons of property, nothing more (less when the children discover that Mr Hick has burnt his own cottage for the insurance). The portraits of

Hick's servants, necessarily suspects, are credible, uncondescending and with their own little dramas whose protagonists are not patronised. Blyton's morality militates in their favour. The little 16-year-old kitchenmaid is in love with the valet fired by Mr Hick, who thus made him a suspect for cottage-arson:[20]

> 'Well, then', she said, 'I'll tell you how I know it wasn't Horace that did it. I know because I met him at five o'clock that day, and I was with him till I got in here at ten o'clock, which is my time for being in!'
> The five children stared at her. This was indeed news.
> 'But why didn't you tell every one that?' asked Larry, at last. 'If you said that, no one would say that Horace burnt down the cottage.'
> Lily's eyes filled with tears. 'Well, you see', she said, 'My mother says I'm too young to say I'll marry any one, but Horace Peeks, he loves me, and I love him. My father said he'd thrash me if he caught me walking out with Horace, and Mrs Minns said she'd tell my father if ever she caught me speaking a word to him. So I didn't dare to go out to the pictures with him, or even to talk to him in the house.'
> 'Poor Lily', said Daisy. 'So when you heard every one talking against him, you were very upset and wrote to warn him.'
> 'Yes', said Lily. 'And, you see, if I tell that I was out with him that night, my father will punish me, and maybe Mrs Minns will send me off, so I'll lose my job. And Horace can't say he was with me because he knows it will be hard for me if he does.'

This is handled with respect for servants' private lives, something unusual in popular fiction by that date. Even Crompton made mild fun of the love-affairs of servants encountered by William, although she made greater fun of those of everyone else, explicitly parodying a maid's love-triangle test for one of his sister Ethel's romances. (The maid's story is potentially tragic, and its end is touching; Ethel's is merely comic.) The child readers are intended to take Lily's part, and feel sorry for her, as the more adult girl Find-Outer Daisy appropriately does. It is not blind pity: Fatty breaks down her concealment of Peeks's return to the house at the key time, but accepts her amended alibi for him. It is an oddly adult moment for Blyton: servant-girls' fathers still beat them for questionable company-keeping (as the Paycock wants to do in O'Casey's *Juno* on hearing that his daughter is pregnant; Blyton gave occasional nods to her Irish ancestry). What the children do not realise is that Lily's father has a point, even if his prohibitions and brutality are contemptible: Horace Peeks is not a particularly reliable prospect for Lily, apart from his refusal to get her into one kind of trouble, however helpful for his alibi. He wears his master's clothes to cut a dash, which suggests that he is less likely to marry Lily than to get her into another kind of trouble. Blyton leaves it to readers to make any such deductions; she simply presents Lily as a likeable human being, deserving reader sympathy, regardless of her social status. Equally, she shows the social gradations among servants coolly: Mrs Mimms is a kindly person to children of the employer class, but a tyrant over poor Lily. Crompton had been at home in that field before her:[21]

> Ever since Violet Elizabeth's disappearance Mrs Bott had been indulging in hysterics in her bedroom and taking it out of Violet Elizabeth's nurse. In return the nurse had hysterics in the nursery and took it out of the nursery maid. In return the nursery maid had hysterics in the kitchen and took it out of the kitchen maid. The kitchen maid had no time for hysterics but she took it out of the cat.

Crompton was a hard-bitten Tory of Marxian realism: she knew who worked the hardest. Over the years, kitchenmaids in great houses were among William's best audiences – thus putting them on a plane with the reader – whether because they liked him, or because they thought he was mad, or both. Blyton may assume some mental retardation in servants lowest in status from time to time, although it strengthens rather than weakens their bonds with children – in her case founded on empathy rather than comedy.

The gardener's boy to whose defence the Find-Outers rally in *The Mystery of the Disappearing Cat* (1944), Luke, is an orphan, living with a brutal stepfather, 'about fifteen, a big lad with a round red face, startlingly blue eyes that looked rather surprised, and a big mouth full of very white teeth'.[22] Those blue eyes are normally a mark of Blytonian favour. The location of the early Peterswood *Mystery* books in the Second World War also makes for more individualism in servant-description than the detective-story norm, as does the distribution of suspects among all classes (in conventional 'Golden Age' detective fiction, the butler may do it, but seldom anyone lower). The usual freeze of the lower classes balances the introduction of the higher, or at least the more moneyed. Crompton's Mrs Bott, for instance, when threatened with wartime destruction, impressively prioritises the feline above the servant creation:[23]

> 'Oh, dear!' she gasped, sinking down on to a chair. 'Oh, dear! oh, dear! oh, dear! Oh, Mrs Brown, what shall I *do*? A hunexploded bomb right in front of my very 'ouse. I daren't go in an' I don't know what's 'appened to poor Pussy, not to speak of the servants.'

Crompton is as usual hilarious, but her message is evident enough: if traditional domestic service is doomed, it is no more than dehumanising employers deserve. Blyton makes Lady Candling a more benign figure but one leaving her vulnerable workers at the mercy of exploitation by malicious superiors only occasionally restrained by her ladyship's fleeting interventions. The head gardener and actual thief, Tupping, makes a confidant and dupe of the local constable, Goon:[24]

> '*And* we found that Dark Queen was gone', said Mr Tupping in a fierce voice. 'Well, Mr Goon – the evidence is as plain as plain, isn't it? Dark Queen was stolen between four and five o'clock – and here's this boy stating that there was no one else near the cats except himself the whole of that time. He took that cat – no doubt about it – and handed her to some friend of his for a bit of pocket-money. He's a bad boy is Luke, and always has been ever since I had him.'
>
> 'I'm not bad, Mr Tupping!' shouted Luke, suddenly finding a little courage. 'I've never took a thing I shouldn't! I've worked hard for you! I've stood things from you I shouldn't stand. You know I'd never steal one of them cats. I'd be too scared to, even if I thought of it!'
>
> 'That's enough, now, that's enough', said Mr Goon fiercely. 'Don't you go talking to Mr Tupping like that. What boys like you want is a good hiding.'

It practically amounts to a conspiracy to stitch the wretched Luke up between them. Crompton, more radical than Blyton, actually did show the local police being ready to frame William as early as 1931, but Blyton's anger in defence of the most underprivileged is deeper. Blyton's treatment of Goon has been made a count in Bob Dixon's indictment of her on the grounds that it shows her hostility to the working class; it says much for Blyton that Marxists accuse her of brutality to the police.

Two books later, Blyton's awareness of the most vulnerable servants took a further turn. *The Mystery of the Spiteful Letters* (1946) introduces a housemaid, Gladys, terrorised by an anonymous letter-writer's revelation that she had come from a reformatory after conviction as a thief:[25]

'You're good now, Gladys, aren't you?' said the little girl. 'You don't look bad. You're good now.'

'Yes – I've not done nothing wrong ever since', said poor Gladys. 'Nor I never would now. They were so kind to me at the Home – you can't think! And I promised the Matron there I'd always do my best wherever I was, and I was so glad when they sent me to your mother's, Miss Bets. But there – they say your sins will always find you out! I guess I'll never be able to keep a good job for long. Somebody will always put it round that I was a thief once, and that my parents are still in prison.'

'Gladys – the person who wrote that letter and threatens to tell about you, is far, far wickeder than you've *ever* been!' said Fatty earnestly.

Blyton clearly wrote the book after studying form in Agatha Christie's *The Moving Finger* (1943), with interesting reversals. The Christie story, characteristically, makes its anonymous letters a smokescreen under which the criminal can conceal his real crime, the murder of his wife. The writer is made to seem illiterate. Blyton's letters are the real thing, and are written by an illiterate person trying to seem literate. The accusations in the Christie letters are ill-founded, as the vicar's wife points out to the convalescent RAF pilot:[26]

'There's plenty of adultery here – and everything else. Any amount of shameful secrets. Why doesn't the writer use those?' She paused and then asked abruptly, 'What did they say in your letter?'

'They suggested that my sister wasn't my sister.'

'And she is?'

Mrs Dane Calthrop asked the question with unembarrassed friendly interest.

'Certainly Joanna is my sister.'

Mrs Dane Calthrop nodded her head.

'That just shows you what I mean. I dare say there are other things –'

> Her clear uninterested eyes looked at me thoughtfully, and I suddenly understood why Lymstock was afraid of Mrs Dane Calthrop.

By 'Lymstock' is meant its middle classes. Peterswood in the Blyton stories means all classes. On the other hand, Christie's anonymous letters' always harping on sex must be elided by Blyton. The nearest we get to it is a letter to a charwoman's sister, which she refuses to show:

> 'She says what's in it isn't for any one to read but me and the police. And I won't say but what she's right, now I've read the letter properly.' . . .
> Mrs Cockles's sister was a fat, untidy woman, who breathed very loudly through her mouth and talked through her nose.
> ' 'Tain't fit for a child to read', she said. 'It's a right down spiteful letter, and not a word of truth in it, neither!'
> 'I'm not a child!' said Fatty, making himself as tall as he could. 'You can trust me to read the letter and not say a word to anyone. I'm – er – I'm investigating the case, you see.'
> Mrs Cockles was very much impressed. But she still agreed with her sister that the letter was not one for him to read.

This is a different matter from sex on the Peeks–Lily front, and Blyton may simply have thought of rude remarks about 'a dirty, untidy' house and owner. But it shrewdly disposes of the main theme of anonymous letters, and is never cleared up. Blyton recognised that the normal range of discovery in an adult detective story must be seriously limited when reworked for children. Where Blyton bettered Christie was in the reality of servants, in sharp contrast to the figures of fun in *The Moving Finger* (even the one who is murdered). Blyton could improve on her models (*The Mystery of the Missing Necklace* (1947) uses Poe's 'The Purloined Letter' device far more credibly), and she saw the need for the range of suspects to cross class divides. The housekeeper, Partridge, in *The Moving Finger*, is only fleetingly a suspect in a firmly middle-class story. Blyton (who in reading the Christie story may have suspected Partridge) makes the housekeeper the crook. Misanthropy, merely amusing in Partridge, becomes tragic and frightening when exposed in the Blyton story:

> 'You're all against me, you are!' wailed Mrs Moon. 'Not a friend have I got in the world! You're all against me!'

'You have only yourself to blame, my good woman', said Inspector Jenks sharply. 'You yourself are apparently filled with spite against a great many people – and you cannot be surprised if you have no friends. . . . Mrs Hilton, I fear that Mrs Moon will not be returning to you.'

'I don't want her', said Mrs Hilton, with a shudder. 'A cruel, underhand, spiteful woman like that in my house! No, never. Poor Gladys. I'll fetch her back at once. I'm horrified and disgusted, Mrs Moon. You have caused a great deal of pain and grief to many people, and I hope you will be well punished.'

Mrs Hilton is not an attractive figure, even by Blyton standards for parents, but her readiness to hire reformed thieves is clearly intended for emulation. It stands greatly to Blyton's credit, deriving as her mystery stories do from a pre-war culture which usually insisted 'once a crook, always a crook' (Edgar Wallace, for instance, much reiterating the sentiment, however affectionate his stories may show themselves to individual crooks). There is an element of wartime community spirit here, as there is when Frank Richards's leading crook Soames saves Harry Wharton and does his bit for Britain. But Mrs Hilton is also shaken by the thought that, left untouched, Mrs Moon might have extended the reach of her spite beyond her own class. Already Mrs Moon has moved to its frontier by including Mr Goon in her epistolary target-range ('Thinks to put me off, no doubt! Tells me I'm a meddler and a muddler! Ah, wait till I get me hands on them!'). The adult Hiltons, censorious of both children and neighbours, may have their own secrets to keep. And the Blyton letters, reversing the Christie situation, hit home every time. Blyton also recognised that her story-children and her child audience would lack experience in seeing through commonplace criminal bluff. Fatty admits that Mrs Moon 'nearly took me in'[27] by writing herself an anonymous letter, but Christie's Miss Marple expects it:[28] 'The person who writes anonymous letters practically always sends them to herself as well. That's part of the – well, the excitement, I suppose.' In any case, detective stories with child detectives could not function on adequate knowledge of adult psychology, even of the comfortable common-sense variety dear to Christie. Blyton therefore concerned herself more with alibi, which in this story meant pinpointing the passengers on a bus to the neighbouring village whence the letters were posted, and this also made for a much wider class-range of suspects than the Christie norm, all the more so in wartime: Lady Candling's companion Miss Trimble, the sweet-shopkeeper Mrs Jolly, a young female artist, PC Goon, and a permanently unidentified 'thin, dark, sour-faced man, huddled up over a newspaper, with a pasty complexion, and a curious habit of twitching his nose like a rabbit every now and again'. Three other habitual users are later discovered: Mrs Moon; a caravan-dweller in the Rectory Field 'with a hooked nose and a droopy little moustache who goes about muttering to himself ... called Nosey because he's so curious about everyone'; and a dressmaker, Miss Tittle, 'like a lot of dressmakers, you know – full of gossip and scandal – a bit spiteful, ... pulls people to pieces too much for my liking ... Knows a bit too much about everybody!'[29] The country bus in the unmentioned war crossed class as well as parish boundaries, and we can see Blyton's suspects vividly enough, socially and anti-socially. What we cannot see, and are not intended to see, is what made Mrs Moon the mental sadist she has become. It is the Iago question, and Blyton leaves it as unexplained as does Shakespeare. Hitler brought motiveless malignity nearer home.

Blyton was sufficiently influenced by Crompton to make her child detectives frequently confuse the case in hand by contrivances of their own, chiefly their feud with Goon. She was by nature, and teacher-training, a moral storyteller; and, when the dictates of a mystery or an adventure necessitated eliminating moral reproof from author to characters, it might seem to imply approval of anti-social behaviour. Goon's bullying of defenceless lower-class servant boys and girls makes him fair game, but the children waste their own time in attempting to waste his, and their post-war attempts at unprovoked practical jokes at the expense of his nephew Ern or his more likeable fellow-constable Pippin produce ironic retribution of events. The endless mockery of Theophilus Goon, beginning with his name, may hold some authorial revenge for petty bureaucratic tyrannies in wartime (unsympathetic constabulary proclaiming banishment from favourite haunts in Swanage, resulting in her exile from it?), but its more important revelation is the fragmentation and supersession of conventional authority during war. Rivalry between private detective and police is at least as old as Poe, but the wartime atmosphere in which Blyton wrote the first Find-Outer stories simultaneously empowered Goon as a largely unrestrained authority-figure, and left him vulnerable to children themselves less firmly under control. Noel Streatfeild in The Children of Primrose Lane shows a policeman's child, working-class and all, telling a security official where he gets off:[30]

Sitting on the rug in a curve of the shingle were the other five. Dickie was one end of the line and Dave the other. Marge was in the middle with Freda and Sally on each side of her. Their faces were intent and desperate. Mr Oak walked up to them. He looked down the line; his voice was cutting.

'I hope you are proud. Just to amuse yourselves you've played at being detectives, and between you you've aided one of your country's most dangerous enemies to escape from the island.'

The children stared at him as if they had been hit on the head.

'Oh – !' said Sally, but before she could get any further there came a strangled sound, and the children were tossed about, and thrown on the beach; then the rug unrolled and out came the man. Mr Elm blew his whistle and from the shadows came soldiers who gripped him. He cursed and swore in German as he was led away.

Dave looked up at Mr Oak reproachfully.

'I don't like to be rude, but I do think you should be sure of your facts before you scold people.'

That has an advantage on Blyton, being child pseudo-authority by professional inheritance rather than by mere parody or cheek. Twenty years before this, in the Greyfriars stories, Peter Todd (a solicitor's son) sometimes elicited the truth of some mystery by a judicial enquiry in which he proved an able examining magistrate more on French than on English lines. Richards anticipated Blyton's mockery of the police by irreverence at the expense of the legal profession, never gently handled in his pages. Smithy, about to be justly convicted of treachery to Redwing, states that Peter[31]

'has the true professional instinct for brow-beating a witness, making the worse appear the better reason, and so forth. I have no doubt that he will have a brilliant career in the future, proving the innocent guilty, or the guilty innocent, according to the fees he gets and –'

'Ha, ha, ha!'

Peter was crimson with wrath. The Bounder's description was not Peter's idea of a legal career. Peter, of course, was young yet.

Blyton ultimately made Goon's nephew Ern supplant Fatty's bourgeois comrades in the Find-Outer series, admittedly with an embarrassing deference to Fatty which the stories are too thin to bear as easily as *The Lord of the Rings* can bear Sam's to Frodo.

Snobbery in Blyton is generally a post-war phenomenon. If her fairies called social conventions into question less formally than Gandalf upset Bilbo's in *The Hobbit*, she was attracted by the nomadic tradition, and that of the learned native. Hence the bourgeois children in *The Adventurous Four* follow the leadership of Andy, whose status in Blyton's Home Counties would be commonly deemed inferior to theirs in wealth, nationality, education and class. Andy at least has a father and a home, however. Jack in *The Secret Island* has only a grandfather and a home, both of which he discards to lead the displaced bourgeois young Arnolds. Barney in *The Rockingdown Mystery* (1949) has nobody other than a monkey. The Blyton series of the Second World War also deprecate wealth, especially for children: Fatty is looked down on because of his money and his boasting, although the later the date of each book, the less the populist ridicule. Jack wins equal status in adoption by the Arnolds and placement in Mike's boarding-school (to whose educational demands he must have risen with spectacular natural ability); thereafter, his origins win only initial allusion, if any. Barney in his fourth adventure, *The Rubadub Mystery* (1952), finds his father; and in his fifth, *The Rat-a-tat Mystery* (1956), he is making nasty remarks about trespassers on his father's property who may be doing no more than snatching a night's sleep as he himself had so often done in bygone days. But four years separated the publication of these two, and Barney's last epiphany as a nomad is his most sympathetic. Blyton's version of *Robin Hood* (1930, 1949) was naturally not in the Marxist pattern of Geoffrey Trease's *Bows Against the Barons* (1934), but it differed from many versions of the day in making nothing of Robin's supposed Norman aristocratic birth and very little of his Saxon socman origins, her emphasis being on dispossession, outlawry, comradeship – and ultimate loyalty to King Richard (but not to his successor King John). It made few concessions to Robin's redistribution of wealth, beyond firmly stating that he robbed the rich and fed the poor. 'They were all outlaws, but the common people loved them, for Robin Hood did them no harm but only good.' Her version of his oath ran:[32]

> I swear to honour God and the King,
> To help the weak and fight the strong,
> To take from the rich and give to the poor,
> So God will help me with His power.

Maid Marian is not congruent with the Five's George, but has hints of her – or perhaps ancestral anticipations. What this means is that

Blyton identified herself with Maid Marian, a useful way to write a Robin Hood book. None of this is socialism; but it is populism, and as such indicative of Blyton's own ideological antennae. King Richard makes Robin Earl of Huntingdon,[33] but when the King dies Robin repudiates his successor John and returns to Sherwood. He also repudiates his earldom and forgets about London, apart from kind thoughts about the deceased Richard. The poor are limited to an admiring chorus (like the fisher-boy of uncertain name who helps George from time to time), but their enemies are the villains.

'Class', as E. P. Thompson said, 'is not a thing: it is a happening.' The one serious blip in Blyton's moderately progressive trajectory on class before the 1950s arose from bad feeling developing between herself and her gardener, Old Tapping, as he was known. He was a very good gardener, but he and Blyton apparently disliked one another from the start. Tensions may have increased with Blyton and her daughters endeavouring to do their bit in the 'Dig for Victory' campaign (which doubtless embittered relations between many a patriotic employer and professional gardener), and the dissolution of Blyton's marriage in 1941–2 also heightened her unhappiness, and with it her irritation. On the other hand, Tapping's daughter-in-law was the cook, whose husband was a soldier, killed in North Africa in 1942; and their son Kenneth was brought up in the house, Green Hedges, playing as best he could with Blyton's younger daughter Imogen, his senior by three years. After Old Tapping was dismissed, apparently for bringing some garden products home, he went to work in an adjoining garden, and occasionally would lift his grandson from the garden whence he had been driven into that where he now reigned. Imogen Smallwood (as she later became) co-ordinated her recollections with Kenneth Tapping to tell us of their having watched a dogfight between planes, and (in his case) taking part in a souvenir-hunt when a German plane crashed in nearby woods. But when he brought back a German soldier's armband, his widowed mother was angered. Frances Tapping was still employed as cook by Blyton in 1946. Blyton was divorced in December 1942 and married Kenneth Waters in October 1943.

Blyton wrote so close to the subconscious that she was often unconscious of writing. In 1943, before the unquestionable reassurance that she obtained from marrying Kenneth Waters (difficult though he was for everyone else), she was evidently suffering from repressed anger against her ex-husband Hugh Pollock (however unjustified) and against the woman he would marry a few days after she married Waters. Blyton's three major books published in

1944 and thus probably written in 1943 showed great hostility to servant figures with authority, though expressed in very different ways. Old Tapping supplied two names – one, the gardener, Tupping, in *The Mystery of the Disappearing Cat*, and the other, the Stick family, in *Five Run Away Together* – could word-associations be more obvious?

The third workman villain is Jo-Jo in *The Island of Adventure*. None resemble the others. 'Horrid Mr Tupping' sounds like Blyton's version of Old Tapping. Her daughter and his grandson paint him as moustached, always wearing a trilby hat and 'breeches with shiny hard brown leather gaiters with buttons all the way down . . . a fob watch in the pocket of his waistcoat, which he wore under a jacket, or over shirt sleeves if the weather was warm. Always, in the pocket of his breeches, he kept a pruning knife.'[34] In brief, a man of dignity, pretension and authority. Imogen Smallwood remembers her sister and herself being beaten for stealing and eating newly ripe tomatoes, a crime that required an informer: apparently the tomatoes were much beloved by Hugh Pollock, so that Blyton may have retrospectively equated that punishment as Tapping's incitement to Pollock, thus demonstrating Pollock's unfitness for parenthood (on which otherwise she would have found it a little hard to build much of an indictment). *The Mystery of the Disappearing Cat* turns on Tupping falsely informing on Luke. The signs of social pretension in Tapping are partly reflected in Tupping, who for various reasons establishes himself in respectability by a friendship with PC Goon. But the effect of Tupping's guilt was not at all anti-labour: Tupping, with or without Goon, has definite middle-class status. His is, in fact, a middle-class crime, kidnapping a prize cat, knowing where its market could be found, using turpentine and paint to make substitutions and alibis (she knew Conan Doyle's 'Silver Blaze' from the *Memoirs of Sherlock Holmes*), and above all seeking to frame a working-class boy by specific arousal of class prejudice in the imbecile but bourgeois Goon. The book is a good one, the better for its anger against class-victimisation.

Jo-Jo in *The Island of Adventure* is more complex since he is a very intelligent criminal trying to appear like a stupid, half-crazy misanthrope. His relevance would seem to be that he is very much his own man, criminal or crazy, spending much time on his boat and doing what jobs he does in his own time even if he has to fulfil certain requirements for Aunt Polly. He is moreover the only adult powerful male on the premises, since Philip and, when he takes up residence, Jack are aged 13 to 14, and Uncle Jocelyn, for all of his enthusiasm for old unhappy far-off things and battles long ago, is physically irrelevant. Blyton at no point suggests that anyone in the house is in physical danger from Jo-Jo, apart from the boys when he decides on a spot of corporal punishment *in loco magistri* – his attempt to drown Bill and the boys at the end is professionalism, having affirmed his criminal identity – but Old Tapping's contribution may have been Blyton's thought that a household of women (with Pollock gone and Waters as yet unarrived) had little means of asserting authority over the zealous and accomplished gardener. Physically he was the strongest person on the premises, and Blyton's dismissal of him over the alleged theft of vegetables for home use may have originated in the fear that he was involved in criminal activity at her expense on a much wider level. She may also have had fears that he was becoming mentally abnormal, especially if she was working herself up to believe anything against him. So, from her anxiety about the over-powerful servant, she fashioned Jo-Jo. If he did owe something to Old Tapping, he was a most impressive character in his own right – or rather his own two rights, mad and bad. Blyton may never again have produced a criminal with better dialogue.

The Sticks demonstrably derive from Old Tapping's name, and the extraordinary hatred with which Blyton handles them must also derive from deep-seated anger against Tapping and more vaguely his relatives; but there is no sign of the Sticks having had models as Tapping was for Tupping. While Blyton in creative writing might allow a wild suspicion (that the Tappings were operating in unison) to help her create the Sticks, she seems to have had no rational proof that Frances Tapping even liked her father-in-law (her readiness to stay with the employer who had fired him does not suggest particular affection, and she would have had little difficulty in getting another wartime job). *Five Run Away Together* has been ruthlessly dissected by Edmund Wallace Hildick, himself an author for children but much superior as critic to other children's authors-turned-critics such as Barbara Euphan Todd, John Rowe Townsend or Geoffrey Trease, especially in his ability to see the value of Blyton and thereby explain something of her appeal:

> it is fully in line with a number of the strongest requirements of readers [from 8 to 11]. It is a long story – a children's novel – running to some 190 pages, thus satisfying the demand for more prolonged immersion or escape, . . . Then it carries exploration of the familiar to the running away, fending for oneself stage, as the title proclaims. . . .

. . . the author never loses sight of the fact that she is unfolding a tale: hardly a page passes without the dramatic insertion of a piece of necessary information or the sounding of a bugle-note of alarm. The basic situation is exquisitely prickly: Georgina's mother's illness and her being rushed with her husband to the hospital miles away, shortly after the girl's three cousins arrive for the holidays, leaving them for over a week in the company of the unpleasant Mrs Stick and her equally unpleasant husband, son and dog. The timing here is, as in most parts of the book, excellent, the reader being given just enough time before the bombshell of the parents' departure to begin intensely to dislike the Sticks, and the child characters equal time to show their dislike and so lay themselves more fully open to retributive unpleasantness. As a band, the characterization is . . . quite brilliant. Here we have fully portrayed the nasty, snobby, cruel selfishness that most children are capable of when they collect in packs of this sort – a dark side to children that very, very few children's authors ever touch on, and then usually only in their hero's and heroine's adversaries.

This analysis, as Hildick would say (writing before the adjective was inflated out of meaning), 'is quite brilliant'. He has taken the Blyton creations intended for admiration, and accords the admiration to their repulsiveness. He takes the example of the Five off for a picnic:

On the way they met Edgar, looking as stupid and sly as usual. 'Why don't you let me come along with you?' he said. 'Let's go to that island. I know a lot about it, I do.'

'No, you don't', said George in a flash. 'You don't know anything about it. And I'd never take you. It's my island, see? Well, ours. It belongs to all four of us and Timmy, too. We should never allow you to go.'

''Tisn't your island', said Edgar. 'That's a lie, that is!'

'You don't know what you're talking about', said George, scornfully. 'Come on, you others! We can't waste time talking to Edgar.'

Hildick ignores Blyton's evident assumption that, for all her allowance in her first pages for new readers in George-was-a-girl-not-a-boy-but . . . (and so on) passages, her audience knew the plots of the two earlier books. He is quite right that the above quotation[35] in its nakedness, is all the moral brutality of a certain almost universally experienced phase of childhood. And it is all the more convincing because the writer – probably unconsciously – shows approval of the brutality. Note the authentic ring of merciless, petulant, childish viciousness in the authorial '. . . Edgar, looking as stupid and as sly as usual'. So characters, readers and author become one in their pack-hunting, and if it is somewhat nauseating it must also be allowed that it is absolutely true, far truer to human nature than the work that would present Edgar as the normal child hero and the spiteful ones as his abnormal antagonists, or the Four as normal 'nice' children, with Edgar as the spiteful outsider.

But the constant readers are Blyton's foremost audience, and her concerns with the first six 'Five' books were with the totality of their strategy, charting George's battle against her father's selfishness and tyranny. It is basic to the series that, while we are on George's side, we notice how like her father she is in temper, in single-mindedness, in selfishness and in natural intellect. So, however much Blyton is stacking the cards brutally against the Sticks, her own apparatus for the reader warns us that George is sometimes no more an acceptable moral yardstick than is her father. The passage even allows us to reconsider her ownership of Kirrin Island: in *Five on a Treasure Island*, the question becomes a standard child ethic – you promised us a gift and 'went back on your promise' – and so we support George. But *Five Run Away Together* tells us that, as child-property owner, George is as grasping as Richards's Sir Hilton Popper. She is moreover foolish: had she conciliated Edgar, she might have found out *what* he knows about Kirrin Island and *why* he knows it, which would bring the criminal intentions of the Sticks to light much earlier. And it raises another matter. If Richards could make Bunter out of Falstaff and Coker from Coriolanus, could Blyton have made George not only from herself, but also from Caliban?[36]

> This island's mine, by Sycorax my mother
> Which thou tak'st from me.

This in essence is her quarrel with her father, whose science admirably counterpoints Prospero's magic. Prospero is of course not Caliban's father (though it requires little plot variation to make him so); yet, if in *Five Run Away Together* George is merely an ungracious Miranda, Edgar as Caliban-come-lately can in his turn complain of unfairness, or at least of want of hospitality. In one respect, *Five Run Away Together* takes its place in the indictment against George's father after his previous betrayals of her to crooks who would only steal the island treasure instead of buying the island, and then to spies wanting to steal his own designs. Symbolically, in this book he has followed the fairy-tale degradation of the princess, and placed her under the rule of the kitchen staff. In fact, he has far better justification now, since his concern is justly with his dangerously ill wife. And, on any normal use of Blyton's moral measurements, that should far outweigh George's grievances.

The fact that it does not suggests that Blyton's own anger against old Tapping has blinded her moral judgement. In publication order, *The Mystery of the Disappearing Cat* came out on 13 July 1944, and *Five Run Away Together* in August 1944; so it is likely that work on the latter promptly followed, concluding the former. Blyton was irrigating her anti-Tapping bile among a much more imaginary family, individually perhaps owing a spat or two to tensions sparking momentary hostility dividing Blyton and her daughters, or some of them, from Kenneth and/or his mother. Beyond that, her anger had made her aware of a hardening of class hostilities by 1943. Hildick points out that the nastiest aspect of the Five versus the Sticks is the persecution of the Stick dog (Tinker, whom George and cousins noisily nickname 'Stinker'), especially by the encouragement of cannibalistic instincts in Timmy; the whole Blyton canon should have arisen and screamed its horror at such gratuitous unkindness to blameless animals, and it appears to be entirely at variance with everything else that Blyton wrote before and after this. But Hildick only confirms her value as historical witness: this is child hostility and anti-servant prejudice in its naked ugly reality – as ugly as the physical descriptions of the Sticks either by Blyton or by George and her cousins (and Timmy, whose supposed thoughts are as bad as his humans').[37]

Blyton's ill-temper with Old Tapping is thus instructive in showing the roots of composition, but Hildick's shrewd conclusions bring out what good source-material her form of writing from the subconscious could provide. Even in the more ordered world that her bourgeois families inhabit (as distinct form the runaways, circus-dwellers, evacuees and so on), she brings out the isolation, moral as well as intellectual, in which they are mired. We must assume that she read her scripts before committing to publication, or else did so in proof; but, at the speed which her deadlines forced on her, she was hardly likely to quarrel with much that her subconscious had provided for her. Intention is probably exceptionally remote from composition in her case: 'my own way of imagining . . . really consists of a kind of opening of "sluice-gates" and allowing a flow of cinematograph pictures and sounds to flood into my conscious mind, from the "under-mind" '.[38] Tactics were left to the subconscious once the overall strategy of George versus her father had been pinned down to its precise point of development (culminating in the *amende honorable* of *Five on Kirrin Island Again*). After the first six 'Five' books, even that was now irrelevant, and she could write one of their later novels in four days. But the earliest Find-Outer novels must have required more careful plotting than most. Her researches in Poe, Conan Doyle, Christie and others warned her not to take the detective-story medium for granted. These stories had to parade their clues, alibis and – a little dauntingly for Blyton – adult suspects. Fatty might derive in part from Poe's Dupin, from Holmes and Hercule Poirot (as well as from Falstaff and Billy Bunter), but he had to be established credibly in his own right as both absurd and authoritative. Hence, if ever Blyton wrote with her eyes and ears open, as it were, it was in the first half-dozen or so of these books. Figures like Lily, Luke and Gladys were very carefully intended by Blyton, and her didactic purposes in these stories included sympathy and support for lower-class servants. She virtually agitates for protection for vulnerable workers (all the more necessary in a wartime situation, with normal social links and old acquaintance sundered). She demands that the repentant criminal be given another chance – if need be, in your back garden or kitchen. E. Nesbit's *The Railway Children*, another obvious influence on her (as also on Streatfeild, Mary Norton, C. S. Lewis and so on) turns on Father being in jail but (essentially for the story) wrongly so, with the unjust sentence ultimately quashed. The wartime populist Blyton is more radical than the Edwardian socialist Nesbit: Gladys is a thief, and her parents are criminals. And the reader is intended to be (and under Blyton's narrative skills probably will be) absolutely on her side, belittling her criminal offence as Fatty belittles it, by contrast to the crime of the poison-penman. The critical child might well agree with Fatty while finding touches of pomposity and patronising even here, when he is blazingly right in his ethical judgement. Similarly, Crompton had her snobbish and affected Wing Commander catch the 'bird-man' spy. But the conclusion has to be that Blyton was firmly on the side of the vulnerable underman or underwoman, in her 'over-' as well as her 'under-mind'. It was a philosophy highly consistent with her *Naughtiest Girl in the School* series, with its search for fairness and devotion to a just community sense. Even Julian was forced to apostatise from his imperial arrogance after *Five Run Away Together*. In *Five Have a Wonderful Time* (1952), a circus man tells Julian: 'Us-folk and you-folk don't mix', to which Julian, still a tad arrogant, but very much changed in social philosophy, answers: 'There's a lot of that sort of feeling about these days, and it's so silly. We're all the same under the skin' (or, to put it another way, no class is exempt from being patronised by Julian).[39]

Hildick finds a fascinating parallel for *Five Run Away Together*:[40]

> Reading it, I was put in mind time and again of another children-on-an-island story: a story in which the quality of the writing is much higher but many of the attitudes portrayed are just as primitive. The only difference in this last connection is that William Golding did not present the gleeful witch-hunts and elated self-righteous viciousness of his *Lord of the Flies* children in a favourable light, with his full approval, and for the approval of child readers.

Lord of the Flies was apparently written in 1952, and we cannot say how much of it was shaping itself into being in Golding's mind during his Second World War service (ranging from helping to sink the *Bismarck* to D-Day operations). Certainly, he studied form from children's island stories and owed them a good deal more than either he or his supportive critics and annotators would admit. The genre was ready for the taking when he got it. R. M. Ballantyne's *The Coral Island* (1857), which he was specifically caricaturing, had seven different editions between 1931 and 1937 respectively; and, when the paper shortage eased off, it had six more between 1947 and 1949. Stevenson's *Treasure Island* (1883) had about twenty between 1929 and 1939. *Robinson Crusoe* had four in the 1930s and six more from 1945 to 1949. They duly inspired disciple works, Richards producing two fine *Magnet* series involving South Sea island drama for Grey-friars boys (1927, 1938), and Johns a splendid one in October–December 1939, the last months of the *Gem*, book-published as *Biggles in the South Seas* (1940).[41] Blyton had made her own initial raid (or homage) in *Five on a Treasure Island*, but one heavily subordinated to the earliest and bitterest hostilities between George and her father: the criminals are walk-on parts, most unlike the well-observed portrait of the unscrupulous tutor-cum-spy Roland who capitalises so well on generational strife (*Five Go Adventuring Again*). *Five Run Away Together* turns on the children leaving

George's home, Kirrin Cottage, under the pollution of the Sticks and camping on Kirrin Island, where they ultimately discover the Sticks once more, now on their kidnapping enterprise. This is an island drama instead of merely featuring an island as contested prize between children and criminals, and, more abrasively, between George and her father. Kirrin Island is not in the South Seas – but neither, in any sane sense, is Golding's island. Professors Gregor and Kinkead-Weekes, for instance, held that Golding produced 'an island and boys that are more convincing than Ballantyne's';[42] the boys perhaps (though Ballantyne's Peterkin Gay has a sense of schoolboy humour conspicuously absent from Golding's creations), but Golding's island is a second-hand jigsaw with missing pieces where we get full sets from Ballantyne, Stevenson, Wells, Barrie, Richards and Johns. In some respects the best desert-island story ever written, *Lord of the Flies* dismally violates Orwell's law of the genre – 'none is altogether bad when it sticks to the actual concrete details of the struggle to keep alive' – unless we add the words 'from each other'.[43] But to bring in formerly civilised humanity as red in tooth and claw as this, Golding (like Stevenson in *Treasure Island* before him) has to pacify Nature. It is so surgically done that the rock which kills Piggy is the clone of that which nearly kills Peterkin, one by human hand, its predecessor by natural accident possibly induced by human disturbance of the environment. The one major victory of humanity over obdurate Nature described by Golding, the use of Piggy's glasses to make fire, is incorrect: Gregor and Kinkead-Weekes point out that myopic vision like Piggy's requires glasses which cannot concentrate the sun's rays (Ballantyne's fire-creation was also suspect, according to Orwell). As to the island, how are its flora and fauna so favourable? Where is it? Gregor and Kinkead-Weekes, with more charity than clarity, try to fix it somewhere off Java and Sumatra – for an aircraft to crash after a flight which refuelled at Gibraltar and Addis Ababa. It would be entertaining to hear Biggles on its geographical credibility.

Golding set himself a task to perform on which he delivered magnificently; but he was not building a cathedral and did not pretend that his Meccano construct was anything of the kind. It could as easily be set like Agatha Christie's Nigger Island (*Ten Little Niggers*, 1939) or Blyton's Kirrin Island off the Devon or Dorset[44] coast, provided that it can be inaccessible for the necessary timespan and has a sufficiency of pigs and fruits. The Christie precedent anticipates Golding on quite a few useful instances of Crusoe degeneration;[45] Wells's *The Island of Dr Moreau* makes human degeneration a scientific necessity since all (save the three who had been born humans) derive from the animals to which they are naturally returned (while the human-born are killed or isolated); and Richards plays with the problem in his quiet way, using the two Greyfriars heroes known to have dark sides to their characters to which they succumb, Harry Wharton occasionally, Herbert Vernon-Smith frequently:[46]

> He realised . . . that he had roused a fierce and implacable spirit in his rivals for the treasure: the captain of the Greyfriars Remove had intended both bullets to hit, and only the difficulty of the range had saved Soames. . . .
> 'You're the fattest, and the least use', said the Bounder sardonically. 'It will be your turn after the grub is gone, if we don't get out of this. There's enough of you to last us a week.'

Similarly, Ginger's idyllic existence with the South Sea Islanders is interrupted by murderous enemies:[47]

> Ginger had never hated any one quite as much as he hated the smooth-tongued Corsican. . . .
> The girl drew her knife and laid it on the coral beside her. 'I cut Atanelli's throat bymeby', she announced casually. 'Maybe I eat him', she added pensively as an afterthought.
> In his overwrought state, the picture of Full Moon eating the fat Corsican made Ginger laugh immoderately. The grotto echoed with his laughter.
> 'You no laugh that way', scolded Full Moon sharply. 'You laugh that way you get debil-debil in head.'

One might argue that Golding's environmental deafness lost him the chance of having his degenerate boys make a logical turn to cannibalism. But, in justice to him, this – symbolically, like all else he does in the book – is just what he achieves. The bodies of both Simon and Piggy disappear into the sea poetically, but they have gone through the equivalent of cannibal consumption by their own comrades. Piggy derives from Peterkin (the assumption that Peterkin becomes Simon derives from most Golding commentators' condescension to *The Coral Island* inducing carelessness):[48]

> we heard a most appalling shriek, which was followed by a chorus of yells from the hogs, and a loud hurrah!

'I do believe', said I, 'that Peterkin has met the hogs.'

'When Greek meets Greek', said Jack, soliloquizing, 'then comes the tug of –'.

Both the name and the hunter cult of *Lord of the Flies* have Ballantyne origins here. But Golding worked with many more models from the genre. His Jack is 'Merridew' where Ballantyne's was 'Martin'; and 'Merridew', a rare surname, is that of Richmal Crompton's Ginger.[49] Many of Golding's critics find themselves using the words 'Billy Bunter' in slightly uncertain description of Piggy. And this Richards serial anticipates Golding, by revisionism of Barrie's *The Admirable Crichton*. When the Polynesians are instructed by Samuel Vernon-Smith's homicidal ex-valet Soames to deal with Bunter, Bunter's offensive treatment of anyone whom he can regard as an underling makes him a certain target for retribution:[50]

'Jacky!'

'Yes, sar.'

'You get um rope and knock seven bells outer fat feller plenty quick!'

'Yes, sar.'

Jacky the boatswain cheerfully provided himself with a rope's end. Then he grasped Bunter by the collar.

The Owl of the Remove twisted his head round to blink at the black boatswain in alarm and amazement.

'Hands off, you black beast!' he yelled.

Jacky grinned.

He had been very unwilling to handle Harry Wharton & Co. at Soames's orders. But he was more than willing to handle Bunter. It was Bunter's happy way to inspire in everyone he encountered a desire to kick him. Not more than two or three times had he ever spoken to the boatswain; but each of those times his remarks had been unpleasant. Jacky was more than ready to give Bunter what he had asked for.

'White marster say give um five-five!' grinned Jacky.

'You black idiot!' howled Bunter. 'That fellow isn't your master – he's our servant.'

'There has been a little change on board this schooner', smiled Soames. 'You will now become aware of it, Master Bunter.'

Bunter is made a galley-slave to the cook, and Jacky is shortly afterwards killed by Soames, whom he is trying to kill in a rescue bid. There is little of Bunter's obnoxious character in Piggy, but Piggy's fat and his dissidence induce hostility, passively from Ralph, then actively from Jack. Golding, from the first, intended to transmute to mutual hatred the spirit Ballantyne had declared for *The Coral Island*:[51]

> There was, indeed, no note of discord whatever in the symphony we played together on that sweet Coral Island; and I am now persuaded that this was owing to our having been all tuned to the same key, namely, that of *love!* Yes, we loved one another with much fervency, while we lived on that island; and, for the matter of that, we love each other still.

That is the innocence for whose loss Ralph weeps at the end of Golding's novel, but arguably it never gets a chance in *Lord of the Flies*. Ballantyne's trio know and are fond of each other on board ship before their shipwreck; Golding's Jack, Ralph and Piggy have never met before, although they have crashed in the same aircraft. Ralph's refusal to learn Piggy's real name, his discovery of the loathed nickname 'Piggy', and his treacherous revelation of it to the rest, begin the ugly things that are to happen – and here Golding is at his least explicable. Why does Ralph reject Piggy at the start? – so much so that his beautiful epitaph for Piggy at the end owes some of its grief to his failure to love him when he was alive. Fatness will not do it, and there is no indication that Piggy was known for selfishness, snobbery, greed or other anti-social attributes revealed on the plane, as Bunter's were shown to the Polynesians on the boat. Richards is perpetually on the alert against class or racial contempt, with Bunter there to express it so that heroes and readers can repudiate it. Piggy does not stand in that dock. Golding's intention, expressed crudely, might be to have Ralph as some sort of Neville Chamberlain, Jack and his choristers by Hitler out of Wagner with Simon sideline into mysticism; Piggy would then be the Jews, persecuted by the Nazis but previously victimised and to some extent ostracised by the English ruling class. But the actual Piggy of the novel is not Jewish, however much the name invites us to remember the despicable pig/pork taunts radiated at Jews by anti-Semites of the early twentieth century. Admittedly, allegories were more common in mid-twentieth-century British literature than unhistorical critics allow for. John Masefield, in an attack on Munich and what he took to be its inertia/ideology, introduced an imaginary white kingdom in Africa in *Live and Kicking Ned* (1939), virtually anticipating a defeatist Pétain and very clear about Germans in relation to Hitler:[52]

> 'I am one who likes the M'gai very much. They are good straight people; when they say a thing they do a thing. It's only lately that they've got this idea of grab and kill. This isn't the people; it's the brute who rules them, and his little gang of murderers. But they're like children or like sheep; they obey; they do just what they are told to do, and believe every tale as true.'

Live and Kicking Ned was held not to be children's literature (the hero is unsuccessfully hanged in the precursor novel *Dead Ned*, 1938), but would have been prescribed as children's literature had it appeared in the 1950s, when *Lord of the Flies* and *The Catcher in the Rye* were. One major effect of the Second World War on children's literature was that the post-war child was deemed less squeamish.

Golding, in his lecture 'Fable', said: 'I did not want a Marxist exegesis. If disaster came, it was not to come through the exploitation of one class by another.' He was very conscious of Orwell's *Animal Farm*, another fable for the time (and one which Golding, with unconvincing arrogance, said that 'children do not like').[53] But class hostility like Five versus the Sticks does not turn on exploitation (apart from the Five demanding food from Mrs Stick, who serves them inadequate meals which they discard in favour of better ones raided from her, or rather from Uncle Quentin's stores). Piggy is quite definitely presented as a Cockney whose speech inspires ridicule rather than being recognised as wit, the two commonplace middle-class reactions to Cockney. Piggy's first words label him: 'Hi!' (not then English middle-class usage, but perhaps indicative of working-class child response to US armed-forces vocabulary during the Second World War) and 'I can't hardly move with all these creeper things', while Ralph, not yet seeing him, 'jerked his stockings with an automatic gesture that made the jungle seem for a moment like the Home Counties'. Shortly, Ralph will be jeering at Piggy's allusions to his 'ass-mar' and his 'auntie'. When the others appear, there grows up 'tacitly . . . the opinion that Piggy was an outsider, not only by accent, which did not matter, but by fat, and ass-mar, and specs, and a certain disinclination for manual labour';[54] but the accent clearly does matter, whatever hypocrisies the Home Counties may have schooled. It is not Bunter (apart from the specs, fat and laziness); Bunter is the greatest snob in Greyfriars, and his speech is that of an adult bourgeois. Could it be Blyton?

Blyton establishes her cast of *Five Run Away Together* on the mainland; in a way, her 'island' includes Kirrin Cottage ashore. George knows and dislikes the Sticks before the opening, but their first mention is on Mrs Stick's 'sour-faced' appearance to help Julian, Dick and Anne with their luggage on arrival.

> 'Who's she?' they whispered to George.
>
> 'The new cook', said George. 'Joanna had to go and look after her mother, who broke her leg. Then Mother got this cook – Mrs Stick her name is.'
>
> 'Good name for her', grinned Julian. 'She looks a real old stick! But all the same I hope she doesn't stick here for long. I hope Joanna comes back. I liked old fat Joanna, and she was nice to Timmy.'
>
> 'Mrs Stick has a dog too', said George. 'A dreadful animal, smaller than Tim, all sort of mangy and moth-eaten. Tim can't bear it.'
>
> 'Where is it?' asked Anne, looking round.
>
> 'It's kept in the kitchen, and Tim isn't allowed near it', said George. 'Good thing too, because I'm sure he'd eat it! He can't think what's in the kitchen, and goes sniffing round the shut door till Mrs Stick nearly goes mad.'
>
> The others laughed.

The hint of cannibalism to start us off is most unpleasant, all the more from a dog perpetually presented as a human colleague with human attributes exaggerated but by no means all invented by George. The only other notable cannibal dog in favourite books read by children at this time was the hound of the Baskervilles, whose story ends with the discovery that he had eaten Dr Mortimer's curly-haired spaniel – and the Holmes stories were a recent source for Blyton. The cannibal motif continues, when the cousins meet the boy Edgar Stick (Julian's contemporary, but – intentionally or otherwise – sounding retarded):

> 'Georgie-porgie', began Edgar again, a silly smile on his wide red face. Julian made a step towards him, and he at once disappeared into the house.
>
> 'Shan't stand much of *him*', said Julian, in a decided voice. 'I wonder *you* do, George. I wonder you haven't slapped his face, stamped on his foot, bitten his ears off and done a few other things! You used to be so fierce.'

It is hardly surprising, after this encouragement, that George is slapping Edgar's face within a few pages, and Julian promptly denounces him for wanting to retaliate. Overtures of civility on Edgar's part are repulsed with ignominy. And so on until the author's farewell to Edgar at the end of the story:

> The Sticks went quietly, Edgar sobbing away to himself. He imagined his mother and father in prison, and he himself sent to a hard and difficult school, not allowed to see his mother for years. Not that that would matter, for the Sticks, both mother and father, were no good to Edgar, and had taught him nothing but bad things. There might be a chance for the wretched boy if he were kept away from them, and set a good example instead of a bad one.

This is not hypocrisy from Blyton, who within two years would be defending the rights of prison graduates in *The Mystery of the Spiteful Letters*. But the Five, from the first, had been of no better use than the Stick parents towards Edgar's redemption, and any reservations by Blyton about their behaviour were not transmitted to her child readers. It is of course Edgar's inferior class status and accent, not his intellect, that prefigure Piggy. So does Edgar's nickname, 'Spotty-Face', with which the Five saddle him. At the end, the kidnapped little girl Jenny Armstrong joins the Five for a week's holiday, a fairly astounding permission to be granted by the parents to whom she has just been restored. The remarks about Stick parental inadequacy uttered almost at the same time ring curiously in the context. Edgar is at one point substituted by the Five as a prisoner in place of little Jenny, a preliminary emasculation having been hinted at by George in her instruction to Timmy:[55]

> 'Now you listen, Timothy – if this boy shouts, you just go for him! Lie here by him and show him your big teeth. Bite him wherever you like if he yells.'
> 'Woof!' said Timmy, looking really pleased. He lay down by Edgar, and the boy tried to move away. But Timmy came nearer every time he moved.

Hildick would seem to have tapped one source for Golding's novel, enabling us to see that Golding was not really imposing a new interpretation on the desert-island adventure but in fact releasing forces which by war's end implicitly were already there. As evidence on British mentality in 1943, *Five Run Away Together* would also seem to show that the vanishing of the servant class had sundered some of the sense of community to which writers had clung ideologically in the war's early years. Other instances of such disillusion followed by counter-attack appear in Johns, not through servants but in another, equally disruptive occupation – the commandos.

Blyton produced as a children's book a serious sociological reflection on Britain at the war's end: The Put-Em-Rights (1946). She had recovered her ethical balance, and presumably her emotional balance with it. It took her back to her literary roots, specifically E. Nesbit's works: directly The Wouldbegoods (1901), indirectly but more profoundly, The Railway Children (1906). Sheila Ray's generous but over-zealous professional didacticism finds that The Put-Em-Rights 'lacks an anchor figure. One of the children should be a totally sympathetic character with whom the readers can identify as they can with Oswald'[56] Bastable in Nesbit. This is to miss Nesbit's ironies. Oswald attracts sympathy in spite of his leadership rather than because of it: his bossiness and self-satisfaction keep the reader laughing at him, unless of course the reader is bossy and self-satisfied. Blyton has far less irony than Nesbit, at least formally: Julian would be much improved by a little of Nesbit's treatment of Oswald, but George's general challenge to him gives him a chance to stay human. Julian was Blyton's first major attempt at child leadership from within a family; her two memorable leaders to that point, Jack and Andy, had been from classes lower than those they led, their expertise from hard economics giving them authority and attractiveness in the eyes of their less experienced followers. (Nesbit, for all of her socialism, had kept leadership within the bourgeois family, however fluctuating its economic circumstances.) Jack and Andy would have been exemplars for evacuees to bear in mind when confronted with rural children knowledgeable in lifestyles unknown to the new arrivals. Fatty, when finally he achieved leadership, was an interesting variant: the rich boy has to prove himself and, for all of his achievements, remains a figure of fun, whose wealth and independence of parents always seem vaguely wrong, and who ultimately finds his best same-sex relationship with the working-class nephew of Goon, his bitterest enemy. Crompton's William was from the same economic bracket as the other Outlaws, but in the Second World War for the first time his family income and lifestyle are shown as decidedly below that of the hated Hubert Lane, whose father has access to black-market food supplies and whose mother takes him to West End films demanding a late train 'partly to show their superiority to people who bought "cheap day tickets" . . . partly in order that Hubert could say', when the film arrived in Hadley later, 'That old thing! Good Lord! I saw it in London ages ago!'[57] But William's successes in any story were as a rule uncertain enough to hold the audience without diversion of sympathies. Blyton's adventure stories were committed to plots where the children would win, if not always without some attrition: therefore she frequently followed the Conan Doyle principle of a somewhat inaccessible leader with much of the progress of events seen through a more sympathetic and more vulnerable supporter, usually the younger and more feminine girl. Ray's demand for a 'totally sympathetic character' misreads 1930s and 1940s children: as a rule, they did not want paragons, goody-goodies or eternal reliables, and their sympathies were the greater when the hero and/or the sidekick occasionally made fools of themselves, when the lion's folly required rescue by the mouse. Blyton had produced innumerable moral tales for *Sunny Stories* in which the protagonist meets some appropriate nemesis (with a sporting chance of recovery and reform).

The Put-Em-Rights is in fact a development of Jesus Christ's instruction to pluck out the beam in one's own eye before looking at the mote in one's brother's, and Blyton works it out by detective-story surprises. Her protagonist who is going to set all in order, as we can see, begins the action: Sally Wilson, the capable if bossy daughter of the capable if bossy headmistress of the village school – not the school Sally goes to, whence a class division is asserted from the first. It might be thought from this that Blyton will give her her comeuppance before we are through; but, instead of labouring the point, Blyton, Christie-like, conceals the clue having momentarily flourished it, and we are brought into an extraordinary epiphany. Sally and her two friends from the Rectory and their two friends from the big house (pastor's children, squire's children) are brought to listen to 'the Tramping Preacher', a charismatic figure, addressed affectionately by the Rector (who presents him) as 'Tramp':

> He looked like a gipsy. He was burnt a very dark brown, his eyes were intensely blue, and his thick shock of hair was black, streaked with grey. He wore corduroy trousers and a blue shirt, with a fairly respectable jacket over it.

('Corduroy' was workman's, or rough, garb in those days.) He is exclusively a preacher for children:

They rose when the Tramp came down the high street. Some of the bigger boys looked sulky. They had wanted to play cricket, not listen to a preacher. But in two minutes the Tramp had them all under his spell in his usual easy way. There was not a sound to be heard as he talked. He told them stories. He made them laugh, and he made the tears stand in their eyes. He stirred their hearts and their imaginations; he made them feel that they were strong and could do anything, anything!

It is a convention used by Crompton, whose wartime preachers are dealt with mercilessly (the wealthy Mrs Dayford lecturing Violet Elizabeth's guests on the need for self-denial, the manic puritan Mrs Sedley-Mortimer daubing her face with cosmetics to inculcate 'the virtues of industry, obedience and self-control'). Blyton is both more reverential – the Tramp is clearly a modern version of Christ – and more disturbing. The children resolve to form a band and tell the Tramp so:

He looked at their serious faces and seemed pleased. Already he knew he had thousands of children working for him, carrying out his ideas, trying to make the world a better place for everyone.

'Well, I wish you good luck', said the Tramp when he left. 'I'll be back again, I hope, and then you shall tell me how you've all got on. Watch and pray and work – those are the things to do.'

But in fact he never reappears (presumably until the Second Coming). He does not produce versions of the mote and the beam in his advice, but the story shows how each of the children set out patronisingly to put their neighbours to rights, and find much more than they have bargained for. The mean boy Micky has to persuade the jobbing gardener not to ill-treat his 'dirty, mangy little mongrel' Midge (very definite, and perhaps self-reproachful, shades of Tinker/Stinker), and finds himself paying for the dog's licence and collar, and the dog itself – after which the gardener becomes fond of the dog, and repays the boy, who insists on the collar being a present. The careless, wealthy boy Claude ('Podge') discovers that the landlord who is about to evict the Tupps is his own father, who is convinced that Mr Tupp has stolen Podge's bicycle, which in fact was grabbed from where Podge had left it by the Tupps' retarded child (shades of Edgar?), and the angry, ashamed landlord ends by denouncing his own son's carelessness in putting temptation in the imbecile's way. The landlord's brother, a surgeon, then cures the brain damage retarding the child, and in facing the angry Tupps during negotiations the surgeon's daughter loses her normal fear, although initially hostility across the class divide makes for great fear. The snobbish boy from the 'village children', Bobby, who has ingratiated himself into the band, takes soup to the Peppers, a village family, because he thinks their father is in prison; the mother pours the ('lukewarm') soup on his head, and it turns out that his own father is in prison. Sally then calls on the Peppers to instruct them to keep quiet about it:

> 'You'll be sorry, Mrs Pepper, if you do this thing, and bring shame on Mrs Jones and Bobby. I am sure everyone will think badly of you if you tittle-tattle about such a matter.'
>
> Mrs Pepper never had tittle-tattled. She was a kind and generous-hearted woman, who always stopped any unkind talk if she heard it. It made her furious that Sally should think she was a tittle-tattler. She went red in the face, and rubbed her hands up and down her soapy arms. She made up her mind to give Sally a shock.
>
> 'Now, look here, Miss Bossy', she said, 'you've come to the wrong house if you think *you're* going to order someone about. Your mother runs this village, and good luck to her – but *you're* not going to run it too! One Wilson running this place is quite enough! And let me tell you this, Miss Bossy – I wasn't going to say a word about Bobby's father, not one word, see? But now you've interfered and tried to boss me round, I've changed my mind! I shall tell every single person what I know about Thomas Jones!'

Sally's subsequent attempts to tell Mrs Jones she should now move out of the village results in Mrs Pepper joining forces with the hitherto snobbish Mrs Jones:

> 'I'm sorry for you, Mrs Jones – it must be hard to have your man in prison, and hard for your boy to know it too.'
>
> Mrs Jones felt the tears coming to her eyes again, and she hastily dabbed them away. 'Yes', she said, 'it's been hard, but I hoped Bobby would never know, and maybe I could bring him up to be better than his father was – and so be proud of my son, if I couldn't be proud of his father.'

Her method of doing this had included jumping to the conclusion that Mrs Pepper's husband was in jail and telling Bobby, so that Mrs

Pepper's reply showed a fine charity – coming from the intended recipient of the Put-Em-Rights' benevolence:[58]

> 'Well it seems to me you're going the wrong way about it', said sensible Mrs Pepper. 'Filling his head with all kinds of grand ideas, instead of letting him make friends with the children he knows. You let him come to tea with my twins sometimes; they'll be good for him! And he'll be good for them, too, for he's got nice manners, your Bobby has. I've always said he was a nice boy, if it wasn't that he sucked up to children who probably didn't want him!'
>
> The real kindness in Mrs Pepper's voice, and the common sense in her words warmed Mrs Jones. She began to feel almost happy. She needn't leave the village! She could still hold up her head. No one would point their fingers at her Bobby. Things suddenly seemed very much brighter.
>
> 'You've done me good', she said to Mrs Pepper. 'That Sally properly upset me.'
>
> For a few minutes the two talked vigorously about Sally and her failings. Then Mrs Jones put the kettle on to make a cup of tea for herself and Mrs Pepper. She found herself liking the sensible, kindly little woman immensely. How could she have been so silly as to hold herself aloof from everyone, and look down on them. Why, Mrs Pepper was a far better person than she was!

Jane Austen it isn't, but Blyton had evidently read *Emma* to some profit: her moral is the same, in its hostility to unthinking condescension to lower orders and better results in seeking support from one's own social equals. Nor is the disciple despicable, even from the lonely heights where Austen's genius reigns. As Sheila Ray observes:[59]

> Most readers must find Mrs Pepper's reaction to Sally most enjoyable and we are given a convincing and sympathetic insight into Mrs Pepper's thoughts as she tells Sally what she thinks of her. Mrs Pepper continues to develop as a character, one of the most convincing adult characters in the whole of Enid Blyton's work . . .

It is also a startling leap of the generation and parental gap. Crompton, Evadne Price and others had given their child readers many satirical eavesdroppings on adult conversations, and Brent-Dyer, or even Richards, might make the reader develop some sense of life from the schoolteacher's view; but this is serious appreciation of adult error and trial. It is also the working-class female hero in children's literature, and one of the best to emerge from the Second World War. (Mrs Pepper's dog, by the way, is called Tinker.) But, although Bobby will be touched when all the other Put-Em-Rights apart from Sally rush to comfort him with little gifts they know he would prize, on hearing his tragedy, he determines to drop out of the little circle of friends when the next holidays came. 'The others wouldn't really miss him, he knew that.' He looks forward to a 'natural' friendship with the Pepper twins (to whom he has been hitherto ' "Stuck-Up" Jones'), 'far more natural than he could ever be with Podge or Micky'. Trying 'to suck up to children just because he thought they were richer or better than himself . . . was a silly thing to do . . . it made him a stupid little snob, without any character at all, because he was always afraid of airing his own opinions in case the others laughed at him'.

Yet *The Put-Em-Rights* did not reject real friendship across class lines, arising from triumph over mutual hostilities or partnership in tough work. Amanda, the lazy child, assumes that she is to tell the supposedly slovenly Mrs Potts how important it is to keep a clean house. It turns out that Mrs Potts is ill, and grieving for her husband in the navy, and unable to cope with a small baby ('Yes, I know what everyone says about me! Now you'll go back to the Rectory and tell everyone what a filthy place this is. I know you and your kind!'). In fact, although unstated, she has post-natal depression. Shamed, Amanda starts to help, discovering how to wash clothes en route ('Can't you wash clothes? How old are you? My, when I was your age I could do all the family wash and iron it too. It won't do you any harm to wash out those curtains, will it? I'd do them myself only I feel that ill'). Many middle-class children presumably had some such baptism of fire – or of soap-suds – when evacuated, but the irony of the reformer being introduced to work shows Blyton's study of Dickens as well as of her contemporaries. Blyton also gives her child audience another taste of war attrition, when Amanda has to call in Mrs Potts's mother, who shows one effect of a husband far away in the navy, almost never writing:

'A better girl than Rene you couldn't see, and a right smart boy Ted is too. Poor girl, she got so down never hearing from him. She let herself go to pieces, and the house too, instead of seeing the doctor and getting things put right. Obstinate, that's what she is. Always afraid of having to go to hospital, though I must say when I was there I properly enjoyed myself. Only time in my life I've ever been fussed round.'

(Blyton was proving a cool and not at all condescending auditor of lower-class speech where most of her contemporaries were content to drop an aitch or two and leave the rest to reader snobbery.) Mrs Potts has to go to hospital, and Amanda is conscripted to supervise Francie, a younger sibling or niece, in putting the house to rights:

'I shall come back this afternoon', she said. 'And I shall come to-morrow, too. In fact, I shall go on coming till the kitchen is fit for Ted to come back to.'

'Well, it'll be nice to have company', said Francie, finishing her tea. 'But I guess you won't stick it after this morning. Anyone can see you're not used to work like this. You'll be tired out and fed up – and that's the last I'll see of you.'

'I don't know why you have such a bad opinion of me', said Amanda, half angry and half hurt. 'I dare-say I don't know how to do things in a house as well as you do, but I can do them if I know.'

'Don't go and get high-and-mighty again', said Francie, grinning at Amanda. 'I like you.'

Amanda suddenly felt pleased. She didn't know why she should be glad that this rather sulky, lazy girl should like her, but she was. She began to like Francie, too.

'Do you help your mother, like I have to help mine?' asked Francie. 'You've only got one maid, haven't you, in that big Rectory? I reckon there's a lot to do.'

Amanda said nothing, because she didn't help mother at all: she didn't even make her own bed. Her mother had said she must, but all that Amanda did was to drag the sheets and blankets up each day, so Alice now did it for her. She didn't like to admit to Francie that she didn't help her mother at all.

Eventually the house is in good shape, Rene (Mrs Potts) comes back from hospital, and Ted comes home from the navy. The war had not been mentioned (readers would know why Ted has been away so long in the navy), but Blyton with assistance from Nesbit managed a fine vision of sailor, from the wars returning:[60]

He stopped at the little gate and looked with pride and joy at his house and garden, both so trim and neat. He saw the rose-tree in the middle full of red roses. He walked in, went to the rose-tree and picked the biggest red rose there.

Then he went to the open door of the cottage to find Rene. She was there to meet him, her face radiant. What a day, what a wonderful day! She had got back her home, her baby and her husband all at once, and she looked lovely with happiness.

'Come on. Let's go', said Francie, in a low voice. 'They'll not want us hanging around here. We'll slip out of the back door. Come on, Amanda!'

Amanda, her eyes taking in the happiness of the two people, seeing Ted give his wife the red rose to show he loved her, hearing Hilda crow with delight to see yet another visitor, was quite lost. She sat there, staring, and Francie had to give her a sharp nudge.

'Come on, Amanda, I tell you! They don't want us. We've done our bit, and we must go.'

'Yes', said Amanda, sighing, and got up to go. The two girls slipped out of the back door, and went across the field there. They looked at one another.

The working-class child knows more about sex than the middle-class one, and thus it is she who has the greater delicacy and refinement here. The departure of the observers derives from Nesbit's *The Railway Children*, whose last lines follow the pardoned convict's return to his family, as the author turns her readers away:[61]

He goes in and the door is shut. I think we will not open the door or follow him. I think that just now we are not wanted here. I think it will be best for us to go quickly and quietly away. At the end of the field, among the thin gold spikes of grass and the harebells and Gipsy roses and St John's Wort, we may just take one last look, over our shoulders, at the white house where neither we nor anyone else is wanted now.

Blyton could take a genial authorial farewell of characters at the end of many a story, though never with this delicacy. But within *The Put-Em-Rights* she has appropriated the Nesbit endgame, handed it to her little proletarian Francie, given Amanda the unspoken regretful sigh of Nesbit's reader, and captured the sublime moment of war's end. Streatfeild remarks of the scene earlier in *The Railway Children* when the mother says goodnight to the children in the unknown, new, remote house to which poverty and shame have driven them:[62]

how truly she had written that scene, not for one brave mother at the beginning of the century, but for brave mothers everywhere in the nineteen-forties, who knew that security, though non-existent, could be built by words. It might have touched her had she been alive and able to visit a shelter, to watch mothers making home out of a hard bench, and to have heard them, in words very similar to those used by her mother in *The Railway Children*, assuring their offspring that while they were around there was nothing of which to be afraid.

It was appropriate for the future author of a fine post-war novel about the Blitz, *When the Siren Wailed* (1974). But Blyton's appropriation was no less justified: nobody had worked harder than she to comfort the children of faraway parents, for all ages from all classes, until demobilisation day – and, of course, after.

The vanishing servant and the divided classes took rather different forms in the hands of children's writers from – and for – overseas. Evadne Price (1896–1985) and 'Pamela Lyndon Travers' (1889–1906) were Australian-born, settled in England, both young actresses becoming journalists, both responding to the Second World War with new self-discovery, Travers working for the UK Ministry of Information in the USA, Price among the first British correspondents to reach Berchtesgaden in the war's last months and subsequently reporting the Nuremberg trials for the London *People*. Mary Norton (1903–92) was English-born but lived in Portugal (after being an actress) from 1927 to 1939, and then worked in the UK (in the War Office) and in the USA (probably for British Intelligence). Their blend of exile, of acting, writing and spying was heady stuff, but their storybook Englands were traditionally nostalgic with wildly inflated eccentricities. For Travers and Norton, magic was only just around the corner;[63] for Price, realism was pushed beyond possible limits. All of them responded to the Second World War by depiction of trusted servants departing, Price and Norton in different ways blaming evacuees, Travers (with story still firmly pre-war) by the wind or the weather changing, since the 'servant' is Mary Poppins, previously met in two earlier books (1934, 1935). But Travers's sole Mary Poppins story from the Second World War ends with her final departure; the later books to follow *Mary Poppins Opens the Door* (1943) are retrospectives. Mary Poppins, like Harold Macmillan, knew a wind of change when she saw it and whether it was temporary or permanent; and the wind of change in the Second World War was the effective removal of the class whose most triumphant symbol she had embodied. In one way, her very advent in *Mary Poppins* (1934) was an omen: her first formal action was to inform her potential employer that letters of reference from former employers were old-fashioned, and to make it clear that it was she, and not her charges' parents, who would decide whether she would stay and when she would go. By the time of her last return in the Second World War those conditions were general.

Norton ends *The Magic Bedknob* (1945) by having the evacuee children sent back to their mother in London ('war job or no war job') for allowing their bed to become waterlogged, and persisting in the true but incredible explanation:[64]

> 'What I still don't understand', reiterated Aunt Beatrice, 'is from where you got the water.'
>
> 'From the sea', said Paul suddenly. 'Carey told you.'
>
> Aunt Beatrice raised her almost hairless eyebrows. She picked up her pen and turned back to her desk. Her thin smile was far from reassuring.
>
> 'No matter', she said. 'I have wired your mother, and Elizabeth is packing your things – the last service Elizabeth will perform for me. After all these years she has given me notice.'

And that is enough reason for the children to be sent back to take their chances with bombs, regardless of their father's absence from home in the armed forces or their claim of blood relationship. They are dismissed, to be driven to the station by the milkman, since taxis are no more. Their aunt gives them no more, and no further farewell, not even a handshake. The sequel, *Bonfires and Broomsticks* (1947), is still set in wartime, but Aunt Beatrice's death scarcely matters to the children. We never learn whether Elizabeth repented her decision on the news of the ouster of the children, or whether Aunt Beatrice made do as best she could with such new servants as the wartime labour conditions would permit. Certainly Elizabeth's notice, even withdrawn, dissolves their social contract. Aunt Beatrice may have symbolised the old guard that dies but never surrenders; she certainly symbolised the old order that remained unchanging even when being displaced by the new. The imperial gaze beneath the almost hairless eyebrows daunted, but for all of its icy authority blanketed youthful conviction with little more substance than the emperor received from the new clothes that he flaunted with such pride. When Elizabeth concluded that neither length of service nor feudal spirit would keep her in a house where the younger generation immersed beds in water allegedly from the (South) seas, Aunt Beatrice's only remaining resources were the milkman, and death.

At the same time, P. L. Travers was also confronting servant power with magic. In *Mary Poppins Opens the Door*, Mary Poppins's cousin Mr Twigley is threatened with marriage by his ruthlessly faithful housekeeper. The story is set before the Second World War, and this idea is old in fact and fiction. But wartime necessities may have given it rather more immediate terror:

> The owner of the head stood before them, glowering. She wore large black boots, a blue-and-white checked apron and a black shawl round her shoulders. Jane and Michael thought she was the ugliest person they had ever seen. And they felt very sorry for Mr Twigley.
>
> 'What – you again!' the huge woman shouted. 'I told you he wasn't in. And in he is not, or my name's not Sarah Clump!'
>
> 'Then you aren't Mrs Twigley!' exclaimed Michael, with relief.
>
> 'Not yet', she remarked, with an ominous smile. 'Here! Down you come, all of you!' she added. For Mary Poppins, with the speed of a serpent, had slipped through the doorway and was dragging the children up the stairs. 'Do you hear me? I'll have the Law on you, bursting into a decent woman's house like a set of Vampires!'
>
> 'Decent!' said Mary Poppins, snorting. 'If you're decent I'm a Dromedary!'

Ultimately, Mary Poppins – no enthusiast for servant power over-turning convention in her own family – clamps Sarah Clump's feet magically to the floor, after which Mr Twigley shrinks her to dwell in a tiny Golden Palace where to live on Peacock Pie. Mrs Clump's moment of repentance between the two enchantments, for all its flickering pathos, is ignored:

> she flung out her arms with a cry of anguish:
>
> 'Mr Twigley!' she begged. 'Please help me, sir! I've always cooked you tasty meals. I've always kept you clean and tidy. You won't have to marry me, I promise. If you'll only wish something to set me free!'
>
> 'Be careful, Fred!' warned Mary Poppins . . .

Mrs Clump's final state admirably captured the museum condition of the idea of the old reliable, or master servant.[65]

Evelyn Price's identity as a children's author did not survive the war, although her last book of loosely linked short stories about the calamitous Jane, *Jane at War* [1947], did not appear until the war was over. None of its content seems subsequent to 1941, and the last event in UK history to be mentioned was clothes-rationing, described here as unexpected by quite watchful local committees, and introduced in fact on 1–2 June 1941. Even when war is accepted as inevitable, Jane's unspeakably snobbish mother, Mrs Turpin, cannot bring herself to refer to a head of state without giving him a prefix when she is in the presence of social inferiors, telling the hospitalised Jane that her elder sister's young man is 'going to the war to be a soldier soon, in uniform, and fight that naughty Mr Hitler'.[66]

Price was an even more savage though less subtle social observer than Crompton, but there must be some uncertainty as to how far she intended *Jane the Patient* (1940), in particular, to exhibit class warfare quite as dreadful as it reveals. Her little heroine in this volume is loathsome to a primary degree, though certainly outstripped by her own family, who win doctoral status in snobbishness, with no reservation. *Jane the Patient* is a useful book for the working historian, describing as it does the operation of a village or small-town hospital ward on the eve of the Second World War. It lacks the breadth, the compassion or the sheer felicity in character-study of Monica Dickens's *One Pair of Feet* (covering the early months of the war and more factually based as a book for old and young adults), but it contains data which Dickens either did not know or might not print. Lady Metwall bullies the hospital to admit protégés of her own, despite the pressure on beds, and insists that possible patients accept her offers of pressure to get them into hospital for operations or other special attention they might not want or need. Price described an appalling waste of hospital resources to facilitate snobbery and jobbery while the nursing staff were being stretched to the limit preparing for possible major casualties with a war-declaration imminent. The book highlighted eve-of-war bourgeois horror on the social mixing of patients into general wards. Jane's mother complains in a loud voice about the disgrace of her daughter being put in a bed with elderly charwomen on either side, who 'look like gypsies or street hawkers . . . That is the worst of public institutions, they are so heartless.' On visiting day, Jane's sister Marjorie is shrieking with laughter at the endless jokes of her friend Willie at the expense of the two charwomen; admittedly, he is finally silenced when one of them tells him: 'Yer want yer trousers smacked, my lad'. Jane is embarrassed by this, and understandably defends her family against its well-justified critics to her left and right, but then engages in lengthy campaigns against the two old women so that one swallows an appliance, Jane pours soup over the head of the other, and so on. The charwomen are unscrupulous malingerers; nobody admits that they might be entitled to some rest after a lifetime's floor-cleaning with the inadequate equipment and pay of those times. One is a swindler, the other a thief. They have some cultural attainments, appropriately citing *Little Lord Fauntleroy* and the play of *East Lynne* in the context of Turpin dress ostentation: it suggests interest in the theatre, but nobody makes anything of it. Although the ward sister has been disgusted by Mrs Turpin's snobbery, demands for special privileges, refusal to recognise the bed famine on the eve of war, and above all insistence on calling the sister 'Nurse', she sees Jane as an innocent child, and perpetually supports her against the charwomen, one of whom ably sums up:[67] 'No, there's one law fer the rich an' one fer the poor in Duppery 'Orspital, an' no justice for them as don't talk la-de-dah . . .' But this is merely felt to be unintentionally funny.

The servant situation in the Turpin household by the Second World War is dominated by 'Vilet', whose phonetic spelling may not have been condescending so much as natural, since – like many another sound – it happily encompassed both the Cockney and the Australian speech. This is a useful key. When in the Antipodes, Australians, like New Zealanders, might have their superfluidity of gentility in the cult of 'Home' (which emphatically meant the Home Counties); but Price, having cut her sharp teeth in London popular journalism, and before it on the London stage, knew all too much of the permanent social victimisation of the returned colonial. The Canadians could take refuge in a North American sound of wealth; the South Africans might betoken even greater wealth, less widely apportioned; the New Zealanders might pass for South Africans; the Anglo-Indians meant Kipling – and Kipling, however vulgar, was patriotically unassailable. But Australians sounded Cockney, and Cockneys meant lower-class comedy. 'Vilet' is sometimes the author's voice. Price and Travers celebrate the female servant as the outstanding mind of the household, devaluing the prevailing social conventions however much she may pretend to conform to them. 'Vilet' is Jane's ally rather than wielding any but an immediate moral authority. Jane will obey her from motives of respect as well as of common interest. 'Vilet' is married, living out the convention that the love-lives of servants are essentially comic (a useful means of sidelining moral responsibilities arising from them):

there was Arnie, her husband, who had been jointly engaged with her, and who was probably the world's worst gardener and odd-jobman. No other household would tolerate Arnie, Vilet knew, and give him good wages for it – wages which were far above the average.

Since the story is largely told within a child's world, although reflecting well beyond a child's articulate thought, we do not know whether Vilet retains Arnie as husband only from motives of respectability; we must assume there was a Lawrentian sex-appeal to start with, however unimaginable it may be now. In general, Vilet's pre-eminence as a cook keeps Arnie employed, but the war calls this into question, especially as his main task is now the building of the Air Raid Shelter which seems to combine Sisyphus's stone and Penelope's web, perpetually reducing itself, or reduced by its maker, back to its initial chaos. Mrs Turpin 'had come into the kitchen to tell Vilet that war economies would compel the master to dispense with Arnie', whence Vilet tries to make Arnie enlist:

'That's what I been expectin', you lazy work-dodger. Never happy unless you're drinkin' at the Spotted Duck. I knew this Air Raid Shelter would lose us this job. Years you been on it. Well, I'm not going to keep you. Just you go and enlist at the recruitin' office and make me proud of you. You go off an' die for your country.'

Arnie didn't want to die for his country, but he didn't dare tell Vilet so in the mood she was in. He finally slunk to the recruiting office and joined the queue, and when his turn came he was received with shocking sarcasm by the brawny sergeant, who said to his partner in crime, ''Ullo! Here's one of the ruins that Cromwell knocked about a bit!' Arnie told him he had come to enlist, and the sergeant's voice became insultingly soothing, and the other soldier rocked with mirth. 'Mind', said the sergeant, 'I'm not sayin' as Hitler mightn't get such a shock at the sight of them knock-knees of yours in riding-breeches, and that saggin' tum-tum of yours in a tunic that he mightn't fall dead on the spot, an' finish the war. We'll send for you if things get really desprit, shall we?'

Vilet won't believe Arnie, and drags him back:

And when the sergeant had seen her he had got very fresh indeed. 'Ah, brought Granpa back, miss?'

'Don't you call my husband names, please. You just shove him into kharki and make me proud of him.'

The sergeant said he couldn't work miracles, much as he would like to. 'You let him die for his country with a pint pot in the Spotted Duck nice and peaceful, missus', he had said. And that had torn it.

'So that's why you turned him down, because he's a drunkard, is it?' Vilet had asked, and even when the sergeant had stuck up for him, she wouldn't listen. Off she stalked home, with Arnie in her backwash. . . . 'Out an' finish that Air Raid Shelter and don't stop till pitch dark or you go to bed supperless as well as tealess.'

'I wish I was in Russia', Arnie muttered. 'I'm sick of bein' a British Wage Slave, an' I 'ope the Germans drops a bomb on the kitchen an' frightens 'ell out of Vilet. I'd drop one meself if I 'ad one.'

This seems as close as the British child got to the Nazi–Soviet pact in domestic operation (as opposed to Biggles's encounters with it in Finland), and in practice it meant Jane and friends shouting 'Hell Hitler!' satirically at Arnie with Nazi salutes. They denounce him to Vilet as a spy:

'Married to a dirty German spy, me with a cousin Ted in the Navy. You never liked cousin Ted, did you?' asked Vilet with sudden venom. 'Proberly tryin' to sink cousin Ted's battleship, I shouldn't wonder, 'cause 'e's too straight for you.'

'I would not, Vilet –'

'As well as set fire to the munition works. Proberly you done all them explosions in the Undergrounds in London an' blew the cloakrooms to bits. Yes, you done that.'

'I never, that was the I.R.A.', protested Arnie.

'It's all the same', said Vilet recklessly, 'sinkin' ships an' droppin' bombs on civilians an' ruinin' people's luggage in cloak-rooms. What's it matter to you, you low-down spy, tryin' to do my poor cousin Ted in?'

Eventually, Mrs Turpin discovers that no other gardener would be available: 'there wasn't even a jobbing one to be had and what they would do for vegetables . . . "No, I shall not economize by getting rid of Arnold, Cook, I promise"' (Mrs Turpin's snobbery not only perpetuates the dehumanising 'Cook' as a mode of address, but is also so wilfully ignorant of Cockney – and Australian – vowels that she takes 'Arnie' to be diminutive for 'Arnold' instead of 'Ernest').[68]

The identification of Communist sympathies with chronic lay-abouts had been prominent in popular literature since the Russian Revolution. Children's literature made less of it, if only because the Bolshevik theme was expected to expectorate heartless psychopaths and fanatical world-subverters. The Nazi–Soviet pact brought various traditional targets together, and just as Arnie's laziness now acquired a satisfactory political and propaganda context, much less amusing writers such as Percy F. Westerman came into their own. Westerman's *When the Allies Swept the Seas* (1940) was a navy story set shortly after the start of the war. It concludes after heavy fighting with ironic epiphanies of propaganda posters back in England. Our hero's railway carriage is invaded by an undesirable:

> The door was pulled open and a weedy, flatchested lout of about twenty, with a stained cigarette sticking to a pendant lower lip, shuffled into the carriage, and, taking a corner seat, put his feet up on the opposite one.
>
> Before the war, specimens of that sort were common enough, hanging round street corners in every town in the country. Now most of them were in khaki; their chests filled out and their ideas broadened under the influence of discipline and comradeship.

(The merit of war as receptacle for unwanted surplus population does not seem to have survived the Blitz, which took care of enough people without preliminary induction.)

> Brian thought he'd seen the fellow before. Yes, he remembered; he'd been brought up before a Juvenile Court on a charge of maliciously injuring a younger boy. Sent to an approved school for two years. That would make him about twenty.

The lout seeks conversation, and Brian asks if he has been conscripted:

> 'Not me', declared the fellow, with a sly glance. 'I'm a conchus objector.'
> 'Conscientious objector, I suppose you mean?'
> 'That's right. The blokes said as 'ow I was to go on the land. I can see myself doing that, I can.'
> 'You prefer to sit tight and draw the dole then?'
> 'Dole? Unemployment benefit, you mean. That's right.'

'Sorry! Then you don't mean to do anything to defend your country?'

'Why should I? What's it done for me? I didn't ask to be born in the bloomin' country, did I?'

'And you're such a pacifist – that's a peace-at-any-price person – that if someone smote you on one cheek you'd offer him the other?'

The lout's knowledge of scripture being of the sketchiest character he could only look at Brian uncomprehendingly and apprehensively.

Westerman's ice was a little thin here: by reminding his audience of the scriptural origin of the quotation that he was using for purposes of ridicule, he risked their remembering that Jesus Christ was the author of the sentiment 'whosoever shall smite thee on thy right cheek, turn to him the other also' (Matthew 5:39). That pacifism is His creed makes it less easy to conscript Christianity, save by the usual expedient of ignoring the doctrine.[69]

'Wot's that?'

'If I punched you on the nose, you wouldn't attempt to defend yourself?'

'None of that, mate', protested the 'conchie', visibly alarmed.

'Don't worry', continued Brian. 'I suppose you had breakfast this morning; tea or coffee?'

'Tea, same as I allus have.'

'Well, then', continued Brian, 'neither tea nor coffee is grown in this country. Nor is tobacco and I see you're smoking. All that comes from overseas at the risk of men's lives and if it weren't for the navy this country would be starving. Men – men, I say – are fighting to feed white-livered rats like you, who only develop what they call a conscience when they're afraid for their miserable hides!'

'This is a free country, ain't it?' rejoined the lout aggressively.

'Yes, and we're supposed to defend freedom with all our might, I believe', replied Brian, mindful of the slogan he'd noticed at the last station. 'All the same, I'd keep quiet over your rotten conscience if I were you or you'll land yourself in trouble!'

The fellow slunk out of the carriage into the corridor.

Brian let down the window.

The intensity of class hatred revealed in this passage was an ominous message for the community spirit on which Britain would need to rely for the months that followed its publication. Price's Arnie is funny, and the Nazi–Soviet pact was a most appropriate target, although the idea of a work-shy gardener as a permanent feature of a child's short-story series shows the outlook deemed suitable for the middle-class child. Mary Mouse and her beloved Whiskers are an appropriate new gospel for the war years when the absence of male labour, as Price frankly asserted, would teach the employer class circumspection. Even when Westerman wanted to show the spirit of England and her Empire flocking to the navy when the book begins, the working class had to appear somewhere between the comic and the brutish:[70]

> One man looked as if he had come straight from a boxing-booth. His flattened nose, square jaw and cauliflower ears gave him that appearance, to say nothing of a livid bruise under his left eye. His answer to a fellow-recruit's questions gave his reason for electing to fight for the freedom of the seas: 'I'm a stoker down at the gas-works, I am. The missus an' me don't hit it off, so I'm on this lay for a little peace and quietness. She didn't 'arf dot me one, she didn't', and his hand went up to the bruise on his heavy features.

Thus Westerman in briefly benevolent mood in the class war.

Colonials might observe such sentiments and perhaps share them, but were hardly at ease in proclaiming them. Evadne Price dug herself in between the snobbery she loathed and the anti-worker hostility which (apart from treasured exceptions like 'Vilet') she evidently shared. Her senior, Violet M. Methley, may be a simpler case, all the more as by the 1940s she usually pursued directly Australian subjects and/or locations. *Vackies* (1941) is an exception. It begins realistically enough – former governess awaiting evacuee children of former charge while erroneously assuming them to be little more than infants in arms – and throws in the conventional tough servant with heart of hidden gold being charmed by small child. But we are quickly shown that 'vackies' come in two kinds, middle and lower class. Middle-class names may be odd, and invite nicknames ('Moon' for 'Mona', 'Oke' for 'Kay'); but workers give their offspring absurd names ('Geranium Bloggs'). Then the lower-class evacuees would return to bomb-threatened areas, notably London, unless the middle-class children make them want to stay in the places to which they had been evacuated. To this laudable exercise they commit themselves for the rest of the book, saving the working class from itself, as it were. The middle class philanthropically seek to develop the interests of the lower class above their absorption in Philistinism:

> 'You see, I do want to find things for them to do', Moon said earnestly. 'Not only the cinema – they'd like to be going to *that all the time*. But they can never have seen anything like your garden and collections.'

But it seems impossible to reform them in matters of taste, and hence concessions must be made en route:

> Only Ireen's face was quite red and raw with soap-scrubbing and she wore a new woollen cap, several sizes too small and in colour a peculiarly hideous shade of royal blue.
>
> Seeing Geranium's eyes fixed stonily upon her, Moon hurriedly praised the baby's smartness and was rewarded by the slow, unwilling smile which made the elder sister's peaked face quite pretty for the moment.
>
> 'I'm so glad she's pleased', Moon thought. 'It just shows that sometimes lies are a good thing – small, white ones anyway. Because, really, I think that cap's simply frightful, only it would have been hateful to say so.'

Ultimately, Moon's brother Kevin throws a spy's time-bomb into the sea while being fired at, and he becomes a hero to the lower-class evacuees while gaining credit for the evacuees as a whole. Equally, Moon saves little Ireen from drowning. Moon salutes Geranium as a heroine for a lesser achievement, but Geranium dutifully acknowledges Moon's pre-eminence:[71] '"Don't talk ser silly", she said. "What abaht you swimmin' aht an' savin' our Ireen? It's not me – it's you what's a hero-een. Greeta Gerber ain't in it, not wiv you."' It rather neatly shows the lower-class standards as irredeemably fixed on what Orwell's *1984* would know as proletfeed, while satisfactorily determining evacuees as winning acceptance for all once middle-class leadership and superiority had been accepted by all. Clearly, Methley saw this as desirable; but what is more important is that she saw it at all and was prepared to record it, which she did with a directness showing her excessively colonial antecedents. It probably reflected a very widespread middle-class superstition.

Australian writers came from sufficient remoteness to describe class edges more clearly, if more crudely, than might be expected of

English authors, in part because the Australians often yearned for acceptance in gentility while suspecting that they were secretly classified among the lower ranks, especially from their accent. Attack on class divisions came from different sources. We have noted the vehement assaults on class privilege in the D. C. Thomson comics. The single most powerful work showing the revolutionary potential of class conflict was a historical novel, and American. In the early 1940s, the USA appeared on Britain's Left. In 1943, the American Newbery Medal (whence the British Carnegie Medal had been conceived) was awarded to Esther Forbes's *Johnny Tremain*, republished the next year in London. The book had striking advantages. Forbes in 1942 had won the Pulitzer Prize for history for *Paul Revere and the World he Lived in*, taking the subject of the USA's most famous poem commemorating the American Revolution, Henry Wadsworth Longfellow's 'Paul Revere's Ride', and biographically contextualising it. She then fashioned her only novel for children from her materials: Boston's Johnny Tremain is trained as a silversmith, Revere's trade. Injured, his vocation is destroyed and he becomes involved in press agitation against British rule, making the valid point that potential rebels come naturally from frustrated people. The book's British publication seems to have been a casualty of British ignorance of America: Chatto and Windus left the *Times Literary Supplement*, for one, under the impression that the book was intended for an adult audience. Its notice concluded:[72]

> What is most conspicuous of all, however, is the more than naive history of the tale. The rabble-rousing Whig case is advanced in the crudest and most solemn terms, with the English inveterately insolent and overbearing, the loyalists dupes, and Sam Adams the soul of patriotic vision. One had thought the time had gone by for this sort of thing.

To the contrary, it seems doubtful if one had thought at all; but the ignorance of the reviewer is instructive. The *TLS* itself reviewed the book again in far greater detail on its republication in Britain by Constable fourteen years later. It retreated systematically from most of the earlier strictures, granted its fairness, found it partisan but 'not prejudiced', acknowledged the pity that Johnny acquires for the fate of his bitterest enemies as revolution ruins them, or the liking he finds for 'such agreeable British . . . as Lieutenant Stranger', and concluded that Johnny[73] at last knows the meaning of James Otis's words: 'We give all that we have, lives, property, safety, skills . . . we fight, we die, for a simple thing. Only that a man can stand up.' When Miss Forbes wrote *Johnny Tremain*, in 1943, these words had a particular topicality. That they have a meaning still is just one reason for welcoming this fine, thoughtful and entirely absorbing book.

Certainly, Forbes had done a great thing: as David Hackett Fischer pointed out fifty years later, her *Revere*'s 'sustained interest in social history was far in advance of academic scholarship',[74] thus endowing herself with the fundamental strength needed for a historical novel for children. She had reached for the Second World War topicality, giving Dr Joseph Warren in her last pages the crucial lines spoken to Johnny:

'You remember that night', he said, 'that last meeting of the Observers. James Otis came, although we didn't want him. I can't remember much of what he said, but I remember how his words made the gooseskin on my arms.'
   'I'll never forget it. He said . . . so a man can stand up.'
   'Yes. And some of us would die – so other men can stand up on their feet like men. A great many of us are going to die for that. They have in the past. They will a hundred years from now – two hundred. God grant there will always be men good enough. Men like Rab.'

Rab is Johnny's older friend, more intransigent in the revolutionary cause than he, and now mortally wounded in the first volley at Lexington (which began the war of the American Revolution). The novel ends with Warren about to operate on Johnny's maimed hand and, we assume, cure it in what we know will be the extreme pain of operation without chloroform, a symbol of the suffering that the rebellious colonies must face to win freedom. (The real Warren would be killed on 23 August, four months later, at the battle of Bunker's Hill.) Otis is terrific: that he was the most radical and the longest-battling among the thinkers who led to the American Revolution is unquestionable, and his madness from 1769 left him to Forbes to do with what she would. In classical literature, his place would be that of the blind oracle Tiresias in the Oedipus legend and Sophoclean plays; in children's literature, it is that of Ben Gunn in *Treasure Island*: a person known to have special knowledge, but easy to dismiss and despise, and yet destined to be the pivot on which the resolution of events turns. It is a part with a special appeal to children because of its apparent powerlessness and its actual potential, as the children themselves want to be. Forbes used Otis to cry her case for the Revolution and proclaim an American inheritance leading to the USA's crusade in the Second World War. If it were not as easy for the British to claim it, Forbes's Otis gave them a formula applicable to their Second World War, and Forbes's Warren the assurance that they were serving it. And the second *TLS* critic (Denis Brogan?) was right in seeing her benign treatment of the British. But Esther Forbes had nonetheless declared the causes of the American Revolution to include class hatred.

The Loyalists in the American Revolution would naturally include persons of wealth and power in the years before the outbreak of fighting. What frequently gave the Revolution teeth was local anger against the wealthy and privileged who ultimately became identified with the defence of Lord North's government, although many of them might initially have been its critics and enemies, or at least the critics and enemies of its predecessors. The height of a carriage-wheel, the power of a legal writ, the break of an old friendship, the lash of a controversialist's disdain might all be marks by which Loyalists became known – and Patriots declared them their enemies and the enemies of Boston, of Massachusetts and of something beginning to be called America. Men of wealth and power had been able to exercise their will and whim with greater freedom by being so far from the government with whom they were increasingly identified. Forbes introduced such a Loyalist in the making through what might seem a clumsy sub-plot when Johnny seeks recognition and possible rights from a supposed kinsman, Jonathan Lyte, who in return seeks to have him convicted of theft, hanged for it, kidnapped, shanghaied or otherwise obliterated – and, in the cutting edge of that power and the frailty of its opponents, class becomes a clear factor in the making of Revolution. It would also make sense as symbol: Lyte as current British rule, Tremain as colonial concern with claims which later disappear in significance as the resultant dispute eclipses them and breaks the shell that once seemed all-important. If the war of 1939–45, or 1940–5, or 1941–5, was to inherit the spirit of 1773–6, it must be with the same class anger that showed Johnny Tremain that his physical survival might depend on his skill and zeal in standing up to those ready to use privilege to crush him. Perhaps, after all, the first *TLS* reviewer had scented that lesson from the pages which he had noticed so carelessly, and thus condemned for its relevance, not its obsolescence. His/her use of the adjective 'rabble-rousing' asserts that a 'rabble' exists, that it is in the public (i.e. the reviewer's) interest not to rouse it, and that *Tremain* sought that arousal. Forbes had cleverly used a fairy-tale convention (dying mother telling orphaned son that when all hope had gone he must claim kinship with Lyte by virtue of a silver cup) and then (in place of the traditional acceptance once tests have been made and the hero's courage and ingenuity established) Lyte claims the cup as his own, stolen, and its possessor therefore its thief. His evidence in court is that of a man who takes the state to be his accomplice:[75]

> Mr Lyte . . . entered as though he owned the court, calling a cheery good morning to Mr Justice, interrupting the mumbled explanation of a shabby bakeress accused of selling mouldy bread. . . .
>
> Mr Lyte was talking as informally as though he and Mr [Justice] Dana were alone together, sitting at a tavern, cracking walnuts, drinking Madeira. He told how his great-grandfather, Jonathan Lyte, Mayor of Causeway, Kent, England, had had six identical cups made . . . On the night of the twenty-third, a thief . . . had broken a pane . . . too small to admit a grown man, so that it was a half-grown boy who had slipped in and taken only one of the famous cups.
>
> . . . Then he went on to tell, with considerable humour and a bright sparkle in his slippery black eyes, about Johnny's visit to his shop, his claims of kinship, and how he had lured him to his house with the stolen cup.
>
> . . . He believed that the case of the theft, all that interested him at the moment, was 'dead open and shut against the boy'. And might he ask the death penalty? There was too much thieving going on in Boston. Poor apprentices were getting out of hand. The gallows had been too long empty.

This is very neatly managed, making it clear that the Loyalist was no idle aristocrat relying on patronage and position to see him through: this is a working merchant, knowing exactly when to flaunt upper-class hauteur and when to be the affable bourgeois, respected in business. Lyte loses this case thanks to Johnny's good fortune with witnesses; but pre-Revolutionary Boston is Lyte's Boston.

Class in Second World War Britain still included aristocratic landholders justified by inheritance; and there is some charm in the Carnegie Winner for 1942, the year before *Johnny Tremain's* Newbery, being partly in celebration of that power and privilege. Writing as 'B.B.', but illustrating his work under his own name,

Denys J. Watkins-Pitchford produced a charming tale of three tiny gnomes trying to find an errant fourth. It was not wholly English – the gnomes have an Irish resonance (as a sequel emphasises), and its American derivations sparkle in the major gnome, Dodder, an obvious cousin to Grumpy in Walt Disney's film *Snow White* (1937). But its English relatives included Jerome K. Jerome's *Three Men on a Boat* and Kenneth Grahame's *The Wind in the Willows*, never quite reaching the comedy or artistry of either, but able to confront them unashamed. The story at first names Man as the 'greatest enemy' that the gnomes 'have to fear'. The gnomes tell a hostile pheasant: 'There's no such thing as private property in nature! The woods and fields belong to the earth, and so do we.' These tenets fire a feud with a gamekeeper, known to the gnomes as Giant Grum, who kills their friend Otter, and who with the aid of Pan is killed by Dodder stuffing leaves into the barrels of his gun. The gamekeeper has been very successfully demonised, and most of the child readers would rejoice in his death: 'B.B.' knew how to capture loyalties and inflame hostilities by cunning economics of tension. Then a lovable small boy, Robin Clobber (the 'b' repetition seems suggestive), sees the gnomes and aids them, even to forgiving their appropriation of his toy boat (with which he had been playing the Battle of the Atlantic). He is the heir of Clobber Court with a nice Daddy and Mummy; his birthday is described (including the gift of a toy Spitfire, the book's other concession to the Second World War), and we last see him riding back from his first fox-hunt, where they have killed (the boy is now eight). The sound of the horn had stopped the fox from killing two of the gnomes, Dodder drawing his attention to it:

> 'Listen again – listen well, Red Stinker to Heaven.'
> The fox's ears switched abruptly.
> Far away came the sound of a horn and the faint 'tow row' of hounds.
> He snarled once, looked down at the motionless figure of Sneezewort, then at Dodder, stood irresolute, swung round and vanished like a shadow!

After the hunt, Robin tells his father that he found his 'first run with hounds' 'Ripping': he is 'almost speechless with happiness'. We are not told that he actually saw the fox's death, but it is contextually logical that he did. Human deaths, however, are kept from him:[76]

'Purkis has gone away on a long holiday, Robin, and I . . . well, I don't think he will be coming back.'

'I'm glad, Daddy; I didn't like him.'

The worker may therefore be murdered to everyone's satisfaction, provided that we are suitably appreciative of his employer and enraptured by the employer's son (and Robin – at least until he tastes his first vulpine blood – is a heart-warming child).

To assess the Second World War child's encounter with the working class in less prejudiced literary hands than those of a Rugby schoolmaster sentimentally defensive of agrarian aristocracy, which 'B.B.' was, requires another look at war fiction. For W. E. Johns, the class division always remained that between officers and men. Johns himself was a non-commissioned officer in the army when he got his great chance, relinquishing his Lance Corporalship on 25 September 1917 on appointment to a commission and on 26 September granted a temporary commission as Second Lieutenant, Royal Flying Corps, at which point he began to learn to fly. Johns's father and grandfather had been tailors. Biggles is from a professional family and first appears as an RFC Captain; and Algy, whom he initially dislikes, is his cousin from Norman-Welsh aristocracy. Ginger, first encountered as a runaway son of a miner, is adopted by Biggles, which gets him into the British officer class from class origins lower than Johns's father. Ginger, early in the Second World War, recalls discarded skills when they are marooned and starving on the Russo-Finnish frontier: ' "There was a time years ago, before you found me wandering about without visible means of subsistence, when I was pretty good at foraging for food", he said quietly'. *Biggles Sees it Through* was written post-Dunkirk when Britain was most anxious for cross-class solidarity against Hitler. Johns evoked the same spirit in *King of the Commandos*, recounting Cub's history after Dunkirk in occupied France, although there – significantly – public-school boy joins up with lower-class boys, adopting rather than recovering anti-bourgeois attitudes. Two years had elapsed – 1941–3 – and class-consciousness was returning with variations.

The one Second World War Biggles novel written before Dunkirk, *Biggles in the Baltic*, offered an unusual complement of non-commissioned personnel whose parts, while small, were not mere walk-on. Flight-Sergeant Smyth, Biggles's wartime fitter and rigger, represents the pre-war type of old faithful retainer, exceedingly proficient within his competence, but no challenge in the leadership or sidekick stakes: in army batman style, Biggles remains 'sir' to him at all times, and he seldom speaks even when rescuing the others. Algy pays him a rare tribute at the close of *Biggles Sees it Through:*[77] 'Good old Smyth; trust him to be in at the death . . . That man's a treasure. He doesn't talk much, but he's on the spot when he's wanted.' A 'treasure' (James Bond's housekeeper would later be so described) is a hard-working servant who does not complain about exploitation; and Smyth is an uneasy character, his NCO status giving him a servant style. His name is curiously pretentious, but possibly derived from Johns's calling him 'Smith' and then fearing identification with a real Smith. He is married, but we never meet her; his brother-in-law, and his son Roy, make guest appearances. He reflected Johns's lack of confidence with class questions, although Smyth's curriculum vitae, however sketchy, had more in common with Johns's than did any other among his creations. Smyth was conditioned by one or more originals, many of whom had turned grey in the RFC as they watched officer after officer depart and fail to return – a father figure from a lower rank, not inarticulate, but functioning with his commissioned offspring only by formal address. Bringing in his actual son, Roy, into *Biggles in the Baltic* to begin the Second World War, proclaimed dynasty in the RFC giving birth to the RAF, but in a new world where aircraft maintenance may be of less importance than aircraft wireless. Roy 'had entered the Royal Air Force as a boy apprentice and had passed out as a wireless operator mechanic', and the story briefly becomes his as he discovers the Germans in control at the base and saves the British and (captured) German code-books from them. The sergeant's son thus becomes for a moment the key to British success or failure; Johns, whether he knew it or not, had highlighted the key factor in the war. The sergeant may have been a silent supporter, but his son inherits the future, although in fact his self-appointed solo mission ends 'in a sheet of purple flame' as he hits his head on a rocky floor and (temporarily) loses consciousness. The story then falls into the hands of his father and the garrulous Cockney cook, Briny, up the tunnel ahead (but unaware) of him, and here we are firmly suspended between past and present, as the sergeant worries and Briny reminisces:

'You know, this reminds me of a place I once struck with my old shipmate, Charlie –'

'I'll sock you on the jaw and give you something else to remember if you don't shut up remembering things', snarled the Flight-Sergeant, whose nerves were on edge.

But this is at the moment when his son, the future, has been the one to take the memorable, obliterating blow, while the past, as perpetually celebrated by Briny, continues to prattle irrelevantly (for the characters) and hilariously (for the readers).

Briny Salt is servant (Raymond's yacht-cook), lower rank, and spirit of the British navy: as a character, he embodied Edwardian traditions about servant garrulity, and lower-class absurdity contrasted with stiff-upper-lip officer taciturn heroism. Yet his purpose in this, unique, appearance is more complex. Johns never used him, or anyone like him, again. Why here, at the beginning of the war that Johns had so long expected Britain to have to fight? Certainly, there is the comic-relief element, the elderly windbag free with comment but in practice a potential disaster area. But, apart from cutting him off in his anecdotage, the comrades clearly become very fond of Briny, and there is genuine affection in Biggles's bullying him to make the parachute-jump off the top of the island which alone can save him. If Johns was giving way to a gerontophagous impatience, he revoked it as Briny took hold of the book and became its best character. Whatever they were fighting for, it was human. Yet the silent Smyth balances the loquacious Briny when his son, also without previous parachute experience, is to follow Briny into the void, and elicits his one recorded expression of paternal affection – characteristically wordless:[78]

> Roy stepped forward, and waited until Algy had dragged the dripping Briny into the flying-boat. Then he jumped clear.
>   His father gasped his relief as the parachute mushroomed out.
>   'You go next, Flight-Sergeant', ordered Biggles.
>   The N.C.O. jumped without a word.

Whatever the uses of the lower classes as symbols – a lovable but useless past, a perilous, unknown present, a dark, exciting future – they had to wait until *Spitfire Parade* and Tug Carrington to provide a character instead of merely a 'character', a figure of mind who was more than a figure of fun, a proletarian hero whom Johns's readers might not merely enjoy but also emulate. His sole reappearance after the war when he acts as a special agent for Biggles, pretending to be a pilot in quest of a job, produces replies to an advertisement:

> In the course of the morning he received three calls. The first was from a man who advised him to give up flying and invited him to

sell his vacuum cleaners. Tug made some pungent suggestions as to what the man might do with his vacuum cleaners, and hung up.

This is absolutely surplus to the story, and must have delighted a youthful audience with few illusions about the nature of the pungent suggestions. Tug reconnoitres his wealthy criminal adversaries with the class-war perspective:[79] 'Fairly studded with diamonds, and reeks like a chemist's shop of scent and hair oil – makes you sick'.

Tug was posted to Biggles's squadron by Air Commodore Raymond with doubt that he should have been given a commission, a natural reaction from a pre-war private yacht-owner. Raymond's diagnosis of Tug's inferiority complex notes that the war 'is a personal matter with him; his parents were killed in one of the first raids on the East End'. It is evidently an obituary for war as a gentleman's game. Once people take things personally . . . Tug roars into action from the first, contesting every point with Biggles, complaining about airmen's readiness for booze to Algy, trying to pick a fight on suspicion of ridicule from Bertie, shooting down a Junkers 88 in mid-conversation, and all the time implying that people are not permanently preoccupied by war as they should be. Biggles in the preliminary interview asks:

'How many enemy aircraft have you shot down?'
   'I dunno, sir.'
   'Why don't you know?'
   'I've never bothered to count them, and that's a fact. Why trouble? There's always plenty more.'
   Again Biggles's eyes met Algy's. They were twinkling. 'It's a great thing to have a sense of humour', he said softly.
   'What's that?' asked Tug.
   'A sense of humour? Haven't you got one?'
   Tug shook his head. 'Not that I know of.'
   'I mean – to be able to see the funny side of things', explained the C.O.
   'Funny?' There was frank incredulity in Tug's voice. 'Do you see something funny about this war, with women and kids –'
   'No – no, of course not', broke in Biggles quickly.

This is Johns's superb reply to the upper-class thesis that the lower classes would collapse under bombing. The points are at Biggles's expense; Johns is on Carrington's side.

Biggles swallowed hard. 'I'll give you a day or two to get the hang of things', he promised.

'I shan't need 'em', announced Tug simply. 'I'm ready as soon as you like. I came down here to shoot Huns, so the sooner I start in the better.'

Biggles dislikes Tug's style of flying:

'All right, Carrington. As you like. But if you go on flying as you've started it's only a matter of time before you do the enemy a good turn by wriing yourself off.'

'That'll be my funeral, sir, won't it?'

He has a sense of humour, but where he comes from it isn't called that. And, after he has shot down the Hun:

There was a faint murmur, like the rustle of autumn leaves, as the others allowed long-held breath to escape from their lungs. The face that Biggles turned to Algy was white and wore a curious expression, an expression that was something between relief and frank disbelief.

'In all my experience I never saw anything quite like that', he said slowly. 'Carrington's flying may not be the sort taught at the best schools, but it works – yes, it certainly works.'

The intent was not permanently to empower the Cockney Carrington at everyone else's expense; the squadron is brought up to strength, and recognisable figures were built from Biggles's own First World War adventures, recycled. Tug's most obvious antipathy is turned against obvious representatives of privilege – Lord Bertie Lissie, or the Oxford undergraduate Henry Harcourt. Johns, no doubt aware of the sneers of Oxbridge-educated critics, made Harcourt's book-learning bow to experience, his comeuppance usually from Ginger rather than Tug. Tug's last appearance is but a singleton in post-war adventures, whereas Lord Bertie becomes one of the gang, having more or less crashed the usual triumvirate by joining the search for Biggles in Biggles 'Fails to Return', presumably because Johns needed a Monte Carlo veteran. Bertie is a comic figure, born of Bertie Wooster and Lord Peter Wimsey, of Scarlet Pimpernel stock; but he is to receive our respect as well as our affection. Initially, the farcical element is uppermost, notably when his dog's warm greetings to its master cause Biggles to overbalance and sprain his wrist:[80]

Biggles regarded him reflectively. 'You know, Bertie, there are times when I find myself wondering if you're a bigger fool than you look, or look a bigger fool than you are.'

'I say, sir, that's a bit steep – absolutely vertical, in fact. After all, Towser's only a pup. When I was in India there was a chappie who kept a tiger –'

'I hope it bit him', cut in Biggles coldly.

'Matter of fact, it did.'

'Fine. The animal evidently had some sense.'

Bertie subsided.

But he goes on to undertake the mission from which Biggles is now invalided (actually taking over the role that Biggles had in the original story), and, when he rescues it from a worthless agent, merely complains on return that the successful explosion lost him his 'beastly eyeglass in the dark'. The memory of Munich and the 'phoney' war probably hardened public opinion against aristocracy: Neville Chamberlain might have been self-evidently bourgeois, but his Foreign Secretary, Lord Halifax, radiated supposed upper-class attitudes (including obvious distrust of the workers). The outbreak of war had been followed by English-language broadcasts from Berlin in what appeared to be an aristocratic accent, promptly nicknamed 'Lord Haw-Haw' by British listeners. The comic weekly *Radio Fun*, in early 1940, ran 'Lord Haw-Haw' as a savage lampoon on 'the Broadcasting Humbug from Hamburg' or 'Broadcasting from Stations Ricebag and Humbug'. The Haw-Haw of the strip wore striped pants (stripe absurdly broadened), said 'nevah' for 'never', and sported a monocle. (He spent much of his time chumming with Hitler, whom he called 'the greatest man in the world' while Hitler shouted 'Heil Me' and 'More Heil for me with Swastikas on', an allusion to 'same to you with knobs on', which was popularly endowed with a phallic connotation.)[81] Inter-war comics had sought to humanise the aristocrat, the *Beano* in 1938 by the invention of Lord Marmaduke, a.k.a. 'Lord Snooty' the Duke's son who sneaks out in disguise to play with alley kids; in wartime, these were sharing his castle and punishment deprivations.[82] Halifax and Haw-Haw made 1940 a bad year for monocled idiots. (Churchill, in reality from much older aristocracy than Halifax, was too individual for class-labelling.) Yet, to apply Kingsley Amis's test, Bertie and Tug are the only two members of Squadron 666 whom one can hear (apart from cod-Welsh, cod-Scots and cod-American voices for Taffy, Angus and Tex). Near the end of the Second World War, Bertie and his dogs change from a joke to an icon, not in the Biggles stories but in the Gimlet ones. Biggles is getting Gimlet, his supporting trio and 100 British troops away from wartime France in *Gimlet Goes Again* and is exchanging information as to plans with Gimlet, who enquires:[83]

> 'By the way, is Bertie Lissie with you?'
> 'Yes, but he's in a hurry to get back – got a foxhound bitch due to whelp to-night, and won't trust the vet to handle it.'
> 'Quite right. If the bitch knows him she'll probably do better than with a stranger. Tell him I hope he gets some nice pups.'
> 'You'll probably see him yourself when he gets back.'
> 'I might give him a hand.'
> 'He'd be glad, I'm sure.'
> 'We shall need the pups. Be pretty sickening, by gad, if after all this sweat there was no huntin'.'
> Copper nudged Cub. 'Blinkin' marvellous, ain't it? Foxhound pups. That's all they think about. How's yer horses? What's the fishin' like? Strike me puce! One day they'll wake up with a jerk and discover there's a war on.'
> 'Don't let them kid you, Copper', returned Cub. 'They know there's a war on. Lord Lissie's pack of hounds means as much to them as the Old Kent Road does to you. It's just a matter of taste.'
> 'Maybe – maybe, but I'd sooner go to the dogs at Clapham stadium and do my fishin' with a pile o' chips', growled Copper.
> Biggles was still talking to Gimlet. 'I'd better get along to keep an eye on things. See you presently.' He strolled away.
> Gimlet turned to Copper. 'Don't stand there dreaming, corporal. There's plenty to do.'
> 'Aye aye, sir.'

This is in part a rerun from the endgame of the only previous Gimlet story, *King of the Commandos*, when Cub is worried that they are about to be trapped by a Messerschmitt, and Gimlet keeps on talking to Freddie, a fellow-sportsman (currently a British secret agent disguised as a rural French innkeeper), about a 'grey mare with a rat tail and flea-bitten hocks'. But it is much more blatant here. The earlier story justifies it:[84]

> Cub . . . began to understand dimly how it was that Britain had survived that dreadful year of the war when she stood alone, outnumbered in men, planes, tanks and guns [when Cub himself has been in occupied France]. Men like these were responsible,

men like Gimlet, Freddie, Bigglesworth, Copper . . . all of them. They did their jobs, and went on doing their jobs whatever happened, calmly – yes, that was the point – without losing their heads. It was not merely bravery, but downright thoroughness.

Both as propaganda and as analysis, that is not bad; and, if two aristocratic fox-hunters against one Cockney (with Biggles, significantly, midway) seems inequitable, it is in keeping with First World War officer preoccupations. It is the later text, written after D-Day, that invites suspicion of a political agenda. Yet Gimlet's gratuitous and habitual rudeness to Copper for far less time-wasting than he has been doing might be read, and be intended to be read, as subversive in the reaction that it prompts. Biggles's own view on Bertie's dogs we have seen. He pointedly declines to join a shooting party while on leave in *The Camels are Coming*. Johns, much later in the Biggles series, expressed distaste for hunting animals. Bertie himself shows no sign of wanting to resume the fox-hunting life. Johns did introduce a fox-hunt into the second post-war Gimlet, *Gimlet Mops Up*, when Freddie leads the hunt and is nearly kidnapped by Nazi 'werewolves' still swearing vengeance on a blacklist of former British operatives: the bifurcation of the chase between the Master chasing the fox and the Nazis chasing the Master, one of them in drag, is managed with some irony, the fox being arguably the most sympathetic figure. We also see something of Gimlet's other peacetime preoccupations:[85]

'I happen to be the President of the Lorrington Cottage Garden Society, and they're expecting me down on Monday to judge the exhibits, and, in the evening, distribute the prizes at the village hall. Of course, I could get out of it, but this is the first post-war meeting, and as many of the competitors are my own tenants I don't like letting them down. . . .'

It's possible that this was a serious attempt to show upper-class, or at least gentlemanly, leadership of the commandos. As a keen gardener, Johns presumably considered it useful. Gimlet has been alleged to derive from Simon Fraser, fourteenth Baron Lovat, who headed a crack commando unit on D-Day; but a glance at Lovat's memoirs belies the charge. Lovat was a courteous man, of broad interests, with a wholehearted hatred of snobbery (as he makes angrily clear in his discussion of Evelyn Waugh). And, whatever Johns intended by it, Gimlet's conduct to Copper, in and out of

war, is snobbery personified. Johns claimed that Gimlet's tough-
ness meant that he was given 'a bunch of wildcats to command',
although in practice we only come to know two (Cub having been
acquired on a mission). Trapper he frequently has to order not to
use torture (which means that Trapper must keep quiet about it
when he does use it), but otherwise he never pulls him up; Copper,
the one lower-class Englishman, he perpetually nags, belittles,
ridicules and tells to get his hair cut; Cub, although far younger
than the others, receives the courtesies of potential membership of
the officer class, a landed family and a public-school education.
Why did Johns create Gimlet so much against the spirit of wartime
egalitarianism? Was it on a hint from the War Office when inviting
the series?

The best explanation seems that Johns was divided in facing the
post-war world, his training taking him one way, his experience the
other. His military identity, all the more as it receded in time, required
him to evangelise for the old-style officer class to which he had never
adhered: having been neither of them nor with them, he now felt it
necessary at a time of disintegrating values to be for them. Yet he
found them hard to tolerate, and hence could never make Gimlet
likeable, although he did make him real. This becomes more credible
when we take into account the last Biggles books, written by Johns in
the 1960s: the criminals or other agents of anti-social behaviour often
prove to be disgruntled upper-class persons. Gimlet is not one of
them; but he could be.

Yet if Copper and, more directly, Tug enabled Johns to make it
fractionally a people's war, his sidelining of the sergeants lost him its
best chance. His one real exception is Sergeant Gray in *Biggles in the
Orient*, whose devotion to his squadron leads him to be deemed a
drunk and then made a murder victim to protect the saboteur. The
scene where Raymond, Biggles and Johnny Crisp all stand over him
telling him he is drunk, regardless of his denials, is as neat an
instance of officer lordship as could be sought.

'Come on, Gray; pull yourself together', rapped out Biggles tersely.
  'Wash-washer matter?' gasped the sergeant.
  'You're drunk', said Johnny bitingly.
  The sergeant was indignant. 'Thash a lie. Not drunk.'
  Biggles gave him more coffee.
  'He says he isn't drunk', said Johnny, looking at Biggles and the
Air Commodore in turn.
  'Of course he does.' The Air Commodore laughed lugubriously.

'Did you ever know a drunken man admit that he was tight? I
didn't.'

'If you tell him he's drunk he'll spend the rest of the night trying
to prove that he isn't', put in Biggles wearily.

The sergeant's eyes were clearing. 'Wash wrong?' he demanded
in a dazed voice, and then was violently sick.

'Tight as an owl', muttered Johnny. 'You won't get any sense out
of him till he's slept it off.'

'I'm afraid you're right', agreed Biggles sadly. 'What a nuisance.'

These sentences are in fact death sentences: had the three officers
been less wise in their own conceit, Gray would have been taken
away for examination and, being under scrutiny, might have survived. Johns celebrates his own methodology in the story (through
Biggles's words) in insisting that the detective plot be unravelled by
Biggles one-third of the story before the end – but he puzzles his
readership skilfully en route, the issue of Scrimshaw's drinking and
Biggles's former alcoholism valorising the officers' judgement
against Gray. In passing, the youthful readers are thereby reminded
of the ease with which censorious children may pass ruthless
judgement on middle-aged drinking, and of the injustice that they
may cause – no bad lesson to preach in the unsettlement of ordinary
families in the Second World War. For Gray proves innocent of
drinking at all, and Biggles's exposition has to record how unjustifiably he and his fellow-officers doomed the Sergeant:[86]

'The person . . . had good reason for caution. He went to kill Gray,
for fear Gray would talk. Gray, had he lived, would have insisted
he was not drunk. He could have proved it. This would have led to
the question, were the other cases of drunkenness on the station –
there had been some, you know – really that, or were the men the
victims of a mysterious malady? The saboteur did not want that
sort of talk, we may be sure. . . .

'. . . Johnny never touches gum. A week ago he came back with a
piece of gum still in the pocket of the aircraft where it had been
planted. Gray, looking over the machine, as he was bound to,
found it. He chewed it, and passed out. Everyone thought he was
drunk. He wasn't. He was doped. . . .

'. . . Dash it, poor Gray almost *told* us what had happened. He said
he had been sitting there *chewing* the thing over, but no one took him
literally. He became unconscious. It was known that we were waiting
for him to come round to ask him questions. That hadn't happened on

the previous occasion. It was realised that he might mention the chewing-gum to us. So he was quietly murdered. . . .'

The real potential for air warfare as class catalyst went to the *Rover* comic, the most clearly working-class-directed among the D. C. Thomson non-tabloid weeklies. It was realised during the war and afterwards in the person of Sergeant-Pilot Matt Braddock, VC and bar:[87]

> He got into the corridor and I pulled the door shut. The train began to move. He peered into a compartment in which there were two RAF group captains, an army colonel, a major and two vacant seats.
>
> He pulled the corridor door open, entered the compartment, dumped his kitbag on the rack and sat down. Then he gestured me in.
>
> 'Take the weight off your feet', he growled.
>
> I'd come down from Scotland and was train weary. I went in and sat down. The major glared at us.
>
> 'This is a first class compartment!' he exclaimed.
>
> Braddock yawned.
>
> 'I can read', he said.
>
> The major went red with indignation.
>
> 'I'm ordering you to get out!' he snapped. Braddock stretched his legs.
>
> 'When did you buy the railway?' he inquired.
>
> The major shot an infuriated glance at him. The group captains shifted uncomfortably.
>
> 'I shall report you to your commanding officer for disobeying an order and for insolence', the major rasped. 'What's your name?'
>
> 'Rhymes with haddock – Braddock!'
>
> The Air Force officers both gave a start. They looked at each other and then at Braddock.
>
> As the train roared under a bridge, one of them spoke to the major. I could not catch what he said, but the major didn't have another word to say. In evident confusion, he opened a newspaper and hid himself behind it.
>
> Braddock winked at me and then put his head back and closed his eyes.

The air force shared one basis for revolution with the navy: the man at the joystick and the man on the bridge are in supreme command of the vessel that they control, and no other officer, however superior to them in rank, may gainsay them. If the distance between a non-commissioned officer and supreme command is the greatest, the revolution will be at its most extreme at that point: hence Braddock made for greater revolution than Tug Carrington. Equally, to a child, the more extreme the revolution, the greater the parallel with a child suddenly given control over adults. Braddock celebrated flying mastery, but his readers more naturally celebrated what that mastery ensured – the rise of the lower ranks, an event within the bounds of possibility, where the rise of the underman in civilian life was not. The underman, or rather the underboy, was assumed to read the Rover. The Rover celebrated air as a force for democratisation much more dramatically, crudely and unrealistically than Johns (or Crompton with her transition from the snobbish Wing Commander Glover to the friendly if godlike beings who called William 'Old Bill' and made eponymous jokes about Ginger, between April 1940 and February 1941).[88] Part of Braddock's success was because the Rover knew that a comic had to be comic. It is also Dick Whittington's elevation by his cat, or Puss-in-Boots's status advancement of his master, the cat in both places supplying the exogenous factor which in Braddock's case is the air. Braddock runs foul of various air 'brass-hats', but the convention is that their air achievements are bogus; in the above extract, his humiliated adversary, significantly, is ground personnel, with the group captains embarrassed spectators. It has to be assumed that the revolutionary who thus successfully challenges the class conventions would be a rebel even without his cat or his aeroplane. When Raymond tells Biggles (who knows it quite well already) that 'The ass on the ground is often the ace in the air', he acknowledges the basis for such status-displacement (which partly explains his doubt expressed in the same letter about Carrington's appropriateness for a commission). Braddock is self-evidently impossible in all senses from a brass-hat view, just as Johns's Worrals, flying aircraft on spy missions, was impossible – but Johns, and, one suspects, the Rover author, wrote them in hopes that their myths would make new sex and class equality possible. They are war-flying as dream, but dream intent on its own realisation. They also remind us that the revolutionary spirit made for different priorities: Johns's Carrington was a slight blow on behalf of working-class aspirations, while the Thomson heroines showed powers of successful rivalry over appropriate heroes; but feminism came first for Johns, class challenge for the Rover.[89]

Class was the quality of British life in the 1930s which most impressed itself on foreign observers ('British', not 'UK', the central tenet of Northern Ireland identity being religious sectarianism). Equally, the result of the 1945 general election allows us to see a drastic change from its passive acceptance by so much of the public. No such tests are available for gender or race. Children's literature itself shows at least temporary return to some forms of racialism in the early 1950s (the era of Mau Mau horror stories from Kenya) and reversion to sex-object status for women in the post-war era (caught by Cadogan and Craig in their chapter-title 'Girl Sleuth to Brainless Beauty').[90] But, on class, we can be specific if not precise. The first-time voters of 1945 would be aged 21–30. The *Magnet* was read by 200,000 per weekly issue around 1930, at which date those voters would have been aged 6–15. Copies borrowed should be allowed for, and probably doubled the sales figure. The most obvious reader age would be 11, but in many cases stretched to inclusion of late teenagers, some of whom were in the armed forces. Thus lessons of anti-authoritarianism, valorisation of working-class secondary heroes, respect for the leader but acknowledgement of his weaknesses notably in pride or over-emphasis on his own indispensability and hence need for his temporary displacement, suspicion of ruling-class personnel or decisions – all these would harmonise with Richards's *Magnet*, with Johns's fiction in other Amalgamated Press papers, more vaguely with Richards–Johns imitators in the D. C. Thomson comics and elsewhere. We have no way to judge how many read what, how far and in what degree of acceptance they retained it, and with what effect. But we do have the repudiation of the popular Churchill and the retention of his wartime cabinet colleagues (Labour); and, if children's literature had any political effect in the voting behaviour of former readers, few of whom still read it, then it contributed to the 1945 débâcle for the Tories. With every possible allowance for error, it still seems that Orwell was right – the *Magnet* and its colleagues did influence the political judgements of readers who thereafter may have read little else, and that Orwell was wrong: its effect, however great or small, must have been, on balance, leftward. This does not need to assume a politics for most ex-*Magnet* readers taking them to the left of Attlee, with all respect for at least two of their number in the persons of Aneurin Bevan and Michael Foot. The revolutionary content noteworthy in the *Hotspur* in 1940, and in other products of that year, is unlikely to have influenced many first-time voters in 1945, few of whom would have read their *Hotspur* beyond the age of 14. The same is even more true of the many pro-USSR products from late 1941 to 1945, although these included not only the populist *Rover* and (by 1945) the more conservative *Wizard*, and the feminists rejoicing in USSR women with wings such as in Dorothy Carter's *Comrades of the Air*, but even the editor of the *Boy's Own Paper*:[91]

> Here's news concerning the heroic Soviet Army – and of a grand opportunity by which you may show your admiration for the magnificent part which Russia is playing in the World War.

This backed an Anglo–Soviet Youth Friendship Alliance bid to send 25,000 parcels 'from the youth of Britain to the soldiers of the valiant Red Army', parcels to include shaving soap, razors and blades, pencils, notebooks, 'writing paper and envelopes, gloves, socks and unbreakable mirrors', all to reach the Russians by 25 February 1943, when 'the Red Army celebrates the 25th anniversary of its establishment' (viz. 1918, after which it quickly found itself in conflict against British troops). The editor, Leonard Halls, was no dewy-eyed infant seduced in mid-combat by the new *Zeitgeist*: he was 48, with thirty years' work for the Amalgamated Press behind him. Nor was there any misreading of the wartime alliance's needs: the Russian front was an even greater hell than the Russian prison camps, and one hopes that many soldiers got the packets. In their way, these were the logical successors for the parcels sent to British troops in France and Flanders twenty-five years earlier, a conclusion that older minds may have reached in 1942–3. But few parcel-senders are likely to have been voters in 1945. And few British voters would have learned to cut their class-war teeth on *Johnny Tremain*. Yet any such reading encounter may have swung a vote – and, as Brent-Dyer reminded us by having her Chalet schoolmistresses read William, God knows how many adults swiped a late-night read of their offspring's literary addictions. I have seen no source showing that Queen Elizabeth (born in 1926) read the *Boy's Own Paper* – but her mother did. It was also read by at least one prisoner-of-war in a German camp. The *BOP* rejoiced in its cover of March 1914 which showed a schoolboy reading it while a middle-aged gentleman on one side and an elderly gentleman on the other surreptitiously read over his shoulders. Whether such unity of purpose would have attended comradeship with the USSR soldiers is another matter; but nostalgia in parcels to the front – and some guilt that there was not yet a second front – may have played its part. Children's literature testified to the absence of a second front, shown in so many aspects from the early recycling of First World War stories to the need for fighting stories being met by new fictional battlegrounds whether in eastern Europe or in English country houses where Quisling squires dreamed of new deference under the New Order.

One result of Second World War fiction for children in relation to class would seem to be that the old snobberies vanished or became threadbare. The return to Tory governments from 1951 did not produce much revival of Tory juvenile fiction, partly because, from Churchill down, Second World War imagery had repudiated the pre-war assumption that men in power know best. In displacing Chamberlain, Churchill embodied successful Tory rebellion, hence one which could not afford the usual Tory weapon of requiring deference to radiate unquestioning acceptance. Blyton's inculcation of the community ideal in the *Naughtiest Girl* series and her championship of victimised servants (however affected by her war with the possessive gardener), and Richards's demonisation of snobs as the most odious boys in his canon, would seem two cases of Tory revolt – though the political allegiance of both authors is not wholly clear throughout their lives. But the most lethal crusader against snobbery of them all, Richmal Crompton, was a Tory by political allegiance, and in her Second World War stories she seethed with ironic rage against the self-serving of wealth – whether Mrs Bott's use of her own local philanthropies to block allotments in her parklands, or the Lane family's black-market transactions to humiliate their more austere neighbours. She made the Land Girl, and the Cockney sergeant, and the AT needing cosmetics to keep her fiancé, become William's comrades-in-arms against snobs and petty dictators. If the William stories had one abiding message, it was in favour of the child's demand – fairness, and the consequent destruction of privilege that such a demand means. That message was at its clearest from Crompton throughout the Second World War.

Notes

1. Orwell, 'The Art of Donald McGill', *Complete Works*, XIII, 28–9.
2. Tolkien to W. H. Auden, 7 June 1955, *Letters*, 213–14.
3. Tolkien, *The Lord of the Rings*, 397.
4. Trease, *Tales out of School* (1948), 120. Having attempted a Marxist version of Robin Hood, Trease felt entitled to lecture his fellow-authors on their ideological inadequacies, in the best finger-wagging socialist Sunday-school manner. This may have been partly camouflage; any decent Robin Hood story is Marxist or (as in Scott) proto-Marxist, or (Blyton) populist.
5. M. Pardoe, *Bunkle Butts In* (1943), 17; *Bunkle Went for Six*, 17, 37, 99.
6. Gorman, *Jack Frere of the Paratroops*, 155. The Greene story, 'The News in

English', originally appeared in the *Strand*, 99 (June 1940), but was not published by Greene in book form until its inclusion in *The Last Word and Other Stories* (1990). The theme, with further elaborations, is worked out in Kurt Vonnegut, *Mother Night* (1961).

7. Crompton, *Just William's Luck* (1948), 15–16. The book followed the making of the eponymous film starring William Graham as William, Audrey Manning as Violet Elizabeth and Jane Welsh as Mrs Brown, directed by Val Guest (*Just William's Luck: Story of the Film in the Making*, n.d. [1948]). Muriel Aked played Emily. The invention of Emily would seem a film-maker's device to soothe the audience by mythologising what was known as 'the servant problem' into an illusory nostalgic past.

8. Crompton, 'The Perfect Little Gentleman', *Happy Mag* (May 1927), and (as 'Georgie and the Outlaws') *William the Outlaw* (October 1927).

9. Richards, *Billy Bunter's Postal Order* (1951), 44.

10. Brent-Dyer, *Lavender Laughs in the Chalet School*, 21.

11. *Mystery at Witchend*, 19–20.

12. Trease, *Tales out of School*, 164.

13. Severn, *Waggon for Five* (1944), 51.

14. Atkinson, *The Nest of the Scarecrow*, 108; *The Monster of Widgeon Weir*, 242.

15. Attenborough, *A Living Memory: Hodder & Stoughton Publishers 1868–1975* (1975), 111–12, 132, 142–3, 154. Stoney, *Blyton*, 125–6, 143.

16. *Mary Mouse and the Doll's House* appeared from Brockhampton in 1942 on Blyton's usual book-per-year fulfilment of series until 1949, after which further volumes came out less regularly. In 1942, Evans published the first of *Enid Blyton's Little Books*, with six stories (one twice as long as each of the rest), nine full-page illustrations and some page-fillers, twenty-one pages of text, 5.3″ × 4.5″, six volumes by Christmas 1943, but with stories often unlinked with one another and any series material (for example Brer Rabbit) being traditional Blyton fare, and with content little different from *Sunny Stories* 8″ × 5″, thirty-two pages for twopence) it was unable to compete with the fortnightly traditional, despite exceptionally fine pictures by Alfred Kerr.

17. Margery Fisher, *Who's Who in Children's Books* (1975), 216.

18. [T. B. Macaulay], 'Dryden', *Edinburgh Review* (January 1828), sixteenth paragraph (the essay was not included in Macaulay's *Critical and Historical Essays* and hence is often placed in miscellanea among his collected works).

19. The wartime titles after the first were *More Adventures of Mary Mouse* (1943), *Little Mary Mouse Again* (1944) and *Hallo, Little Mary Mouse* (1945). Each book had 124 captions (64 pp.) by Blyton for individual pictures. 10,000 copies were sold in 1942.

20. *The Mystery of the Burnt Cottage* (1943), 106–7.

21. Crompton, 'The Sweet Little Girl in White', *Happy Mag* (May 1924) and *Still William* (April 1925), 48.

22. *The Mystery of the Disappearing Cat* (1944), 6.

23. Crompton, 'William Helps the Spitfire Fund', *Modern Woman* (March 1941) and *William Does His Bit*, 198.

24. *The Mystery of the Disappearing Cat*, 48.

25. *The Mystery of the Spiteful Letters* (1946), 61–2.

26. *The Moving Finger* (1943), 45–6.

27. *The Mystery of the Spiteful Letters*, 96–7, 163–4, 122, 158.

28. *The Moving Finger*, 157.

29. *The Mystery of the Spiteful Letters*, 74, 107, 104–6.

30. *The Children of Primrose Lane* (1941), 248.

31. *Magnet* 859 (July 1924).
32. Blyton, *Tales of Robin Hood* (1930), *Robin Hood Book* (1949), 9.
33. A useful test of snobbery v. populism in Robin Hood versions is whether the outlaw leader is taken to be the wrongfully ousted Earl of Huntingdon, reinstated by Richard I, or the newly created Earl, the former making Robin a Norman, the latter usually a Saxon. Scott, *Ivanhoe*, makes his Locksley a man of the forest, and untroubled by any nobility of origin or elevation. During Richard I's reign, the actual Earl of Huntingdon was the Scots King William I. Robin Hood was probably early thirteenth century, if he existed.
34. Tupping may not be based on Tapping in looks, but the possessiveness about the employer's garden is evidently identical (p. 12): 'It wasn't a bit of good telling Mr. Tapping that it wasn't his garden. He felt that it belonged to him; he felt that every flower was his, every pea, and every smallest currant', Imogen Smallwood, *A Childhood at Green Hedges* (1989), 24–7, 41–5, 54, 71–2, 78, 95. Reviewers described this book as embittered and hostile to Blyton; in fact, it seems to me an astonishing triumph in objectivity – moving, charming and inspirational.
35. Wallace Hildick (normally signing his books 'E. W. Hildick' – 'E.' being 'Edmund' not 'Edgar', but we will leave *King Lear* out of this), *Children and Fiction* (1970), 85, 86; but see also 87–9, 134–9. Apart from want of historical context, this is one of the finest works of its kind. Perhaps unconsciously, it too testifies to Blyton's power over her audience by becoming so furious with the dictatorial Julian that it ends by accusing him of Roman imperial grandeur and of bullying Blyton ('we know that the broader human aspects will never be allowed to develop, that Mrs Stick will remain the puppet she has been most of the time. So has the Emperor Julian decreed it, and his creator humbly submits', p. 138).
36. Shakespeare, *The Tempest*, I. ii. 331–2. Edgar is on thin ice in questioning George's title to the island, since her father specifically denied it two books ago, so her breaking off the conversation has some justification even if her general hostility has much less excuse – but she has never been one to seek excuses for hostility.
37. The Sticks prove to be kidnappers in the end, their victim being a little girl whose distraught parents the Five then persuade to leave the restored infant in camp with them on Kirrin Island: this may have been Blyton's compensation for so much hostility to Edgar, also a child junior to them.
38. Blyton to Peter McKellar, 13 May 1957, Stoney, *Blyton*, 213; but the entire correspondence is invaluable (pp. 205–15).
39. Kipling, who died in 1936, was one of the leading common sources for almost all books published for children in Second World War Britain, as well as being extensively read himself; but Blyton was perhaps tapping her source at a curious point here, since 'The Ladies' (1895) is supposedly a meditation on sexual reminiscences by some Tommy Atkins back from India: 'For the Colonel's lady and Judy O'Grady | Are sisters under their skins!' Certainly the innocent Blyton meant no sexual innuendo, however much Kipling did. But Julian is sometimes a male counterpart of Judy.
40. Hildick, *Children and Fiction*, 139.
41. *Magnets* 1,017–26 (August–October 1927), 1,589–98 (July–October 1938).
42. Ian Gregor and Mark Kinkead-Weekes, *William Golding: A Critical Study of his Novels* ([1967] 2002), 7.
43. Orwell, 'Charles Reade', *New Statesman and Nation*, 17 August 1940, *Complete Works*, XII, 233: Wells's leading desert islands are *The Island of Dr Moreau* and 'Aepyornis Island', Barrie's in his plays *The Admirable Crichton* and *Peter Pan*.

44. Norman Wright, *Famous Five: Everything You Ever Wanted to Know* (2000) is an excellent companion to the Blyton Five series, and deals ably with the locale in Swanage and the Isle of Purbeck, whose limestone underground passages so greatly influenced Blyton's writing about her beloved holiday resort closed to her by war. He points out that Kirrin Island was largely based on recollection of Jersey, where she spent her honeymoon with Hugh Pollock in 1924. But Kirrin Island, by being placed so close to the mainland, had certain distinctive Dorset features and seems to have owed a little to the Isle of Purbeck.

45. All ten invitees to Nigger Island die, two by suicide, the girl from personal guilt and atmospheric influence; the old general is killed but sank into a fatalistic torpor before what in his case was release; the girl suicide has initially shot a man who had been intending to shoot her before going upstairs and hanging herself.

46. *Magnet* 1,025 (8 October 1927).

47. *Biggles in the South Seas*, 220, 222–3.

48. R. M. Ballantyne, *The Coral Island* (1858), 118 (chapter 10).

49. Cadogan, *The William Companion*, 67 (which notes two or three stories where the name becomes Flowerdew).

50. *Magnet* 1,022 (17 September 1927).

51. *The Coral Island*, 165 (chapter 14).

52. Masefield, *Live and Kicking Ned* ([1939] 1970), 283. The book was unfavourably reviewed in the *Spectator* by Graham Greene (10 November 1939) in one of his less perceptive moments.

53. Golding, 'Fable', *The Hot Gates and Other Occasional Pieces* ([1954] 1984), 89, 86.

54. Golding, *Lord of the Flies* ([1954] 1962), ed. Gregor and Kinkead-Weekes, 11, 13, 18, 81.

55. Blyton, *Five Run Away Together*, 14–15, 17, 191, 154.

56. Sheila Ray, *The Blyton Phenomenon* ([1982] 1983), 189.

57. Crompton, 'Hubert's Party', *Modern Woman* (June 1942) and *William Carries On*, 243.

58. Blyton, *The Put-Em-Rights* (1946), 15, 17–18, 21, 39, 21, 118, 143, 150.

59. Ray, *The Blyton Phenomenon*, 191. Ray's useful analysis (pp. 189–92) ends by finding the book's 'weakest feature . . . the almost complete lack of humour'. Blytonian humour, yes, but in its place is a rarity for her, Cromptonian humour, as the frauds encounter Nemesis.

60. Blyton, *The Put-Em-Rights*, 165, 164, 51, 56–7, 69–70, 92, 160.

61. Nesbit, *The Railway Children* (1906), last page(s) of all editions.

62. Noel Streatfeild, *Magic and the Magician: E. Nesbit and her Children's Books* (1958), 124.

63. Both Norton and Travers make their agents of magic spinsters – the social group traditionally associated with witchcraft, and most frequently victimised. But in each case the agent looks like something of unimpeachable respectability – the secretary of the Women's Institute, in the case of Norton's Miss Price, and a 'Nannie', in that of Mary Poppins. In Frank Baum's *The Wizard of Oz*, especially as filmed, the respectable spinster *becomes* a witch, but only when dreamed. Does this differentiate England and Kansas?

64. Norton, *The Magic Bedknobs* (1945), 106–7.

65. Travers, *Mary Poppins Opens the Door* (1944; Travers having made her way to the USA (*I Go by Sea, I Go by Land*, 1941); the new Poppins was first published in the USA, 1943), 30–1, 44.

66. Price, *Jane the Patient* [1940], 70. The Jane saga began in the late 1920s with *Just Jane*.
67. Ibid., 47–8, 71, 65–6.
68. Price, *Jane Gets Busy*, 54; *Jane at War*, 30, 31, 45, 48.
69. Westerman, *When the Allies Swept the Seas*, 220–2.
70. Ibid., 214–15, 11–12.
71. Methley, *Vackies* (1941), 99–100, 104, 253. The book was published by Oxford University Press, but no copy appeared in the catalogue of the British Museum (later Library), to which every British book should be sent. It reminds us of the confusion caused by the war, and the lacunae it caused in official records as well as deposit copies. The BM lost stock from Nazi bombing, but books destroyed were listed in the catalogue.
72. *Times Literary Supplement*, 6 January 1945. Sam Adams in fact ends looking slightly dingy.
73. *Times Literary Supplement*, 11 April 1958.
74. Fischer, *Paul Revere's Ride* (1994), 339.
75. Forbes, *Johnny Tremain* (1944), 247, 79–80. The Constable edition is a simple reproduction of text, plus a gun on the title page.
76. 'B.B.', *The Little Grey Men* (1942), 86–7, 188, 133.
77. Johns, *Biggles Sees it Through*, 210, 248.
78. Johns, *Biggles in the Baltic*, 197, 251.
79. Johns, *Biggles Hunts Big Game* (August 1948), 105, 180.
80. Johns, *Spitfire Parade*, 11, 29–30, 31, 36, 32, 171.
81. *Radio Fun* (March, April 1940), reproduced in Denis Gifford (ed.), *Comics at War* (1988), 131, 130.
82. During the war, Snooty was formally presented with a sword for services rendered, to put him on the same level as the people of Stalingrad, to whom, as Snooty read, George VI presented a sword as 'Every Man, Woman and Child fought to save the city!' (*Beano*, January 1944, reproduced in Gifford, *Comics at War*, 119). Orwell, 'Boys' Weeklies', *Complete Works*, XII, 65.
83. Johns, *Gimlet Goes Again*, 182–3.
84. Johns, *King of the Commandos*, 186, 190.
85. Johns, *Gimlet Mops Up* (1947), 92.
86. Johns, *Biggles in the Orient* (November 1944), 81–2, 118, 120, 121.
87. George Bourne, *I Flew with Braddock* [1959?], 11–12.
88. Crompton, 'William and the Bird Man', *William and the Evacuees*; 'The Outlaws and the Parachutist', *William Does His Bit*.
89. Gifford, *Comics at War*, 112, noted that for comics 'the ladies came into their own in World War Two' but rightly singles out 'Pansy Potter the Strong Man's Daughter who really liberated girl readers of the *Beano*', and supplies appropriate reproductions. In one (August 1940), a Nazi submarine torpedoes Pansy's model boat, annoying her sufficiently to cause her to open up the submarine with a tin-opener, hook worms on to the pants of every crew-member, and incite sharks to obtain the worms from the appropriate anatomical portions (Freudian papers please copy). In another (July 1943, the strip now in colour in place of its initial black and white), Pansy is parachuted into Germany as a spy and gets into a U-boat crew by shaking the captain until he capitulates, then loading a torpedo backwards so that it sinks its own submarine, whose captain she then delivers in mid-ocean to the British ship that he was trying to sink (Gifford, ibid., 115, 117).
90. Cadogan and Craig, *You're a Brick, Angela!*, chapter 17.
91. On the *Wizard*, see Cadogan and Craig, *Women and Children First*, 234–5. *BOP*,

vol. 65, no. 4 (now 9d in place of 6d three years earlier), 3. There is a useful history of the *BOP* by its last editor, who died with his work almost completed: Jack Cox, *Take a Cold Tub, Sir!* (1982), as well as a good anthology by Philip Warner, *The Best of British Pluck* (1976). Needless to say, nothing is said of Second World War Russophilia. Another image of Russophile young Britain appears in Angela Brazil, *The School in the Forest* ([1944]). Miss Murray, a shrewd spinster lady, is knitting while a group of boys and girls round a Christmastide fire tell stories: her 'knitting makes me think of a marvellous story' in which a political prisoner in nineteenth-century Austria gets free by unravelling woollen clothes into a ball sent through his window to the ground, where friends attached a strong rope to it: 'Perhaps the Russian you're knitting that woollie for will use it in the same way?' suggested Marjorie. 'I hope he won't have the need' (p. 199). But this was to acknowledge that, after the war, he might, as many heroes of the Russian fight against the Nazis did – if they lived long enough to be imprisoned.

FIGURE 10 Homicidal (but actually white) native about to miss Biggles
(Capt. W. E. Johns, 'The Adventure of the Golden Shirts',
afterwards in *Biggles – Charter Pilot*) – see pp. 373–4.

Race

In the middle of the night, Johanna woke from a horrible dream – a muddly, awful dream, in which she was being tortured, and knew she was going to be burnt alive.

She opened her eyes . . . And she was being tortured, she had a most horrible pain.

Johanna finished up some intimate questions and answers by saying, 'I suppose it was those things on sticks – toffee-apples – that the peasants gave us!'

Hans stood stock still. 'It was nothing of the sort', he said crossly. 'We were poisoned, of course!'

Josephine Elder [Dr Olive Gwendoline Potter],
Strangers at the Farm School (1940)[1]

'Oh yes, I know all about how Jews are treated in Germany. That's why you've come sneaking over here. In England we're nice to everybody – until we get tired.'

Mary K. Harris, *Gretel at St Bride's* (1941)[2]

You only know your class when it is assigned to you, whether by friends, enemies or unknowns. Your gender you should be able to decide with less assistance, although it is likely that its full implications will be discovered with the aid of someone else – genuinely friendly assistance, let us hope. Your race may seem even more certain, but its implications for you are greatly affected by the attitude that you find it invites. Martha Hoden in the *American Historical Review* (February 2003) entitled a remarkable essay 'The Mercurial Nature and Abiding Power of Race', and this classification is crucial to any study of the matter with respect to the Second World War. The Jews were murdered by Germans, a people whom their ancestors, fifty years earlier, would have deemed less hostile than their neighbours either to east or to west (France in 1894 having the Dreyfus affair, and Russia under Alexander III having launched anti-Jewish persecutions since his accession in 1881). For that matter, their future fellow-victims in the Holocaust, homosexual men, knew themselves to have friends in court when Hitler came to power. Josephine Elder's *Strangers at the Farm* has a little gypsy girl say of Germany, supposedly in 1938 but in a text written after the Second World War has begun: 'My Dada say 'e's goin' back there, soon. It's a better life for gipsies there than 'ere. I shan't be sorry –' and the homesick little Jewish boy to whom she speaks is convincing himself that the same would be true for him, even to believing that his life is less endangered in Nazi Germany. And Hitler's invasion of Russia, whose peoples he would also order to extermination, was done while the Russian government was still convinced that he would observe his non-aggression pact with them. Few of the victims foresaw that genocide was a Nazi priority, not simply a resort.

The British writers for children between 1939 and 1945 inherited racialist traditions of various kinds, some of them both exceedingly mixed and readily available in reprints when the war began. Gypsies had had vastly varying English literary fortunes. George Borrow's celebrations *Lavengro* and *The Romany Rye* were almost a century old but were still being read and quoted by children's authors. Matthew Arnold's 'The Scholar-Gypsy' was still being learned by heart in school. Toad's horse-dealing with a gypsy in *The Wind in the Willows* was an indispensable part in the Odyssey of children's favourite jail-breaker. More literary children could still thrill to the curse of Meg Merrilies and its complex fulfilment in Scott's *Guy Mannering*. Frank Richards introduced a gypsy kidnapping almost at the commencement of the *Magnet*, the victim being his future heroine Marjorie Hazeldene, more lachrymose than she would ever be again; and later he would briefly and hilariously domicile 'Mick, the Gypsy' at Greyfriars. In summer 1936, Richards's series about the Muccolini circus featured one of the most beautiful women he ever imagined, Zara, the gypsy equestrienne, Queen of the Ring, saved by Harry Wharton, courted by Billy Bunter, and ultimately married to Bill Williams, otherwise Marco the lion-tamer. Evadne Price introduced an exceedingly light-fingered gypsy (possibly her most attractive male character ever) on the eve of the Second World War in 'A Small Matter of £1,000,000' (*Jane Gets Busy*), where he saves Jane's beloved dog Popeye at considerable risk to his own neck, and Jane innocently enables him to escape from the victims of his endless thefts and to force apologies for their attempted arrest of him. By the end of the war, Saville had brought three likeable gypsies into friendship with Peter Sterling and the Mortons. On the other hand, Josephine Elder's gypsies, in what is one of the more sensitive racially preoccupied novels for children of its time, handles gypsies with hostility and, significantly, has its otherwise enlightened father-figure, Mr Forrester, make a great compliment of departing from what he makes clear is his habitual classification of gypsies as liars. The Jewish refugee children have concealed themselves from the gypsies while travelling with them, and the blameless gypsies are told:[3] 'We'll believe you, this once . . . since the young lady bears you out. You shouldn't go talking to other people's children, this is the sort of thing it leads to. Come along, you two . . .' In fact, the condemnation of gypsies to a status of liar was one which Jews (and Catholics) also suffered, though Elder neither hints such a thing of Jews herself nor shows any anti-Jewish feeling by her British characters. Elder, in common with Mary K. Harris, Olive C. Dougan and others, saw how Jewish children's experience of Nazi persecution must leave them in frequent terror that their troubles would resume in some comparable form in Britain. Elder collides these fears in the boy Hans with problems in gender and class: his well-to-do European background has meant that he sees a community school with farmwork obligations as a forced labour-camp.

> 'although they call us pupils, we are really labourers who work for them and get no pay. Whoever heard of a boy darning his socks and making his own bed? Yet we have to do it, as though we were in prison!'
> Johanna had still spirit enough left to retort, 'I don't see why boys shouldn't make their beds the same as girls! Darning socks I think they would be so bad at that it would not be worth while!'
> Hans rolled an eye at her and said in lordly tones, 'It is not work suitable for a boy. But that is not important. What I mean is that it is not suitable for the children of a great German lawyer such as our father to live with poor English people and clean out their hen-houses for them!'

Hans has in fact assimilated to Germany so well that he thinks as a German more than as a Jew. He takes patriotic pride in his family's service in the First World War: 'Hans was scowling. "The English", he announced, "are our enemies. Did they not kill my uncle and wound my father, so that he goes lame? How can you say they are kind?"' It is his sister who remembers

> a crowd in the road. Some were young Nazis, some were ordinary people, and in the middle a dozen or so men were on their knees, scrubbing the path. Hans was just asking what on earth they were

doing, scrubbing the muddy path in their ordinary indoor suits,
when one of them looked up, and they saw it was their own father
– their sleek, dignified father, his hair hanging over his face, his
glasses awry, scrubbing that path. A red-faced young Nazi gave
him a kick as they passed, and Johanna remembered hearing Hans
scream, and trying to force her way through the crowd to kick the
Nazi, scratch him, bite him, do him any injury she could. But the
governess had seized her and dragged her, protesting, away and
indoors.

They had never seen their father since then. He was, they were
told, safe and well – in a Concentration Camp.

It would be Elder's last book before the war demanded that she take
over two other medical practices in addition to her own, which ended
her career as a writer for children. After the war, she wrote some
novels for adults; it may have been that she, like Jeffrey Havilton,
found the themes in her last school story too powerful for her to
resume with the genre in quieter times. As it was, she gave her
readers the happy ending of reunion with parents on the last pages,
a common feature of refugee tales, including those by Brent-Dyer,
Gwendoline Courtney and Johns himself. It may have unintentionally
induced child illusions as to the chances of Jews getting out of Nazi
camps; it certainly showed how unthinkable extermination camps
still seemed to the British public in the first months of the war. As for
the anti-gypsy passages in a book so aware of the psychological
sufferings of Jewish children, it may be a conflation across time:
Elder's 'Farm School' was apparently based on a family farm of long
ago, so that the anti-gypsy attitudes may have been a Victorian
farmer's irritations. It does not gainsay the irony.

Deeper into the Second World War, Angela Brazil replayed the
theme of the long-lost child stolen by gypsies, which made for a
sensitive balance between the anti-gypsy heroine's wallows in her
own prejudice and attraction to a gypsy child who proves to be her
own sister. The School in the Forest (1944) also went out of its way to
tell a story of Scottish children, 350 years earlier, being condemned to
live in kennels and feed in pig-troughs:[4]

'Oh, how dreadful! Do these things happen now in the occupied
countries and Russian villages?' asked Maud.

'Something of the sort, I'm afraid, especially to Jewish children.
We must send out all we can to help them, through the Red Cross.'

Blyton's gypsies tended to be rather dirty and devoted to a male protagonist of the series (as usual, her innocence enabled her to sail closer to sex than anyone else could). They are presented as inferiors, but are shown to have terrific courage. The endlessly courageous racial inferior with specialist skills is a standard convention of children's book and comic fiction of the early twentieth century; but, since the prime commodity in most of these stories is courage, the portraits are friendly and, within limits, admiring. Blyton's use of analogous characters gave her an African equivalent of her gypsies, the boy Mafumu in *The Secret Mountain* (1941): the eldest white boy, Jack, is 'adored' by him, fairly demonstratively, and while embarrassed is 'secretly rather proud' of it. It is not a relationship of equals (as, say, Vernon-Smith and his Kikuyu hunter become), nor one of master–servant (as Bunter attempts, with ludicrous effects, in the South Seas adventure of 1938). It is much more physical in expression than Richards or Johns would ever employ, Mafumu sleeping as near to Jack as possible, sometimes lying 'almost on top of him'. Mafumu calls Jack 'King of Boys', and there may be some recollection of Gaelic bard devotion to a chieftain, if the part-Irish Blyton knew of it. It's important that the action in these stories is briefly (and heroically) seen through the gypsy/African child's mind. Mafumu is, if anything, more intelligent than the white children: he is very quick in language-assimilation, for instance. He is treated with maternalism, but with no sign of racial hostility, and the white children greatly regret leaving him at the end of the adventure ('He seemed quite one of us.'[5] – the 'quite' seems to capture both the admission of fellowship and the slight surprise in doing so). This particular group of children are not an average middle-class crowd, Jack being originally a working-class orphan, Paul a Ruritanian Crown Prince, and Mike and the two girls former unpaid servants to brutal relatives – Mafumu meets them under both heads, being a nephew to a bullying African conscripted for paid servitude, and being himself clearly destined to become chief of his people, for his part in the adventure.

This indicates an element of Blyton giving a largely child-performed *King Solomon's Mines*, as Sheila Ray noted (*The Blyton Phenomenon*, 168–70); but the character of Mafumu (and he has one), and his final reversal of his subordinate role to his tyrannical uncle on the strength of his (genuine) heroism, also suggest Blyton's awareness of J. M. Synge's *Playboy of the Western World*.

Gypsies were indigenous to Britain. Many Africans had imperial 'protection' (though God knew where Mafumu's country was; Enid

Blyton certainly did not). But many English on the eve of the Second World War were instinctively hostile to 'foreigners', as Stanley Baldwin was. Inevitably, imperial literature, like North American frontier literature, carried out savage warfare at the expense of obstreperous aborigines – the Greyfriars boys took their tolls of South Sea cannibals – but there was surprising divergence from the United States near-genocidal literature at the expense of Amerindians.[6] Richards, who was never prepared to forgive the USA for the Declaration of Independence, and perhaps more personal wrongs, renewed his attacks as late as April–May 1938 in the *Magnet* for American victimisation of the original inhabitants.[7]

But, as the Jews faced genocide nearer home, responses were sometimes less certain. John Buchan's early apportionment of anti-Jewish remarks among his more sympathetic characters came to a sudden end when Hitler came to power, and his *A Prince of the Captivity* (1933) featured a Jew as second hero, shot by the Germans in the First World War, while the main hero is murdered by the Nazis at the book's close. But Richmal Crompton, with no such antecedents to expiate, took a startlingly callous view of Jewish sufferings under the Nazis the following year, in 'William and the Nasties' (June 1934). The story was purged from the canon by Crompton's niece and literary advisers when the series was reprinted in 1986, but remained in print throughout the war, its book *William the Detective* reaching its fourteenth reprint in 1947, when the paper shortage was at its worst. And, on 31 October 1936, Richards produced another grossly insensitive performance, 'Harry Wharton's Amazing Relation', turning on anti-Jewish sentiment. Crompton may not have used Jewish characters before, and the only one in this story ends up unexpectedly likeable; Richards had a strong track record over a quarter-century of pro-Jewish writing, savagely denouncing anti-Jewish attitudes. One of Greyfriars's closest friendships is that between the scholarship boy of shoemaker parentage, Dick Penfold, and his wealthy Jewish study-mate Monty Newland, who has to conceal his financial rescue of Penfold's family from his proud friend; and Newland as protagonist of this 1936 story remains strongly likeable. But one of the most alarming qualities of both stories was that sentiments critical of Jews in general come from characters with whom readers would normally identify or whom at least they would see as their own ideals or comrades: William and his Outlaws, Harry Wharton and Bob Cherry. Both Crompton and Richards were probably trying to make pro-Jewish points – certainly, in both cases, anti-Jewish conduct is shown to be self-destructive – but, whatever the cause, the execution revealed clumsiness seldom evident from two such practised wordsmiths. Official Nazi government persecution of the Jews had begun in April 1933, and the Nuremberg Laws outlawed the Jews in September 1935. It may be that neither writer could quite cope with the implications of what was happening and was about to happen – and they would have been representative in that.[8]

In a pre-war Jane story, Evadne Price made merciless game of Jewish refugees and their exploiter-benefactors (appearing in book form in 1940, but presumably written and serially published before the outbreak of war). The refugee traffic is coolly represented as a means for hypocritical pseudo-philanthropists, led by Jane's mother, to save labour with slave labour:

'If the women of Duppery can help one poor creature to escape to Freedom from Persecution, we shall not have lived in vain. Especially', added Mrs Turpin with unconscious humour, 'as we can't get servants in this district and Austrian refugees work for nearly nothing and don't mind being on their feet from dawn to midnight, and hardly eat a thing.'

One prospective refugee telegraphs the vicar's wife: 'I will put up with what you offer', a slightly laboured joke about the unintentional accuracy of linguistic ineptitude. This would not be bad social criticism – the overseas generosity of domestic misers is an old historical phenomenon – and it is clear that the alleged local labour shortage lies in the future: the charwoman is promptly fired by the home-makers for refugees. But the portraits of the refugees themselves are very ill-natured, with strong implications of fraud all round. The refugee for the vicarage defects before arrival to employment in London. Her counterpart for Jane's family proves equally disillusioning: 'Mrs Turpin was looking for a thin, dejected, pathetic refugee and Fritzi was fat and hilarious and being the life and soul of a a bevy of excited relatives, who had met her'. Fritzi proves a bad housekeeper, a dreadful cook, a vile laundress, a user-up of hot water in long baths, and an ingrate: 'Really, thought Mrs Turpin, for a woman who had been hounded and persecuted by Hitler, Fritzi seemed singularly unappreciative of everything that had been done for her in England, the land of the free'. Eventually, Fritzi discovers that a former Austrian now domiciled and married in the village is a Nazi supporter flourishing a swastika ornament, and chases her with a knife, howling 'Nazi! Nazi!' while her victim apparently screams 'Yude! Yude!' and Jane shouts 'Go it, Fritzi! Go it, Petrarka!', 'cheering on both sides with impartiality'. Petrarka proves to be a spy once the war is on, and decamps, abandoning her postman husband, but in the pre-war story one seems to be as bad as the other: we are evidently meant to share Jane's bloodthirsty neutrality. Eventually, Jane steals the Nazi ornament and surreptitiously sticks it on Amelia Tweeddale's paper hat when forced to go to her birthday party, so that Fritzi, now in service at the vicarage, will react, which she does, Amelia being 'well and truly up-ended and spanked by the infuriated, strong-armed, horny-handed Fritzi Wasservogel'. This last touch (sic) shows the immigrant Price's readiness to conform to the fashionable British obsessions with bottom-spanking ('I doubt whether my poor child will be able to sit down comfortably for weeks to come').[9] But the overall message seems to be that the Jewish refugees are tiresome, useless troublemakers best left where they are. Price's open and somewhat Anglophobe cynicism hardly offsets a message of isolation in one of its most pernicious forms. Jews would die because of such anti-refugee sentiments, sufficiently diffused among British (and Irish and American) civilians to encourage the instinctive government policies of exclusion.

It is tragic that a touch of this new racial hostility in the post-Munich months invaded Crompton. If 'William and the Nasties' has been somewhat unfairly criticised, no excuse of good intentions may be offered for the Jewish detail in 'William Gets His Own Back' (November 1939). It is improbable that it was written after the outbreak of war; it more likely reflects a general post-Munich feeling that anything, Jews included, likely to impair the Chamberlain Peace must be discredited. The story near its end involves Hubert and Queenie Lane betraying an alliance with William against a gang of school-leaving-age campers (probably from London), as a result of which William is locked up in an empty house

> owned by an old man called Daniel Smith, who had a flat bald head, Jewish nose, cross eyes, and a wispy grey beard. He lived in another derelict but smaller house nearby and looked almost as tumble-down as his property. He earned his living (apparently) by renting a few bad meadows, a few worse cottages, keeping poultry and buying and selling everything from house property to old iron. He was known to the Outlaws as Cross-eye Smith and had always been a virulent enemy of theirs. His son, Rube, helped his father in the business and shared fully his dislike of boys in general and the Outlaws in particular, chasing them away with stones and bricks whenever they approached his property.

The devil is in the detail: it is all standard caricature of Jews as low-level profiteers, with stops pulled out in a performance as crude as Crompton ever orchestrated: the description of Cross-eye Smith (irrelevantly to the story, where he is heard but not seen), his nose being labelled Jewish, his son being Rube, and his general malevolence. Ginger (who has come to rescue William) sees Cross-eye and Rube 'comin' here. They'll *murder* us if they find us. Let's hide, quick.' And they overhear the Smiths 'talking in thick strident voices', exulting in evidence of the campers having lit fires and smoked. 'And all the wood's as dry as tinder. The windows are all broke, too. That'll make a good draught. The place is insured for £2000, and I couldn't get it off my hands if I tried to *give* it away.' Later that night, the Smiths duly fire the place; and William's and Ginger's evidence – heard by the insurance agent during their recriminations against the Lanes the following day – wins bicycles for them (and, presumably, respite from prosecution for their hated enemies the campers). Apart from the poisonous use of Smith's Jewishness, it is a well-told story, the climax turning elegantly on the boredom of the insurance agent waiting for his train:

> So he loitered about, deriving what entertainment he could from the limited resources of the place. He had watched a hen scratching the surface of the road for about ten minutes and was tiring of the spectacle. This first-class juvenile row, springing up suddenly on the highway under his nose, was a welcome diversion.

The Smiths do not, of course, attempt to murder William and Ginger, although we have a slight frisson at William's peril should Ginger not have realised that he had been captured. The insurance man is alerted by what is presumably Queenie's line:[10] 'Wish you'd still been in that ole house when it caught fire. You'd've got burnt up an' jolly well serve *you* right.' Queenie's vindictiveness is centre-stage and duly closes the story by her fury at seeing her enemies rewarded as a result of her treachery; but the background thought of William incinerated by the Jewish Smiths' arson darkens what is already a fairly bitter comedy.

Crompton did not withdraw the story, but her conscience was not easy. It is one stage more anti-Jewish than *Jane Gets Busy*: the Jews under attack are British-domiciled and almost certainly British subjects. In an adult novel, *Weatherley Parade* (1944), written when the fate of the Jews in Germany and Poland was becoming known in Britain, Crompton included a pre-war scene in which Jim and his daughter Jo return in 1937 from Germany, where her anti-Nazi husband Karl had been tortured to death in a concentration camp:[11]

> Jo opened her eyes. 'I had a miscarriage', she said.
>   'Tell them the whole bloody story', burst out Jim in a white heat of rage that made them all turn to look at him in amazement. 'They'll have to know sooner or later. . . . The devils were kicking an old woman in one of their filthy Jew-baiting orgies, and, when Jo tried to interfere, they knocked her down and kicked her, too. . . . And I had to soft-soap the bastards and cringe to them. God! I wish I'd had the guts to stick a knife into one of them!'

The symbolism is straightforward: the murders of Jews bring about the deaths of our future children. It is a variant of Donne's Sermon quoted by Hemingway to entitle *For Whom the Bell Tolls*, but it is a more personal one. Crompton was too honest and too clear-sighted to deny her part in the Jewish tragedy, however infinitesimally small. It has a frightening loneliness about it. Laments for the fate of European Jews were very few among the writers for children; still fewer were the self-indictments.

Orwell's dark forebodings as to the intent of Lord Camrose in controlling boys' papers may have had some basis in Amalgamated Press house policy on combustible public questions in 1939, during which year Camrose was in the Ministry of Information. Anti-German propaganda was probably more firmly stifled in the months before war than at any time previously. The war actually broke out during the serialisation of *Biggles – Secret Agent* as 'Castle Sinister' in *The Modern Boy* between 12 August and 14 October 1939, and its place in a Camrose weekly may explain W. E. Johns's necessity to set it not in Germany but in a German-controlled imaginary 'Lucrania', German-speaking, Germany-surrounded, and German-staffed up to and including Erich von Stalhein as Chief commanding trigger-happy storm-troopers of Police. Its Jewish policy is firmly Nazi, even if the word is not used. Unlike 'Sapper', Sydney Horler, Lynn Brock and thriller-writers sometimes viewed as adult fare for the Johns graduate, Johns supplied no promiscuous anti-Jewish moments nor any of the more elegant malice in the same line available from Chesterton, Buchan, Sayers or Christie. It's possible that Paul Cronfelt, the businessman who double-crosses Biggles and von Stalhein in *Biggles & Co.*, was originally Jewish: if so, all signs of it were dropped. The Nazis might have used a Jew for business profit (many anti-Semites had ludicrous notions of Jewish capacity for financial success), but it hardly made sense to recruit them in a criminal enterprise demanding absolute silence. The (non-speaking) cosmopolitan banker Klein, who assists the treacherous 'Maltovian' General Bethstein in *Biggles Goes to War* and shares his fate, was probably intended for a Jew; but that was natural casting, and the refusal to name him as a Jew was consistent with the coded but obvious message that Lovitzna, to whom Bethstein and Klein are betraying Maltovia, is Germany. Steeley helps rob the wife of a sausage king with a Jewish name in *Sky High*, but they are not named as Jews, and his 'fortune out of overworking underpaid men and women' could be as much an allusion to Ogden Armour of Armour Star (whose factory inspired Upton Sinclair's *The Jungle*, 1906) as to a Jew. In sum, Johns was not anti-Jewish – and as some of his allusions to non-whites show, he was not circumspect on racial questions – but he was not pro-Jewish. Possibly he was pro-Arab, pro-Egyptian or pro-Muslim – not nearly as much his regretted subaltern T. E. Lawrence, but enough to go on with. The hero of *Desert Night* (1938) has a bosom friend in an Arab sheik whose place he takes (sheik friends and substitutes were commonplace from the early 1920s in the movie roles of Rudolph Valentino, in the fiction of P. C. Wren and even among the boys of Greyfriars). The occasional guest role on the Biggles team is taken in *Biggles Flies South* by a charming and learned young Egyptian archaeologist, Kadar ('a native, but obviously one of the better class, and his skin was not much darker than that of a sunburned white man').[12] Enemy tribesmen are disposed of ruthlessly enough, but they are often figures of dignity, and even sympathy: 'White men are all the same. They bring death to where there was only peace'[13] observes a Touareg chief, immediately after the Second World War, in *Sergeant Bigglesworth, C.I.D.* (1947). Johns claimed to have served in Iraq; no trace of this has been found, but he clearly had desert experience of some kind – and, whether official, Secret Service or private, it left him with a great love, though also a shrewd respect, for the desert.

The Jew in *Biggles – Secret Agent* is unique, both as a Jew and as a victim: nothing equal to its horror is evident in any of Johns's other writing, even in the penetration of Nazi-occupied Europe at its worst. It is in fact a portrait of the world that the Munich agreement had left to take care of itself:

Ginger regarded with a mixture of disgust and sympathy an old man whose back was bent by years, by labour, or by suffering, or, perhaps, by a combination of all three. His hair, had it been clean, would have been white; long and tangled, it hung far down over the back of his collarless neck, and down his cheeks until it became part of the unkempt beard that concealed the lower part of his face. His old-fashioned jacket and shapeless trousers, once black, were green with age, and dirty beyond description, as were his hands and that part of his face which was not covered with hair. His movements were slow and uncertain; indeed, his fingers trembled to such an extent that it was only with difficulty that he brought the wick of the candle and the flame of the match together.

Biggles caught Ginger's eyes.

'Observe what persecution and the fear of death does to a man in time', he said softly, in English. 'Poor devil. He is just an animated piece of terror.' Then, more loudly, he went on in German, 'Do not worry about us, Father. You have nothing to fear.'

Biggles needs information, but that 'Father' is one of his finest moments.

'What can I do for you?' he asked nervously, looking from one to the other.'You were not wise to come here.'

'Why not?' asked Biggles.

'I am a Jew.'

'Do they treat Jews so badly?'

'You have seen', said the old man simply.

'Why do you stay here and suffer?'

'How can I go? I have no money – none.' The old man's eyes darted from door to window, and back again to his visitors. 'They have had it all', he said softly, but there was a world of hate behind his tremulous voice.

Again: 'He was nearly inarticulate with terror, and Ginger marvelled that a man could be reduced to such a lamentable condition'. And again, when it is clear that they are overheard:[14]

The Jew's terror was pitiful to behold. A faint moan broke from his ashen lips, and he nearly collapsed. His eyes, saucer-eyed with fear, stared at the door. His lips moved noiselessly.

Biggles's mouth set in a hard line. He motioned to Ginger to remain still. 'Thank you very much, Father', he said in a loud voice. 'I think we shall be able to find our way now.'

Biggles and Ginger have just parachuted illegally into the country, but it is clear that if the eavesdropper is anti-Jewish (as it is clear

from the story that private as well as public individuals are), the
supposedly innocuous purpose of the visit is flanked by an expression of comradeship defying the prevailing persecution, regardless of
its dangers to them and to their mission. The money he has already
given the Jew, it is hoped, will get him away to a daughter in
Switzerland. But the whole passage put any future war on the
anti-racialist basis that it required.

Yet, when Johns wrote about the Second World War, the Jews were
hardly mentioned in his pages. The Palestine issue may have been
one cause. 'The Jew of Unterhamstadt' supplied the title of the fourth
chapter of *Biggles – Secret Agent*, thus flagging the issue to the
hesitating purchaser; and perhaps government officials looking over
recent Johns titles may have said a word to this effect in prompting
books on Worrals and on Gimlet. Johns did not take kindly to
censorship; but, if he was at least somewhat pro-Arab on Palestine,
he might have been ready to accept such a tip. Certainly, both before
and during the war, the British authorities were exceedingly anxious
to discourage Jewish settlement in Palestine, and therefore even to
disapprove Jewish emigration from Austria and Germany, many
Jewish refugees being interned in the UK when war broke out. Johns
did introduce another, wealthier Jew in the second half of *Sinister
Service* (a thriller about the brothers Lovell whose first half had
originally been the last 'Steeley' story (*War Thriller*, 27 April 1940),
now slightly amended with new heroes for 1942 publication). Johns
apparently realised that the only Jews with some chance of safety in
the Nazi regime (*Biggles – Secret Agent* having virtually predicted
Jewish extermination) would be those of some means with specific
Nazi protection (such as the geopolitics expert Karl Haushofer, an
old friend of Hess, and his half-Jewish wife, who in former days had
given hospitality to the unknown, disgraced and indigent Hitler). The
Jew in *Sinister Service* is a British agent, much concerned when
fugitives with a refugee inventor invade his house ('It was never
suggested that I should have to do this sort of thing. My work lies in a
different direction'). He quickly disillusions his optimistic guests
('You don't know our Gestapo') but agrees to put them up ('I've been
living for months on the edge of a precipice and my nerves are
beginning to suffer"'). Our heroes are somewhat insensitive ('"I'm
afraid that fellow's nerves are on the jump", remarked Lance. "It's a
pity, but it can't be helped. I hope they'll hold out for another couple
of days"'). Their host provides a bottle of light Rhenish, bread,
cheese, and sausage (not an orthodox Jew, unsurprisingly), cold
potatoes and apples ('"That's the best I can do for the moment",

he said. "Food is getting scarce" ").[15] While they are in hiding, the agents discover that their Jewish host has been arrested and killed on a charge of sabotage and that his wife has committed suicide in her prison cell. The brothers and their charge of course escape. The whole business is handled with little compassion; Johns seems to imply a separate Jewish agenda, temporary allies though the doomed host and the unbidden guests may be, and this may symbolise the divergent interests that the British government (though not necessarily the British Premier) regarded as dividing it from the Jews in Europe, Britain and Palestine.

And that, incredibly, is all. Johns would make much mention of Nazi atrocities, notably in the two wartime Gimlet books and in the post-war *Biggles Hunts Big Game, Biggles Takes a Holiday* and *Worrals in the Wastelands*. Jews are never mentioned. In its way, it mirrors the adult reading: concentration-camp emphases were quickly directed to prisoner-of-war camps and their famous escapes. The public read *The Colditz Story* or *The Wooden Horse*, not the Belsen chronicles. Irma Grese, tried as the Beast (or the Bitch) of Belsen and found guilty on 17 November 1945, and hanged on 12 December 1945, is mentioned as being executed 'for her crimes at Belsen Murder Camp' in *Worrals in the Wastelands*, whose arch-criminal Anna Shultz is clearly based on her. Worrals speaks of Shultz's 'ghastly record. I could hardly bear to read the details; there's a limit to what I can stand in the way of horrors. Don't call her a woman. She's a Gorgon. Her wretched victims used to call her the Devil's Sister . . .' Yet, despite the majority of Grese's victims having been Jews, they were omitted when the book cited her quite real trial, or in any facts stated against Shultz. The report that 'Rumey was ignorant of the dreadful things his fiancee was doing in the Stenberg Internment Camp' is all too evocative of the famous German ignorance of the fate of the Jews; but Jews receive not a word. Shultz's husband (as he proves to be), Dr Wolfe, is reported as 'wanted by the War Crimes Commission' for his 'experiments on prisoners, many of whom died in agony'; but this could simply be captured Allied personnel. No doubt their fate would be vivid for Johns, with memories of his own capture in the First World War; but this verges on denial of the Holocaust. Shultz is described as being in 'a woman's internment camp', but in context there is nothing to say what women they were, and the words appear after mention of 'a man's camp, for British prisoners of war'.[16] During the years between Grese's trial and the publication of *Worrals in the Wastelands*, the Jewish revolt against the UK took on a terrorist quality, notably when British headquarters at the King David Hotel in Jerusalem were blown up by a Zionist murder gang on 22 July 1946, with ninety-three deaths. This may have made the difference, and may indeed account for the extraordinary delay between the real and supposed events in the book (1945–6) and its appearance (1949). Johns may have boycotted Jews as a topic in view of the fate of British troops, some of whom he may have known; and this could have forced extensive rewriting. If so, it was to the book's literary, although not to its moral, advantage: time in its gestation may have helped to lift it above its fellows. It must also be assumed that similar circumstances accounted for the elimination of Jewish sufferings from countless other Second World War books and comics appearing in the immediate aftermath.

The Jew of Unterhamstadt in *Biggles – Secret Agent* is a most unattractive figure, Biggles rightly stressing that his surrounding squalor stems from terror and persecution: to save himself, he has to appear beneath contempt. It does not save his son, a more able-bodied Jew, conscripted as an undertaker to dress a fake funeral and then apparently eliminated – another firm warning of the probable fate lying ahead of German Jews. Brent-Dyer in *The Chalet School in Exile*, appearing at more or less the same time of book publication, April–May 1940, can present its persecuted and doomed Jewish goldsmith as a figure of more dignity and honour – the Chalet schoolgirls who try to save him are long-standing residents, not recent, secret arrivals, and are even called Fräulein by the Austrians annoyed at being checked in their homicide. Jewish generosity in crisis is recalled not simply as self-protection or gratitude, but as altruism: if Johns may have reflected the influence of Scott's Isaac in *Ivanhoe*, Brent-Dyer caught the spirit of his Rebecca:

> 'Last winter, when you were all starving, didn't Frau Goldmann send soup and coffee every day to your home? And didn't Herr Goldmann give you a job so that you had a regular wage? And is this the way you show your gratitude? You *deserve* to starve!'
>
> 'He's a Jew! Jew have no right to live!' declared Hans Bocher sullenly. 'Give place, Fräulein Bettany, and hand over old Jew to us! Better take care, or you'll be in trouble for this. Let him go! We'll see to him!'

Ivanhoe has another relevance. Isaac and Rebecca are threatened by a variety of elements – popular hostility, Norman extortion, Templar lust – until last of all the supreme authority, the Inquisition, determines on burning the girl alive. Brent-Dyer comparably linked the popular lynch-mob to ultimate governing authority, though now secular rather than clerical. She transmitted the message that in Nazi territory mob victims who escaped would be pursued with state reprisal, not protection: 'Miss Wilson ... knew from her daily reading of the papers that the girls would not be safe an instant, once the authorities at Innsbruck heard of this'. The dying priest would be marked down by the state if he recovered:[17] 'Vater Johann knows he is dying. But if he lived, it would mean prison for helping you to escape. He prefers death to a Nazi gaol.' Almost on cue from Brent-Dyer, Worrals and Gimlet produced comparable priests at risk from the Nazis while saving Allied personnel in hidey-holes, as Vater Johann had done; but there, at least, the authorities (had they known) could have charged them with aiding the wartime enemy. Biggles and Miss Wilson in peacetime learn that it is a crime against the state simply to show humanity to a Jew. It is the state which endangers the life of the Jew of Unterhamstadt; but windows of his premises have been smashed and the door is chalked 'Jude', making Lucrania what Biggles terms[18] 'one of the places under the influence of anti-Jewish propaganda'. It was exactly the point that should have invited stronger reassertion once the Second World War had begun; but it did not receive it.

Johns may have half-hidden another Jewish theme in *Biggles – Secret Agent*. The quest is to recover a missing British scientist, originally Lucranian and mysteriously returned to his birthplace, Professor Max Beklinder, research chemist in extra-lethal poison gas and other explosives, whose prime product is named Linderite. Britain and the USA were by now well stocked with refugee Jewish and Jewish-wed scientists, headed by Einstein, who coincidentally during the story's serialisation wrote to President Roosevelt to set on foot research into what would eventuate as the atomic bomb. This was not a very remarkable or even original prophecy.[19] But its use in the story is dramatic enough: Beklinder holds up a bottle to von Stalhein, and discusses it and handles interruptions professorially.

'It is an explosive infinitely more powerful than Linderite', announced the Professor. He almost purred the words as he held up the bottle again and gazed affectionately at the contents.

Von Stalhein's hand crept towards his pocket, but the Professor saw the movement. 'Shoot – shoot by all means', he said calmly. 'Doubtless you are aware of what happens when nitro-glycerine is dropped – or even moved violently. It explodes. I believe the compound in my hand to be so deadly that any severe vibration

– such as would occur if I allowed it to fall – would be sufficient to cause it to detonate. If such a thing occurred I should have only one regret – not that there would be much time for regrets, you understand? I should not live to see exactly how devastating would be the result. But it would be considerable, I assure you. Very little would be left of the castle. As for you and me, why, nothing would remain to show that we had ever been. A fitting end for a research chemist like myself – and for a liar like you'.

There is nothing to show Beklinder as Jewish; his abandonment of his wife and son in Lucrania without subsequent contact conflicts with common assumptions of Jewish family solidarity. If anything, it seems a flicker of autobiography, Johns having left his own wife and son; Biggles cuts unusually deep on a personal issue with allusion to Beklinder's 'fit – a belated fit you will think – of remorse over the unfortunate wife'.[20] But well-informed child readers would associate refugee scientific discoverers with Jews fleeing from Nazis, and the acknowledged Jew in the story would prompt the idea. It was probably Johns's way of showing what really lay behind refugee research for possible future anti-Nazi war. And Beklinder's bleak stoicism may connect with what Johns knew of the hard courage of Jews emigrating to Palestine. Certainly, the cowardice so often alleged against the Jews by their persecutors had no place in Beklinder.

Johns's most immediate inspiration may have been the invalided Major Charles James Louis Gilson (1878–1943), whose thirty-five-year career as a writer for boys followed extensive service in the Far East, and was interrupted during the First World War when he joined the navy and served at Antwerp. Gilson's *Out of the Nazi Clutch* (1940) posited a schoolboy deprived of his last year to learn his father's shipping business as a trainee in Nazi Germany, where he rescues a younger boy (a quarter Jewish) from being stoned. Gilson may have had some Jewish ancestry. In any event, he firmly identified anti-Jewish attitudes as part of Nazi beliefs interlocked with Anglophobia. His readers were told on the eve of the rescue:[21]

Provided you were an Aryan and a German, provided you had neither a sense of proportion nor a sense of humour, so long as you marched in step, waved flags and *heiled* Hitler, you belonged to a heavenborn, invincible race, and all other peoples were inferior, fit objects for hatred and contempt. And they hated, as they did everything else, to order. They hated whom they were told to hate:

first, the Communists; then the Jews; then the Roman Church, and the Austrians, and the Czechs, and finally the Poles – and it was this succession of hatreds, and the misery and persecution that resulted therefrom, that led to the outbreak of war in 1939, when the accumulated hatred of all these years became centred against England.

Gilson was Victorian enough to sermonise his audience with little embarrassment; and this passage warns the reader to read a story initially set in 1937 with a clear focus on 1939. It also taught that no man was an island via the as yet undescribed rescue: 'by saving little Otto Spohr that evening from further persecution, he saved his own life in years to come'. But if the form was crudely traditional, both in adjuration and in anticipation, the grim sequence itself anticipated Pastor Martin Niemöller's warning against thinking only of one's own:[22]

> they came for the Communists and I didn't speak up because I was not a Communist. Then they came for the Jews and I didn't speak up because I was not a Jew. They they came for the trade unionists and I didn't speak up because I was not a trade unionist. Then they came for the Catholics and I didn't speak up because I was a Protestant. Then they came for me . . . By that time there was nobody left to speak up.

The rescue is accomplished by beating the leader of the stone-throwers in boxing (Gilson had been at Dulwich College, whose boxing record was immortalised in the school fiction of P. G. Wodehouse): skill defeats strength, although the young Nazi 'like every German . . . took a pride in physical courage'. The hero sees young Spohr home, but later finds him and his father in a state of siege after the anti-Jewish boycott is proclaimed:

> The Nazis had broken into the shop and had looted everything. Both Otto and his father had been manhandled and beaten with sticks; and they had passed that night on a refuse dump outside the city. They were bruised, miserable, and well-nigh frozen by the cold wind – for the winter was drawing on. Before dawn they had returned to their wrecked and ravaged home, because there was nowhere else to go. They had crept through the streets like two stray and starving dogs; but, in the end, they had got back safely and without being seen.

Since then they had been to all intents and purposes imprisoned in their own house. Fortunately the Nazis had not thought of going down into the cellar, or – what was more probable – they had failed to find the entrance.

This anticipates the future existence of Anne Frank; the Niemöller argument is anticipated by the English boy hero's adult host (whose own son is already wholeheartedly in the Nazi youth):

'It is terrible, a disgrace to our country! But what can I do, what can anyone do, about it? These people seem unable to discriminate. Undesirable aliens ought to be turned out of the country – everyone agrees with that. But this little grocer! Only half Jew by birth, a Christian by religion, and a hard-working, peaceable citizen. All the same, Walter, I most strongly advise you not to have anything to do with it. We Germans can do nothing but look on, and regret and feel ashamed. It seems cowardly advice, I know, and I am even more ashamed to have to give it; but, if you are wise, you will leave these poor people to their fate, as you may get into serious trouble yourself. Even your passport may not protect you.'

Walter manages to save the Spohrs from Buchenwald, where Nazi officials are taking them. Once again, Gilson interrupted his narrative to explain:[23]

'I've got orders to take them to Buchenwald, where they'll be treated as they deserve.'
Walter was unable to conceal his consternation. News of what was happening in the concentration camps had already leaked out. Some of the guards in these huge modern torture-chambers surrounded by barbed wire had the ordinary instincts of civilized human beings. There may have been comparatively few of them; but these few were horrified by the brutal treatment meted out to the unfortunate prisoners by their comrades, and they had made no secret of it to their friends. There were many Germans who were horrified at what they regarded as a disgrace to their country. Others stolidly refused to believe a word of it. Others, again, would merely shrug their shoulders, and declare that the inmates of the concentration camps got no more than they deserved.
Their so-called crimes were no more than that they had Semitic blood in their veins or that they had in some way offended the Nazis. That was enough. No trial was necessary, for there was no

recognized offence with which they could be charged. An order was given by someone 'higher up' – and they were hustled away, to be beaten, scourged and kicked, many of them never to be seen again alive.

It is startling to remember that this is a passage written before the Second World War was a year old. Gilson (although himself a bedridden invalid for much if not by now all of the time) must have had good sources of information. He lacked Johns's artistry: apart from the Kailyard Scots Captain MacAndrew, who helps Walter get the Spohrs to Schleswig-Holstein and (when war has broken out) to England, the characters are walk-on figures intended to illustrate the fine sentiments of the author. His happy ending, at least for the Spohrs and the heroes, depends excessively on coincidence. Brent-Dyer's grim doom for the Goldmanns and the priest is much closer to reality. But, when introducing and analysing his fictions, Gilson was both memorable and singular in his isolation.

A. J. P. Taylor pointed out one ugly fact on this in his *English History 1914–1945*. Leslie Hore-Belisha was proposed by Neville Chamberlain in January 1940 for the Ministry of Information and then vetoed by Halifax because he was a Jew. This is certainly evidence of exclusion of possible pro-Jewish propaganda. Harold Nicolson later banned a broadcast talk by Bernard Shaw from the BBC because its excoriation of Hitler's crimes against the Jews might alienate potential allies who were themselves anti-Jewish.[24]

We cannot say whether wartime fiction for children was restrained in content by pressures on its publishers through paper quotas: officialdom certainly did not want agitation of the Jewish question for fear of Palestine complications, British immigration officials did not want potential re-emigrants to Palestine, and American authorities were hostile to Jewish entry from the UK or anywhere else (demanding certificates of birth from German Jews, which few had and no German government officials would give them). Saving the Jews was not an Allied war aim, despite individual personal regard for the Jews by such figures as Churchill, Eleanor Roosevelt and so on. Orwell's belief that anti-Jewish sentiment was on the increase in Second World War Britain is not altogether convincing as an explanation for the disappearance of Jews from children's literature. His own experience with *Animal Farm* indicated how effective censorship pressure from the old-boy network might be, even though neither public-school types in the civil service nor, say, T. S. Eliot in Faber & Faber seemed likely Stalinists. Anti-

Catholicism in Britain was vigorous in the 1940s, and many of the
anti-Jewish remarks quoted by Orwell could as readily have been
made about Catholics (and Orwell himself would have been much
more likely to make them about Catholics). Yet continental Catholics
were frequently represented as automatically anti-Nazi characters by
writers for children in the Second World War where continental
Jews (a more likely anti-Nazi type) were ignored. Orwell in early 1945
said that nobody who still wrote about Jews in the anti-Jewish
manner of G. K. Chesterton could be published; but the converse
might also have applied. A year earlier, Orwell had told Roy Fuller:
'by my own experience it is almost impossible to mention Jews in
print, either favourably or unfavourably, without getting into trouble'.[25] Quite apart from HM Government Palestine policy discouraging emotive pro-Jewish sentiments among writers for children, there
may have been a feeling among publishers themselves that allusions
to Jews were to be discouraged.

The most notable allusion to Jews to be found in a fictional work
of relevance to children, composed during the war, is in J. R. R.
Tolkien's *The Lord of the Rings*. It is now a very public work, but
its wartime gestation was a very private one. Its reflection of its
author's scholarship and imagination should not obscure that of his
spirituality, centred as it is on a meditation on the Lord's Prayer
(irresistible temptation vanquished by forgiveness for injury). The
wholehearted Catholicism naturally affected the ground where
Catholics had so much to unlearn and to learn: their view of the
Jews. Tolkien's original inspiration of the Jews as a model for the
dwarves in *The Hobbit* gave that story its greatest tragic strength
(Gollum only acquired his tragic character when *The Hobbit* was
revised after publication of *The Lord of the Rings*). Bilbo's acceptance, rejection and forgiveness by the Dwarf leader Thorin give him
what seems *his* only tragic moment, and transmit a long, remote grief
to *The Lord of the Rings*. The dwarves, among whom so much of the
comic glee as well as tragic depth was given to *The Hobbit*, are
obliterated much more thoroughly in the successor book. Thorin dies
a tragic but romantic death in *The Hobbit*, his nephews Kili and Fili
meeting appropriate chivalric ends at his side. Balin, Ori and Óin die
ugly deaths in the dark, far from the comrades among whom they had
once mourned Thorin. Their attempted return to the former land of
dwarf glory, Moria, seems to have been inspired by Zionism, but the
fate that they shared may have been prompted by what Britain was
gradually learning about the Holocaust. Balin's death is only known
for certain when the Fellowship of the Ring find his inscribed tomb

and subsequently fragments of record all too reminiscent of the real-life destruction of the Jews:[26]

> 'The last lines run *the pool is up to the wall at Westgate. The Watcher in the Water took Óin. We cannot get out. The end comes,* and then *drums, drums in the deep.* I wonder what that means. The last thing written is in a trailing scrawl of elf-letters: *they are coming.* There is nothing more.'

Posthumously – that is, when the victims of ethnic cleansing were dead, and the soldiers and civilians who would also die were dead, and Hitler was dead, and the war was dead, and the worst criminals at the Nuremberg trials were dead – posthumously, the war became a war against racism. It was a valuable, indeed invaluable, legacy, however unhistorical. The one place where such an interpretation had validity at the time was in Asia, where it existed as propaganda for the other side. The Japanese were anxious to make the most of Asian resentment against the white imperial powers, and the most obvious expression of racial victimisation would have been in individual colonial experiences. Allied propaganda reactions to the Japanese themselves were often highly racialistic, thus handing the Japanese a grievance to share in common with the former victims of white empire, not to say an agenda for encouragement of revolt. British child readers were not presented with comparable hate-objects as the war in the Pacific began to dominate. There were bad jokes in their reading-matter about the divinity of the Emperor Hirohito, but seldom acquiring the demonic image won by Hitler, or that of the more absurd bully associated with Mussolini. Tojo was probably unknown in name to most little Britons, and even little Americans may have forgotten him after his resignation in July 1944, though his execution in 1948 no doubt recalled him to their memories. But the command level in combat stories was another matter. Germans were human, even when being despatched by Gimlet or some equally recriminatory public servant: they might be monsters of cruelty, not necessarily always an exaggeration even with Jews omitted from the story, but they were at worst human distortions. Japanese were generally rendered as sub-human. In the midst of his eloquence against the persecution of the Jews, the Far East veteran Gilson used the Japanese as a symbol to show how low the Germans were falling:[27]

> 'Buchenwald!' Walter gasped.
>   'You cannot take them there!'

The man grinned. He looked rather like a Japanese; and when he showed his protruding teeth, the resemblance was even more marked.

The traditions of mutual regard between classic opponents are very old and inspire subsequent generations: Hector and Achilles, Cuchulainn and Ferdia, Caesar and Pompey, Sir Gawain and the Green Knight, Coeur de Lion and Saladin, du Guesclin and the Black Prince, Clive and Dupleix, Montcalm and Wolfe. They were triumphantly reinvoked in the most chivalric theatre of the First World War, the air – and while Johns in the Second World War etched many anti-Nazi portraits, occasional German male pilots can provide attractive cameos. Conspicuously, von Stalhein is at his most heroic when playing an airborne role (*Biggles Flies East*, *Biggles & Co.*), and his descent into war crimes is on the earth as well as earthy. But even when the German enemy is evil, it is the evil of a double, one who in heroic fantasy is the victim who so easily might have been the killer, an image realised by Housman and Owen in verse. The poets preferred to make such an adversary a lovable one, once he was dead. Prose made him more ambiguous; and, in writers as varied as John Buchan and Sydney Bowen, there is the element of shame before the villain master of disguise who might be one's double (if he chose) and conceivably might be oneself gone to the bad, when he appears to have won. It is not simply the hero's anger at the enemy's victory, or at his own discomfiture, but something akin to horror at the triumph of our evil selves, our damnation by giving our Mr Hydes the control of our future. Buchan effectively realises this profound shame in *Mr Standfast*, and in its derivative banality Bowen does ditto in *Dave Dawson on Convoy Patrol* (1943) a quarter-century later. But, however hated these villains, revulsion from Buchan's von Schwabing and Bowen's von Khole deepens from their facility in becoming English. The same applies to the sadistic Nazi female pilot Hylda passing as the daughter of an American archaeologist in *Worrals Goes East*. No such role is possible for a Japanese in these stories. One might have a Japanese friend (as in John Finnemore's Edwardian school stories) or even a Japanese hero (as in E. Phillips Oppenheim's *The Illustrious Prince* and John P. Marquand's Mr Moto series). One might pass for Japanese, as for a time the protagonist of Jan Maclure's *Escape to Chungking* (1942) does. But a Japanese in such fiction cannot pass for English. Algy's interrogation in *Biggles Delivers the Goods*, when captured by Admiral Tamashoa, shows it clearly:

the admiral was a smooth-faced, foppish-looking little man of barely middle age, absurdly overdressed by European standards. His uniform was as impressive as that of a cinema attendant. The breast was hung with medals and studded with orders. When the prisoners entered he was reading a document – or for effect, making a pretence of doing so. This he continued to do for a full two minutes, during which a silence, embarrassing in its intensity, persisted. At length Tamashoa deigned to look up. He laid the paper aside and with his elbows on the desk looked at Algy.

'Answer questions', he said, in fair English. 'What were you doing in airplane?'

'Flying', answered Algy.

Tamashoa appeared to see nothing facetious in the answer. Not a muscle of his face moved. 'Quite so. What were you doing in sea?' he asked.

'Swimming', replied Algy.

'Quite so. I mean, what are you doing here?' queried Tamashoa.

'Standing', replied Algy evenly. He did not smile.

'Why?' asked Tamashoa.

'Because no one has offered me a seat.'

Algy later calls him 'that poodle-faking admiral' despite the fact that any intentional music-hall notes or echoes of the Edwardian Dolly dialogues of Barry Pain come from Algy himself, and could not come from Tamashoa:[28]

Tamashoa's next question showed an unbelievable lack of understanding of the Anglo-Saxon mind. 'If you will tell me why you were flying, and why British are on Elephant Island with the pirate Li Chi, you shall have your life.'

Algy shook his head. 'Has no one ever told you that we do not buy our lives from our enemies?'

This derives clearly enough from Sir Francis Doyle's Victorian verses about the private of the Buffs who died rather than kow-tow to the Chinese, despite the capitulations of his Burman fellow-captives; and Frank Richards had sent it up rotten in the gyrations of Billy Bunter to save his fat life during his Chinese adventures (*Magnet*, summer 1930). To borrow another moment from Richards, it is intended to show (in the words of Hurree Jamset Ram Singh) 'as your extremely bad poet has remarked, east is east and west is west, and never the twain shall meet' (*Magnet*, 14 February 1931). Biggles indeed manages to suggest that the Japanese violate that taboo with heinous effects:

'I know what war is like against the Nazis, and I've had some experience of trouble with plain unvarnished savages from whom one doesn't expect anything but murder; but these semicivilized Japanese seem to be the worst of the lot. . . .'

This is in *Biggles in Borneo* (1943), set in summer 1942, the first of the three novels pitching Biggles's Squadron against Japan. Japanese flogging of prisoners is emphasised, but Johns reserved its most vivid epiphany to show the treatment of an Asian. If any British boys were to be influenced by Japanese exploitation of anti-imperial arguments, this should open their eyes:[29]

Ah Wong appeared . . . With him was a huge Malay foreman. Ginger happened to catch sight of the man's back, and shuddered. It had recently been flogged to ribbons. The man glanced round and saw Ginger staring. For a moment their eyes met, and at the expression of sullen hate in those of the native Ginger felt his blood run cold. He guessed who had done the flogging, and Ah Wong confirmed it.
   'Kayan ask Japanese not to burn his home', he said evenly.'They flog him plenty much. He no like Japanese.'
   'I can understand that', answered Biggles grimly.

The passage has integrity: Kayan's hatred seems against all imperial figures, though specifically – and, shortly, spectacularly – turned against his immediate oppressors, the Japanese. Nevertheless, both *Biggles in Borneo* and *Biggles Delivers the Goods* seek to show the Asian peoples as loosely united against Japan, including renegade British driven from army service for marrying an Asian. Even in that, there is a certain unease, a hidden reminder of where the Japanese had learned their imperialism. An excellent introduction for children to human life, published in 1942 by the septuagenarian Frederick Kirkman (1869–1945), *Ages and Ages Ago*, concluded by pointing out the five races of men, of whom the British were made from three – Dark Long-Heads, Fair Long-Heads, and Round-Heads – the others being the Negroes and the Mongols; the purest Mongols were the Chinese, the Japanese being a mixture of Mongols and Dark Long-Heads. The enemy who ought to be remote seemed uneasily nearer.

Major Gilson in *Sons of the Sword: A Tale of the Sino–Japanese War* ([1941]) had written sympathetically to, and from the standpoint of, young Chinese resisters of the Japanese invasion – the Second World War for East Asia included most of the 1930s – but his Japanese were 'these brutal oppressors, aping the dictators of Europe as they had always imitated others'.[30] Johns capitalised on this as a clue for Biggles in his pursuit of the Japanese secret weapon in *Biggles in the Orient*:[31]

> 'The first thing that struck me about this weapon was that the Japs had invented it', he began. 'The Japanese don't invent things – at least, not mechanical devices. They're good at copying other people's. They'll copy anything – they even copied their language from China. It would be a strange thing, you must admit, if they had produced a mechanical device, like a death ray, for instance, that has baffled Western scientists. . . .'

But Americans, who had had more to do with Japanese, were sometimes much less sure. Frederick Nelson Litten's protagonist in *Sinister Island Squadron* (1944 [US], 1946 [UK]) is an American brought up in Japan who enlists after Pearl Harbor in the US Navy: 'the treachery of Japan had been a personal experience. These four cadets knew the Japanese as polite, funny little men who could imitate, but not invent; stupid, inferior in every way. A dangerous fallacy, Gil knew.'

It was comforting to assure oneself that the Japanese could win over nobody they did not buy. Rutherford Montgomery's *Thumbs Up!* (1942 [US], 1943 [UK]) also sought to show American combat troops in the wake of Pearl Harbor, this time in the Philippines, where they hear reports of large pay and bribes leading 'a few' to support the imminent Japanese invasion. Equally, the suave Larapindi, grand enabler of the secret weapon in *Biggles in the Orient*, proves to have been promised 'a high political position in India should the country be taken by the Japanese', although he has to use obscure religious rites to consolidate his supporters. Larapindi showed that he could at least join the native penetration of the British imperial establishment, while the son of his innocent business partner, at Oxford, is apparently thus above suspicion. The Americans were less certain of their universities as forcing-houses of loyalty than was Air Commodore Raymond. Litten (in what seems the most thoughtful of the contemporary American juvenile fictions on the war against Japan to win British republication) knew better:

The [Japanese] Captain watched Gil for a long moment, then suddenly began to laugh.

'I am having humorous fun with you, Mr Warriner', he said. 'After the manner of Sherlock Holmes. I read him when I attend in Harvard. . . .'

Lower levels of US education are even less reassuring:[32]

'What puzzles me', Gil said, 'is the way you speak American.'

'You're looking at a graduate of Iolani High', answered the corporal. 'I was born in Honolulu.' . . .

When Gil didn't answer, the corporal took a knife from a sheath in his canvas belt, ran his thumb along the sharp blade. But he shook his head.

'No, I'll let Intelligence take care of you. Commander Tonoye was born in Frisco; the mobsters in that town are tough, and he learned their system.'

Frederic Kummer's *The Perilous Island*, another story in which the USA hears of the Pearl Harbor attack, prematurely hinted of the menace in charming Japanese fellow-students:[33]

Saito was well liked by the other students because of his invariable cheerfulness, his amiable disposition, his never-failing smile. . . .

'Very happy, always', he said, 'to give assistance to American friend. Our two great countries preserve long-time honourable peace.'

He put on his coat, went out, still smiling his dental smile, and Steve, thinking of the efforts then under way at Washington to harmonize the difference between America and the Mikado's people, concluded that the Japanese as a race were peace-loving and friendly, in spite of the suspicion with which they were regarded by most residents of the Pacific Coast.

If Biggles trusted no non-white in the security crisis of *Biggles in the Orient*, US forces in the Pacific after Pearl Harbor might feel the same, but found it less easy to maintain control. In Rutherford Montgomery's *Thumbs Up!*, two Japanese, disguised as sugar labourers from the cane fields, emerge from hiding when two US Marine pilots are aloft in their warplane and hold them up with sub-machine-guns: 'The precise English of the yellow man indicated he had been educated in an American school'. Details of the flight (a patrol between Luzon and Taiwan) have evidently been passed to them by other Japanese agents. 'For so boastful a race, you Americans are, as you would say, dumb.' A little later, they instruct their captives to parachute into the South China Sea with no chance of reaching land, but the two marines overcome them and later offer characteristic self-congratulation on their more humane methods: 'If we're shot down I'll loosen your hands and feet just to show you what a white man does even for a rat'. This in some ways reflected an observer as well as a partisan. In 1943–4, Montgomery was familiar to thousands of British child readers of Puffin Books for his Jack-Londonesque *Carcajou*, very much a kill-or-be-killed tale of Arctic wildlife. The heroes of *Thumbs Up!* begin by being ordered from an imaginary 'Paris Island' some hundreds of miles east of the Philippines, whither they have to fly with despatches while their superiors and comrades are last seen facing annihilation from the Japanese immediately after Pearl Harbor, and end by facing a similar fate themselves on Bataan Peninsula a few weeks later.

A common note in Pacific-theatre American tales republished in Hutchinson's six-shilling 'War Adventure Series' in 1943–6 is of American vague good nature towards Japan before Pearl Harbor. The first marine reactions, even when finding themselves at war, are genial enough, in Montgomery's hands. A US pilot, shot down and parachuting out, is fired at by a Japanese pilot himself then shot down by anti-aircraft gunnery. Although the narrative speaks of 'the diving assassin' and 'the diving killer', Montgomery gives his ex-footballer marine a more kindly reaction:[34]

> Marty watched the little fellow fighting to get out. He found himself hoping the fellow would make it. He managed to get clear and took to his silk. A moment later he was sailing down close to Marty. Marty grinned across at him and shouted:
>
> 'I thought you birds were supposed to commit suicide?'
>
> 'Next time, but not this time', the Jap called back in perfect English.
>
> 'Happy Landing!' Marty shouted.
>
> The Jap did not answer. He was busy working his lines, trying to land at sea instead of on the island.

Despite genial appearances, all the American authors make it clear that this kind of chivalry exists purely – and transiently – on their side. In the process, they record very bitter Japanese hatred of the whites, frequently from experiences of white racial contempt, although few of them conjured up anything quite equal to Johns's vision of it:[35]

> They were ordinary Japanese soldiers, infantrymen, dirty, with the usual twigs attached to their shoddy uniforms for camouflage purposes. Both carried rifles and were smoking cigarettes. No other sounds came from the forest so it was fairly certain that they were alone.
>
> Their immediate reaction to the spectacle before them was not unnatural. They broke into an excited jabber as they walked on to the fuselage. When one of them pointed at the dead pilot and burst out laughing, after a momentary look of wonder Biggles frowned: friend or foe, to European eyes the sight was anything but funny. When one of them kicked the body every vestige of colour drained from his face. His lips came together in a hard line; his nostrils quivered. Still he did not move. But when one of the men, with what was evidently a remark intended to be jocular, bent down and inserted his cigarette between the dead pilot's lips, and then, shouting with laughter, stepped back to observe the effect, Biggles' pent-up anger could no longer be restrained.
>
> 'You scum', he grated. The words were low, but distinct.
>
> The two Japanese spun round as if a shot had been fired. They stared in goggle-eyed amazement, no longer laughing, but fearful, as though confronted by a ghost – the ghost of the body they had violated. Superstitious by nature, they may have believed that.

This may not be entirely racial in origin. When Biggles is captured on the last day of the First World War in his first book, *The Camels are Coming*, an ordinary German soldier kicks his live body after his crash; and Johns himself, threatened with death after this, may have been physically humiliated in ways that he did not fully disclose in public. He had initially served in France in ground troops, and his stories testify to ordinary soldiers' hatred of enemy pilots who rained death and destruction down on them and their families. British and German troops he recorded as having similar reactions. Johns transferred them to Ginger as a soldier on the Aragon front fighting for the Spanish Republicans:[36]

> Ginger had fired at several enemy machines, and his inability to check their progress had aroused in him a wholehearted hatred of

the enemy pilots who – so it seemed to him – dealt death with little risk to themselves.

This does not mean that Ginger, the surrogate reader, would have made fun of dead pilots more than feeling that some unduly vicious strafer or bomber come to grief deserved his fate.

Johns was using these nuances in *Biggles in the Orient* to pile hatred on the Japanese and to make his British child readers detest their Asian enemy (who had not bombed Britain) as much as their European (who had). The British boy, who might in a short space of time be the British soldier, had to be made to feel that he would be fighting an evil thing in Japanese military might as much as in Nazism: put another way, while the secret-weapon fears in *Biggles in the Orient* isolate that book for Biggles's refusal to trust non-whites (he does trust several in the other tales of war against Japan), it is still a demand for solidarity in defence of the Empire, however much it is ridden by self-doubt. Symbolically, the air battle of Calcutta so vividly described in the chapter 'The Blitz that Failed' is made to take the place of the Battle of Britain, which Johns never really rebuilt around Biggles. Pearl Harbor gave the Americans a meaning for their war against Japan; the British, as Johns saw it, had only the dwindling and almost bankrupt memories of imperial solidarity to keep their heart in the Asian struggle. Johns was later to give Biggles a sub-Kipling birth and early life in India, but he shows little sign of it here. Biggles tells his pilots: 'For the benefit of those of you who haven't been to India before, we don't use the expression *natives*. It's discourteous.'[37] It would not have been considered so by most white residents in his infancy. Johns was thus writing with awareness of an Indian as well as a Japanese agenda indicting attitudes of the ruling whites; but, however much the Japanese treatment of the dead British pilots was deployed by Johns to rally hostility against them, the laughter ascribed to them at the cigarette in the dead man's mouth is shrewd. Living white men issued their commands to Asians with cigarettes between their lips that they pointedly would not trouble to remove: a native (*sic*) being given orders was expected to understand them whether or not the accent was articulate or the intonation unclear through lips firm enough to keep the tobacco-fire burning.

We can do no more than glimpse a third dimension to Johns's anti-Japanese rhetoric; but Litten for one agonised openly about the extent of American righteousness in their quarrel with the foe. At the outset of *Sinister Island Squadron*, a Japanese mate tempts his

Filipino captain against the Americans, who 'hate all Orientals, and Greed is their god, they will take any risk for money'. He continues:

> 'When we are safe I will show you how to deal with the Americans. *Banzai!* Asia for the Asiatics!'
> The Captain repeated, 'Asia for the Asiatics!' Suddenly he frowned. '*You* are giving orders – but *I* am the master of the vessel!'
> Yoshida shrugged again. 'What matter? The co-prosperity of five hundred millions is at stake. "Yellow monkeys" they call the Japanese. And the Philippines, "Moon-face." For fifty years you have been slaves of the money barons of America.'
> 'Yet they have now set us free', said Sandor, doubtfully.
> 'Free!' exclaimed Yoshida. 'Free to starve! . . . But the god-Emperor is paternal, kind. *He* has a plan by which you shall not starve, but be administered.'

This might be self-evident fraud, but the American characters tried to be honest about its meaning:

> 'They're proud, over-sensitive, and America has caused them to lose face. We've barred them from citizenship, condemned them for the occupation of Korea and Manchuria, and the Chinese incident. And they *have* been an aggressor nation. But if you'll read history you'll see our territorial expansion hasn't always been above reproach. It's not a hundred years since we gobbled up a chunk of Mexico, using the same tactics.'

What Messrs Hutchinson's young British readers made of this when it reached them in 1946 is a moot point, since, in the state of British education in those days, few of them in any school or university would have heard of the Mexican War of 1846–8. (D. C. Thomson's comics had some anti-Mexican versions of it.) That the analogy was just would no doubt have passed them by, especially as the pro-Japanese speaker has become fanatically anti-Japanese by the end of the novel, when he has been rescued from over two years' captivity in Japanese military hands. It is even less likely that the young British would have seen parallels with their own imperial legacy. On the other hand, any who did would have made more sense of the growing pressure for Indian independence. Litten at least set up a critical apparatus for such reader exercises. The protagonist is an American boy raised in Japan, indignantly volunteering for the US forces after Pearl Harbor. He meets Colt, a Texan:

'So you were raised a Jap? There was a settlement of Japs at a town called Orange near Beaumont. They raised garden truck, sold it to the oilfields. One thing about Japs, they know where they belong. They work hard, too, Not like the shiftless, impudent niggers. In my burg in Texas, we got signs on the main street, "Black Man, don't let the sun go down and find you in this town!"'

. . . Gil couldn't let Colt's remark pass.

'Are you boasting about those signs?' he asked. 'I thought this was a free country.'

Colt turned on him, chin out-thrust. 'What was your job in Japan, Kiwi – missionary?'

. . . He thought suddenly of a trait possessed by the Japanese, a national unity, not present in America. There was Bernstein, who complained of unfair treatment because he was a Jew; McCoy, telling how his Union had whipped management into line . . . And now Colt, proud of the race discrimination practised in his home town. . . . Could Americans call themselves united against such evidence?

Litten was a professional writer, good for his annual book for boys most years since 1929 (he missed none from 1937 to 1946 inclusive), a pilot's fellow-traveller in the spirit although not the standard of worshipful literacy that Kipling breathed through his *Soldiers Three*. But *Sinister Island Squadron* seems to have been a special effort. It began with acknowledgements to several navy commanders, an air cadet, a 'four-striper', a medical corpsman, a coast guardsman, a navy pilot, and a Mrs Cora Ball of Evanston, Illinois, 'who lived for many years in the Islands of Nippon'. Some of their reminiscent footage preceded the war, and one cannot disentangle early wartime self-doubts in Litten's mind from those of his relevant sources.

Despite civil-rights demonstrations on the eve of America's entry into the war and the implication of an end to racial hatred in Roosevelt's 'four freedoms' speech to Congress on 6 January 1941 (for, if Freedom From Fear meant anything, it must mean that), anti-Negro discrimination was still an active regret for only a small proportion of whites, with a somewhat larger proportion vaguely feeling that it was too bad and something must be done about it sometime. British recipients of US troops domiciled in their neigh-bourhoods at some point between Pearl Harbor and D-Day were frequently surprised, and in many cases dismayed, by their segrega-tion and by broad British official hints that the American custom should not be challenged. (Readers of the *Gem* and the *Magnet* would have been less surprised: Richards had used every opportunity to denounce United States celebration of freedom as hypocrisy when judged by its treatment of Mexicans, blacks and Amerindians – most recently in the *Magnet* in May 1938.) It was not until 1948 that the momentum of the fight against Nazism and against Japanese exploitation of American racism percolated into high politics, and on 27 July 1948 Truman announced the desegregation of the US armed services.

Litten pursues the black–white case into one episode. Colt and two other cadets refuse to work on an operation involving two blacks as fellow-workers, Gil upbraids them as 'quitters', Colt fights him and is knocked out by judo methods, the building begins to collapse, one of the blacks (Albert) is injured and all have to work with one another. Gil is angry enough at the moment of fighting ('The man who stood there taunting him was a symbol of a nation that, even after Pearl Harbour [sic], could not submerge the petty hatreds that would destroy her') – but, when Gil saves them all, Colt remains formally hostile to him while making 'weekly visits to the mill village joining Chapel Hill, where Albert was convalescing. Visits out of the precious "liberty" which every cadet hoarded. . . . Those signs in the home town didn't mean much after all.' This is no doubt edifying, and not unreal. Hard-bitten white Southern segregationists were frequently on much more genuine social – no less than anti-social – terms with their black neighbours, with a depth of common understanding absent from northern white cross-racial forays however good-natured. The interest in the health and welfare of blacks whom somehow they had come to work with was genuine, if somewhat condescending. And, intentionally or otherwise, it contrasts with the more tolerant whites in the recent episode, none of whom seems to visit the convalescing Albert. But the conclusion that everything was therefore all right is all too accurate, as a measure of subordination of liberal instincts to national priorities. Gil ultimately decides that American diversity makes for true unity, and even earlier draws the lesson that

> The whole theory of totalitarian war was built on hurling masses of men and planes into battle on a plan unknown to any but the master mind. The strategy had won in Poland, Russia, France and Holland. . . . But over England, the Luftwaffe had been turned back. By a handful of British flyers, men of initiative, trained to follow orders, but each pilot capable of thinking for himself.

As an analysis of the Battle of Britain, this merits serious consideration, and it was an important lesson to draw for the use of British and
American children. The assumption was that the Americans would
share the British advantage. It agrees with Johns's view, born of his
memories of the First World War. But it had vanished by the war in
Vietnam.

The sense of Japan deepened as a society sinking everything into
total obedience to the state and conformity with its dictates (rather at
variance with the intense controversies among the ruling Japanese
élite on the eve of the war against the USA and on that of its end).
Above all, this became symbolised throughout Anglophone children's literature by the act of hara-kiri. Litten used it almost at
the end of Sinister Island Squadron both to rescue his heroes and to
etch a final portrait of the enemy on the reader's mind:[38]

> the captain's voice came through the gale; he was ordering his men
> to make prisoners of the white men and to kill the imposter who
> called himself Yoshida. When they did not obey he stepped out to
> meet them, arm raised. It was a hand grenade he held, and he tossed
> it into the squad. . . . A blinding flash, a hammering concussion –
> and there were only pieces of men writhing on the rocky flat.

Biggles bitterly obituarises the mess waiter whose hara-kiri has
broken his best clue to the enemy spy headquarters:[39] 'He'd never
dare to tell his boss that he'd failed. That would mean losing face,
which is worse than death to a Jap.' Close readers, or subliminal
reception, might take the message that Biggles sandwiches the
verdict in self-reproaches for not having realised that this would
happen, while not having the slightest intent of committing suicide
because he has failed. Variations on the theme of unquestioning
fanatics versus soldiers of free will ran through books and comics
beyond the war. Litten sought to pinpoint less violent contrasts but
did little more than pose the question:

> He thought of the noisy mobs that watched the State U. games in
> Seattle – and of the silent crowds at the wrestling tournaments in
> Meiji Stadium in Tokyo, where the people hissed politely when
> their favourite won. . . . Different – and yet his friends at Kyoto –
> Joe Karai and the rest – had the same ideas as the gang at the
> Sigma Chi house . . . Or did they? He shook his head, there was a
> difference – something deep down in these people that no Amer-
> ican could touch. . . .

That was before Pearl Harbor:[40]

> Pearl Harbour bombed – but it couldn't be! 'Treacherously' was the
> word the broadcaster had used. . . . But the Japanese were an
> honourable people, . . . Pearl Harbour – Kaneohe – bombed,
> destroyed! But the Japanese had wanted peace. . . . The face of
> the mate, Yoshida, rose before him, and Dr Hoyo's face – and the
> faces of his friends at Kyoto. All different, but in each one some-
> thing that shut out the white man. Something unfathomable and
> sinister.

Kummer was a little less subtle:[41]

> 'The success of an honourable friend', he murmured,'always
> brings joy to humble Japanese boy's heart.'
>   Steve left him, completely baffled. It seemed impossible that this
> young student's friendly smile could mask black treachery, and yet
> the Oriental mind held depths that were beyond understanding by
> those of the West. It was quite possible that Saito had been
> responsible for the attack on him the day before, and could still
> meet him with a pretence of warm friendship.

All of this sort of thing offered both justification and incentive for the
internment of Japanese Americans, the stress on Japanese use of
American education being particularly relevant. (The actual injustice
to large numbers of Japanese Americans was not acknowledged with
regret until the beginning of the Clinton administration, forty-five
years later.) In general, the British did not use their fictions to justify
violations of civil liberty – Brent-Dyer courageously attacked internment – but the finest schoolboy confrontation of belligerent Japan,
Jan Maclure's Escape to Chungking (1942), came to much more
constructive conclusions about the relevance of Japanese culture
to the World War. In fact, it even recruited a little of it on the Allied
side.
  Maclure is a mystery. No other book can be found under that
name in the National Union Catalog or the British Library Catalogue; Oxford University Press, the publishers, have destroyed their
records; we cannot even be sure of the sex of the writer from what
may well be a pseudonym. It is dedicated 'For S.H. who has not
escaped – yet', which in the context may be a friend – possibly a
Japanese friend – still in Japan in 1942, the year of publication.
Maclure was evidently by then in Britain, since s/he cites The Times

in the prefatory note as a source of Japanese official statements transmitted by Reuter or Domei agency messages. But s/he knew Japan well, especially Japanese theatre. The book's learning is unusually well filtered through schoolboy perceptions with less evident authorial complicity than in Richards or Blyton, or authorial intervention than in Johns or Crompton. Its quality was recognised by critics and public, and it was reprinted within the year. The reader-identification figure, Christopher Maddison, may have taken a few pages to win acceptance in his audience's mind, since few British children would have White Russian mothers and an upbringing in Japan. But the 15-year-old Christopher's linguistic powers would not alienate the sturdiest monoglot – that kind of skill is as easy to imagine as magic beanstalks or Blytonian wishing-chairs at earlier stages of development. Although we first meet him being impudent in Japanese to a policeman, the impudence enables us to accept his proficiency. The device is clever: it is agreeably like William's perpetual figure-skating between defiance and diplomacy, especially with the schoolboy's mother mollifying irritated Authority. Simultaneously, we are alert to the false goodwill shortly to be shattered (by Pearl Harbor, as usual). But it is not quite as tranquil as the cheery 'Banzai!' with which the Japanese sailors speed the Swallows and Amazons on their way to begin *Missee Lee*; no other product of 1941 on Brits among Japs could approach the peace of that (broken only, if a little tactlessly, by the pet monkey 'chattering angrily at a couple of Japanese sailors', zoologically a touch too close to American epithets after Pearl Harbor).[42] It also prefigures what is to come: the schoolboy must forget the luxury of impudence – and in this context, its parent, condescension – to make what terms he can with an enemy power with whom he will be at secret war.

The novel is transformed by an epiphany refected in the frontispiece: 'For the third time Christopher bowed politely and in real homage' to a regal, Japanese, female figure in authority. This proves to be 'Makino Sozaemon III, the world-famous actor and dancer, unequalled for his feminine roles, third in a great tradition of players, and an ally of England', to whom Christopher's mother has sent the boy for instructions on getting out of Japan with secret-weapon particulars. Christopher's un-English deference (on hands and knees in Jack Matthew's frontispiece) is 'to the brilliant dancer and to the man who was prepared to risk his life for a greater loyalty than that of country'. Sozaemon welcomes the 'child of Nina Nevensky . . . She has always admired what is best in the Japanese nation, though we both grieve over the spirit of domination and cruelty that is changing her nature . . .' It is a philosophy of Art against War:

> The actor's face grew increasingly grave, . . . and the contrast between the thought of war and deadly explosive and his own picturesque, fragile appearance, suggestive of ladies enclosed in feudal castles, where their lords defended themselves with bow and arrow and sword, struck Christopher with sudden irony.

This is to argue that the spirit of the true Japan is on the Allied side (the beneficiaries of Christopher's possible escape with a vital document taken from a dying British spy). It is akin to Johns's use of the Catholic priests as automatic supporters of the British agents in Nazi-occupied France, once again the seemingly feminine non-soldier giving practical and, symbolically, spiritual aid. But Johns's priests can also claim patriotism, as their France, however collaborative with Nazism, is clearly conquered against its will. This is a higher Japan against a baser. Woodrow Wilson used the same device in his war message to Congress on 2 April 1917 when he took words of Martin Luther to justify hostilities against Luther's Germany. Sozaemon holds that Japan's present rulers are Japan's real enemies:

> He went on to speak of the great perils that threatened the East, of the preparations for war on a scale and of an audacity and ruthlessness for which England and America were completely unprepared; of the unspeakable darkness that would overwhelm a hemisphere if the brutality and aggressiveness, the self-deception and warped judgment of Japan's present rulers were unchecked, sacrificing their own country as well as the rest of Asia in their establishment of the New Order.

This was propaganda of the finest draft, leaving Montgomery, Kummer and Litten puerile by contrast. Johns's method of letting the local victims testify was wiser, although still weaker than Maclure's. The chapter is entitled 'Modern Might and Ancient Chivalry'. Litten's unease at racial hostility to the Japanese, although succumbing to it, is answered here: Maclure condemned the Japanese by celebrating their culture. But there is no comfortable reassurance that behind the Japanese war machine, a true Japan is doing its bit for the Allies in or out of drag. Sozaemon disguises and trains Christopher into passing as Japanese (Litten also assumes that metamorphosis can occur in *that* direction), but the last we hear of him is eavesdropped on the conversation of two Japanese business-men on a train:

> one of them glanced again at his *Osaka Mainichi* and gave a whistle.
>
> 'I say – what *do* you think? – Sozaemon of all people – have a look at this – would you have believed such a thing?'
>
> ('Come to the point, can't you?' breathed Christopher, as he tried to gaze unconcernedly out of the window.)
>
> 'Mā, mā, who would have thought it? A man of his reputation. Tck, tck! It's an uncertain world we live in. Well, well! I've taken my family to the Kabuka Theatre many a time, and never expected to hear of Makino Sozaemon's arrest . . . for "dangerous thought" wasn't it?'
>
> 'Yes – you know, he had been on tour with his company in England once. It must be the influence of those dastardly British . . .'

The foster-brother to whom Sozaemon sends Christopher is also arrested, and the alternative, a coal-merchant, also proves unavail-able:

> 'Is the master of the house at home?'
>
> 'The *master!* Did you ask for the *master?* Lord preserve us, is this impudence or ignorance?'
>
> 'I beg your pardon. I have just arrived in Moji from Tokyo, and my friends asked me to look up Kobayashi San while I was here. . . . I'm very sorry if . . .'
>
> 'Tell your friends that the master put an end to his life yesterday. He is an honourable man, and would only do such an act from the highest motives. It is a great loss for us all, and if your friends in Tokyo are anything to do with the reason that made him kill himself, you had better keep out of my way for good and all. Get along with you!' And with a harsh jarring sound the heavy door was pushed back into place.

Hara-kiri becomes much more chilling when presented not simply as alien but as the only recourse for one's friends. It is all the more effective wrapped in a prejudice common to east and west: provincial contempt for the metropolis. Nevertheless, while cut off from Japa-nese Fifth Columnists (as counterparts of such figures would have

been called in Spain or Britain), Christopher notes potential sources
of disaffection, feeling 'desperately sorry for the thousands of inhabitants of this crowded and sordid city [Osaka], living in an almost
inconceivable poverty'. Conservatives reacted against effects of
Japanese industrialisation, as Christopher discovers through his
own inadequacy as a boatman's helper:[43]

> 'You're a good-for-nothing creature, aren't you? Dishonest, idle,
> impudent, gutless – like all your generation. Never learnt to handle
> a boat or a horse, I don't suppose – all you think about is
> aeroplanes and cars! Well, you mark my words, there'll be a time
> when you'll be glad enough to be able to do the simple kind
> of things we old folks were brought up to do. Planes and cars
> won't run without juice, and with this mighty war going on I'm
> a-thinking we're going to run out of that altogether. . . . Why, if it
> hadn't been for these modern inventions you're all so proud of, the
> war might never have happened, and we'd all be a lot happier than
> we are now. . . .'

The fugitive's natural allies in fleeing from an oppressor power are
its permanent victims. Johns optimistically traded on this principle
with the conquered French (he seems to have been rather more
doubtful about the Norwegians and Belgians); and Wilfrid Robertson in *Dunkirk Dunes to Libyan Sands* (1941) got his hero out of one
difficulty when the train bearing him from capture at Dunkirk is
derailed in Germany:[44]

> 'Why should you want to help – you, a German?'
> The other gave a mirthless laugh. 'A German once, perhaps', he
> replied, 'before we became a race of outcasts in this fatherland of
> ours. I am a Jew.'
> 'Ah!' Martin raised his knee from the man's chest and stood up,
> helping the other to his feet. The word 'Jude' disspelled all his
> doubts about treachery; if the man were a Jew he could be trusted
> not to betray him to their mutual enemies.
> The man's fingers plucked at his sleeve. 'Come', he urged, 'here
> on the road anyone may pass. Trust me, trust Isodore Rosenbaum;
> if the Nazis are your enemies, are they not ten times more his?
> Come, I have a safe hiding place that none have yet found.'

Christopher is rescued by a boy from the 'rumpen', wasteland-
dwellers of Korean origin 'keeping alive the ancient resentment

against the conquering race', and here also his passport is his status as a fugitive from the authorities. He passes for a time as Korean, and, when his very likeable rescuer is killed, takes his place as horse-servant in the Japanese army. (His Korean boss sees through his disguise but, having surprised him by the detection, keeps silence.) That many other people were alive to diplomatic necessities in exploiting implicit hostility to the Japanese among their subjected peoples was shown by John Hampson, in the Tory *Spectator* for 18 December 1942, whose citation of his favourite niece's rapturous ' "You do get your money's worth!" . . . having devoured the book in one evening' was offset by his complaints of 'the contempt expressed by the hero for small nations and other ways of life than our own'. Hampson's point is a little difficult to sustain with any realism: a privileged youth suddenly forced to welcome hospitality and accep-tance among 'this lowest stratum of society' is hardly likely to relish it. In fact, Christopher seems very fond of the Korean family who so generously share 'their improvised home and miserable meals' with him, and one of his few moments of tranquillity comes in listening to their 'nostalgic songs of their homeland . . . watching the camp fire-light flickering on their mobile faces'. When his friend Ei-ko Kin is killed while sharing a lonely hut with him during an earthquake, Christopher finds his body in the darkness:

> He found one hand and rubbed it frantically, trying to persuade himself that he heard faint breathing; but after a while he realized there was no possible chance of the boy being alive after such injuries. Almost too shocked to feel anything now, he lay there, holding Kin's rough hand as if to give him comfort.

He even speaks to his dead friend when he steals his identity papers:[45]

> He saw that Kin must have been killed outright, but his lips wore their habitual amused expression, and Christopher was glad there was no fear on his face. Ashamedly he felt for the papers in Kin's waistband, put them in his own, and then broke out, 'I'm sorry, Ei-ko, I'm sorry. I'd do anything to bring you back again – but you do understand, don't you?' . . .
>
> Feeling a complete beast, but afraid to face any inquiry or inquest, Christopher turned to go up the mountain, with a last salute to the merry vagabond.

(The boys have left Kin's family to become horse-servants, and Kin's people will not expect to hear from him for a long time, if at all; Christopher ultimately gets a message back to them in their wasteland at the edge of their city – Nagasaki.) Hampson's hyperactive political correctness is more instructive in its existence than in its content; the *Spectator* would not be conspicuous for it later.

Escape to Chungking's ideas about an older Japan being ready to betray its brutal supplanters have ironic echoes for one of the most successful historical novels for children published early in the war, Geoffrey Trease's *Cue for Treason* (1940), in which two gallant Elizabethan teenagers find a plot to assassinate the aged Elizabeth during a command performance of *Henry V* (in which the children's friend Shakespeare plays the Archbishop of Canterbury). Trease (or his publishers, Basil Blackwell of Oxford) was sufficiently aware of the sensitivities of book-buying Roman Catholics not to state that the conspiracy detected among the Cumbria squirearchy was in the Catholic cause, but it clearly is so. Trease still retained his Popular Front priorities, if less rabidly than during his days of publication by the Communist Lawrence & Wishart (1934–7); but in his boy-now-adult narrator's hands they slid into fairly standard English Whig historiographical conventions:[46]

> If the Queen lived, all would be well. The rising would wither away as other rebellions had. If the Queen died, God alone knew what would happen. England would have lost the keystone which had held the kingdom together for more than a generation. We might go back to the days of the religious struggles, back to the civil strife between the great nobles which had wasted England in the Wars of the Roses. Back . . .? Yes, back. Whatever might be said about the old Queen – and I've come to realise in these latter years that she had many faults – at least she looked forward. England changed and grew under her hand, even though the growing pains brought many an agony. Many of the old country families hated her, and especially in the North, because she stood for the new ways and they for the old.

How far the now adult narrator's former friend Shakespeare would have agreed with this is unknown – he was hostile to foreign aggression, Papal probably included, so far as his plays are evidence, but the same evidence puts him doctrinally non-Roman Catholic – but, having got the children into the Globe, he is mercifully exempted from secret-service stuff. Mr Secretary Robert Cecil is the character for that, coping manfully with a conspiracy of which, for once, he is not the ultimate author. If Jan Maclure had read Trease's popular story to study form, s/he might have wondered if Shakespeare was a less sure standard-bearer for the new than for the old, and thence reflect on the theatre as custodian of values under attack from forward-looking regimes as brutal as the Japanese New Order – or the later Tudors. Many of Trease's reviewers had little difficulty in analogising between security crises during the last days of Elizabeth and the first days of George VI. The local Cumberland squire seemed a most appropriate petty tyrant as well as high traitor. We have seen how John Mowbray's *The Radio Mystery* and the film *Went the Day Well* featured the apparently trustworthy squire as Quisling.

Hampson, who had suffered childhood poverty and parental brutality, served a brief prison sentence and lived a solitary homo-sexual life, may have reacted against Christopher's mixture of gratitude to the Koreans and occasional bouts of genocidal hatred against Japan and all who lived in her:

> his heart failed him when he heard of British confirmation of the withdrawal from Ipoh; he was sickened by the reports of the destruction done at Manila, and the evasive argument that 'Japan does not recognize Manila as an open city because the decision was taken by General MacArthur without consultation with the Filipinos'.

(Rutherford Montgomery's Marty and 'boll weevil' in *Thumbs Up!* saw that policy at first hand before their final stand in Bataan.)

> The words of the Lion [Sozaemon] came back to him as he bent over the vegetable chopper, slicing *daikon*, and he wondered how much longer Britain and America would be forced to be on the defensive, instead of taking the initiative against this treacherous enemy. Looking round at the unattractive customers in the café, he sometimes felt that it would do no harm to wipe out the whole race, but back again among the merry *rumpen* he repented of his disgust.

Hampson may also have disliked the concern about horses which wins Christopher his place in the Japanese forces embarked for China (where he hopes to make his final escape), and which firmly fixes him among the better-class British children where horse meant status:

For company he much preferred the merry and shiftless Kin tribe to the dour sailors and the coarsened troops. The way the soldiers had treated the horses had been bad enough, but when any duty took him through the army quarters he was far more appalled by the way the N.C.O.s treated their men. The thick atmosphere of stabled humanity sickened him, and it was with great secret pleasure that he remembered his *Gulliver's Travels*, contrasting the khaki-clad yahoos with the gentle, well-mannered Houyhnhnms packed into the hold, and suffering patiently the degradation of life at sea.

Maclure's idea of the Japanese army may be little more flattering than Johns's, but it was aware of their universality.

Individually they were as mixed a lot as any conscripted army: some foul-mouthed and sadistic; others bewildered young peasants or ex-students, home-sick for a heavily-thatched farmhouse in a remote valley of Ibarakiken, or a narrow street in the suburbs of Nagoya, bright with electricity and noisy with gramophones.

Once in China, the Japanese also echo other imperial peoples:

'What pig-sties the Chinese live in!' grumbled one of the men. 'Ugly, filthy, and no electric light! Compare this with even the poorest cottage at home – and see what we have to teach them.'
    'A lot of illiterate peasants they are, too' chimed in a second. 'See how the British have exploited them and kept them under, and think what we could do to give them culture and civilization, if only their stupid leaders would give in.'
    'Perhaps they like living like this', put in Christopher innocently.
    '*Like* it! What's that got to do with it? People oughtn't to be allowed to live like beasts, at the mercy of bandits and landlords and money-lenders. We'll change all that, once we get proper control of the country.'
    Christopher's mind flashed back to the opium-dealer . . .

The opium-dealer had been back in Japan, encountered just after hearing of the suicide coal-merchant:

'I'm in the opium business – no need to keep it dark these days. The Government encourages us to open up new dens in Manchu-kuo and North China; once the Chinks get a taste of that stuff they're not going to bother any more about sabotage or guerilla tactics – and there's a nice little profit in it for us.'

This also is an echo of other imperial peoples, somewhat less pointed against the actual British record, especially since the opium-dealer meditates on Hong Kong's potential as a future market 'with all those Chinese starved of the drug by the British'.

By the end, Christopher has become a trusted attendant on a brigadier and a major, to whom he ministers when their headquarters are bombed. He then puts on the half-conscious brigadier's uniform, apologises for it and thanks them for their kindness, but says he must do his own job. The major, trapped and almost certainly dying, fires two shots at him, now realising he is a spy:[47]

as Christopher wheeled round the Major's revolver clattered to the floor.

'Oh – fine – work', breathed Christopher involuntarily, '– and I deserved it . . . But I should think he's done for himself.' Then, pulling himself together, he turned back to prevent the Brigadier reaching out for another weapon, and slowly felt his way backwards through the wreckage. For a second his eyes lifted to the two small holes in the plaster in front of him, and he realized by what a fine margin the shots had missed his head. As he reached the threshold he flickered his eyes again – this time towards where the Major lay. He lifted his left hand in salute.

'Good-bye, Major – I'm sorry, but – shigata ga nai – it can't be helped', and with this characteristic Japanese phrase he broke with the language he had spoken from childhood, and found himself outside.

Even the sound of the last syllable echoes Housman's[48]

In blood and smoke and flame I lost my heart.
I lost it to a soldier and a foeman,
A chap that did not kill me, but he tried;
Then took the sabre straight and took it striking
And laughed and kissed his hand to me and died.

Very properly, the story then becomes black comedy as Christopher uses the Japanese uniform and a white flag to overcome his linguistic deficiency: he does not know Chinese and is thus in mortal danger from his own side. He is saved, and at last manages to find Allied

Authority ready to listen to his story with its vital secrets: a Chinese officer who had served in the Red Army and thus knew Russian. *Escape to Chungking* now faced whatever realities would be known to its readers, but not as yet to its author as it went to press. Many war books faced that problem, but few did so as frankly as this. A Percy F. Westerman simply exhorted his audience at the close, as with the last sentence of *With the Commandos* (1943), magnificent in mixture of metaphor:[49] 'He'd put his hand to the plough and there was no turning back – not until the foul beasts had been finally and crushingly defeated and swords beaten into plough-shares in a sane and enlightened world'. Jan Maclure said it like it was, the very upbeat, even comic upbeat, of Christopher's final breakthrough needing contextualisation in the disasters for the real-life UK he had so resourcefully represented:

> It was only then that he realized how much he had counted on the Japanese reports being exaggerated, and his heart sank to hear the truth. As he listened to the accounts of the enemy's advance through Malaya, and of the immediate and overwhelming threat to Singapore, he felt again the nightmare oppression that had come over him on the evening he spent with the Lion. Now it had come true – that immense and long-premeditated drive against the foundations of the Empire in the East, the clouds of tanks, barges and planes, the hordes of tenacious, ape-like [!] jungle-fighters, the unseen army of traders and fishermen who had made ready the way for the invading forces. . . .

Whatever else *Escape to Chungking* might be, it would not be escapist, or at least not escapist alone. It had to cope with the vision of the child reader closing it, thrilled that Christopher is safe, but knowing that countless others (such as the unknown dedicatee S.H.) were not, that many of them were British, and that however remote the Empire it had meant security for kith and kin. And what were they fighting? It was folly simply to write them as monsters in the hope that this might write them off: 'Christopher . . . was wrestling with the insuperable problem of how a nation can be decent, kindly and courteous as individuals, and yet devilish in the mass'.

Kith and kin are evidently subliminal to the story, symbolised in a singular way. Christopher is called 'Kit' by his Russian mother; his doomed Korean saviour is 'Kin'. Their unity, and its replacement by Kit's assumption of Kin's identity, touch on child *Döppelgänger*, even child Calvinist tales of the industrious and idle apprentice (both are in fact industrious but must pretend idleness – or at least vagabondage – to appear innocuous); also the fairy-story siblings in which only the last survives or at least succeeds. But more to the point are modern forms where two youths represent a privileged background and a hardier, the latter perishing: Edward Waverley and Fergus Mac-Ivor Vich Ian Vohr, in Scott's *Waverley*; David Balfour and Ransome in Stevenson's *Kidnapped*; Alleyne and Ford in Conan Doyle's *The White Company*. In all cases, the most notable difference is in usage of speech – Fergus's language being Gaelic, Ransome's blasphemous, Ford's iconoclastic, Kin combining something of all three. In all cases, the survivor has had to learn something of the lifestyle and survival methods of the doomed companion. It is particularly identified with Scottish writers; be it so. All we know of Jan Maclure was that s/he either had or chose a Scottish name.

But, in itself, the obvious source of *Escape to Chungking* is undoubtedly Rudyard Kipling's *Kim*. Both Kit and Kin embody aspects of Kim, above all his multiplex identities, evasions of authority, embodiment of pieties, mockeries, masquerades. The later story even ends on a Kiplingesque meeting with the cousin of the British agent Francis at whose death Christopher had become guardian of the McGuffin or vital document. The tutorial from the Lion, Sozaemon, is foreshadowed by Kim's devotion to the lama. Kipling might have been made a little uneasy by the gender-bending, both for his reasons and its, but he had died in 1936. The imperial purpose is common to both, and the mortal peril to the Empire, if far greater in 1941–2, is at least in the Kipling tradition. *Kim* had had innumerable imitators in its first decade, whether in short story or full-length novel or serial (for example John Comfort's (i.e. Bessie Marchant's) *The Heart of a Hero*, which ran in *Little Folks* in 1905). In general, however, they went for the *gamin*'s secret identity being his abduction from a British military family in early youth. Christopher's identity is settled from the outset, and so in its way is Kin's, but between them (on a Kipling-scale of race) lies the ghost of Kim, Irish-Celtic probably on both sides. Kit as a name has another origin: Maclure had a light touch with her/his literature, but was firmly literary all the same:[50]

'He doesn't like my calling him "Kit"' put in Nina [Mother]. 'He thinks it sounds affected, but I like it – Kit Maddison makes me think of Kit Marlowe, and he's a person I've always admired.'
    'Kit Marlowe – atheist and wastrel – stabbed in the back in a

tavern brawl', said Francis lightly, as if to break the strange, grave intimacy that seemed to bind the three of them together.

'Kit Marlowe – poet and patriot', countered Nina softly, adding in a tone so low that her son hardly caught it, 'and don't *you* go letting yourself be stabbed in the back!'

He does, of course. Whether Marlowe's third – gay – identity is relevant is moot; it harmonises with the gender frontiers elsewhere. But Marlowe's association with secret service on behalf of Elizabethan government is appropriate; though Geoffrey Trease was no doubt wise to make Shakespeare rather than him the hero's friend in *Cue for Treason*, it may be further evidence as to its influence on *Escape to Chungking*. Both books mixed escapism with a realistic moral for their young readers in Britain. The future might seem very dark, and one may be left very self-dependent, but the national cause (however remote its expression in time or place) is worth the work, the risk and, if need be, the death. The readiness to introduce a comrade's death again reflects the conventions of Kipling's golden age rather than the inter-war years and after. Kipling would have regarded his adventure stories as ultimately riveting his youthful audience to their duty rather than ways of escape (which they certainly also were), but the times for which *Escape to Chungking* was written ensured that any such moral was inescapable. Orwell was in fact far more correct in seeing the permanence of Kipling's influence than his mishits with the *Magnet* might suggest; but it was a Kipling looking firmly into the hostile eye of the Second World War at its most demoralising. Britain hailed Dunkirk as a victory, and the Battle of Britain as a triumph, but there was only one way to read the fall of Singapore. *Escape to Chungking* might be comforting reading, but it ran *towards* disaster, and faced it, and brought its reinforcement for it. Escapism did not have to mean running away.

Kipling was also apposite in another sense. He can sound repulsively racist, yet race in Kipling can be very ambiguous, and Maclure shared with him the ability to respect individuals from a hostile culture. Yet, cumulatively, the effect was one asserting racial superiority: Kipling would have considered Kit as superior in race to Kin, but also to Kim, although he might have preferred Kin, and certainly preferred Kim. But en masse it was, if necessary, British racial superiority that must be vindicated; and, give or take a Russian mother, Maclure seems to remain there.

British children were thus told by British writers during the eve and morning of the war that it was a war against racists (not, save for

Brent-Dyer, Gilson and one or two others, against racism); by its end, they were getting something much closer to a racist justification. This did not mean racism being more evident at home. The brunt of anti-Japanese writing for British children in 1944–7 came from American writers, most of whom had junior US citizens rather than younger British subjects in their sights. Anti-Japanese sentiment among British authors of domestic dramas for children emerged, if at all, as a reflection of stories brought back by British soldiers from Japanese concentration camps. Blyton – not a consciously racist writer – introduces what the normally good-natured Lucy-Ann calls 'the nasty little slinky Japanese servants' into the entourage of the mad King in *The Mountain of Adventure*, but then Lucy-Ann disliked being seized by them, seeing the boys hurled around by jiu-jitsu, and watching them manhandle paratroopers towards probable deaths. Blyton says vaguely at the end that 'they probably had bad records', which sounds like Blytonese for concentration-camp guards.[51] By this point, 1949, Americans were shortly to look more dubiously on Chinese than Japanese, and it might be suggested that Blyton anticipated the forthcoming diplomatic revolution by confusedly endowing the Japanese with the Chinese 'l' for 'r' instead of the Japanese 'r' for 'l'. More intentional signs of ecumenism could be found around this date in the *Mickey Mouse Weekly*, whose resident 'special agent', the Hon. Monty Carstairs (monocle, toothbrush-moustache ('Ronnie') and three (non-public) schoolboy Watsons), had a Japanese servant for the statutory valet. Since his name was 'Mr San', meaning 'Mr Mr', the thrilling author's hold on his Orient seems no stronger than chez Blyton.

Race in Blyton is unimportant in general. Her use of golliwogs derives from Edwardian models and shares their place in a moralistic bestiary. They are, like small children, on the whole good, but sometimes bad. The same is true of toys, fairies and so on. Much was made (a much that showed how little else there was to denounce) concerning a story of a black doll who became gratifyingly pink, originally in 1937: but the vigilante indignation as usual indicated indigence in research – Blyton, short of ideas for a plot in what was still her nonage, consciously or otherwise drew on Walter de la Mare's 'Sambo and the Snow Mountains'. Since de la Mare's ambiguities have confused his critics on every other subject, they would probably baffle them on race as well. A late Blyton story in which Noddy is mugged by three golliwogs probably elicited a passionate, and no doubt anti-social, sense of gratitude to the golliwogs in many parents forced to read Noddy to their offspring.

The clean-up squad in Blyton's publishers have nonetheless been zealous in the removal of potentially offensive material; since their motives are mercenary rather than meritorious, little sense has been attached to the activity. The king villain in *The Island of Adventure*, Jo-Jo, has been whitened and monosyllabled, which eliminates first the useful point that black servants obtained undesirable menial work for bad pay in the wartime years, and secondly Blyton's uninhibited tribute to the superior intelligence of her black villain, cleverly exploiting patronising dismissals of his supposed stupidity or sub-normality. He is probably the best villain she produced, and his doomsday chat is in the best blood-curdler vein:

> 'We just want to say a fond good-bye you', said Jo-Jo, his black face gleaming in the lamp-light. 'We've finished up our business here. You came in at the end, Bill Smugs the cop, too late to do anything. We've got all the notes we'll ever be able to use now.'
> 'So you're clearing out, are you?' said Bill, quietly. 'Smashing up the machines to hide your tracks – taking away all your stores and your packets of dud notes. You won't escape so easily. Your machines will be found all right, smashed or not, and your . . .'
> 'Nothing will ever be found, Bill Smugs', said Jo-Jo. 'Not a thing. The whole police force can come to this island, but they'll never find anything they can trace back to us – never!'
> 'Why?' asked Bill, unable to conceal his surprise.
> 'Because we're flooding the mines', said Jo-Jo, smiling wickedly and showing his white teeth. 'Yes, Bill Smugs, these mines will soon be flooded – water will pour into every tunnel, every passage, every cave. It will hide our machines, and all traces of our work. I am afraid it will hide you too.'
> 'You're not going to leave us here, surely', said Bill. 'Leave me, if you like – but take these boys with you.'
> 'We don't want any of you', said Jo-Jo, still in the same horribly polite tones. 'You would be in the way.'
> 'You couldn't be as cruel as that', cried Bill. 'Why, they're only children.'
> 'I have my orders', said Jo-Jo. He did not seem at all the same stupid, half-crazy fellow that the boys knew before – he was a different Jo-Jo altogether, and not at all a pleasant one.

Jo-Jo seems derived from Injun Joe in Mark Twain's *Tom Sawyer*: like every British writer for children onwards from Stevenson who brooded about adventure stories (especially treasure stories), that was the prime source. Twain's portrait is frankly racist, from the nurture of revenge which speeds the murder to the intent of nostril-slitting on the Widow Douglas, all fully linked to Joe's Indian antecedents ('an Injun! That's different!'). The closest Jo-Jo gets to racial dictates of anti-social conduct is in the poetry of the doom that he pronounces. The use of race to excite disgust by derogatory physical description is utterly absent: when Jo-Jo pretends to be stupid-crazy, he rolls his eyes, but here the abiding memory is the attractive one of 'his amazingly white teeth'.

There is no implication that the undersea forgers (thought up by Blyton's contemplation of underground tunnels at Swanage) were operating in the Nazi interest, a theme worked by other wartime fictionists. Blyton would have heard of Nazi humiliation when the blond beasts were routed by the black American, Jesse Owens, at the Nazi Olympics in 1936 to know that the Nazis were unlikely to select a black man as their *Oberhaupt* in masterminding financial chaos, however appropriate submarine printing-presses might be for Operation Sea-Lion. There is perhaps a touch of German deliberation and irony about Jo-Jo nonetheless:[52]

> 'We have mined part of the passage through which you came from Craggy-Tops, under the sea-bed. When we are safely above ground, you will hear the muffled roar of a great explosion. The dynamite will blow a hole in the roof of that undersea passage – and the sea will pour through. As you will guess, it will rush into these mines, and fill them up to sea-level. I am afraid you will not find things very pleasant then.'

It could be read as an answer to the hostility that the boys have shown Jo-Jo throughout the story, though this is clearly no more than the resentment they would have shown to any servant who obstructed and failed to oblige them. Blytonian children are told not to be selfish, but their adventures require them to be very self-centred.

The black fugitive paratrooper in *The Mountain of Adventure* is much more in the yes-massa tradition ('You not say I here. I poor nigger, little missy, lost and all alone'); but, although fleeing for his life, his first instinct is to protect Lucy-Ann more than to save himself. Blyton evidently knew that, if Uncle Tom is self-abasing, he gives his life to protect women. It is hardly realist dialogue for a paratrooper, but black persons knew all too well the value of deference to the omnipotent whites, however much they might detest it or them. The Stowe precedent (in print as a child's classic in

Britain) led naturally enough to the pursuit of Sam, the black man, across the mountainside by Alsatian dogs, Lucy-Ann's tears for him, Philip's capture in attempting to rescue him and their joint captivity. Lucy-Ann no doubt milks a little Eva sentiment from Stowe; but, in the security of the mid-twentieth century, her own life is in small danger. But Sam's is forfeit:[53]

> 'They had these queer wings fitted to their arms and were given orders to jump from the helicopter at a given moment – or else be pushed out', said Philip.
> 'What happened?' asked Jack.
> 'Sam doesn't know', answered Philip. 'You see, none of his mates came back. He's pretty certain they fell to their death. *He* didn't want to do the same – so he got away.'

The children and the paratroopers are duly rescued by Bill Smugs and his co-pilot Johns.

But the Johns who presumably inspired this baptism was more complex and less clear in his racial attitudes than the stay-at-home Blyton. The role of non-whites in the Johns fiction showed some response to changing attitudes – we noted Kadar in *Biggles Flies South* as a valued if not heavily used team-mate, where many previous figures were unpleasant and racially accentuated nasties, though only minor characters. The Second World War produced quite a number of attractive non-whites playing central roles. The first of these had certainly been created in peacetime: the brown Polynesians Shell-Breaker and Full Moon in *Biggles in the South Seas*. Shell-Breaker is simply a sort of Polynesian Ginger, but Full Moon is a remarkable figure, Johns's first successful female protagonist. Johns was quite aware of what he was doing in going beyond the norm of racial and gender conventions, and even satirises them at a moving moment when Ginger is unable to find words to thank her for saving his life:[54]

> 'Full Moon, one day I thank you for this', he said at last huskily. 'I think you're wonderful!'
> Full Moon laughed.
> 'What for wonderful!' she asked naively. 'Me no run away when plenty trouble. Me glad when you go overboard; no longer wonder how save you from schooner.'
> 'Well, I reckon you're a brick!' declared Ginger.
> 'What is brick?' inquired Full Moon curiously.
> Ginger could not find an adequate answer.

Dusky in *Biggles in the Jungle* is the much more stock faithful-native figure, triumphantly valorised and mercilessly lampooned by Frank Richards in different adventures (Kicky, Smithy's idolised Kikuyu (*Magnet*, August-October 1931); Popoo, Bunter's disillusioned Kana-ka (*Magnet*, August 1938)). Johns could work inter-racial affection heterosocially, but not homosocially, certainly not to Richards's stature. Certainly, the principle of environmental leadership being best in native hands is once again vindicated, and Uncle Tom also gets his innings:

> 'Dey shoot at us. Dey kill my brudders and capture me, and say me work for dem. Dey make me slabe.'
>   Biggles frowned. 'Slave? Do you mean that seriously?''
>   'Sure I do, massa.'
>   'But slavery was done away with long ago.'
>   Dusky shook his head sadly. 'Not up *dis* ribber, massa.'

This, for Johns, is quite a mordant turn of irony. The reader's conventions are deliberately mocked by the use of the stereotype which it symbolically overturns: *Uncle Tom's Cabin*, read during the Second World War as Dickens was read with all the comfort of eighty years since agricultural or industrial slavery. If slavery is dead on the Mississippi, it is alive and well on other rivers where to go up is as bad as it once was to go down the great US mother of waters. And the profit in this new slavery is shared by Americans. Johns, like Hergé in the 1950s (*Coke en Stock*, translated as *The Red Sea Sharks*), was urgently anxious to belie the supposed death of slavery, and very rightly so for the education of his youthful audience. The killing of the American slavers by the revolted slaves conscripts the readership on the black side, with deliberately threadbare face-savers about Authority being too far away to prevent the end that the audience demands.

The story is set in the inter-war years, the last major retrospective apart from forays into Biggles's schooldays and boyhood, but it has an ominous sign of both Second World War present and post-war future. The half-caste 'King of the Forest', supported by American adventurers looting their wealthy colleague, can rely on intelligence reports from the Acting Governor's head clerk. It does not greatly seem as though the head clerk is enjoying life under any regime:[55] 'a tall, emaciated-looking man whose skin, yellow from recurrent bouts of fever, seemed to be drawn tightly over the bones'. Among other things, he attempts to kill Biggles by aeroplane sabotage, which suggests either extraordinarily high devotion to the King of the Forest, not very likely for a sophisticated urban civil servant, or a shrewd belief that British servants needed insurance policies. The story is half a world and several years away from the fall of Singapore, but it was written in its immediate aftermath, if not during the event itself. Translated into the actual war against Japan, it shows us how high motives for imperial protection of natives could easily become a suspicious hostility to every native while British power falls from the skies. Racialist attitudes in Johns seem primarily the product of fears about security, which in itself was very much the main concern of his political thought in the 1930s. This is not to deny the possible impact of emotive response: his first noteworthy political activity – being a soldier in the Great War – assumed British–French friendship (not simply alliance) as a security condition. Everything relevant that he wrote reflected aesthetic as well as scientific support for this to the end of his life. It persisted, in fact, throughout the Cold War, when he became bitterly hostile to the arms race and fearful of mutual nuclear destruction. But he does not seem to have hated any people for the sake of hating them; although he seems to have taken Nazism as a natural consequence of being German, he was fond of showing a German however exceptional as chivalrous enemy. The Japanese came closest to becoming a national antipathy, but only from 1936 (*Biggles – Air Commodore*) to 1946 (*Biggles Delivers the Goods*).

But the Japanese shared with the half-castes the security problem of being partly within the British world, and partly able to draw on primitive enemies outside it. This in fact accounts for much of the hatred of racial mixing in literature: Injun Joe was dangerous because he combined knowledge of white strengths and weaknesses with that of Amerindian. It is an English imperial fear going back at least to William Wallace, Robert Bruce or Hugh O'Neill, all of whom were at various times courtiers and aliens, multilingual and localist. Johns was not notably hysterical about it. *Biggles Delivers the Goods* revives the figure of Li Chi, the Oxonian Chinese pirate, whose reappearance may have owed something to Ransome's Cambridge-educated female pirate Missee Lee, but whose first epiphany in *Biggles Flies Again* could well have helped to inspire her. The figure itself owes something to white models. *Gem* and *Magnet* readers were well accustomed to Rafflesians (or, as the original put it, Raffleites): Richards's own Talbot, Lancaster, Jim Valentine, Valentine Compton (all ultimately reformed, thanks to the love of good schoolboys). Johns worked in the genre through Steeley, in their stablemate the *Thriller*, where the leading house crook was the Saint, Simon Templar, whose creator, Leslie Charteris, was the half-Chinese Leslie Charles Bowyer Yin. Li Chi's original appearance in *Biggles Flies Again* in 1934 coincided with the initial hegemony of the Saint, whose adventures had poured forth from 1930, and was probably somewhere between a homage and a joke, given the name links, the Englishness of the Charteris stories and the Chinese antecedents of their author. The Saint won a free pardon for saving the life of George V from a train on a line where bombs had been planted, as Talbot back in 1914 had won his pardon from the same king for saving the king's troops from having their train bombed by a saboteur. But, unlike Talbot, Steeley and Co., the Saint never really reformed until the Second World War drove him into the arms of the (American) goverment. Li Chi followed the same course. The Air Commodore expresses it gracelessly but forcefully:

> 'Whatever else he may or may not be, he's a Chinaman, and to say that he hates the Japs for what they have done to China is to express his feelings mildly. He says – and it may be true – that the Japs in Shanghai decapitated his father for refusing to give them certain information. When you kill a parent in a country where ancestor worship is a religion, you start something, and I imagine that Li Chi's one ambition in life now is to do a spot of decapitating himself. . . .'

It enables Johns to sympathise with some Chinese criticisms of European culture, as in different ways Richards had done. When Biggles, Li Chi and his native followers capture a ship,[56]

> 'I will go to see what happens below decks', decided Li Chi.
>
> Biggles nodded. 'From what I could hear your fellows won't need any help from us. I think we'll stay here. I have a feeling that things will be a bit messy downstairs.'
>
> 'War is always a messy business, my friend, no matter where it is; and the *parang* is no more barbarous than the bomb, the tank or the flame thrower, such as the civilised peoples of Europe use', said Li Chi, with emphasis on the word civilised.

This was written shortly after Hiroshima and Nagasaki.

Li Chi is successively a joke, an irony and a wartime ally, plus various minor roles such as the Voltairean in the last paragraph. *Biggles Delivers the Goods* makes him the mediator and conduit between civilisation and barbarism, with his meanings of these in mind: Johns may have agreed with the 1935 Low dual cartoon which showed peaceful hut-dwellers in Ethiopia living contentedly followed by the same village reduced to a bombed, lifeless wilderness, respectively headed 'BARBARISM' and 'CIVILIZATION'; Johns time and again expresses anger at the destruction of pre-white societies by imperial or commercial incursion.

Li Chi, Chinese mediator reflecting an English education and speech superior to those of Biggles and (probably) Raymond, tells them (with 'a ghost of a smile') of 'Major Marling . . . an unusual member of that unusual race – the English'.

> 'Twenty years ago Major Marling was one of the most popular officers of the British army in India. He was handsome, wealthy – but not wise, for he committed the most unpardonable indiscretion which a British officer in India can commit. He fell in love with a native girl – a princess to be sure, but still, a girl of the country. There was a scandal, as a result of which he was invited to resign his commission – an invitation which he was bound to accept. Then, in the face of the powers that be, he married the girl. He could not stay in India. He would not return to England. So with his beautiful young wife he retired to the most inaccessible part of Lower Burma, a tract of land reached only by a dangerous river.'

The ironies are multifold. Johns was partly musing on his own need to conceal his common-law marriage, and his own resentment of the higher command which had endangered his life by illegal orders, and of the British conventions which forced him to deny the woman when he called his wife the right of legal marriage, to say nothing of the pusillanimous British government which had cost him his editorship. There seems a personal note in:

> 'Then, soon after the war began, prompted perhaps by a whim, or pride of race, or it may have been by a sudden burst of patriotism, or defiance of the enemy, he resumed his British nationality – in his dress and his mode of life.'

But the use of inter-racial marriage as a metaphor for his own situation is an astounding change for Johns, much deeper than Ginger's fervent but apparently sexless romance with Full Moon. Marling must be partly based on the White Rajahs of Sarawak (to whom Johns elsewhere made allusion); but Lalla, his child by the princess, is another matter:

Ginger gazed with curiosity on a young fellow of about his own age, slim, straight as a lance, dark-eyed, with skin the colour of café au lait and smooth as that of a girl. His dress was part European, part Eastern. A khaki shirt was thrust into well-worn riding breeches of the same colour, clipped tight into the waist by a belt which carried a heavy hunting knife with a jewelled handle. Mosquito boots encased his legs. On his head he wore a turban of blue silk, fastened across the front with a gold pin on which was mounted a ruby of considerable size. In the crook of his arm he held a light sporting rifle. He smiled half shyly, half sadly, at the visitors.

The major himself, having reverted to his former manners, shows little sign of the intervening years when he refused to see any white man and wore Asian costume. Lalla must have been brought up to view British officers with suspicion. Li Chi tells Raymond and Biggles that at that time it amused Marling 'to help me cheat the government which he always felt had used him badly'. Ginger is not prepared to write him off as merely heroic and comic, telling Biggles: 'The fellow I'm sorry for is Prince Lalla. . . . I had a long talk with him . . . Nice lad. He's burning to get into the war. It's a pretty lonely sort of life for a chap of his age, stuck up here at the back of beyond.' Lalla plays a brave though not very prominent part in the story, but it ends with Biggles taking him back to India, Lalla 'having obtained his father's consent to join the RAF'. The major also sends valuable rubies to be sold for the Red Cross, which he terms 'from loyal friends in Burma'. It is one of the most profound uses of 'loyal' in Second World War literature. Lalla seems a statement that any future for the British Commonwealth depends on the recognition and celebration of a multi-racial society. Since the prejudice against a 'half-caste', a figure sexually challenging white confidence, ran old, wide and deep in children's literature, Lalla is an important as well as a welcome figure: his existence was a rebuke to British military traditions all the more severe in being conveyed by an Oxonian Chinese pirate, thief and opium-smuggler, speaking to senior officers at the Air Ministry. He is almost entirely irrelevant to his story's plot. Marling's rejection and resumption of his Britishness could have been managed simply by allusion to his dead wife, who, being dead, could figure in a conventional plot provided that there were no descendants. Marling could have simply been a paternalistic Lawrence of Lower Burma.[57]

Biggles in the South Seas is the first revolt of the primitives on the side of Biggles, an interesting foretaste of the war: the revolt is independent of Biggles, although in sympathy with him. Although the war-party forms on its own momentum and its chief's decision, the larger civilisation is clearly white-ruled, shown at the beginning of the novel when Biggles is told of the realities by a Polynesian skipper when the villain of the piece enters:[58]

> Namu had half risen to his feet, but he dropped back again into his seat and touched Biggles on the arm. 'Castanelli', he whispered nervously.
>
> 'What about it?' asked Biggles.'You've nothing to be afraid of, have you?'
>
> 'Maybe you not understand. If Castanelli go for me I do nothing.'
> 'Why not?'
> 'Castanelli white man. Me hit Castanelli I get into bad trouble.'
> 'Ah, I understand', nodded Biggles, counting out some change to pay the bill.

The symbolism of the white man's economics making the pace is apposite. Well might Biggles understand, since up to now he has approved of, and profited by, such white supremacy. *Biggles in the Jungle* ends with the full-dress slave revolt culminating in the welcome murder of the treacherous white exploiters of slavery.[59]

Professor John Morton Blum, in his masterly study of US politics and culture during the Second World War, *V was for Victory*, notes an assessment of American comics made by two psychologists for the US Office of War Information under Elmer Davis in 1942. Most comic-strip heroes had donned uniforms (other than Superman and Li'1 Abner, who from somewhat different perspectives would have lost too much identity in discarding their customary apparel), but 'did not understand global war . . . [Their] Americans won their battles alone, allies were nonexistent or subordinate, the enemy was a pushover'.[60] One notable exception was Milton Caniff's *Terry and the Pirates*. Well might it be. It had been going strong since 1934, featuring a boy named Terry Lee and Chinese pirates led by a Dragon Lady. (Is it possible that the *crème de la crème* of the Second World War British writing for children, socially speaking, the Swallows and Amazons series of Arthur Ransome, could have had its Missee Lee derive her surname and Chinese pirate leadership from fusion of Terry's name and the Dragon Lady's occupation? One hears a thousand index-cards fall from the nerveless fingers of a hundred librarians heading children's departments of the 1940s at the thought

of Arthur Ransome in tandem with an American comic.) From the
Japanese invasion of China in 1937, the strip became increasingly
critical of Japan (where it was nonetheless reprinted until Pearl
Harbor). Terry had by now grown up, and in 1942 entered the US air
force. The pirates were forgotten as his original enemies, and their
retention in the title, no less than the place of the Chinese as much-
vaunted allies in both strip and war, created an illusion of pirates as
wartime allies. Similarly, Major Marling gets Li Chi to take charge of
'several Chinese and Lascars, the crew of a ship sunk by the enemy in
the Gulf of Siam . . . I shall be glad to get rid of them. They're an ugly-
looking crowd':

> They were, Biggles remarked to Ginger, as tough-looking a pack of
> pirates as he had ever seen in one place. 'No wonder the major
> wanted to get rid of them', he concluded, smiling.
>   Li Chi, who overheard the remark, surprised Ginger by obser-
> ving, casually, that in his opinion they *were* pirates. He smiled at
> Ginger's expression and added: 'Oh yes, there are still plenty of
> pirates in the China Sea'.

Constant readers (well flagged to the first Li Chi story by footnote
both to *Biggles Flies Again* and to its Penguin edition) would recall
what Ginger, not in the series then, does not know, that Biggles first
hears of Li Chi himself as a pirate (his informants being the local
English-language newspaper and Li Chi himself, pretending to be his
own victim). It symbolises the idea of Britain, mistress of the seas,
finding allies among the less official rulers of the waves: a culture
whose children were having their sinews stiffened by stories of
Elizabethan daring-do could find something to celebrate in a modern,
albeit Chinese, version of Sir Francis Drake. Just as the Drake legend
required official disapproval but covert sympathy for his piracy,
Biggles is required to express distaste for his allies' more bloodthirsty activities, but the readers are given every encouragement in
crossing the ethnical and ethical frontiers. When the pirates under
Biggles's increasingly nominal command raid Victoria Point to
rescue Algy and Marling, the Major is amused by his attempts to
impose order:

> 'You'll never stop them now; they're berserk', said Marling casually.
> 'The trouble with these chaps is they tend to get out of hand.'
>   '*Tend* to get out of hand!' cried Biggles with bitter sarcasm.
> 'They're like a lot of wild animals.'

'Why not? That's just what they are', said Marling cheerfully. 'They're having the time of their lives', he added. 'Leave 'em alone for a bit – they'll mop the place up for you.'

Algy burst in, eyes wild. 'Where's Tamashoa?' he demanded belligerently. 'I can't find the skunk. I want him.'

'Okay, help yourself', said Biggles, 'I give up.'

The British officers, whether among the rescued or the rescuers, are drawn into the massacre. Even Ginger, who observes most of it, starts firing at the interpreter when he tries to flee:

Jumping to the window hoping for a second shot, looking down he saw that the wretched interpreter could not have chosen a worse moment for his attempt. Ayert and a number of his men were on their way to the *kabangs* and the Jap landed in the middle of them. His cry of fear was cut off by fierce yells of exultation. Ginger turned away quickly. There was nothing he could do about it.

'He didn't get far', he told Biggles. 'He nearly jumped on top of Ayert. He'd have done better to jump on a tiger.' He glanced at the major. 'These natives are savages', he observed.

'Of course they're savages, my boy', replied the major sharply. 'So would you be a savage had you lived here and seen your friends carved up by this Japanese scum. Why, half an hour ago that infernal rascal stood calmly by and watched Melong's son decapitated.'

When the raiders are making their way back to base:

To Biggles' annoyance, the unruly native commandos, flushed with success, abandoned all restraint, and from time to time the forest rang with wild laughter as some man described a personal adventure.

'Don't worry', said Marling to Biggles. 'Any odd Japs who happen to be about will run the other way when they hear this din. They don't like *parangs*. I do. It's a nice weapon, particularly for jungle work, and it takes a good man to face up to one. The War Office might do worse than make an issue of them to commando troops. It's the head they're laughing at.'

'Head?' queried Biggles. 'What head?'

'They've got a head for a trophy, a souvenir of the occasion. They're passing it round . . . great joke.'

'What!' For the first time Biggles really grasped what the major was talking about. 'I'll stop that', he declared.

'I wouldn't try – you might lose your own. They do things without thinking when they're in this mood.'

Biggles steadied himself and walked on.

Schoolteachers probably did not care for Biggles, officially (though the magisterial reading of confiscated copies in secret would be a nice statistic); but, if the books had been officially recognised, would children have given an honest answer to questions of their support for Biggles or Marling in this exchange? And if so, would it have been on Biggles's side? And if not, was that the author's view? Perhaps honours were left even with the final exchange:[61]

'Everybody fights a war his own way', asserted Marling. 'That's the Malay way. This is their theatre as much as ours, so who are we to quibble?'

'There's something in that', acknowledged Biggles. 'But I don't like loose heads about.' He marched on.

Johns had earlier versions of it in *Biggles in Borneo*, where the allies are not pirates but head-hunters.

Despite Biggles's fastidiousness (or because of it), some regard between British officers and savage allies is evident. The *mentalité* may be compared to that of General ('Vinegar Joe') Stilwell who despised his officer allies among the Chinese in the real war taking place to the north, but who had high admiration for the ordinary Chinese fighting man. The assumption seems to have been that the less like white men they became, the more worthwhile they were: if they were to participate in white culture, it must be absurdly. In Borneo, for instance, Biggles remarks:[62]

'When I submit my report on the operation, remind me to call attention to the outstanding work done by Suba. He ought to get a medal.'

'He'd probably prefer a tin of sardines', opined Rex drily.

'Then give him a couple with the compliments of the British Government', ordered Biggles, smiling.

In the Mergui Archipelago, Li Chi's bos'n, Ayert, is 'a tall, gaunt Malay, minus one eye, and a face so scarred that Ginger shuddered when he looked at it'; but later Ginger finds him chuckling while reading a film paper:

'For the love of Pete', he murmured, turning an astonished face to Li Chi. 'Where did he get that?'

'He bought it.'

'*Bought* it – where?'

'When we were in India. He has a stack of them.' Li Chi smiled. 'Didn't you know that Ayert was a film fan?'

'A *film* fan!' Ginger was incredulous. 'Do you mean he goes to films?'

'On every possible occasion. In fact, before the war it was no uncommon thing for him to go hundreds of miles out of his way to visit a picture palace at Calcutta, Singapore, Penang, Renong, Rangoon – or any place within reach. He adores the films.'

Ginger blinked. 'Ayert at the flicks – that's a knock-out. It's a picture I can't visualise. Can he actually read that paper he's looking at?'

'No, he can't read English, but he loves to look at the pictures. He recognises the actors and actresses. Indeed, he knows all the stars by name.'

'What's his favourite?'

'Ask him.'

Ginger spoke to Ayert. 'Who's your favourite actor?' he asked.

'Donald Duck', returned Ayert without hesitation. 'Very clever wise guy.'

Ginger looked at Biggles. 'That beats cock fighting.'

'In the thriller section he prefers westerns', volunteered Li Chi. 'I make him leave his pistol with the cloakroom attendant, otherwise he's liable to take part in the shooting.'

Ginger smiled. 'I'd like to go with him with some time. It should be fun.'

Apart from its sardonic enjoyment of showing a common hobby as a means of eroding antipathy among persons of different races and cultures (Ginger is a film addict endlessly spouting American slang in the first stories where he appears), the passage has problems. Johns had a strong sense of humour, apparently more schoolboyish than the ironic amusement to which Biggles rises on occasion (for example, his entertainment at finding a coffin whose corpse proves to be a collection of books headed by *Grimm's Fairy Tales*). Donald Duck (whose speech was somewhat incomprehensible to Anglophones by first language, let alone Malay pirates) sounds like a Johns joke, possibly arising from the thought that Donald frequently behaves like the popular idea of a berserk Malay. But the passage in general sounds like the product of air-force club gossip. It was also a means of mockery of Americanisation and its critics in wartime Britain. It is irrelevant to the story, apart from the capture of the ship *Sumatran*, when Biggles and Ginger reach the bridge:[63]

> Ayert and Li Chi were there. Ayert was calmly wiping his *parang* on his sarong. Two Japs, an officer and a rating, lay on the floor in a widening pool of blood. Ginger shuddered.
> 'Foolishly they aimed their pistols at us', murmured Li Chi, as if this was all the explanation needed.
> 'Hit 'em. Like Clark Gable, *tuans*', said Ayert, grinning, showing his yellow teeth.

Ayert may be specifically referring to the MGM movie *They Met in Bombay* (1941), starring Gable, Rosalind Russell and Peter Lorre, where crooks become embattled against the Japanese, which may reveal one of Johns's sources as well as sprinkling a little covert self-satire. (Li Chi has touches of Peter Lorre.) But the main effect is surely intended as 'brothers under the skin': Ayert and Ginger – naturally extended to Ayert and the reader – prove to have pleasures in common, and, however incongruous to think of a Malay pirate with one eye as one's alternative self, his claims on Gable-status are (as he shows) rather better than ours. Children identified with Hollywood heroes in performance much more readily in those days; in our voyeuristic day they want to know *about* them, fifty to eighty years ago they wanted to *be* them. The first story in the first William book celebrates such identification. The effect would be to make children identify with Ayert as well (the more class-conscious might prefer to be Li Chi). So too would the pursuit of *Photoplay* or whatever Ayert was reading: the older among Johns's readers would be graduating to that. For the younger film addicts among them, there was *Film Fun*, still produced by the Amalgamated Press among the few children's weeklies to survive its slaughter of the *Magnet* and its stablemates in May 1940.

This was not incompatible with Johns's increasing witness to the need to leave people alone. A few years later, 'The Adventure of the Luminous Clay' (*Biggles' Chinese Puzzle*, 1955) turned on some east Pacific islands, of which the Air Commodore tells Biggles:[64]

> 'The group happens to be one of those to which, in these days of radio and aircraft refuelling stations, several countries now lay claim. If it were known that one of the islands had a particular

value, and we had made a raid on it, there might be an international rumpus, and we don't want that.'

'I would have said that the people who have most right to the islands are those who live there', asserted Biggles.

If ever an author needed protection from his friends, it was Johns. One adventure, *Biggles and the Lost Sovereigns* (1964), ended with Biggles about to run home Chintoo, his Malay interpreter-become-friend with the comment: 'When you find yourself working with a reliable chap like that it makes nonsense of the colour-bar argument'.[65] But when Johns was dead, the book was reprinted, largely unchanged, in 1978, by Knight (paperback) Books; that sentence was deleted. No doubt the officious publishing hand thought it was being 'politically correct'. In so doing, it revealed the degree of racial prejudice underlying political correctness, much deeper and more pernicious than was ever intended by Johns, even in his worst days. He regretted his bad actions; his revisers regretted his good ones.

Notes

1. Elder, *Strangers at the Farm School*, 103, 105.
2. Harris, *Gretel at St Bride's*, 48.
3. Elder, *Strangers at the Farm School*, 84, 131, 88–9, 76–7, 30. Whether Elder realised that the benevolent Mr Forrester's insistence on gypsy observation of apartheid towards gentile children was what she had described being forced on the Jewish children in Nazi Germany is unclear, but the presumption in view of her sensitivity and her intellect must be that she did.
4. Brazil, *The School in the Forest*, 258. Lest it be deemed yet another English crime, it was a vengeance by George Gordon, first Marquis of Huntly, against the Farquharsons of Deeside. The rarity of the Jewish analogy for such horrors, in children's literature in the Second World War, is chilling: all the more credit to Brazil. Being Brazil, they get up a Bluebell Fête and raise £6 8s 3d – but, however pathetic, morally it was much more than most.
5. Blyton, *The Secret Mountain* ([1941] 1982), 55–6, 71, 152. What this means is that the usual lazy libel that Blyton was racist is simply impossible: no racist could take pleasure in the thought of a black child sleeping as close as it could to a white; and she clearly did. As Wilde said of the sins that his critics ascribed to Dorian Gray, he who finds them has brought them.
6. The Newbery Medal for 1940 was won by James Daugherty, *Daniel Boone*, which children of today, invited to review it for the Newbery website, seemed unanimous in finding genocidal in its attitude to Amerindians. Extracts quoted are not covered by excuses such as the need for defence, security and so on. It was not reprinted in the UK.
7. *Magnets* 1,576–8 (April–May 1938). Another strongly pro-Amerindian story, this time against pre-Revolution soldiers in British service, may be found in 'Cecil Fanshaw' (C. H. Dent), 'Running Horse's Vengeance', *Champion Annual, 1939* (1938).

8. 'William and the Nasties', *Happy Mag* (June 1934) and *William the Detective* (June 1934). *Magnet* 1,498 (31 October 1936). For later attacks on anti-Jewish attitudes, see *Magnet* (9 April 1938).

9. Price, *Jane Gets Busy* ([1940]), chapters 3, 5 and 12.

10. Crompton, 'William Gets His Own Back', *Happy Mag* (November 1939) and *William and the Evacuees* (May 1940), 225, 228, 228–9, 232.

11. Crompton, *Weatherley Parade*, 219–20.

12. Johns, *Biggles Flies South* (May 1938), 28.

13. Johns, *Sergeant Bigglesworth, C.I.D.*, 131.

14. Johns, *Biggles – Secret Agent* (May 1940), 57–8, 58–9, 62, 65.

15. Johns, *Sinister Service* ([1942] 1949), 145, 146–7.

16. Johns, *Worrals in the Wastelands* (1949), 10, 23, 24, 60, 59.

17. Brent-Dyer, *The Chalet School in Exile*, 120, 121, 131.

18. Johns, *Biggles – Secret Agent*, 53.

19. Cf. Richards, Reply to Orwell, in Orwell, *Complete Works*, XII, 85.

20. Johns, *Biggles – Secret Agent*, 167, 15.

21. Gilson, *Out of the Nazi Clutch*, 20.

22. Martin Niemöller, Foreword, *Children of Light and Darkness* (1944).

23. Gilson, *Out of the Nazi Clutch*, 47–8, 92–3.

24. Michael Holroyd, *Bernard Shaw* (1991), III, 433.

25. Orwell to Fuller, 7 March 1944, Orwell, *Complete Works*, XVI, 116.

26. Tolkien, *The Lord of the Rings*, I, *The Fellowship of the Ring*, Book Two, chapter 5, 314. 'I do think of the "Dwarves" like Jews: at once native and alien in their habitations, speaking the languages of the country, but with an accent due to their own private tongue' (Tolkien to Naomi Mitchison, 8 December 1955, *Letters*, 229).

27. Gilson, *Out of the Nazi Clutch*, 93.

28. Johns, *Biggles Delivers the Goods* (April 1946), 111–12. 'Admiral Tamashoa' must have been intended to make the reader think of Admiral Tojo, the premier who ordered the attack on Pearl Harbor which brought the USA into the war. Japan must have been close to defeat when this was written, if Hiroshima had not already intervened (6 August 1945).

29. Johns, *Biggles in Borneo* (July 1943), 50–1, 124–5.

30. Gilson, *Sons of the Sword*, 15.

31. Johns, *Biggles in the Orient*, 115.

32. Litten, *Sinister Island Squadron*, 67, 38, 178. Litten, born in 1885, published about one book a year for boys, usually about the US armed services, between 1929 and 1961. Hutchinson of London republished four.

33. Kummer, *The Perilous Island* ([1944]), 12, 20–4, 28–9.

34. Montgomery, *Thumbs Up!* ([US edn 1942] 1943), 24–5.

35. Johns, *Biggles in the Orient*, 60.

36. Johns, *Biggles in Spain*, 100.

37. Johns, *Biggles in the Orient*, 34.. I was so strongly impressed by this as a boy that, when as a university Americanist I learned that one was now expected to refer to Amerindians as 'native Americans', I was horrified and still cannot bring myself to use it.

38. Litten, *Sinister Island Squadron*, 18, 24, 75–6, [5], 83, 84, 94, 67, 194.

39. Johns, *Biggles in the Orient*, 130.

40. Litten, *Sinister Island Squadron*, 27, 62.

41. Kummer, *The Perilous Island*, 61.

42. Arthur Ransome, *Missee Lee* ([1941] 1957), 20.

43. Jan Maclure, *Escape to Chungking* (1942), 45, 45–6, 46, 69, 71, 57, 92.

44. Robertson, *Dunkirk Dunes to Libyan Sands* (1941), 23.
45. Maclure, *Escape to Chungking*, 110, 114, 118, 120.
46. Trease, *Cue for Treason* ([1940] 1973), 210–11.
47. Maclure, *Escape to Chungking*, 112, 133–4, 134, 16–61, 73, 169–70.
48. A. E. Housman, *More Poems* (1936), 37.
49. Westerman, *With the Commandos*, 302.
50. Maclure, *Escape to Chungking*, 175–6, 176, 19–20.
51. Blyton, *The Mountain of Adventure*, 264, 324.
52. *The Island of Adventure*, 303–4, 305, 304.
53. *The Mountain of Adventure*, 136, 186.
54. Johns, *Biggles in the South Seas*, 213.
55. Johns, *Biggles in the Jungle*, 29, 38.
56. Johns, *Biggles Delivers the Goods*, 11–12, 96.
57. Ibid., 17–18, 59, 19, 66, 114, 151, 73, 181.
58. Johns, *Biggles in the South Seas*, 44.
59. Johns, *Biggles in the Jungle*, 178.
60. Blum, *V was for Victory* ([1976] 1977), 37.
61. Johns, *Biggles Delivers the Goods*, 71–2, 73, 151–2, 154–5, 156, 157.
62. Johns, *Biggles in Borneo*, 97.
63. Johns, *Biggles Delivers the Goods*, 33, 49–50, 96.
64. Johns, 'The Adventure of the Luminous Clay', *Biggles' Chinese Puzzle* ([1955] 1973), 92–3.
65. Johns, *Biggles and the Lost Sovereigns* (1964), 183–4.

FIGURE 11 British menace in Belgian nightmare (Hergé, *Le Crabe aux Pinces d'Or*, serialised in *Le Soir*, 1940–1) – see pp. 368–9.

Epilogue

'What else did happen in history?'
'They were always killin' people for one thing', said Henry.
'Who were?'
'People.'
'Why?'
'They had to. How d'you think there'd've been any hist'ry if they hadn't?'
This seemed unanswerable.
'Well, we can't kill people', said William decisively. 'We've gotter find something . . .'

Richmal Crompton, 'William the Conspirator'[1]

Do not despair
For Johnny-head-in-air;
He sleeps as sound
As Johnny underground.
Fetch out no shroud
For Johnny-in-the-cloud;
And keep your tears
For him in after years.
Better by far
For Johnny-the-bright-star,
To keep your head,
And see his children fed.

Squadron-Leader John Pudney, 'For Johnny',
written on the back of an envelope
during a London air-raid, 1941[2]

Hell came down from the sky, and Death made itself at home. Daddy went away and was killed or maybe wasn't, but you didn't know. Mummy often went away too, and maybe she was killed as well, and maybe you didn't know one way or the other about her either. You were on your own, all the more when then there were endless people milling around you. Sometimes they worried about you and sometimes they didn't, and you found it hard to say sometimes whether it was worse when they didn't worry about you or worry you, or when they did. Sometimes you didn't know where you were, and now and again you didn't know who you were. You had trouble knowing if you were still real. It was easier when you had brothers and sisters still with you, because they were real, and if they were, so must you be. There was a man in Germany who was real, because he was sending aeroplanes over to kill you, if they could, and there was a man in England who was real, because you could hear him on the wireless telling you that you must all stop the man in Germany. People weren't as real as they had been because now other people were doing jobs you remembered the first people doing, and the other people didn't seem to be as good at it, or else they were older or younger or women or something, and sometimes you were somewhere else and the people there didn't seem as real as the ones you could remember from what seemed longer and longer ago.

But some things were real. The people in the comics, whether as pictures or as stories. The children or animals or fairies you read about in Enid Blyton. Biggles and his friends flying somewhere out there. William and the Outlaws somewhere down the road from you. The Chalet School. The Lone Piners in Shropshire. Children somewhere, anywhere, having quests, ordeals, adventures, and winning over ugly odds and uglier criminals or Nazis or Japanese. You were safe when you were with them, even if you were all killed by the next bomb. You could not lose if those nice people went on writing stories for you about people whose companionship made you happy. Hitler might have had Wagner. But you were better off. You had Enid Blyton. If you did know anything about Wagner, maybe with his stories retold by J. Walker MacSpadden, you would know that his gods died, and his heroes did stupid things and couldn't escape from the results. But in Enid Blyton people did stupid things and did escape, if they were nice. Nice but stupid and occasionally clever. Like you.

When it was over, the books changed, but not as much as you might imagine. The First World War had had a sudden end, effectively symbolised in the last Biggles story of the first batch, *The Camels are Coming*, where the embittered hero is captured by recriminatory German soldiers, and on being rescued from their attentions by a German officer Biggles regrets his own absence from a raid scheduled for that afternoon. He evidently saw himself going down with all flags flying, but –

'Yes? But there will be no raid this afternoon', replied the German smiling.

'Why not?'

The German laughed softly. 'An Armistice was signed half an hour ago – but of course, you didn't know.'[3]

That story-ending was written fourteen years after the event, but it is historically invaluable. There is a touch of the same thing at the close of *Biggles Sees it Through*, when the Russians rejoice at the end of the Finnish Winter War, eliciting the unusually enlightened comment from Raymond: 'Most sensible people would rather cheer than shoot each other'.[4] But there were no German smiles or Japanese rejoicings visible after the Second World War, and no doubts but that a war had been won. Firm, decisive events were proclaimed: German surrender, V-E Day, Hiroshima, Nagasaki, V-J Day. Biggles's first meeting with a German after this war gets the reaction:[5] ' "You won the war, so I suppose you can do what you like", almost spat the German.' The war is in fact not over for him (though the ex-Nazi crooks with whom he is working seem animated only by greed), and several villains in successive stories up to 1949 do their best to prolong it. But there is little aerial combat from any of them, or in the post-war Worrals stories. It is simplest to say that if Johns faced his problems in revving up his First World War reminiscent footage to Spitfire standards, he would not try its luck in the jet age. In effect, it drew a line after the Second World War which had not existed after the First. Johns's refusal to look back, fictionally, to either World War after the 1940s hardened that line. He was even prepared to tinker with Biggles's schooldays and pre-school years, but Biggles' days as a war pilot or an inter-war pilot-errant were now sealed within imaginary history, apart from one or two old acquaintances.

Others would look back, but after firm breaks. War fiction had been declining in some quarters. Strip-cartoon comics in particular lost interest in it, and D. C. Thomson initially excluded any war matter from its products once it was over, although it would rapidly return in the strongly prole-centred *Rover* with Braddock, and *Adventure* also reran reworked Second World War material. The Amalgamated Press were less drastic. The *Girls' Crystal* had featured the occasional war story well into 1945, and Elise Probyn's Shirley Preston (with flickering support from 'her father's staff in the British Secret Service') revisited its pages with her devoted Chinese friend Ming-Su and their ruthless foe, the Japanese master spy Kokani. (Elise Probyn's real name was John McKibbon: it is tempting to endow him with a Scots linguistic origin which could have supplied 'Kokani' from 'ca' canny'.) Publication of Christmas annuals in early autumn meant that addicts were regaled in the 1946 *Girls' Crystal Annual* with Denia (a.k.a. Enid or Horace) Boyten's 'The Secret of Menagerie Isle' (where Corinne's 'amazing discovery . . . brought her right up against the grim realities of the war against Japan' and where Boyten's use of Fifth Column conspiracy in pro-Allied South America grasped the Argentine dilemma in early 1945). But the next year was warless apart from mayhem in the Upper Fourth and generally keeping a stiff but comely upper lip against the threats of the Phantom Viking, the Haunted Manor, the Pirate Isle and the pompous Cousin George. The new school-story publishers Gerald G. Swan specifically excluded all war content from accept-ability in unsolicited manuscripts from 1943, which did not prevent girls in May Sullivan's *Diana of Cliff End School* (1945) from scaring rival relatives away from a treasure-box by writing 'the ominous word "Gunpowder" on one side':[6]

> Fenella smiled, but her eyes had darkened ominously.
> 'Listen to me, my charming cousin', she said. 'If you so much as lay a hand on the box, I will kick it with all my might, and blow you to smithereens!'
> 'The gunpowder!' shrieked Pamela.

As Ronald Searle's post-war cartoons would indicate, school stories might reverse Clausewitz by becoming the continuation of war by other means.

Sometimes there was no break, and the *Champion*'s Rockfist Rogan kept his Second World War exploits going long after peace until they were allowed to fade into the war against crime where Biggles had taken refuge. But this was rare. Frank Elias's First World War story resurrected with face-lift to take an early place in the fiction of the Second World War, was not going to have future equivalents. In post-war austerity, it was hard for weekly papers to restore careless would-be upper-class insouciance, much though they sometimes tried. More and more teenage characters were depicted as taking unappetising jobs to eke out their dwindling substance. The weeklies also had to make occasional references to the effects of war's end quite shortly after that event. Paper shortage prevented the last wartime Worrals from appearing until December 1945, while *Biggles Delivers the Goods* did not reach its readers for at least eight months after Hiroshima. The *Girls' Crystal* as early as

1 September 1945, in contrast, had Heather Granger (John Wheway) tell 'her' readers of 'Not Wanted at Seaview Villa' how Dorrie and Tommy Elmore had not seen their uncle Major Dean 'since his return from the war'. Even earlier, on 25 August, Enid (or Horace) Boyten confronted the readers of 'Claudine and the Whistling Tower' with the perils of wartime collaborators with the Nazis when peace returned to the Channel Islands. Boyten naturally pulled 'her' punches: no mention was made of forcible head-shaving any more than of collaboration having possibly taken a sexual form, although the former was being imposed in Belgium and elsewhere in punishment for the latter (the Nazis' allies, the IRA, would adopt such punishments to terrorise Northern Irish Catholic girls for friendships with British soldiers some thirty years later). The genre itself received wide celebration from the Twentieth-Century Fox movie *His Affair* (US title *This is My Affair* (1937)) in which Robert Taylor played a US undercover man passing for a crook to everyone apart from President William McKinley, and hence highly embarrassed by that statesman's assassination in 1901. Graham Greene in *Night and Day* (26 August 1937) had hailed it as 'the best American melodrama of the year . . . admirable acting by Mr Robert Taylor and Mr Victor McLaglen and quick and cunning direction'. No doubt it inspired his *Strand* story 'The News in English' and J. T. Gorman's *Jack Frere of the Paratroops* with their British agents disguised as Nazi propagandists; but Boyten was closer to *His Affair* in having the agent-disguised-as-Nazi-collaborator being dependent on a Resistance hero, Paul, under whose orders she (Claudine) had passed for pro-Nazi and who had now disappeared. Boyten simply has him kidnapped and held prisoner by a Nazi disguised as the hero's sidekick (*Girls' Crystal* readers were accustomed to well-shuffled cards of identity in or out of school). Naturally all ends up hotsy-totsy with the warm handshake to which Amalgamated Press protagonists were obliged to restrict themselves (save under the mistletoe):

Her vision was blurred a little as Paul gripped her hand in a warm clasp.
'You've been true-blue from first to last, Claudine', he told her.
And perhaps those simple words were her best reward.

But did any readers wonder about other alleged collaborators unable to prove their true patriotism in the absence of dead or 'missing' control-figures? And did they realise that the punishment they faced was likely to be a great deal worse than not being invited to celebration suppers or being barred from competition for the prize for the best decorations?

The Channel Islands might have their special collective and individual traumata, born of occupation, guilt, innocence and yearnings for uncertainly directed revenge. One suspects that Mary Treadgold was representative in returning the English child characters of *We Couldn't Leave Dinah* to their imaginary Channel isle after the war, with the problematic protagonists whom it had left on the island conveniently forgotten. Recrimination against lukewarm patriots in Britain made little impact on children's fiction in the immediate aftermath of the Second World War. Even the war's impact on the landscape was elided, seaside stories returning in bulk with no allusion to the preliminary clearance from mines. In fact, many writers ignored the bans on beach-bathing: Blyton's Five had frolicked around Kirrin Island with no thought of the restrictions keeping their author from her beloved Swanage, although undertones of war determined some of their plots. Paradoxically, Blyton captured the most brutal impact of war in *The Valley of Adventure* in the burnt-out dwellings and bombed mountain-passes surrounding the children suddenly finding themselves in post-war Austria. As they do not at first know where they are, there is almost a time-travel element:

> 'Two burnt houses – and nobody to be found anywhere', said Jack. 'Very curious. What's been happening in this valley?'
>
> Higher up still they could see yet another house – would that be burnt out too? They laboured up to it, and gazed on it in despair.
>
> 'Quite burnt out', said Dinah. 'What an awful thing! What's happened to the people who lived here? There must have been war here, or something. I do wonder where we are.'

Blyton's affection for her Austrian asylum-seeker Maria Engler, whose name she used for the persecuted cardiac patient befriended by Jack, induced her implication of Austrian resistance to Nazi conquest, although the more thoughtful child might have realised that any bomb damage was probably Allied. Friendship for her refugee had evidently led Blyton to some research. There certainly was Austrian anti-Nazi resistance, notably in 1944–5, although much of it was Communist or socialist. Her assumption of Nazi exploitation was fair enough:

> 'Julius . . . lived in the big farm-house not far from here. But our enemies burnt it down, and all the other farms too, and took our

cows and our horses, our pigs and everything we had. Many they killed, and only few of us escaped.

'. . . Ah, Julius worked against the enemy all the time. Everyone knows Julius. He should be a great man now among his people – but times are strange and maybe he is no longer great, now that we have peace. . . .'

Another survivor, found later, reaffirms Julius (perhaps vaguely based on the tradition of Andreas Hofer via Brent-Dyer, and others, earlier publicists of supposed Tyrolean anti-Nazism):

'Ah, what a great man! How he worked against the enemy, even when they were shooting and bombing and burning in our valley. It was he who discovered that the enemy was using our mountain caves to hide away these treasures – treasures stolen from our churches and many other places.

'. . . one day Julius Muller . . . ordered us to come here, by a way he knew, and guard the treasure – not for the enemy, no – but for him and the people! He said that one day the enemy would be defeated and would flee away – and then he and the others would come back to find the treasure – but he has not come.'

'He can't', said Jack. 'The pass is blocked. No one can get in or out of this valley now – except by aeroplane. The war has been over a long time. . . .'

(Notwithstanding future hints of Japanese brutality to British girls in *The Mountain of Adventure*, reinforcing post-war anecdotes of Far Eastern campaigns, Blyton categorically told readers of the now fortnightly *Sunny Stories* on 15 June 1945: 'Now the war is over'.)

Blyton could follow Brent-Dyer's formula in stressing the anti-Catholicism of the Nazis, even if the anti-Nazism of the Catholics was sometimes less certain. She also assumed that the Catholics venerated the statues and regarded even security arrangements involving temporary removal of their jewels as blasphemous.

'Not do that! Ah, bad boy!' cried the old man, removing a brooch from Jack's hand.

'We only want to hide the things from those men', protested Jack. 'They'll be back and steal these things soon.'

'They belong to these', said the old man, waving his hand towards the statues. 'They must not be removed by anyone. It is against the law of the Church.'

Their theology might have been defective, and their iconolatry more Greek than Roman, but Austrian peasants might very well have guarded Church treasures with such assumptions. Blyton captured what reactions to Nazi despoliation would have been. She was brief, but effective:

> The old man and woman had rushed to the rescue of their beloved statues when the men had begun to strip off the jewellery. The men had struck the poor old things and shouted at them. The old man had taken his weeping, trembling wife away, and the children had done their best to comfort them.

The old woman is also deeply moved when she sees Lucy-Ann (Blyton realistically making Lucy-Ann 'surprised and not very pleased' by such demonstrative affection from an unknown):[7]

> 'We had a little granddaughter', he said. 'So like this little girl, with red hair and a sweet face. She lived with us. And one day the enemy came and took her away and we never saw her again. So now my wife sees her little lost one in your sister. You must excuse her, for maybe she really thinks her small Greta has come back.'

The year of publication, 1947, was also that which saw the first publication of Anne Frank's diary. It is just possible that this is its very indirect acknowledgement. At least it bears witness to the Second World War as a child-killer – and here Blyton seems to have been a pioneer. If she had protected, and in some cases heavily guarded, her child readers from the horrors of war, she was ready to make them face up to the fate of their little European contemporaries in its simplest form – once the war was over.

Johns made far less of post-war misery in *Sergeant Bigglesworth, C.I.D.* for all of its being set at war's end, not after what Blyton's Jack would call 'a long time'. (Both appeared in 1947's crop to compete in the Christmas trade.) Augsburg is briefly witnessed, with local transport being horse-cab rather than taxi, but that seems the limit of privation described. The town has 'an insalubrious thoroughfare in a poor quarter' to which the airmen go to find a witness who proves to have been murdered; but there is no sense of the wretched destitution.[8] It would have formed part of the American Zone of occupied Germany from 5 June 1945, but Biggles only encounters a blasé British Wing Commander; and his indifference to possible ex-Nazi seizure of lethal aircraft and covert operations on the airfield that he supposedly controls is so marked that Johns seems to be warning against Nazi survival exploiting British 'demob fever'. The story's impossible chronology is also useful to us. Biggles and his squadron had their last adventures in the war against Japan, so that they would have remained in service until after V-J Day and the start of American rule at Augsburg. There is no hint of this. The war is a war the British have won. *Biggles in Borneo* did feature some Americans, including a general, rescued by Biggles and his squadron from Japanese pursuit and prison-camp, victims of the fall of the Philippines: the Americans were thus suppliants for British aid and beneficiaries of British courage and skill. Biggles's squadron itself is ultimately saved from extinction by the Australians, not the Americans, and of the rescued prisoners the important initiative is taken by a Chinese. Tex O'Hara is American but serving in Biggles's squadron chiefly in hopes of finding a good war to fight in, having been exiled by the pusillanimity of the New York police; he does not return to the US forces (unlike R. Sidney Bowen's Dick Dawson). Johns was annoyed that his books did not sell in the United States as being too British; he was not prepared to put Biggles in a US-ruled world. In post-war stories, Biggles's main – and very close – working relationship outside the UK is with a Frenchman, Marcel Brissac, and his American counterpart is only introduced much later and given much less efficiency. Fleming's Bond was more ready to admit American predominance, although Britain (embodied, somewhat unfairly, in Bond) is the more resourceful, more subtle, more attractive (presumably the origin of the image that Mr Tony Blair's spin-doctors sought to project in his otherwise devoted subordination to President G. W. Bush). The Biggles stories' exclusion of the USA was unrealistic, a new form of cocooning the British child against world realities (in stark contrast to Johns's stories from 1935 to 1945, exaggerating but not distorting British potential).

Violence in children's comics and in their books in general was bound to be deepened by the war, however convenient it might be to blame the Americans. People gave themselves excuses. Johns, quite absurdly, wrote to Geoffrey Trease in answer to a letter soliciting data for the (subsequently anti-Johns) *Tales out of School* (1948) on 2 February 1948:[9]

> I teach sportsmanship according to the British idea. One doesn't need blood and thunder to do that. In more than forty novels about my hero Biggles he has only once struck a man, and that was a matter of life and death.

It may have been that Johns, uneasily seeking to guard himself against what he rightly diagnosed as a hostile enquirer, played a game which many English writers associated with the Jesuits (who were believed by Elizabethans not to give honest answers under torture): on the average, Biggles had struck a man only once in each of the novels. Oxford University Press artists had been a little over-fond of the moments. Biggles, in a comment made about the same time as Johns was writing to Trease, improved on his creator:[10]

> 'I've been accustomed for so long to settling arguments with guns that I've forgotten how to use my hands. Besides, I dislike hurting my knuckles . . . Tug seems to know of a way of hitting people without hurting himself. It struck me that he was just the sort of chap to – discourage, shall we say – this specious seller of newspapers without putting us all into the dock on a charge of homicide. . . .'

This, of course, was for the benefit of the audience whom Johns held in higher regard than he did Trease: his readers. But, however elegant Biggles's mockery on the theme, Johns worried about it, and adver-tised the Gimlet stories with some apology:[11]

> His methods are not always as gentlemanly as Biggles'. When things get rough he's apt to get tough. Which is why, of course, he was given a bunch of wildcats to command. After all, kid gloves are about as useful to a commando on his job as roller skates would be to a steeplejack.

That was all very well while the war was on – but what to do with the commando, or any other trained killer, when government had no further need of his services was an ugly peacetime riddle, all the more because it could not be much discussed or even much admitted. Georgette Heyer, the historical novelist, conceded the point in her modern detective story *Duplicate Death* (1949) by providing an ex-commando prominently among the murder suspects while promptly drawing the likelihood's teeth by also making him the former school-boy who had so charmed her readers by pestering her police in her *They Found Him Dead* (1936). But in general, unease about the ex-commando and his literature was scapegoated on the American. Percy F. Westerman had acknowledged their proximity during the war itself in his *With the Commandos* (1943):[12]

During the forenoon the Commandos mustered for inspection – two hundred well-conditioned men who bore more resemblance to American gangsters than to troops of the British Army. They wore uniform of sorts, mainly much worn and soiled battle-dress with close fitting head-dress. Each seemed to have armed himself according to his own choice. Most had knives in sheaths tucked into their right outside trouser leg. Some carried loaded sticks and truncheons made of rubber piping filled with sand.

If this really was what Westerman and his publishers thought American gangsters looked like, it indicated a latitude in sartorial standards that might have won reproof from Al Capone. Perhaps this helps explain Johns's extraordinary emphasis on Gimlet's aristocracy from his first appearance as a wartime commando. A Gimlet product is restrained by archaic British traditions of deference; a Gimlet product is not an American, accustomed to a liberal capitalist freedom in violence.

The contrast (it was hoped) lay in stories of Nazis who had not surrendered but in one form or another continued their war against society. The ugly, and frankly frightening, vision of post-war Nazi assassins taking vengeance on their wartime enemies, notably commandos and spies, firmly identified the British ex-commandos with preservation of law and order (in *Gimlet Mops Up* [1947]), and the post-war enemies of society against rather than among them. The Nazis were appropriate scapegoats. Considered in themselves, Johns's commandos were not absolutely reassuring: Gimlet primarily pledged to his class rather than his country, Copper with his criminal record, Trapper with his preference for torture in interrogation, Cub with his two years' life among outlaw juvenile delinquents. But, once welded together, they were much more amenable to discipline than, say, Biggles's Ginger, pre-war and in wartime, or, when the feminist bit is between her teeth, Worrals. In all of this, it is worth recalling the US post-Vietnam Rambo movies, notably the first, in which a returned Vietnam veteran, while fanatically loyal to the USA, more or less demolishes an entire American town with his bare teeth in justifiable irritation with officious local Authority. The discontented veteran trained in anti-social skills may be all the more dangerous to society if he retains his patriotism after the war. Post-war British children's literature needed to juggle rather nervously between admiration for the patriotism and restraint over the skills. One did not want their new post-war freedom to make them British versions of Anna Shultz, or the Nazi Werewolves sworn to kill

Gimlet, or the suave ex-Nazi Gontermann who invites Biggles to join forces with him for[13]

> 'Money, my dear chap; and the satisfaction of exerting power over those who think they can run civilisation their own way for their own ends. The world is bursting with wealth. Why not have some of it? There are two sorts of people in this world, my dear Bigglesworth – the mugs and the others. The mugs accept what is doled out to them. The others, to which class we belong, help themselves. . . .'

Some of Johns's youthful readers may well have lived long enough to wonder if those ethics, repudiated by Biggles, won control of Britain in the later twentieth century. But the problem of the ex-commando and his ethics when alive and well and in post-war society was one which had been present before, if previously somewhat muted in edifying literature for children. The Black and Tans and the Auxiliaries had played a little of that game in the Ireland of 1920, even if they had not been sent out to live on the land. Fighting guerrilla armies, they resorted to unauthorised and unorthodox actions, with the usual result of counter-terrorism becoming terrorism itself. The standard device in boys' fiction was a livewire teenage local supporter (cleverly reworked by Johns through making Cub a French Resistance boy forced out of an English origin). The Black and Tans had had such a local helper in Mayo and Galway, William Joyce, hanged on 3 January 1946 for collaboration with the Nazis in the Lord Haw-Haw broadcasts. But most graduates of extra-curricular warfare found better fulfilment after the war, since unorthodox activities would be required of soldiers in Kenya and other points of imperial weakness to terrorist revolt. In this climate, commando stories returned to the comics during the 1950s, for what were the last days of word-narrative in children's weeklies. D. C. Thomson's *Adventure*, for instance, gave away with one issue *Commando at War*, with front cover showing huge, ferocious, face-blacked commando having evidently climbed cliff with knife-blade between teeth and grenade in hand, planes performing ballet in background and ship ablaze. It acknowledged the coming suzerainty of the picture-comic with the series title in top right corner 'THE BIG SHOW PICTURE ALBUM!', apparently seeking to conceal the fact that its content was largely text (the companion volume *War in the Air* being comparably camouflaged). It went to some pains to show that the subjects were unique, but was careful to add that they were also commonplace civilians:

the finest fighting unit the warring world had ever seen. They were
COMMANDOS!

The troops who filled the ranks were not, as many people
imagine, a collection of wrestlers and bruisers, of weight-lifters
and boxers, of toughs and thugs. The opposite was the case. It was
the ordinary man in the street, the baker, the butcher, the mechanic, the clerk,

– this began to resemble the crew in Lewis Carroll's 'The Hunting of
the Snark', possibly an unconscious derivation –

who in war wore the word 'Commando' on his battledress sleeve.
But he differed from the ordinary soldier because, of his own free
will, he had chosen to 'become specially trained to perform duties
of a hazardous nature'.

Adventure formally acknowledged assistance in the writing from
Captain Murdoch C. McDougall, author of *Swiftly They Struck*
(1954), an account of his experiences in No. 4 Commando (with
introduction from Lord Lovat). *Commando at War* put a cheerful
construction on its events: the Dieppe raid of 19 August 1942 was a
'short and bitter fight' which had proved that 'Combined Operations
could pay rich dividends, and that the fighting men who wore the
green beret had no equal . . . that the enemy coast was not invincible,
and the Commandos had laid the foundations for the Allied invasion
of Europe'. Percy F. Westerman had never hesitated in declaring a
victory; and, having made a hospital case of his hero, *With the
Commandos* ([1943]) had rallied morale in his best man-to-boy
propagandist manner:

It showed that, with the command of the sea and the complete
mastery of the air it was feasible to land an enormously strong
force at almost any part of German-occupied Western Europe.

In short, a formidable Second Front could be formed to free the
enslaved countries from Hitler's yoke; but where, when and how
could only be known to the military commanders of the allied
nations until the opportune moment arrived.

The raid on Dieppe had added yet another page to the fighting
traditions of the British Commonwealth of Nations. It had proved
that, even in the face of enormous odds, the will to do and dare
and, if needs be, die, was as strong as ever in the hearts of the men
of the Armed Forces of the Crown.

He might have outrun his propagandistic lines of supply as regards the Second Front, had he not previously removed his ideological skirts from the unwelcome proximity of Aneurin Bevan and other premature advocates of the offensive:[14]

> People who clamoured unthinkingly for a Second Front, failed to take into consideration the fact that landing on the Normandy coast, especially from shallow-draught invasion barges, is only practicable at infrequent periods. There is also the big range of tide to be taken into consideration.

Historians are doubtful about Dieppe's efficacy, with 1,000 killed and 2,000 prisoners, and rude remarks from Hitler about the British having had the courtesy to cross the sea to present their opponent with samples of their latest weapons.[15] Johns made Gimlet's retrospective comments on it exceptional (for him) in their humility, apologising to a corporal for having 'lost' him at Dieppe (when they meet again during a later raid).[16] That was in *Gimlet Goes Again*, when the Second Front was well and truly open by the time of its publication in November 1944. But former commandos at war felt free to mythologise when the heroes were once again bakers and (commercially) butchers.

Westerman shared a few of Johns's reservations about the Americans, but his criticisms were more historical. Johns was happy with Herodotus, but left more recent history to others. Westerman was ready enough to blame the First World War for the Second. In *One of the Many* ([1945]), he targeted humanitarians readily, through the lips of a grounded (and curiously Americanised) squadron-leader, and indirectly preached the unrestrained bombing of Germany:

> They saw an English city scarred by enemy air action. For the first time they could realize the tremendous effects of modern warfare as introduced by the *kultured* Hun.
>
> 'Aw! forget it, you guys! . . . Wait till you see what *we've* done to *them*. And by the time you boys have been over to stoke up, well I guess Old Goering won't have much of his outfit left. Unless –'
>
> He paused.
>
> 'Unless what, sir?' asked Whangi, unable to restrain his curiosity.
>
> 'Unless there's a let-up in high places amongst the Allied Nations. In the last war a dignitary of the Church proclaimed, "Don't humiliate Germany" and "Let us humiliate ourselves". [The

allusion is to the courageous Randall Davidson, Archbishop of Canterbury.] The British followed this advice and landed us in a Second World War. Just now, there are other parsons starting to butt in and denounce the bombing of Germany. [The comparably brave George Bell, Bishop of Chichester, thus destroyed his own prospects for Canterbury.] They say it is inhuman and contrary to all Christian principles. I'm not saying that it isn't, but we're forced to do it to save ourselves from enslavement.'

This had the merit of combining several alternative (if somewhat mutually contradictory) defences of the bombing of German people — which in fact stiffened their resistance, as with the British reaction to the Blitz. Further discussion among the pilots first elicits (inaccurate) agreement on the Germans having begun aerial bombardment, trumped by a South African pilot 'who owed many of his strong religious beliefs to the teaching of his [Boer] grandfather':

'the Lord raised brimstone and fire upon the cities of the plain and all the inhabitants. Isn't that something to go upon to justify the extermination of Nazi-ism?'

'Gee, I believe you're right', declared the other. 'I'd never thought of that! Someone ought to write to the Press suggesting that the parsons should study the points raised. But this isn't the time or place for a theological discussion. . . . No. 3 Flight — attention!'

A former RFC pilot of the First World War and subsequent pacifist, Rupert Atherton, looks at the war-demolished village of his upbringing and tells his son:[17]

'There, but for the War that was supposed to end war but didn't, you might be living to-day. It's but one instance of hundreds of thousands of British homes destroyed because we didn't learn the lesson of the last war. That is to finish the job properly. And if we — the United Nations — don't smash Germany and Japan so that they will never become Great Powers again, we'll have all this beastly business for the third time, only far worse, within the next fifteen years. . . . Let's get out of it, Dick, I've seen enough!'

Artistic use of entry and exit (save in cases of presumed death) is not conspicuous in Westerman, but it may be intentional that we never again see or hear from this senior protagonist in One of the Many, although his son's adventures occupy another twenty-five pages.

Two years later, the avowedly post-war *Trapped in the Jungle* ([1947]) enabled Westerman to explain the revolution in Japanese–UK relations after 'British sympathies' in the Russo–Japanese war of 1905 having been 'ninety-nine per cent pro-Jap' and Japan's having been 'Great Britain's ally in the struggle against Imperial Germany':

> The Washington Treaty [of the early 1920s], limiting British, American and Japanese capital ships to a 5:5:3 ratio, altered entirely the hitherto good Anglo-Japanese relations.
>
> The War Lords of the Land of the Rising Sun secretly but efficiently prepared for a war designed to make Japan supreme in the Pacific and the Far East and, later, ready for wide world domination.

The second paragraph is characteristically crude and implicitly chauvinist, as usual, but the first is startlingly perceptive. It at least hints that Washington had wanted the abrogation of the Anglo-Japanese alliance, having remarked that the previous wartime links between the three powers bore 'no degree of enthusiasm towards the yellow men' on the part of the USA. And the Washington Conference's tactical generosity towards Japan in naval power ratio could not offset Japan's future exclusion from its valued partnership with Britain. But this was the limit of Westerman's hints of American responsibility, and youthful readers might well assume that it censured the Americans for letting Japan have so good a naval ratio, not for isolating Japan. Westerman quickly turned to the effects:[18]

> Quickly the veneer of western culture disappeared from the face of the Japanese Empire. Rumours, soon to be proved to be only too true, came in, and continued to do so, of unspeakable barbarities being committed upon helpless British and American soliders and civilians, men and women alike, by the bestial toops of the Mikado.

Westerman heartily applauded Hiroshima.[19] Johns gave Biggles misgivings at science's gifts of destruction in place of benefaction. Blyton had been reacting along the same lines in *Five on Kirrin Island Again* (1947), her redemption of George's father:[20]

> 'I'll tell you what my experiments are for, George – they are to find a way of replacing all coal, coke and oil – an idea to give the world all the heat and power it wants, and to do away with mines and miners.'

'Good gracious!' said George. 'It would be one of the most wonderful things the world has ever known.'

'Yes', said her father. 'And I should *give* it to the whole world – it shall not be in the power of any one country, or collection of men. It shall be a gift to the whole of mankind – but, George, there are men who want my secret for themselves, so that they may make colossal fortunes out of it.'

It was only a few years since Blyton had been founding her wider reputation as an imaginative writer on *Adventures of the Wishing-Chair* (1937) and *The Enchanted Wood* (1939). She demonstrated what historians of science later came to recognise, that tales of magic are the earliest form of tales of science. But if Uncle Quentin is only slightly evolved from an uncertain-tempered enchanter, his intentions are a remarkable political comment – welfare world versus unbridled capitalism. It was published when the Labour government found its national welfare proposals challenged by private business interests. If Blyton seems a startling recruit to the ideal of the welfare state, she is a significant witness on social rethinking prompted by the Second World War. But George's father (never before so termed so frequently) is global in his ambition.

The Lord of the Rings confronted the idea of Sauron's potential profiteers surviving, when the returning hobbits find the defeated Saruman exploiting the Shire. Fears of Nazi survival (specifically Hitler, a myth that H. R. Trevor-Roper's arrogant and amusing inquest helped to dispel) and of Japanese non-surrender percolated in the years after war. Westerman's *Trapped in the Jungle* dealt with repatriating Japanese prisoners:

'When we were in a Jap prison camp', replied Mr Miles grimly, 'I've seen more than half-starved men tearing at a carcass as putrid as that one, with the Jap guards shaking with laughter at the sight. And we're feeding those yellow blighters down there with two good meals of *clean* rice a day, sir. It don't seem sense to me, with millions in India nigh on starvation; makes me wonder what those Sikhs think about it.'

'I'm afraid what we think or say won't help matters', rejoined Captain Carr. 'We're obeying orders and that's all there's to it. . . .'

But it also assumed extensive Japanese survival in the jungle with opposition from guerrillas also ignorant of the war's end, less incredibly than the guerrilla-leader turning out to be the schoolboy protagonist's long-lost cousin. (Coincidence seems to have been regarded by the author as a Westerman's best friend.) This particular story also targeted the problem of post-war readjustment for morally damaged soldiers more seriously than most: four hi-jack a passenger aircraft after having robbed a rent-roll in Britain, and ultimately expiate their crimes in being killed by the unsurrendered Japanese. At one point, the leader becomes a companion of one of his passenger victims, the schoolboy. Westerman drew on an old tradition here, the veteran frequently of dubious and sometimes of criminal past in alliance with the supposedly likeable and potentially redemptive youth: Ballantyne's *Coral Island* with Ralph Rover's pirate Bill, Stevenson's *Treasure Island* with Jim Hawkins's initial friendship and later linkage with Long John Silver (and at other times with Ben Gunn), Conan Doyle's *Micah Clarke* with its hero's vicissitudes anent the Puritan adventurer Decimus Saxon, John Masefield's *Jim Davis* on and off with the smuggler Marah, even Richards' Harry Wharton being saved from the Nazi spy by his old enemy James Soames. Westerman turned that key when hi-jacker and victim reach the lost guerrilla cousin:

> Bud Millicane, although a self-confessed gangster and bandit, had more than once saved his life. To have to tell Roy that Bud had made him jump from the flying-boat seemed like sneaking, and that went hard against Kenneth's code of schoolboy honour. It would also be decidedly awkward if Bud told his version and it differed materially from his. He wished he could have waited until Bud awoke and could be present before he gave his guarded version of his adventures. Then Bud would see he didn't sneak!

Westerman seldom did much with character – Johns by contrast seems positively Austenian – but this makes good use of the traditional glimpse of the void between innocent Youth and the all-too-experienced Age. Its hard-bitten *envoi* to the hi-jacker when killed (in saving the boy's life) is no less realistic:[21] 'He was sorry about Bud's end, though, perhaps, it had been the best way out. It wouldn't have been much of a bright outlook to go through the rest of his life branded by the hand of Justice.'

Presumably Westerman might have given Bud more of a chance had he been in the officer class; presumably also he would have given him no chance of any redemption had he been Japanese. The reconciliation with old enemies was most obviously asserted (as one might predict) with fellow-whites. Biggles's conflict with von

Stalhein did not end until 1958, to be followed by cautious flickers of friendship. Yet some of the hardest words against Nazi Germany were written after the war's end, and some *amendes* eluded realisation. *Adventure* revived a wartime story of a one-man submarine piloted by 'The Human Torpedo': he began by protesting against the brutality of his Nazi superiors but ended as an implacable instrument of revenge, only aborted when 'something snapped' in his brain and he rode on a torpedo to blow up a British vessel until his own submarine got in his way.

Nonetheless, D. C. Thomson of Dundee had celebrated the advent of peace, through the graceful artistry of Dudley D. Watkins at his most benevolent. To Oor Wullie, the imminent end of the war means the prospect of knocking off PC Murdoch's helmet with a 'hauf-brick' and telling 'wir heidmaster' to 'go and bile his fat heid'. But first he has to thank a soldier, a sailor and a pilot on behalf of himself and his masters 'for a' ye've done!!! – pit it there!', and the handshakes of congratulation are followed by the headmaster's 'Well, William! The war's over! Shake hands!' And when that is done, Murdoch wants to follow suit, and each confesses to the other:

'Shak' haunds, P.C. Murdoch! I wis goin' tae knock yer helmet aff wi' that [half-brick] – but I canna dae it!'
'Wullie, ye're a wee imp! But I wish I had a laddie like ye!'

So his friends accuse him of being 'feart', and he fights them both, and so can then honourably shake hands with them, and they ride off in an army waste-disposal truck ahead of pipers and drummers, Union Jacks waving. This was V-E Day (appearing in the *Sunday Post*, 13 May 1945). But the *Post*'s other favourites, the Broons, still had their menfolk in the army throughout 1945.[22]

However much the ordinary people in the recent Allies might differ as to who had won what, the Americans and the British were at least aware of each other. Crompton, characteristically, struck a more brutally realistic note than the infectious peace spirit permitted elsewhere. Her work at the Toc H canteen for men and women in the armed forces may have cut down on her time for writing. She was now also turning out William scripts for radio broadcasts in 1945–6. In any case, only two William stories appeared in 1945, one starring Mrs Bott's clothes coupons, without which 'In rags, I am. Hardly a stitch to me back. I could have cried me eyes out, I was that upset . . . when I think of myself goin' about for the next six months with me clothes droppin' off me back.'

This dependence would continue for many more months. And the second, first published in *William and the Brains Trust* (April 1945), had William enthusiastically and very successfully raising money for the prisoners-of-war. Crompton was mocking in manner as usual ('Things had been dull in the village lately, and, rather to the Outlaws' surprise, the youthful members of the community seized eagerly on the idea'), but, for all of the comedy of the main themes – the sales and purchases, in alliance and recrimination, among the children, and the absurdity of William's Aunt Florence's attempts to knit toys – the profits appear to be the largest in William's career (Aunt Florence's toy camel eluding all attempts at sale and then, in competition, at identification). The story in magazine publication was held over until November because of the paper shortage, as happened in many other outlets ('This isn't the post-War Christmas number that I'd *hoped* to provide', stated the *Boy's Own Paper* for December 1945 grimly, 'there's no more paper available yet'), but it seemed to reflect a continuing conviction that Red Cross Funds were needed to bring many of the recently liberated home. (In fact, the medical condition of some camp survivors sometimes delayed their being either repatriated or redomesticated.) Actual peace celebrations under William's aegis had to wait for 1946, first appearing as 'The Pageant' in *Modern Woman* for May, and revised as 'The Battle of Flowers' in *William – the Bold* more than four years later. For the first time in over twenty years, it included both little girls recurrent in the stories – Violet Elizabeth Bott, and Joan Parfitt, who (in keeping with Crompton's view of war as a means of greater female achievement) was now much more than a female adjunct, saving William from criminal charges in 'Joan to the Rescue'. But 'The Pageant' has her once more as clinging and dependent in contrast to the permanently critical and unwelcome Violet Elizabeth – with whom she unexpectedly forms a feminist alliance at the end.

Having decided to rehearse their victory pageant in Marleigh Manor, whose owners they believe to be in Scotland, the Outlaws quarrel with Violet Elizabeth, whom they decide should be Germany, and Crompton suggests the uncertainty with which the defeated Germany was visualised:

'What thould I wear?' said Violet Elizabeth. 'It dependth on what I'd wear.'

They considered the question.

'Swashtikas', suggested Henry.

'No', said Violet Elizabeth firmly. 'I don't like thwathtikath!'

'Sackcloth', said Ginger.

'No', said Violet Elizabeth still more firmly. 'I don't like thackcloth'.

She insists she wants to wear 'a fanthy dreth of a rothe'.

'And I muth ride in the chariot and I muth go on firtht in front of Britannia.'

She smiled at them radiantly, as if she had completely solved the problem.

'You can't do that if you're Germany', said William.

'Why not?'

''Cause — 'cause you've gotter be sorry for all the wrong you've done.'

'Well, I'm not', said Violet Elizabeth with spirit, 'and I haven't done any wrong.'

'You started the war.'

'I didn't', snapped Violet Elizabeth. 'I wath in bed with a biliouth attack the day the war thtarted. Athk the doctor if you don't believe me.'

Crompton kept William about eleven years of age for his fifty years of literary life, but while Violet Elizabeth was officially 'thix' she frequently showed all too much maturity in cunning and repartee, and for this story she was evidently extended in age to about ten. Crompton had clearly heard the frequent excuse reported from Germany that ordinary Germans were guiltless of starting the war, and gleefully reached for her scalpel. She kept it unchanged when revising for book publication: the excuses were if anything more audible by 1950. Violet Elizabeth withdraws from the Outlaws' councils 'with an impressive air of dignity which did not quite desert her even when she turned at the door and put out her tongue at them'. But she then horrifies them by persuading Hubert Lane and his followers to hold a pageant to put the Outlaws' efforts in the shade ('though they would not have admitted it, they felt wounded and betrayed. That Violet Elizabeth, their most troublesome but most loyal follower, should have joined the Hubert Laneites was almost too monstrous for belief'). Initial rehearsals reflected something of the inter-service rivalry of which William was ignorant but Crompton was not: 'William tried to divide them into groups of soldiers, sailors, airmen, commandos and paratroops, but the free fight would break out again immediately and the ranks would become inextricably mingled'. Arriving for their dress rehearsal at Marleigh Manor grounds, they find an audience of bored-looking children sitting in rows, to whom William, recovering, introduces 'our Vict'ry pageant' beginning with Joan as Britannia reading her poem prophesying peace. But, before the supposedly peaceful victorious troops commence their usual sanguinary manoeuvres,

> Violet Elizabeth, dressed in her pink silk rose costume, appeared at the head of the Hubert Laneites and led them up to William, smiling radiantly.
>
> 'I wath only teathing you, William', she said. 'I've got a lovely thuprithe for you.' She turned the radiant smile on the audience and, striking an attitude, proclaimed:

> > 'I am ole Germany, Beat in the war,
> > A goothe that won't go goothe-thtepping any more.'

> She pointed at Hubert, who wore a row of medals on his coat.

> > 'Here'th old Goering,
> > He ithn't purring
> > Any more.'

In the book text, Crompton dropped Violet Elizabeth's 'poem' and merely had her turn herself in ('I am Germany, an' thethe are German prithonerth'), judging that new readers would have forgotten the Nazi personnel by 1950. But the 1946 text had its fidelity. Goering had meant the Blitz, and the most obvious sound of the invading bombers had been the broken purr of the Junkers 88.

> She next pointed at Bertie Franks, who had a short moustache corked upon his upper lip.

> > 'Here'th the ole Führer
> > He won't go to Nürnberg any more.

> Next she waved her hand airily at Claude Bellew, a thin, undersized member of Hubert's gang.

> > 'Here'th old Goebbleth the liar.
> > He won't say London's on fire
> > Any more.'

Crompton was speaking for the Auxiliary Fire Service, among whom she had served. The deep satisfaction it evidently gave her is shown by forgetting to make Violet Elizabeth lisp in the second line. (Goering was still alive and a prisoner at Nuremberg as she wrote; Hitler and Goebbels were dead.)

A wave of both hands included the rest of the Hubert Laneites.

> 'And here'th the ole German prithonerth,
> Their generalth, too,
> Looking juth like the monkeyth
> You thee in the zoo.'

Crompton was elsewhere writing of her horror at the fate of the Jews, and her anger at the extent to which British appeasement had betrayed them. This was not simple schoolgirl vindictiveness. Moreover, she had an account to settle with the war profiteers and self-servers who had dishonoured wartime Britain, a role for which she had previously cast the Lane family. Mrs Bott had complained, and co-operated under duress, but Mrs Lane had hoarded, and sought to humiliate organisers of co-operative work which sidelined her:

> The Hubert Laneites stared at her, speechless with fury, aghast at the trick that had been played on them.
> For Violet Elizabeth had joined them, offering to organise their pageant, act the part of Britannia, and even help them capture the Outlaws for German prisoners. She had cast Hubert Lane for the part of Churchill, stipulating that he must have a row of medals, which, she assured him, Churchill always wore. So Hubert, who was rather stupid, procured the medals.

Goering's medallic sheen was permanently reflected in the minds of his more satirical enemies, notably Charlie Chaplin's The Great Dictator, where Adenoid Hinkel – its Hitler – pins one on him and then tears all of them off, thus debagging him. Churchill was an exhibitionist also, but one of much more originality. (Thomas Henry's illustration recalled the Churchillian boiler suit.)

> She had assigned to Bertie Franks the part of Mr Eden and had corked his moustache herself, assuring him that the likeness was now so perfect that no one could tell the difference. Claud Bellew, she said, must be Monty, Georgie Parker and the rest of them

> British soldiers. Instead of which, she had shamelessly delivered
> them into the hands of their enemies, making them play the hateful
> and humiliating part themselves in the Outlaws' pageant.
>   She stood there, smiling proudly.
>   'Ithn't it a lovely thurprithe, William?' she said.

Crompton's celebration of women in the armed forces, while recognising those other women keeping the home fires burning, helps us to
see her transformation of the male pageant, with purely national-
symbolic female accessories, into a metaphor for British female
intelligence and leadership. Time and again, the Worrals stories
turn on male stupidity being exploited in the British interest by
women whom Germans take to be their dupes or servants.

> The infuriated Hubert Laneites flung themselves upon the Out-
> laws. The Outlaws flung themselves upon the Hubert Laneites.
> The battle spread to the audience, and the audience, losing its air
> of listlessness, flung itself upon both sides impartially.

And then Lady Markham appears:[23]

> For she was smiling in unmistakable welcome. She held out her
> hand to William and clasped his warmly.
>   'Thank you, my dear boy', she said. 'Thank you.'

It turns out that the Markhams had been let down in the entertainments they had planned for an annual party for slum children, and
thought William's intervention had saved the day with what Lady
Markham took to be a 'Battle of Flowers'. And so recriminations and
humiliations are traded, offloaded and finally dispersed in making a
happier day for slum children – under aristocratic auspices (Crompton was a Tory).
    Propaganda? Certainly – and a challenge to the welfare state to
make such charity needless. Escapism perhaps – but the greatest
problem likely to have been created by escapism was not that of
preventing children from facing the war – the war, after all, faced
them, whether or not they read about it – but that of leading them to
escape *towards* the war, wanting to do their bit and making the bit
too great a mouthful. Johns supplied the classic case of it in Nigel
Norman Peters approaching a party of commandos whom he tells
that their leader has been captured, and then leads to his rescue –
surely almost every Second World War British child's pet fantasy –

after which we are told of his having run away from school to rescue
his father from Dunkirk, where he was isolated on the bombing of the
pleasure-craft manned by 'three unshaven longshoremen' on their
third rescue voyage bearing him as stowaway (like Westerman,
Johns made it clear that Dunkirk was evacuated with ugly casualties
and unknown fates among the rescuers).[24] Norman Dale's *Secret
Service!* (1943) ventured on more dangerous ground in having two
evacuees run away from their foster-parents (too nice rather than too
nasty) to join the navy and fight against submarines. As with
William and Biggles, the hero's most conspicuous friend is called
Ginger. They do ultimately capture a U-boat commander, although
not before he orders their destruction:[25]

> 'Quickly!' said the German. 'I cannot waste time. There is no one at
> the wheel, and we are off our course.'
>   'I don't like to put 'em overboard – just a couple of kids',
> muttered the skipper.
>   'You English are fools', said the German. 'It does not matter if
> you do not like it. It is the only sensible thing to do. What do two
> children matter anyway? We have wasted time enough.'

This is tolerably authentic German-style English:

> The skipper came uncertainly towards them, with a queer expres-
> sion on his face; and Peter was so filled with horror that he could
> not move. He could not believe that this was really happening. To
> be flung into the sea and left to drown! It could not happen to him –
> not to Peter Rudd! He tried to say something, but could not speak.
> But Ginger shouted:
>   'Come on, mate! We aren't done for yet!'

Peter and Ginger are ten. But an even more dangerous form of
escapism is described in Josephine Elder's *Strangers at the Farm*
(1940), where little Jewish refugees just before the war mistake
school duties for slave labour and try to run back to Germany in
the belief that it will be better. As for the actual fate of children
homeless or lost, few among the Second World War authors seem to
have braved it, although it was necessarily a traditional theme in pre-
war publications. One notable use of it during the war was by 'B.B.',
otherwise D. J. Watkins-Pitchford, who in 1944 followed the success
of *The Little Grey Men* with *Brendon Chase*, in which three brothers
run away from home and live in the forest like Robin Hood, as they

think. The date is presumably before the First World War. Marcus Crouch picked up the uneasiness that it induced when, in *Treasure Seekers and Borrowers*, he noted its 'amoral quality':[26]

> B.B. made the irresponsible life of *Brendon Chase* so appealing that he was forced conscientiously to point out throughout the story that this was a story of the past and that it could not happen again.

In fact, it *was* happening, with fugitive children capable of looking after themselves in the new jungle of Blitz-torn London. But, while Elinor Mordaunt's *Blitz Kids* caught touches of it, no writer penetrated the realities of the real waifs of the war. B.B.'s story, granted its authentic scents and rural freedom, tells the whim of a self-indulgent group of privileged children; their unknown counterparts in far less idyllic surroundings stayed alive as best they could, probably in ways that the fashionable book-publishing houses would not have wished to know. The Victorians had more hard-bitten attitudes, and in popularising the term 'street-Arab' they conveyed all they needed about a nomadic, homeless, urban infant population. If it had apparently died out in the inter-war years, the Blitz brought it back. Norman Dale captured a little of the mind of evacuee administrators who might in themselves prompt flight into oblivion:[27]

> 'I'm sure you love the country now you've got used to it. So much nicer than smoky old London. I think you're really a very lucky little boy.'
> Once again Peter said nothing. He now knew that he did not like Mrs Chater a bit. He didn't see why he was so lucky, and he hated her for talking like that about 'smoky old London', as though it weren't the finest place in the world.
> 'And your father's in the Army, isn't he?' said Mrs Chater.
> 'Yes, lady.'
> 'Isn't that splendid? And what does your mother do?'
> 'She works in a factory.'
> 'Ah! Making munitions?'
> 'No', said Peter. 'Making boots.'
> Mrs Chater was silent.

D. C. Thomson's *Rover* met the challenge with a splendid serial in 1943 featuring half-nomadic children in blitzed London, necessarily not utterly bereft of personal links, as many must have been.

Crompton, Richards and countless other writers of same-character series accommodated the war after it became clear that it was, so to speak, here to stay. But some new writers made efforts to get along without it, only to take it on board in later voyages. Agnes M. R. Dunlop, a native of Ayrshire, wrote her first book for children as Elisabeth Kyle on the theme of English arrivals in Scotland (*Visitors from England*) in 1941, covering some of the same mutual suspicions that Blyton had studied in *The Children of Kidillin*, but unlike Blyton she avoided the war. But its successor, *Vanishing Island* (1942), talked of blackouts and petrol restrictions on the second page, and noted that the school bell was no longer rung for fear that the coastline Scots village folk might take it for an invasion signal; and the English children's mother is driving an ambulance in London (although the story itself is about a long-ago abduction of a child from an island and his rescue after many years' confinement in another one). Virginia Pye started her series about the Price family and their friend Johanna with *Red-Letter Holiday*; but, although published in November 1940, it had no word of war. Yet, by 1943, they were thoroughly and most amusingly warbound. It shows how authority can be transferred from adults to children in wartime as a result of the jobs to be undertaken as servants are called up or depart, and comments favourably on 'one of the very few good things that come out of war, that people of every conceivable kind and age and upbringing are being expected to do things they never dreamed of.' But noblesse continued to oblige (the author was Lady Pye):

Miss Matthews was seventy-two and had had snow-white hair for twelve years, but a life long habit of doing everything for herself and everyone else within sight had caused her to harbour an inward conviction that she had remained about thirty. Noticing the porter looked somewhere around fifteen and was probably still growing she had automatically seized the heaviest case from him.

The protagonists encounter the youthful proletariat on a wartime train:

'Let's breave on all the windows', said Jimmy, 'and I'll show the kids how to draw 'itler. I learnt it off a chap in the Secret Service.'
He puffed hot blasts all over the window and with one grubby finger began his sketch.
'There you are . . . make a round and then a scoop for 'is fancy cow lick. Two blobs, a line and a smudge and you 'ave it to a T.'

It allows for schoolboy suspicions of a military-age schoolmaster being 'a communist agent or a nazi spy'; and in best Richards tradition he proves to be CID, but another master is a saboteur (afterwards 'found head downwards in a boghole'). The class element is interesting, aristocracy as usual ready to make tactical and not unaffectionate alliance with lower-class youth while sneering its head off at the bourgeoisie. Lady Pye was Irish by antecedent, and this was a vigorous literary convention (Lady Gregory, Somerville and Ross, Wilde, Shaw, Synge); she also had the slightly chipped confidence to be expected from the younger sister of a best-selling novelist (Margaret Kennedy, author of *The Constant Nymph*). Gay and Priscilla find Gay's Grannie reading Catherine Sinclair's *Holiday House* (1839) to her evacuees:

> a cheerful giggling little girl of eight called Mary Potter shepherded in two boys of six and a nice solid little party of four called Eunice (pronounced to rhyme with Tunis, which Granny had found difficult to remember at first) who clambered on to Granny's knee and demanded in the deepest huskiest voice that Gay had ever heard, if she could wear Granny's brooch during reading. . . . No one could have guessed that Granny, these days, toiled nearly all day long in the kitchen or vegetable garden. It was all so serene and peaceful. Other people's houses looked so crowded, as if they had blitzed furniture belonging to relations tucked into every corner, and other people's blackout always seemed to depend on drawing pins and stamp paper. . . .

And the fact that she was 'Grannie' on p. 108 and 'Granny' on pp. 110–11 must not lead us too strongly to censure T. S. Eliot and his colleagues in Faber & Faber: don't you know there was a war on? In any case, what Grannie lost in orthography she gained in Greek pronunciation, and however delicious its pretensions it provided one of the most charming vignettes in evacuee literature. But it is otherwise when they encounter proletarian attempts at bourgeoisi-fication:

> There was a knock at the door and in flounced the most horrible looking apparition Gay had ever seen. She bore an armful of clean towels, and was dressed in a mob cap and a long mauve gown with criss cross lacing down the front. She was much made up with plucked eyebrows, had a gimlet eye, a discontented smirk, and dirty finger nails, a quarter of an inch long, enamelled blood red.

She was finished off with high-heeled shoes with a hole for the toe (a very ugly bulging toe in this case) to come through.

'Good evening, Modom, er, Miss', she said in an affected drawl, and smirked at Priscilla who said, 'Good evening', in a very stony voice.

The maid departed and Priscilla giving a haughty sniff, remarked:

'Little does she think I'm going to sleep bare. Let's go down to the lounge or whatever it's called.'

Sleeping in the raw is terribly aristocratic, if a little too strong for most writers (and probably most publishers). The diatribe against the maid may have inspired M. E. Atkinson in her sneers against Rosie in *The Nest of the Scarecrow* a year later. But Pye linked the class conflict in sexual awareness to guest-house augmentation of regulations in wartime:

'Guard your conversation' . . . 'Mind the step' . . . 'Please switch off the light', said the first landing.

'No baths after nine-thirty' . . . 'Use hot water sparingly' . . . 'Meals served in rooms 1s. extra', said the second.

'No dogs allowed' . . . 'Wireless only to be used for news' . . . 'Please sign the register', said the hall.

Their noses led them to the refectory, a low beam-festooned room with a luxuriant crop of warming pans on the walls. Two dank females dressed again in mauve gowns waited on them. Gay, in an attempt to rally Priscilla's flagging spirits, added to the bottom of the menu a note which read 'The management regret that owing to the increased cost of living a charge will be made for the use of the cruet.'

All of these things enhanced a good story, disparate, yet making its own Canterbury pilgrimages through wartime England with work in what it saw, wit in what it heard, warmth in what it told. It was unusually generous to national enemies:[28]

'Fearfully risky job', said Alan. 'I wish spies never got caught.'

'I know', said Susan, 'it makes me sick the different way we honour our own Secret Service people. I don't mean that, because of course they're all equally brave, but it's so dishonest to speak of brave people on the other side as "spies" and talk as if they were sneaking thieves.'

This is rare. Johns has Biggles in considerable self-loathing when a spy's role is thrust on him in *Biggles Flies East* and *Biggles Defies the Swastika*; he shows some bleak sympathy for von Stalhein once he has defeated him in the former, and there is a good-humoured gallantry in the German spy exposed in the last First World War novel, *The Rescue Flight* (published May 1939), but no trace of it is evident in the portraits of Second World War spies. William's spies are the most frightening people he ever meets. One or two of Saville's are attractive, but only in deception. In general, Second World War spies such as in Dorita Fairlie Bruce's *Dimsie Carries On* are so unattractive as to invite reader suspicion long before the heroes are aroused. Blyton faced up to the problem more fair-mindedly than most in *The Castle of Adventure* when the master spy is described:[29]

> 'He's a brave man', said Philip [who has been knocked about and threatened with flogging and shooting by him].
> 'Yes – most spies are brave', said Bill.

But the theme of regimentation continued in Pye after the war, as it did in Johns's *Gimlet Lends a Hand* and various other post-war narratives from authors either Tory or swinging back to Toryism. Pye herself in her *The Prices Return* (1946) seems anxious to declare her Toryism, if in slightly coded form: Mrs Price, irrelevantly to anything else, writes to tell her husband of a letter in the Tory *Spectator* 'he'd be interested to read'. The story is very much about the fate of the Prices as the new poor; and despite, or perhaps because of, Pye's regarding it as 'my favourite', it has a more introverted, smaller world than the community-conscious canvas of *Red-Letter Holiday* or *Half-Term Holiday*. But its elegaic sense gave it the nerve to confront the war-ravaged capital as few other writers for children did:

> During the war, when the Prices thought of their return to London, they always saw it as a grand adventure, beginning with the move itself, which was to be a glorious entry into a new life. Their house in West Kensington had been bombed and many of their possessions lost, and though they minded very much about this at the time, they had come to feel that it was rather nice to make a new start. They didn't talk much about the disaster, and perhaps they didn't often think about it, but sometimes, someone would say: 'When we go back to London. . .' and the company would fall silent, each busy with his or her own thoughts.
> Mrs Price, who had been in London more often than the children

during the war, had the least rosy picture of the future. She had seen how dreary the nice parts of London had become and how the pre-war dreary parts were now desolate and gloomy beyond words. However she did not believe in crossing bridges before she got to them, and thought, therefore, less than anyone about the return and, when she did, she scurried quickly past an unpleasantly clear picture of herself with an enormous shopping basket, in a fish queue.

The children thought the new life would contain all the things they hadn't had before the war.

They are wildly and luxuriantly unrealistic; but Susan, the eldest girl, thinks of a fridge – and, for all their reduced circumstances, her mother is doing so by the end of the book, having to ask her husband 'whether they should try to have a fridge, or put up with rancid butter when the summer came round again'. Some post-war Americanisation was inevitable, even if it was not called that: the 'labour-saving device' had been talked of too freely in British women's ears (although not noticeably in Mrs Price's) for them simply to sigh for re-enactment of life in 1938. And real children often did not even remember 1938. The ageing of London and of Britain after the war was as problematic a theme as the ageing of child characters. Pye, via the Prices, took it on by confronting the housing shortage, first at long distance: 'I rang up your Aunt Price to ask her advice about house hunting. It's all most gloomy, she said there just aren't any houses to hunt.' Mother prospects in London while children see to provisions in Berkshire:

'I wish Tom joy at the food office', said Susan. 'The girl there is the kind who cancels everything in your book and everything on your card, and leaves you nothing but your ration book to eat for a week.'

'Hints for using up ration books', murmured Johanna, dreamily. 'Mash seven pounds of potatoes to a firm pulp, and add page three and four, finely shredded, of ration book J.B.2.'

'Could you be quiet?' said Mrs Price, patiently. 'Johanna and Alan will go to the fish queue, and will stay there until they have procured enough of anything to feed us to-morrow night.'

'That's a tall order', protested Johanna.

'If they sell out before you get your turn, you can try Mr Blocksome for offal and if that fails you must just do a shop-to-shop scrounge.'

Alan Price overhears Maidenhead residents denouncing the whole process ('This place is completely ruined, since the war. People have no manners, and no morals. It's all these evacuees').

> Susan and Alan got the milk on the way to the bus. They failed to persuade the hag at the dairy to allow Alan any milk, until he could produce an emergency card.
>
> 'Here he is', said Susan, 'in the flesh, and here's his identity card, and he's obviously under eighteen, and therefore gets half a pint, and we'll give you the card to-morrow, so can't we have the milk to-day?'
>
> 'Not without you're registered here', said the woman, with the well-known air of satisfaction which some people wear when they feel they have a water-tight case to be disobliging.
>
> 'Good morning', said Susan, flouncing out with the meagre allowance of milk for the family which she hid, with Alan's help, in a shady ditch near the bus stop.

It was possible, of course, that brash gentility from London might not immediately win the hearts of Maidenhead traders by the mixture of *droit de seigneur* and regulation-evasion which Lady Pye described, more particularly if her word 'hag' hovered in the air at such diplomatic exchanges. As an observer, Pye may have been a more accurate witness than her case necessitated. But the milk motif enabled her to explain why the Price children saddled themselves secretly with a goat when the return to London was assured. The goat (which in the event turns out to be pregnant) is obtained from another returnee to London, whose case showed Pye's common touch when not waging class war:

> She had arrived, four years earlier, wheeling an ancient pram on enormous wheels, and in the pram were most of the things that she had been able to save when the front half of her house caught the blast from a bomb a little way up the street. She had been brought up as a girl in the country, and, after sixty-three years in Hackney, seemed undaunted at the prospect of setting up in a very remote spot by herself. Mrs Furbolt looked after her until she was over her recent shock, and the Bell family had set to and tidied up a very ruined cottage, put in some necessary bits of furniture and installed her with some misgivings. Mrs Roost, with sturdy independence, had immediately planted spring cabbage, and knocked the garden into shape, and before long she had several

hens and a beloved goat whom she called Mrs Callagan. Mrs Roost 'popped up' to give Mrs Furbolt a hand twice a week, and the wage and the generous meal she received, together with many little presents, kept her going. Moreover, Mrs Callagan was a good milker and often Mrs Roost was able to sell her milk.

This celebrates the Cockney heart of London, a just object of general veneration since the Battle of Britain. Dickens had begun the veneration with the obvious superiority of Sam Weller to his masters (save in innocence), and it was realistic and generous veneration even if it also condescended. The condescension had become institutionalised in its literary usage (although even before the Blitz Crompton, for one, handled Cockneys with a hard-bitten respect), but the Blitz shamed away some of the condescension. In their hearts, many of the better classes (as they still saw themselves, even when no longer the better-off classes) had believed the Cockneys likely to crumble under the bombing, though they were in fact unmatched for resilience and defiance against Hitler. The celebration of Cockneys, the sudden urge to identify with the Old Kent Road, spread far and wide from the cartoons of Low and the story reportage of Elinor Mordaunt to the media in general. Tug Carrington was Johns's initial reaction: no longer the working-class figure of fun that Briny in *Biggles in the Baltic* had been, but the implacable answer to the Blitz, and, right down to his last appearances in war and peace, the answer also to the toffs who had made it possible for Hitler to have the Blitz. By the time he created Copper, and subordinated him so painfully to Gimlet, Johns was cooling, and the character synthesises the condescension with the veneration. Pye is another version of this, all the more notable for its expression in post-war writing. Mrs Roost is the Cockney heart of London, with the frank implication that her spirit lay at the heart of British survival. But she is ring-fenced. She can be enshrined, and then bundled off stage to leave a goat as comic relic. The ring-fencing enables Pye to harden the rediscovery of her own class sentiments in the post-war disillusion and equalisation surviving without war's justification. More subtle than Evelyn Waugh, it gives hostages to the working-class cult.

The apex of class war surfaces in the dream of Pye's Johanna in hospital after an accident on a hayrick:[30]

Johanna woke from a very long and peculiar dream, in which she was trying to hide from someone with red hair called 'The government'. This man bore a strong resemblance to the great,

long-legged scissor man, and, as she shrank behind the coal
scuttle, he advanced with a menacing prance across an immense
parquet floor.

The National Health Act came into force on 6 November 1946, the
year in which the book was published; its writing was presumably
taking place while Aneurin Bevan, so often denounced as a Red, was
in vehement battle against the more conservative doctors. The
allusion is to Heinrich Hoffmann's *Struwwelpeter* (1845, translated
from German to English, 1848), whose 'great tall tailor' dashes in, on
almost stilt-like legs, to cut off Conrad's thumbs when he sucks them.
Resurgent Tories liked to liken the Attlee government legislation to
Hitler's National Socialist decrees and an anti-Nazi version of
Struwwelpeter had circulated in Britain during the war. One had
to be a sophisticated and deeply read child to get all of Lady Pye's
allusions, but this one might have struck home to a few small Tories
in reinforcement of paternal apoplexy. Yet it is crude in its turn by
comparison to an artist of the quality of Noel Streatfeild. Streatfeild's
war thrillers, the Ruritanian *The House in Cornwall* and the proletarian *The Children of Primrose Lane*, are works of value, but more
within Blyton's grasp than hers. But, with *Party Frock* (1946), she
was back with the rural professional classes from whom she was
herself a refugee. Pye's crabbing could never strike the sympathetic
chords that Streatfeild thrummed effortlessly. Streatfeild's doctor's
children win permission to stage their pageant at the Abbey from its
Colonel, whose reduced circumstances force him to leave it – until
the book's climax saves him – and who lives in style much reduced,
rather like white Southern old families after the Civil War, butler and
housekeeper faithfully staying at their posts like Mammy and Uncle
Peter in Margaret Mitchell's *Gone With the Wind* (1936), a highly
probable influence:[31]

> Mrs Day was thin and tall and looked her best on a horse. She had
> never been taught to do housework, and was not really good at it,
> but she tried very hard. Trying very hard in her case meant doing
> things fast, but not always in the best way, so that she usually had
> at least three burns and four cuts on her hands. She had three
> fingers tied up now; she held them out to John and Phoebe as she
> went to get them some cocoa.
> 'Fat. Tipped it over. Told me to be careful, didn't you, Partridge?
> Never was good at taking advice.' John said he hoped her fingers
> were not painful. Mrs Day had, at one time or another, broken most

of the bones in her body hunting and thought nothing of a few burns. 'Don't hurt at all. Waste of the fat we mind, isn't it, Mawser?'

Partridge and Mrs Mawser had been in service at the Abbey since they were children. . . . Both Partridge and Mrs Mawser had liked it better when Mrs Day kept to what they called her own side of the house. It was not, in their opinion, at all a good idea her sitting at the kitchen table having snacks with them. Even if it made more work they would rather that she let them take the covers off the drawing-room furniture and had sat down in there and done nothing. . . .

'Pack of nonsense', Mrs Day said. 'New world, new ways, never too old to learn.'

Neither Crompton nor Richards was likely to be restrained by the pieties of post-war butler survival. Richards in *Billy Bunter's Christmas Party* (1949) posits a partly bombed stately home where the butler hangs on even when the youthful and impoverished heir sub-lets to Bunter's hotelier uncle; but it turns out that the butler, disguised as a ghost, is scaring the guests away so he can grab the missing hoard of his deceased miser master, while the heir, operating as the local chauffeur, is also still on the scene. Crompton's *Just William's Luck* (1948) includes a chauffeur who is in fact the gangster boss of his nominal employer. The realistic Elisabeth Kyle in *The Seven Sapphires* (1944) has its villainous chauffeur haunting bombed sites in ironic parody of the notion of post-war fidelity, this time in pursuit of treasure originally stolen by himself. Kyle uses youthful Scots discovering what in date should be wartime London, but what eerily seems to be post-war. The chauffeur is now in the merchant navy, but hopes to flee with his ill-gotten gains to Rio de Janeiro, with intent to desert at that point. Britannia was apparently ruling the waves, in the estimation of her crooks, long before Grand Admiral Dönitz laid down his U-boats and surrendered. Presumably the story was set slightly in the future, since its Christmas timing had to be 1944, to accommodate Antwerp's being free from summer onwards (1944) as a landing port for the Allies, and the chauffeur's proposing to sail from there to Rio.

Yet, although bombing in *The Seven Sapphires* is so remote from the story that even the war might be ended, its long-term impact is ruthlessly brought home, as a nine-year-old Scot on arrival in London hears from a coeval:

'I told you. It was a bomb. The blue stones were threaded in a sort of necklace and they were left at the shop the day the bomb fell. Father was to mend the necklace. I saw it lying on the counter myself, just before Aunt Mina took me away to spend the night with her and Uncle Sam. It was the first time London was bombed, and nobody expected the Germans to come that very night, not even the lady who left the necklace. But it was.'

'Ay. I see noo. So the shop was smashed, and your faither was killed, and all the gold and silver and jools –'

'They managed to pick quite a lot of things out of the rubbish next morning, but not the blue stones. Do you know how much they're worth? Two thousand pounds!'

'Losh, Maggie, yon's a fortune! Nae wonder ye're spending your time huntin' for it. But' – here a horrid thought struck Walter – 'if the stones *are* found they'll no be yours onyway, they'll be the wumman's that lost them.'

To his surprise Winkle shook his head. 'No, they won't. The money would be mine. Dad hadn't a very good head for business, that's what Aunt Mina says, anyway. He'd forgotten to renew the insurance on the things in the shop –'

'Whit's insurance?'

'It's money you pay every year or so that if anything gets stolen or lost you get paid for it. When Dad died he'd just about two thousand pounds in the bank to leave to me, and the lawyers belonging to the lady who had the blue stones made the bank pay the money to them, as copen – compensation.'

Eventually, Walter asks:

'Whit wad ye dae wi' the money if ye had it?'

Winkle's eyes grew large and round as they fixed themselves on a bush. 'First I'd have a thorough blow-out. Fish an' chips an' peas in vinegar, and cocoa – mugs and mugs of it, with lots of sugar. And then I'd run away from Aunt Mina and pay someone else to look after me. Someone that's not always casting up how much I cost them –'

'Is your Uncle Sam no' ony better?'

Winkle's eyes contracted suddenly like a cat's. 'He's all right when he hasn't had a drop too much. When he has he beats me.'

'Never!' Walter moved closer along the seat, staring.

'Look here!' Winkle shoved up his sleeve and thrust a skinny arm under the other's nose. There was a long blue mark on it.

Walter looked at it, fascinated. Then he gulped and his face grew red with anger. 'Tell me why ye think the blue stanes are hereabouts and I'll help ye find them!' he cried.

It was a Dickensian fate, but not with Dickensian direction. The boy's deprivation of his middle-class professional inheritance in wealth and hence in society confines him to an ugly lower-class world into which his improvident father's embittered sister has married, and Winkle finds no redeeming Joe Gargery in the uncle in whom sober hypocrisy alternates with drunken brutality. Other proletarian figures in the story share a capacity for temporary benevolence to cloak ugly and rapacious intentions. Kyle could be strongly anti-snobbish, especially in a Scottish context, but the fear of loss of class and what it would entail is much stronger here than in less observant writers – and the Scottish perspective of both author and main protagonist sharpens the stakes. Thus saving Winkle from brutality activates Walter, but the reader of whatever age knows that positive gains will also follow the escape: the happy ending restores the boy to the bourgeoisie. At the same time, the effect of the bombing is remorselessly laid out in its capitalist impact: the sapphires' owner only survived their disappearance by a few hours, and her executors held the estate of the dead jeweller liable utterly regardless of the bomb damage being part of a national emergency. Walter's English host Peter finds Dolphin Alley with the aid of his mother's solicitor friend Mr Marple and digs out some details from the verger of the now desolate St Ermine's Church of the events of 24 August 1940. There is a quick but firm indication of what the bombing of the shop had involved:

'our air warden was Mr Leathers, the stationer over the way. Very prompt 'e was on the spot, blowing 'is whistle like anythink. Worked like a navvy, 'e did, tryin' to save Wimpole's stock arter 'e'd pulled the poor fellow 'imself out o' the ruins. 'E stayed to the last, too, and did his best, I must say.'

The old verger was naturally more upset about the loss of St Ermine's stained glass:

'Late Perpendicular both o' them, and a lovely enamel, so the experts say. Massacre of the Innocents on yonder side o' the porch, and Tree of Jesse on t'other. Facing west both o' them, as you can see, and in summer with the sun setting through them the colours thrown on the floor was like a carpet o' butterflies.'

'They must have been very fine. I suppose they got smashed in the blitz you had here?'

. . . 'One o' them was, but not t'other. I'm sure I did my best to get the authorities to take notice of them, but there, St Ermine's isn't what you might call a show place, and these ' 'ere windows got left to the last. Then they sent some hexperts fit to take the glass out, lead by lead, and put it away in a place of safety. But they'd only managed the Massacre of the Innocents by the night we got our first bombs 'ere. Tree of Jesse was smashed to smithereens.'

In the event, two of the sapphires are recovered from the fragments of the Tree of Jesse, with which they had been accidentally swept up (the other five are caught on the person of the chauffeur before he can take them to Antwerp). The covert symbolism of the Tree of Jesse being destroyed comes into the open at the end of the book when (once again implying the war's end) the surviving window is replaced in the old church:[32]

'Who's yon man wearin' a crown?' Walter demanded. 'And why's he egging on thae fellies wi' the swords in their hands?'

'Don't you remember the story of Herod and the Innocents?' Margot said. 'You know, when King Herod was told that a greater king than himself was born, and he ordered all the Jewish babies to be killed –'

'Like Hitler', Walter said, awed.

We must put away our story-books and do sums, as most children in these islands then termed elementary arithmetic. In abstracting the figures from the *Bookseller* (8 March and 18 October 1945), I limit comparative data to the highest twelve categories from the fifty listed. The 1939 figure is for the twelve months, and acts almost as a normal figure since attrition to the book trade only began to make itself felt by the end of December 1939. The 1945 figure covers only January to September. Digits in brackets show league-table position.

CLASSIFICATION	1939	1940	1941	1942	1943	1944	9 months 1945
Total Book Titles	*14,904*	*11,053*	*7,581*	*7,241*	*6,705*	*6,781*	*4,759*
Fiction	4,222 (1)	3,781 (1)	2,342 (1)	1,559 (1)	1,408 (1)	1,255 (1)	901 (1)
Children's Books	1,303 (3)	973 (2)	520 (3)	595 (3)	671 (2)	785 (2)	452 (2)
Educational	1,350 (2)	658 (3)	340 (6)	384 (5)	312 (6)	374 (5)	269 (5)
Politics & Economics	704 (5)	551 (4)	556 (2)	678 (2)	596 (3)	576 (3)	369 (3)
Religion & Theology	763 (4)	519 (5)	446 (4)	495 (4)	425 (4)	467 (4)	332 (4)
Biography & Memoirs	689 (6)	444 (6)	356 (5)	295 (7)	281 (7)	252 (7)	168 (9)
Poetry & Drama	535 (7)	310 (8)	286 (7)	249 (8)	329 (5)	328 (6)	193 (6)
Medical & Surgical	498 (8)	374 (7)	238 (8)	303 (6)	212 (9)	238 (8)	180 (7)
History	387 (9)	279 (9)	199 (9)	213 (10)	192 (10)	161 (10)	102 (13)
Oriental	337 (10)	144 (12)	76 (18)	60	34	49	23
Travel & Adventure	311 (11)	209 (11)	112 (14)	108 (15)	102 (16)	78	61
Essays & Belles Letters	298 (12)	252 (10)	112 (14)	158 (11)	124 (13)	127 (14)	110 (11)
Naval & Military	59	139 (14)	158 (11)	246 (9)	229 (8)	160 (11)	87 (16)

These data throw fascinating light on the mind of the British Isles in the Second World War. It is difficult to see where Eire figures would have inflated totals beyond the average, apart from 'Educational' where the Eire totals would include Irish-language materials, other than translations, and hence I leave them out of account. But translations themselves produce more figures of importance. Translations accounted for 2 per cent of the British total of published books in 1939, of which children's books numbered seven of the overall 305; 1940 showed five out of 168; 1941 two of 131; 1942 three of 109; 1943 four of 129; 1944 five of 101. 1945's nine months produced six of eighty-nine, two in September alone, out of fourteen. The figures are astoundingly low, and suggest a publishing fraternity in miserable cultural isolation: if it does include Irish Gaelic translation of children's books, the exposure of the wartime British child to the cultures of war-torn Europe must have been almost non-existent. No doubt there was much unease about rights of authors in countries under Nazi rule or supervision; but the figures for 1939 are worse than any save for 1941, the worst year of the war for publication of children's books. The September 1945 improvement was prophetic, especially as Puffin Books began to produce books translated from all across Europe: *Afke's Ten* from the Dutch, *Flaxen Braids* from the Swedish, and so on. But the British child before the war had been starved of the culture from which s/he was about to be cut off. When Jean de Brunhoff, Erich Kästner, Père Castor, H. J. Kaesr and J. H. Johansen have been subtracted, what was left? During the war itself, what provision was made for little refugees from occupied Europe? Lucyna Krzemieniecka's *The Three Little Sisters* was published by Collins in 1942 in translation from the original Polish, originally published in Warsaw by Bluszcz and 'adapted to English by the Polish Library'. It was a pleasant little story about three daughters of a poor seamstress whose headaches prevent her from sewing, from which they rescue her by hard work, generosity and mostly by rescuing a wealthy beauty from enchantment (the only male in the story is an oleaginous nasty baker who refuses the sisters employment). There were engaging turns of phrase from author and/or translator: 'Misery sat in the corner and began to make more mischief'. 'Yes, I was once a rich lady, with great estates, but my heart was cold, even colder than a hangman's.' It was charmingly illustrated, many of the pink-and-black-and-white drawings taking up more than half of the book's fifty-four pages. And it constituted one-third of the totality of translated books for children in its year.[33]

The *Bookseller* showed fluctuation in children's book-reprints over the war years to run at approximately one-quarter of the category's total in 1939, one-third in 1940, one-quarter in 1941, one-seventh in 1942, one-sixth in 1943, one-tenth in 1944 and one-fourteenth in 1945. This testified to the worsening of the paper famine year by year as the war drew nearer its end, corresponding to the unmentioned comics and magazines reduced to appearances fortnightly up to 1948–9. The figures would include reprints of items whose first editions had been noted within the period: thus *William and the Evacuees*, originally published in May 1940, was reprinted in October and November 1940 (possibly covering destruction of stocks in the Blitz), in November 1941, January 1942 and November 1944, the November dates obviously with an eye on the Christmas-present market. It's easy to see, therefore, how classics plentiful in every major bookshop in the 1930s had completely disappeared by September 1945.

But the figures testify to exceptional publishing goodwill towards original books for children, written in English. One-eleventh of the entire British publishing product went to children's books in 1939, and 1940; one-fifteenth in 1941; one-twelfth in 1942; one-tenth in 1943; one-ninth in 1944; one-tenth in 1945. We may note the bad dip in the aftermath of the Blitz, when Politics and Economics (actually classified as 'Politics, Political Economy & Questions of the Day') shot from under one-twentieth of the total British and Irish product (1939 and 1940) to one-fifteenth (1941), and one-eleventh (1942–4): the Question of the Day was clearly the Morrow and its form of government. But Children's Books edged back to second place in 1943–4. Educational publishing, by contrast, collapsed: parents were buying to keep their children quiet, amused and secure for the duration of the war, but training the child mind fell far below the need to absorb it. In 1939, Educational publishing had forty-seven titles more than Children's Books; in 1943 it had much less than half their number. The steady standing of Religious books may surprise a more secular society half a century later; in fact, while its league-table position remained constant, its relative strength rose substantially, moving from one-twentieth (1939 and 1940) through one-sixteenth (1941) to one-fourteenth (1942), where it more or less remained. The preoccupation with God harmonised with the predominance of children's authors who kept God as First Reserve, so to say, not a heavy presence as in Victorian works, but a friend at hand or a visible institution. But the slump in matter of Oriental preoccupation also matches the mood, if not the material, from writers for children. The erosion from tenth place to twelfth to eighteenth and thence from sight, and the falling numbers from 337 to twenty-three, carry the same implication as *Biggles in the Orient*: it may be a war theatre, but, from the fall of Singapore, it has ceased to be a British institution in any reliable sense. British readers would again follow Johns in returning to post-independence India nostalgically: Biggles was given an Indian birth in *Biggles Goes to School* (1951) – rather against the evidence of the first Biggles books – and in his post-war returns made some impressive Indian friends (notably in *Biggles in the Terai*). But this was a very different matter from the beleaguered and subverted Raj – emblematised as the RAF in *Biggles in the Orient*. It is one of the war's finest books for children – 'a marvel of deft plotting', as Professor John Carey has said, and the clue to oriental penetration of occidental defences ('a scrap of pepperminty paper') which Carey so rightly calls 'a brilliant touch', gaining affinities, perhaps literary obligations, in William Golding's *Pincher Martin*. But it left little hope of a post-war future for the British in India; and the lack of British confidence in the orient in Johns's pages was mirrored by the lack of British interest in it at home. Like Biggles, the British readership wanted to win and get out of the orient, culturally – and hence, whether it recognised it or not, politically. But this was not a retreat from reality. Fiction, the spoiled child of the publishing trade, held its own at one-third of the whole trade from 1939 to 1941, but in 1942 and 1943 was well under a quarter, and in 1944 well under a fifth, with little improvement by September 1945. Naturally, the war had produced its rise in Naval and Military books, and Aeronautics followed a little behind (ninth and eleventh respectively for 1942, eighth and twelfth for 1943, both falling from 1944). The Christmas trade of 1945 saw a collapse in war-book sales, although the children were still getting their plenty from Hutchinson's and (on the Westerman front) Blackie's. War-related fiction was given reviewers' attention, where the war fiction was frozen off most review-lists. Kitty Barne's *In the Same Boat* (1945) faced the international consciousness that so many were avoiding, by throwing together two boarding-school girls whose first acquaintance was on a torpedoed liner, and whose nationalities were English and Polish, the Polish girl being no solitary suppliant but the niece of a dashing young Polish paratrooper. Mary Norton's *The Magic Bedknob* notoriously celebrated modern-day witchcraft from a magnificently human and very funny witch, but its origin was evacuee and its social setting an ironic commentary on the sufferings of the over-privileged. Even Johns's offering, *Worrals of the Islands* (1945), was more war-related than action-centred, although the last Second World War Biggles had yet to appear.

But the most obvious post-war effect here was not in content preference so much as in the mixture of rediscovery and new world. Sales were up and stocks were lower; some booksellers thought the public had found new ways of discrimination, others thought they would buy anything. But, with children, the chief impression at Christmas 1945 was that they had become readers – often because of having to give up so many non-reading habits from toys to cigarette-cards – and they would stay readers. Children came back to London with renewed zeal for its bookshops after managing as best they could in the remoteness of evacuation. Miss Christina Foyle, not the most likely member of the 'world's largest bookshop' to engage in day-to-day chit-chat with *hoi polloi*, told the *Bookseller*: 'For the first time in my experience, they are buying second-hand books as presents'. In fact, with the paper shortage, the mass delivery of innumerable works for wartime salvage, and the hold-ups on favourite authors' latest promised for Christmas, it was no wonder. George Newnes, indeed, took out advertising space for a picture of Malcolm Saville and an encomium for his attainments as a package for the information that, while his latest story of David Morton and his twin siblings, *The Gay Dolphin Adventure*, set in Rye, had been *published* in time for Christmas, it might not be in your bookshop until January. It, too, was war-related, being chiefly concerned with the financial difficulties of a widow trying to run a newly acquired hotel slinkily managed by the Dickensian-named Mr Grandon. Another publisher had more success in getting out Saville's less adventure-bound narrative of Londoners doing their best as evacuees in rural surroundings, *Trouble at Townsend*. Top sellers were still Enid Blyton and Arthur Ransome, Cape congratulating themselves on having maintained the latter a priority to keep in print through (or rather despite) thick bureaucrats and thin supplies.

But how far did series by their nature weaken child standards while strengthening addiction? They certainly became far more prevalent, even the comics running series of serials about the same characters where once they were confined to their house detective or the resident school. From the war, the *Adventure* had its succession of football stories about Baldy Hogan, manager of Burhill United (when not unfairly ousted), year after year. The *Champion* had Danny of the Dazzlers, who during the cricket season became Danny the Downshire demon (bowler). True, the *Wizard* had long boasted the super-centenarian Wilson (born 1795), whose extraordinary diet made him the fastest runner in the world; and his saga must at times have seemed as durable as himself in terms of prospective longevity: it seems to have originally been inspired by Kipling, the *Wizard* having started its existence on 23 September 1922 with a jungle story of a lad rescued in infancy from the wolves and known as 'Mowkeela'. Rockfist Rogan, RAF, in the *Champion*, went on non-stop from one world war to the next, and may have been the only war series to continue far beyond V-J Day. But these had been single spies, and the serials-into-sagas now became battalions.

The comics were not likely to shine in subtlety of character-depiction. But Melvyn Bragg rightly recalled them: 'Wilson, Alf Tupper, Limp Along Leslie, Baldy Hogan, Cannonball Kid, Sergeant Braddock – each one clearly defined by a few notes and able to play variations on simple themes for ever and a day, it appeared'.[34] It was the books where decline was evident as the series stretched out to the crack of doom. Conan Doyle, however lethal his intentions for Sherlock Holmes in 1893, has the distinction of having written sixty stories about Holmes and Watson between 1886 and 1927, within which it is possible to trace a consistently deepening love of Holmes for Watson until he weeps on fearing that Watson is dead ('The Three Garridebs', *Strand*, January 1925). But lesser persons followed him, good as many of them were. In many ways, the natural writer of innumerable series was Percy F. Westerman, who did virtually nothing with character. His material was organised like a gigantic soap-opera, in which personnel strayed from one series into another, gritting their jaws and stiffening their upper lips more or less indistinguishably (unlike Johns, whose leads differed greatly from one another). Westerman's *Trapped in the Jungle*, for instance, included five (out of thirty) chapters about Captain Alan Carr of the navy, previously the title-role of five other books; Carr never makes contact with the protagonists of this story, and his connection with its plot is of the flimsiest. But constant Westermaniacs would rejoice, and neophytes would hardly be impeded. Presumably, Westerman readers would have the sense of his entire œuvre constituting a steady succession of reliable protagonists whose names were their only variation. It is unlikely that Blackie interfered much with the personal arrangements of their prize author, leaving him to hurl forth his manuscripts from his houseboat off Portsmouth at the rate of three a year. His annual total stayed there until he turned 80, thereafter dropping to one per year for his remaining four years of life, both author and booklist ending in 1959.

The other great septuagenarian, Richards, had written many more words than Westerman. But, where Westerman saw publication of his 147th book for boys in 1947, the year produced Richards's first. Thanks to the success of Orwell's *Animal Farm* in 1945, 'Boys' Weeklies' was rescued from the obscurity of *Inside the Whale* and the third issue of *Horizon*; and, as its content won nostalgic comment from reviewers of the resultant *Critical Essays* in 1946, a young publisher named Charles Skilton thought that there might be a market for Greyfriars books. There was. He published the second, *Billy Bunter's Banknote*, in 1948 with a run of 11,000 copies, and had to reprint with 12,500 in January 1949. The titles expressed the drawback. Bunter had been Richards's finest creation, as Orwell had seen, but his best work was done as a sort of *chaos ex machina*: a clear story and dramatic plot would work their destiny out among several characters, and for the most part Bunter would intervene, violently distorting the pattern and perturbing the orbits until a very different outcome confronted the several strategists and tacticians. An occasional story might be all about Bunter; but in most cases, even when he was the apparent protagonist, events were worked out through other eyes, usually those of the Famous Five. Similarly, his great original, Falstaff, is a lord of misrule in the *Henry IV* plays, but the central focus is on Henry and namesake son. The post-war books gave Bunter an excess of limelight, partly because Bunter, in most inadequate artistic hands, had been made a strip character in the *Knockout* with little left of the Greyfriars cast. Richards would have repudiated any suggestion of paying any lip service to the abomination, but he did not quarrel with the argument that the book market wanted Bunter centre-stage. And so it proved. Some books did chiefly concern themselves with persons other than Bunter. *Bunter Does His Best*, for instance, was Richards's final confrontation of the ghost of his own familiar friend who had broken off relations with him in the early 1890s: it once more staged Harry Wharton's break with his four friends, which had corroded two bitter series in the *Magnet* in 1924–5 and in 1932. But, where the former series were really grim studies in human mutual destruction, the book's shorter length dictated a more circumscribed break, and Wharton is reconciled to the others by swallowing his pride when told to do so by Marjorie Hazeldene. The books followed the convention of the interwar *Magnets* that Bob Cherry alone was in love with Marjorie, so that Richards made excellent work of showing mutual respect of boy and girl without sexual complications. Bunter's eavesdropping clears Wharton of a charge which had blackened his name, but her advice enables Wharton to win back support from many of those who had broken with him for his obstinacy, ill-temper and arrogance, and to do so before his name is cleared. But inevitably the books became permutations for the scapegrace Bunter, and the canvas was reduced, some of its best characters vanishing. It was the choice of anti-hero celebrated in his individualism in place of the earlier chronicles of community. It might be argued that Crompton's William was another such figure; but there was little common ground, and less after the war, when William conspicuously worked endlessly for British victory, local improvement, support of ill-treated war-deployed personnel, removal of injustices suffered by others, fund-raising for war-related charities, and so on. In the First World War Bunter used the war to serve his own greed and laziness; in the Second World War William seems perpetually if often disastrously at work for anyone but himself. And in social reality Bunter is a lone predator, William is ruler of a communal republic, the Outlaws. Crompton always sought to make William's village bear some resemblance to reality, notably to her own Bromley. Richards's Greyfriars began as a version of public schools which really existed, but as the decades advanced it became more and more a satirical comedy at the expense of the system: after the war, Greyfriars, like Wodehouse's Blandings, was only as real as Peter Pan's Never-neverland. Richards, like Wodehouse, had grown more kindly about what had once been a target for his satire, and he was much better informed about Latin and the howlers that it might spawn. But it no longer claimed any existence either as public-school cult or as its caricature. It certainly celebrated comradeship, courage and comedy, and in that was in the spirit of the wartime fiction for children which Richards began but could not continue.

The *Bunter* series was an important reversal: he was continued in fine prose, happily spewing its appropriately inappropriate classical similes and literary quagmires, where during the war he was limited to bad strip-cartoons. As such, Bunter reversed a degenerate sign of the times. Tabloid comics had fluctuated – the *Wizard*, for instance, had begun with strip-cartoon material as well as print in 1922, but it was the print alone which survived – but in the 1950s print gave way to picture in comic after comic. Nor was there any erosion of quality in the *Adventure, Rover, Wizard* and *Hotspur*: their anonymous scribes were demolished by the now irreversible tabloid march, but they went down with all colours flying. Those colours were never of Richards's ultra-violet, but they did their work well, glorified the working class (in the *Rover*), mocked the pretensions of dubious wealth (in the *Adventure*), celebrated the austere life (in the *Wizard*) and satirised absurd authority (in the *Hotspur*) while also preaching the eternal verities of comradeship, courage and comedy more as standing by your mates and having a good laugh. They too could claim to stretch the imagination: they lacked Johns's mordant hatred of war (coming back to it as they did, and he refused to do, even removing air combat from almost all of the later Biggles stories), but they were quite prepared to introduce benign extra-terrestrials as correctives of Earth's more obvious social evils. They were much less revolutionary in message than during the war but more widely working-class in sympathies (even the public-school 'Red Circle' stories in the *Hotspur* acquiring a working-class hero, Sam Webster). They would never match the finesse which the septuagenarian Richards still brought to his execution. If Richards himself was not the equal of Conan Doyle, he was not prepared to ossify his characters, and he pursued the development of several of them as best he could in his last, near-blind, years. But the market wanted Bunter, and it was Bunter who continued to devour most of his space until his death in 1961.

Series rescued Richards, albeit restricting him. Series imprisoned Johns until he died in harness in 1968. Series as the product as well as the descendant of wartime established Blyton but would later weaken and destroy her, in the judgement of her daughter Imogen. Her readiness to bring the 'Five' and 'Adventure' books to an end showed the shrewd business mind behind them but the market was stronger than the shrewdness – or, as Blyton liked to put it, 'you' insisted on keeping the series going, and, as a good sport as well as a good professional, she insisted she was glad that 'you' had. Her school stories – three for the community-ruled Whyteleafe School of the *Naughtiest Girl* books, six for each of the more conventional variety, St Clare's and Malory Towers – ended their series by being nominally harnessed to the progress of one or two specific children, and their quality remained high, the complexities of character-sketching and social motivation belying the usual complaints of her simplicity. But Blyton's capitulation to mass production meant inevitable lowering of her high standards – and the standards of the wartime stories *The Naughtiest Girl in the School*, *Five Go Adventuring Again*, *The Mystery of the Disappearing Cat*, *Claudine at St Clare's* and *The Island of Adventure* were high. To Marcus Crouch's defensive 'at their most considerable they could not perhaps be called very good', the historian must answer that some could, without 'perhaps'. They were numerous – we may accept his figures of sixty-seven for '1942–5, lean years generally' – and critical notices supported high ranking.[35]

But the change came in 1945, when Kathleen Dowding joined the *Times Literary Supplement* with special responsibility for children's books, rising to assistant editor in 1948 and resigning in 1955. Crouch noted 183 titles for Blyton in 1946–50, followed by sixty-six in 1951 alone; in these six years, the *TLS* noticed five of her books. Its historian Derwent May pays tribute to Dowding's build-up of the children's books supplements 'with many well-known children's writers contributing anonymously'. This made for masked lynch-mob conditions: the less successful would be employed to stifle comment on the more successful. Johns, Crompton and Richards were also boycotted in these years, thus defying the purpose for which the then editor Stanley Morison had hired Dowding: 'Any worth-while book published in the country should be at least mentioned . . . the weekly chronicle of books should be restored, thus affording mention automatically'. Whatever else might be charged against Blyton, she had systematically fought against snobbery, and had sought to foster in her readers both physical and moral courage. It was appropriately ironic that she should now be the victim of snobbery and of cowardice. The *TLS* and fellow-critics ran away from Blyton. If they saw her as their enemy, they left their guard-duty when she appeared. If, as her critics were later to charge, on very inadequate citation, her books were deleterious to child education, then the journals which failed to show how had abandoned all claim for respect. The same was true of their treatment of the other major sellers. The books supplements built by Dowding into what May terms 'an incomparably wide and well-written survey of a genre that was at its peak in Britain in these years' were incomparable above all in what they left undone. May admittedly is a little mixed in his plaudits: elsewhere, his history has Dowding's supplements 'produced mainly, it must be said, at the instigation of the advertising department' – and Blyton, Crompton, Johns and Richards needed no advertisement.[36] But the want of any positive criticism drove them all back upon their citadels, discouraging diversification. Students of Blyton in the 1940s would recognise in the Noddy series, which began in 1949, a reduction of Blyton's own work to extreme simplistics. It still played the great part of teaching children to read, and of offering them affection, involvement and absorption. But by her standards it was a decline, quickly becoming an institutionalised decline. It was the war that had first led her to spread her protective wings so wide, and the sense of mission induced by that service proved inescapable for the future. In that sense, she was not only a war hero but also a war victim.

Some authors struggled against the enslavement by series, Saville by exploring new places with new characters, Brent-Dyer by opening up a historical dimension in her contemporary fiction for children, Crompton by trying out a new character as well as reverting to her career as an adult novelist. Dorita Fairlie Bruce, at the war's end, leaped into the eighteenth century with *A Laverock Lilting*, stressing families and locality (around Largs in south-west Scotland): her best-known heroine, Dimsie, became sidelined by a war plot as an Argyll lochside doctor's wife in *Dimsie Carries On* (much as her occupa-tional precursor Anne of Green Gables also faded out in the First World War story *Rilla of Ingleside*). The Second World War also ended her other two school series, on Toby and on Nancy, although ten years later she returned to school stories for her last three books. Crompton created a smaller boy, 'Jimmy', with a brother the same age as William, but this almost came under the heading of new skins for old wine. The adult novels continued, with sometimes acid social observation now, significantly reflective of the war changes, parti-cularly in *Westover* (1946). Fourteen years later, Crompton was remarking, after the appearance of her last novel for adults to be published: 'there's not much call nowadays for quiet stories about families and village life – that's rather a vanished world' (William, whose appeal happily roared on, was presumably the subject of noisy stories about families and village life).[37] Yet *Westover* had shown how the expected erosion of class-consciousness never arrived.[38]

Derek was a tall fair good-looking young man who had been a pilot in the Air Force during the war and was now working in his father's business.

'It's an odd thing', he said, looking round, 'but, you know, all this peace-time stuff still seems unreal to me. Only the war seems real.'

'It's the opposite with me', said Hubert. 'Even while the war was on, it didn't seem real. It seems like a dream now. I'm not keen on my job, but I was jolly glad to get back to it.'

'I always wanted to go into the old man's business', said Derek, 'but, now I'm in it, it's all as flat as a pancake. This working *against* people gets me down . . . trying to 'do' the next man instead of giving him a helping hand as one did in the war. The old man says you must have competition, and the essence of competition is to knock the next man out, and heaven knows the old man's straight enough. It isn't that there's any funny business about it. It's that – well, when for five years you've been working with people – all pulling together – it sorts of gets you down to have to start working *against* everyone, trying to queer their pitch. All decent chaps, too. . . . Gosh!' he ended, 'I sometimes think I'd give the rest of my life to have one day of the Battle of Britain back. . . .

'My mother says that the real heroines of the war were the housewives', said Derek, 'who went on dusting and scrubbing and waiting in fish queues and cooking up odds and ends of rations every day. She says it would have been much easier to be a commando.'

Sometimes the conservative proves the most faithful guardian of revolution. Streatfeild tried a little of the same thing in her end-of-war adult novel *Saplings*, which the hilarious detective-novelist V. C. Clinton-Baddeley told *Spectator* readers (7 December 1945) 'would do some parents a power of good to read'. He summed it up as

a study of the war-time development of four children, shocked by the death of their father, wronged by the incomprehension and selfishness of their lovely silly mother, an under-bred over-sexed silver-plated female whose only principle in bringing up her children has been to insist that they should find her charming. Miss Streatfeild is here demolishing the charwoman's easy belief that 'at any rate, the children haven't suffered'. The lives of these children were very easily broken by the blast of a bomb they never heard themselves.

Yet, without the bomb, the lover or the brandy, Blyton's *Claudine at St Clare's* could prove as salutary a text for parents. We meet the mother of the Honourable Angela Favorleigh (presumably Lady Favorleigh or Lady something-in-the-peerage, but Blyton never wasted time on surnames):[39]

> The complaining voice of Angela's mother could be heard very often indeed that afternoon. Beautiful as she was, attractive and exquisite her dress and looks, the lovely face was spoilt by an expression of discontent and boredom.
>
> She complained of so many things, and her voice was unfortunately harsh and too loud! She complained of the hard bench that she had to sit on to watch the tennis-matches. She found fault with the cup of tea that Angela brought her. 'What terrible tea! They might at least provide China tea. You know I can't drink Indian tea, Angela.'
>
> She complained of the cake she took. 'Awfully dry', she said. 'I can hardly eat it.'
>
> 'Leave it then', said Angela's father. And to Angela's horror her mother dropped the cake on the ground, where it could be trodden underfoot. The sharp eyes of the other girls noted all these things, and Angela began to feel rather uncomfortable.

Claudine was written when rationing was omnipresent, and when merchant shipping was still endangered. Blyton did a great service in pointing out to children that bad behaviour in scarcity was likely from persons of wealth and social position, much as Crompton had done in satirising the obstructionism of Mrs Bott and the hoarding and illicit buying by the Lanes. As regards Blyton's anti-social consequences, Wendy Cope, an avid Blytonian in her youth, reflected sweetly: 'I don't know if Enid Blyton did me any harm. I keep meaning to re-read some and find out what's wrong with it.'[40]

The size of children's books was a permanent casualty of the Second World War. In the later 1930s, Oxford University Press published its Biggles stories in standard thick paper, with 255–6 pages per title at about a possible 260 words per page, and with striking colour frontispiece by Johns's common-law wife Doris's brother Howard Leigh, usually featuring an aircraft in dramatic flight, as well as six or so black-and-white drawings by different artists of varying quality (usually Alfred Sindall). *Biggles in Borneo* (1943), the last Biggles title with Oxford, reached 185 pages at a possible 350 words per page, with four line-drawings and colour frontispiece, all by Stuart Tresilian (later Blyton's illustrator for *The Island of Adventure* and so on). The jacket was by now very striking, in this case showing Suba, Biggles's Punan ally, leading his friend Kalut and an impressive party of befeathered spear-carriers with a fighter plane (RAF-marked) supportively above their heads. The hard cover bore another illustration on the front, showing plane, ship and palm tree (although in 1941 *Biggles Defies the Swastika* had most helpfully shown a map of Scandinavia, marking Oslo, with an unmarked flying-boat in transit away from it, presumably the Dornier stolen by Biggles, Algy and Ginger to make their exeunt). Oxford's meanness to their authors did not extend to their production, despite maintenance of the officially logotyped war-economy standard. Thickness of paper was shrinking. *Biggles – Secret Agent* (1940) was still 1½″ exclusive of covers; *Biggles in Borneo* was about ⅓″. After the war, the entire corpus of Oxford Biggles titles was produced in identical jackets (showing Biggles in flying kit with a mildly what-do-they-want-now? expression, aircraft in the remote background patiently awaiting him), without frontispiece, still at the wartime five shillings. But Hodder celebrated their new acquisition with attractive colour plates by Leslie Stead as frontispieces in the mid-1940s, and interesting use of single colour across two facing pages amid text as well as occasional line-drawings, selling at six shillings. Content was about 60,000 words in place of the pre-war Oxford 70,000. By the end of the 1960s, Johns's Biggles books were down to over 50,000 words, but the decline was more precipitate in pace, incident and characterisation than in extent: plots often remained engaging, but the aromatic red herrings of earlier years now fizzled out. Similarly, the size of book declined for the surviving comic annuals. *The Rover Book for Boys* for 1934 held 172 pages with twelve stories, selling at half a crown (two shillings and sixpence, £0.125). It rose to three shillings for 1941, then three shillings and sixpence for 1942, and disappeared during 1942 (when comics were forced to go fortnightly), not resuming until 1949, for 1950, at five shillings. Its stories were now down to eight, its colour illustrations (four in 1934) now down to one, its pages 125. In content, it lost about a quarter. The 1950 *Rover* fiction quality was if anything better than the 1934, and its sympathies much more firmly with the underdog and the worker, reflecting the impact of war on its parent journal. The *Hotspur Book for Boys*, also from D. C. Thomson, rose from half a crown (£0.125) for the years 1935–40 to three shillings (£0.15) for 1941, then five shillings (£0.25) for 1943, did not appear until 1948 or 1949 at the same price, and

vanished until 1966 (the *Rover Book* disappearing until its issues
from 1956 to 1969, while the *Wizard Book* made the same progress
from its 1936 issue, made its 1942 offering at three shillings and
sixpence (£0.175), and appeared again in 1949 only, at five shillings). The *Hotspur Book* for 1941 had nine stories and 125 pages at
a possible 700 words per page, and that for 1949 the same contents
total, pagination and wordage, but the width had fallen from 1¼" to
⅓". The *Rover Book* for 1950 was also ⅓" where its 1934 predecessor
had been over 1⅔". The paper scarcity rather than the production
cost was the killer, well beyond the war.

After fighting off the initial attempt at purchase tax in 1940, books
held their prices down impressively, all the more impressive when
one notices the despair with which the July imposition of the tax was
met by writers, such as Streatfeild in her diary for the 23rd:[41]

> Most people think it doesn't go far enough. To me, with a 12% tax
> on books, and a shilling on the ordinary income tax, it went
> paralysingly far. There are moments when I think the struggle is
> too great, and relapse into dreams of the beauty of sudden death
> by bombs.

But purchase tax was dropped under fire from writers, printers,
publishers and booksellers. The comic remained a twopenny for the
1940s. The rise in annuals' prices apparently met with market
resistance: the post-war Richards annuals kept going because they
were seen as a spin-off, not of twopenny comics but of seven-and-
sixpenny books. Various authors had comparable arrangements:
Blyton from 1946 produced a series of twelve *Enid Blyton Holiday
Books*. Brent-Dyer, anxious to divert to *Laura at Wynyards* (1947)
and other non-Chalet works, pleased her Chalet faithful by three
annual-type Chalet books in successive years from 1947. The *Daily
Mail* produced its *Annual*, whose gifted cartoonist Trog (afterwards
a hilarious visual demythologiser (and remythologiser) of politics)
gave wider scope to the activities of his (or their) daily cartoon
character Flook (an animal with a trunk whose end occasionally
went red-hot, who could fly, and whose anchor-man was a boy
named Rufus). Streatfeild and Blyton were among the contributors,
Blyton at one point making the startling political contribution to 'The
Little Girl Who Cried' that she model herself on a little girl 'in a far-
off country' where enemies beat her to make her reveal the whereabouts of her father and brothers:

'Then they burnt down her house, but even when she saw the flames Anna would not give away her father and brothers, nor beg for mercy, nor cry. . . .

'The enemy said that they were sure the little girl did not know where her father and brothers were, or she would certainly have told them, or cried bitterly. . . .'

The end of the war led Derek McCulloch ('Uncle Mac') of the Children's Hour into some spin-off volumes enshrining some of the programmes, chiefly in 1947. Uncle Mac might reasonably have felt that his programmes had fed reading during the war, not undercut it (as television would later do). Crompton's work based on the William stories, with John Clark as William, began reaching 18 million listeners in 1945: 'Just – William!' was both title and opening line for each episode, thus reproducing the title of the first book. It created a myth by which William became generally known as 'Just William' – but it had no origin in the stories, any more than the appropriation of Richards's thirty-year-old title 'the Famous Five' for Harry Wharton and Co. had any existing place in Blyton's saga of Timmy, George and her cousins. The best-known persons known as 'the Just' in children's literature seem to be the reformed traitor Edmund (allegory for the human race) in C. S. Lewis's Narnia stories, and Louis XIII in Dumas's The Three Musketeers (where the term is denounced as rank hypocrisy on the part of its user). Neither has much in common with William, who would have given both Richelieu and the White Witch of Narnia very short shrift. The William series (five in all) went on until 1952. Violet Elizabeth Bott was played by Anthea Askey, daughter of 'Big-Hearted Arthur' Askey, with whom she enlivened the strip-cartoon pages of Radio Fun (where they roamed the world, going broke in post-war Japan, finding vampires in Franco's Spain and so on). This may have cast against type – though either as herself or as Violet Elizabeth she could bewitch her way through any crisis – but even more startling was the voice of Charles Hawtrey for the odious Hubert Lane, familiar as it must have been as that of Children's Hour boy detective Norman Bones. Norman and his cousin Henry detected over 130 problems and won the hearts of the infant British public from their first articulation on air on 17 July 1943 (Henry being played by Patricia Hayes). The 29-year-old Hawtrey at that point was a veteran schoolboy survivor of the Will Hay films, whose best literary realisation was by Richards, writing under his own name, Charles Hamilton, Will Hay at Bend-over and The Barring-Out at Bendover (both 1938). But Hawtrey could assert an innocent profundity – and here he did, beginning with 'Mystery at Ditchmoor', set in August 1940 three years before transmission, when Norman Bones becomes suspicious of a painting supposedly by an artist who has left it to be called for, but showing a church's flagpole whose original had blown down many months before, proving that the picture was not the work of a few days before as the alleged artist had claimed, but an old painting, shop-bought, and in fact a repository for the plans of Britain's most secret aeroplane concealed at the back of the picture-frame. The original story was, like all its successors, the work of a preparatory school-master, Anthony C. Wilson, who had begun his first in answer to a demand from his charges for a story.

It is possible – indeed probable – that the name derived from the *Spectator*'s elegantly breezy detective-story critic Norman Blood (who was in fact Rupert Hart-Davis, now serving in the Guards). Blood leads to Bones. But the Bones convention was one according with the Blytons, the Cromptons and the Johnses (viewed during the hegemony of Ginger, Cub and recent-head-girl Worrals): that children would take command where adults failed. It was an excellent protection for years in which the world was falling to pieces and children had to take control of themselves, of their diplomatic relations, of their family survival, of their infant juniors and geriatric seniors, and of their future. Blyton's *Daily Mail Annual* story of Anna expressed awareness of the need for exemplars: that was what she and her colleagues were doing in print, and what Norman Bones and his cousin Henry did more insidiously on the radio, communicating through the use of one sense and thus intensifying concentration. Nor were any of these children super-children (if we except the animal attraction of Jimmy Brown in Galliano's circus and Philip Mannering in *The Island of Adventure*). The greatest of them, William, is notoriously wrong more often than not and triumphant, when he does triumph, by luck rather than judgement. Wilson similarly wrote of his heroes Norman and Henry. Other detectives sailed the airwaves, such as Johnny Britten, the messenger and boy detective in Harry Alan Towers's 'Boy Wanted' in 1942. Barbara Sleigh adapted Saville's *Mystery at Witchend* in tandem with its proof stages at the publisher, Newnes, in 1943. The father of British child detective fiction, at least from translation in 1931, was Erich Kästner's *Emil and the Detectives*, banned and burnt by the Nazis in its author's Germany; Hedley Goodall adapted it for BBC Children's Hour in 1941. It was a particularly fine case of child evangelicalism in time of war, because it captures two child-types all too relevant to the children of Second World War Britain, the victim as well as the saviours. Emil is robbed, bewildered and humiliated, and then is unexpectedly befriended by other children who take the lead in rescuing him.

And the wartime child needed its unexpected child-protectors and allies, as all around were signs that Justice was brutally rationed like everything else. Brent-Dyer's local authorities, whether Nazi or Tory, talk their prevailing clichés of courage and purity, or whatever may be the word of the day, in bullying tones of hollow men. Even the norms of security in the series disintegrate under wartime pressure: Mrs Bott, formerly a good-natured if snobbish figure of fun, tries to have William jailed; von Stalhein, in peacetime trying to avoid killing Biggles, in the Second World War sets an assassin's price for his head; the headmistress of the Chalet School is hospitalised and her successor is a tyrannical careerist; and after 18 May 1940 there is no *Magnet*. Graham Greene, who would write of 'the Lost Childhood', found enough evidence himself of what was happening to the authors whom children read once the Second World War had begun. It was he who would salute the first Worrals, while noticing that this latest heroine killed her country's enemies. It was he who, in reviewing John Buchan's last novel, *Sick Heart River* (1940), recalled the first appearance of its dying hero Edward Leithen running 'like a thief in a London thoroughfare on a June afternoon' in *The Power House* (1913), whence Greene quoted: 'Now I saw how thin is the protection of civilization', which, in 1940, 'certainly we can all see now'. And the world of the United Kingdom in the Second World War must often have seemed to its child readers 'a small cramped place'.[42]

In some ways, the Second World War may not have been cramped enough. A Scottish, Welsh or Irish child might quite well imagine their William with their own accent, until they heard wireless or cinema get at him. But it was possible for local radio to unite as well as divide society. English wireless depended on the BBC accent, whose superior tones intimidated those who lacked them. Scottish wireless privileged the Scottish voice. (Welsh wireless needed linguistic proficiency in the language, and Irish wireless persecuted anyone deemed to employ the King's English accents, save for buffoonish purposes.) Hence Lavinia Derwent's *Tammy Troot* (1945) might seem in writing merely substitution of the Kailyard by the Kailburn, but it legitimated the speech of its child listeners. It retained enough of the ancestral Scots to intimidate the stranger, thus comforting the user (where Mummerset, derisively comprehensible, merely condescended to rural England). It even allowed its anthropomorphic hero to take cognisance of international conditions:[43]

> just then a gleam of light flashed down on the water and seemed to turn the little fish into silver.
>
> 'Oh, mexty me! I'm caught in a searchlight', cried Tam in alarm.
>
> 'Naethin' o' the sort. It's only a moonbeam', scoffed Rab [the Water-Rat].

What elevated Tammy rather above the excessively human herd of beasts for bairns was his Granny, whose symbolism as repository of folklore is expressed by her prowess in mimicry. 'She even imitated Froggy doing his song and Rab Rat reciting "A Rat's a Rat for a' That".' Froggy's opening song at the concert had been 'A Frog who would a Wooin' Go', presumably apposite for the Scots traditions of coronach and keening, in view of its tragic outcome. It would have been open-ended which child spotted that (though the broadcast may have included the text in whole or part; and at least Willie Joss, the reader, should have sung the first line). But all young listeners in Scotland were evidently expected to know the allusion to Rabbie Burns's 'A Man's a Man for A' That' so well and so affectionately that they would relish the parody and the poet's transmigration into a friendly water-rat (they would also be expected to know his 'To a Mouse'). In creating Rab Rat, Derwent managed the Burns motif with the allusiveness which warms by its recognition rather than freezes by its condescension, and its obvious derivation from the poetic Water-Rat in Kenneth Grahame's The Wind in the Willows was strengthened by Tammy Troot's creation in 1942, with Gordon Crier's wireless adaptation of Grahame's masterpiece heard on Boxing Day 1941 in tandem with Crier's version of Grahame's fellow-Scot J. M. Barrie's Peter Pan.

For a people who supposedly did not celebrate Christmas, the Scots did themselves well in their offerings for the entertainment of the natives under their cultural colonisation. Even Uncle Mac, one suspects, passed for Scottish in most English child minds, although his loyalties were Cornish when not Sussex. It seemed that Scots national unity strengthened as English class-division hardened after the war, although politically the Labour Party in power defected for the first time from its promise of devolution. (When devolution did arrive, in 1999, Scottish broadcasting was excepted from it, and subsequently declined after an excellent half-century.) The BBC

liked working with Scottish locations for children's stories and
plays; and, as Blyton during the war and Johns after it could
demonstrate, Scotland united the known and the mysterious. Blyton
and Kyle showed that initial antagonism was a good way to start the
story rolling, or alternatively such a figure as Blyton's Andy made for
a more interesting friendship as a contrast in age, authority, education, language and nationality. (He also legitimised more rational
forms of dress.) The BBC status of Scotland offset a sense of Scots as
second-class citizens, and the wartime dependence on regions had
played into the hands of ethnic zealots wanting to raise Scots and
Welsh profiles. The same was true of Northern Ireland, depending on
how Irish or Ulster it wished to assert itself: it made for a three-tier
culture, British, Ulster Protestant, Ulster Catholic, common ground
possible among any two but seldom all three. Ursula Eason produced
Patricia Lynch's *The King of the Tinkers* in 1940; but Northern
Ireland officials would not have looked too kindly on her work after
the wartime publication of her *Fiddler's Quest* punctuated by the
hazardous comings and goings of its heroic IRA outlaw, however
vaguely set some ten to twenty years previously. Scottish patriotic
sentiment was so much safer, when kept in the comfortable bounds
of Elisabeth Kyle's *Behind the Waterfall*, adapted and broadcast in
1944, or Kathleen Fidler's radio play of the same period, *Fingal's
Ghost*. Fidler was Leicestershire-born in 1899, Lancashire-educated,
and at college in North Wales; but as a former headmistress, she was
a scriptwriter on the Authors' Panel for Schools Broadcasting in
Scotland. Her first stories of the Brydons, celebrating horticulture in
wartime Britain, were broadcasts about English children made into
books; *Fingal's Ghost* was her first Scottish foray, once more the
Blyton–Kyle formula of English children ill-at-ease with a strange
Scotland which Fidler exacerbated by putting them among Gaelic-
speakers in Tobermory at the north end of the Isle of Mull (familiar
ground to devotees of *Kidnapped*, where the shipwrecked David
Balfour had made his miserable progress). It preached diplomacy:

> 'And who might your uncle be, now, who was meeting you?' asked
> the porter.
>   'Gosh! What impudence!' muttered Jane. . . .
>   'Ssh!' Frank cautioned her. 'Everyone knows everyone in these
> islands. He may be able to help us.'

The uncle is the local minister, which makes the doctor's boat-rowing
son an appropriate companion and upmarket shade of Blyton's Andy,

with whom to become suspicious of a boatman (Peter McQueen) and his mysterious visitor client (Bain), who duly prove German spies:

> 'if we surrendered, what would our chances be! They daren't let us go back to Ulva to tell the tale. That submarine would be doomed at once, if we ever got home again.'
>
> 'Jane's right', agreed Frank. 'The Germans would either have to bump us off or take us for a trip to Germany in that submarine, and I don't relish either prospect.'

Nature naturally aids them:

> 'Frank! Jane! Do you realise what this means? Only one man at a time can come through that hole, and he's got to come feet first! And we'd be waiting for him with a few hefty stones. What a place for a last stand!'

The Nazis prove nasty: 'Floodlight the whole place and fix your machine gun to let them have it if they throw a single stone'. And even worse:

> Bain took a look along the cleft till he came to the narrow bend in it. Then he gave a sinister laugh.
>
> 'If we can't get 'em out, there's something else we can do.'
>
> 'What's that, sir?'
>
> 'Keep 'em in, *for good*! You, Heinrich, get back to the boat and fetch that charge of high explosive and a fuse. It won't take much to bring down a fall of rock here. Once they're behind that, they'll never be found.'
>
> Even McQueen was appalled at the thought of such a horrible deed.
>
> 'But that's awful, sir. Ye couldna' do that to a bit lassie like Miss Jane.'
>
> 'Couldn't I?' sneered Bain.

But they get away, and prove that modern children are ghostproof:

> 'And how did you find out all this?' demanded Doctor Mackinnon.
>
> 'We watched Peter McQueen come with his boat to the cave. He was painted up with phosphorescent paint to look like a ghost ship with Fingal in it. We knew at once there was something fishy.'

And the minister's housekeeper duly unleashes the Kailyard's awful vengeance on the miscreant:[44]

Elspeth stood up with dignity and advanced with a threatening mien towards Peter McQueen, who backed a step or two till he was gripped by the strong hands of the bluejackets.

'It is just this, Peter McQueen. If anything had happened to my little lassie, I wouldna' hae rested, neither here nor in my grave, till I'd brocht punishment on ye. Traitor and coward that ye are, ye're no' fit tae be called a man, when ye mak' war on helpless bairns. 'Tis no Scotsman ye are, tae dae the like, nay, nor no decent Englishman either! 'Tis mair like the German devils ye herd wi'. And it gies me the greatest pleasure tae pluck at your glaring red beard and ca' ye a German!'

With that Elspeth tweaked at McQueen's red beard. McQueen put up his hands to his face, but Elspeth tweaked again. Suddenly the beard came away in her hand! Startled she fell back and McQueen clapped his hand to his rough black chin.

'Good heavens! Hans Danckner!' cried the Commander. 'The man the Navy have been hunting for in every port!'

'Do you mean a German?' asked Elspeth sharply.

'He is, madam. And a dangerous one, for he has lived many years in this country as a spy.'

'Then, thank Heaven, he's a German. I was richt! It went tae ma soul tae think yon image o' a man was a Scotsman! I micht hae known he was ower vile!' declared Elspeth with triumph.

'Lurking in Ulva and ca'ing himself an Islander. The shame o' it!'

If it worked at all on the wireless, it would have worked well. It would have fallen flat, or it would have been heroic. Text – all the more as novelised script – cannot tell us. Fidler has been supplying the now familiar device of children saving the state but an elderly, Oban-reared, Ulva-domiciled, secluded old spinster, Scots Doric rather than Gaelic in speech symbolised intransigence and resistance to the ultimate degree and at the ultimate point of the UK. It is of course intended to be comic anti-climax, to ease us down from the mortal peril of the children, frightening enough on BBC drama, no doubt. The Nazis had to be more menacing than in Blyton, Saville, Johns or Crompton to make an impact: like Shakespeare's Macbeth, if more passively, British children by 1944 had 'supp'd full with horrors'. The lesson from Richards and from the D. C. Thomson comics must also be applied: evil must be ridiculed as well as defied. The irony of the need to cater to expectation of fear in the era of the V2 brings us a little closer to understanding the role of reading in child survival. The pursuit of laughter in children's reading was a natural means to counter fear; but the pursuit of fear in it must have acted as inoculation. The best work – in which so many of the children's writers shared – mixed both. Are you hungry? Hitler is hungrier – see the *Beano*. Moreover, your hunger may be frightening but his hunger is funny, although you must feel the need to be brave about being hungry – or at least bereft of things you want, like sweets – to be able to laugh about how hungry Hitler is. From the beginning of the war, bombing-raids were easier to face because of Bunter's inability to face them (*Magnet*, 4 May 1940):[45]

> 'Buck up, Bunter!'
>   'Beast!' howled Bunter. 'Help me on with these trousers! Find my gas-mask! Don't knock that cake off the table, you ass! I want to take that cake with me. Can't you see my shoes? Where are my socks? I think you might find a fellow's socks for him, after all I've done for you! You want me to be bombed and gassed, and blown to bits – that's what you want, you beast! Wow! If you kick me again, you beast, I'll – yarooooooooop!'
>   Billy Bunter, half dressed, with one sock on, and another in a fat hand, rolled out into the gallery, with the help of Harry Wharton's foot.

Streatfeild made sure that spycatching was funny too:[46]

> 'Who wrapped him in that rug?', asked Mr Elm.
>   Freda flushed.
>   'Sally and I.'
>   Mr Oak's voice was full of admiration.
>   'Wrap him in a rug and sit on him. As sensible a way to catch a spy as I've seen.'

Children knew the value of the commonplace as reassurance, as Enid Blyton acknowledged in giving the week's prize for verse in *Sunny Stories*, 31 May 1940, to June Burton (age 6) of Woodlawn Road, Sherwood Hall Estate, Mansfield, Notts:

> I like balloons to hold in my hand,
>   But when they go pop
>   I don't like it at all.
>
> To rise in the air must be ever so grand,
>   Like those barrage balloons
>   Watching over our land.

Burton is the youngest writer quoted by me in this book, and in saluting her – the word 'watching' shows fine artistry and observation – we may see how once again Blyton diversified her forms of reassurance to wartime children, fighting fear by encouraging creativity. Blyton herself showed how to meet fear with laughter and courage most effectively through Kiki the parrot:[47]

> The water rose to their waists and then more rapidly to their shoulders.
> 'God Save the King!' said Kiki, in a horrified tone, looking down from Jack's shoulder at the restless black water below her.

Johns had always mixed humour with his most dangerous moments (I beg his pardon, perilous passages) when he could, as when Algy, pursued by the head of the Italian secret police in Monaco as he searches for a possibly dead Biggles, seeks information from François, who misleads him to protect his own former employer, who is in fact Algy's fellow-agent Bertie:[48]

> 'I am a stranger in these parts', he explained. 'Tell me, does the word Castillon mean anything to you?'
> The man considered the matter. 'It may – and it may not', he replied.
> Algy perceived that he was not likely to learn much from this churlish fellow. He had one last try.
> 'Is it a place – a village perhaps?'
> 'It was', replied the man. 'Are you thinking of going there?'
> 'Yes.'
> The man laughed. 'The cats will be pleased to see you', he observed.
> 'Cats?' Algy began to think he was dealing with a madman. 'Is this a village of cats?' he queried.
> The man nodded. He seemed to be enjoying a private joke. 'That's right – a village of cats. The cats eat the birds. You will be able to eat the cats.'

Further particulars are to be found in the chapter which resumes Algy's adventures in Biggles 'Fails to Return': 'XI. The Cats of Castillon'. And William, at perhaps the moment of his greatest wartime challenge when he follows two spies into hiding, alerted because of his fears of them, is able to save the situation unwittingly when the policeman whom he manages to get in cannot spell and has to use a rubber, which proves to be the cache for which the spies had been searching and whose discovery will convict them:[49]

> William suddenly remembered his newly acquired rubber and brought it out proudly, wiping the crumbs from it.
>
> 'Here's a rubber', he said.
>
> The policeman took it, rubbed the offendings, then scowled suspiciously at William.
>
> 'None of your tricks!' he said. 'This ain't no rubber. It don't rub, anyway.'
>
> 'I thought it was', said William apologetically. 'I found it in a tea-cake.'
>
> Then, for the first time, he noticed Miss Smith and the soldier. Their eyes were fixed in frozen horror on the rubber. Their faces had turned a greenish white.

Fear, courage, laughter – and beyond it (seldom daring to express itself anywhere near mawkishness) love of friends, community, country. The famous stiff upper lip, the terror of the British child at soppiness, the lesson taught as early as Kipling's *Stalky & Co.* that the most heartfelt sentiments must not be prostituted – instinctively the mass of British writers for children in the Second World War followed their dictates.

Tom Harrisson, in his Mass-Observation-derived *Living Through the Blitz*, reported children as less affected than adults by what they went through:

> Evacuation, country life and general war dislocation certainly played a larger part than any blitz, where the young were con-cerned. Of those who stayed put with their parents, a few were continually nervous and a few constantly exhilarated. The greater part adjusted as well as their parents or mildly 'better'. At no stage did they present a special problem as compared, for example, with old ladies or stray pets.

(The last sentence is self-deceiving. Orphaned, lost or nomadic children did not 'present' a problem when they went into hiding and joined small gangs. They lived how they could and, from the little we know of them, seem to have ducked official attention, which in any case had enough to deal with. Many were no doubt ultimately wiped out in bomb raids or were sent into evacuation when picked up, without much time or inclination from those who found them to sort out previous history.)[50]

This very broad conclusion was confirmed by the psychologist P. E. Vernon in a post-blitz review of data from all sources where he concluded: 'All observers seem to agree that raids have even less effect upon children than adults.' The chief psychiatrist of Guy's Hospital in South London could not find a single case of 'acute emotional reactions among children' bombed. A Surrey Child Guidance Clinic recorded two cases of 'siren-fright' where the children had not been subject to bombing.

And his footnote cites Celia Fremlin's 'independent analysis' of London blitz evidence finding only 'a tiny majority' of children affected by bombing, children in general showing 'a *tremendous* capacity for adaptation'. We may accept this, while noting that wartime conditions were not precisely conducive to pursuit of child mental problems. But, if we do accept it, it is not enough simply to do so and leave it. The historian must pursue causes of the traumas that did not happen – what Sherlock Holmes might analogise to the dog that did nothing in the night-time when the horse was stolen ('Silver Blaze'). We can say firmly that the despised and butchered comics, the *Girls' Crystal*, the *Rover*, *Adventure*, *Wizard*, *Hotspur*, *Champion*, the *Beano*, the *Dandy*, *Radio Fun*, even the *Knockout* stood friends to the bereft and frightened children. The *Magnet* and others which would perish in May 1940 helped them through the first evacuations. The children's surroundings, even the bombed sites on which so many played, presented them with phenomena likely to traumatise; yet the world of the imagination, consumed by the readers, retailed to their associates, gave them the means of survival.

In their various ways, the writers and books discussed in this history will have played parts, the most fecund probably the most valuable: Westerman, Brent-Dyer, Johns, Saville, Crompton; and above all the children must have owed so much of their solace to the towering shoulders of Enid Blyton. It would also seem that, against the destructive element of child life in wartime, namely lynch-mob persecution of other children for supposedly patriotic reasons, Blyton was probably the most effective writer. Irish or Irish-named children may have been endangered by understandable popular fury over the IRA Coventry explosion of 1939 and other attempts; Blyton gave her heroines of the St Clare's school stories an Irish surname, and, after the series had taken off, the second was probably her only title of her 600 to bear the surname of a child character, *The O'Sullivan Twins* (1942). Italian-born or Italian-surnamed children were hounded once Mussolini had entered the war in June 1940, and

Blyton's *Circus Days Again* (1942) closed on the stage-Italian Galliano apotheosised by the grateful circus-folk whom he has saved from disintegration, and in some cases family disruption and contract slavery. She even took account of the possibility of ganging up against children with German Christian names, popular since the early Georges and Victoria's Albert and liable to persist as parental duplication. The Alberts could and did flourish without thought of their Teutonic provenance, but it was less easy for Adolphs (for all of Queen Victoria's uncle Cambridge, whose son she made her commander-in-chief). On Empire Day (24 May) 1940, undoubtedly the most terrible in the Day's history, *Sunny Stories* opened with Blyton's 'The Boy who Changed his Name':

> There was once a boy whose name was Adolph Jones. Poor Adolph! It was most unlucky, as you can guess, that he had that name, because all the children teased him about it and made him very unhappy.
>
> 'You can't be English if you're called Adolph', said George. 'We don't want to play with you.'
>
> 'Don't be so mean', said Adolph fiercely. 'I can't help my name, can I? My father was called Adolph, and so was my grandfather and my great-grandfather. It just happens to be a name in our family, like the name George is in *your* family.'
>
> But it didn't matter what Adolph said. The others teased him about his unfortunate name, and pretended he was an enemy.
>
> It was horrid! It was very unkind too, because Adoph was a jolly boy, and loved being friendly.

The other children tie Adolph to a tree:

> 'Adolph the enemy! Adolph the enemy!' sang the children, as they ran off to paddle in the river. They were not really as unkind as they seemed, for if just one of them had said 'I say! It's hard luck on old Adolph to treat him like this!' they would all have been very sorry, and would have set poor Adolph free. But nobody said it, and so they went on being unkind without thinking about it at all.
>
> Adolph was left behind, tied to the tree. He was very angry and very unhappy. He thought he would ask his mother to move somewhere else. He thought he would run right away and be a boy on a ship and change his name to Kenneth or George or Harry. He thought lots of fierce, miserable thoughts as he struggled to free himself.

Ultimately, he gets free and sees his persecutors drowning:

> Adolph saw what was happening, and his heart beat fast. He was glad!
>
> 'Serve them right!' he said. 'Serve them right! They said they were my enemies, and now they are being punished. I'm glad!'
>
> But he wasn't really glad. He was frightened for Jane, George, and Harry. He started to run towards the river.
>
> 'They're not my enemies!' he thought. 'If I leave them to drown, I would be a real proper Adolph. I'd be behaving like a wicked enemy. But I'm British! And I'll jolly well show them I'm British too!'

To be British meant to forgive your enemies (at least, for the moment, the British ones). It was in its humble way what Tolkien in those days was bringing into being as the turning-point of *The Lord of the Rings*. But the initial reaction ably reduced to child language what the Adolph in all her readers' minds was saying at that very moment as his armies swept to victory in the Netherlands, in Belgium and in France. Before *Sunny Stories* had its next number (still weekly), Belgium had capitulated, and the British were beginning the evacuation of Dunkirk. Blyton was taking the opportunity to get her name on any Nazi hit-list should Britain fall in the wake of France: the real proper Adolph, the wicked enemy, would have ways of making her silent, and she knew it. Her little Adolph managed his Dunkirk before the real thing began, throwing the rope that had bound him to his persecutors clinging to a log, and drawing them to shore with skilful directions. Blyton knew that the next stage of war would be naval:

> '*We* behaved like the enemy, not you, Adolph', said Harry. 'I see that now. You behaved more like a Britisher than any of us. Let's change your name for you, shall we?'
>
> 'Well, I wanted to, but you wouldn't let me', said Adolph, suddenly feeling very happy.
>
> 'Let's call him a great name', shouted John, 'Let's call him Nelson. He was a great Britisher. I've seen his statue in London, higher than anyone else's. Let's call him Nelson!'
>
> So they changed Adolph's name to Nelson, and wasn't he proud! He ran home with them, laughing and talking, friends with them all, as pleased as could be.
>
> 'Good-bye, Nelson!' they shouted. 'See you this afternoon, Nelson! Mind you come and play early, Nelson! Good old Nelson!'

That was the end of Adolph Jones, and the beginning of Nelson Jones. And what I would like to know is – if you had been the Adolph of this story, would you have ended up as Nelson too? I'm quite sure you would!

The last exhortation was a characteristic coda for *Sunny Stories* but seldom delivered with the same confidence as to audience behaviour (not that she denounced her readers). But it also reminded the reader that it was all too easy to end up as the target of a lynch-mob, and that today's bully (and she preached incessantly against bullies) could be tomorrow's victim. And it was a subtle hint to take heart from invocation of Nelson in the weeks ahead.

If any of Blyton's future critics had performed a tithe of her services to the children of Britain in their time of greatest need, they would have deserved medals. There were, of course, exemplars without end, and one wonders whether George Orwell's boy hero, invented by Winston Smith for propaganda purposes, had anything to do with the edifying stories of boy heroes of the war somewhat breathlessly written up in works like James W. Kenyon's *The Boy's Book of Modern Heroes* (1942). Professor Bernard Crick points out that Smith's manufactured cult figure was Comrade Ogilvy, and that the Director-General of the BBC in Orwell's time there had been Sir Frederick Ogilvie, whose knighthood in 1942 might be recalled in Smith's debating 'with himself whether to award Comrade Ogilvy the Order of Conspicuous Merit'.[51] If Orwell thought that some of the BBC or related wartime propaganda used bogus cases, or that real ones were given obsessional dedication to the war effort beyond conceivable reality, he may have had some basis. But there were quite enough child deaths in the cause of war without anyone's invention, many of them from age-deceptive volunteers. And the writers of formal fiction knew the merit of winning their readers by mutual grins. William shows phenomenal courage, objectively, in proposing to remove the bomb from outside Joan's door and put it outside Hubert Lane's; but Crompton makes it clear he is convinced that a saucepan on his head and a tin tray to use as a shield 'if it starts explodin'' are all he needs to immunise himself from its effects. It is useful evidence on the unreality of bomb danger in the minds of children in places suffering only one raid or none. It also suggests that child heroes might be heroic from sheer ignorance – again a useful corrective to propaganda. Crompton was more trustworthy than the Ministry of Information, as instinctively her readers may have suspected. Johns, catching the spirit of virtual surprise among

Second World War air pilots at their own popular status, uses his perpetual-boy pilot Ginger to comparable effect, for instance in *Biggles in the Orient*. Missing after a very ugly dogfight preventing a monster Japanese air raid on Calcutta, Ginger naturally leaves Biggles in anxiety (not particularly alleviated by the Air Commodore's 'Oh, dear! Isn't he back?'). When he does return, his explanation is admirably anti-heroic:[52]

'I blotted my copy book', he confessed. 'I got a brace of bombers and went out for the hat trick. One of my little ambitions has always been to get three birds with one stone, so to speak. Unfortunately I hadn't much ammo left, so to make sure I went in close.' Ginger smiled lugubriously. 'I went too close. I thought the rear gunner was looking the other way, but he couldn't have been. As soon as I opened up he handed me a squirt that nearly knocked my engine off its bearers. I had to bale out.'

'Did you get *him?*' demanded Ferocity.

Ginger shook his head sadly. 'That's the irritating part of it. I don't know. I couldn't hang around long enough to see.'

There was a titter of mirth.

'I got down all right – in the middle of a thousand-acre paddy-field. The rice was growing in mud. I never want to see rice again. That's all. . . .'

Comparison with actual reminiscences from British Second World War pilots indicates that this tone was authentic enough, and what children heard of air combat from its survivors was likely to be in the same strain. There is no reason to think that children of sixty years ago were any more appreciative of being patronised than they are today, even if they were less explicit to their seniors about it.

The Carnegie Medal for the most outstanding contribution to children's literature has been handled a little roughly in these pages, not for the awards it made – Linklater's *Wind on the Moon* for 1944 with its mingling of fun, fantasy and fear was a perfect choice – but for those it shirked. Its own conduct from the very first award, Arthur Ransome's *Pigeon Post* (1936) to salute his series to date, all the way to that for 1947, Walter de la Mare's *Collected Stories for Children*, all published before the war, invited as a consistent choice the twenty-five William books from Richmal Crompton honoured in *William and the Brains Trust* (1945, second year of no award). But Crompton, like Blyton, was too popular. One is reminded of the schoolteacher in Harper Lee's *To Kill a Mockingbird* (1960) who objected to children learning to read because they had not been started on it by her methods. Crompton seems to have let it worry her no more than it seems to have troubled Blyton: their concern was their readers, not committees which Crompton could all too easily see staffed by book-world equivalents of Mrs Monks, Miss Milton, General Moult, Mrs Bott and the rest of the adult villagers she had dissected in the intervals of subjecting to the mercy of William. But the choice for 1946 – Elizabeth Goudge's *The Little White Horse* – was appropriate as an end both to the war and to this book. It was set in 1842, not 1942, yet its metaphors of ancient feuds, lovers' ruptures, the war of good and evil, the dog that proves a lion and the horse that proves a unicorn, the need for atonement and restitution for ancestrally ill-gotten wealth, the old and new in child behaviour, the ex-atheist as more penetrating pastor, the boy in dreams emanating from reality, and the little girl who discovers she must take command, were apposite. In her autobiography, *The Joy of the Snow* (1976), she wrote:[53]

> In our hearts every one of us would like to create a new world, less terrible than this one, a world where there is at least a possibility that things may work out right. The greatest writers are able to do this. In *The Lord of the Rings* Professor Tolkien has created a world that is entirely new and if the book ends in haunting sadness Frodo and Sam do at least throw the ring in the fire; if it had been in this world that they embarked on their terrible journey they would have died half-way up the mountain. And so, even with lesser writers, a story is a groping attempt to make a new world, even if the attempt ends in nothing better than the rearrangement of the furniture.

If the war had sent Crompton to the fire-fighters, and blasted Streatfeild's home, and shattered Blyton's marriage, and made Johns come out as feminist, and made a novelist of Saville by driving his children to Shropshire, and impoverished Richards, Goudge saw it in her native West Country:

> The cuckoos and the air-raid sirens shouted together and once, just after the sound of a distant bomb explosion had died away, I remember that I heard a hen in the next-door garden cackling with satisfaction because she had just laid an egg. I found that extremely comforting. Whatever happened nest-building and egg-laying would go on and the earth would continue to pass through

the seasonal changes of her beauty. . . . near us in Devon there was a direct hit on a church packed full of children for a children's service. That I think was Devon's first big tragedy. I suppose that my mother and I suffered less in the war than most people did, and we often felt ashamed because of our comparative immunity. . . .

The American army was now everywhere and gradually all of us in the village began to realise that some hidden undertaking was going on around us. Lanes where we had been accustomed to walk were sealed off, certain orchards and woods could not be entered and the heavy traffic of lorries was heard at night. My mother and I were slow to realise what was happening until one day a neighbour, a man with a mind more enquiring than ours ejaculated, 'It only needs an air-raid and a few bombs on this village to blow us all sky-high!' Then we realised that all our leafy and shady country places were filling up with stored ammunition. . . .

There was still much more to come, the doodle-bugs and the shattering horror of the dropping of the atomic bombs. People have grown used to the thought of atomic warfare now, the present generation have grown up with the bomb, and so it is hard for them to realise how appalled we were then. And the dropping of the bombs seemed to tarnish victory. When it came at last most of us felt almost more shame than joy. . . .

Elsewhere, she wrote:[54] 'Of all the nightmare horrors created by man for his own undoing the beast of war is the most unmanageable. The beast seemed to control the man far more than the man controlled the beast.' And the Second World War was in one way summed up by her as were the wars of imperialism that preceded and in part induced it: 'There is no vengeance so cruel as the vengeance of a new age that has been checked and hindered in its progress by an older age that will not die without a fight'.

The maturing of the heroine, so uneasy a topic in so many hands, is managed in The Little White Horse with a hilarious economy. Loveday Minette points out to Maria how her enjoyment in 'being as aggravating as she knew how to be', to send her beloved Robin into a temper, could have driven them both into a quarrel which in the story's convention would 'wreck not only your own happiness but the happiness of the whole valley'. It is a perceptive piece of child psychology, noting (as had Blyton, in the Adolph story) that child quarrels can begin with a child simply taking pleasure in starting one, as though it were a new toy train, and could be stopped or derailed at will. But when Loveday Minette tells Maria how she quarrelled, apparently irreparably, with Sir Benjamin, Maria affirms Child Power with the magnificent authority that we might expect from a pupil of her governess Miss Heliotrope: ' "I've not time now, Mother Minette, to tell you how dreadfully silly I think you and Sir Benjamin have been", she said severely, "but I'll tell you later" '. The story plays pleasantly with the convention of ending in all living happy ever after; and indeed we are ultimately told that they did, although the end of the story is after that, when the older couples 'took off their bodies and laid them aside and went joyfully away into the next' world, and at the very end we are told how Maria knows that when she is a very old woman the unicorn will return:[55] 'He would come towards her and she would run towards him, and he would carry her upon his back away and away, she did not quite know where, but to a good place where she wanted to be'.

Goudge herself used her metaphor of peace and reconciliation in her own Anglican context, which she inherited from an evangelical father while herself being so High Anglican that the story bitterly denounces the suppression of English monasteries. The evil Black Men in the tale are descendants of Norman supporters of William the Conqueror; Maria's own family only go back to Edward I, when with the king's aid the then squire drives out the monks, thus making Sir Benjanim and his cousin Maria heirs to tainted wealth. The evil are not irredeemable; the good are far from perfect. Any person interpreting the leader of the Black Men as Hitler is answered when Maria finds his redeeming quality: 'Somehow Maria did not doubt that if she kept her part of the bargain, Monsieur Cocq de Noir would keep his. The wickedest of men have good in them somewhere, and, remembering the direct look in his eyes, she felt quite sure that he was not a man who would break his word.' After Munich, Hitler was identified in the British public mind as a man who would. Goudge evidently felt her own affinity more with the Roman Catholic Tolkien than with the Anglican Lewis, and her notion of reconciling the heritage of social division in the English past anticipates, almost certainly without inspiring, the 'scouring of the Shire' passage at the close of The Lord of the Rings. Both of them recoiled with horror from the dropping of the atomic bombs on Hiroshima and Nagasaki, and both repudiated the idea of a victorious country simply preening itself. Tolkien, the anti-allegorist, would indignantly repudiate any more specific a reading of the passage than that; but it is enough. Maria may convert Cocq de Noir, but not by becoming like him; to welcome Saruman is to invite his Pride to rear its head in one's own places, the Pride with which Saruman became infected by the contemplation of Sauron. To conquer Hitler always carried the danger of growing like Hitler.

What happened to those British and Northern Irish children who survived their long wartime suffering and privations is easier to tell, because being adult they left more records; their reading, however, will tell us less, and television had now come to devour much of their leisure. But we are entitled to steal our last word from Goudge, since we are doing no more than giving our final apposite quotation from our last document:

'I should like this story to be like all the best stories and to end in "Happy ever after". . . .'

Notes

1. *Happy Mag* (February 1935) and *William the Detective*.
2. Brian Gardner (ed.), *The Terrible Rain*, 77. I first heard it when it was recited to me by Mrs Carolyn Peploe, whose father was a fighter pilot in the Battle of Britain.
3. Johns, *The Camels are Coming*, last words.
4. Johns, *Biggles Sees it Through*, 186.
5. Johns, *Sergeant Bigglesworth, C.I.D.*, 28.
6. Sullivan, *Diana of Cliff End School* (1945), 189.
7. Blyton, *The Valley of Adventure*, 38–40, 179–80, 246, 270, 283, 244, 248.
8. Johns, *Sergeant Bigglesworth, C.I.D.*, 45. Johns's first post-war novel, *Gimlet Comes Home*, pitches Gimlet and co. against American gangsters.
9. Johns to Trease, in Trease, *Tales out of School*, 94.
10. Johns, *Biggles Hunts Big Game*, 35.
11. Johns to 'every boy who reads this book', n.d. but printed on cover and included on loose sheet with all Biggles books from Hodder & Stoughton, c. 1950.
12. Westerman, *With the Commandos*, 42.
13. Johns, *Sergeant Bigglesworth, C.I.D.*, 90.
14. Westerman, *With the Commandos*, 300.
15. Adolf Hitler, *Hitler's Table-Talk 1941–1944* ([1953] 2000), 663.
16. Johns, *Gimlet Goes Again*, 177. The apology may be exceptional, but its manner is not: 'Gimlet tossed him a greeting'.
17. Westerman, *One of the Many*, 249–50, 263.
18. Westerman, *Trapped in the Jungle*, 100. He had spoken of the unspeakable barbarities in *One of the Many*, 134–5.
19. Westerman, *Trapped in the Jungle*, 91.
20. Blyton, *Five on Kirrin Island Again*, 142. He denounces the atomic bomb on p. 49.
21. Westerman, *Trapped in the Jungle*, 112, 204, 241.
22. *The Broons and Oor Wullie at War 1939–1945*.
23. 'The Pageant' was published in *Modern Woman* (May 1946) and then republished in *William at War*, ed. Richmal C. Ashbee (1995), 215–39, while the revised text renamed 'The Battle of Flowers' first appeared in *William the Bold* (1950).

24. Johns, *King of the Commandos*, 17–18.
25. Dale, *Secret Service!*, 101–2.
26. Crouch, *Treasure Seekers and Borrowers*, 93.
27. Dale, *Secret Service!*, 9–10.
28. Pye, *Half-term Holiday*, 26, 27, 34, 185, 111, 108, 110–11, 112, 112–13.
29. Blyton, *The Castle of Adventure*, 303.
30. Pye, *The Prices Return*, 7–8, 19, 20–1, 25, 36, 84, 92. For Pye's dispassionate verdicts on her own stories, see D. L. Kirkpatrick, *Twentieth-Century Children's Writers* (1978), 1,020.
31. Streatfeild, *Party Frock*, 31, 36–8.
32. Kyle, *The Seven Sapphires*, 14–17, 17–18, 58–9, 96, 92–4, 228.
33. Krzemieniecka, *The Three Little Sisters*, 7, 49.
34. Carey and Bragg, in Antonia Fraser (ed.), *Pleasure of Reading* (1992), 109–10, 169 respectively.
35. Crouch, *Treasure Seekers and Borrowers*, 97, 92.
36. May, *Critical Times*, 403, 276, 322, 298.
37. Mary Cadogan, *Richmal Crompton* (1986), 145–6.
38. Crompton, *Westover* ([1946]), 79–80.
39. Blyton, *Claudine at St Clare's* (1944) 66–7.
40. Cope, in Antonia Fraser (ed.), *Pleasure of Reading*, 190.
41. Noel Streatfeild, Diary for 23 July 1940, quoted in Angela Bull, *Noel Streatfeild* (1984), 173.
42. Greene, *Spectator* vol. 166 (18 April 1941), reprinted in *The Lost Childhood and Other Essays*, 104–5. Greene, *The Ministry of Fear*, 89–90.
43. Derwent, *Tammy Troot*, 38.
44. Fidler, *Fingal's Ghost*, 6, 42–3, 47, 51, 52, 58, 63–4.
45. *Magnet* 1,681.
46. Streatfeild, *The Children of Primrose Lane*, 182.
47. Blyton, *The Island of Adventure*, 312.
48. Johns, *Biggles 'Fails to Return'*, 109–10.
49. Crompton, 'William and the Tea-Cake', *Modern Woman* (January 1943) and *William and the Brains Trust*, 103–4.
50. Harrisson, *Living Through the Blitz* ([1976] 1990), 319.
51. Orwell, *1984*, ed. Crick, 196–7.
52. Johns, *Biggles in the Orient*, 123–4.
53. Goudge, *The Joy of the Snow* (1976), 8, 222, 223, 235, 236.
54. Goudge, 'For Consideration', in Rose Dobbs (comp.), *At the Sign of the Dolphin: An Elizabeth Goudge Anthology* (1947), 505.
55. Goudge, *The Little White Horse* ([1946] 1965), 192, 187, 195, 270.

Sources, Guides and Regrets

'Mickey, the most important words in the language are "Please",
"Thank you" and "Sorry".'

Carolyn Peploe to my son

The origin of this book lay in a conference at the University of
Edinburgh, organised by Paul Addison and Jeremy Crang, then
Director and Assistant Director respectively of the Centre for Second
World War Studies (now broadened to include the First World War),
on the Battle of Britain. The Centre is attached to the Department of
History, whose staff included them and me, and they asked me to
contribute to the conference and to the resultant book, *The Burning
Blue* (2000), on the Battle of Britain and on children's literature. My
conference paper elicited many useful comments, and the ensuing
text was most carefully edited by the organisers-become-editors. It
was a joy and an honour to appear among their contributors, and this
was many times redoubled when they brought me into their series for
Edinburgh University Press. Their wisdom, strength, judgement,
encouragement and sheer hard work have been the perfect foundation for this book. Both of them are great teachers, and profoundly
inspiring as such to me; and our belief that teaching and research are
each other's essential partners, not rivals, is admirably borne out by
their work as editors. No contributor to a series can ever have had
more cause for gratitude to editors than I have to them. (The series
itself – Societies at War – necessarily diminished detailed analysis of
some fine writers with other preoccupations, such as Violet Needham.) Their books have provided me with instructive background –
Paul's *The Road to 1945* and *Churchill on the Home Front* in
particular, and Jeremy's *The British Army and the People's War
1939–45* – and appropriately the history book which has meant most
to me in writing this work is *English History 1914–1945* by Paul's
teacher, A. J. P. Taylor, whose beautiful prose and perpetual challenge are as vital for successor historians as is his wealth of

information. I also found his *Essays in English History* invaluable to relax the mind when self-exhausted by wrestling with textual problems of Enid Blyton and her fellow-sources.

My fellow-historians, whether students or colleagues, have been innumerable founts of inspiration, beginning with my former chief, Professor George Shepperson, whose enthusiasm for my interests has been generous as always. The present Director of the Centre for the Study of the Two World Wars, Professor James McMillan, guided me in European and especially Belgian history. The History Department in general aided me greatly in seminars and conversations. I am particularly indebted to Professors Rhodri Jeffreys-Jones, Jill Stephenson and V. G. Kiernan; to the late James Maclean, the late Esmonde Robertson, the late George Hammersley, the late Maurice Larkin – and to his widow, Enid Larkin, for deep insights and helpful reflections; and to very many students at all levels down the years, from Professor Tony Aldgate who has taught me so much about film, though Colin Nicolson, with parental as well as historical insights, to Tristan Redman who presented me anonymously with an invaluable book, and Constance Woodhouse who produced a fine term paper for me on *Little Folks* in the First World War. Dr Jennifer Litster has been an admirable commentator and critic especially on Canadian literature, and her external examiner, Professor Mary Rubio, has been generosity itself in sharing her unrivalled knowledge of L. M. Montgomery. Dr Tom Webster is a fund of common sense on new historiographical approaches, and in various ways Finn Pollard, Keith Mears, Jeff Nelson and many other graduate students have been fine compasses for their ancient mariner. Professor Tony Goodman and Dr John Gooding aided me greatly with their example in the use of literature as historical sources, and Professor Robert Anderson's use of school stories in teaching the history of education was of major benefit to me when I had the good fortune to be his second marker. Dr Tom Barron and Miss Patricia J. Storey have opened up several rich fields for investigation with the zest and humour which have been unflagging in their goodness to me over almost forty years.

Apart from drawing in the aid of Europeanists by speaking to our Modern History seminar on Tintin and the Nazis, I found towards the end of my research and writing that I needed another seminar discussion to contemplate what seems a very new subject in children's history. The most remarkable discovery that this threw in my way was the realisation that the subject was set on its feet by Jesus Christ – but His followers here as elsewhere have fallen short. He seems to have been the only person in the Bible who really liked children – as opposed to the many whom it presents as children, with charm and interest – and His emphases on looking to children for leadership, on welcoming children among us, and on realising the immense advantages provided by child innocence, are foundations of the subject. History tends to be written with the assumption, unconscious or otherwise, that the historian's perspective is the desirable norm towards which history should properly move. For the historian of children, this means assuming that the desideratum in a child is ceasing to be a child, and hence a child's life is studied to welcome all indications that s/he has less and less of a child about her or him. This is as sensible as looking at medieval history solely for signs that modern history is taking over from it. Obviously, continua in human life – as in human history – are worth considering, but only as aspects, not the totality, of the story. Equally, a sudden cataclysmic event may end a childhood: few of the books mentioned here assert such an event, but it is clear that childhood is over for Christopher when he has finished his Odyssey from Japan in Jan Maclure's *Escape to Chungking*; and Elinor Brent-Dyer shows a similarly harsh break with a comparably unreal and protected past when her perennial hero Jo flees from Austrian Nazis in *The Chalet School in Exile*. In her case, the book does not end on that violent ageing; but it breaks in time, and Jo is married in the interval. One of our few real-life figures in this book, Colin Ryder Richardson, suffered such childhood's end by the ordeal through which he survived the sinking of the *City of Benares*; and I am most grateful to him for what he let me and others know about it. But, as he shows, it is dangerous for children suddenly to lose their childhood; and it is dangerous for the historian to view the childhood waiting for its end, like a detective-story reader losing enjoyment, appreciation and meaning in what is read, through hunger to know the murderer.

The readiness of historians to generalise about children should necessarily be caught short by war, especially when the country in question suffers war on its own soil, is occupied by an alien army, and/or is subjected to regime-change or the threat of it by war, revolution or both. The UK had no invaders other than in the special case of the Channel Islands, alien armies on her soil were friendly invitees, and any revolutions in thought or act shed no fellow-citizens' blood. But British and Ulster blood was being shed at home and abroad, more of it civilian and child blood than in any war in Britain's or Northern Ireland's history. Similarly, social disruption was more drastic than at any time since the seventeenth-century civil wars overwhelmed the entire archipelago. Apart from what Edith

Sitwell called 'the terrible rain' killing and wounding the children and their elders, efforts to save their lives – and the children were paramount in that agenda – drove countless numbers from their homes and familiar environments into strange and often ill-prepared refuges, sometimes overseas, and many more into air-raid shelters of their own or provided locally as underground as possible. Government history is a frequent object of subsequent historians' suspicion, but in this field the UK produced a masterpiece within five years of the war: Richard Titmuss's *Problems of Social Policy* (1950). There is a wealth of literature on evacuees, one way or another, such as Ben Wicks's *No Time to Wave Good-bye* (1988), notable for its evidence on children's books as reassurance familiar or inviting in a shattered world. Angus Calder's *The People's War: Britain 1939–1945* (1969) is invaluable, as is his *The Myth of the Blitz* (1991), albeit its realities outweigh its myths, much to our advantage. American and other social observers analysed in its pages are worth pursuit in their own books for what they say of children. Juliet Gardiner, *The Children's War* (2005), is an indispensable contribution from a distinguished historian well experienced in the world of books. Norman Longmate, *How We Lived Then* (1971, 2002) has a useful chapter about books (including children's) 'Out of Print'. Individual regions are adding their reminiscences more and more to the general stock with excellent material, not always fruitful on what children read, but fascinating in their differences and similarities. I have cited only a few of an increasing wealth, some by individual memorialists like Jim Davidson's *A Bairn's War* on Peterhead, some by multi-author reminiscences such as Paul Rason ed., *Memories of the Many* (1995) for Bromley, and Mary Walton and J. P. Lamb, *Raiders Over Sheffield* (1980), some through city or town museums to whose courtesy I am much obliged from Sheffield to Redruth (which commemorated the impeccable behaviour of one of its evacuees who later became a Great Train Robber). Very many colleagues and friends gave me invaluable assistance on where they went and what they read, John Fowler the former literary editor of the Glasgow *Herald* contributing a most helpful bibliography, the late Neville Garden of BBC Scotland providing recollections of reactions to fictional characters (invaluable if not always repeatable). Yet Robert Westall, *Children of the Blitz* has much validity including its 'There was a whole children's war, never recorded'.

But to write children's history by means of assessment of their reading matter, even if limited to a cataclysmic period of national upheaval and isolation, can do little more than process and stack the clues whence inferences may be drawn with more likelihood of greater value when accompanied by other evidence. We can suggest *mentalités* from books written and read during that time (uneasily aware that, in the Second World War, large print-runs and second editions are far less certain indicators of popularity than usual and may merely reflect Nazi arson and resilient publisher optimism). We may also acknowledge that notice of major work being written or inspired during the war may augment our findings, since our story is necessarily about the impact of war on writers as well as the impact of writers on readers, and that it is sensible as well as agreeable to take account of genius such as Tolkien, Golding and Lewis and to see where they fit into the world of writing for children of more immediate output in the war itself. But, however enjoyable and perhaps even useful, our work here is even more limited than the above.

It has not been possible to make more than a brief survey of comics during the period, partly because snobbery and questionable wartime crusades for paper-saving meant that archives of comics are almost impossible to find outside the British Library – and I could only make brief forays there, for enabling which I am most grateful to Library officials in St Pancras and Colindale, and to Professor Peter and Ms Liselotte Marshall. I had participated in Paul Harris's *D. C. Thomson Bumper Fun Book* (1976), whose ribald title disguised serious studies of one publisher's products and whose contributors found themselves much more favourable to so austerely right-wing an imprint than they had expected; but it was not until now that I had realised how very left-wing wartime Thomson comics became. Taken into account with Blyton's advocacy of school communism and child leadership from lower-class expertise, Johns's feminism and Crompton's attacks on anti-social privilege, all flourishing in 1940–2, we have something like a revolutionary moment and one which braced children for war transformations and post-war reconstruction. But it was not without warning. The *Magnet* reprints by Howard Baker make it possible to see how far Frank Richards, for one, had been laying down long traditions whose depiction of privileged but frequently ill-used schoolboys and resourceful schoolgirls made wartime psychological readjustment less unexpected. These reprints, including some *Gems*, were sometimes assembled in very illogical fashion; but the student is put at ease by first-class bibliographical guides to original publication order and titles and to their ultimate volumes when reproduced: George Beal (ed.), *The Complete Magnet Companion 1996*, and *Magnet and Gem Facsimile Editions* (1994).

Richmal Crompton's magazine publication is also conveniently assembled with much additional relevance in Mary Cadogan with David Schutte, *The William Companion* (1990); and Cadogan, *Just William Through the Ages* (1994), is a useful supplement. Cadogan's name is a hallmark of reliability, as is the bookseller Norman Wright's for Blyton and Johns data, notably bibliographies of Blyton's Sunny Stories, topographical studies of 'Five' stories and so on. My own investigations of Blyton's beloved Swanage, whence the war exiled her, were made possible by the hospitality of Pat and Anne McDonald, who were tireless in helping me to prospect everything from the local golf club, which Blyton eventually adopted, to the entrances to limestone underground passages inspirational to the author but now closed to the public. Norman Wright has now removed to Swanage, but his good nature, advice and wisdom have been given generously for many years to me. I am deeply grateful also to Professor Jeffrey Richards, whose vast learning and profound wisdom I value so much, whether personally given or enshrined in the best book on English school fiction, his *Happiest Days* (1988), and in his various works on film with Tony Aldgate, notably *Britain Can Take It* (1986, 1994), which has been forever in my hands for comparative purposes during the period. I am most grateful to my former student Michael Coyne for endless ideas on film; and my old master at BBC Critics' Forum, Philip French, film critic for the *Observer*, has been an endless explorer of new critical frontiers, beckoning me forward in his Wenceslastic footprints.

On the school-story front, Robert J. Kirkpatrick's annotated bibliography *Bullies, Beaks and Flannelled Fools* (1990, 2001) is now the supreme state of the art, as are his *Encyclopaedia of Boys' School Stories* (2000), and the companion volume for *Girls' School Stories* (2000) edited by Sue Sims and Hilary Clare. I am greatly obliged to Robert Kirkpatrick and to Brian Doyle for their joint help in biographical enquiries, and also to Brian Doyle's *The Who's Who of Children's Literature* (1968). The constructive and positive tone of these works yields much more understanding of transmission of values than can be claimed by censorious rivals whose Procrustean beds lop off what they miss. We get back to Jesus's reminder: to get anywhere, we must let the children be heard, be seen and move, and we must accept their leadership – in this case, if we are tempted to evaluative judgements. This is not merely, nor primarily, the argument of numbers sold (even when bombing and fires do not make nonsense of print-runs or copies-diminution); it means getting hold of child reactions at the time if possible, in retrospect if not (much less trustworthy, since former children often forget much about having been children, as would-be critics all too clearly often reveal – and, where they remember, their memory can be warped by the subsequent need either to accept or to rebel against adult conventions). One of the best critical tools available to the historian is thus the Second World War book coverage in *Time and Tide*, where in addition to its many intelligent adult critics – probably more than in any other weekly apart from the *Times Literary Supplement* – scores of children contributed their opinions of new books, gave their ages and showed strong signs of independent verdicts, in addition to other infant conclusions filtered through adult reviewers.

What you do not get is much indication of a child's dawning sexual responses, in any direction, although a few personal recollections have confided memories of being attracted to Blyton's George, or Crompton's William. Johns's Ginger seems in my view to have been intended not to have been seen sexually aroused by Full Moon while obviously loving her, though he clearly is by Jeanette Ducoste – but Professor John Carey recalls being excited with some sexual implication by Full Moon (presumably in imaginary self-substitution for Ginger), as he mentions in Lady Antonia Fraser's admirable compilation *The Pleasure of Reading* (1992), which gives us far more than one book has ever done about author recollections of youthful literary discovery and addiction. One of my own very best sources on this was Sean Mac Réamoinn, editor of a book of similar title on Gaelic poetry; he died a few days ago as I write this.

The literary reviews during the war are a first-class source for the cultural historian; and, however limited the value of their adult reviews of books for children, they involuntarily convey much of the nature of the world in which the children had to grow. Thus the Orwell v. Richards debate was acknowledged as having begun with Orwell's 'most original' essay in *Inside the Whale* by V. S. Pritchett (*New Statesman and Nation*, 16 March 1940), albeit to Queenie Leavis in *Scrutiny* (September 1940) 'not altogether original', while 'P. M.' in the *New English Weekly* proclaimed that

> Many hours of intelligent curiosity and alert social interest must have been spent by Orwell upon these superficially insignificant publications, and many remembered since his school days; and now his effort to extract their human and social meaning amounts almost to a thrilling journey through some darkest Africa of the world of letters, of which he is the only Livingstone!

and wondered:

> Why do not more of our young writers get similarly interested in
> something that is happening just under our noses, such as this
> vast stream of juvenile literature, and bring it to our notice?

In noticing the *Horizon* for March 1940, the *New Statesman and
Nation* had anonymously hailed the essay as 'a fascinating, surprising
and disconcerting piece of research' (24 February 1940) and declared
that Richards's 'spirited reply demonstrates how ably he can write
and how fatuously he can think' (27 April 1940), which did little more
than police the proceedings with no desire to participate. The *Times
Literary Supplement* found Orwell 'amusing and instructive reading'
but felt that he 'ignores the element of pure mental play in such
reading' and doubted whether the *Magnet* would convince boys from
12 to 18 of the impeccability of *laissez-faire* capitalism, the risibility of
foreigners and the immortality of the British Empire, while Robert
Herring in *Life and Letters Today* (June 1940) felt that he forgot 'the
adolescent routine of living through several stages of civilization; to
read *Gem* and *Magnet* is no more than the traditional pulling of wings
off a fly' – surely the most revolting response that the debate can have
received.

But, however these commentators might pull their punches, their
notices were but part of intense argument on public schools and the
desirability of their future (while apparently ignorant of any others),
as the journals masticated Morris Marples, *Public School Slang*
('Children are much less inventive in the use of words than in other
directions, and it does not appear that a single one of the slang
phrases that have enriched the English language . . . is of public-
school origin', *New English Weekly*, 16 May 1940); J. T. Hankinson,
Choosing and Using a Public School ('I am afraid that intelligent
parents . . . would find . . . alarming . . . the blend of naivety and
timidity in his more positive utterances . . . [such as] On Sex:

> Doctors and educationalists hold a variety of views concerning the
> possible harm that may come from masturbation, but whatever that
> may be, a Housemaster must also look at it from an additional angle
> (Thomas Smallbones, *New Statesman and Nation*, 20 January 1940));

S. P. B. Mais, 'A Public School in Wartime', *New Statesman and
Nation* (2 March 1940); 'Cheironax', *Sketch of a School* and so on,
culminating in *Horizon*'s outraged editorial comment (August 1940):

For a hundred years the public schools have fought Imagination, and with so much success that they have almost succeeded in extinguishing it in the ruling class. We are even faced with the extraordinary situation of fighting Germans who have more imagination than we have, for imagination combined with efficiency has characterized all the actions of the enemy in this war, and it is because Churchill has imagination that he is the one indispensable leader at the present time.

But was not Imagination the origin and the recipient of Richards's work, and that of so many other writers noted in our pages as read by the Second World War's children, and deplored where noticed by its adults? At least, Horizon's spokesman, Connolly or Stephen Spender, acknowledged that the debate was pivotal to the war; but it left unanswered the question of Richards's being supportive or otherwise to the public school – or, for that matter, of whether Churchill was. The historian today is at least made aware of the passions and pinpricks behind which authors wrote and children read – and, even now, it should be clear that the range of sources continually opens wider. The Spectator, for instance, at the beginning of the Second World War had Graham Greene as its literary editor, greatly advancing its critical value on Worrals and much else; and he had edited the most literary volume of critiques on the public-school question, The Old School (1934).

The literary argument and the historian's landscape were conspicuously enlarged in May 1940 by the publication of A. J. Jenkinson, What Do Boys and Girls Read? Jenkinson's study, with its many tables of child preferences in comics and certain books, won plaudits from Orwell, who reviewed it for both Life and Letters (July 1940) and the Listener (a good journal of criticism as well as storehouse of significant broadcast talks) for 8 August 1940; its main interest today is more for the historian of methodology. Jenkinson, remarked Orwell in Life and Letters, concluded 'that the less literature is taught as an examinable "subject" the better', and Orwell felt that he underrated 'the improvement in literacy and intelligence that is unquestionably taking place' (Complete Works, XII, 205; see also 204, 224–5). T. R. Barnes in the Leavisite Scrutiny (June 1940) was appropriately pessimistic, taking Jenkinson's questionnaire sample of 2,900 as 'large enough to be fairly representative' but regretting that his judgements usually erred 'on the side of tolerance'. T. C. Worsley (New Statesman and Nation, 25 May 1940) wondered whether schoolchildren might not be examined on 'material which performed the psychological function of the present bloods [comics] in a less debased form', in which case the Thomson near-monopoly 'has to be broken'. (Clearly, Thomson's progress to Red Russia in Romania was an utterly unexpected evolution – except among Thomson readers, we may suspect.) The *TLS* (1 June 1940) gave Jenkinson a second leader, and showed one insight as to the morrow:

> Children of the future, it seems, may be allowed to shape their course of reading without prohibition – because in spite of appearances to the contrary it will be recognized that they know better than their elders what is good for them. . . . If a voice is raised to demand a veto against the monstrously successful 'bloods', it will not obtain Mr Jenkinson's unqualified support. Without upholding the poor values and the shallowness of thought which are the obvious features of those works, he points out their importance as fantasy material . . .

What ailed the book was the pejorative term 'bloods', by now as completely antiquated as the slang in the *Magnet* (where, however, a 'blood' meant a first-class cricketer and footballer like Blundell of the Fifth); and, since it grouped text-bound papers from *Magnet* to *Adventure* with the tabloids from *Beano* to *Film Fun*, snobbery was as usual eating away at the vitals of science. And Jenkinson did not know what to make of Crompton: it was as though William had arisen from her pages to confuse Jenkinson by his highest-motivated chaotics.

STORIES OF HOME LIFE

This category was inserted, in the first place, at the instance of a Head mistress who maintained that girls read numerous books like Alcott's *Little Women*, and that these might usefully form a separate section in classification. Her impression turned out to have a substantial basis. Even in boys' schools *Little Women* and its kind are frequently read at the lower ages. However, it was a consequence of a single decision of the investigator [i.e. Jenkinson] (which he had to make early and before its full consequences were apparent) that stories of home life take such a prominent place amongst the twelve categories. This was the decision to include the works of Richmal Crompton under the heading 'stories of home life'. Books by this writer are prodigiously popular at the ages of 12 +, 13 +, and 14 +. One boy of 14 + entered '14 William Books' as part of his month's reading! As he did not specify the titles the investigator (quite arbitrarily) entered five. Smaller entries – of 7, 5, and 3 – are common with all the titles specified. At 15 +, practically no boys read Richmal Crompton [or were prepared to admit it, but poor Jenkinson's Imagination did not stretch that far]. The avidity with which these books are read, up to the age of 15, is a most remarkable testimony to the immaturity of the Middle School boy . . . (pp. 24–5)

– and indeed to the immaturity of God knows how many of the rest of us.

Dickens turns out to be highly popular at all ages in both Secondary and Senior Schools – to a degree which may, indeed, cause some surprise. (p. 25)

(Less, perhaps, when the sets of Dickens given away to readers of the Labour Party newspaper the *Daily Herald* are borne in mind: they were in the house, so children seeking reading-matter found them.)

He does not enjoy the almost delirious patronage bestowed on Richmal Crompton; he does stand the test of time as she does not, for he is still highly popular at 15 +. (p. 25)

Eventually, Jenkinson seems to have given up on classification of Crompton, as when noting that thirteen boys in a form specified having privately read twenty-six books, including:

one history book, two technical books, one by Richmal Crompton, seven detective stories, and twelve adventure stories. Four may be said to reach a creditable standard of literacy: Conan Doyle's *Sign of Four*, Rider Haggard's *King Solomon's Mines*, H. G. Wells' *Short Stories* and the *Invisible Man*. (p. 59)

(What on earth was the history book which failed Jenkinson's 'creditable standard': *1066 and All That?*)

One or two of the Senior Schools keep considerable stocks of informational books for quiet reading, mostly popularized science or engineering. No doubt they hope that the boys will 'pick up something useful' or have an interest 'awakened'. Even these schools have to let in Richmal Crompton . . . (p. 62)

In reporting the results of his questionnaires, Jenkinson found a high proportion of girls still declaring readership of Crompton (in fact, of the secondary-school 15 + group, one-fifth named themselves as her readers, in contrast to the boys' official collapse of readership at that age, and lower age-groups of girls, registering one-sixth or lower).

> The 'William' books are all entered in the category of stories of home life; the girls themselves frequently describe them otherwise. Many of the younger girls call them 'adventures'; many of the older girls describe them as 'humorous'. This suggests an interesting change in point of view (which may perhaps partly account for the fluctuation at 14 +); the younger girls thrill at the audacity of the 'William' books, the older ones laugh at the absurdity; the younger ones laugh, but they laugh in triumph, the older ones laugh at the humour. (p. 178)

This was as far as Jenkinson progressed in seeing the conjunction between children and humour; it was more than most of his critical contemporaries. It made his misadventures among the 'bloods' comparatively easy-going:

> For the sake of convenient and rapid reference, the term 'bloods' is here used to mean 'the weekly, fortnightly, or monthly adventure and story papers and magazines for boys and girls'. It includes the Boy's Own Paper, and the Magnet, Rainbow, and Comic Cuts. This may do violence to the prejudices of some readers, since certain periodicals such as the Rainbow and the Boy's Own Paper are in some quarters held to be worthier and nobler than the Magnet, Comic Cuts, and their peers. The distinction seems to be a class distinction; similar appetites are satisfied in what is regarded as a more refined way. (p. 64)

Perhaps. One is left wondering if Jenkinson had ever read one of these journals, much as countless future librarians, editors, critics and so on would denounce Enid Blyton without sullying their eyes with her works. Certainly, Richards's classical similes and psychological enmeshings bore about as much relationship to Comic Cuts as Admiral Lord Nelson resembled a pantomime Dame – a touch of kinship in the theatricals, perhaps, but little fundamental proximity. No doubt Greyfriars would repudiate refinement – oddly enough, the only possible aspirant for it might be Bunter if he felt that it could result in solid refreshment – but, once war had begun, the Boy's Own

Paper began to run Biggles, who on being invited to formal dinner with a cabinet minister threatened to gurgle over his soup. The nearest Johns got to it was having the post-war Gimlet invite his former subordinate commandos to the Ritz, to its considerable regret.

This, then, was the state of the scholarly art and its critical environment when the Second World War began; and it continued largely on similar lines, with much useful information misapplied and ill-directed. The historian thus has much to harvest from authorities with much more to divulge than their judgements suggest. Marcus Crouch, for instance, produced in *Treasure Seekers and Borrowers* (1962) a splendid litany of chldren's books published within the war, and benefited the present work in countless ways, while insisting that the Second World War took place in a literary trough of writing for children. Equally, in *Chosen for Children* (1957, 1967, 1977) he provided an account of the Carnegie Medal Awards invaluable in its documents, while apparently assuming that it went to the organisers' credit however much they shirked their work. Other standard works made fewer citations and louder comminations. Fred Inglis, *The Promise of Happiness: Value and Meaning in Children's Fiction* (1981), might have been retitled *I Was a Teenage Blytonian*, but at least it makes fewer attempts to disguise personal pique or cultural crowd-following as objectivity. Alec Ellis, *History of Children's Reading and Literature* (1968), drove its unoriginal theses home with chapter-titles hammer-blowing: 'Years of Decision in Education 1918–1945', 'Mediocrity and Escapism in Children's Literature 1920–1945', 'Libraries for Children 1919–1945' – and, since the war bombings make the last title seem a tasteless joke and the second a reproof that might startle a Spartan mother, it seems somewhat self-defeating. Complaints that 'the results of wartime evacuation proved overwhelmingly retrogressive, . . . rumours that many children lost their ability to read due to lack of practice' and 'the majority still monopolized the descendants of penny dreadfuls and other trivia of the 19th century', seem to report famine conditions while insisting that the public ought to eat cake instead of the available bread. If D. C. Thomson's *Adventure*, *Rover*, *Wizard* and *Hotspur* supplied vast amounts of print for twopence and the purchasers read it, we ought to be grateful for their fine fight to keep down illiteracy. It is high time that Thomson's (who in my view have nothing to lose by it) encouraged graduate students to undertake histories of their wartime services to Britain with use of all available company records. My own insufficient reading of their products suggests that the quality of most of their stories was surprisingly high, and often better than many books in hard covers priced for much wealthier children. As it is, Thomson's have issued useful and tasteful anthologies of Oor Wullie, the Broons, Lord Snooty, Desperate Dan and the first issues of the *Dandy*, *Beano*, *Magic*, *Adventure*, *Wizard*, *Skipper*, *Rover* and *Hotspur*, and have greatly helped historians by showing dates of all reproduced comics or individual pages. One support for an argument of the high quality of comics' reading-matter is that made by Rupert Hart-Davis on detective fiction (*Spectator*, 20 October 1939): 'either the plot or the style must be superlative, which will hold the attention of one waiting or enduring a *Blitz*-krieg'. Superlative they may not all have been, but they certainly held attention in times worse than any public prediction had hinted.

Several publishers have written memoirs or permitted histories, which will have various uses however much they seek to conceal; but the primary source for the book trade is its own magazine, the *Bookseller*, which required to be read extensively, as did the children's fare in the *Radio Times*, and the weekly journals' children's reviews (in both senses). My readers will notice individual judgements on specific weeklies or particular reviews; but, while grateful for the entertainment and education that the historian will get from all, I must express my deepest debt to the *Bookseller*, crammed with information not always intended to reveal as much as it did and does (beginning with Eleanor Graham's 'The Season's Children's Books' (7 September 1939), where she told the booksellers 'to give full weight to the one award made to children's books', the Carnegie Medal, and 'do what you can for it. Have a card printed, perhaps, and make a little show of the first three winners' (in fact, the runners-up (if any) were no longer disclosed). 'It will increase sales, and help, too, to establish the medal at its real value' (with awards being made by an inquorate committee – but Graham did instruct her audience to read the books they sold.)

I first learned the value of the *Bookseller* when I was a temporary assistant at Hodges, Figgis, 6 Dawson Street, Dublin, and owe much to what I was taught by S. E. Allen Figgis, J. Frank Murray, Michael O'Neill Walshe, Robert Twigg, George Marshall Hodgins, John Mason Hudson and Gerald Blake. The main impact of the war by then, the mid-1950s, was occasional libel actions (military), commercial travellers from London (including the sardonic survivors of the military pep-talk that Montgomery insisted on giving the salesmen when their firm published his memoirs), and Mr Brendan Behan, whose hilarious visits to the shop (hilarity much intended, in his case) were, as his *Borstal Boy* (1958) revealed, those of a former child who had spent much time in wartime Britain having been rightly sentenced to Borstal for intending to plant explosive devices in civilian Liverpool and who became deeply and even romantically attached to some of his fellow-inmates, appropriately eroding his hatred in love. The book was banned in Ireland.

Initially, the prolonged life of many wartime authors' writing overshadowed their abrupt departure from wartime subjects; and the former mass audience (now aged between 35 and 40) may have acknowledged the end of an era when Johns, Blyton, Crompton and Brent-Dyer died in 1968–9, to have their place in history (if not necessarily in literature) admitted by the presence of all save Brent-Dyer in the *Dictionary of National Biography*; the latter was also included in the more professional *Oxford Dictionary of National Biography* (2004), whose work was aided by biographies, all four being well served. The *Dictionary of Literary Biography*: vol. 160, *British Children's Writers 1914–1960* (1996) is useful if over-evaluative. The star biography of a writer for children went, with his usual luck, to Ransome, Hugh Brogan's *Life* (1984), which Brogan followed with Ransome's letters *Signalling from Mars* (1997), Sir Rupert Hart-Davis (who trained me in biographical research) having edited Ransome's *Autobiography* (1976). The literature showed that, however much Ransome avoided the Second World War, his productivity warred with his bellicose wife, once Trotsky's secretary, who prevented the publication of *The Picts and the Martyrs* for a year by insistence on its cultural inadequacy (thus subjecting Ransome to the same bourgeois snobbery whereby critics boycotted Crompton and then Blyton). I am proud to be a member of the Arthur Ransome Society, whose exhilarating deliberations by land and sea continually deepen Ransome studies, and have taught me much.

Much more needs to be done biographically, and the *ODNB* should greatly broaden its catchment area as it recruits subjects in self-revision: Saville was not included, for one, although he now has a biography by Mark O'Hanlon (2001). Some valuable work has been done in D. L. Kirkpatrick (ed.), *Twentieth-Century Children's Writers* (1983) and its successor (fourth) edition, if sometimes tempted to challenge the whirligig of time in its attempts at critical judgements. Margery Fisher, frequently censorious, found a good way to sugar her pills in *Who's Who in Children's Books* (1975), with articles on the major characters, the less friendly the less accurate. Her *The Bright Face of Danger* (1986), on adventure stories, is fun to argue with. I've mentioned Geoffrey Trease, *Tales out of School* (1949,

1964), in the text; its numerous citations are useful even if a competitor disguised as a critic may be suspect, and Trease was much more open about it than was, say, Barbara Euphan Todd in pseudonymous hatchet-work in *Punch*, which, like Richards's outlets, circulated far beyond its sales. Wartime *Punch* had early versions of Geoffrey Willans's diaristic bad boy, Nigel Molesworth, collected for post-war epiphanies in *Down With Skool*; they never quite found wartime feet, though they were certainly good enough for *Punch*.

Mary Cadogan wrote good lives of Richards (1988) and of Crompton (1993), and her *Women with Wings* (1992) is a splendid introduction to the world of Worrals (and other leading airwomen, fictional and otherwise). Her enthusiasm keeps her a little starry-eyed, which thus blends effectively with the more hard-bitten Patricia Craig in their work on girls' fiction, *You're a Brick, Angela!* (1976, 1986), and its sequel, the leading precursor of my book here, *Women and Children First* (1978), looking at the fiction of both world wars, and a splendidly illuminating pathfinder. Cadogan, in art and insight, has the advantage over W. O. G. Lofts and D. J. Adley, *The World of Frank Richards* (1976); but we are all indebted to their prosopography, *The Men Behind Boys' Fiction* (1970). Gillian Freeman, *The Schoolgirl Ethic* (1976), nets Angela Brazil faithfully while perhaps less ready to concede resilience in the last works than I would. Jack Cox, *Take a Cold Tub, Sir!* (1982), is an insider's sketch of the *BOP*, but necessarily a jet-travelling glimpse of a journal famous for leisurely thrills. Bob Dixon, *Catching Them Young* (2 vols, 1977), might be entitled *Tell the Children to Stop Laughing, Comrade!*: it makes a lightning raid as a pseudo-Marxist press-gang and indicts for racism, sexism, class warfare, political reaction and so on practically any book noted for popularity with children. Ironically, for all of its screaming generalisations on lazily gathered evidence, prejudging its targets guilty, it asks useful questions worth considering while discarding the instant answers. Vehemence is usually in proportion to ignorance: Robert Leeson, a Marxist who reviewed fiction for children for Communist newspapers, produced in *Reading and Righting* (1984) a truly instructive study of juvenile fiction, informed and elegant. For example:

> What [Johns] had, and what superior writers often seem to lack, is the will to communicate with young readers. He liked sharing a story with them. So did Blyton. The will to tell a story that will rivet the audience, rather than the award panel, is the first gleam the critic needs to look for in a book. (p. 148)

For him, 'The Second World War ... caused some of the old snobberies to be discarded' (p. 118). E. S. Turner, *Boys Will Be Boys* (1948, 1975) is a far-cutting literary pathfinder.

Some of the controversy has inspired further research. E. Wallace Hildick, a post-war writer for children, attacked Blyton's *Five Run Away Together* in his *Children and Fiction* (1970), having clearly read it and greatly admired the author's technique; but, in contrasting her morality with that of Golding's *Lord of the Flies*, he appropriately invited a question of two of Golding. As Wilde pointed out, creative work is the best critical response: thus J. K. Rowling's Harry Potter stories embody profound critical comment on school stories, particularly in their hostility to racism. The vast range of children's fiction needs guidance; and Humphrey Carpenter and Mari Prichard edited *The Oxford Companion to Children's Literature* (1995), in general a tolerably informative companion but more Mr Standfast than Mr Valiant-for-Truth when it comes to conventional critical verdicts. Robert Druce, *This Day Our Daily Fictions* (1992), investigates how Blyton and Ian Fleming became best-sellers, but is weakened by Fleming's primary appeal to cruder instincts than Blyton. Peter Hunt straddles the field with his cautious histories such as *An Introduction to Children's Literature* (1994), yet is capable of finding that what he calls 'one highly thought of book', *The Little Grey Men* by 'B.B.', 'demonstrates the woolly thinking of some critics', which 'overlooks the rather unsavoury murder by the gnomes of the gamekeeper'. What is a 'savoury' murder? (Possibly in *William Carries On* when William, with the best of motives, put lemon soap in mistake for lemons into soup and a sweet to be consumed by the editor of a magazine catering for culinary tastes?) Brian Thompson, *Keeping Mum* (2006) has a much more positive memory of *The Little Grey Men*, a wartime gift to the boy from his father's RAF crew.

One of the most fascinating qualities about a study such as this set in the Second World War is that to pursue the literary output and biographical experience of a number of writers may seriously contradict common assumptions about their lives and works as totalities. Johns's feminism flared up, then dwindled and vanished, within the Second World War decade, and is ignored in the usual thumbnail sketches of his life. Some commentators seem to feel that the war was in bad taste (as Wilde said, when war came to be regarded as vulgar, it would cease to be popular). John Rowe Townsend's *Written for Children* (1965, 1974) proclaimed that 'The war itself inspired curiously few worth-while adventure stories. In the main, the best writers hung back.' Thus fortified to make his qualified assessment, it is hardly surprising that he takes Streatfeild's *The Children of Primrose Lane* to be about evacuees; it is one of the four books produced in the Second World War that he mentions. And a certain creepy feeling can chill the reader of criticisms: Catherine Storr, for instance, told readers of the *Sunday Times* (7 March 1971): 'I believe that children should be allowed to feel fear. And I believe that they must also be allowed to meet terror and pity and evil' (reprinted in Nicholas Tucker (ed.), *Suitable for Children?*, 1976). Was the war so remote that this doctrine could be asserted twenty-five years later without an apparent thought on the children who had had no choice about feeling fear or meeting terror and pity and evil?

The questions of literary quality and educational value are important, and we need expert guidance (in small supply for children's literature). But, for the historian, these are not initially the most important questions. The first question is: how did these books help the children to live through the presence of the Second World War and its terrible rain, its disruption and its privations? If we find ourselves saying that they were able to preserve their mental health because so many of their writers were of literary quality, that becomes immediately important. We can see why the BBC broadcasts of *The Wind in the Willows* during the war could have played their part in strengthening the threatened children, if we turn to the fascinating critical essay by my late mentor and friend W. W. Robson (in his *The Definition of Literature*, 1982), or learn how another friend, the zoologist Aubrey Manning, was led by childhood reading of the book to his vocation (as well as to his literary relaxation, which inspired me so much in writing this book). Alistair Fowler's *History of English Literature* (1987, 1989) has given me an admirable context in which to see where child reading found itself, and throughout my work I have been spurred on by the sharpness of his critical judgements as we talked. But perhaps the supreme gift he gave me was his reflections on why he had liked the *Magnet*: suddenly a great critic was unified before my eyes with a captivated child. Andrew Hook gave me the strength of his recollections of comics and their self-destruction when the miles of print were finally jettisoned for drawings. Roger Savage remembered crucial radio and film programmes from the war years and after, and sparkled with bibliographical and other inspiration. All save Aubrey are academics in English literature, but in all of them were the children they had left behind who still had a word to be remembered about their lives and likes. (Roger put me onto Francis Spufford (2002), an exceptional linkage of child memory to critical reflection, for a later period than ours.)

I am their pupil, but I had had earlier teachers also. At the *Scotsman*, the late Allen Wright gave me Edinburgh Festival Fringe assignments to review plays for children whence I derived much, especially from Jim Hutton and Leicestershire Youth Arts, and from my child companions whose critical judgements were always invaluable to me – my own children and, after they grew up, several others, notably Adam Brown, and Emily and Christopher Green, and later Edward and Sofia Cogliano, and from those students concerned with child reviewing in the *Festival Times*, particularly Tim Willis and Jamie Donald. Before that, Harry Reid and Julie Davidson, then on the *Scotsman*, drew me into writing about Enid Blyton. Brian Fallon commissioned for the *Irish Times* my obituary article on W. E. Johns (entitled 'Biggles Flies Home'). In my undergraduate years in University College Dublin, Dr Lorna Reynolds chaired a paper (in kindly bewilderment) in which I sought to tell Irish undergraduates in English literature of what I regarded as more appropriate fodder for their critical powers, and my friend Michael Williams intervened from the floor with apophthegms on the Celticism of Wilson, bicentenarian athletic hero of the *Wizard*. I and my fellow-students of Second World War writers, when I was in secondary school at Belvedere College Dublin, were encouraged to try our hands at commando fiction by the late Rev. Eamonn Egan SJ, and particularly enjoyed the ironic stimulation of Michael Gallagher. At home, Joan, Nancy and Pat Buchanan, our doctor's daughters, started me on William, my next-door neighbour Michael Gerald Little, and my friends Conan Rafferty and Niall Gibbons, lent me and discussed fictions now but a few years after the Second World War, and my cousins Patrick and Francis Wall and my sisters Mary and Ruth supplied their various reactions to what we were reading. With them, I shared what other impressions we could pick up about the war north and east of us in the recent past; and my father told me about history and my mother about the books she liked reading – which, long, long ago, had included a supply of the *Magnet*.

But learning is without end, on children's literature as on everything else. The best way to start on the subject when you are grown up is to find a good bookshop, as I found in Edinburgh in the Old Children's Bookshelf, well down the Royal Mile before you reach Holyrood, where Shirley Neilson's stock and personal enthusiasm, and her Ransomian assistant Kirsty Taylor, whet any appetite and have enabled me to find books of whose existence I would never otherwise have known, including the mysterious Jan Maclure's *Escape to Chungking*. The Internet can of course find specific items, above all birth and death dates (and my thanks to my colleague Robert Mason in guiding me through its intricacies), but there is no substitute for rows of books, nor any time machine more capable of delivering you back into history. The unwary must be warned that first editions of children's authors are essential unless a later edition when collated proves identical. Later editions of Saville and Johns were weakened by deletions, Crompton and Brent-Dyer truncated in paperback, Blyton drastically rewritten since her death. Some publishers' failure to print publishing dates make detection of first editons hard.

My most recent major debts are to my grandchildren Owen, Rosie and Sophie, whose existence and perceptions have been instructive and refreshing however unintended for the matter in hand. To my children Leila, Sara and Michael my debts are endless, including their wisdom at all ages in discussing the subject and guiding my ideas on it; and their friends and ours in the Spode Family Weeks have been constant aiders and abetters and their schoolmates' parents Carolyn and Charles Peploe. I have to thank a myriad host of friends and colleagues for talking about their youthful reading and about their lives in the Second World War, among whom I want to single out the late R. P. Stephenson, whose gentle reminiscences brought a lost Yorkshire world before me. Morag Bruford and her late husband Allan lent valuable relics of their infancy to me, and gave me even more valuable folk memories. Lucy Kiberd was a most helpful retrospective critic. John Havard gave me rich memories of Tolkien. Paul Bailey cleared up a Chinese question. David Batchelor made me think wireless. Dorian Grieve was a sparkling confidant. I have benefited in all kinds of ways from the superb editorial work of Roda Morrison of Edinburgh University Press, and from the Argus-like vigilance of my magnificent copy-editor, Ivor Normand. I must thank Esmé Watson for many aids in needful quests, and Eddie Clark, our endlessly patient production editor, scion of an illustrious publishing family.

Librarians in the University of Edinburgh, especially Marjorie MacGregor, have been patient and generous in the extreme, and it is with deep grief that I record my appreciation of our late Librarian and my former student Ian Mowat. The National Library of Ireland has never yet failed me in its readiness to produce its unique treasures at momentary notice; the National Library of Scotland is enshrined in my heart forever, and no words of mine can do justice to the warmth, kindness, good-humour, resourcefulness and tolerance light-years beyond the call of duty of its Reading-Room staff, its stock-fetchers, and its servitors; mentions by name would be as endless as my thanks to them must be.

And my greatest obligation of all is as always to my ever-loving wife Bonnie, ever since we met once upon a time and lived happily ever after.

O.D.E.
University of Edinburgh
St Valentine's Day, 2007

Acknowledgements

Grateful acknowledgement is made to the following sources for permission to reproduce material previously published elsewhere. Every effort has been made to trace the copyright holders, but if any have been inadvertently overlooked, the publisher will be pleased to make the necessary arrangements at the first opportunity.

Our thanks are due to David Higham Associates for permission to quote from Graham Greene's article in the *Spectator*, 29 November 1940, 'The Unknown War'; for permission to quote from Muriel Spark, *The Prime of Miss Jean Brodie* (Macmillan and Penguin); for permission to quote from P. L. Travers, *Mary Poppins Opens the Door* (HarperCollins); for permission to quote from Richard Hughes, *Don't Blame Me! and Other Stories* (Chatto & Windus); for permission to quote from B.B./Denys Watkins-Pitchford, *The Little Grey Men* (Oxford University Press); for permission to quote from A. J. P. Taylor, *English History 1914–1945* (Oxford University Press); for permission to quote from Elizabeth Goudge, *The Joy of Snow*, from her *The Little White Horse* and from her 'For Consideration'.

Our thanks are due to Councillor Jim Davidson (SNP) for permission to quote from his *A Bairn's War*.

Our thanks are due to the estate of Margot Pardoe for permission to quote from her *Bunkle Butts In*, and also to Fidra Books.

Our thanks are due to Magnus Linklater for permission to quote from Eric Linklater's *The Wind on the Moon* and *The Art of Adventure*.

Our thanks are due to Girls Gone By for permission to quote from Dorita Fairlie Bruce, *Dimsie Carries On* and *Nancy Calls the Tune*; for permission to quote from Elinor M. Brent-Dyer, *The Chalet School in Exile*, *The Chalet School Goes To It*, *The Highland Twins at the Chalet School* and *Gay from China at the Chalet School*; for permission to quote from Malcolm Saville, *Mystery at Witchend* and *Seven White Gates*; for permission to quote from Josephine Elder, *Strangers at the Farm School*.

Our thanks are due to the Society of Authors for permission to quote from George Bernard Shaw's review of *The Prisoner of Zenda* in the *Saturday Review*, 11 January 1896.

Our thanks are due to the Ardizzone estate for permission to quote from Edward Ardizzone, *Little Tim and the Brave Sea-Captain*, and personally to Laura Cecil for biographical advice.

Our thanks are due to Laura Chalmers, granddaughter of B. G. Aston, for permission to quote from Jeffrey Havilton, *School vs Spy*, and also to Malcolm McNaught, Director of External Relations, Glasgow Academy, for his courteous aid.

Our thanks are due to the C. S. Lewis Company for EXTRACTS by C. S. Lewis © C. S. Lewis Pte. Ltd. Reprinted by permission.

Our thanks are due to A. P. Watt for quotation from the works of Richmal Crompton by permission of A. P. Watt Ltd, on behalf of Dr Paul Ashbee. Our thanks are due to A. P. Watt for quotation from the works of W. E. Johns by permission of A. P. Watt Ltd, on behalf of W. E. Johns (Publications) Ltd.

Our thanks are due to Chorion and particularly to Helen Mills for permission to quote extracts from the works of Enid Blyton.

Our thanks are due to A. M. Heath & Co. Ltd for the Noel Streatfeild estate.

The Lord of the Rings, *Letters* and 'On Fairy-Stories' reprinted by permission of HarperCollins Ltd © J. R. R. Tolkien, 1954–1955, 1981 and 1946.

Animal Farm by George Orwell (copyright © George Orwell, 1945)
Nineteen-Eighty-Four by George Orwell (copyright © George Orwell, 1949)
The Art of Donald McGill by George Orwell (copyright © George Orwell, 1941)
Phantom Patrol by George Orwell (copyright © George Orwell, 1940)
The Saturday Book 5 by George Orwell (copyright © George Orwell, 1945)
Little Men by George Orwell (copyright © George Orwell, 1941)
by permission of Bill Hamilton as the Literary Executor of the Estate of the Late Sonia Brownell Orwell and Secker & Warburg Ltd.

Index

Although these books and names here are source-lists in their own right, the index does not include 'Sources, Guides and Regrets'. Dates for book-titles refer to first British publication. Surname-prefixes ('Mac' [and its variants treated with it], 'O', 'de', 'de la', 'du', 'des', 'van', 'von') commence names as required. Definite and indefinite articles are ignored in initial order.